Praise for Ruth Rosen and *The World Split Open*

"Thoroughly absorbing"
—*Chicago Tribune*

"Ruth Rosen has produced an indispensable history of the contemporary women's movement. Her book should be required (and enthralling) reading for women and men who want to understand recent developments shaping the longest revolution in American history."
—Sandra M. Gilbert, co-author of *The Madwoman in the Attic*

"Superb . . . tough-minded, fair, finely written and exhaustively documented, *The World Split Open* offers stunning amounts of information that can enlighten even those who've been immersed in the women's movement for the last thirty years and more. . . . *The World Split Open* is a model of its kind—at once intensely personal and intellectually solid."
—*The Dallas Morning News*

"Comprehensively researched and exquisitely written, *The World Split Open* is destined to become a classic for teachers and students of U.S. history."
—Kathryn Kish Sklar, Distinguished Professor of History, SUNY Binghamton

"As an activist herself, Rosen is particularly adept at capturing the passion that motivated many participants in the movement . . . a noted feminist academic, in *The World Split Open* she creates a narrative account that should appeal to non-academic readers as well."
—*Bookpage*

"In this brilliant history of recent decades in the feminist movement, Rosen gives us views both panoramic and close up, authoritative and lively. She reviews our triumphs, our mistakes, and the vision we need for the years ahead. Must reading for those who've been in the thick of it, those who've gritted their teeth through it, and those who've done neither."
—Arlie Russell Hochschild, author of *The Second Shift* and *The Time Bind*

PENGUIN BOOKS

THE WORLD SPLIT OPEN

Ruth Rosen, a professor emerita at the University of California, Davis, teaches history and public policy at U.C. Berkeley. She is the editor of the highly acclaimed *Maimie Papers*, amd author of the classic *Prostitution in America*. An award-winning journalist, she is a former columnist for the *Los Angeles Times* and editorial writer and columnist for the *San Francisco Chronicle*. A co-founder and senior fellow of the Longview Institute, she writes for a wide variety of magazines and journals, including TomDispatch.com, *The History News Network*, TomPaine.com, *The American Prospect, Dissent, The Nation*, AlterNet.org, and is a regular contributor to the online political Web site *Talking Points Memo Café*.

THE WORLD SPLIT OPEN

HOW THE MODERN WOMEN'S MOVEMENT CHANGED AMERICA

Ruth Rosen

PENGUIN BOOKS

PENGUIN BOOKS
Published by the Penguin Group
Penguin Group (USA) Inc., 375 Hudson Street, New York, New York 10014, U.S.A.
Penguin Group (Canada), 90 Eglinton Avenue East, Suite 700, Toronto, Ontario,
Canada M4P 2Y3 (a division of Pearson Penguin Canada Inc.)
Penguin Books Ltd, 80 Strand, London WC2R 0RL, England
Penguin Ireland, 25 St Stephen's Green, Dublin 2, Ireland (a division of Penguin Books Ltd)
Penguin Group (Australia), 250 Camberwell Road, Camberwell, Victoria 3124, Australia
(a division of Pearson Australia Group Pty Ltd)
Penguin Books India Pvt Ltd, 11 Community Centre, Panchsheel Park, New Delhi – 110 017, India
Penguin Group (NZ), 67 Apollo Drive, Rosedale, North Shore 0632, New Zealand
(a division of Pearson New Zealand Ltd)
Penguin Books (South Africa) (Pty) Ltd, 24 Sturdee Avenue, Rosebank, Johannesburg 2196, South Africa

Penguin Books Ltd, Registered Offices: 80 Strand, London WC2R 0RL, England

First published in the United States of America by Viking Penguin,
a member of Penguin Putnam Inc. 2000
Published in Penguin Books 2001
This edition published in Penguin Books 2006

17 19 20 18

Grateful acknowledgment is made for permission to reprint the following copyrighted works:
"An Answer to a Man's Question, 'What Can I Do About Women's Liberation?'"
by Susan Griffin. By permission of the author.
"Poem: That Chick Is So Revolutionary" by Alta Gerrey. By permission of the author.
"If Men Could Menstruate" by Gloria Steinem. By permission of the author.

THE LIBRARY OF CONGRESS HAS CATALOGED THE HARDCOVER EDITION AS FOLLOWS:
Rosen, Ruth.
The world split open: how the modern women's
movement changed America/Ruth Rosen.
p. cm.
Includes bibliographical references and index.
ISBN 0-670-81462-8 (hc.)
ISBN 978-0-14-009719-1 (pbk.)
1. Feminism—United States—History—20th Century. I. Title.
HQ1421.R68   2000
305.42'0973—dc21   99-054439

Printed in the United States of America
Set in Bodoni Book
Designed by Betty Lew

IN HONOR OF WOMEN—
PAST,
PRESENT, AND
FUTURE

AND
FOR WENDEL

If anything remains more or less unchanged,
it will be the role of women.

> —David Riesman, sociologist, Harvard University
> *Time*
> July 21, 1967

If we do not know our own history,
we are doomed to live it as though
it were our private fate.

> —Hannah Arendt, political theorist

Contents

❧

PREFACE: THE LONGEST REVOLUTION

❧

Bursts of artillery fire, mass strikes, massacred protesters, bomb explosions—these are our images of revolution. But some revolutions are harder to recognize: no cataclysms mark their beginnings or ends, no casualties are left lying in pools of blood. Though people may suffer greatly, their pain is hidden from public view. Such was the case with the American women's movement. Activists didn't hurl tear gas canisters at the police, burn down buildings, or fight in the street. Nor did they overthrow the government or achieve economic dominance or political hegemony. But they did subvert authority and transform society in dramatic and irrevocable ways; so much so that young women who come of age in the twenty-first century would not even recognize the America that existed before the feminist revolution came about.

Before the revolution, during the 1950s, the president of Harvard University saw no reason to increase the number of female undergraduates because the university's mission was to "train leaders," and Harvard's Lamont Library was off-limits to women for fear they would distract male students. Newspaper ads separated jobs by sex; employers paid women less than men for the same work. Bars often refused to serve women; banks routinely denied women credit or loans. Some states even excluded women from jury duty. Radio producers considered women's voices too abrasive to be on air; television executives believed they didn't have enough credibility to anchor the news; no women ran big corporations or universities, worked as firefighters or police officers, sat on the Supreme Court, installed electric equipment, climbed telephone poles, or owned construction companies. All hurricanes bore female names, thanks to the widely held view that women brought chaos and destruction to society. As late as 1970, Dr. Edgar Berman, a well-known physician, proclaimed on television that women were too tortured by hormonal disturbances to assume the presidency of the nation. Few people knew more than a few women professors, doctors, or lawyers. Everyone addressed a woman as either Miss or Mrs., depending on her marital status, and if a woman wanted an abortion, legal nowhere in America, she risked her life, searching among quacks in back alleys for a competent and compassionate doctor. The public believed that rape victims had probably "asked for it," most women felt too ashamed to report it, and no language existed to make sense of marital rape, date rape, domestic violence, or sexual harassment. Just two words summed up the hidden injuries women suffered in silence: "That's life."

Long before the women's movement began, American women's participation in both the labor force and the sexual revolution had dramatically altered their lives. But it took a women's movement to address the many ways women felt exploited, to lend legitimacy to their growing sense of injustice, and to name and reinterpret customs and practices that had long been accepted, but for which there was no language.

One day in the fall of 1967, soon after I arrived at the University of California, Berkeley to begin graduate studies, I noticed a small card tacked to a bulletin board in the student union: "Women's Liberation Group forming—all are welcome." At the time, I was also working as a journalist and photographer in the antiwar movement and was quite certain that I didn't need any more emancipation, thank you very much. "But it could be a great story," I thought. On the appointed day, I entered a small room in the student union and announced I wanted to write a story about the group. They agreed, but insisted that I participate. Two hours later, my world began to turn upside down. As with so many in my generation, feminism cast a new, sometimes thrilling, sometimes unnerving light on my own personal and intellectual past. I lived on the edge, experienced the trauma of a kind of rebirth, and emerged with a sensibility and intellectual commitment that has shaped the rest of my adult life.

Fast-forward to the waning weeks of the year 1979, when media pundits declared—with a collective sigh of relief—that the women's movement was dead, and that the entire decade had been nothing but a political and cultural black hole of self-absorption, populated by hedonists and narcissists who spent their time in cults and hot tubs. Already the media had dubbed the people who came of age during the 1960s and 1970s "the Me Generation." To put it mildly, I was flabbergasted. I wondered if they and I had lived through the same years. Had they really missed the not-so-quiet revolution in women's—and therefore men's—lives? True, the media had eventually tuned out, demonstrations had gradually diminished, but the women's movement had ignited a cultural war that raged for decades. As an historian, I was appalled that pundits had already packaged the decade, without recognizing the birth of a revolution that would irreversibly transform American culture and society.

One day, in the early 1980s, I was standing at the front of a cavernous hall that passes for a classroom at the Davis campus of the University of California. I gazed out over hundreds of my students, many of whom were no older than I'd been in 1967. I was just about to give a lecture on the roots and impact of the contemporary women's movement. On an impulse, I began by asking the class what they knew of the world of women before the movement had taken off, the era of their parents. And what issues, I also asked, had the women's movement redefined?

Eyes glazed over. Their main political memories focused on cars waiting in long lines for gas, and helicopters fetching a disgraced president into retirement or lifting Americans out of Saigon. What in the world was I talking about? What issues? I stood there listening to the silence and then spontaneously began to sketch out that world. I began to cover the blackboard with short catchphrases that reflected some of the ordinary but invariably painful female experiences that the women's movement had excavated and exposed to public view. Then, noting their growing amazement, I paused, took a deep breath, and stared at my own sprawling list.

Every life, I suppose, is allowed at least one epiphany. I could have been depressed by how little they knew. Instead, I felt a strange sense of elation. It wasn't just the enormity of all that women had challenged that still seemed breathtaking. What stunned me was that the changes in women's lives had been so deep, so wide-ranging, so transformative. I realized that the women's movement could not be erased, that it had brought about changes that these young people now took for granted.

That realization led, through many unexpected twists and turns, to years of archival research, interviewing, and analysis for a book on the origins and impact of the contemporary women's movement. I wanted to evoke the remarkable passion and accomplishments of that powerful moment in our history—and perhaps the future history of women worldwide—without romanticizing it, or ignoring the many mistakes, squandered opportunities, and failures of imagination that are part of every life and every movement.

Research for this book proved to be a pleasure, as well as an exercise in frustration. Sometimes, I sat at clean desks with a pencil in tidy, well-organized archives. Often, I sat on dusty floors, in attics or in library stacks, examining cartons filled with uncatalogued documents, yellowed letters, and undated flyers. I interviewed people who lived in penthouses with wrap-around terraces, in suburban homes with decks and pools, and in sixth-floor walk-up apartments, where bathtubs sat in the middle of kitchens, surrounded by armies of roaches.

This is not a book just about an isolated section of society. Dissident movements provide a microcosmic view of the dominant culture's values, assumptions, and social structure. American political culture shaped contemporary feminism, and the women's movement, in its turn, has transformed that political culture. Many readers, I suspect, probably know that American feminism was shaped by the political culture of the fifties and sixties. But it also developed out of much longer and deeper political traditions—such as the disestablishment of religion as a state force and a profound distrust of centralized government; the celebration of individual enterprise and initiative; a class politics expressed mostly through race and gender; a long evangelical tradition that has existed outside political parties and government; and a deep and abiding belief that in America, one can always reinvent oneself.

Since this book covers the entire second half of the twentieth century, I knew my first task was to explain how Cold War culture and its ideas about gender patrolled the boundaries between men and women, gay and straight, patriotic and subversive. For those who weren't there, it's necessary to grasp how much the immediate postwar era suppressed dissent, glorified motherhood, celebrated women's biological difference, and sanctified the nuclear family, all of which led to a revolt against that decade's cultural icon of motherhood.

But movements are made by people, not simply by ideas. The more I interviewed women, the more I understood that the movement arose from two generations of women who recognized, with considerable anguish and anger, that neither traditional liberalism nor the politics of the New Left was addressing what equality could mean for modern working women. And this was just the beginning. As these women activists learned to see the world through their own eyes, the feminist movement fragmented, and new populations of women—trade unionists, the old, the young, racial and ethnic minorities, some of whom had initially spurned feminism—began to assert different priorities. With that broadening constituency, many different feminisms began permeating American society.

Such a threatening movement spread to the general public through familiar sources of media and popular culture. Feminism became palatable to American mainstream culture by addressing the individual woman, rather than women as a group. What I began to call "consumer feminism" and "therapeutic feminism" had enabled a small political movement to enter daily life. Eventually, the idea of "sisterhood" gave way to the image of the Superwoman, who, with her hair swept back, briefcase in one hand, baby in the other, tried to have it all, by doing it all.

A backlash was inevitable, though few anticipated its religious and political ferocity. With its rallying cry of "family values" in the 1980s, the Republican Right successfully tied up the Equal Rights Amendment (ERA) in state legislatures and took the first steps to curtail the right to an abortion. So many hard-won gains of the women's movement seemed under siege. But the backlash, I eventually realized, masked another reality. By the end of the twentieth century, feminist ideas had burrowed too deeply into our culture for any resistance or politics to root them out. Meanwhile, women in other parts of the globe, fueled by international conferences, began challenging different forms of patriarchal authority and inventing feminism all over again.

The women's movement changed lives in ways that are rare in the history of social movements. Living life as a feminist was—and is—an intensely personal and dramatic experience. Naturally, there will be some people who will be disappointed not to find their particular memories and experiences in this book. All of us experienced the women's movement from our own perspectives, at different distances, and at varied ages. Some of us never experienced it at all. There were many stories; there are many memories. I hope there will be many more histories.

I did not write this book only for my generation, those of us raised to live as traditional women, whose lives were dramatically disrupted and transformed by the power of feminist insights. Although I believe present and former activists need to rethink the past, to know where we have been and how we arrived there, I have always kept a much broader audience in mind. This book is also written for those women and men who did not participate in the women's movement, who were too busy trying to survive, who felt excluded or estranged, who were too scared, were too old or too young, were not yet born, are still not born.

Ruth Rosen
Berkeley, California

CHRONOLOGY

(Signs of backlash in heavier type)

1848 Married women allowed to own property.

The First Women's Rights Convention, held in Seneca Falls, New York, produces the "Declaration of the Rights of Woman" and the demand for women's suffrage.

1872 Victoria Woodhull is the first woman to run for president, even though she cannot vote and is in prison for violating the famous Comstock Law by sending obscene literature through the mail, in this case, about free love.

1893 Colorado is the first state to allow women's suffrage.

1919 Congress passes the Nineteenth Amendment, called "The Susan B. Anthony Amendment."

Three-fourths of the states ratify it on August 26, 1920.

1923 The Equal Rights Amendment is first introduced in Congress.

1953 The National Weather Service begins naming hurricanes after women.

1954 In *Brown v. Board of Education*, the Supreme Court declares that separate but equal facilities for the races are not constitutional.

1955 The first lesbian organization, the Daughters of Bilitis, is founded.

Rosa Parks refuses to give up her bus seat to a white man, igniting the Montgomery Bus Boycott.

Daisy Lee Bates, President of Arkansas NAACP, leads nine African-American teenagers to integrate Little Rock High School.

1957 The Soviet Union launches the first space satellite, Sputnik, spurring a demand to train women in math and science.

1959 Barbie doll is introduced to girls.

1960 John F. Kennedy is elected president.

Four young men sit-in at a Greensboro, North Carolina, lunch counter after they are refused service. Their action ignites youthful civil rights activists all over the South.

The Student Nonviolent Coordinating Committee (SNCC) is founded.

Young Americans for Freedom founded.

1961 President Kennedy appoints Eleanor Roosevelt as chair of the first President's Commission on the Status of Women and Esther Peterson, who had a long history of improving working women's lives, as head of the Women's Bureau, making her the assistant secretary of the Department of Labor.

Fifty thousand women in sixty cities, mobilized by Women Strike for Peace, protest aboveground testing of nuclear bombs and tainted milk.

Birth control pills approved in 1960 and made available in 1961. Patricia McGinnis and Lana Phelan start the Society for Humane Abortion in California to demand access to abortion as a woman's right. In 1966 McGinnis sets up the Association to Repeal Abortion Law in California, which provides lists of abortion doctors and offers free classes in self-abortion.

1962 Helen Gurley Brown publishes *Sex and the Single Girl*, which gives single women permission to enjoy sex outside of marriage.

Students for a Democratic Society (SDS) launches the student protest movement with "The Port Huron Statement," a critique of American domestic and foreign policy that also decries the powerlessness of ordinary people.

Rachel Carson publishes *Silent Spring*, which attacks the reckless use of toxins and pesticides.

Dolores Fernandez Huerta helps Cesar Chavez start the Farm Workers' Association (Later the United Farm Workers). The Union's first woman organizing in the field is Jesse Lopez de la Cruz.

1963 The report from the President's Commission on the Status of Women, *The American Woman*, is published.

Some 200,000 people rally in Washington, D.C., and hear Martin Luther King, Jr.'s "I have a dream" speech.

Betty Friedan publishes *The Feminine Mystique*.

Congress passes the Equal Pay Act.

1964 Congress passes the Civil Rights Act, including Title VII, which prohibits discrimination in employment—not only on the basis of race, color, religion, and national origin, but also on sex. The Equal Employment Opportunity Commission (EEOC) is created to enforce Title VII, but women's complaints are ignored and ridiculed.

Freedom Summer: One thousand northern students join SNCC workers in the South on voter registration and Freedom School projects.

Congress passes the Tonkin Gulf Resolution, which allows funding for the Vietnam War.

The Mississippi Freedom Democratic Party tries, but fails, to replace the all-white Mississippi delegation at the Democratic National Convention in Atlanta. Disillusionment within the civil rights movement deepens.

Casey Hayden and Mary King circulate a memo about sexual inequality within the civil rights movement.

The Beatles take the U.S. by storm on their first tour of the country.

1965 Executive Order 11246 is signed by President Lyndon B. Johnson, requiring companies doing business with the government to undertake affirmative action in hiring minorities.

Casey Hayden and Mary King send "A Kind of Memo" to fifty women in the antiwar and student movements. At an SDS conference in 1965, the first group of women meet alone in order to discuss the "Memo."

In *Griswold v. Connecticut*, the Supreme Court declares that married couples have a right to birth control based on their "right to privacy."

Dorothy Height leads the National Council of Negro Women to address problems of women.

1966 At the Third Annual Conference on the Status of Women in Washington, women realize that the EEOC will not enforce the Civil Rights Act of 1964 and discover that their attempts to pass resolutions are foiled. The National Organization for Women (NOW) is founded.

NOW petitions the EEOC to end the sexual segregation of classified advertisements for employment.

The call for Black Power begins.

1967 At a press conference, Betty Friedan, president of NOW, announces that federally funded child care centers for working mothers and a full income-tax deduction for child care costs are central to NOW's goals.

President Johnson extends affirmative action to women.

The Conference for a New Politics ridicules young feminists' demands.

The Chicago Women's Liberation Group begins meeting.

New York Radical Women also forms.

Barbara Avedon and other women organize Another Mother for Peace with the slogan, "War is not healthy for children and other living things."

NOW adopts a Bill of Rights for Women.

Women on welfare begin to organize. In California Alicia Escalante starts the East Los Angeles Welfare Rights Organization and later founds the Chicano National Welfare Fights Organization. Black activist welfare recipients such as Johnnie Tillmom, Etta Horn, and Beulah Sanders join forces in the National Welfare Rights Organization to educate women about applying for benefits and lobbying for respect within the system as well as for job-training and day care programs. By 1969 there are 22,000 members, but the NWRO lacks funds to continue beyond 1975.

1968 January 15. New York feminists bring a dummy of "Traditional Womanhood" to the all-women's Jeanette Rankin Brigade demonstration against the war in Vietnam in Washington, D.C., and state their intention to bury her. For the first time, feminists use the slogan "Sisterhood is Powerful."

In Chicago, over two hundred women from thirty-seven states and Canada meet for the First National Women's Liberation Conference.

New York Radical Women begin process of "consciousness-raising."

Shirley Chisholm is elected first African-American woman representative (D-NY) to Congress.

New York NOW members picket the *New York Times* to end sex-segregated classified advertising.

The Women's Equity Action League is formed by women who leave NOW to pursue feminist goals other than abortion.

The National Abortion Rights Action League is formed.

Martin Luther King, Jr., and Robert F. Kennedy are assassinated. Students and young people in Mexico, France, Germany, and dozens of other countries rally, protest, and demand social and economic change.

In August, U.S. students are beaten in Chicago at the Democratic National Convention, and Soviet troops trample "Prague Spring."

Voice of the Women's Liberation Movement, first newsletter from WLM, is published by Joreen (Jo Freeman) in Chicago. In New York, radical feminists publish *Notes from the First Year*. Feminist publications sweep across the nation. Between 1968 and 1973, five hundred publications appear.

IRS allows widows and single or divorced women over thirty-five to receive head-of-household status with deductions.

Dorothy Lee Bolden organizes the National Domestic Workers Union.

New York women's liberationists protest against the Miss America Pageant in Atlantic City. Ground zero for myth of bra burning.

1969 Gay men resist police raid at the Stonewall Bar in New York City, launching the gay liberation movement.

The Boston Women's Health Collective publishes a pamphlet, *Our Bodies, Ourselves: A Book by and for Women*. In 1973, it is published as a book.

Accuracy in Media (AIM), a right-wing watchdog on "liberal bias," is formed.

Members of Redstockings disrupt a hearing on abortion laws of the New York State legislature when the panel of witnesses turns out to be fourteen men and one nun. They demand repeal, not reform, of abortion laws.

NOW celebrates Mother's Day with the slogan "Rights, Not Roses."

The Federal Bureau of Investigation begins widespread infiltration of the women's movement at all levels.

1970 The great media blitz begins, with stories all year long on the new women's movement.

Pat Mainardi offers a proposal for "wages for housework."

California is first state to adopt "no-fault" divorce, which ends up impoverishing older women who have no skills.

The North American Indian Women's Association is founded.

Toni Cade publishes *The Black Woman*.

Bella Abzug is elected to Congress.

Feminists stage sit-ins at *Newsweek* and *Ladies' Home Journal* and file an antidiscrimination suit against *Time*, *Life*, *Fortune*, and *Sports Illustrated*. The Feminist Press is started.

Major classic works appear in 1970 and 1971: Germaine Greer, *The Female Eunuch*; Vivian Gornick and Barbara Moran, editors, *Woman in Sexist Society: Studies in Power and Powerlessness*; Shulamith Firestone, *Dialectics of Sex*; Kate Millett, *Sexual Politics*; Robin Morgan, *Sisterhood Is Powerful*; Celestine Ware, *Woman Power*.

In Wisconsin, the first AFL-CIO conference meets to discuss the status of women in unions. It endorses the ERA and opposes state protective legislation.

On August 26, fifty thousand women march to commemorate the fiftieth anniversary of the suffrage amendment in New York. Feminists drape a huge banner over the Statue of Liberty that says "Women of the World Unite." In forty-two states, women participate in the "Strike for Equality."

Maggie Kuhn forms the Gray Panthers to fight for older citizens' rights.

NOW sues 1,300 corporations.

WEAL files class action suit against more than one hundred colleges and universities.

The Lutheran Church in America and the America Lutheran Church allow women to be ordained.

The Episcopal Church permits women deacons, but not ordination for women.

Barbara Herman is the first woman cantor, in a Reform Jewish temple in New Jersey.

National Right to Life Committee is established by the Catholic Church to block liberalization of abortion laws.

Hawaii, Alaska, and New York become the first states to liberalize their abortion laws.

Barbara Seaman and others disrupt the Senate subcommittee's hearing on the Pill, protesting that most witnesses are male doctors and that women are being used as "guinea pigs" in testing.

Forty-six editorial staff women win a settlement in their suit charging sexual discrimination at *Newsweek* magazine.

Women on the staff of RAT take over the New York radical underground newspaper.

Sit-in at *Ladies' Home Journal* by one hundred women leads to a special supplement in the August, 1970, issue.

The Congress to Unite Women meets in New York City. Lesbians stage the Lavender Menace Action, one of the first asserting the right to be public lesbians.

Chicana feminists in California found the *Comision Feminil Mexicana Nacional.* They start a model service center for working women. Founders include Gracia Molina Pick, Francisca Flores, Graciella Oivares, and Yolanda Nova.

Singer Janis Joplin dies of a heroin overdose.

1971 New York Radical Feminists hold a "Speak-out on Rape," in which women disclose their personal experiences.

New York NOW forms a "Baby Carriage Brigade" to demonstrate its support of women's right to deduct child care expenses. "Are Children As Important As Martinis?" is their slogan.

Norman Mailer's *Prisoner of Sex*, a sophisticated and highly publicized attack on the women's movement, is published.

On her first day as representative from New York, Bella Abzug demands that all U.S. troops be withdrawn from Vietnam.

Bella Abzug, Shirley Chisholm, Betty Friedan, Gloria Steinem, and others help found the National Women's Political Caucus to support more women candidates.

First Feminist Women's Health Center founded in Los Angeles by Carol Downer and Lorraine Rothman.

The National Press Club allows women to become full members.

Berkeley, California, initiates women's studies in primary schools.

The Professional Women's Caucus files a class action sexual discrimination suit against every law school in the country receiving federal funds.

President Richard Nixon vetoes the Comprehensive Child Development Bill, passed by both houses of Congress, which would have provided $2 billion for child care.

Three hundred and forty French women sign a petition, "Manifesto of 340 Bitches," declaring they have had an abortion.

The FBI reports that the increase in women's crime rate is up sharply over that in men's.

1972 Puerto Rican women hold their first national conference.

The Equal Rights Amendment passes both houses of Congress; ratification is necessary by 1979.

Congress passes Title IX of the 1972 Educational Amendments to the Civil Rights Act to enforce sex equality in education, which forces educational institutions to support women's sports.

Congress passes the Equal Employment Opportunity Act, which prohibits sex discrimination in employment.

Ms. magazine is launched.

Representative Shirley Chisholm runs for the Democratic Party nomination for president of the United States and loses.

In San Francisco, Margo St. James organizes COYOTE (Call Off Your Old Tired Ethics) to improve the working conditions of prostitutes.

Phyllis Schlafly attacks the ERA in her newsletter and forms a new organization, "StopERA."

Midge Decter, neoconservative, publishes an attack against the women's movement in *The New Chastity and Other Arguments Against Women's Liberation.*

Jesse Helms is elected to the U.S. Senate.

The country debates whether Maude, a fictional character in a television sitcom, should have a late-life abortion.

NOW launches an attack on sexism in schoolbooks, with its pamphlet *Dick and Jane As Victims.*

For the first time, a girl wins a soap box derby. She apologizes.

The Equal Pay Act of 1963 is extended to cover administrative, professional, and executive employees.

The Feminist Press starts the *Women's Studies Newsletter.* (In 1977, the National Women's Studies Association formed; by 1978 there are over 15,000 courses.)

Women's issues, including the right to abortion, are included in the platform of La Raza Unida, a Mexican-American political movement.

Marlo Thomas and friends produce the record *Free to Be . . . You and Me,* the first record of nonsexist, multiracial songs, poems, and stories for children.

Judy Chicago, Miriam Shapiro, and members of the Feminist Art Program of the California Institute of the Arts open a seventeen-room *Womanhouse* exhibit, viewed by 4,000 people.

The first conference of Older Women's Liberation (women over thirty) is held in New York City.

1973   In its *Roe v. Wade* decision, the Supreme Court establishes a woman's right to abortion.

Congress allows the first female page in the House of Representatives.

Singer Helen Reddy wins a Grammy Award for her song "I Am Woman," which becomes a kind of informal anthem of the movement.

AT&T agrees to end discrimination in women's salaries and to pay retroactive compensation to women employees.

The National Black Feminist Organization is formed.

More than three hundred women from twenty-seven countries attend an International Feminist Planning Conference in Cambridge, Massachusetts. Their goal is to create an international movement through global conferences.

Conservative Judaism permits women to be counted in making up the minyan, or ten people necessary for congregational worship.

Dr. Mary Daly's book, *Beyond God the Father*, rejects male divinity and questions all received religious wisdom.

George Gilder's *Sexual Suicide*, a sustained attack against the women's movement, is published.

Billie Jean King's efforts succeed when the U.S. Tennis Association announces that the U.S. Open will award equal prize money to women and men.

Bernice Reagon Johnson forms an a cappella group, *Sweet Honey in the Rock*, which emphasizes songs about civil rights and social justice.

Redwood Records, a women's music record company, is founded, and issues Holly Near's *Hang in There*.

In Los Angeles, the first West Coast Lesbian Feminist Conference is held.

Office workers form Women Employed in Chicago, Women Office Workers in New York, and 9-5 in Boston. Union Wage in San Francisco had been formed in 1971.

First U.S. battered women's shelters open.

Attorney Marian Wright Edelman founds Children's Defense Fund.

Billie Jean King defeats Bobby Riggs in the "Battle of the Sexes" tennis match.

The Supreme Court outlaws sexually-segregated classified ads.

The AFL-CIO National Convention endorses the ERA.

The Government Printing Office style book accepts Ms. as a prefix.

Dr. Benjamin Spock renounces his earlier views on child care and revises his classic book.

Stewardesses for Women's Rights formed to support job rights, a dignified public image, and health issues of female flight attendants.

The National Association for the Repeal of Abortion, founded in 1969, changes its name to the National Abortion Rights Action League and makes its goal the preservation of the 1973 Supreme Court Decision.

1974 The Freedom of Information Act passes.

Congress passes the Equal Credit Opportunity Act, which allows married women to get credit in their own name for the first time.

Over one thousand colleges and universities offer women's studies courses and eighty have full programs.

Helen Thomas, after covering Washington for thirty years, is finally named White House reporter for UPI and becomes the first woman to hold this position.

Little League, for the first time, allows girls to compete in baseball.

Diana Russell publishes *The Politics of Rape.*

The Mexican American Women's National Association (MANA) is founded. It is pro-choice, against forced sterilization, and starts a successful Hermanitas ("Little Sisters") program.

Domestic workers covered by the minimum-wage law.

First Lady Betty Ford and Happy Rockefeller, wife of New York's governer, speak openly about their own mastectomies.

Class action suit against the *New York Times* is settled in 1978 in favor of five hundred fifty female employees.

First National Women's Music Festival is held.

Paul Weyrich receives funds from Joseph Coors to organize the Committee for the Survival of a Free Congress, and Richard Viguerie becomes the organization's direct mail fund-raiser and establishes the Conservative Caucus. The National Conservative Political Action Committee established by John "Terry" Dolan is created one year later.

The Washington State Court grants a lesbian mother living with her lover custody of her children.

Passport Office allows use of maiden name.

The National Women's Football League is formed and the All-America Girls' Basketball Conference is held.

More than 3,000 women from 58 unions attend a Chicago meeting where the Coalition of Labor Union Women (CLUW) is formed. The group is made up entirely of union members; the goals are to combat sexism within unions, to push for legislation addressing female workers' needs, and to organize the thirty million women workers who are not in unions.

After a three-year campaign by women's groups, New York no longer requires a rape victim to give independent corroboration from witnesses of the crime.

1975 The United Nations sponsors the First International Conference on Women in Mexico City.

For the first time, federal employees' salaries can be garnished for child support and alimony.

National Right to Life PAC organized.

Phyllis Schlafly organizes Eagle Forum as an alternative to "women's lib," in support of voluntary school prayer, law and order, and a strong national defense, and against busing, federally funded child care, and abortion.

Tish Sommers, chair of NOW's Older Women Task Force, coins the phrase "displaced homemaker."

The Vietnam War ends, after fourteen years and the deaths of 56,559 Americans and millions of Vietnamese.

Susan Brownmiller's *Against Our Will* on the ubiquity of rape is published.

NOW sponsors "Alice Doesn't" Day, and asks women across the country to go on strike for one day.

Joanne Little, who was raped by a guard while in jail, is acquitted of murdering her offender. The case establishes a precedent for killing as self-defense against rape.

Mississippi court rules that women cannot be systematically excluded from jury duty.

Ten California Chicanas file a suit, charging they were involuntarily sterilized at a county medical center.

The first National Women's Health Conference, sponsored by the

Our Bodies, Ourselves Collective, is held at Harvard Medical School; four thousand women attend.

Time magazine breaks tradition in naming the Man of the Year by designating ten women for cover honors.

The National Congress of Neighborhood Women forms to upgrade the status of working-class women through education, community program training, and college studies. The Sisterhood of Black Single Mothers in Brooklyn brings two hundred women together to run a clothing and baby-sitting cooperative and to share information.

1976 *Redbook* magazine polls its readers about sexual harassment. Ninety percent of young women say they view the situation as "serious."

The nation's first Center for Displaced Homemakers opens at Mills College, Oakland, California, inspired by Tish Sommers.

A bill that defines a "person" as "a human being" from the moment of fertilization is signed by Louisiana's governor, but does not survive court challenge.

The United Nations Decade for Women begins.

A movement to repeal a gay rights ordinance in Dade County, Florida, is led by singer Anita Bryant.

ERAmerica is launched to promote the ratification of ERA.

The National Alliance of Black Feminists organizes in Chicago.

The Organization of Pan Asian American Women forms for women of Asian and Pacific American Islander descent.

Barbara Jordan becomes the first African-American and first woman to give the keynote speech at the Democratic National Convention.

Supreme Court decision agrees with General Electric that the company's failure to cover pregnancy-related disability is not discriminatory.

Both the House and Senate pass the Hyde Amendment, which prohibits the use of federal Medicaid money for abortions.

Many professional and women's organizations decide to boycott those states that have not passed the ERA and to hold their conferences elsewhere.

Sarah Caldwell is the first woman to conduct at the Metropolitan Opera after Beverly Sills refuses to sing unless Caldwell conducts.

The International Tribunal on Crimes Against Women is held in Brussels.

NASA announces it will accept women for astronaut training.

New research gives hitherto unacknowledged credit to geneticist Rosalind Franklin for her work in solving the riddle of the DNA molecule.

French prostitutes stage nationwide strike.

Women in Iceland hold a day-long strike to show their importance to the economy, virtually shutting down the country.

1977 Houston, Texas, witnesses the First National Women's Conference, at which twenty thousand representatives, women from all states, gather to pass a far-reaching National Plan of Action.

National Association of Cuban-American Women formed.

National Coalition Against Domestic Violence established.

Eleanor Smeal, president of NOW, demands that homemakers should have their own Social Security accounts.

The American Civil Liberties Union asks the Rhode Island Supreme Court to allow women to use their own names, rather than that of their husbands.

Joanie Caucus, the runaway wife turned feminist made famous in *Doonesbury*, graduates from law school.

The Air Force graduates its first women pilots.

AT&T announces its willingness to allow dual listing of married people in phone books.

1978 Congress passes the Pregnancy Discrimination Act that prohibits discrimination against pregnant women in all areas of employment.

Laura X founds National Clearinghouse on Marital and Date Rape to lobby for changes in state law.

Proposition 6 in California attempts, but fails, to prohibit gays and lesbians from teaching in California schools.

Women Against Pornography is founded in New York City.

Congress extends ratification deadline for ERA to June 30, 1982.

Over 100,000 people demonstrate in Washington, D.C., to support ratification of the Equal Rights Amendment.

More women than men enter American colleges and universities.

Congress passes a bill prohibiting the introduction of the victim's reputation in cases of rape or attempted rape.

New York is the first state to pass a bill to locate the children of women who have taken the synthetic hormone diethylstilbe-strol (DES).

Women sports writers are no longer barred from major league baseball locker rooms.

Congress allocates $5 million to the Department of Labor to set up centers for displaced homemakers.

The first national feminist conference on pornography is sponsored by Women Against Violence in Pornography and the Media in San Francisco. They sponsor the first "Take Back the Night" march to draw attention to a woman's right to walk the streets at night without fear. Soon thousands of women across the country stage similar marches.

John Rideout, the first man charged with raping his wife while they were living together, is acquitted by an Oregon Court.

1979   The Moral Majority is founded by Jerry Falwell, television evangelist.

President Jimmy Carter fires Bella Abzug from the Advisory Committee on Women because she insists that unemployment, the federal government, and inflation are all women's issues.

The National Weather Service decides to follow a new policy of naming hurricanes after *both* women and men.

National March in Washington, D.C., for lesbians and gays draws 100,000 participants from all over the country.

Judy Chicago's collaborative art work *The Dinner Party,* with thirty-nine place settings for famous women, creates a stir in the artistic community.

Rose Kushner, author of *Why Me?,* persuades the National Institutes of Health to endorse a two-stage breast biopsy procedure, enabling women to have a choice in their breast surgery for cancer.

1980   Ronald Reagan is elected president of the United States in the first demonstration of the "gender gap," with more men than women voting for Reagan.

Copenhagen, Denmark, hosts the UN's Second World Conference on Women.

National Judicial Education Program to Promote Equality for Women and Men in the Courts begins to educate judges about gender bias.

The EEOC publishes new guidelines on sexual harassment.

For the first time, the Republican platform no longer supports the ERA and goes on record as being against abortion. The National Women's History Research Project is established and Molly Murphy MacGregor is named as executive director. Its goal is to promote the multicultural study of women's history in the k–12 classroom. It lobbies successfully for the National Women's History Week in 1981.

1981 Sandra Day O'Connor is the first woman appointed to the U.S. Supreme Court.

Jesse Helms introduces Human Life Bill, in order to make abortion illegal.

1982 The Equal Rights Amendment is unable to gather the necessary number of states for ratification.

The Family Protection Act is introduced in Congress. It would have established prayer in the schools, forbidden federal funding for schoolbooks that depicted women in unconventional roles, repealed federal laws against child and spouse abuse, and prohibited coed sports. It doesn't pass.

1983 Sally Ride becomes the first American woman in space.

Congress passes the Retirement Equity Act that gives equal benefits to women in private pension systems.

In *City of Akron v. Akron Center*, the Supreme Court upholds parental consent requirement for minors seeking abortions.

U.S. feminist peace activists establish Seneca Falls encampment against nuclear arms.

Alice Walker receives Pulitzer Prize for *The Color Purple*.

1984 Walter Mondale chooses Geraldine Ferraro for his vice-presidential running mate. They lose to Ronald Reagan and George Bush.

Mothers of East Los Angeles organize to oppose violence and to battle against environmental racism.

Leontyne T. C. Kelly becomes the first African-American ordained as a bishop in the United Methodist Church.

1985 The UN's Third World Conference on Women is held in Nairobi, Kenya.

The American Psychiatric Association removes homosexuality from its category of mental illnesses and disorders.

Bella Abzug founds Women's Foreign Policy Council, which, along with Women for Meaningful Summits and the Jane Addams Conference, struggles to promote women's interests in foreign policy.

Amy Eilberg becomes first woman Conservative Rabbi.

Ellen Malcolm starts EMILY's List to give financial backing to pro-choice Democratic women candidates for state and federal office. EMILY stands for "Early Money Is Like Yeast."

1986 The Meese Commission produces a list of all the films it deems to be pornographic "social menaces."

The Supreme Court rules in *EEOC v. Sears* that Sears did not discriminate.

Margaret Atwood publishes her dystopian novel *The Handmaid's Tale*, in which the religious Right has won electoral power and creates the theocracy and republic of Gilead.

The *New York Times* finally agrees to use Ms. instead of Miss or Mrs.

Barbara Mikulski, from Maryland, becomes first Democratic woman elected to the U.S. Senate who hasn't succeeded her husband. The number of women in the Senate doubles from one to two.

A *Newsweek* poll reveals that 56 percent of women consider themselves feminists; 71 percent say that the movement has improved their lives; only 4 percent describe themselves as antifeminist.

1987 Eleanor Smeal and others found the Fund for the Feminist Majority, in part to encourage feminists to run for office.

Congress declares March "Women's History Month."

Court rules against Mary Beth Whitehead in "Baby M" case, highlighting the issue of surrogate mothers.

1988 In *Webster v. Reproductive Services*, the Supreme Court allows Missouri's prohibition of the use of public funds for abortion.

Toni Morrison receives the Pulitzer Prize for all her work, including *Beloved*.

Methodists create a gender-neutral hymnal.

Congress approves a memorial for the 10,000 women who served in Vietnam.

1989 African-American Barbara Harris is ordained as the first female bishop in the Episcopal Church.

1990 Congress passes the Americans with Disabilities Act, which prohibits discrimination on the basis of disability.

1991 The country is mesmerized by the confirmation hearings of Clarence Thomas, who is accused by his former special assistant Anita Hill of sexual harassment.

The American Association of University Women publishes a groundbreaking critique, *How Schools Shortchange Girls*.

The Supreme Court rules that the U.S. government can deny foreign aid to any overseas health organizations that promote abortion.

The president of NOW, Patricia Ireland, is vilified when she reveals that she lives with a female companion.

NOW sponsors a Young Feminist Conference in Akron, Ohio, which draws eight hundred young women, who also rally against the Gulf War.

The Senate overturns the "gag rule" that bars federally financed family planning clinics from discussing abortion with women.

Susan Faludi publishes *Backlash*, which documents how and who helped create a backlash against the women's movement in the 1980s.

The film *Thelma and Louise* strikes a nerve among women viewers that baffles film critics.

1992   In *Planned Parenthood of Southeastern Pennsylvania v. Robert P. Casey*, the Supreme Court affirms a woman's right to abortion but allows certain restrictions based on a state's "compelling" interest in potential human life.

Colorado and Oregon pass antigay ordinances, which are overthrown by the Supreme Court in 1996.

Some 750,000 women, men, and children turn out for the Pro-Choice March in Washington, D.C., with the slogan "We Won't Go Back! We Will Fight Back." The march attracts labor unions, celebrities, and students from six hundred campuses. A similar march is held in Los Angeles the next week.

EMILY's List, the Women's Campaign Fund, and other groups raise money for a record number of women running for electoral office.

Barbara Bush and Marilyn Quayle try to promote "family values" at Republican National Convention.

Five major women's clinics in Buffalo become the target of Operation Rescue.

Vice President Dan Quayle attacks the fictional television character Murphy Brown for having a child with no husband.

The State Farm Insurance Company agrees to pay $157 million to 814 women who were denied jobs as agents in the largest sex discrimination settlement in U.S. history under the Civil Rights Act of 1964.

"The Year of the Woman" in politics results in more women elected than in any prior year.

1993   Congress passes the Family and Medical Leave Act, which gives men and women protected unpaid leave to respond to family emergencies.

Bill Clinton appoints a record number of women to his cabinet and as heads of agencies, but withdraws the candidacies of Zoe Baird and Kimba Wood for attorney general because of the "Nannygate" issue.

The Tailhook scandal, in which naval aviators are accused of sexual harassment and lewd behavior, is exposed.

The United Nations World Conference on Human Rights meets in Vienna and, after hearing the testimony of women from all over the world, accepts the "Vienna Declaration," stating that violence against women or girls is a violation of their human rights. The General Assembly accepts the resolution.

1994   The Supreme Court rules that obstructing the entrance to an abortion clinic is illegal.

Congress passes the Violence Against Women Act, which provides funds for services for victims of rape and domestic violence, allows women to seek civil rights remedies for gender-related crimes, and trains police and judiciary.

The United Nations Conference on Population and Development in Cairo passes a resolution that education for women (instead of industrial development) is a precondition for population control.

1995   Beijing, China, hosts the United Nations' Fourth World Conference on Women. The conference calls for women's rights as human rights, and endorses a far-reaching and radical plan for peace and equality for women.

The Glass Ceiling Commission reports that white men hold 95 percent of senior management positions.

The O. J. Simpson trial, in which he is accused of killing his estranged wife and her friend, results in his acquittal, but the lengthy drama also teaches the nation about domestic violence.

The University of California Board of Regents ends affirmative action in admissions, hiring, and contracting on all campuses.

At the UN's Fourth World Conference on Women in Beijing, First Lady Hillary Rodham Clinton speaks out against abuse against women. "It is a violation of human rights when women are denied the right to plan their own families, and that includes being forced to have abortions or being sterilized against their will."

1996 Rape as an instrument of war is defined as a war crime as Serbian military and police officers are indicted on rape charges.

President Clinton is elected for a second term, partly due to women's expectations that he will improve their working and family lives.

President Clinton signs a bill that does away with the national entitlement to welfare for mothers with dependent children, without providing for training or child care. States receive block grants for whatever programs they want to keep or begin.

1998 Independent counsel Kenneth Starr and the far right-wing keep up relentless attacks against Democratic president Bill Clinton. Clinton's affair with Monica Lewinsky provides them with ammunition and ignites a national debate that ends up in the impeachment of the president in 1999, but the Senate acquits him. The vast majority of Americans try to return personal behavior to private life, and support the president. Pundits notice that Americans now seem to be able to distinguish between sexual harassment and a sexual affair. The political Right denounces feminists as hypocrites for their perceived support of Clinton.

1999 The UN reports that women and children still constitute the overwhelming majority of the world's poor and that women are two-thirds of the world's illiterate.

The newest users of the Internet are middle-aged women.

The U.S. women's soccer team battles an evenly matched Chinese team and wins the World Cup trophy by one point in overtime penalty kicks. The nation is suddenly mesmerized by women's soccer.

Boys Don't Cry, a film about a teenager, born a girl, who lives as a young man, with lethal consequences, introduces Americans to a growing transgender civil rights movement.

2000 The Beijing Plus Five meetings at the United Nations assess the progress that each nation has made in implementing the 1995 *Platform for Action*. Activists successfully defend against a well-organized backlash launched by various nations and orthodox religions. Evidence of a global backlash is clearly present.

Violence against clinics that provide abortions continues unabated.

Bangladesh reports that in one year there have been 177 cases of men throwing sulfuric acid in women's faces to express their feelings of anger or rejection. Only a handful of men are jailed. Some women's rights advocates regard it as violation of women's human rights. Others think their society has become too permissive and advocate the return of veiled faces.

Twenty-two million single, divorced, and widowed women, who mostly voted for Democrats due to their relative economic insecurity, do not vote. George W. Bush becomes president.

New Yorkers elect Hillary Rodham Clinton as U.S. Senator.

The Federal Drug Administration approves mifepristone (RU-486) for use in medical abortions, twelve years after its first use in France. At the same time, the number of abortion providers shrinks to a historical low.

On Mother's Day, a "Million Mom March" gathers in Washington, D.C., and in other cities, to end gun violence.

A UNICEF study reports that half of the world's female population has experienced violence or abuse during their lifetimes, and describes it as a "global epidemic."

During a Puerto Rican day parade in New York City, young men grope, strip, and molest at least fifty female bystanders.

2001   President Bush reinstates the Reagan-era global gag rule that prevents any international agency from receiving U.S. funds if it mentions or provides abortions; strips contraceptive coverage from federal employees (which Congress restores); prevents taxpayer funding for additional stem-cell research; and closes the White House Office for Women's Initiatives and Outreach.

For the first time in world history, an international criminal court successfully indicts three Bosnian soldiers for the war crime of raping women during wartime.

Barbara Ehrenreich's *Nickel and Dimed* exposes the poverty of low-wage female workers and remains on the best-seller list for the next five years.

A class-action sex discrimination suit, *Duke v. Wal-Mart Stores*, is

filed in the ninth U.S. District Court and eventually represents
1.6 million former and current female Wal-Mart workers.

Terrorists fly planes into New York's World Trade Center and the
Pentagon on September 11. President Bush declares a "war on terror," and invades and overthrows the Taliban government in
Afghanistan, citing the Taliban's brutal treatment of women as one
justification. Rep. Barbara Lee (D-CA) casts the only vote against
giving the president authority to "use all necessary and appropriate
force" against suspected terrorists.

2002 **The Bush administration withholds $34 million appropriated
by Congress to the U.N. Population Fund for birth control,
arguing (incorrectly) that the money will be used for "coercive
abortions." The U.N. agency estimates that this withdrawl will
result in 800,000 more abortions and 2 million more unwanted
pregnancies. The U.S. State Department freezes $3 million
in funding for the World Health Organization because it
conducts research on mifepristone.**

HBO broadcasts Eve Ensler's play *The Vagina Monologues* and
800 events promote V-Day around the world to fund shelters for
abused women, anti-rape campaigns, and women's centers.

Women who work as painters, steamfitters, plumbers, carpenters,
bricklayers, and other trades form the first nationwide female
trade union—Tradeswomen Now and Tomorrow (TNT).

Halle Berry becomes the first women of color to win an Academy
Award for best actress.

A new international study reveals that hormone replacement
therapy for post-menopausal women does not decrease the danger of heart disease, prevent Alzheimer's disease, urinary incon-
tinence, major depression, or osteoporosis.

The National Organization for Women names Wal-Mart a "Mer-
chant of Shame" for its exploitative working conditions, sex
discrimination, low wages, and unaffordable health benefits.

California becomes the first state to require employers to provide
half pay for six weeks of parental leave. It also obliges accredited
medical schools to offer abortion training, permit nurses, physicians assistants, and midwives to prescribe mifepristone, and
protect abortion rights if *Roe v. Wade* is overturned.

Rep. Nancy Pelosi (D-CA) becomes the first female House
Democratic Whip.

The New York Times begins including same-sex unions among its wedding announcements.

The National Cancer Institute Web site posts an unproven link between abortion and breast cancer and the Centers for Disease Control and Prevention Web site casts doubt on whether condoms effectively protect against pregnancy and sexually transmitted infections. Critics argue the Bush administration is politicizing science.

Time magazine names three women—Enron accountant Sherron Watkins, World Com internal auditor Cynthia Cooper, and FBI agent Coleen Rowley—as "persons of the year" because, as whistleblowers on corporate corruption, they upheld "American values."

President Bush withdraws his support for the U.N. Convention on the Elimination of All Forms of Discrimination Against Women (CEDAW), adopted in 1979 (and signed by 180 nations by the end of 2005).

The U.S. Health and Human Services department announces new rules that make unborn fetuses, but not pregnant women, eligible for prenatal care.

2003 A UNICEF report reveals that the United States still has the highest teen birth rate among the twenty-eight most developed nations. The Bush administration increases spending by $60 million on abstinence-only programs that do not permit discussion of birth control.

Hans Blix, head of the U.N. weapons inspection team, finds no evidence of weapons of mass destruction in Iraq or links between al-Qaeda and Iraq. For the first time in history, some 10 million people on five continents, with many women in leadership positions, march against a war that has not yet begun.

The United States invades Iraq on March 20 after arguing that Saddam Hussein's regime possesses weapons of mass destruction, which are never found.

Joe Wilson, former ambassador to Niger, writes an op-ed publicly critizing the Bush administration for inaccurately stating that Iraq tried to purchase uranium from Niger. Through leaks to the media, unknown top White House officials expose that Wilson's wife, Valerie Plame, is an undercover CIA agent, which endangers national security.

U.S. propaganda casts Private Jessica Lynch as a heroine who fought off Iraqis and was beaten and raped. But she tells the public she did not engage in combat and was well-cared for by Iraqis. Dr. Sally Ride, who became the first female astronaut in 1983 in space on the shuttle Challenger, is inducted into the U.S. Astronaut Hall of Fame.

The Supreme Court strikes down as unconstitutional a Texas law banning sodomy.

A feminist worldwide campaign, which includes many American activists, influences Nigerian courts to overturn a stoning sentence against Amina Lawal for a conviction of adultery.

President Bush signs the so-called "Partial-Birth Abortion Ban" act, banning many late-term terminations.

Shirin Ebadi, an Iranian defender of women's and human rights, is the first Muslim woman to win the Nobel Peace Prize.

The U.S. Census' "American Time-Use Survey" finds that the average working woman spends more than twice as much time on household chores than the average working man.

A study of female cadets at the U.S. Air Force Academy reveals that 70 percent reported sexual harassment and nearly 20 percent were sexually assaulted.

According to a *Ms.* magazine report, more than eight out of ten women feel favorably toward the accomplishments and goals of the women's movement.

2004 Newly elected mayor Gavin Newsom of San Francisco issues marriage licenses to more than four thousand same-sex couples. The Massachusetts Supreme Court, which had held in 2003 that same-sex couples are entitled to the "protection, benefits, and obligations of civil marriage," starts issuing same-sex wedding licenses.

President Bush calls for a constitutonal amendment banning same-sex marriage. The legislation fails in Congress.

Revelations about the torture of detainees at Abu Ghraib and Guantánamo shock the nation. Although Lynndie England and other low-ranking soldiers are found guilty, no high-level administration officials are accused of war crimes or of violating the Geneva Accords.

President Bush signs the Unborn Victims of Violence Act, intended to confer legal personhood on the fetus.

The March for Women's Lives, thought to be the largest protest in the nation's history, draws more than a million people to Washington, D.C., to defend women's rights to reproductive health and abortion. **Ignoring the scientific recommendations of its own panel of experts, the FDA denies women over-the-counter access to Plan B emergency contraception.**

Women's wrestling is added to the Olympic games and transsexuals are permitted to compete for the first time.

Congress denies funding for abortions to female soldiers, even for victims of rape or incest.

Wangari Maathai, an African activist famous for planting trees as part of the Green Belt Movement, and a strong advocate for a sustainable environment, peace, and women's rights, becomes the first African woman to win the Nobel Peace Prize.

PBS anchor Gwen Ifill stumps both Vice President Dick Cheney and Senator John Edwards during a vice presidential debate with a question about how they would address the AIDS epidemic among African American women.

The Census Bureau reports the wage gap between women and men widening in 2003, with women earning only 75.5 cents on men's dollar.

The four "Jersey Girls," widows of 9/11 victims, prod a reluctant White House, after 441 days, to create an independent panel to investigate the terrorist attacks of September 11, 2001.

A congressional report says that two-thirds of the federally funded "abstinence-only" programs contain "false, misleading, or distorted information about reproductive health."

President Bush is reelected. The gender gap (the difference between male and female votes) shrinks to 7 percent, partly due to fears about security and terrorism. The youth vote increases by 9.3 percent.

2005 Condoleezza Rice becomes the first female African American Secretary of State.

Lawrence Summers, president of Harvard University, ignites a national controversy when he speculates that women may be inferior to men in the field of science. (By February 2006, he is forced to resign.)

Islamic women hold the first women-led, mixed-gender Islamic prayer in New York, sparking a worldwide controversy among Muslims.

South Africa becomes the fifth country—joining the Netherlands, Belgium, Spain, and Canada—to legalize same-sex marriage. England and New Zealand legalize civil unions.

The Baltimore Symphony Orchestra hires the first female conductor to head a major American orchestra.

Cindy Sheehan, the mother of soldier Casey Sheehan who died in Iraq on April 2004, reinvigorates the antiwar movement when she camps outside President Bush's ranch in Crawford, Texas, until he will explain why her son died.

China officially outlaws sexual harassment and family violence.

Women in Silicon Valley hold a conference to address their relative invisibility in the blogosphere and in cyberspace.

At the U.N. Beijing Plus Ten Conference, delegates reaffirm the 1995 Beijing Plan for Action, a broad platform that asserted women's rights as human rights. Many view the U.S. rightward political turn as a major obstacle for improving women's status around the world. Activists call for mainstreaming gender concerns into development, diplomacy, and peacemaking.

Hurricane Katrina causes catastrophic destruction of the Gulf Coast. The people most affected are those households headed by African American women, among the poorest in the region.

Network television broadcasts *Commander in Chief*, the first series about a woman assuming the presidency of the United States.

Rosa Parks, who ignited the Montgomery Bus boycott when she refused to give up her front bus seat in 1955, dies at age 92. She is the first female African American whose body lies in state in the Capitol rotunda.

Access to abortion becomes a serious problem: One-third of American women live in areas where there are no providers.

The film *Brokeback Mountain* challenges an iconic image of American masculinity by showing ranch hands whose love endures throughout their marriages and adult lives.

Mukhtaran Bibi, gang-raped in Pakistan on a local council order for crimes committed by her brother, is honored by *Glamour* magazine as a "woman of the year." With funds from compensation and *New York Times* readers, she builds girls' schools in her village, but fears assassination.

The Sundance Channel broadcasts an eight-part documentary series, *Transgeneration*, that follows four transgender college students for a year. A feature film, *TransAmerica*, tells the story of a transgender woman who discovers she has fathered a teenage son.

Forty years after the modern women's movement began, women make up 15 percent of both houses of Congress, at least 50 percent of those enrolled in law and medical schools, and 46 percent of the U.S. labor force.

Ellen Johnson-Sirleaf, elected president of Liberia, is the first female leader of an African nation; Angela Merkel becomes the first female chancellor of Germany.

2006   Betty Friedan, author of the groundbreaking 1963 *Feminine Mystique*, dies at age 85.

Coretta King, who took up the nonviolent civil rights campaign of her assassinated husband, dies at age 78.

Effa Manley is the first woman elected to the baseball Hall of Fame. A white woman who passed as an African American, she co-owned (with her black husband) the New Jersey–based Eagles, who won the Negro Leagues World Series in 1946.

Progressive Michelle Bachelet wins the presidency in Chile. Serious speculation about Senator Hillary Rodham Clinton's presidential aspirations suggests that an American woman president is no longer unimaginable.

South Dakota passes legislation banning all abortions in the state, including for victims of rape and incest, setting up a direct challenge to *Roe v. Wade*.

The 2006 American Time Use Survey released by the Labor Bureau finds that women, regardless of marital status, spend more time on housework and child care than men. More specifically, women report spending one hour a day on housework and three-quarters of an hour on food prepartion, while men do fifteen minutes on each task. More than half of the women surveyed said they had done housework in the past twenty-four hours, while only one in five men had; 66 percent of women had prepared meals versus 37 percent of men. Additionally women with children spent twice as much time caring for them as men with children.

Democrats win both houses of Congress in the midterm elections and Nancy Pelosi (D–San Francisco) becomes the first female speaker of the House of Representatives.

Part One:

REFUGEES FROM THE FIFTIES

Chapter One

❧

DAWN OF DISCONTENT

"Until I was twenty-eight," wrote the poet Anne Sexton, "I had a kind of buried self who didn't know she could do anything but make white sauce and diaper babies. I didn't know I had any creative depths. I was a victim of the American Dream, the bourgeois, middle-class dream. All I wanted was a little piece of life, to be married, to have children. I thought the nightmares, the visions, the demons would go away if there was enough love to put them down. I was trying my damnedest to lead a conventional life, for that was how I was brought up, and it was what my husband wanted of me. But one can't build little white picket fences to keep nightmares out. The surface cracked when I was about twenty-eight. I had a psychotic breakdown and tried to kill myself."[1]

Anne Sexton was a deeply troubled artist, but many housewives shared her depression and her demons. More than a few women secretly experienced the fifties as a private nightmare, something observant daughters of the time noted with alarm. Sensing the bitterness and disappointment of so many adult women, these daughters came of age eagerly mapping escapes from what they regarded as the claustrophobic constraints of the fifties. "As we grew older," one woman explained, "we saw our mothers—our role models, the women we were to become—thwarted in their efforts toward self-realization and expression. A deep and bitter lesson, this one—and one we couldn't take lightly. It reverberated through the core of our beings, and we resolved not to let it happen to us; we resolved to be different."[2]

WOMEN AT HOME

In 1963, a housewife and former labor union journalist named Betty Friedan published the results of interviews she had conducted with other women who had been educated at Smith College. In the privacy of their suburban homes, these housewives had revealed the depths of their despair to her. Blessed with good providers, nice homes, and healthy children, they puzzled over their unhappiness. Not knowing that other women shared their troubles, they experienced them as personal and blamed themselves for their misery. Friedan called this inchoate unhappiness "the problem that has no name."

To quell their conflicts, some of the interviewees gulped tranquilizers, cooked gourmet meals, or scrutinized their children as though they were rare insects. In search of stimulation, some housewives had sought out sexual affairs or volunteered their time to churches, schools, and charitable organizations. Some women stuffed their houses with shiny new laborsaving devices. Yet, despite these material comforts, something still seemed to be missing. Many of these educated women, Friedan discovered, had nurtured dreams that were never realized, but also never forgotten. The postwar conviction that women should limit their lives exclusively to home and hearth had tied them to the family, closed other opportunities, and crushed many spirits. Friedan dubbed this powerful belief system "the feminine mystique," and her book *The Feminine Mystique* became an instant best-seller.

In many ways, Betty Friedan's background made her an ideal person to expose such domestic unhappiness to the American public. Born and reared in Peoria, Illinois, Betty Goldstein graduated from Smith College in 1942, already well versed in left-wing ideals of social justice and economic equality. After college, she joined the swirling intellectual and political world of leftist politics, worked as a journalist, and in 1947 married Carl Friedan. When she became pregnant with her second child, she was fired by her employer—not an unusual experience for working women at the time.

She and her husband then settled into a suburban life in which she experienced firsthand the isolation of a housewife. But even as she raised three children, she continued to write for mainstream women's magazines. To ease her own burdens as a mother and a writer, she hired a housekeeper, but when other housewives described the isolation and narrowness of their lives, she clearly understood their frustration. She also had the political savvy to see the significance of their complaints and the skills with which to describe them movingly on paper. Readers of her book, in turn, imagined her as a sister housewife, trapped in the gilded cage of a suburban home, restless and impatient to lead a life of her own.

In fact, Friedan already had a life of her own, one far more politicized than that of the average housewife or magazine writer. As a longtime activist on the antifascist Left and in union struggles, and as an experienced labor journalist for the *UE News*, the newsletter of the United Electrical, Radio and Machine Workers of America, Friedan had early targeted the plight of women workers. In 1952, she wrote a manual titled *UE Fights for Women Workers*, which described how one of the most Communist-influenced unions of the postwar era had fought against the discrimination of women workers.

Although she continued to write about women's problems throughout the fifties, Friedan never thought of herself as a feminist. "By the time I got to college," she explained, "the first century of struggle for women's rights had been blotted out of the national memory and the national consciousness." True enough. But to women in and around "the popular front" of the 1930s (the loose political alliance among Communist, Progressive, and labor groups against Fascism), the very word "feminist" conjured up images of spoiled bourgeois ladies who voted Republican. Women of the Left instead debated "the Woman Question" or the plight of female workers, but certainly not the problems of middle-class housewives.[3]

When Friedan wrote *The Feminine Mystique*, she chose to omit her radical past from her account of her life. Early drafts of the manuscript reveal a far more daring vision, including a proposal for national legislation to create a "GI Bill" to promote women's education. But in a country that had only recently passed through the violently anti-Communist convulsion known as "McCarthyism," Friedan feared her ideas would be discredited if she focused on the problems of working women or advocated government intervention in the affairs of women. So she settled on a safer strategy, that of addressing middle-class white housewives as a sister suburbanite.[4]

Gerda Lerner, a longtime activist and future historian of women, worried about this decision: "I have just finished reading your splendid book and want to tell you how excited and delighted I am with it. . . . You have done for women . . . what Rachel Carson [author of the pioneering ecological exposé *Silent Spring*, 1962] did for the birds and trees." But she also criticized Friedan's exclusion of black, poor, and working women, anticipating what would become a widespread criticism of *The Feminine Mystique*, as well as of the contemporary women's movement. But Friedan made a choice to be heard, not to be "Red-baited," and in America, that meant addressing the middle class. So she concentrated on the power of the feminine mystique, creating a concept through which she then accused the entire society and culture—the media, science, psychiatry, education, and social sciences—of a mass conspiracy to limit the lives of women.[5]

Not surprisingly, Friedan's accusations incited widespread hostility. "Many were violently outraged," she later wrote, "at the charge that American women have been seduced back into the doll's house, living through their husbands and children instead of finding individual identity in the modern world. I was cursed, pitied, told to get psychiatric help, to go jump in the lake and accused of being 'more of a threat to the United States than the Russians.' " But many American magazines and journals also reviewed *The Feminine Mystique* positively. Excerpted in several women's magazines, read by three million people, debated in the *Boston Globe*, the book reached a huge population of American women and men.[6]

Using the language of personal growth, Friedan challenged women to live an examined and purposeful life. With the publication of *The Feminine Mystique*, each housewife, at last, knew she was not alone. "We can no longer ignore that voice within women that says: 'I want something more than my husband and my children and my home.' " With phrases as simple as that, Friedan opened a Pandora's box and out tumbled the unnamed complaints that would mobilize one potential constituency of the modern women's movement.

For some housewives, Friedan's revelations came not a minute too soon. Letters arrived by the hundreds, as housewives poured out their confusion, despair, self-contempt, or determination to change. Readers came from backgrounds that bore little resemblance to the college-educated housewives whose complaints filled the book. Written by hand, sometimes in crayon or pencil, some letters were barely literate, and not the products of college graduates, but these women, too, knew that something was seriously wrong with their lives. They blessed Friedan, asked her for advice, described their despair, and begged for advice about how to change their lives. "Help!" pleaded one woman. "I have read your views on woman's emancipation and thoroughly agree with you on all accounts—but—how does one go about it?" Some women painfully revealed their sense of hopelessness, the arrogance of psychiatrists they had consulted, the indifference of their husbands. Still others wrote of the changes they were in the process of making: the return to school; the search for a new job; even simple symbolic acts like the purchase of a toy stethoscope for a baby daughter.[7]

From Florida, a mother of four wrote Friedan, "I have been trying for years to tell my husband of my need to do something to find myself—to have a purpose. All I've ever achieved was to end up feeling guilty about wanting to be more than a housewife and mother." A housewife from Massachusetts questioned the very meaning of her existence: "I have for the past ten years now been asking myself: 'Is this all there is to life?' I am a housewife and mother of five children. I have had a very poor education. I am 38 years old, and if this is all there is for me to look forward to, I don't want to go on." A Wyoming woman wrote that "few books have had such an impact." Wondering how to pull her life together at age thirty-seven, she confided to Friedan,

> My secret scream as I stir the oatmeal, iron the blue jeans, and sell pop at the Little League baseball games is "Stop the World, I want to get on Before it's too late!" I love my family dearly and wouldn't trade them, or my life with them, for *anything*. But as they go out each day to meet, and get involved in this great big wonderful world, I yearn to tag along!

A female politician wrote that her career had blessedly kept her from feeling "trapped." An unhappy housewife who described her daily obsession with changing her life wrote, "I owe you a debt of eternal gratitude." Like many readers, she had passed her copy of the book on to friends. From one radicalized housewife arrived these encouraging words: "If you ever need partisans for your revolution or endorsements for your product, you can count on this 'saved' housewife for undying support."[8]

For all its insights, *The Feminine Mystique* was not without shortcomings. Well-acquainted with social and economic analysis, Friedan nevertheless focused on the psychological search for a new identity outside the home. She ignored the different obstacles faced by working-class and minority women, championed careers as though women could easily find well-paid, meaningful work in a sex-segregated labor force, and failed to question the presumption that women bore responsibility for all domestic work. In short, her book, which emphasized the claustrophobic character of domesticity, was a call for self-realization, not a statement of feminist public policy. Still, she had broken the silence and had begun unmasking the reality of women's lives.

COLD WAR CONTAINMENT

The fifties was an age of cognitive dissonance: millions of people believed in ideals that poorly described their own experience. The decade quarantined dissent and oozed conformity. On the pages of *Life* magazine, on the new television screens, Americans—the white and well-fed variety—radiated wholesomeness, cleanliness, fecundity, and fidelity. Liberated by shiny new appliances, apron-clad mothers played with their boisterous broods. Rosy-cheeked fathers jauntily swung their briefcases as they strolled off to work. On Sunday afternoons, families on television and in magazines gathered around their barbecues and celebrated their good fortune. It was as though someone had banished poverty, prejudice, and pain from public culture.[9]

But just beneath the surface, many real Americans, unlike their media counterparts, experienced anxiety and confusion. While the media painted a roseate portrait of suburban motherhood and the happy nuclear family, growing numbers of women actually entered the labor force, lesbians and gays cracked open the closet door as they created underground organizations, leftist activists brought a progressive agenda into mainstream organizations, domestic discontent simmered, urban poverty and racial segregation increased as whites began their flight to the suburbs, and the young quietly began crossing over an unbridgeable generational divide.[10]

Far from being a shelter from the storm of American life, the family proved to be the storm itself. Despite lip service to age-old verities, values had indeed shifted. The men and women who married in the late forties and fifties entered a changing culture as if they were sailors at sea in uncharted waters. Reared in the Depression, most had grown up in a culture that valued duty, thrift, long-term commitment, and an old-fashioned work ethic. But they married and bore children in a culture of abundance that prized planned obsolescence and disposability, glamorized leisure, and promised individual happiness through the purchase of products. Ironically, the very consumer culture that celebrated "togetherness" also addressed husbands, wives, and children as individuals with promises of personal freedom and autonomy.[11]

Though divorce was still rare, Americans began getting a bad case of the marital jitters. *Ladies' Home Journal* regularly published a column titled "Can This Marriage Be Saved?" Marital counseling became more popular in the late 1950s as couples tried to avoid the even worse stigma of divorce. Schools offered special programs on "marriage and the family." The 1957 founding of Parents without Partners, an organization dedicated to providing emotional and social comfort for newly divorced parents, signaled the growing problem of familial disintegration.[12]

The setting for such family life, was, of course, the newly built suburbs that altered the social landscape, leaving the poor, minorities, singles, the childless, lesbians and gay men, and bohemian culture behind in the cities. The suburban population doubled in one decade from thirty-six million to seventy-two million people. By the end of the fifties, one-fourth of all Americans had found a small, sunny oasis of open space in the suburbs. Ironically, at the peak of anti-Communist fervor, few Americans seemed to realize that what made this exodus possible were public subsidies for higher education for veterans, low-interest home loans for GIs, the private automobile, and interstate highways, all paid for by the federal government in the name of containing Communism.[13]

If a storm was brewing unexpectedly within the sacred confines of the family, there was another storm out there in the world that directly endangered home and hearth. The Cold War pitted the United States against the Union of Soviet Socialist Republics, capitalism against Communism, one nuclear-armed superpower against the other. It was a "war" that could not be fought directly for fear of causing global nuclear extinction. To contain Communism and to win the "hearts and minds" of Third World and unaligned nations, the U.S. government threw a circle of strategic bases around the globe. The two superpowers settled into a policy of deterrence, which, if it worked forever, would prevent Mutually Assured Destruction, dubbed, appropriately enough, MAD. Then, instead of annihilating each other, the two countries embarked upon a series of "proxy" wars, some of which threatened to turn the Cold War into a scorching conflagration.

On the home front, demonic images of the Soviet Union unleashed a moral panic, a "great fear" that penetrated all aspects of American culture and society. Like the Devil, Communism seemed to lurk everywhere, capable of inhabiting the soul of any individual. Vigilance, the government insisted, was essential. The search for Communists in American life became an obsession. Loyalty oaths, indictments, and blacklists crippled thousands of lives. Fear of internal sabotage and subversion crushed dissent. In 1950, Joseph McCarthy rose to power on a tsunami of anti-Communist hysteria, proclaiming Communists to be in every nook and cranny of American life, and at the very highest reaches of the American government. He fell only when his futile attacks against the United States Army—broadcast to millions of Americans in their living rooms—exposed his hateful persecution of innocent people. But to true believers, political treason, like religious heresy, endangered the nation's moral covenant with God. In the name of that covenant, Ethel and Julius Rosenberg, convicted of espionage, were executed in 1953.

The red-baiting witch hunts that Joseph McCarthy came to symbolize and that took his name—McCarthyism—coincided with what might be characterized as a national emotional breakdown. The Cold War recruited everyone and all resources into the national battle against the Soviet Union. Like a colonial jeremiad, a 1950s civil defense pamphlet warned, "Our nation is in a grim struggle for national survival and the preservation of the world."[14] Americans mobilized the military, the civilian population, the economy, education, and even children for what seemed like an interminable war. *My Weekly Reader*, a scholastic news magazine, unleashed a barrage of anti-Communist propaganda at elementary-school students in order to produce another generation of Cold Warriors. The Boy Scouts, worried about American men's growing "softness," pledged to toughen boys' physical and psychological strength to fight Communism. Universities shifted their attention to the kind of basic research and defense projects required to counter Soviet expansionism. The military sent families to join soldiers at strategic bases, as ambassadors for a superior way of life.[15]

Anti-Communism also helped contain the storm brewing within the home. American women could be mobilized without a single woman leaving her suburban home for work. The belief that American superiority rested on its booming consumer culture and rigidly defined gender roles became strangely intertwined with Cold War politics. In 1959, at an American National Exhibition in Moscow, Vice President Richard Nixon and Soviet Premier Nikita Khruschchev engaged in a bizarre "kitchen debate." As historian Elaine May has noted, "The two leaders did not discuss missiles, bombs, or even modes of government. Rather, they argued over the relative merits of American and Soviet washing machines, televisions, and electric ranges."[16]

As they toured model American homes, Nixon boasted of the labor-saving devices that gave American women time to cultivate their charms as wives and to care for their children. "What we want is to make easier the life of our housewives," said Nixon. Khrushchev testily retorted that the Soviet Union had little use for full-time housewives. Its women workers were busy building an industrial society. Tracking this bizarre debate, the American press compared the "bedraggled drudges" of the Soviet Union, who lost their looks at an early age and neglected their children, with the well-groomed American housewives whose leisure allowed them to care for themselves, as well as their families.[17]

The advertising industry quickly geared up to instruct new home-makers in the ways they could help fight Communism. In 1954, a *McCall's* magazine editorial coined the ideal of "togetherness," a concept designed to slow the centrifugal forces that were already spinning members of the family in different directions. Speaking before the Wilmington City Federation of Women's Clubs, a director of Du Pont reminded his female audience that they were no longer just housewives. "You are 'Managers of Destiny,'" he told them, "perfectly positioned to fight socialism."

> This is where you women can be of tremendous help—by everlastingly teaching and preaching the values of individu-alism and of personal freedom, and by keeping alive a burn-ing faith in our philosophy of incentive and free choice. . . . Socialists have tried to relieve the individual of all responsi-bility. . . . Only women, with their "independence," can fight for individual liberty.[18]

Simply put, the nation needed women to fuel the growing consumer economy. Anita Colby, an author and consultant, lectured businessmen on how to decipher the mysterious ways of the female consumer:

> She, too, gets restless . . . but unlike you, she can't head for a bar alone at night to spend a few hours of relaxation. No, re-stricted to home and children, she takes it out in a new color of hair—or calls in a decorator to do over the house—and

may even surprise you when you come home one day with a ripped-up lawn bearing all the ear-marks of a swimming-pool in embryo! At the very least, she'll buy herself a new hat. This is bad, you think? Well, all you cosmetic manufacturers, makers of textiles, furniture, housewares, plumbing appliances, and millinery experts think about your annual sales-figures!! Honestly now, where would you be without the little woman's rebellion?[19]

It didn't take much to convince postwar men and women that the United States, and not the Soviet Union, offered the good life. Between 1945 and 1960, the gross national product leaped 250 percent. In 1955, with only 6 percent of the world's population, the United States produced half the world's goods. By 1960, 60 percent of Americans belonged to the middle class, and owned their own homes; 75 percent of farmers owned their own lands. The discretionary income of the middle class doubled: 87 percent owned televisions, 75 percent owned washing machines, and ten million citizens owned shares in American companies.[20]

The growing middle class had to ignore a great deal as they celebrated their material success. Racial segregation and discrimination still ruled the South. As the middle class expanded, the rich grew richer, while the poor slid further into grinding poverty. The nation's wealth, moreover, rested, as one observer noted, "on Hydrogen bombs, B-52 bombers, a nuclear navy, guided missiles . . . the potential Armageddon . . . death supporting life." The American Dream—a wife, children, ownership of a home, a car, and "the good things in life"—had finally come within reach of a critical mass of men.

After the political demise of Joseph McCarthy in 1954, Americans caught their breath and began to settle down to enjoy the domestic affluence they had purchased—or so they thought—through such extremities of vigilance. But McCarthyism had seeped deep into the culture, like toxic waste that poisons the earth long after officials declare a hazardous accident is over. Dissent—supposedly the touchstone of a democratic society—became linked in the popular mind with Communist sympathizers. Anti-Communism also cast a shadow of self-censorship across the intellectual landscape, destroying a credible non-Communist Left, squelching intellectual and political opposition, and forcing a political consensus that glossed over America's simmering racial, gender, economic, ecological, and social problems.[21]

In such an atmosphere, even marriage and childbearing became politicized. A majority of Americans judged men or women who did not marry as "sick," thinking them either immoral, selfish, or neutrotic. As "difference" became synonymous with "deviant," people began to regard such men or women with suspicion, their refusal to mate hinting at some "antisocial" secret like homosexual or Communist tendencies. FBI director J. Edgar Hoover even encouraged women to marry early and have children to fight "the twin enemies of freedom—crime and Communism."[22]

Young couples married and bore children with an enthusiasm that confounded demographers' predictions of a falling birthrate. Fueled by a pent-up desire for family life after the Depression and war, they married earlier, slowed the rising divorce rate, and reversed a century's decline in the fertility rate by producing the biggest baby boom in history (from 1946 to 1964). At its peak in 1957, American women gave birth to over four million babies a year. A parade of baby carriages and bulging profiles transformed the landscape of America's parks, leaving one stunned foreign observer to note that "every other young housewife I see is pregnant."[23]

The feminine mystique also had a profound influence on popular culture. An unmarried woman was an embarrassment. Hollywood scripts of the time required career women to acknowledge marriage as the source of all happiness. In the 1955 film *The Tender Trap*, Debbie Reynolds successfully auditions for her first big acting job. Dismissing congratulations from her agent, Frank Sinatra, she dutifully repeats the catechism of those years: "Marriage is the most important thing in the world. A woman isn't really a woman until she's been married and had children." Later, the poet Adrienne Rich would express the pressure that so many actual women felt at the time.

> As soon as I was visibly and clearly pregnant I felt, for the first time in my adolescent and adult life, not-guilty. The atmosphere of approval in which I was bathed—even by strangers on the street, it seemed—was like an aura I carried with me, in which doubts, fears, misgivings, met with absolute denial. *This is what women have always done.*[24]

Fashion played an important role in constructing and constricting the new feminine and maternal image of the postwar era. The simple, broad-shouldered, man-tailored clothing of the war years gave way to

Christian Dior's "New Look," a style that exaggerated feminine curves and a womanly silhouette. Lacquered bouffant hairdos and starkly outlined eyes and mouths advertised an exaggerated if untouchable female sexuality. "Fifties clothes were like armor," the writer Brett Harvey recalled:

> Our clothes expressed all the contradictions of our roles. Our ridiculously starched skirts and hobbling sheaths were a caricature of femininity. Our cinched waist and aggressively pointed breasts advertised our availability at the same time they warned of our impregnability.[25]

"Experts" rushed to reposition homemaking as a profession. *Life* magazine praised the "increasing emphasis on the nurturing and homemaking values among women who might have at one time pursued a career." Standards of cleanliness steadily climbed as industry redefined laborsaving devices as necessities rather than luxuries. Advertisements mercilessly attacked women's insecurities as mothers, wives, and housekeepers. To protect their children, mothers had to scour and sanitize their homes. A *professional* homemaker sewed her own clothes, preserved her own fruits and vegetables, developed the arts of an experienced chef, and decorated her home with the skills of an interior designer. Add in the nearly eight hours a week that many suburban housewives spent in a car chauffeuring about their brood and doing errands, and it becomes clear why suburban housewives spent more time consumed by housework, broadly defined, than had their grandmothers.[26]

The professionalization of the housewife turned the act of consumption into a patriotic act and kept American industry humming. Industrial psychologists advised manufacturers on how to make a housewife feel professional: "When a housewife uses one product for washing clothes, a second for dishes, a third for walls, a fourth for floors, a fifth for venetian blinds, rather than an all-purpose cleaner, she feels less like an unskilled laborer and more like an engineer." Later, one disgruntled fifties woman quipped, "The Good Housekeeping seal of approval was the brand of the slave."[27]

More important than her homemaking skills or her appearance was a woman's role as a mother. Dr. Benjamin Spock, the author of the 1946 best-seller *The Common Sense Book of Baby Care*, the child-raising bible of that era, insisted that babies needed constant attention. Without a mother at home, children languished or, worse, became juvenile delinquents. A good mother always greeted her children after school with affection and nourishment. "More important than any meal," remembered one daughter of the fifties, "the after-school milk and cookies were akin to Eucharistic substance, symbolic of nurture and love."[28]

Spock, a paragon of child permissiveness, strongly encouraged mothers to stay at home with their children. "If a mother realizes clearly how vital this kind of care is to a small child," he explained, "it may make it easier for her to decide that the extra money she might earn, or the satisfaction she might receive from an outside job, is not so important after all." When child care became too overwhelming, the distraught mother was advised to "go to a movie, or to the beauty parlor, or to get a new dress or hat." But mothers, it turned out, could also do too much. Four years before Spock, Philip Wylie's bestselling book *Generation of Vipers* set the tone for blaming mothers for everything that seemed wrong in the postwar era. Economic disaster, religious apathy, and the nervous breakdowns of soldiers during and after battle were all attributable to mothers' overly protective domination of their sons, which he dubbed "Momism." America's mothers now had to walk the fine line between neglect and smothering overprotection. If they worked outside their homes, they risked creating a generation of juvenile delinquents. If they stayed home and smothered their children, they risked producing a generation of denatured, sissified young men.[29]

THE BIG LIE

After her children were asleep and her housework was done, it was hardly time for a woman to fall into bed, exhausted or depressed. A housewife still needed to exchange her apron for an outfit that would rekindle her husband's sexual interest in her. The expanding consumer culture depended heavily on women's repeated purchases of beauty products. But the formula didn't always work. Behind closed doors, many marriages seemed deeply troubled, and at the heart of those troubles was the nature of female sexuality.

The war years had witnessed increased teenage prostitution, greater sexual activity among both heterosexuals and homosexuals, and escalating marital infidelity. After the war, Americans tried to "contain" such disorderly sexual behavior. But it turned out that sexual expectations had, in fact, changed. Panicked social critics encouraged early marriage, hoping it might put a brake on youthful sexual experimentation. And sometimes it did, but when it couldn't, sexual hypocrisy became a way of life. Society still expected men to have experience and women to have none. The same culture that increasingly exploited sex to promote products still insisted on the appearance of virginal innocence in its girls and women.[30]

After the war, dating turned into a highly elaborate form of courtship in which male aggression and female passivity were carefully prescribed and encoded. "In the fifties," one woman remembered, "the only thing worse than sleeping with a man was to telephone him." Every step in male commitment permitted freer sexual activity, as kissing escalated into necking, necking slid into petting, and heavy petting stopped only a technical step before "going all the way." "We started dating," recalled one woman, "and we kept on dating until we got married my junior year. In between we did the whole bit. First, he gave me his class ring, then the lavaliere—the necklace with the letters of his fraternity. Next came the fraternity pin, until, da-dum, the engagement ring." Although a bevy of experts and teen magazines strongly advocated "saving oneself for marriage," one woman later admitted, "Everybody was doing it. But it was the Big Lie that nobody was."[31]

Couples expected an "eroticized marriage" and looked for advice from experts. Eustace Chesser, the author of the widely read *Love Without Fear* (1947), kept in print in paperback through the fifties, popularized the idea that marital bliss required mutual orgasm. The most widely read marriage manual of the decade, *Ideal Marriage: Its Physiology and Technique*, written by the Dutch physician Th. H. Van de Velde in 1930 and reprinted thirty-two times between 1941 and 1957, went a step further, declaring, "Every considerable erotic stimulation of their wives that does not terminate in orgasm, on the women's part, represents an injury, and repeated injuries of this kind lead to permanent—or very obstinate—damage to both body and soul."

The growing popularity of the simultaneous orgasm, however doctrinaire, also presumed that women should experience orgasmic fulfillment. Yet, that was not what women's magazines reported. They brooded about American women's frigidity—the decade's term for everything from sexual boredom to nonorgasmic sex. The medical and psychiatric community, heavily influenced by Freudian doctrine, blamed women for refusing to accept their true feminine identity. They insisted that two kinds of orgasms existed, vaginal and clitoral, but that only one was of value. For them, a clitoral orgasm was, by definition, the immature response of a neurotic and frigid woman who willfully refused to surrender to her feminine destiny. Achieved by male penetration, the vaginal orgasm demonstrated a woman's true affirmation of her feminine maturity.[32]

No one knows how many women spent those years doubting their femininity because they had never experienced the much-touted vaginal orgasm. No doubt there were many. In one study of white middle-class couples, one-third of women claimed they had never achieved orgasm. Some of these women perhaps mistook emotional emptiness for sexual dissatisfaction. Betty Friedan grew bewildered when housewives gave her "an explicitly sexual answer to a question that was not sexual at all." Could it be, she wondered, that they viewed sex as a substitute for a "forfeited self"?[33]

It was difficult to know. "Frigidity" probably had many causes, including guilt. Over 80 percent of the women Alfred Kinsey interviewed for his study of female sexuality expressed moral objections to premarital sex, but half of them nevertheless violated their own values. One divorced woman later explained the source of her sexual problems:

> My experience *being with* my to-be husband succeeded in conditioning me to utter subservience to *his* satisfaction and he never thought mine could be other than automatic upon his (else I was "frigid" or wrong somehow). And he is and was a psychoanalyst! I remain as I was—unfulfilled.

After marriage, some wives who had engaged in premarital sex wondered if their husbands still "respected" them.

> I feel this gradual introduction to the sex experience has advantages over being plunged into it suddenly on the wedding night. However, it carried with it for me a high sense of guilt, which still bothers me after all these years. I am forever grateful that we did finally marry because I probably wouldn't have felt free to marry anyone else. This feeling of guilt may be why I am unable to respond sexually as I wish I could.[34]

Ignorance of anatomy and sexuality was also widespread. One woman, who had saved herself for marriage, wondered "whether or not the lack of sexual experience before marriage marred our early days of marriage . . . but I believe a better understanding of woman's nature on the part of [my husband] . . . could have helped considerably. After seventeen years, this understanding is still lacking." Another woman revealed that she "didn't know anything about orgasms":

> The first time . . . we were in his room in his dorm. It was fast—he came in and he came out. It was a sharp, poignant pleasure that had no resolution. It stayed like that, it never got any better. He would come in and then pull out and come into a handkerchief. I was always left hanging. I used to come back to my dorm and lie down on the floor and howl and pound the floor. But I didn't really know why I was frustrated. I felt so lonely.[35]

The truth is, it was difficult to switch from virginal bride to sexy wife. As Barbara Ehrenreich, Elizabeth Hess, and Gloria Jacobs have argued, women—not men—made the sexual revolution. Between the fifties and the eighties, men's sexual behavior changed very little. They still enjoyed premarital sexual experiences in their youth, married, and afterward perhaps strayed with other women. But during the same period, as Ehrenreich has pointed out, women moved "from a pattern of virginity before marriage and monogamy thereafter to a pattern that much more resembles men's."

Even before the sixties, a sexual revolution simmered, but it had not yet boiled over. Women received confusing messages from a culture in transition. Society still divided the female population into "good" and "bad" women. The spreading use of birth control—diaphragms and condoms—helped rupture the historic tie between sex and procreation, but they were for planning babies, not for pleasure. Despite the expectation of an "eroticized" marriage, many people still felt shy about discussing sexual matters in public or, for that matter, in private. Advice manuals emphasized the desirability of female orgasm but assumed the woman would remain passive and stressed the man's effort. Marriage manuals encouraged men to satisfy their wives but faulted women for being "frigid." A Freudian-saturated culture promoted the crackpot notion that women achieved sexual satisfaction exclusively through vaginal penetration. Private behavior contrasted sharply with public pronouncements of marital fidelity and sexual innocence. Some women felt guilty if they had sex before marriage and guiltier still if they had too few orgasms afterward. Sexual advice had changed, but traditional attitudes had not. The fact is, women really weren't sure what they were supposed to feel. Some women, not surprisingly, felt nothing at all. The result: too many women "faked it" and too few men noticed.

Many men, too, felt suffocated by the self-conscious "togetherness" demanded of the suburban family. By the mid-fifties, a few Beats and playboys began to search for escape routes from the traditional obligation to support families. But most men didn't flee. As one husband explained, "You stayed with the decisions you made in your early twenties. You stuck with your job. You stuck with your wife. You stuck with everything." And if life became too hard, men used liquor or other women to cope with their dissatisfaction.[36]

The manly courage so powerfully portrayed in the Westerns, detective stories, or war films of the era mocked the actual lives men led as suburban husbands. Growing numbers of them worked in industries and corporations that stripped them of autonomy, dictated the terms of their work, and rewarded conformity and teamwork more than personal initiative. Despite the popularity of a tough-fisted masculinity in the popular media, American men were also becoming more liberal and more open-minded. In 1959, a poll revealed that more men than women said they would vote for a woman president. And just as men were losing authority at work, growing numbers of mothers and wives were expanding theirs by joining men in the labor force.[37]

WOMEN AT WORK

Although the image of the American housewife dominated popular culture, "the most striking feature of the fifties," as historian William Chafe has noted, "was the degree to which women continued to enter the job market and expand their sphere." Between 1940 and 1960, the number of working women doubled, rising from 15 percent to 30 percent, and the proportion of married working mothers jumped 400 percent. By 1955, more women worked in the labor force than had during World War II, when women had been mobilized to support America's fighting men.[38]

This was not what government policy had intended. Even before the war's end, public planners had tried to wean American women from their wartime jobs. A job manual written for female war workers reminded them that "the mother stands at the heart of family life. She it is who will create the world after the war." Apparently, some working women disagreed. A survey conducted immediately after the war by the Bureau of Women Workers revealed that 75 percent of women workers preferred to remain employed outside their homes.[39]

But as military industries wound down, they laid off women who had earned high wages as skilled workers during the war. Newly converted civilian industries gave preferential treatment to demobilized veterans or simply refused to hire women for what was now redefined as "men's work." Faced with shrinking opportunities and reduced pay, some working women looked forward to starting or resuming family life. One woman who worked six days a week during the war knew that "the idea was for women to go back home. The women understood that," she said. "And the men had been promised their jobs when they came back. I was ready to go home. I was tired . . . I knew that it would be coming and I didn't feel any let-down. The experience was interesting, but I couldn't have kept it up forever. It was too hard."[40] But many women had no choice but to seek other work. Rosie the Riveter, the widely celebrated wartime heroine, put down her welding tools and resumed her work as a waitress, barmaid, dishwasher, salesgirl, or domestic.

A decade later, literate, educated housewives discovered that new opportunities had opened up to them. In 1956, the United States officially became a "postindustrial society," with the number of white collar workers exceeding that of industrial laborers. As nonfactory, service-oriented jobs mushroomed, businesses and corporations began to search for single women to hire as secretarial and clerical workers. Since they were in short supply, educated middle-class married mothers, who turned out to be ideal employees, were sought out by business. With their children in school, mothers provided a cheap and fluid labor force whose willingness to accept low wages for part-time work without benefits substantially increased corporate profits.[41]

As a result, the most powerful challenge to the feminine mystique came not from women bored by domestic life, but from a corporate sector that successfully drew women out of their homes and into the workforce. By 1960, married women accounted for 52 percent of the female labor force (up from 36 percent in 1950), double-income families had jumped 222 percent since 1940, and a third of working women were mothers with children under eighteen years of age.[42]

An aspiring middle class had also changed its definition of "economic necessity." Couples now dreamed of a new home, two cars, a college education for their children—both boys and girls—with discretionary income left over for leisure pursuits and vacations. But rising inflation, coupled with higher expectations, meant that many men simply could not provide "the good life" on a single paycheck—although the myth was that they were doing just that. The great irony of the decade was that working mothers—those villains of popular culture—very likely contributed to the relative prosperity of the postwar years. The rise in women's wages (though still low compared to men's), according to some economists, may have even increased the cost of women staying at home. When mothers worked, countless families were able to climb into the middle class and assure their children a college education.[43]

Naturally, some of these working women worried about protecting their husbands' feelings. Children of the Great Depression, they knew exactly how to justify their work outside the home to men and their families; they were "helping out." One working mother knew that "husbands feel bad enough about not being able to handle the whole job without our help."

> Do you think we're going to say right out, "My Joe just can't put five kids through college, and then Sue needed braces last year, and Johnny will need them too, and the washer had to be replaced, and Ann was ashamed to bring friends home because the living room furniture was such a mess, so I went to work"?[44]

Working women also tried not to disrupt family life. One woman recalled how carefully she tried to ensure "that there would be no disruption of the service . . . the cooking, the cleaning."

> We had our family evenings together every night . . . I could have taken a full-time job . . . with benefits and a better salary. I discussed it with my husband and I told him, if I take on this full-time job, I will be taking away something from you that you have to have. You are the breadwinner and . . . I will not take that away from you. To work full-time, I felt I would be taking away his manhood, his feeling of being the head of the household. I never regretted it. We had a good, loving relationship for thirty years.[45]

Although few women at the time admitted that they worked because they were bored, many later confessed that homemaking had left them desperate for greater stimulation and that, after the isolation of the home, they loved the camaraderie of working with other people. Estelle Shuster began working in 1950, when her daughters were twelve and eight. "I went to work, because I was bored in the house."

> My husband was a CPA, he was never home, and when he was, it was the nose in his tax papers or the newspaper over the face. My mother thought it was scandalous that I went to work. And my husband said, "What you're trying to do is make everyone feel as if I can't earn a living for you." Belittling, that was the word he used, he said I was belittling him by working. I said, I don't care how anyone feels, I have to get out of the house.[46]

Some women viewed employment as an insurance policy against an impending empty nest. Women born in 1900 lived on the average 50.8 years. Without birth control, many women kept bearing children until the last decade of their lives. The baby boom, which reversed a century's decline in women's fertility, masked how much a longer life span and fewer children would change women's lives. Daughters born in 1957, who resumed the pattern of late marriages and fewer children, could expect to live 72.8 years, giving them thirty or forty years to reinvent their lives after their last child left home.[47]

Like housewives, working women faced formidable obstacles and problems for which there existed no language. At age twenty-five, Doris Earnshaw, a married graduate of Middlebury College, who had already taught in a French college, decided to apply to graduate school in French literature at the University of California, Berkeley.

> The Chairman of the Department said to me (in French), "I am sorry, madame, you are very well qualified, but we do not take married ladies." The words still ring in my ears. I felt shut out (and effectively was shut out) of the academic career I felt ready for and now I wonder why I didn't protest. . . . I took a job as a maid in a wealthy home; we lived over the garage; I had a day uniform and a party uniform, and in my spare time read through French literature in a thorough self-imposed course of study.

A few years later, Earnshaw worked in the Library of Congress ("No discrimination there; an old-time woman martinet supervisor hired me to catalog Russian periodicals using my Russian language skills") and then in the Bancroft Library at the University of California, Berkeley ("Again no discrimination") while she raised her children. Looking back on these years, Earnshaw said:

> I think young women in the fifties were like the returning sol-
> diers; eager to find new paths, but shunted into the domestic
> life while the men were helped to earn college degrees. The
> war had affected us, too, and we were frustrated by the clash of
> our ideals with the lids placed on achievement. Betty Friedan's
> *The Feminine Mystique* hit me with full force. I understood it
> immediately, and began my first steps of recovery. . . . Eventu-
> ally, in a time of extreme frustration (screaming by myself when
> no one was around), trying to be the perfect fifties model wife
> and mother, I was invited into the Comparative Literature
> Ph.D. program, which I was thrilled to start, and finished in
> 1981. During those ten years I was part of the group of women
> who pioneered the study of women poets of the world.

A happy ending, but Earnshaw never forgot the decades she had lost.

> The initial discrimination when I was twenty-five (and my un-
> thinking acceptance of it) resulted in a missed career, and a
> damaged sense of self-esteem, but not altogether; by age fifty-
> five I had the Ph.D. and then followed eighteen rewarding
> years of teaching at the lecturer level in the university that
> once turned me away.[48]

Working women also commonly encountered predatory male supervisors and coworkers whose hands groped where they were not wanted.
Here was another problem without a name. "That's life," women said to
each other. Maria O'Connor, whose husband's salary was insufficient to
support their daughters, worked at a supermarket where she daily tried
to avoid such roaming hands. "At work, everybody was always making a
remark, or touching you," she recalled.

> Now they call it harassment. We had a lot of harassment from
> the supervisors, the managers. One time I bent down to pick

up something and the manager put his hand on me. You know, you couldn't wear pants in those days, you had to wear a uniform, a dress. I was so mad, I had a cup of coffee in my hand and threw it. The man ducked and the cup hit another young guy, but I didn't care. I yelled at him, "You just keep your goddamn hands off me." He said, "If you don't like it, work somewhere else." So he fired me.

O'Connor decided to take her grievance to her union. The man swore he had done nothing at all, and another woman employee backed him up. The union insisted he take her back, but O'Connor, completely disgusted, said, "Take your job and . . ."

Then she worked for a butcher. "Those years, it was tough to be a woman on the job."

> If you didn't want to go out with them, they'd say you were a tramp, you were no good. Some of the girls, they'd feel like they had to go out with them. [The supervisors] used to say, come on Maria, we have to go upstairs and get something from the storeroom. And moron that I was, I would go up there and first thing I know he's got me crushed up against the wall. So I say, stop it, take your hands off me and he says, oh you can go work at the other store. Spiteful. You know, he was going to transfer me because I wouldn't let him get near me.

Meanwhile, Maria had to deal with an extremely jealous husband who resented the fact that she worked with men all day. Then, when she returned home, "he would start in on me about the guys at work. I'd say to him, 'If I leave the store at six and I'm home at twenty after six, when am I gonna have an affair?' "[49]

The nightmare for working mothers was finding adequate child care. Eighty percent of them relied on the vagaries of relatives, friends, and sitters. One out of thirteen children turned into an unsupervised "latchkey" child. Social critics blamed working women for creating an "epidemic" of juvenile delinquency, but stubbornly refused to consider the idea of government-sponsored child care. In the United States, as opposed to the Soviet Union, patriotic American women raised their own children.

Working women naturally returned home to the same tasks of cooking, shopping, and cleaning expected of a full-time housewife. "Believe me," explained one disgruntled wife,

> a modern woman of today would have to be *four* women to be everything that is expected of her. My husband wants me to work not for the satisfaction I might get out of working, but for the extra money *he* will have for himself. . . . *But*, how about the extra burden it would put on me. I would go out to work if possible, but I cannot do that and come home to a house full of screaming kids, dishes piled in the sink, and mountains of laundry to do. It is no fun to come home and see the sweet, dear, lazy bum asleep on the couch after being on my feet all day. He still likes his home-made pies, cakes and appetizing meals. He thinks he would lose some of his masculinity if anyone saw him hanging out the wash, or washing dishes. And if he *had* to give up any of his fishing or hunting or running around visiting his buddies to keep an eye on the kids, well, I'm not killing myself for the almighty dollar.[50]

In fact, American men *were* helping out more than ever. In 1954, *Life* magazine announced in an article titled "The Domestication of the American Male" what many social commentators already suspected. But there were limits. As the authors of *Modern Mothers' Dilemma* warned, men "can't be asked to take over much. It is more than unfair to expect him to do half the housework as well as carry the load of a full-time job; it prevents him from doing his best work and keeps him from enjoying his home as he should."[51]

Working women also encountered a sex-segregated labor force. Discrimination in wages and jobs was so common that many didn't even notice. A woman opening the daily newspaper found the help-wanted ads divided by sex. On one page were jobs open to men. On the opposite page were jobs that funneled women into domestic service, waitressing, sales, and the expanding world of "pink collar work," where they shuffled, typed, and filed the avalanche of paper required by bureaucratic organizations. By 1960, 59 percent of women employees worked in occupations defined as "women's work."

Even when women did the same work as men, they received substantially lower wages. Though few working men had ever earned an adequate family wage, employers insisted that women simply worked for "pin money." While her children were in high school, one mother worked in a travel agency where she accidentally discovered that her boss paid her far less than men who did the same work. Like many women of the time, she griped privately but said nothing, grateful for the money she did make for her children's college educations.[52]

Where could women find help? They mostly worked in nonunionized jobs. With few exceptions, weakened labor unions in any case refused to deal with women's employment problems. By the end of the fifties, not surprisingly, women's wages had even decreased. In 1960, women earned 61 percent of men's wages, a drop of 3 percent since 1955. In 1959, a white male with a high-school education earned on average $4,429, while his female counterpart earned only $3,458. For blacks, it was worse: black college-educated men earned $4,840; black college-educated women, $3,708.

Meanwhile, a small army of social critics blasted working women for many of America's ills: alcoholic husbands, homosexual children, and juvenile delinquency. In their influential anti-Communist best-seller, *The Modern Woman: The Lost Sex* (1947), Ferdinand Lundberg and Marya Farnham typically laid society's problems on women's defiant determination to pursue outside interests and careers. The authors argued that an "independent" woman was an oxymoron, single women were sick, and childless women were "emotionally disturbed." "All spinsters," they concluded, "[should] be barred by law from having anything to do with the teaching of children on the ground of emotional incompetence."[53]

"Only in America," noted a foreign observer as late as 1962, "is 'Career Woman' an obscene phrase." Caught between the myth of the happy housewife and the reality of their working lives, some working women refused to acknowledge that they worked. Alice Quaytman, a leftist political activist before, during, and after World War II, raised her family and worked as a child psychologist during the fifties. But when anyone asked what she did, she elusively described herself as a "mother who works with children." Another mother, a salaried president of a national philanthropic organization who put in eighty hours a week, explained her full-time housekeeper and lengthy absences from home as the result of her "volunteer" work. Many suburban women worked full-time, without pay, as part of the female voluntary army that created the libraries, schools, charities, and religious organizations that turned suburban developments into communities. This, they could brag about.[54]

Fearing social and political ostracism, career women downplayed their independence. Frances Perkins, former secretary of labor, denounced feminism and argued that the "happiest place for most women is in the home." Journalist Dorothy Thompson argued that women who engaged in demanding intellectual work cheated their husbands and children. Even Margaret Mead, the great anthropologist who had introduced Americans to the very idea that gender roles were flexible, publicly worried about women who searched for status in a "competitive world rather than a unique place by a glowing hearth."[55]

Even without an organized women's movement, a virulent strain of antifeminism saturated the culture. Psychiatry pitted the healthy, submissive, patriotic mother and wife against the neurotic and strident feminist, whose determination to ruin other women's lives originated from her own sick unwillingness to surrender to feminine fulfillment. Critics associated feminism with an un-American godless Communism that forced women to work outside the home. A few former suffragists—like the repentant ex-Communists of the time—publicly recanted their youthful ways, belatedly took their husbands' last names, and dutifully bowed to the idea of man's natural superiority.[56]

WOMEN'S POLITICAL LIFE

At the same time, a very small circle of former suffragists, members of the conservative National Woman's Party (NWP), did keep alive the dream of an Equal Rights Amendment, which they had first submitted in 1923, soon after women gained the right to vote. The ERA would have given women equality in every arena of public life, but was opposed by labor and working women who feared it would destroy the protective legislation women enjoyed. Still, the NWP exerted very little influence on the dominant culture.[57]

After the passage of the Susan B. Anthony amendment in 1920 that granted suffrage to women, the activists who worked together in a successful coalition—now called the First Wave of Feminism— scattered to work on a variety of different issues—child labor protection, prenatal care for mothers, and peace. In the international arena, as historian Leila Rupp has shown, Jane Addams and others founded the Women's International League for Peace and Freedom and organized a women's global movement dedicated to universal disarmament. But, domestically, these activists had ceased to exist as a single mass-based

social movement. During the thirties, women activists made unioniza-
tion, the fight against poverty, and Fascism their highest priorities. In
the early forties, activists organized radical industrial unions, joined the
anti-Fascist Left, enlisted in the burgeoning civil rights movement that
fought tenant evictions, and demanded jobs and health care for urban
African-Americans.[58]

After the war, many of these female activists resumed their political
work. On May 8, 1946, International Women's Day, a group of leftist
women founded the Congress of American Women (CAW). It was to be
the U.S. branch of the Women's International Democratic Federation
(WIDF), a global organization that included tens of millions of women
in forty-one countries whose goal was to achieve peace and gain full political, economic, social, and legal rights for women.[59]

CAW's members successfully linked women's issues, social justice,
and peace with racial equality and economic justice. At its peak, CAW
boasted 250,000 women members and prided itself on its progressive
and interracial social agenda. Their feisty slogan was "Ten women anywhere can organize anything." CAW's agenda prefigured much of the
modern women's movement that emerged in the sixties. It called for a
Commission on the Status of Women, federal training programs for poor
women, national health insurance and child care for working women,
equal pay for equal work, and access to professional schools. Members
also protested negative stereotypes of women.

CAW never hid the fact that some of its leaders were members of the
Communist Party. In 1950, the House Un-American Activities Committee (HUAC) required CAW to register as an agent of a foreign organization. In fear, many liberal and union members promptly fled the
organization. Faced with a protracted and costly legal fight, CAW dissolved and its history remained invisible for nearly four decades.

During the late thirties and forties, Popular Front activism inspired
countless women like Betty Friedan to work for class and race equality.
Like her, many of these activists married and raised small children in
the fifties, unaware of the change that domestic life would bring. Ruth
Friedman, for example, went from full-time activist to fifties housewife
within a few short years. At New York's City College, she had been immersed in radical politics and later worked as a union organizer in
Hollywood. In 1946, she and her husband started a family.

> We didn't talk about it much. What's to discuss? We were mar-
> ried so we should have babies. I'd always assumed I'd have

children, even though I never had any particular feeling for children. . . . So we started to build a nest. Suddenly, my life was different. I couldn't work, couldn't do my political stuff, couldn't even make phone calls without being interrupted.

Soon after the birth of their second child, Friedman's husband began a Ph.D. program.

There was no discussion about which one of us would go on for further education. It was just taken for granted that it would be Ben. It wasn't until some time around the late fifties that I began to feel unhappy being at home alone with the kids and seeing that he was advancing himself intellectually and in every way. He was *out there* and I was *in here*.

After some discussion, she decided to return to work.

When I first started back to work, there was a regular chorus, when I left in the morning, of tsk, tsk, tsk all around the courtyard. I was the only woman who went to work in that development, even among those progressives. They were staying home with their children. People would say things to me, they would allude to the fact that "you're never around." There was not a morning that I went out that I didn't feel conflicted about going. Not conflicted about *wanting* to go to work—I *knew* that was what I wanted. But about whether or not it was the right thing to do.[60]

Many leftist mothers found a way to continue their political activities as an extended part of their domestic routine. They brought their skills and values into the PTA, the YWCA, volunteer organizations, community activities, and local politics. In one New York City neighborhood, a local PTA became the battleground on which Stalinist and Trotskyist factions fought each other. Adeline Brunner, a longtime leftist activist, joked about how she "infiltrated" the PTA in El Cerrito, California, to improve her children's school's commitment to minorities and the poor. Later, she founded a preschool that educated some of the boys and girls who would emerge as New Left activists in the sixties. Alice Quaytman brought a similar progressive agenda and background into her PTA in the Bronx in New York City. Committed to racial equality and economic justice, she fought the school board and administrators to ensure that no children experienced discrimination. She, too, helped start a nursery school to give children a head start in life.[61]

Like Betty Friedan, none of these leftist women ever described themselves as "feminists" before the sixties, but the issue of women's subordination was often on their minds. Life on the Left provided shared values and a community committed to economic justice. But the "woman question," as it was called, although it permeated most leftist organizations of the thirties and forties, did not necessarily change everyday behavior.

Stella Novicki left her family's farm at age seventeen and found a job working in a packinghouse. There she became an active member of the union. "Women had an awfully tough time because men brought their prejudices there," she recalled.

> Some of my brothers who believed in equality and that women should have rights, didn't crank the mimeograph, didn't type. I did the shit work, until all hours, as did the few other women who didn't have family obligations. And then when the union came around giving out jobs with pay, the guys got them. I and the other women didn't. It was the men who got the organizing jobs.

Novicki also resented the fact that the "union didn't encourage women to come to meetings."

> They didn't actually want to take up the problems that the women had. I organized women's groups, young women's groups. They liked to dance and I loved to dance and we went dancing together. I talked to them about the union. The women were interested after a while when they saw that the union could actually win things for them, bread and butter things. . . . We talked about nurseries . . . we tried to show the community that the union was concerned about the welfare of the young people; we raised the problems of women; we raised the problem of inequality.

Despite her frustration with union men's prejudices, she still felt "it was a privilege and a wonderful experience to participate in the excitement of those times."[62]

Many women activists experienced the same combination of excitement and resentment. One woman complained to her husband, " 'While you sit on your ass making the revolution, I'm out there in the kitchen like a slave. What we need is a revolution in this house.' But, of course, he simply ignored me, and I simply went on doing it." In 1946, another woman wrote to the Communist newspaper the *Daily Worker* that her husband "could give an excellent lecture on the necessity to emancipate women," but never thought of helping with housework, cooking, or child care. Bea Richtman, a member of the Communist Party, later asked, "What I want to know is how come so many people were thrown out [of the Party] for white chauvinism [racism] but not one goddamned Communist was ever thrown out for male chauvinism?"

Although these women were well acquainted with the "woman question," only a handful aired their personal resentments. In 1947, Betty Millard, a leftist feminist, penned an article in the magazine the *New Masses* in which she described "the quiet, more veiled lynching" of American women. "Many of the thirty-eight million American housewives," she wrote,

> are doomed to circumscribed, petty lives, to the stultification
> of whatever abilities and interest, outside of motherhood, they
> may have had. The 15,400,000 women wage-earners are dis-
> criminated against in almost every field of employment, are
> notoriously paid less than men for the same work, and are the
> first to be laid off.

Twenty years before young feminists would redefine rape as an act not of aggressive sex but of violence against and control over women, Millard called it "a violent expression of a pattern of male supremacy, an outgrowth of age-old economic, political and cultural exploitation of women by men." In a footnote, she added, "It might be interesting to consider the question of rape as a form of violence practiced against women."[63]

As a young activist in the Communist Youth League, Alice Quaytman had fought tenant evictions in Harlem during the Depression. Soon the Party sent her to an institute to prepare her for a greater leadership role. At meetings, she persistently raised the "woman question," but her male comrades routinely dismissed her grievances as "bourgeois concerns." At one point, she missed several classes due to illness. Her teacher, a distinguished Party intellectual, invited her to retrieve copies of his lectures at his apartment. When she arrived, he tried to throw her down on his bed. She successfully fought him off, but told no one; she knew leftist activists would not consider sexual assault worthy of political discussion. "Also, as mad as I was," she added, "I couldn't imagine harming the reputation of such an important and famous Party intellectual."

Although male chauvinism infuriated Quaytman, it wasn't until the late sixties that, in her view, she really "got" feminism. One evening in 1968, she cooked dinner for her family and several young friends active in the antiwar and women's liberation movements. When her husband asked her to bring him some butter from the kitchen, she began to rise, but was stopped cold by a young feminist who stood up and bluntly asked the husband, "Why can't you get it yourself?" Alice Quaytman sat down, stunned. It had never occurred to her that shared housework might be a political issue. "Suddenly, I realized what they were talking about. For us, politics had been about changing the world, but we hadn't even noticed the politics of the intimate world in which we lived."[64]

Black women activists were not terribly troubled by the feminine mystique, which, they knew, was mostly directed at white middle-class women. For them, racism and discrimination were the greatest obstacles they faced. Jean Williams, a descendant of escaped slaves, joined the Communist Party and worked in a settlement house in a Nashville ghetto. By 1950, she married, moved to Brooklyn, and had two daughters. Her husband, a Party official, was indicted, like a number of Communist Party leaders, under the Smith Act of 1940. The charge was advocating the forcible or violent overthrow of the American government, for which he faced a sentence of five or more years in jail. Like other persecuted radicals, he went "underground," leaving Jean to raise their children. She did not see him again for five years. Meanwhile, she worked as an assistant to a doctor who had been a Spanish Civil War veteran. While the FBI terrorized her children, following them everywhere they went,

> the black community in Brooklyn where I lived was a great source of support for us. . . . We didn't run from it [the FBI presence]. Some people lived in communities where their neighbors turned on them and isolated them and they were forced to move. We tried to organize our whole neighborhood about what was happening, and what my husband was, and

what he believed. Our only problem was that a woman on the
first floor of the building was running a numbers operation
and she was sure this was interfering with her business.

Williams understood that her main responsibility, like that of most
women, whether or not they were Communist activists or suburban Re-
publicans, was to keep her family together. "There weren't that many
women in the leadership," she recalled, "so the people most in danger
of being indicted were men. Besides, someone needed to stay and take
care of the children."[65]

The incipient civil rights movement of the late forties and fifties produced many experienced female activists, some of whom would influence younger women or turn into important feminist leaders themselves.
Fannie Lou Hamer and Ella Baker, two of the great orators and organizers of the civil rights movement, inspired a generation of young civil
rights activists to feel proud of powerful female leadership. Dorothy
Height, president of the National Council of Negro Women, lawyer
Pauli Murray, and union leaders Aileen Hernandez and Addie Wyatt all
played decisive roles in explaining the double jeopardy that black
women faced in American society as women and as minorities. Jesse De
la Cruz, a Chicana farmworker who early joined Cesar Chavez's United
Farm Workers, later organized women in agricultural communities.

Among their many contributions, activists in CAW gave a new generation of young women the gift of women's history. Eleanor Flexner, the
author of *Century of Struggle* (1959), the first accessible study of the
suffrage movement, had worked in the Communist Party during the thirties, organized workers into radical labor unions during the war, and
then worked in CAW. Interviewed near the end of her life, Flexner credited the Left movement with opening up the fields of both African-
American and women's history in universities. "I can definitely trace
the origins of my book," she explained, "to some of my contacts with
Communists like Elizabeth Gurley Flynn and Claudia Jones (who was
quite unknown to the larger white community)." Another major contribution to women's history that grew out of CAW's membership was "The
Lady and the Mill Girl," a seminal article written by Gerda Lerner,
which described the ways in which the Industrial Revolution had affected women of different classes. Her work, and Flexner's, both of
which emphasized the class dimensions of women's lives, would soon
become urtexts for a new generation of women activists and historians.

Later, Aileen Kraditor, another Left activist, wrote *Ideas of the Woman's Suffrage Movement* (1965), an intellectual history of the nineteenth-century women's movement that would help jump-start the field of women's history.[66]

Some of these women kept a very low profile during the fifties. But through their local activism, they helped preserve a spirit that would prove crucial to the rebirth of the modern women's movement. Women like Betty Friedan, Gerda Lerner, Esther Peterson, Bella Abzug, Eleanor Flexner, Dorothy Haener, Claudia Jones, Aileen Kraditor, Dorothy Height, Eve Merriam, and Mildred Jeffrey, to name just a handful, were among the many women who gained invaluable organizing, oratorical, and writing skills as activists in labor unions, civil rights movements, and other Left movements. We will never know their numbers; we may never know their names. McCarthyism drove many of them into silence and anonymity, but they kept the "woman question" alive in tough times, and taught a new generation of daughters "their mother tongue." Rosalyn Baxandall, Bettina Aptheker, Jackie Goldberg, Linda Gordon, Barbara Epstein, Kathie (Amatniek) Sarachild, Angela Davis, Ann Froines, Dinky Romilly, and Sharon Jeffrey—just some of the activists crucial to the women's movement of the sixties and beyond—were "Red-diaper" babies whose mothers had passed on, consciously or not, the historical memory of women's radical activism. The continuity between women of the Old Left and the rebirth of feminism among both the middle-aged and the young is part of an important story that still needs to be recovered.

THE DISCOVERY OF DISCONTENT

In 1947, *Life* magazine published "American Woman's Dilemma," an article that described both the discontent of housewives and the growing participation of women in the labor force. Two years later, another *Life* article mysteriously announced that "suddenly and for no plain reason the women of the United States were seized with an eerie restlessness." Still tracking the "woman problem" in 1956, *Life* devoted a special issue to women's problems that began with this astonishing statement: "Historians of the future may speak of the twentieth century as 'the era of the feminist revolution.' " The magazine nonetheless concluded that women suffered mostly because they had fought for their rights instead of enjoying their privileges—femininity, child-rearing, and devotion to beauty. In the same year, *McCall's* published a piece called "The Mother Who Ran Away." To the amazement of the editors, it generated a deluge of letters from besieged mothers. "It was our moment of truth," a former editor confided to Betty Friedan. "We suddenly realized that all those women at home with their three and a half children were miserably unhappy." By 1960, when the mass media, including almost all the women's magazines, suddenly discovered what they dubbed "The Trapped Housewife," the woes of the suburban housewife were already less than a well-kept secret. But it took Friedan to put that secret onto the national political agenda.[67]

It took far longer for working women to puncture the official reality that American women didn't work outside the home. In 1957, the National Manpower Council seemed positively stunned to "discover" that an invisible army of working women, many with children, had entered the labor force. Two books published by the council, *Womanpower in Today's World* and *Work in the Lives of Married Women* (1958), first publicized the hidden realities of working women's lives. Shocked by the statistics they uncovered, the authors repeatedly described the situation as a "revolution."[68]

It was. By the end of the decade, before Betty Friedan wrote about it, the feminine mystique—as a description of women's actual lives—was becoming more myth than fact. But myths die slowly, especially when they serve a useful purpose. For war-weary women and men, the feminine mystique, with its illusion of clear gender roles, brought with it a sense of social order. But the feminine mystique also crippled the lives of many American women. Rather than face social ostracism, some women gave up their dreams and lashed themselves to home and hearth. Millions of women learned to interpret their dissatisfaction as evidence of individual madness. Millions more—whose lives never began to resemble that of a middle-class housewife—suffered unnecessary guilt as they worked around the clock to ensure the survival of their families.

Insecure in their separate worlds, women privately sniped at each other: housewives blasted activists as unpatriotic; working women derided housewives as spoiled and lazy; and housewives accused working women of neglecting their children. A local Girl Scout troop leader shocked one mother who worked as a civilian specialist for the Air Force by refusing to admit the daughters of "working women" to her troop. Housewives in one neighborhood decided to prevent their daughters from visiting the home of a high-school teacher who never greeted her own two teenage daughters with milk and cookies.[69]

And yet, these adult women had a great deal in common: wherever they worked, whatever they did, they were treated as subordinates. Observing this fact in a 1960 issue of *Ladies' Home Journal*, the journalist Dorothy Thompson asked, "Women have had the vote for over forty years and their organizations lobby in Washington for all sorts of causes but why, why, why don't they take up their *own* causes and obvious needs?"[70]

They would, but American women did not yet possess a common language with which to express their shared subordination. "I did not set out consciously to start a revolution," Betty Friedan insisted. But she already knew that successful movements require group solidarity. She understood that labor struggles only flourished with broad class consciousness and that civil rights movements required race consciousness. To publicize their private and public injuries, women would need to expand their gender consciousness and find a language with which to express common grievances.

This they were not yet ready to do. But the demands made by the feminine mystique paradoxically intensified their gender consciousness. By politicizing women's lives in the battle to contain Communism, the 1950s deepened American women's awareness of how their identity as females had become the basis for their exclusion. Within a decade, housewives, working women, women activists—whose experiences, disappointments, and hopes would set the agenda of the modern women's movement—would launch a scathing attack on the very culture that had blamed them for everything. By then, they would know how to use their identity as women as a weapon in the battle against discrimination and in the struggle for equality.

Chapter Two

FEMALE GENERATION GAP

"When I was growing up," wrote Anna Quindlen, a *New York Times* columnist, novelist, and mother of three who was born in the 1950s, "motherhood was a kind of cage."

> You stayed home and felt your mind turn to the stuff that you
> put in little bowls and tried to spoon into little mouths and
> eventually wound up wiping off of little floors. . . . By the time
> I was a grown-up, the answer, if you were strong and smart
> and wanted to be somebody, was not to be a mom. I certainly
> didn't want to be one.[1]

After she read *The Feminine Mystique*, another young woman picked up her pen and wrote Betty Friedan: "My mother has stayed at home for twenty-three years and raised four children. . . . The emptiness of her life appalls me; her helplessness and dependence on my father frightens me."[2]

Paula Weideger, a feminist who chose not to have children, later tried to explain why so many young feminists had feared marriage and motherhood: "The desire to have children, along with good feelings about motherhood, was buried because women were so scared."

> They were afraid they would turn out like their own mothers,
> most of whom were housewives and housewives only. Women
> like me who grew up in the 1950s had been made edgy and
> claustrophobic by the narrowness of the life laid out for them

from birth. To give mother-feeling any place in your heart
might mean being lost to mothering forever—or at least "till
the kids are grown."[3]

With one foot firmly planted in the world of their mothers, daughters
of the fifties viscerally feared the constraints experienced by the adult
women around them. Those daughters who were "war babies," born between 1941 and 1945, became the leaders and shock troops of the
women's liberation movement, stamping its political culture with their
specific experiences and fears. By the time the movement began, many
had finished college, married, and borne children. Their younger sisters, baby boomers born between 1946 and 1950, joined the movement
as college students. The youngest baby boomers, born after 1950, came
of age in an atmosphere saturated with media images of protest, of the
sexual revolution, and of the counterculture. Maturing while the women's
movement was a rising tide, they took for granted freedoms that had em-
blazoned their older sisters' banners. Some spawned women's groups in
their high schools, but many became pioneers of a different sort: they
would be the first women to shape adult lives amid the new opportunities and burdens created by the modern feminist movement.[4]

As the new decade of the sixties began, social and cultural critics began worrying about a "generation gap" that suddenly seemed to have
severed the connections of the young with their parents. But the media
viewed the generation gap largely through the lens of the male experience. *Life* magazine's 1968 cover story "The Generation Gap" typically
concentrated on the tension-filled relationship between a nephew and
his uncle. The *New York Times* repeatedly described it in terms of a
young man's alienation from the adult world. What everyone failed to
notice was that *two* generation gaps existed, side by side, each with its
own gender-specific fears and dreams.[5]

Whatever created a male rebel, journalists and scholars assumed,
also shaped his female counterpart. And they were partly right. On the
surface, rebellious young men and women did seem strikingly similar.
Both rejected the popular music of their parents, savored the riffs of
jazz, and gyrated to the urgent, rhythmic beat of rock 'n' roll. Together,
they criticized the excessive materialism and conformity of their parents' world, feared the madness of nuclear deterrence, and denounced
the anti-Communist obsession that led to proxy wars like the one in
Vietnam. Both reproached America's poverty and racism, condemned
the hypocrisy of a democratic society that daily violated its own ideals,

expressed contempt for the military and economic "establishment," vowed to change "the system," and favored direct action over the stodgy, hierarchical, bureaucratic ways of the adult world.

But there was a profound difference as well: the belief in a single "generation gap" hid the quiet desperation experienced by daughters of the fifties. Sociologists Richard Flacks and Kenneth Keniston both discovered that a majority of young male activists, however strongly they rejected adult society, nonetheless sought to live out the ideals of their liberal parents. Instead of becoming a lawyer, banker, teacher, or businessman, a male rebel might choose to join the Peace Corps, or work as a community, labor, or movement organizer. A rebellious son might reject material success, but not his future as a father. Young male activists knew they could combine a life as an activist with fatherhood. Many did just that.[6]

For activist daughters, the generation gap was far more complicated. The immediate past conjured up images of claustrophobic marriages, coercive motherhood, and constrained chastity. Whatever their age, these young women had personal acquaintance with the power of the feminine mystique, sometimes in the person of their mother, but definitely with the fifties' cultural icon of the housewife. The ghost haunting these young women wore an apron and lived vicariously through the lives of a husband and children. Against her, the women's liberation movement would be forged.

Fear of becoming an "ordinary housewife"—in the words of feminist writer Susan Griffin—is what fueled the female generation gap. Could a woman in her twenties mate and bear children without turning into a domestic drudge? They didn't know. As they rejected the world of their mothers—but not necessarily their mothers' secret dreams—daughters searched for an identity based on something besides marriage and motherhood. And for that, there were precious few role models.[7]

If critics detected a certain hostility toward men, marriage, and motherhood in the women's liberation movement, little wonder. As feminist psychologist Phyllis Chesler later explained, "Psychologically, we had committed matricide." But critics did not understand the source of these fears. Ranting against the Equal Rights Amendment in the 1970s, the antifeminist activist Phyllis Schlafly charged that feminists

> hate men, marriage and children. They are out to destroy morality and the family. They look upon husbands as exploiters, children as an evil to be avoided (by abortion if necessary),

and the family as an institution which keeps women in
"second-class citizenship" or even slavery.[8]

Schlafly (willfully) mistook symbols for substance. There are reasons
why movements target certain enemies, flash particular symbols, choose
to use particular metaphors, and set the goals they do. Activists' images
of the past naturally shape their view of the present and how they imagine the future. The ubiquity of the feminine mystique, which had politicized the lives of adult women, also politicized some young women's
resistance to a domestic life. The subject of motherhood shadowed the
women's movement. Sometimes young women talked incessantly about
motherhood, but as an institution, rather than as part of their futures.
Some feminists celebrated motherhood as a way to finesse the differences between straight and gay women or to create a basis for solidarity
among women of all races and backgrounds.[9] However they talked about
mothering, they still sought something beyond a life devoted exclusively
to domesticity. As Barbara Berg has observed:

> Surely this was not the first time in American history that
> daughters yearned to live lives different from their mothers,
> to forge new paths, to go in new directions. What was unique
> to us—the generation coming of age in the sixties and
> seventies—however, was that we had the *opportunity* to act on
> these dreams and inspirations and to make them a reality.[10]

EDUCATED FOR WHAT?

One of those opportunities was higher education. By the late fifties, liberal middle-class families expected that their daughters would attend
college. But many girls felt confused about the purpose of their education. Experts warned that every year a girl spent developing her mind
"reduced the probability of a woman marrying." One critic suggested
that women should not receive the same training as men. "Their place is
in the home and their education should concentrate on homemaking
and fitting them for their special roles as wives and mothers. It is more
important that they put a good dinner on the table than that they talk
Greek."[11]

In 1950, Lynn White, president of Mills College and the author of the widely read book *Educating Our Daughters*, announced that education actually "frustrated" women. Rather than straining to absorb science and philosophy, college women should, he proposed, learn the "theory and preparation of a basque paella, of a well-marinated shish-kebab, lamb kidney sauteed in sherry, an authoritative curry." The president of Radcliffe College suggested that the college alter its regular curriculum because it only served to "equip and encourage women to compete with men." In a 1955 commencement address at Smith College, the liberal Democrat and presidential candidate Adlai Stevenson explained how much young women could accomplish during this "historical crisis" (the Cold War) by assuming "the humble role of housewife—which," he added, "is what most of you are going to be whether you like the idea or not just now—and you'll like it!" In 1956, *Life* magazine acknowledged "that [women] have minds and should use them . . . so long as their primary interest is the home."[12]

Some colleges and universities bowed to such pressure by altering parts of their curricula. Mills College fielded a "Marriage" major and introduced a course on "Volunteerism." The University of Chicago, in a striking departure from its highly intellectual course of study, offered its students a course called "Parenthood in a Free Nation." The New School in New York City offered a new course entitled "Modern Woman's Dilemma," taught by a man, which emphasized individual rather than social solutions. Naturally, such an educational atmosphere affected women students. "We don't want careers," explained one coed. "Our parents expect us to go to college. Everybody goes. But a girl who got serious about anything she studied—like, wanting to go on and do research—would be peculiar, unfeminine. I guess everybody wants to graduate with a diamond ring on her finger. That's the important thing."[13]

Veteran educators couldn't help but notice the change. In 1954, a retired female professor from the University of Illinois observed, "For these last ten years, I felt increasingly that something had gone wrong with our young women of college age." Women faculty cringed when coeds characterized them as "bitter, unromantic old witches"—despite the fact that many had married and raised children. In 1959, Mabel Newcomer's book *A Century of Higher Education for Women* provided a devastating statistical portrait of how American society's ambivalent attitude toward women's education had eroded their educational progress. Though the overall number of women in college had soared, the percentage of college women had dropped from 47 percent in 1920 to 34.2

percent in 1958. In 1920, women had earned half of all bachelor's degrees, one of every six doctorates, and by 1940 women had received 13
percent of all doctorates. Yet, by the mid-fifties, they received only 24
percent of the bachelor's degrees and 10 percent of the doctorates.
Other signs of slippage worried those who cared about women's education. In 1956, three out of every five women in coeducational institutions were preparing for a future in nursing, home economics, and
secretarial work. The United States was the only industrial country in
which the percentage of women in universities had decreased over
twenty years.[14]

Ironically, one of the many Cold War panics helped rescue young
women from this downward spiral. The Soviet Union's launch of the first
space satellite, Sputnik, in 1957, shocked the nation. Were Americans
behind Russians in science and technology? It seemed inconceivable,
but the evidence was overhead. Government and educational leaders
knew that the Soviets educated both sexes in math and in the sciences.
Reeling from the enemy's technological feat, the United States decided
to educate not just boys but girls, too, in math and science. "A great national resource of feminine brain power is being lost," officials now proclaimed, "because potential mathematicians, scientists, writers and
artists marry early, have large families, and never put their higher education to public use." To contain Communism, the nation suddenly
needed women in the laboratory more than at home.

Girls quickly sensed the change. Guidance counselors suddenly
pushed them into physics and calculus classes in high school. Such
classes did a great deal to enhance young women's educational aspirations. But math and science still could not help them figure out how to
escape the ghost who wore an apron. As they entered college, some
young women imagined following in the footsteps of their fathers—even
though, like their male counterparts, they often rejected the "compromises" associated with their fathers' lives. But for a variety of reasons,
including the fact that they felt they had no legitimate claim to "male"
occupations, patterning themselves after adult men was simply not a
viable option.

The rebellious young women who postponed marriage and childbearing tried on new identities found in teen culture or college life, and perhaps in "the movement"—but only, it seemed, by modeling themselves
after their male counterparts. Within these various youth cultures,
women could make an end run around marriage and motherhood, and

experiment with different kinds of independent identities. But assuming the garb of a male rebel simply postponed the day when young women would have to figure out how to mate and bear children, if at all, *and* still maintain an independent identity. This is one reason why the American women's movement became so engrossed with the question of female identity. As future feminists tried to escape the feminine mystique, they discovered solutions that addressed men's alienation, but not their own.

The female generation gap brought different issues to the surface, requiring different answers. These young women had long sensed "that underneath the busy dailyness of [our mothers'] lives, there was a deep and stagnant well of frustration and sorrow." Sometimes, mothers had openly discussed their sorrows with their daughters. But nonverbal messages—sighing, psychosomatic complaints, unexplained weeping—communicated just as well what a conspiracy of silence often forbade: the expression of profound discontent.[15]

MOTHERS' MIXED MESSAGES

And many mothers, it turned out, wanted a different future for their daughters. In a 1962 Gallup poll, only 10 percent of mothers hoped their daughters would follow the pattern of their lives. In letters to Betty Friedan, women wrote of their dreams for their daughters. One mother, a self-described "drop-out from Oberlin College" who became "a victim of the Feminine Mystique and the mother of five," hoped her daughter would never experience the "servile feeling" she had felt as a housewife. "How can we help our daughters to avoid making the mistake of following the crowd into early marriage? I would be heart-broken to see any of them make the mistakes I've made."[16]

But mothers also worried about their daughters' future security and encouraged them to marry and have children as well. "Be like me, don't be like me," was the confusing message a good many daughters imbibed along with their milk and cookies. The result was that many young women grew up with a pervasive sense of ambivalence about the future. They feared becoming like—or unlike—the cultural image of the fifties mother. It was an ambivalence felt even by women across (white) class lines. In her research on middle-class and working-class daughters of the era, Kathleen Gerson found that 79 percent of women's families had stressed the importance of a domesticized future. Yet, 45 percent of these daughters developed an early aversion to such a life and had "looked on marriage and children with either indifference or disdain as children. Instead, they gave central importance to work," emphasizing "the dangers of domesticity instead of its joys."[17]

Young black women, in contrast, were more likely to feel empathy for their mothers, whom they admired as the foundation of their families and communities, and viewed as models for their future lives. But they sometimes wanted their mothers' lives to conform to what they saw on television. As a girl, Assata Shakur wished her mother were more "normal."

> Why didn't my mother have freshly baked cookies ready when I came home from school? Why didn't we live in a house with a backyard and a front yard instead of an ole apartment? I remember looking at my mother as she cleaned the house in her raggedy housecoat with her hair in curlers. "How disgusting," I would think. Why didn't she clean the house in high heels and shirtwaist dresses like they did on television?[18]

Alix Kates Shulman's popular novel *Burning Questions*, published in 1978, created an unforgettable portrait of a future middle-class white feminist. Born before World War II, Zane, the heroine of the novel, grows up in Babylon, Indiana, where she restlessly passes her childhood digging holes to China in her backyard. In adolescence, she chafes at the shallow conformity and empty materialism of her middle-class suburban family. A misfit who devours biographies of revolutionaries and plays chess, Zane eventually escapes in the late fifties to MacDougal Street, in New York City's Greenwich Village, where she throws herself into the underground Beat culture. Soon disillusioned, Zane marries, bears three children, and rapidly descends into domestic drudgery. From the window of her Washington Square apartment, an envious Zane watches a slightly younger generation march for civil rights, demonstrate against the Vietnam War, and float to a new consciousness on the drugs and sex of an exuberant counterculture. At novel's end, Zane joins a women's group, where, for the first time, she feels free to explore the "burning questions" of a lifetime.[19]

As sociologist Wini Breines has observed, "coming of age" novels written by such women often turned on fears of replicating the lives of their mothers. In Barbara Raskin's *Hot Flashes*, one character says, "None of us wanted to do any of the things our mothers did—nor the way they did it—during the postwar years." In Lynn Lauber's *White Girls*, the heroine portrays her mother as a frustrated and disgruntled woman. Observing the wealthy WASP women of her childhood, the writer Annie Dillard wrote, "They coped: They sighed, they permitted themselves a remark or two, they lived essentially alone. They reared their children with their own two hands, and did all their own cooking and driving." In each case, the writer focuses on some aspect of her mother's life that she vows not to repeat.[20]

Every generation of daughters is finely attuned to the source of their mothers' unhappiness. Daughters of the fifties instinctively blamed the feminine mystique for their mothers' compromises and disappointments. But not all young women felt a need to declare a generational war on adult women. Most daughters quietly embraced new opportunities in higher education, pursued jobs or careers, married, juggled work and children, or decided to forgo marriage and children altogether. But the young women who created the women's liberation movement both *politicized* and *publicized* their rejection of the feminine mystique.

Those who became feminists had learned to politicize what they observed. Some "Red-diaper babies" (children of Old Left parents) grew up learning the language of social and economic justice. Others, who grew up in conservative homes, often absorbed that language when they befriended young radicals in the civil rights or antiwar movements. Most importantly, a critical number of young women learned, through their experiences in other political movements, how to identify and politicize a personal sense of social and economic injustice.[21]

Those who become leaders, activists, or writers in the women's liberation movement early had observed the lives of their mothers or of other adult women, and, even when they admired their political visions or commitments, knew they didn't want an *exclusively* domestic life. Naomi Weisstein, a major theorist and activist in the movement, described herself as a "polka dot diaper" baby, the daughter of a mother who "had grown up in a Bolshevik family and had become the kind of feminist you could be in the 1920s, not sufficient to pursue her career [as well as] have kids." Before having children, Weisstein's mother had been a concert pianist. With children, her career ended. As a teenager, Weisstein "vowed that I would never get married and that I would never have kids. I was sure it ruined her life. And I still think so."[22] Perhaps it is not surprising that Weisstein, a well-known physiological psychologist, later founded the Chicago Women's Liberation Rock and Roll Band.

Barbara Ehrenreich, too, remembered how "you had to steel yourself as a girl if you didn't want to follow a prescribed role." Her mother's expectations ran low. "Even at a young age, I could understand that the only good thing you could do as a woman was to be a housewife, but you would never have any respect that way. Because I don't think my father respected my mother. She was a full-time housewife, and that's what I did not want to be."[23]

Middle-class girls were not alone in rejecting the feminine mystique. Phyllis Chesler, a product of a working-class home and author of *Women and Madness*, later wrote, "If I had wanted to be anything other than a wife and mother, perhaps an actress, I had absolutely no female role model or mentor. I knew nothing about my feminist history. My generation would not discover our feminist legacy until we were in our twenties, thirties, even forties." Irene Peslikis, a feminist activist and artist, grew up in a Greek working-class family in Queens, New York. Her mother worked outside the home—as a hatcheck girl or as a factory hand—to help the family stay afloat. Still, by the time she reached adolescence, Peslikis had decided "I wasn't going to be a housewife. . . . I didn't think too much about marriage, and when I did I would cringe at the very idea."[24]

Many young feminists grew up in such working-class homes. In fact, a disproportionate number of leaders and activists came from secular, working-class Jewish activist families. Later, the media would describe *all* feminists as white middle-class women, but appearances often deceive. The movement naturally grew from an educated and relatively privileged constituency, but many young women who joined the early women's liberation movement were raised by blue collar parents who wanted their daughters to be the first in their family to attend college. Higher education is what transformed these working-class adolescents into middle-class women. As they mingled with other students, they acquired the social confidence, verbal skills, and appearance that would mask their working-class backgrounds. By the late sixties, many feminists, including Gloria Steinem, Ellen Willis, Marge Piercy, Phyllis Chesler, Susan Griffin, Alta, and Alix Kates Shulman, to name but a few of the better-known activists, spoke, wrote, dressed, and otherwise acted like middle-class women. But they first crossed class lines, gained a sense of middle-class entitlement from their education, and only then turned their attention to the "woman question."[25]

Fearful and confused, these college-aged women—like their male counterparts—sought intellectual, cultural, and political mentors in books or in life to help them understand their alienation. But most of what they found was written by, for, and about men. Authors like Albert Camus, Jean-Paul Sartre, Jean Genet, or Samuel Beckett explored the existential and absurd dilemmas of men's lives. Iconoclastic scholars and critics like C. Wright Mills, David Riesman, William Whyte, Paul Goodman, and Lewis Mumford dissected male conformity, analyzed power relations between men, exposed racial injustice, and condemned the corporate male drone and the bland boredom of his suburban life. But little of this social criticism seemed to directly address young women's lives.[26]

Popular culture even beat the Beats to the punch in publicizing a male desire to flee domesticity. Hugh Hefner's *Playboy* came to life in 1953, encouraging bachelors—for the first time in American history—to enjoy a satisfying sexual life without feeling the slightest guilt for not supporting a wife, children, and home. For the upscale single man, an elaborately appointed apartment—complete with revolving bed, rotating lovers, and reflecting mirrors—offered all the pleasures of sex without the burdens of family. For the first time, your disposable income was yours alone, to spend on anything your heart desired, from stereo to sailboat.

In short, for young men determined to avoid the world of their fathers, freedom meant cutting loose from women and children—hardly a new theme in American culture. Only a tiny number of men, of course, followed the Beats into coffeehouses or onto the road, and even fewer had the guts or money to imitate Hefner's sybaritic bachelor lifestyle. Still, one could always dream. As the alienated sons of the fifties entered a new decade, they had models of revolt, intellectual analyses of their alienation, prophetic mentors, and fantasies of escape, if only they dared.

Their female counterparts had few women mentors. Like educated women before them, these alienated women lived in a dual culture, experiencing life as women, but learning to interpret the world as men. They absorbed critiques of materialism and conformity through men's eyes, learned to view society's failures through men's needs, and convinced themselves to reject the commitment and security that free-spirited men condemned. In the short run, the male literary and cultural tradition of dissent inspired dreams of freedom, unleashed a critical distrust of authority, and encouraged a taste for the unconventional—all of which created a solid foundation for a feminism that would question all received wisdom. In the meantime, young women learned to see freedom through men's eyes, and when it didn't exactly fit, they blamed themselves for insufficient daring, insufficient learning, and insufficient radicalism.

THE BEATS

For a small number of future feminists, the Beats—though mostly men—offered a seductive escape from a conventional life. Allen Ginsberg's shrieking incantation against the madness of modern life and Kerouac's tales of life on the road inspired young women as well as men. The Beats provided no map to transcendent experience; but they did romanticize spontaneous unpredictability. Here, at last, was an appealing alternative to life with an apron or, for that matter, an attaché case.

In 1959, Marilyn Coffey, twenty-two years old, was an aspiring writer juggling headlines for the society page of the *Evening Journal* in Lincoln, Nebraska, a city she regarded as "the epitome of hypocrisy and sterile living. I was a member of the so-called Silent Generation and silent many of us were, back in the fifties, in the aftermath of Joe McCarthy and the Korean War. Speechless. A strange condition for a woman who aspired to be a writer." Then, Jack Kerouac's *On the Road* fell into her hands:

> I didn't understand half what I was reading, but something of
> the life being described was comprehensive to me, foreign as
> it was to the young woman who'd been born and bred in the
> conservative Midwest. . . . The words shot through me like a
> fusillade of bullets. I was undone, a changed person. I bought
> myself a straw-covered bottle of Chianti, a candle, and a pad
> of paper . . . began to write by candlelight, scribbling words
> onto paper as fast as my hand could compose, following instinctively Kerouac's model of Spontaneous Prose. . . . The
> novel liberated me as it did many others of my generation.
> There was that instantaneous recognition of self. For the first

time since I began writing ... I felt free to say anything I
wanted. ... For I, in those blissfully naive pre-feminist days,
felt the equal of any man.

Coffey fled to Denver, "where, in the Greyhound Bus Depot, I twirled a
girlfriend, eyes closed, arm extended, in front of a gigantic map of the
United States. She pointed and we set off."[27]

From the late fifties on, thousands of high-school and college-aged
young women dressed in black descended upon New York's Greenwich
Village and San Francisco's North Beach in search of poetry, folk music,
art, and sexual adventures. Bohemian life offered an opportunity to recast oneself as a misfit, to revel in social disapproval, to elevate an iconoclastic subculture over the dominant culture—all of which would later
prove invaluable experiences to female activists. As one feminist later
wrote, "Our adult lives began born out of these fragments of stolen consciousness. The basic awareness grew that truth, whatever it was, was
something we had all our lives been protected from. Reality had been
kept in quarantine so we could not become contaminated." By experi-
menting with a bohemian existence, some daughters of the fifties, hun-
gry for spontaneity, transcendence, and adventure, chose to end that
quarantine.[28]

In her *Memoirs of a Beatnik*, the poet Diane Di Prima, who enjoyed
sexual relations with both men and women, described how bohemian
life meant "one's blood running strong and red in one's own veins." Di
Prima spent "long afternoons" in coffeeshops on MacDougal Street,
reading and meeting fellow bohemians and artists, "nursing twenty-five-
cent cups of espresso for hours, and drawing pictures on paper napkins." Annie Dillard looked for "life" beyond her sheltered life not just
in books, but in "experience." "I myself was getting wild; I wanted wild-
ness, originality, genius, rapture, hope. I wanted strength, not tea parties." After college, Susan Griffin melted into the Beat scene in San
Francisco, where for the first time she realized she was a writer.

While many young women sought to simulate the Beat sensibility,
only a few actually broke into the inner sacred circle. In a vivid memoir
of her experience as Jack Kerouac's girlfriend, Joyce Johnson described
herself and other female Beats as "minor characters" on a stage reserved mainly for men. Already, at age sixteen, the talented and intellectually ambitious Johnson observed that "just as girls guarded their
virginity, the boys guarded something less tangible which they called

Themselves. They seemed to believe they had a mission in life, from which they could easily be deflected by being exposed to too much emotion."[29]

After she became Jack Kerouac's lover, Johnson again noted this pattern among Kerouac and his pals. Soon she realized that she represented the "anchorage" he needed, when he wanted it, but with no strings attached. Kerouac, whose life alternated between the open road and his mother's home, dropped in on Johnson for "short reunions." She rarely demanded more; hip culture ridiculed the desire for commitment as "uncool." Men defined the nature of freedom and women were required to drop their "bourgeois hang-ups" and accept it. Between their adventures, the men survived by "scuffling"—living off others—and working only when absolutely necessary. Their great accomplishment, Johnson decided,

> was to avoid actual employment for as long as possible and by
> whatever means. But it was all right for women to go out and
> earn wages, since they had no important creative endeavors
> to be distracted from. The women didn't mind, or, if they did,
> they never said—not until years later.

Still, what attracted Johnson to Kerouac and his friends were their spiritual adventures—"some pursuit of the heightened moment, intensity for its own sake." This, she disappointingly learned, was "something they apparently find only when they're with each other."

Of the men who created the world of the Beats, Johnson decided, "I think it was about the right to remain children."[30] True enough, but Johnson also recounts the many freedoms that "minor characters" could enjoy as well. The absence of male economic and emotional commitment freed women from daily subordination to male authority. While the men "scuffled," women like Johnson early on achieved a certain degree of social and economic independence. Female Beats also gained partial entry into an intellectual world previously reserved for men. No other cultural niche permitted a woman to enjoy such a combination of unconventional intellectual, sexual, and economic experiences: academic women were supposed to look asexual; Hollywood sex symbols were required to act dumb. Within the limits of a male-defined aesthetic of freedom, women like Joyce Johnson lived a bohemian ideal of female independence.

SWINGING SINGLES

Few college women ever took up the unconventional life of the Beats; they mostly married. But a significant minority of young women carved out a less exotic alternative lifestyle as "swinging singles" in large cities. By the late fifties, a growing number of college-educated women began migrating to large urban areas, lured by the promise of adventure and excitement. They took jobs as airline stewardesses, teachers, social workers, editorial assistants, or office workers, filling the thousands of new clerical and secretarial jobs created by expanding corporate and state bureaucracies. After a few years of adventure, most of them undoubtedly expected to marry. In the meantime, they shared apartments with other single women and socialized in a singles subculture that their very numbers created.

What distinguished these young women from their predecessors was that they lived neither at home nor in supervised boardinghouses, and that *they* made the rules by which they lived. Some moved casually from one sexual encounter to another, without anyone's disapproval; indeed, often without anyone's knowledge. As Barbara Ehrenreich has argued in *Re-Making Love*, "For young, single, heterosexual women in the fifties and sixties, the city held forth an entirely new vision of female sexual possibility—and the first setting for a sexual revolution."[31]

Unlike the exotic enclaves of the Beats, the embryonic "swinging singles" subculture remained hidden from public view until the publication in 1962 of Helen Gurley Brown's book *Sex and the Single Girl*. Brown gave Americans their first peek inside the swinging singles culture and her lighthearted advocacy of the single life became a national best-seller. By the time that Betty Friedan encouraged married women to combine motherhood with a career in 1963, Brown had already gone on record urging single women to postpone or skip marriage and simply enjoy a fulfilling sexual life.

Brown's ideas mirrored Hugh Hefner's "playboy philosophy." Few single women in the early sixties expected their swinging life to last indefinitely. But while they waited for "Mr. Right," they had Brown's permission to enjoy themselves. In large cities, she insisted, "there is something else a girl can say and frequently does when a man 'insists' and that is 'yes.' . . . Nice girls *do* have affairs, and they do not necessarily die of them." Married couples could keep their diapers, crabgrass, and suburban homes. For the single man or woman, Hefner and Brown now offered an alternative hedonistic lifestyle.[32]

Like the women attached to the Beats, single women soon discovered the fundamental inequality that shadowed their sexually liberated lives. Affairs with married men often brought loneliness and disappointment. Since they earned less than men, they had trouble supporting their lifestyle. In addition, the "value" of an unmarried woman, unlike an unmarried man, depreciated with time. If she waited too long, she risked ending up with no husband at all *and* bumping up against a biological clock. "Spontaneous" sexual pleasures could also be very dangerous. Without perfect contraception or legal abortions, women literally risked their lives if they became pregnant. Fear of pregnancy—or of an illegal abortion—also dampened many a young woman's enthusiasm for the pleasure of sex. The Pill, which would be approved in 1960, was not yet on the horizon.

It is difficult to even imagine what life was like for adventurous young women at a time when abortion remained illegal. A simple mistake, the unwillingness of a young man to use a condom or his inability to use it effectively, the failure of a diaphragm, a vague comprehension of the ovulation cycle, or the belief in coitus interruptus as a failproof method of contraception could, in an instant, change the course of your life. Some women, of course, hastily married, leaving behind their youth and the dream of an education. Others, fearing the loss of their dreams, landed on some quack's kitchen table. If all went well, a young woman returned to her life, perhaps fearful of repeating the experience. If things went badly, a woman found herself in an emergency room, interrogated by hospital personnel, explaining that she had suffered a miscarriage, at the mercy of antibiotics that couldn't always cure an advancing infection. All too often the infection spread, the woman began to bleed profusely, and she died. Advocates of abortion reform estimated that close to one million women had illegal abortions annually before the procedure became legal in 1973, and they attributed some five thousand deaths directly to illegal abortions. The most common kind of illegal abortion was self-induced. Women desperate to end a pregnancy tried an astonishing array of abortifacients. Doctors who examined infected wombs or who performed autopsies became all too familiar with signs of self-induced abortion:

> Air pumped into the uterus left the large blood vessels distended. Turpentine, when ingested or introduced by douche, gave the urine an odor reminiscent of violets; lower abdomi-

nal tenderness was a sign that soap or detergent might have been forced up the cervix. Potassium permanganate tablets, pushed into the vagina to stimulate bleeding that emergency-room doctors might then see as a miscarriage already under-way, left craters of corroded tissue along the vaginal walls, so that suturing them was like trying to put fine surgical stitches into a softened stick of butter.[33]

Large numbers of women knew someone who had gone through the ordeal of having an illegal abortion. First came the agonizing wait for the result of a pregnancy test. Then the search for a doctor. Word of mouth spread the names of "abortionists." But how could you be sure that the "doctor" would use sterile instruments and knew how to per-form an abortion safely? In the dark and dangerous world of illegal abortions, you simply had to take what was available. Women also had to raise enough cash, because most abortionists demanded their fee be-fore starting the procedure. Since the fees were often exorbitant, that meant borrowing from many friends who together put up the money for the abortion.

"Rebecca Thatcher" became pregnant when she was a sophomore at college. She came home and told her parents, who then begged their family physician to perform an abortion. Having known the family for decades, he complied. Such arrangements, hidden from public view, usually took place in the doctor's office. Rebecca's doctor gave her local anesthesia and antibiotics in case of infection. Five years later, she mar-ried and had two sons. "Iris Manning," also a college student, went through a horrible ordeal. Estranged from her parents, she raised enough money to pay a "back alley" abortionist. After she handed over the money, she was told to strip and to lie down on a dirty kitchen table. A friend held her hand. Without anesthesia, she screamed in pain as a leering sadist shoved a rubber hose inside her womb. A decade later, she raised a daughter and son with great satisfaction. But she never for-got the desperation, the humiliation, or the pain.

By the sixties, an underground network of ministers, women activists, and doctors were skirting the law and directing pregnant women to com-petent physicians who had been certified by former patients. "Phyllis Sanders" became pregnant in 1968, her second year in graduate school. Aware of an underground group in San Francisco that provided women with lists of competent doctors, she went to one of those clandestine meetings. There, Patricia McGinnis, a longtime advocate of legal abortion, and founder of the Society for Humane Abortion (SHA), gave her the name of the doctor who performed abortions on the various girlfriends of the chief of police in Mexico City. After raising the money, she and her companion flew to Mexico City and took a taxi to the clinic. There, a nurse fed them and left them alone to sleep in a comfortable room. The next morning, the doctor gave her a thorough medical checkup, and then general anesthesia. When she awoke, her four-week pregnancy had ended. The nurse insisted she rest for a day and gave her antibiotics when she left, just in case an infection developed. The couple spent the next two days engrossed in the archaeology and art museums. She returned to her graduate studies healthy and unscarred. But her enthusiasm for sex, she admitted, had certainly diminished.[34]

By 1969, McGinnis reported that her group had sent twelve thousand women outside of the country for an abortion. Each woman, in turn, had to write an appraisal of the provider and write a letter to her state legislators demanding legal abortion. But Patricia McGinnis was hardly alone in challenging the law. In 1965, Heather Booth, a veteran activist of the civil rights and New Left movements, discovered a doctor in Chicago who would perform abortions for pregnant young women. In 1967, a group of women took over the work and called it first "The Service" and then "Jane." In addition to providing names of abortion providers, they also arranged for "scholarships" and counseling. In some cases, members of Jane did the abortions themselves. Between 1969 and 1973, Jane had arranged for eleven thousand illegal abortions.

The non-Catholic clergy also played an important role in these underground networks. As journalist Cynthia Gorney has documented, there were close to one thousand ministers participating in this illegal and secretive work:

> At the University of Chicago, a Baptist minister named E. Spencer Parson had been sending pregnant students for illegal abortions since 1965. In East Rutherford, New Jersey, an answering machine in a United Methodist parsonage took messages from women who wanted the name of a competent abortionist. . . . In Wisconsin, during the late 1960s, a pregnant woman could walk into the office of certain Baptist or Methodist or United Church of Christ ministers and walk out

an hour later with the name of an illegal abortion provider in Chicago or Juarez. In Pennsylvania, a call to a certain telephone number rang an answering machine in a Baptist nursery school in the town of Wayne; the recorded message left instructions on finding the nearest minister who could provide "counseling" on abortion—and, it was understood, a referral to an abortionist.

If discovered, all these doctors and ministers faced arrest for aiding an illegal abortion. Nonetheless, a group of fifty California ministers and rabbis, committed to helping women find safe abortions, shared this August 16, 1968, memorandum with one another:

> Dr. Madrid is on again. He and his assistants moved all equipment from Juarez to Nogales, Sonora, since we last communicated with you. The new arrangement is as follows: Fly to Tucson, Ariz. Take bus to Nogales Ariz, a 1 hr. 10 min. ride. From the U.S. side of Nogales call 21-70-5 on the Mexican side. Say "this is Mary" and receive the reply "this is Pete," as before. An English-speaking man will be on duty from 9AM to 7PM daily. He will instruct the caller as to meeting place, the driver will identify himself with the green card with our stamp on it, as usual. New prices: $250 to 8 wks. $350 8-13 wks.[35]

In 1960, when the federal government approved the use of the birth control pill, the incipient sexual revolution shifted into higher gear. Growing numbers of unmarried women began to stake out their right to enjoy sex for pleasure rather than for procreation. Those who rebelled eagerly embraced their sexual freedom, happy to explore the pleasures of the body, and seduced by the hope that "free love" would lead to a fulfilling life. But sexual freedom did not directly challenge or redefine either marriage or motherhood. The feminine mystique still seemed to rule life after marriage. After having sex with her boyfriend, one woman recalled, "I started dressing in black and acting more like a Bohemian. But you know, for all this socialism and Bohemianism, I still had this idea that I'd get married and some man would support me and that I ought to get a teaching degree so that I'd have 'something to fall back on.'"[36]

THE SECOND SEX

Young women in the early sixties still lacked a language with which to express their inchoate yearnings and fears. Nowhere in American culture was there an analytic framework or vocabulary suitable for an emancipated woman except in Simone de Beauvoir's book *The Second Sex*. Published in France in 1948, it made its way across the Atlantic in 1953 and quickly gained national attention. As Jean-Paul Sartre's lifelong unmarried companion, de Beauvoir was already notorious for the café-bohemian life she and Sartre popularized in postwar Paris and for her refusal to marry and her decision to remain childless.

Her book was astonishingly subversive. "One is not born, but rather one becomes a woman: no biological, psychological or economic fate determines the figure that the human female presents in society." With these few words, de Beauvoir challenged contemporary views of women's "nature" and began exposing the artificiality of common ideas about gender. Without apology, she attacked the myth of blissful domesticity, describing marriage as servitude and housework as unrelenting drudgery "comparable to the punishment of Sisyphus." Demolishing the cult of sentimental motherhood, de Beauvoir wrote that pregnancy and maternity enslaved as much as they enriched. Maternal devotion, she declared, was only rarely a fulfilling life for most women.[37]

"In the darkness of the Fifties and Sixties before the new women's movement dawned," one feminist later wrote, "*The Second Sex* was like a secret code that we emerging women used to send messages to each other." Quite a few future leaders of the women's liberation movement read it in college or discovered it in the "movement." A professor of philosophy at Ohio Wesleyan University introduced Mary King, a future civil rights activist and feminist, to de Beauvoir's thought. In 1963, she and Casey Hayden, then prominent white women in the Student Nonviolent Coordinating Committee, were working as activists and organizers in southwestern Atlanta. They spent their evenings reading and discussing de Beauvoir's *The Second Sex*, as well as Doris Lessing's *The Golden Notebook*, a powerful novel about women and independence, published the year before. In a memoir, Mary King recalled, "Casey and I had an insatiable appetite for these two authors and especially for de Beauvoir's global perspective." What especially influenced them, she wrote, was the "fundamental existential belief that the human race is responsible for its own destiny," an idea that deepened and reinforced their tireless efforts for civil rights. But de Beauvoir's influence went deeper. From her existentialist philosophy, Hayden and King—central figures in starting the women's movement—absorbed startling revelations about their position as women. "Our copy of de Beauvoir's *The Second Sex*," wrote King, "was underlined, creased, marked up, and finally coverless from our study of it." Eager to spread the message, they began circulating the exhilarating idea that women could define themselves.[38]

When *The Second Sex* was published in the United States in 1953, it entered a culture deeply antagonistic to feminism. Nevertheless, educated women discovered the book and passed it on to friends. Gradually, de Beauvoir's ideas trickled into the margins of American intellectual life. For some women, her work represented pure heresy, properly banned by papal authority. But dedicated thousands felt that on meeting de Beauvoir on the page, they had been struck by the truth and date their transformed consciousness to the discovery of this one book. As feminist writer Susan Griffin explained, "I read de Beauvoir in 1961 and was never the same. Every time I think we have discovered some new idea, I go back and find that de Beauvoir saw it first, that we often are reinventing what she first revealed."[39]

De Beauvoir was not the first person to write of women's subordination. But she was the first to address women's modern dilemma—the fact that they possessed basic political rights yet suffered from extreme cultural, social, and economic marginality. Nor was her work without flaws. She made universal claims based on the experience of French (and some American) girls and women. Ignorant of women's history, de Beauvoir omitted women's historic efforts to transcend their condition, as well as the world around them. Her emphasis on individual choice ignored a movement's need for solidarity and her wistful prediction that socialism would end female oppression underestimated the powerful constraints of class and race, as well as those of religion and global politics.[40]

Still, her brilliant and daring analysis of women's condition encouraged her readers to see themselves and their world through their own eyes. By her own example (even if she did understate the inequalities in her alliance with Sartre), she made personal life the setting for high drama and combined a bohemian sexual freedom with serious intellectual commitment. Through her novels and autobiographical works, she taught a generation of young admirers the political implications of seemingly private matters. Though she offered inadequate answers, she asked brilliant questions, creating a formidable intellectual agenda for a new generation of feminists.[41]

CULTURAL MATRIPHOBIA

Daughters of the fifties had grown up in a highly politicized era, one that celebrated capitalism, vilified Communism, and idealized the feminine mystique. As children of the Cold War, they had learned to contain Communism by assuming their patriotic role as wives and mothers. Permissive parents and higher education had raised young women's expectations, but the feminine mystique blurred any new vision of the future.

Still young at the dawn of a new decade, the daughters of the fifties entered college, bohemian adventures, love affairs, marriage, the civil rights movement, antiwar activities, and the New Left with unarticulated fears of replicating the world of their mothers. In cities, bohemian enclaves and the culture of singles permitted intellectual and sexual adventures, but sexual liberation did not address their fears of traditional marriage. Haunted by their own private demons, they lived a second parallel generational gap, which, until the mid-sixties, remained invisibly subsumed by the entire generation's quest for a different adult future.

At the same time, they drew inspiration from movements for social change that rapidly challenged the nation. As liberal Americans began addressing problems neglected for more than a decade, they inflated the idealistic expectations of these young women, who were just coming of age. The resurrection of a peace movement, the moral drama of the civil rights movement, the rediscovery of poverty, and the exposure of environmental pollution gave new legitimacy to questioning and challenging adults' interpretation of the world.

Interestingly, it was American women activists—white women marching for peace and nuclear safety, black women fighting segregation—who first inspired young women to see the power of female protest. As they matured, elders of the baby boom began to make peace a pressing issue. For many parents, the atomic bomb had mercifully ended a ghastly war. To their children, it had ushered in the threat of planetary annihilation. The bomb became a symbol of the generational divide. Raised in the aftermath of the atomic bombings of Hiroshima and Nagasaki, the postwar generation had grown up in the shadow of a mushroom cloud that threatened to end, in a blinding instant, their lives and their world.[42]

Many "war babies" clearly recall when adult women began protesting American and Soviet aboveground testing of nuclear weapons. In 1961, as a radioactive cloud from a Russian nuclear test hung over the United States, fear of nuclear fallout sparked demands for the two superpowers to sign a test-ban treaty. Women activists argued that strontium 90—a by-product of nuclear testing—was poisoning their children's milk. Suddenly, seemingly out of nowhere, an estimated fifty thousand women in over sixty cities walked out of their homes in an unprecedented one-day housewives' "strike" on November 1, 1961.

Five women who had met while working with the Committee for a Sane Nuclear Policy (SANE) organized the November protest. Weary of SANE's ineffective bureaucratic and lobbying tactics, they had pledged to take direct action against the nuclear threat and called themselves Women Strike for Peace. Former members of CAW and other Left and peace organizations, they organized the strike out of their address books and from their Christmas-card lists. For the first time since the 1920s, women emerged not as part of a mass movement, but *as* that movement, ready to take up the political activism that McCarthyism had interrupted.[43]

But nothing was more inspiring to young women just coming of age than the civil rights movement. Television broadcast into their homes the Montgomery boycott; the violent battles over school integration in Little Rock, Arkansas, and at the University of Mississippi; the sit-ins at lunch counters in Greensboro, North Carolina; the Freedom Rides into the Deep South; the march to Selma, Alabama, and other civil rights struggles. Television also showed stark scenes of racial hatred even as it publicized the bravery of children and adults, black and white, who dared the nation to live up to its ideals. The civil rights movement taught a generation of indoctrinated youthful Cold Warriors that America was hardly a perfect democracy. And it sent a clear message to those restless daughters of the fifties who were heading into college, determined not to become prisoners of the kitchen and nursery. If collective action could destroy racial segregation, which was based on the belief in white superiority, why couldn't women challenge ideas about female inferiority?

Part Two

REBIRTH OF FEMINISM

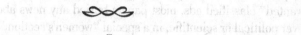

Chapter Three

LIMITS OF LIBERALISM

Much to their amusement, men opened the July 1962 issue of *Esquire* magazine to discover that a middle-aged Caroline Kennedy had won the most recent presidential election. According to the story, crowds of women cheered as the youthful and charismatic politician assumed her fifth term in office. Apparently, when women usurped power in the early years of the twenty-first century, one of their first acts was to abolish the two-term presidency. Then, they rewrote history, substituting Eleanor Roosevelt for FDR. Nationwide, women fitted themselves with surgical skin grafts so that "men were no longer needed." Now, the article reported, men crept cautiously around "women's bars" from which they were legally excluded. They dressed decoratively, spoke softly, lest they displease women and incite their wrath and violent retribution.

This absurdist dystopian fantasy, meant to tickle men's funny bones even as it struck a note of horror, appeared in *Esquire*'s special issue, "The American Woman." To the proposition, "Women of America, Now is the time to Arise," *Esquire* commissioned a "yes" and "no" response. Robert Arthur, who had written this presumably nightmarish satire, assumed that if women gained power, they would simply turn the tables on men and treat them as second-class citizens. Equality between men and women was, for him, unimaginable. Power existed for only one reason: to dominate others.[1]

Not all men shared his anxiety about women's changing lives. *Esquire*'s "yes" article, written by a self-described "unreconstructed male feminist," argued that women deserved no less than full participation in American society. In fact, the *Esquire* issue reflected an existing ambivalence in the country at large. Much of American society still accepted the idea that "separate but equal"—while discredited as policy for the races—suited men's and women's separate social roles rather well. You could see it played out in the daily newspaper. In addition to sex-segregated "help wanted" classified ads, most papers buried any news about women, however political or scientific, in a special "women's section."

It surprised no one, then, when on December 15, 1961, the *Washington Post* tucked the historic news "JFK Seeks Equal Job Status for Women" between two other memorable events of the day: "First Lady Prefers Pastels" and "Skiers to Dance at Ball Tonight," all of which appeared in its "For and About Women" section. The *New York Times* squeezed the same story between book reviews and its "Contract Bridge" column. What these stories reported was John F. Kennedy's decision to create a Presidential Commission on the Status of Women.[2]

When Kennedy won the presidential election of 1960, the very last thing on his mind was to serve as a midwife for the modern women's movement. But decades before the phrase "gender gap" entered political discourse, the idea of a "women's bloc" already worried politicians. Less than two months before the election, the *Saturday Evening Post* had interviewed women leaders in both parties and floated the unsettling idea that women might swing the election. Pleased to be recognized, women in both parties argued that "there is no doubt that if women did vote as a solid bloc, they could swing the election. It is a matter of simple arithmetic: There are 3,500,000 more women than men of voting age—although all of them do not vote. . . . If sex appeal, or appeal to housewifely prejudice or issues that would sway career women or college girls or club ladies were the determining factor, then women could carry any contest." In the weeks before the election, women in the Democratic Party redoubled their efforts to reach female voters through breakfasts and "kaffe klatches."[3]

Kennedy, who only beat Richard Nixon by the slimmest of margins, knew how much women had helped him. Turning his eyes toward the future, he couldn't ignore their growing disgruntlement. One indefatigable female party activist complained that women formed the "hard core" of political organizations but received little recognition for their efforts: "They work at the neighborhood level as block captains, poll watchers, checkers, election-day baby sitters and chauffeurs. They staff party and campaign headquarters. They get out the vote and raise funds. . . . In short, woman power has the same untapped creative potential as atomic energy!"[4]

Democratic women also complained about the "antediluvian male politicians" who "talk down" to the "dear little women" and "try to flatter their looks, rather than their aspirations." "I get awfully tired," explained a former leader of women in the Democratic party,

> of being treated as if I were the English-speaking delegate from another planet. . . . There are too many popular cliches about women. Why must we be typed as fluttery females or bespectacled battleaxes? The public image of women has reached an all-time low—not in fact, but in print. More of us are working, more of us hold better and more responsible positions than ever before—but you'd never know it if you had to depend for information on what you read about women. We are constantly pictured as a limp, indecisive lump, quivering with uncontrolled emotions. . . . Let's insist on speaking and acting as individuals who have a rightful place on the human planet.[5]

Impatiently, these party activists waited for their political payback. But Kennedy disappointed them, offering very few women high-level positions. Margaret Price of Michigan, one of the few Democratic women who had any influence with Kennedy, flooded him with women's résumés, but with little result. When Kennedy appointed no woman to his cabinet, the well-known journalist Doris Fleeson wrote in her *New York Post* column: "At this stage, it appears that for women, the New Frontiers are the old frontiers."[6] Veteran Democratic activist Emma Guffey Miller informed Kennedy that "It is a grievous disappointment to the women leaders and ardent workers that so few women have been named to worthwhile positions. . . . As a woman of long political experience, I feel the situation has become serious and I hope whoever is responsible for it may be made to realize that the result may well be disastrous."[7] Depressed and disillusioned, another party activist predicted that fifty years would pass before the country elected a woman president. Yet another activist grimly joked—as it turned out, accurately—"Man will walk on the moon before there is a woman chief executive."[8]

A PRESIDENTIAL COMMISSION

Esther Peterson, Kennedy's newly appointed head of the Women's Bureau, a division of the U.S. Labor Bureau, quickly mobilized a coalition of women in liberal and labor organizations to pressure Kennedy to create a special commission to explore women's status in the United States. Former First Lady Eleanor Roosevelt, a towering presence, visited the president "to express her concern over the failure of the New Frontier administration to recognize and utilize fully the talents of women." In the view of black activist and lawyer Pauli Murray, that conversation "was the catalytic event which signaled the rebirth of feminism in the U.S."[9]

To Kennedy, a commission seemed a cheap political payoff, a way to reassure the American people that all was well, that women required no drastic or dramatic changes. By creating a commission, he also avoided the far more contentious alternative, that of supporting the Equal Rights Amendment (ERA). After the suffrage amendment was ratified in 1920, Alice Paul, the leader of the National Woman's Party (NWP), submitted the ERA to Congress in 1923, and every year afterward. The members of the NWP, a conservative and relatively well-to-do group of women of means and professional women, sought formal equality with men and argued that a constitutional amendment was necessary to guarantee women's equality with men. With one fell swoop, they argued, the ERA could wipe out all state laws that discriminated against women.

But the amendment, which simply stated, "Equality of rights under the law shall not be denied or abridged by the United States or by any State on account of sex," stayed on the back burner, resisted by labor unions, who were afraid of losing protective legislation for working women. Ever since 1923, women activists remained deeply divided over the ERA, and not until 1970 did female labor and leftist activists give up their strong opposition to the ERA. In their view, protective legislation, which regulated the hours and conditions of women's work, had protected female laborers from extreme exploitation. If the ERA were passed, protective legislation would be eliminated and employers would be free to exploit women. Now Esther Peterson and other women in the Democratic Party, whose roots were in labor, pressed for a commission, rather than the president's support of the ERA. For Kennedy, it was a blessing; labor constituted an important part of his political base.

To justify a commission concerned with women's needs, Kennedy cast it as part of the post-Sputnik Cold War effort to free women's talents for public service. He appointed Eleanor Roosevelt as its chair and charged the commission to "make studies of all barriers to the full participation of women in our democracy."

In 1963, the President's Commission on the Status of Women issued *The Presidential Report on American Women*. Not surprisingly, it mirrored the culture's ambivalence about women's proper place in society. The report reaffirmed their roles as wives, housekeepers, and rearers of children, while documenting the inequalities they faced as workers. Most of the tepid recommendations, as Betty Friedan later noted, were "duly buried in bureaucratic file drawers." The report, a thoroughly political and diluted document, avoided offending any group's sensibilities.[10]

But the commission's report did reveal a great deal about women's place in the American imagination. Amplifying the concern of many social and cultural critics of the day, the report repeatedly decried "the erosion of American family life" and praised those wives and mothers who were holding together the nation's transient families and communities. The report also sounded the alarm that working women would only contribute to the atomization of American social life. The famous anthropologist Margaret Mead even worried that the report had not sufficiently praised full-time mothers and wives and asked, "Who will be there to bandage the child's knee and listen to the husband's troubles and give the human element in the world?"

Here was a serious conundrum. If the nation's female talent were not deployed in universities and laboratories, the Cold War might be lost to a Communist empire that had no scruples about turning its women into workers and scientists, and sending its children to day care centers, as part of its plan to conquer the world. Yet, if American women did work outside the home, who would care for the children, the families, and the communities? This was a dilemma that would haunt the women's movement for decades.[11]

Disappointing as the report may have been, the commission was still an historic convocation. As the first official body to study women's status, the commission collected immense amounts of data, most of which supported the complaints and problems reported by housewives and workers. Press coverage of the commission broke out of the ghetto of the women's section and made the front page of the *New York Times*. NBC's *Today* show broadcast a lively interview with Esther Peterson, the Associated Press ran a four-part series on the final report, and, in 1965, a book of its findings appeared. Most important of all, within a year of its publication, the national commission spawned dozens of state commissions (an idea promoted by Esther Peterson), and the government distributed eighty-three thousand copies of the commission's report, with its invaluable data on women's lives, which was quickly translated into Japanese, Swedish, and Italian. By 1967, all fifty states boasted such commissions.[12]

Charged with collecting local data about women, the state commissions held an annual national conference at which they compared their information and discussed their recommendations for improving women's lives. By 1963, the lives of the women they studied had already changed greatly. Better contraception, more educational and economic opportunity, and the liberalization of attitudes toward divorce were altering a social landscape that had seemed engraved in cement. Later marriages, fewer children, rising divorce rates, and longer life spans meant that more women could expect to spend some part of their lives supporting their families or themselves. Trying to study modern women's status was like aiming at a moving target.[13]

At about the time that the commission started its work, Congress began considering 432 pieces of legislation on women's rights that it would debate between 1960 and 1966—none of which would have appeared on the political agenda without the behind-the-scenes work of hundreds of political women. Activists pushed the Kennedy administration to respond to all kinds of grievances. In 1962, the president revised, by executive order, an 1870 law used to bar women from holding high-level federal positions. The Supreme Court also ruled that states could no longer ban the sale of contraception or exclude women from juries. Shepherded by the Women's Bureau and strongly supported by the United Auto Workers and other labor organizations, the Equal Pay Act was passed in 1963. The original intent—and wording of the bill—proposed equal pay for *comparable* work; the final act required only equal pay for equal [or the same] work. In the midst of jubilant celebration, some women activists knew that the law would have little impact on the vast majority of female workers. Few of them did "men's work"; they were part of a sex-segregated labor force that paid them "women's wages" for "women's work." Nevertheless, an important principle had passed into law, and over the next decade, 171,000 employees would be awarded $84 million for equal work done but not rewarded.[14]

Who were these women who linked the suffrage generation to the generation of feminists emerging in the late 1960s? What kind of leadership and experience did they bring to this job? Who lobbied for the Equal Pay Act? And who used the President's Commission as a way to launch a new women's movement? Veterans in the Left, trade unions, the civil rights movement, and mainstream women's organizations, which demonstrated extraordinary persistence and unfailing commitment, but have remained hidden in history. Most Americans, if they thought about them at all, probably imagined them to be white middle-class professional women. In fact, feminism was resurrected by women whose ideas had developed in a deeply radical milieu.[15]

President Kennedy certainly never intended his presidential commission to turn into what Pauli Murray dubbed "the first high-level consciousness group." But this is what happened. Among its members were leaders from Churchwomen United, the National Association of Catholic Women, the National Association of Jewish Women, the B'nai B'rith, the League of Women Voters, the American Association of University Women, the Business and Professional Women's Clubs, the National Association for the Advancement of Colored People, the Teamsters, and the United Packinghouse Workers. There were also representatives of women in religious orders, professors in universities, schoolteachers, and those who had worked for child welfare, peace, and educational reform.[16]

These leaders brought an incredible range of interests, experiences, and perspectives to the commission. Dorothy Haener, a tireless organizer of women in the United Auto Workers, argued ceaselessly for a higher minimum wage. (Haener later chaired NOW's Task Force on Poverty, a fact that never received as much attention as NOW's efforts to break the "glass ceiling" for professional women.) Addie Wyatt, an African-American leader of the United Packinghouse Workers of America and the NAACP, viewed the commission as a chance for working women to "raise our voice" on a national level and to gain a "sharper focus on women's concerns." She was also the first person to insist that women needed their own civil rights organization, modeled on the NAACP. Kay Clarenbach, chair of the Wisconsin State Commission, first president of the Association of State Commissions, and author of the first handbook for the state commissions, had been a professor of political science at the University of Wisconsin. Later, Clarenbach said that her experience on the commission "not only changed my life, it subsequently *became* my life!" Clarenbach eventually came to see her work in global terms. "Feminism," she said, "is a vision of a different kind of society."[17]

A disproportionate number of these women came from the Midwest, rather than from either coast or Washington, D.C. The heartland, with its progressive political traditions and strong unions, had apparently provided women with greater opportunities to become effective organizers. Dubbed by some politicians the "Wisconsin Mafia," these seasoned veterans transformed the role of the state commissions. Although they were only supposed to collect data and report on it, they quickly turned data into ammunition that could be used for lobbying legislatures. They wrote publications, researched the law, held conferences, and gave endless speeches. In a typical year, the indefatigable Kay Clarenbach gave forty speeches. In her view, they "laid the groundwork that was absolutely necessary" for changing women's lives.[18]

Everything is data, but data is not everything, as sociologist Pauline Bart has warned. To really learn about women's lives, these women would have to learn from one another. And so they did. What Kennedy could not have known was that when brought together, women tell each other stories about their lives. As these commission members began to share grievances and secrets, they began to discover exactly how ubiquitous was sex discrimination.

They also learned a great deal about the diversity of the female experience. Rural women taught urbanites who had never milked a cow about the isolation and precariousness of farm life. African-Americans tried to teach their white counterparts about how racism affected every aspect of their lives. Trade unionists described the conditions under which they worked to professional women. Lawyers and professors revealed, in turn, the kinds of discrimination and ridicule they encountered. Housewives tried to convince union activists and minority women that they, too, felt devalued as individuals. Gradually, they taught each other what women needed. Kay Clarenbach, for instance, recalled how Pauli Murray convinced her during an airplane trip why reproductive control of women's bodies was a precondition for women's other freedoms. Charlotte Bunch's articles—which other members gave her—helped her grasp, for the first time, the problems lesbians faced in society. Recalling those heady years, Clarenbach deadpanned, "Days when you don't learn something can be a drag."[19]

The cumulative impact of these conversations and revelations gave rise to a collective awareness that whatever women did, their work was devalued, and that most women—wherever they worked, whatever the color of their skin, whatever their ethnic or regional background—did not participate in the same educational, economic, or political worlds as their male counterparts.

THE TURNING POINT, TITLE VII

Nineteen sixty-three had been a banner year. The Equal Pay Act, the *Presidential Report on American Women*, and *The Feminine Mystique* all helped to publicize a growing sense of gender consciousness. The next year was no less momentous. After President Kennedy's assassination in November 1963, Congress began considering the comprehensive civil rights bill. Congressman "Judge" Howard Smith, the southern chairman of the House Rules Committee, offered an amendment to add "sex" to Title VII, the section of the bill that prohibited discrimination in employment on the basis of race, color, religion, or national origin by private employers. A longtime supporter of the Equal Rights Amendment, as well as an ardent segregationist, Smith saw his amendment as purely a win-win proposition. A prohibition on sex discrimination would give northern representatives a reason to vote against the act without facing the accusation of being racists. And if it passed, at least he wanted to be sure that "white women" would be the beneficiaries.[20]

At first, Smith's colleagues did not even take the amendment seriously. In an excessive display of chivalric oratory, Smith regaled the House with a letter from a woman who complained of the paucity of men available as husbands. Playing for laughs, he asked the House to take these "real grievances" seriously. The House erupted in riotous laughter. Emmanuel Celler, the liberal New York chairman of the Judiciary Committee, added to the jocular spirit when he announced that it was he—never his wife—who always had the last two words in his household, and those were "Yes, dear."[21]

When the laughter subsided, coalitions began forming for and against Smith's amendment. Prodded by the Virginia members of the National Woman's Party—never known for its progressive views on race—these women now turned to Smith as a natural ally. Democratic representative Edith Green, the sponsor of the 1963 Equal Pay Act, worried that the amendment would gather opposition to the civil rights bill and risk African-Americans' chance to win their civil rights. She decided to vote against Smith's amendment. On the other hand, yes votes came from those representatives who had decided that they would not endure another "Negro's hour"—the post–Civil War moment when suffrage was granted to black men, but not to black or white women. Representative Martha Griffiths, a Republican who had long sought to include a prohibition on sex discrimination in the civil rights bill, helped forge a bizarre coalition of southern congressmen and their feminist supporters who seized the unexpected opportunity. The amendment passed.

Women activists immediately began a lobbying campaign to ensure passage of the entire bill itself. Betty Friedan, Martha Griffiths, Pauli

Murray, members of the National Women's Party, the Business and Professional Women's Clubs, and dozens of other women's organizations invaded legislators' offices, warning of the consequences if they dared vote against half of their constituency. Supported by President Lyndon Johnson's wife, Lady Bird, and various members of the administration, the Civil Rights Act of 1964—including Title VII—passed.[22]

Nearly every American social movement can point to some specific legal victory that decisively raised their members' sense of entitlement. For black Americans, it was *Brown v. Board of Education of Topeka*, the 1954 Supreme Court ruling against "separate but equal" education. For the women's movement, it was Title VII of the 1964 Civil Rights Act. The legislation created a new agency, the Equal Employment Opportunity Commission (EEOC), charged with investigating complaints of racial and sexual discrimination. But women quickly discovered that its director, Herman Edelsberg, considered sex discrimination a joke, or at least a distraction from the more important work of assisting black men. Edelsberg called Title VII "a fluke . . . conceived out of wedlock." "There are people on this commission," he informed the press, "who think that no man should be required to have a male secretary and I am one of them." When it was signed into law at the White House ceremony, no women were present, and the *New York Times*'s account of the bill did not even mention that the new legislation prohibited sex discrimination in employment.[23]

When someone at a White House Conference on Equal Opportunity openly wondered if Playboy clubs would now have to employ male "bunnies," the press quickly picked up the joke and dubbed the sex amendment the "Bunny Law." A *New York Times* editorial coyly suggested that

> Federal officials . . . may find it would have been better
> if Congress had just abolished sex itself. Handyman must
> disappear from the language; he was pretty much a goner
> anyway, if you ever started looking for one in desperation.
> No more milkman, iceman, serviceman, foreman or press-
> man. . . . The Rockettes may become bi-sexual, and a pity,
> too . . . Bunny problem, indeed! This is revolution, chaos. You
> can't even safely advertise for a wife any more.[24]

Title VII remained a joke. In August 1965, the EEOC shocked women activists when it ruled that sex-segregated help-wanted ads were perfectly legal. The *New Republic*, a liberal journal of opinion, agreed. "Why should a mischievous joke perpetrated on the floor of the House of Representatives be treated by a responsible administration body with this kind of seriousness?" The idea of banishing sex discrimination challenged deeply held ideas about gender and elicited much nervous ridicule. The *Wall Street Journal* asked its readers to imagine "a shapeless, knobby-kneed male 'bunny' serving drinks to a group of astonished businessmen or a 'matronly vice-president' lusting after her male secretary." What are we going to do now, asked a personnel officer of a large airline, "when a gal walks into our office, demands a job as an airline pilot and has the credentials to qualify?" In companies that traditionally hired only women, businessmen grew edgy. One manager of an electronics component company lamented, "I suppose we'll have to advertise for people with small, nimble fingers and hire the first male midget with unusual dexterity [who] shows up."[25]

Even if the EEOC had taken sex discrimination seriously, Congress had severely limited its powers. The agency could only investigate individual complaints, issue findings, and seek voluntary settlements. If a company refused to concede race or sex discrimination, the EEOC had to persuade the Civil Rights Division of the Justice Department to seek judicial enforcement. If the division refused, the complainant's only recourse was to file suit in federal court.[26]

Nonetheless, by 1965, working women began flooding the EEOC with their grievances. In some parts of the country, nearly half the complaints came from working women who identified acts of discrimination. Shocked by the volume of these grievances, the EEOC nevertheless remained committed to monitoring only racial discrimination. Mired in the Vietnam War and unsettled by race riots in American cities, neither President Johnson nor Congress gave women's complaints any attention. On June 20, 1966, Representative Martha Griffiths, a tireless fighter for women's rights, denounced the EEOC for its "specious, negative, and arrogant" attitude toward sex discrimination. "I would remind them," she announced on the floor of Congress, "that they took an oath to uphold the law, not just the part of it that they are interested in."[27]

No one seemed to care—except members of the state commissions who had convened for their third conference in Washington, D.C., ten days after Griffiths attacked the EEOC. Within their respective states, the commissions had supported more flexible working hours, the repeal of discriminatory laws, equal pay, and dozens of other "women's issues." The state commissions had also created a national network of women

who, by gathering and sharing data about women in their respective
states, had gained expert knowledge about women's subordinate status
in American society. But by themselves, as delegates to the third conference on state commissions, they were almost powerless. As Betty
Friedan later noted, "It is more than a historical fluke that the organization of the women's movement was ignited by that law, never meant to be
enforced, against sex discrimination in employment."[28]

THE FOUNDING OF NOW

They did have one vital resource to call on—what Betty Friedan called
"an underground feminist movement" that existed in the nation's capital. Friedan was in constant contact with women who risked their government jobs to promote women's issues there. She credited women like
"Catherine East of the Women's Bureau of the Labor Department for
spreading the feminist underground around Washington and acting as
midwife to the women's movement." The network also included Esther
Peterson; Mary Eastwood, a former member of the President's Commission; EEOC commissioner Richard Graham; Sonia Pressman, an attorney in the EEOC; legal scholar Pauli Murray; and congresswoman
Martha Griffiths. Frustrated by the government's unwillingness to influence the EEOC and angered by the EEOC's unwillingness to address
sex discrimination—especially sex-segregated "want ads"—fifteen
women finally agreed to meet one evening during the conference in
Friedan's hotel room to discuss the possibility of starting a new women's
organization.[29]

Some of the women wondered whether they could even trust one another. For some, surfacing in any advocacy group for women was risky.
Friedan later recalled how difficult it was for "women who didn't know
each other personally, who hadn't yet acquired the trust we would later
earn in action together." The McCarthy period had left a legacy of fear,
and many activists had learned to keep their silence on political issues.
The discussion continued past midnight, interrupted by "ladylike rows,"
and filled with suspicion and timidity. When the meeting ended, the
group was still unable to agree on the nature of the new organization or
whether there should even be one. Betty Friedan went to bed feeling the
bitter taste of defeat. "I thought the battle was over before it had even begun, not realizing that the same fear and finally the daring necessary to
act despite those fears were now under way in the others, just as in me."[30]

In fact, the struggle had just begun. At the conference the next day, a group of delegates presented a resolution insisting that the EEOC enforce Title VII of the Civil Rights Act. Conference officials, worried about pressuring the Johnson administration, refused to allow the resolution to come to a vote. The delegates, from various state commissions, grew furious. They were tired of talk; they wanted action.

At lunch, a group hastily gathered around two tables to discuss their next move. Time was running out, because, as Friedan later explained, "most of us had plane reservations that afternoon, when the conference ended, and had to get back in time to make dinner for their families." In conspiratorial fashion, they whispered, passed around notes on paper napkins, and discussed forming a new organization. On one of those paper napkins, Friedan wrote down a name—the National Organization for Women. Its purpose, she scribbled, would be "to take the actions needed to bring women into the mainstream of American society, now" and to fight for "full equality for women, in full equal partnership with men."[31] As they left to catch their planes, the conspirators agreed to call a formal meeting to create the new organization that fall.

The founding of a feminist civil rights organization of some sort was probably inevitable. Women needed a nongovernmental organization that could pressure the government from outside, as an independent movement. But at the time it seemed an audacious act, frightening to many of its potential members. Alice Rossi, the distinguished sociologist, sent membership invitations to thirty or forty sociologists, but few chose to join.[32]

By creating a feminist civil rights organization, NOW members did more than assert their independence from male-dominated liberal politics; they publicly acknowledged that liberal political culture was inadequate to address the reality of women's lives. By declaring their autonomy from a liberal government, they also freed themselves to consider the question of women's rights from a more radical perspective. "Everything was different," Friedan recalled. "The problems *looked* different, the definition of the problems, the solutions sought, once we dared to judge our conditions as women by that simple standard, the hallmark of American democracy—equality, no more, no less."[33] As she drafted a "Statement of Purpose" for NOW, Friedan found herself "forced to spell out in my own mind the implications of 'equality for women.'" One thing was certain, "separate but equal" was out of the question. How should one define equality and liberty for modern women?

While Friedan deliberated, a growing public debate about women was stirring in the media and in the academy. Suddenly, all kinds of people seemed eager to break the spell of the feminine mystique. In 1964, the American Academy of Arts and Sciences helped recast the issue in intellectual terms by publishing a special issue on women in its prestigious journal *Daedalus*. Like the report of the President's Commission, the *Daedalus* collection reflected the cultural ambivalence of the period; it included articles that emphasized women's traditional role in the home and others that challenged received wisdom. Articles by such well-known scholars as Erik H. Erikson and Carl Degler would become classics—later to be embraced or attacked by feminists. The most startling of them, the one that would provide the greatest intellectual legitimacy for a women's movement, was Alice Rossi's article, titled "Equality Between the Sexes: An Immodest Proposal," that both shaped and reflected early feminists' ideas about gender.[34]

A distinguished sociologist and educator, Rossi felt discouraged by the apathy of her female students, noting "there is no overt anti-feminism in our society in 1964, not because sex equality has been achieved, but because there is practically no feminist spark left among American women." Rossi directly attacked the fifties' obsession with sexual difference, and offered an alternative vision of gender equality—androgyny.

> An androgynous conception of sex roles means that each sex will cultivate some of the characteristics usually associated with the other in traditional sex role definitions. This means that tenderness and expressiveness should be cultivated in boys and socially approved in men. . . . It means that achievement, need, workmanship and constructive aggression should be cultivated in girls and approved in women.

Like de Beauvoir, Rossi argued that gender is an artificial construct of culture, adding only, "I shall leave to speculative discourse and future physiological research the question of what constitutes irreducible differences between the sexes." Though Rossi would later emphasize sex differences, rather than sameness in the 1970s, her "immodest proposal" in 1964 had an enormous impact on the rebirth of feminism. In the wake of the fifties, few women activists and intellectuals wanted to rest their case for equality on "sexual difference." For them, sexual difference reminded them of all the reasons why women had been excluded from political, economic, and social life. Rossi's emphasis on androgyny was far more appealing. If both women and men could absorb each other's strongest traits, then they could make choices based on individual talent and temperament, rather than on one's sexual identity at birth.[35]

Like most activists of the time, Friedan shunned arguments based on difference. "The time has come," she wrote, "to confront, with concrete actions, the conditions that now prevent women from enjoying the equality of opportunity and freedom of choice which is their right, as individual Americans, and as human beings." Friedan recognized American women's right to shape their own lives as well as their right to self-fulfillment. These values, she explained, were "simply the values of the American Revolution . . . applied to women." "The logic," Friedan wrote, "was inexorable."

> Once we broke through that feminine mystique and called
> ourselves human—no more, no less—surely we were entitled
> to the enjoyment of the values which were our American,
> democratic human right. All we had to do was really look at
> the concrete conditions of our daily life in the light of those
> lofty values of equality which are supposed to be every man's
> birthright—and we could immediately see how unfair, how
> oppressive, our situation was.[36]

But that wasn't possible without challenging many fundamental aspects of liberal political culture. Women's rights, as it turned out, were not just another ingredient you could add and stir into the American Dream. The citizen whose rights the state protected had always been imagined as a man, and his biological and work lives were dramatically different from those experienced by a woman. The right to pursue happiness, for example, took on new meaning when it included a woman's right to control her own body and reproductive future. Equal opportunity meant something quite different when it involved sharing domestic work, ending sexual harassment in the workplace, and ending all forms of violence against women. When applied to women, individual rights, which most Americans considered the touchstone of American political culture, turned out to threaten men's authority in the family and challenge all kinds of social and cultural traditions. It was not at all clear—to many women and men—that these were "individual rights" that the state should consider protecting. For liberal political culture to recast the citizen as a woman and embrace fundamental economic and social transformations in the home and the workplace required nothing less than an expansion of the definition of democracy.

In 1966, the radicalism of this challenge to American political culture was not yet fully grasped by Betty Friedan, by young feminists in the women's liberation movement, nor even by their opponents. Although feminists would long debate whether to emphasize women's difference from or similarity to men, neither choice fully embraced the reality of women's lives. Women were both like and unlike men. Any society that didn't honor women's ability to bear and raise children was clearly violating their rights to fully participate in society. Any society that equated equality with women living as men could not be viewed as a genuine democracy. A true "gender democracy" would have to honor the life of the family as much as it honored the life of work. Men would no longer be the frame of reference. But nor would women. The revolutionary thrust of feminism required an extensive expansion of democracy at work, in the home, in public, in private. Nothing less would do.

On October 29, 1966, NOW convened its official founding conference in Washington, D.C. Of the three hundred women who became charter members, 120 came from the Midwest, which once again highlighted the indigenous female activism in this region of the nation. Of these three hundred members, only thirty could be present to adopt the "Statement of Purpose" and new bylaws. This small convocation elected Friedan its first president and former EEOC commissioners Aileen Hernandez and Richard Graham its vice presidents. NOW's "Statement of Purpose" declared that women's demands for equality were "part of the world-wide revolution of human rights now taking place within and beyond our national borders." The writers were determined to avoid the kind of separatism just then emerging in black activist organizations, so the first sentence of the "Statement" began, "We men and women," and called for "a fully equal partnership of the sexes. . . ." It also enumerated the dramatic changes that had created the basis for a new surge of demands for women's rights: an extended life span of seventy-five years and the development of technology that reduced the importance of muscular strength.[37]

NOW's statement challenged American society to heed women's grievances. One of those issues was that despite the optimistic social programs of Kennedy's New Frontier and Johnson's Great Society, the economic status of women had actually declined. By 1966, the wages of full-time year-round women workers averaged only 60 percent of those of men, a drop of 3.6 percent in a decade. Black women, burdened by the double discrimination of sex and race, earned even less. In addition, although 46.4 percent of American adult women now worked, 75 percent of them labored in routine clerical, sales, or factory jobs or as household workers, cleaning women, and hospital attendants.[38]

In all the professions, women were also losing ground. Though they constituted 53 percent of the population, they represented less than 1 percent of federal judges, less than 4 percent of lawyers, and only 7 percent of doctors. In addition, since World War II, men had been replacing women in professions once considered "women's fields"—as administrators of secondary and elementary schools, librarians, and social workers. This hidden and "dangerous decline," NOW's "Statement" declared, had to be "recognized and reversed by 'the power of American law' [and the] protection guaranteed by the U.S. Constitution to the civil rights of all individuals." Token appointments were unacceptable; the government would have to stop discriminating against women in all areas of public life.[39]

The "Statement" pointedly criticized the United States for lagging behind other industrialized countries in providing the kinds of social welfare—health care, child care, and pregnancy leave—that supported women's domestic and work needs. Women "should not have to choose between family life and participation in industry or the professions." Nor should "all normal women . . . retire from jobs or professions for ten or fifteen years, to devote their full time to raising children, only to reenter the job market at a relatively minor level." The "Statement" questioned the "assumption that these problems are the unique responsibility of each individual woman, rather than a basic social dilemma which society must solve."

Contrary to later accusations that feminists ignored the issue of child-rearing and denied women the choice of remaining full-time mothers, NOW's "Statement" called for a nationwide network of child care centers, as well as national programs to provide retraining, after their children grew up, "for women who have chosen to care for their own children full-time." The "Statement" also urged recasting traditional gender roles within marriage, proposing that "a true partnership between the sexes demands a different concept of marriage, an equitable sharing of the responsibilities of home and children and of the economic burden of their support."[40]

During NOW's first few years, the press gave the new organization only slightly more respect—and far less attention—than the sexier young women's liberation movement that sprang to life in 1967. To report NOW's first convention, the *New York Times* placed an article headlined "They Meet in Victorian Parlor to Demand 'True Equality' " right beneath exciting new recipes for turkeys and stuffing. The *Washington Post* headlined its report "Neo-Suffragettes on the March: Mrs. Friedan Is Fighting for Women's Equality NOW" and ran it next to an ad for a "fashion clearance" and below photographs of diplomatic wives greeting each other.[41]

NOW also suffered from meager resources. For three years, the organization lacked an office of its own. Nevertheless, NOW members made do, much as those in the civil rights and students' movements had, by borrowing any resources to which they had access. The new secretary-treasurer, Caroline Davis of the United Auto Workers, gave NOW a valuable "free ride" by allowing it to use the UAW's facilities—especially its precious WATS phone line,* as well as copy and mimeograph machines. Betty Friedan's apartment in New York City served as the center of policy-making and organization. Fearful of centralization, NOW quickly developed local chapters to counterbalance the power of a national headquarters. Local leadership identified their own priorities and projects, while the national leadership made policy and coordinated national actions.

With these slim resources, NOW plunged into action. Predictably, its first official act was to pressure the EEOC to prohibit segregated "help wanted" advertising. Such a division of ads, NOW argued, ensured that women would not be able to enter the higher-paid and more skilled occupations reserved for men. To dramatize the issue, NOW members picketed the *New York Times* in August 1967. In December, NOW declared a National Day of Demonstration against the EEOC, mobilizing women to picket local EEOC offices. After tipping off the television networks, small groups of NOW members, in an attempt to demonstrate the worthlessness of sex-segregated want ads, dumped bundles of newspapers in front of EEOC local offices. In August 1968, after years of protracted struggles with the government and the newspaper industry, the EEOC finally barred segregated want ads.[42]

---

*WATS telephone lines allowed either free or deeply discounted calls from institutions like unions and universities. Without them, national organization was far more difficult. All social movements at the time depended upon the use of WATS lines to do what e-mail would do in the 1990s.

Contrary to conventional wisdom, NOW members—although mostly white and middle class—targeted the problems of ordinary working women, not those of professional women. The assault on segregated classified ads, for instance, benefited working women who wanted to enter the skilled blue collar jobs formerly designated as men's work. NOW also waged a successful campaign against airlines that forced stewardesses to resign once they married or turned thirty-two. This requirement had produced windfall profits for the airlines that fired wave after wave of stewardesses, without having to give them raises, pensions, or Social Security payments. "Sex discrimination," observed Friedan, "*was* big business."[43]

NOW next pressed the government, as well as federal contractors and subcontractors, to ban sex discrimination—again, something that did not particularly benefit professional women. In the fall of 1965, President Johnson had signed an Executive Order banning racial (but not sexual) discrimination in businesses and institutions that received funds from the government. Two years later, NOW leaders began lobbying President Johnson for similar treatment. He responded by adding "sex" to the new Executive Order. The results were far-reaching: any university or company that received federal contracts now had to ensure fair employment to women as well as to racial minorities.

During its first year, NOW also pushed for enforcement of Title VII by the EEOC, so that minority women in federal poverty programs would get equal attention and so that child care expenses would be deductible. In its first court action, for which it established its Legal Defense Fund, NOW supported southern factory women who sued Colgate-Palmolive and Southern Bell Telephone for denying women jobs—an action that had been prohibited by state laws. All these campaigns were aimed at improving the lives of ordinary working women.

EARLY RIFTS

NOW certainly experienced squabbles and factions among its members. Tensions between local chapters and national headquarters sometimes erupted into public fights. Political disagreements frequently hid personality clashes. But such tensions were inevitable. How could one organization represent the political and social needs of *all* women?

At its 1967 convention, when NOW proposed a new Bill of Rights, the young organization faced the fragility of feminist solidarity. The Bill of Rights, presented to members for ratification, called for dramatic changes in American society. Although labor still opposed it, NOW members embraced the passage of the Equal Rights Amendment to the Constitution. To improve working women's lives, the Bill of Rights included enforcement of laws banning sex discrimination in employment, maternity leave, equality in Social Security benefits, tax deductions for home and child care expenses for working parents, and child care centers. In addition, it also included the demand for equal and unsegregated education, equal job training opportunities and allowances for women in poverty, and the right of women to control their reproductive lives.[44]

Unanimous approval proved impossible. The Equal Rights Amendment immediately faced opposition from trade union women who wanted to extend protective legislation to men before they ended it for women. Their opponents argued that industry and business routinely used state protective laws to deny women workers promotions or overtime pay. Fighting sex discrimination case by case, state by state, could take another fifty years, whereas a constitutional amendment could wipe out institutional sex discrimination with one law. To women who enjoyed or aspired to professional status, the ERA seemed perfectly logical and necessary. In Betty Friedan's words, "It was a guarantee that would take precedence over those state laws now 'protecting' women from good jobs and pay, that could not be rescinded at a mere whim of Congress or state legislature. With it, the courts low and high, state or federal, could no longer rule that women were not 'persons' under the U.S. Constitution as they have done so frequently over the years."[45]

But that was not the view of labor. When the 1967 convention voted to endorse the ERA, Caroline Davis, respecting the UAW's wishes, resigned as NOW's secretary-treasurer, which caused the organization to lose its precious union mailing and printing resources. But just one year later, the UAW reversed its position and came out in favor of the ERA. Soon after, the entire American Federation of Labor–Congress of Industrial Organizations (AFL/CIO), recognizing the wisdom of extending protection to all workers, changed its position and also supported the amendment. Many feminists breathed a sigh of relief. NOW and labor unions, part of the same political base, would not be locked in a political battle over the ERA.

A woman's right to an abortion created an even greater schism in

NOW's ranks. Nevertheless, after extensive debate and some abstentions from Catholic sisters, this part of the Bill of Rights also passed. A few women, certain that such a controversial issue would offend potential sympathizers, left NOW to found the Women's Equity Action League (WEAL) in 1968. Dr. Elizabeth Boyer, the Ohio lawyer who led WEAL, targeted three areas of sex discrimination—employment, education, and de facto tax inequities. Described as "the far right wing of the women's Mafia," WEAL cultivated a ladylike style to attract more conservative women to join the struggle for women's rights. One of WEAL's liveliest chapters, for example, blossomed in Iowa, where, according to Boyer, "you couldn't sell 'women's liberation' if you gold-plated it."[46]

The rights of lesbians—not included in the original document— proved to be another divisive issue, though one that only surfaced several years later, after the founding of the gay liberation movement. In 1969 and again in 1970, Betty Friedan had labeled lesbianism a "lavender menace" that threatened to taint the women's movement. Angry at being "purged" by her assaults, many lesbians left the organization. In 1971, after years of hiding in the organizational closet, the remaining lesbians demanded that NOW pass a resolution recognizing their civil rights. In response, NOW did so, declaring that a "woman's right to her own person includes the right to define and express her own sexuality and to choose her own lifestyle; therefore we acknowledge the oppression of lesbians as a legitimate concern of feminism." In 1973, NOW established a Task Force on Sexuality and Lesbianism, and passed a resolution that, by defining homosexuality as a civil rights issue, repositioned the granting of rights to lesbianism and sexual preference as but another liberal extension of civil rights. It declared that the organization should "actively introduce and support civil rights legislation to end discrimination based on sexual orientation . . . in housing, employment, credit, finance, child custody, and public accommodation."[47]

Though NOW waged many of its high-profile battles in the courts, its members also educated, marched, picketed, and protested to publicize feminist issues. A broad range of national task forces publicized the need for more child care centers, the repeal of laws that prohibited abortion, more equitable tax and divorce laws, Social Security reform, nonsexist textbooks, and an end to sexual stereotypes in advertising and television programs. To advertising agencies that created insulting images of women, they presented their "barefoot and pregnant in the kitchen" award. On Mother's Day 1967, NOW attempted to organize demonstrations nationwide for "rights, not roses." At the exact spot where a group of suffragists had chained themselves to a White House fence fifty years earlier, activists ceremoniously dumped a huge pile of aprons. Nothing reflected the rejection of the fifties housewife more starkly than that trash pile of aprons.[48]

Many of NOW's public demonstrations targeted sex discrimination in public spaces. After a particularly "tedious lawyerish" discussion at a NOW national board meeting in New York City in 1968, a few members adjourned to the Men's Bar and Grill at the Hotel Biltmore to calm their nerves. There, the bartender informed them that he could not serve female customers. After alerting the media, twenty women moved to stage a sit-in at the bar. The bar decided to close for twenty-four hours. But NOW members picketed anyway in full view of network cameras. To celebrate Valentine's Day in 1968, Betty Friedan led an invasion of the Oak Room at the Plaza Hotel in New York City. Soon afterward, New York feminists invaded that epitome of the male sanctuary, McSorley's Old Ale House. Such demonstrations had their cumulative impact. Gradually, individual states began banning sex discrimination in public accommodations.[49]

A certain wilder spirit of protest began to enter NOW, thanks in part to younger women who by 1967 were creating loosely affiliated small groups collectively known as the women's liberation movement. Though NOW and women's liberation groups often joined forces for specific protests, efforts to form coalitions between the two branches of the movement frequently failed. The demons that haunted the daughters of the fifties never fully disappeared. Meredith Tax, an early activist, realized how much the female generation gap influenced the culture of the young women's liberation movement:

> My friends and I thought of NOW as an organization for peo-
> ple our mother's age. We were movement girls, not career
> women; NOW's demands and organizational style weren't
> radical enough for us. We wanted to build a just society, not
> get a bigger slice of the pie. Besides, we were generational
> sectarians; we didn't trust anybody over thirty.[50]

Influenced by the antihierarchical spirit of New Left groups, as well as by the theatrical thrust of the counterculture, the younger women's liberation movement was not particularly concerned with proving their respectability; on the contrary, they wanted to shake things up as much as possible.

Meanwhile, NOW officials became increasingly worried that the movement would appear too undisciplined or unrespectable. In March 1968, an article by Martha Lear on the new women's movement appeared in the *New York Times Magazine*. Its title, "The Second Feminist Wave," christened the movement with a name that connected it to "first wave" feminism in the suffrage movement.[51] Lear's article also reported that some members were preparing a "black comedy" to dramatize the EEOC's reluctance to take sex discrimination seriously. Twelve women, dressed for cocktails, planned to crash an EEOC hearing, make a commotion, get thrown out and possibly arrested, and then meet with the press to explain their grievances. One of the large, home-lettered signs was to read, "A Chicken in Every Pot, a Whore in Every Home." After some deliberation, some NOW members, worried that the press might headline the demonstration as "Prostitutes Picket EEOC," decided on a different image: two secretaries chained to their typewriters.

The "Valerie Solanas affair" intensified some of the conflicts between older and younger feminists in New York's NOW, where tensions were already high. In 1968, a disturbed artist in New York's avant-garde art scene wrote—by herself—a document she called the "SCUM Manifesto," an acronym for the Society for Cutting Up Men. Her manifesto not only blamed men for every evil in the world, but also argued for their collective annihilation. Shortly afterward, Solanas shot and wounded pop artist Andy Warhol, whom she blamed for her own marginality. She was arraigned for attempted murder and consigned to psychiatric observation.

A few younger feminists turned Solanas into a cause célèbre; others viewed her as a disturbed woman in need of sisterly assistance. When Ti-Grace Atkinson, the president of New York NOW, publicly appeared at Solanas's trial, some NOW members worried about being identified with "man-hating" women. NOW's board consisted of university professors and administrators, state and national labor union officers, local and federal government officials, business executives, physicians, and members of religious orders, all of whom were dedicated to preserving NOW's public reputation and credibility. Atkinson, already dissatisfied with what she considered NOW's "elitist" structure, then resigned to form her own organization, the October 17th Movement (named after the day she left), later renamed "The Feminists."[52]

Collisions between the women's liberation movement and NOW were frequent and probably inevitable. In November 1969, a year not remembered for youthful deference, NOW attempted to gather disparate groups from the mushrooming women's movement at a Congress to Unite Women in New York City. For three days, over five hundred women from a wide range of groups and organizations debated feminist issues, but it was clear that the young women dominated the agenda and that their rebellious spirit ruled the meeting. Betty Friedan, for instance, would never have convened a workshop to discuss "whether women's liberation would end sex or make it better." As she later wrote:

> I didn't think a thousand vibrators would make much difference—or that it mattered who was in the missionary position—if unequal power positions in real life weren't changed. . . . It was the *economic* imbalance, the power imbalance in the world that subverted sex, or made sex itself into a power game where no one could win. . . . I feel like a grim spoilsport sometimes, always insisting to my sisters in the movement on that dull economic basis that had to change for any woman to be able to enjoy her own sexuality, or to truly love anyone. . . . It was so much easier and more fun just to talk about sex, vibrators, women, men, underneath or on top. But to extrapolate sexual joylessness and lonely need, masochism or cruelty as the permanent condition of women is in my opinion to give up the battle. This is the sexual pathology bred by our inequality and the reaction to it.[53]

On the first evening, a group of women from Boston's Female Liberation took the stage and formed a semicircle around one woman who proceeded to cut off the luxurious long hair of another. Wearing short hair, the women explained to the audience, was a rejection of the conventional feminine image cultivated by society. The audience was electrified. Some women shouted that they shouldn't cut their hair, that long hair was lovely and countercultural. Other women denounced the image of the long-haired, hip, radical, movement "chick."

Betty Friedan looked on with horror. To her, the hair-cutting demonstration perfectly captured the differences that separated NOW from the women's liberation movement. To Friedan, as to most other NOW members, the highest priority was to change social policy and to eliminate legal sex discrimination. After women gained economic independence,

NOW members reasoned, they would have the power to make changes in their private lives as well.

To older women, transforming oneself was not, by itself, a political act. Friedan loathed "the abusive language and style of some of the women, their sexual shock tactics and [their] man-hating, down-with-motherhood stance." Their message, she argued, "was to *make yourself ugly,* to stop shaving under your arms, to stop wearing makeup or pretty dresses—any skirts at all." Whether liberals or Marxists, older women viewed politics as a disciplined activity; one changed the system from within in order to give women choices about how to live their lives.[54]

Despite NOW's determination to maintain its respectability, the women's liberation movement continually nudged the organization in new directions. Initially, NOW scorned the idea of consciousness-raising, arguing that feminism was about action, not talking. But as new women entered the organization, unfamiliar with politics of any sort, let alone feminism, older members discovered that "rap groups" helped such novices "catch up" on movement issues.

The truth is, both branches of the movement were essential. NOW activists promoted leadership and the organizing skills that made them effective lobbyists, organizers, and strategists. They also provided the modern women's movement with the staying power it needed to withstand backlash after backlash. Although they didn't always agree—Kay Clarenbach, for instance, recalled that at early NOW meetings, the "decibel level in sessions became unbelievable"—they somehow figured out how to keep NOW alive as a national feminist organization.[55] Some younger liberationists characterized NOW as "liberal" or "reformist," an organization that merely wanted a piece of the pie, rather than entirely new ingredients. But it is much too simple to categorize these two branches of the new women's movement as liberal versus radical, or legislative versus revolutionary. NOW's struggle for equal opportunity, especially in employment and education, required a *collective* solution to individual women's problems. Nor could all members of the organized women's rights movement be described as simply "liberals." Betty Friedan, Bella Abzug, Pauli Murray, Gerda Lerner, Addie Wyatt, and Esther Peterson, for example, were among those whose activism in the labor and civil rights movements brought a working-class and race-conscious perspective to the women's movement.

Young feminists contributed something equally important—a radical critique of patriarchal culture, visions of alternative lifestyles, and the unmasking of the hidden injuries women had suffered. Although they generally chose to work outside established institutions, they created a network of alternative, grassroots, self-help, nonprofit services—rape crisis centers and battered women's shelters, for example—that eventually became established institutions themselves. Sometimes the injuries these younger women unmasked changed laws; sometimes NOW's legislative efforts altered the nation's consciousness. In many ways, the differences were really about the targets and the style in which the struggle was waged. At times, ideological or generational differences bitterly divided feminists, but neither branch of the movement, by itself, could have brought about the staggering changes that swept through American culture during the remaining decades of the twentieth century.[56]

To impatient young women, NOW members often seemed stuffy and stolid. They voted; they elected leaders; they even paid dues. Rather than staying up all night seeking consensus, they relied on Robert's Rules of Order. But young women weren't the only ones who knew how to have fun. In her memoir, *It Changed My Life*, Betty Friedan described a gala celebration in 1973 to commemorate the tenth anniversary of the publication of *The Feminine Mystique*.

> A dramatic celebration of our herstory closed with the song "I Am Woman"; suddenly women got out of their seats and started dancing around the hotel ballroom, joining hands in a circle that got larger and larger until maybe a thousand of us were dancing and singing: "There is nothing I can't do. . . . No price too great to pay . . . I am strong . . . I am invincible. . . . I am woman." It was a spontaneous, beautiful expression of the exhilaration we all felt in those years, women really moving as women.[57]

By the mid-1970s, the challenge to traditional liberalism, waged by attorneys and activists through commissions, class action suits, hearings, and protests, had achieved a stunning series of successes. As the scholar and activist Cynthia Harrison observed:

> They had produced legislation mandating equal treatment for women in education and in credit, eliminating criminal penalties for abortion, changing prejudicial rape laws, banning discrimination against pregnant women, equalizing property distribution at divorce, and offering tax credits for childcare.[58]

The momentum of the women's movement seemed unstoppable. Exploiting its conservative image, WEAL waged an aggressive campaign against American university policies in 1969. Within a year, WEAL filed complaints against more than three hundred colleges and universities, including every medical school in the nation. In 1970, NOW filed a blanket complaint against thirteen hundred corporations that received federal funds, forcing them to give back pay to hundreds of women workers. In the same year, NOW documented Judge Harold Carswell's record of discrimination and helped to derail his nomination to the Supreme Court. In 1971, over three hundred women met in Washington, D.C., to found the National Women's Political Caucus, whose goal was "to awaken, organize and assert the vast political power represented by women." Early members included Bella Abzug, Shirley Chisholm, Betty Friedan, Liz Carpenter, and Gloria Steinem. Within a few years, the NWPC had active local caucuses in every state and began fielding female candidates for political office.

In 1972, Congress quickly passed the Equal Rights Amendment and sent it to the states for what many assumed would be a quick ratification. In the same year, Congress passed Title IX of the Education Amendments of 1972, which denied funds for men's sports unless an equal amount were provided for girls' and women's sports, a piece of legislation that instantly altered women's relationship to athletics and sports. In the same year, *Ms.* magazine made its debut; women for the first time became floor reporters at political conventions; the Equal Pay Act was extended to cover administrative, executive, and professional personnel; NOW and the Urban League filed a class action suit against General Mills for sex and race discrimination; NOW initiated action against sexism in elementary-school textbooks with *Dick and Jane as Victims*; and women theologians called for the "castration of sexist religions" at the largest and most prestigious gathering of biblical scholars in history.

One year later, in 1973, the Supreme Court ruled in *Roe v. Wade* that abortion was constitutionally protected by a woman's right to privacy; Billie Jean King beat Bobby Riggs in a much-hyped "Battle of the Sexes" tennis game; AT&T signed the largest job sex discrimination settlement—$38 million—in the nation's history; the U.S. Printing Office agreed to accept "Ms." as an optional title for women; the Bank of California settled a lawsuit by NOW and minority groups who had charged sex and race discrimination; NOW organized an International Feminist Planning Conference in Cambridge, Massachusetts, which three hundred women from twenty-seven countries attended; a New Jersey court ruled that the state Little League must admit girls; and Helen Reddy won a Grammy Award for the hit record "I Am Woman," an explicitly feminist song that became the unofficial anthem of the women's movement.

In 1974, approximately one thousand colleges and universities offered women's studies courses; the steel industry settled a sex discrimination suit that gave $56 million in back pay and wage adjustments to 386,000 women workers; Congress passed the Equal Credit Opportunity Act, which allowed married women, for the first time, to obtain credit in their own names, and the Educational Equity Act, designed to eliminate sexist curricula and achieve equity for all students regardless of sex; and Helen Thomas, after covering Washington for thirty years, became the first woman to be named a White House reporter.

So many successes in so few years. Yet, the speed of change masked a strong strain of resistance that grew alongside the women's movement. Signs of an instant backlash appeared everywhere. After the election of Richard Nixon in 1968, legal challenges met stiffer resistance from a Republican administration. It was not until 1970, for example, that the Justice Department actually pressed its first sex discrimination case. In 1970, former vice president Hubert Humphrey's personal physician, Dr. Edgar Berman, sparked a fierce national debate when he announced that women were unfit for the presidency because they might be "subject to curious mental aberrations." In the same year, the Catholic Church established the National Right to Life Committee to block liberalization of abortion laws; Billy Graham called feminism "an echo of our overall philosophy of permissiveness"; a group of women in Kingman, Arizona, organized Happiness of Womanhood (HOW), which soon affiliated with the League of Housewives.

The next year, the women's movement suffered one of its most significant defeats. A coalition of feminists and child care advocates had lobbied and nurtured the Comprehensive Child Development Act of 1971, which would have provided child care for all women. Feminists wept with joy when the legislation survived both houses of Congress and was finally passed. But their victory was short-lived. President Richard Nixon vetoed the act and Congress, heavily lobbied by right-wing opponents, failed to override the veto. In his veto message, written by Pat Buchanan, Nixon described it as "the most radical piece of legislation to emerge from the 93rd Congress," and said it would "commit the vast moral authority of the national government to the side of communal approaches to child-rearing" and "would lead to the Sovietization of

American children." It would take years before politicians dared touch the issue of child care again.[59]

In 1972, Phyllis Schlafly attacked the ERA and formed a new organization, Stop ERA; Midge Decter, a neoconservative and wife of conservative Norman Podhoretz, published a diatribe against the feminist movement in a book entitled *The New Chastity and Other Arguments Against Women's Liberation*; and North Carolina voters sent conservative Jesse Helms to the U.S. Senate. By 1973, the EEOC had a backlog of sixty-five thousand uninvestigated complaints; the National Committee for a Human Life Amendment had begun to lobby for a law that would overturn *Roe v. Wade*; the Society for a Christian Commonwealth, a conservative Catholic lay group, called for the excommunication of Justice William Brennan, Jr., for his pro-choice view in the Supreme Court decision; Joseph Coors, looking for a way to fund his conservative political agenda, established the Heritage Foundation, which would become the "think tank" of the Reagan administration—and funded a legal network for the radical Right to protect business and industry from what they termed costly government regulations, such as affirmative action; eighty-six hundred delegates to the Southern Baptist Convention passed a resolution affirming male superiority; Jesse Helms introduced an amendment to the Foreign Assistance Act that prohibited the use of funds for abortion services or research and for abortifacient drugs and devices, which unanimously passed in a Senate that had no female members; and George Gilder published *Sexual Suicide*, a sustained argument against the women's movement.

In 1974, the first "March for Life" took place; Coors funded Paul Weyrich to organize the Committee for the Survival of a Free Congress and Richard Viguerie became the organization's direct mail fund-raiser; militant antifeminists stormed the Michigan House demanding that they rescind the ERA; and the National Conservative Political Action Committee (NCPAC), which became the Right's major tool to oppose feminism, was established and headed by John T. Dolan, a former member of the conservative group Young Americans for Freedom. The next year, Phyllis Schlafly organized the Eagle Forum as "the alternative to women's lib." The race had begun; the antifeminist backlash had as much momentum as the women's movement. Who would emerge the victor was not at all certain.[60]

WOMEN'S STRIKE FOR EQUALITY

For some of that backlash, Betty Friedan believed, the media was responsible. Journalists of all sorts were "still treating the women's movement as a joke." As a result, "Women feared identifying themselves as feminists or with the movement at all. We needed an action to show them—and ourselves—how powerful we were. I sensed that the women 'out there' were ready to move in far greater numbers than even we realized."

To commemorate the fiftieth anniversary of the ratification of the women's suffrage amendment (August 26, 1920), Friedan called for a national "Women's Strike for Equality." Although she hoped that women would abstain from their usual work, Friedan viewed the strike as a symbolic gesture. Word went out that local chapters should decide how to participate in the "strike." After considerable squabbling, feminists finally agreed upon three central demands: the right to abortion, the right to child care, and equal opportunity in employment and education. (Radical feminists, however, carried banners demanding "free abortion on demand and 24-hour child care centers.")

Here, then, were the core demands of the feminist revolution in 1970.[61] Riding high on a string of legal victories and widely publicized demonstrations, for twenty-four hours feminists laid aside their factional differences and mounted the largest women's demonstrations held since the suffrage movement. In cities and towns across the country, women marched, picketed, protested, held teach-ins and rallies, and produced skits and plays. Some women actually refused to work. A common poster urged, "Don't Cook Dinner—Starve a Rat Today." Another reminded women, "Don't Iron While the Strike is Hot."

On Boston Commons, some feminists distributed contraceptive foam and whistled at and taunted construction workers. At the *Washington Post*, women held a teach-in; in Rochester, New York, feminists smashed teacups to protest a lack of female participation in government; in Dayton, Ohio, two hundred women listened to talks by welfare women and hospital union members; in New York City, women built a makeshift child care center on the grounds of City Hall, draped an enormous banner "Women of the World Unite" over the Statue of Liberty, and invaded advertising agencies with medals inscribed, "This ad insults women."

It was an unforgettable day. One twenty-four-year-old woman who didn't consider herself a feminist brought her child to work and was promptly fired. She called NOW and one hundred women marched and picketed until her company rehired her. A female reporter decided to wear a brown and white button that simply read, "Women-Strike, Aug. 26th." After waiters refused to serve her, she ended her newspaper story with these words: "I'll tell you, wearing this little button really has been an eye-opener." The media mostly highlighted the march and rally held in New York City. Linking arms, a huge crowd of women (anywhere from ten thousand to fifty thousand, depending on whether your source was the police, the *New York Times*, or rally organizers) marched down Fifth Avenue, banners and posters bobbing above radiant faces. Radical feminists, high-school girls, mothers with strollers, suburban matrons, domestics, and office workers joined elderly suffragists dressed in traditional white to follow the same route taken by first-wave feminists over half a century earlier.[62]

Extensive media coverage informed a nation still reeling from black power, the counterculture, and the antiwar movement that the fledgling movement for women's rights and women's liberation was not a passing fad. (The media also felt compelled to report that Betty Friedan arrived late, after having her hair "done.") In the aftermath of the march, a CBS News poll found that four out of five people over eighteen had read or heard about women's liberation.[63]

The 1970 Women's Strike was a stunning success. In the months to come, NOW's ranks swelled by 50 percent. Many feminists remembered the day as a peak experience in their lives. Across the nation, feminists in coastal cities, as well as those in the heartland, no longer felt isolated. Unity, if only achieved for a day, filled participants with exhilaration. For a brief moment, the banners "Sisterhood Is Powerful" and "Women of the World Unite" seemed to describe the future. At the end of the day's whirlwind events, Betty Friedan's keynote speech solemnly expressed the spiritual transformation many women experienced that day:

> In the religion of my ancestors, there was a prayer that Jewish men said every morning. They prayed, "Thank thee, Lord, that I was not born a woman." Today I feel, feel for the first time, feel absolutely sure that all women are going to be able to say, as I say tonight: "Thank thee, Lord, that I was born a woman, for this day."[64]

Chapter Four

LEAVING THE LEFT

In May 1964, the *Daily Californian*, the student newspaper at the University of California, Berkeley published the exciting news that "Energetic Women Discuss the Role of Educated Wives." Less than six years later, in January 1970, the same newspaper reported a campus-wide women's liberation conference titled "Women to Break Shackles." Accompanying the announcement was a photograph of a woman on her knees, her mouth open in a silent scream.[1]

In the intervening years, some young women felt as if they had lived several lifetimes. Outward appearance told part of the story. They had replaced matronly shirtwaists, tight undergarments, teased and sprayed hair, and heavily made up faces with miniskirts, bell-bottom pants, granny glasses, long, dangling earrings, unshaved bodies, long, straight hair, little or no underwear, and faces without makeup. Their thinking had changed even more dramatically as their sense of entitlement had grown. By 1965, the Zeitgeist, that indescribable but palpable spirit of the times, was affecting much of college youth. Each year, college-educated young women—as well as the larger public—began to take seriously what was still referred to as the "modern woman's dilemma," shorthand for the debate over women's proper role in modern society.

During the same years that an older generation of women bumped up against the limits of liberalism, a younger generation of women was emerging from the 1950s, shaking off the dust and detritus of that decade, and beginning to question all kinds of received wisdom. They soon began to enter the political, social, and cultural movements then sprouting on college campuses. "The movement," as it came to be

called, not only included the civil rights, student, and antiwar movements, but also a network of friendships, sexual partners, spouses, and
communal living arrangements in which the alienated daughters of the
fifties had taken refuge. For many young women, it would be an agonizing decision to leave this political community. It meant rupturing years
of personal ties to a subculture that, at its most idealistic moments, saw
itself as the redeemer of a nation poisoned by racism, materialism, and
imperialism. What fueled their exodus was the ridicule and humiliation
they experienced from men in the civil rights movement and then in
the New Left and antiwar movements who could not—or would not—
understand that the women's liberation movement would expand the very
definition of democracy. What made it possible was that many of these
movements had already begun a downward spiral into self-destruction.

THE END OF THE AGE OF COMPLACENCY

It's difficult to understand the origins and culture of the women's liberation movement without grasping something of the history and character
of the New Left. In the post–World War II era, any independent radical
critique of American society could be—and regularly was—discredited
by being associated with Communism, and with the Soviet Union in particular. In such a chilling political atmosphere, cultural and social critics of all sorts risked stigma, as well as unemployment. The death of
Joseph Stalin and the censure of the red-baiting Joseph McCarthy
opened up space for new kinds of critical thought. Soviet premier Nikita
Khrushchev's revelations in 1956 of Stalin's monstrous crimes hastened
the collapse of the Old Left, as many of the faithful deserted the American Communist Party. In England and the United States, small groups
of intellectuals began in the late 1950s creating a "New" Left, dedicated organizationally to avoiding the hierarchical, centralized leadership promoted by the Communist Party and ideologically to sustaining a
democratic and egalitarian socialist movement.

This generation of young people, who had grown up under the
nuclear terror of the Cold War, dreamed of creating a different kind of
dissident political culture. In a prescient 1960 essay, "The New Left,"
the iconoclastic sociologist C. Wright Mills caught their mood when he
declared "the age of complacency is ending." In 1962, the leftist activist and author Michael Harrington, in his book *The Other America*,

reminded a generation reared in relative prosperity of the hidden poverty that still crippled the lives of many Americans. World events also inspired New Leftists: Mahatma Gandhi's powerful use of nonviolence in India's struggle to overthrow its English rulers, the newly won independence of African nations from colonial rule, the drama of the Cuban revolution, and the rise of Third World liberation movements. The election of a youthful John F. Kennedy, who urged young Americans in his inaugural speech "to ask not what your country can do for you, but what you can do for your country," helped spur a sense that a new era of social change and "participatory democracy" had begun.[2]

From Kennedy's election in 1960 to the end of the decade, young activists went on a wild political and cultural roller-coaster ride that left many of them with serious cases of vertigo. As the decade began, young southern civil rights workers founded the Student Nonviolent Coordinating Committee (SNCC, pronounced "Snick"), whose goal was to create a "beloved community" while working to end segregation through nonviolence. Two years later, New Left activists on college campuses launched Students for a Democratic Society (SDS), committing themselves, in their founding statement, to persuading their country to live up to its democratic ideals.

Yet, by 1969, the New Left was in tatters. Black-power separatists and young black armed revolutionaries had replaced SNCC's integrationist nonviolent idealists. SDS had splintered into warring Marxist and Maoist factions, each infatuated with its own idealized image of Third World movements, and in the case of the Weather Underground, dedicated to armed struggle. The counterculture and the sexual revolution, which had loosened the fifties' hold on American culture with the promise of, as the catchphrase then went, "sex, drugs, and rock 'n' roll," had degenerated into an urban culture of homeless runaways, pornographic underground newspapers, drug abuse, sexual exploitation, and a crass commercialism that rivaled anything mainstream society was capable of producing. To many activists, "the movement" seemed dead.

The origins of the women's liberation movement are tightly woven into this tumultuous decade.[3] Its story begins in the segregated South, where young white women absorbed ideals, values, and strategies that would eventually shape the women's liberation movement. The initial goal of SNCC was to organize the growing number of students streaming into the civil rights movement after four black college men in Greensboro,

North Carolina, staged a sit-in when they were refused service at a Woolworth's lunch counter. Within two months of their sit-in, thirty thousand students followed their example. By the end of 1960, seventy thousand students had invented kneel-ins and prayer-ins all over the South, and thirty-six hundred young people had been arrested, jailed, and, in some cases, beaten. Ella Baker, a member of the Southern Christian Leadership Conference (SCLC), a civil rights group led by ministers and parent organization to SNCC, decided to call an organizing conference for student sit-in leaders. She soon became known as SNCC's unofficial mother.

SNCC exuded a youthful, chaotic, morally earnest spirit. A young white volunteer described her first impression as she entered one of its offices.

> Papers were strewn across the desk with unstudied abandon. Telephones were ringing, wastebaskets bulged with trash, and file-cabinet drawers gaped open. A mimeograph machine monotonously whooshed paper through its roller in the background, and a radio somewhere thumped a heavy beat. The floors looked as if they had not been scrubbed since installation, and the windows were opaque with dust. I did not see anyone who was white there among the young black people rushing around that day.[4]

SNCC's determination to organize at the grass roots, to develop local leadership, "to let the people decide," and to refuse bail when arrested, clashed with the more conservative church leaders of the Southern Christian Leadership Conference, who preached patience as they tried to preserve their fragile alliances with liberals, politicians, and labor leaders. SNCC's evolving movement culture profoundly influenced every other youthful movement that surfaced in its wake. Through their emphasis on direct action, SNCC activists taught other young people "to put their bodies on the line." By seeking to organize—and live among—the poorest of the poor in states like Mississippi, they lived, rather than preached, a millenarian dream of creating a redemptive and "beloved community." By "telling it like it is," they integrated personal revelation into group politics. By making all decisions through consensus, they gave birth to the exhausting but democratic experience of participatory democracy, which would be most commonly experienced as all-night meetings.

SNCC's redemptive vision was interracial in practice and spirit, even if its members were largely black. The young organization soon attracted strikingly talented and dedicated young southern and northern blacks and whites. During its early years, only a handful of its regular staff members were white women. These women, already committed to changing race relations, arrived fresh from southern church-sponsored civil rights work or from the YWCA, where they had participated in projects to desegregate southern universities and communities. Others had discovered civil rights work through the National Student Association, an organization of college student leaders and peace activists. After 1962, some civil rights workers came from the campus-based Students for a Democratic Society.[5]

Two white women in their twenties, Mary King and Sandra "Casey" Cason (known after her marriage in 1962 to SDS founder and activist Tom Hayden as Casey Hayden), joined SNCC without ever imagining the impact this experience would have on their lives. Like so many young people who would become involved in sixties movements, Mary King came from "a home of high purpose," the daughter of a Virginia minister in a family with five generations of ministers to its name. The influence of her family's tradition led her to work first in the YWCA and then in SNCC. "There was little rebellion in my decision to work in the YWCA and then in SNCC. I was in fact being a dutiful daughter."[6]

Sandra "Casey" Cason was born in 1939 in Austin, Texas. The daughter of the only divorced, self-supporting mother in a small coastal Texas town, Cason grew up in modest surroundings and early "developed a bias against the rich, of whom there were many in this oil rich country." In 1957, she entered the University of Texas, "liberal leaning, slightly alienated," but without a language to express her alienation. By 1960, she, too, had gravitated to the local YWCA chapter, which was trying to desegregate public facilities, and took up residence in the only integrated housing on campus, the Christian Faith and Life Community. Through the YWCA, she also had her first experience with "consensus-forming, non-hierarchical, egalitarian small-groups."[7] In Atlanta, she began working with Ella Baker on a YWCA project to create "race relations workshops" across the South.

One of the important friends she made was Dorothy Dawson, a southerner who had been her roommate at the University of Texas. Born in 1937, Dawson grew up in San Antonio, Texas, in a conservative family that emphasized humanistic values. The constant presence of a black servant made her uncomfortable; the early death of her father forced her mother to provide for her family. As an adolescent, Dawson observed her mother's vulnerability, privately vowing that she would somehow achieve economic independence as an adult.

As a freshman, Dawson wrote a term paper on racism and met Robb Burlage, the editor of the student newspaper, an SDS intellectual and activist whom she married in 1963. With Casey Hayden and Robb Burlage, Dorothy Dawson worked to desegregate social life at the university. She, too, went to Atlanta to set up projects that would prepare students for desegregation on southern campuses.[8]

Through her husband, Tom Hayden, Casey Hayden also met members of the northern student movement who had a penchant for writing position papers. Later, Hayden credited SDS with having "a large influence in the decision to put forward position papers about women" that would be crucial to the formation of the women's liberation movement in the mid-sixties. On a trip North in 1961, Casey Hayden also met members of Women Strike for Peace, who were organizing a massive housewives' strike against aboveground nuclear testing. These women made a lasting impression on her. "In its simplicity and Quaker-like speaking from the heart, this group was much like SNCC or the Y. It was also devoted to direct action, speaking truth to power. It seemed everyone was on the same track, and in the same rhythm."[9]

All these disparate experiences seemed to come together in SNCC. They saw grinding poverty close up, but also the rich culture of black community life. They witnessed the despair of the poor, but also the courage of local black leaders. They felt powerlessness, but also learned the strength of hope. Perhaps most important, they felt like integral members of an interracial group whose immodest goal was the redemption of a racist America through love. "We were the beloved community," recalled Casey Hayden twenty-five years later, "harassed, happy, and poor. And in those little, hot, black, rural churches, we went into the music, into the sound, and everyone was welcome inside this perfect place. We simply dropped race."[10]

SNCC's concern for the poorest of the poor deeply affected both King and Hayden. "We loved the untouchables," remembered Hayden. "We believed the last should be first and not only should be first, but in fact *were* first in our value system. The movement in its early days had a grandeur that feared no rebuke and assumed no false attitudes. It was a holy time."[11]

During these years, white women in SNCC would violate nearly every racial and sexual convention of southern culture. SNCC also granted them extraordinary work opportunities not then open to most women. Within a short time of joining, Mary King became communications assistant to SNCC leader Julian Bond. Armed with a precious WATS line, King briefed the press on pending civil rights activities, reported on police brutality, pushed a recalcitrant FBI to act on threats to organizers' lives, and helped coordinate northern groups of Friends of SNCC to pressure the federal government. Casey Hayden became one of SNCC's most effective staff and project organizers, a legend to younger members.

Constant danger and an atmosphere of terror threw both women, barely out of college, into a combat-zone-like situation. Beatings, jailings, and fire bombings taught them to cope with always-imminent danger. Night riders trailed activists' cars or shot up the "freedom houses" in which organizers lived. The real possibility of vaginal searches and jail rapes during imprisonments tested their commitment and endurance in the face of state-sanctioned violence. Stories of jailers pouring acid on women's genital tissue—which happened after arrests during the Freedom Rides—brought home their double jeopardy as civil rights activists *and* women. And, yet, as Casey Hayden observed, whatever the dangers, "nonviolent direct action was a transforming experience—a new self was created."[12]

By 1964, SNCC leaders realized that the savage violence used against black civil rights workers had still not ignited the nation's indignation. One year earlier, the black civil rights worker Medgar Evers had been assassinated, mourned by blacks across the country, but his untimely death had done nothing to increase government protection of black civil rights activists in the South. White lives, as SNCC leader Bob Moses reluctantly admitted, were far more valued. So SNCC recruited approximately one thousand northern students to help with voter registration and education in Mississippi and other southern states for what was dubbed "Freedom Summer." These young men and women, recruited from elite colleges, had parents and families who were well-placed to pressure the government to protect their children's lives. The immediate disappearance of James Chaney, Michael Schwerner, and Andrew Goodman, three civil rights activists, underscored the dangers these volunteers faced. By the end of the summer, their beaten and mutilated bodies were discovered, reminding volunteers that civil rights work would sometimes require the sacrifice of lives.

The presence of white students, as SNCC activists had predicted, sparked the media's interest in the South's violent treatment of civil rights workers. By the end of Freedom Summer, civil rights workers had witnessed fifteen murders, four woundings, thirty-seven churches bombed or burned, and over one thousand arrests in Mississippi alone. Security precautions became elaborate—organizers carried two-way radios and dared not go out alone at night or even enter a downtown area in interracial groups.

The strong young leadership of black men like Bob Moses, James Foreman, Julian Bond, John Lewis, Andrew Young, and Stokely Carmichael provided models of courage and conviction. Just as impressive were the black women leaders, such as Ruby Doris Smith, who eventually ran SNCC's Atlanta office, and Cynthia Washington, Septima Clark, Joyce Ladner, Frances Beale, Bernice Reagon, Ann Moody, Diane Nash, and Daisy Bates, who worked as project directors or staff members. Jo Ann Robinson, whose activism stretched back to the Montgomery bus boycott, and Ella Baker, advocate of participatory democracy, filled many young women with awe. Fannie Lou Hamer, the youngest of twenty children in her family, was picking cotton by age six, and had worked for eighteen years as a sharecropper before she helped orchestrate the attempt by Mississippi blacks to replace the all-white delegation to the Democratic convention with their own Mississippi Freedom Democratic Party in 1964. Famed for her powerful rendition of "This Little Light of Mine," Hamer proved to be an inspired orator, leader, and singer. Upon meeting her, Mary King thought, "Everything about her suggested strength of character as well as physical stamina, and the more you knew her the more you felt her vitality, warmth, and spiritual strength."[13]

In small communities across the South, white SNCC women observed the remarkable clout black women wielded in their churches and civic organizations. Dorothy Burlage was certain that these local black women who organized church meetings for civil rights work, helped with voter registration, and risked their lives by housing SNCC workers "inspired me to think that women could do anything." Grassroots activists like Unita Blackwell, Annie Devine, and Winson Hudson sustained the movement even as they risked their lives. These black women became, as historian Sara Evans has observed, "substitute mother figures, new models of womanhood."[14]

SNCC also provided a postgraduate education in social and political theory. During the first four years, debates about politics rippled through SNCC's ranks, challenging all manner of intellectual complacency. Mary King and Casey Hayden spent endless nights poring over the works of Simone de Beauvoir and Doris Lessing before passing them on to their male comrades. By 1964, in the face of relentless violence, some had even begun to question the near-sacred conviction that the power of the movement and its path to success lay in Gandhian nonviolence. Debates between advocates of nonviolent direct action and those who wanted to concentrate on voter registration drew from different political or philosophical texts.

Within SNCC, personal life merged with movement culture. As Mary King put it, "Our political, emotional, and spiritual lives were inseparably bound to the movement. There was no line where the movement began and our personal lives left off. . . . In a sense I didn't have a life of my own. The movement was too encompassing. . . . These goals were so close, yet they were so far. They grabbed me up, sucked me in, and took over. . . . Relationships were intense and bonds deep." The community made daily life bearable. Jane Stembridge, another early white female staffer, noted, "When we had nothing, we had community. When our hands were empty, they were held."[15]

These glory years did not last long. By 1964, SNCC had mushroomed into an organization of over 150 paid staff members spread across the South. Some activists thought that SNCC needed order and direction and that funds should be funneled through a centralized office structure in Atlanta. Others, including Bob Moses, Casey Hayden, and Mary King, urged SNCC to retain its decentralized organization, allowing local leadership to make their own monetary and policy decisions.[16] Not insignificantly, a more centralized leadership and rationalized bureaucracy would have imperiled the informal leadership women had enjoyed in SNCC.

Racial tensions soon became tangled up in these thorny questions of structure. Some veteran SNCC workers, influenced by what they were learning of African liberation and by growing black separatist sentiments, felt invaded by an army of well-meaning, but basically naïve, white students from the North. Sexual excitement, as well as tensions, permeated the community. One southern longtime activist for example, recalled with pleasure and no regrets the loving sexual relations she had with both black and white SNCC organizers. Another organizer described how sleeping with black men was simply part of being a member of an interracial family. Yet another veteran organizer recalled how much she enjoyed the adventure of sleeping with different black men as

she visited various projects in the Deep South.[17] In many cases, the
families of these southern women had severed emotional ties with them.
But with male lovers, as one woman put it, they found the "comfort and
release" that eased the tension and fear they experienced every day. As
highly valued members of the SNCC community, they rarely sensed any
disrespect from the black or white men with whom they worked.[18]

FREEDOM SUMMER

During Freedom Summer 1964, when northern college students came to
register voters, the sudden appearance of four hundred northern white
female volunteers pushed sexual tensions to the breaking point. Southern white female staffers habitually dressed plainly, without jewelry or
makeup. But some of the northern women, who were not fully aware of
the tense atmosphere in small southern towns, dressed quite provocatively. "Wittingly or unwittingly," wrote Mary King, "a number of them
found themselves attracted by the sexually explicit manner of certain
black men in the local community and also on the SNCC staff. Many
wore décolleté necklines and dangling earrings, not realizing that these
would be provocative in Southern rural communities, and seemed sometimes to strike an incautious pose."[19]

Most female volunteers were, in fact, serious and committed to hard
work. Still, northern white women and local black men did seem like
exotic creatures to each other. In some cases, sexual liaisons deepened
into love affairs. In other cases, they used each other to taste "forbidden
fruit." For some northern white women, the aggressive attention of
black men affirmed their sexual desirability for the first time. One
woman commented that white men had always "found her too large, but
black men assumed I was a sexual person and I needed that very
badly." Another recalled, "In terms of black men, one of the things I
discovered ... [was] that physically I was attractive to black men
whereas I never had been attractive to white men."[20]

Eager to prove their lack of racism, some adventuresome and anxious
northern women made easy sexual targets. According to Mary King, "Any
number of black men manipulated this anxiety." For some black southern
men, it was an unprecedented opportunity to violate the South's most
powerful taboo—interracial sex. As Staunton Lynd, a white director of the
Freedom Schools that educated young black children, put it, "Every

black SNCC worker with perhaps a few exceptions counted a notch on his gun to have slept with a white woman—as many as possible."[21]

Some of these white northern women felt that black men treated them as just so many conquests. Others resented that they had to conduct their sexual liaisons in secret, lest black men lose face—or encounter danger—if caught sleeping with a white woman. Some women felt they had to pass a "sexual litmus test" before they were accepted into a project. Others complained of a no-win double standard that operated for female volunteers. "If you didn't [have sex] you could count on being harassed. If you did, you ran the risk of being written off as a 'bad girl' and tossed off the project. This didn't happen to the guys."[22]

Sexual exploitation was not the only problem white female volunteers identified during Freedom Summer. In evaluating prospective volunteers, SNCC's male recruiters viewed white women volunteers through conventional eyes. They categorically rejected women who said they wouldn't or couldn't type. They regarded an attractive woman as a potential problem. They rejected one woman because she said she would be willing to sleep with a black man. No man was ever rejected for expressing similar desires for black women. (No man, of course, was ever asked.)[23]

Traditional ideals of womanhood also determined the assignments given to female volunteers. Whatever their job preferences, most women ended up as Freedom School teachers, clerical workers, or community center staff members. More men, in contrast, moved out into voter registration projects that took them into the black community. Common sense as well as sexual stereotyping informed these decisions. To place white women in interracial freedom projects in the Deep South violated every community convention and courted extreme danger. By confining women to schools, offices or classrooms, SNCC staffers could better protect the safety of female volunteers.

But such policies just replicated the conventions that so many of these volunteers hoped to escape. Few young women had signed up for Freedom Summer dreaming of typing or vacuuming. Yet their new lives often looked all too familiar. In the morning, as in any suburban community, men left to face the challenges and dangers of the outside world, while the women stayed inside tending the children, teaching students, or cleaning house. The moral drama of changing the world had brought them South, yet here they were, clerks, teachers, and housewives.[24] Since voter registration workers risked greater danger, men's work was more valued than clerical labor or teaching. When beatings and arrests took place, male recruits faced down danger and earned their manhood. "If we have no incidents, our egos suffer no end," one young man wrote home.[25]

Black women, by their own accounts, experienced SNCC quite differently from white women volunteers. They had early on become leaders of major projects, highly valued within the SNCC community. Sexual exploitation was not what vexed them during Freedom Summer. Rather, it was the way black male staffers gravitated to young white female recruits. During the day, black women would work closely with black men, only to watch them turn to white women at night—behavior that would soon be scorned as "backsliding." Black women, like their white female counterparts, also suffered from a double standard, but of a different nature—they found themselves attacked when they became involved with a white man.[26]

Cynthia Washington joined SNCC in 1963 and became a director of a freedom project in Mississippi, responsible for voter registration and community organization. "I remember discussions with various women about our treatment [by black male staffers] as one of the boys and its impact on us as women," she has written.

> We did the same work as men—organizing around voter registration and community issues in rural areas—usually *with* men. But when we finally got back to some town where we could relax and go out, the men went out with other women. Our skills and abilities were recognized and respected, but that seemed to place us in some category other than female. Some years later, I was told by a male SNCC worker that some of the project women had made him feel superfluous. I wish he had told me that at the time because the differences in the way women were treated certainly did add to the tensions between black and white women.[27]

Despite—or because of—all these sexual and racial tensions, Freedom Summer gave birth to an awareness of women's subordination that would later attack stereotypes of both black and white women. But in 1964, neither the black nor the white women of SNCC could fully grasp how their situation exaggerated stereotypes of weak white women who needed protection and strong black women who needed none. While white women complained that they were being excessively protected,

one black woman observed that "we became Amazons, less than and
more than women at the same time." Washington, for instance, was astonished by such complaints by white women. "I couldn't understand
what they wanted," she explained.

> As far as I could see, being a project director wasn't much
> fun. I didn't realize then that having my own project made a
> lot of difference in how I was perceived and treated. And I
> did not see what I was doing as exceptional. . . . It seemed to
> many of us that white women were demanding a chance to be
> independent while we needed help and assistance which was
> not always forthcoming. We definitely started from opposite
> ends of the spectrum.[28]

Whatever the problems, most white women viewed Freedom Summer
as a transformative experience. During that summer, a network of
friendships between northern and southern women had been created,
one that would last through the years of the antiwar movement and the
New Left. Equally important, SNCC's emphasis on community, the redemption of the powerless, and the promotion of self-determination
would provide much of the structural and ideological foundation for
a new feminist movement. Through Freedom Summer, a number of
women also gained an awareness of the kind of sexual exploitation and
discrimination they would soon encounter in the movement culture of
the New Left.[29]

In November 1964, SNCC held a retreat in Waveland, Mississippi, to
deal with its simmering staff resentments and conflicts. Word went out
that staffers should draft position papers on questions dividing SNCC.
"It was here," Casey Hayden remembered, "that the many threads of
SNCC started to unravel, separately." Crucial to that unraveling was
the growth of black separatism. That August, black activists in Mississippi had suffered a humiliating defeat at the Democratic presidential
nominating convention in Atlanta. Their alternate slate of delegates
from the Mississippi Freedom Democratic Party arrived with high hopes
of challenging the all-white Mississippi delegation. But after days of
internecine fights and compromises, the national party leadership hu-
miliated the Freedom Democratic Party by offering it only two token
convention votes, and no recognition. Fannie Lou Hamer refused the insulting compromise. For many blacks, young and old, it was a profound

disappointment that underscored the growing belief that they could not trust whites to advance their cause.

"We were facing, most of all, the question of what to do next," Casey Hayden wrote, "and SNCC was just as divided as other civil rights organizations."[30] After she wrote a position paper on how to improve communication, Mary King decided to write another one that addressed the future impact of a hierarchical, bureaucratic structure within SNCC. For quite some time, a number of women in SNCC had been discussing women's position in the organization. As King later explained, "Slowly and perhaps inevitably, self-determination was coming to mean not only politics but also literally self. For both Casey and me, this translated into our growing conviction that we had an obligation to find ways to communicate our deepening sense of political definition which included the political identification of ourselves as women." Although neither King nor Hayden felt personally marginalized, they were keenly aware of the experiences of others.

But once at the typewriter, King found herself blocked by self-doubt. "The issue was enormous. I was afraid. . . . My heart was palpitating and I was shaking as I typed it. My fear of a joking response was making me unsteady in my resolve." King drafted the paper, a list of grievances particularly concerning discrimination against SNCC women, to which Hayden added analysis and commentary.[31] Modestly titled "SNCC Position Paper, Nov. 1964," this historic statement prefigured many of the ideas, complaints, and analyses that would shape the women's liberation movement. Among its grievances, the major one may have been the unquestioned nature of informal male authority within the organization. Men dominated all the committees, farmed out most of the clerical work to women, and expected them to take the minutes at all meetings. They cited several examples of discrimination, which were hardly earth-shattering crimes. They studiously avoided the feminist language they had learned from de Beauvoir's The Second Sex because "within the framework of the civil rights movement and the field of human rights and civil liberties at the time . . . women's rights had no meaning and indeed did not exist." Instead, they self-consciously chose to rely on the movement's own rhetoric of race relations and relied on "clear-cut analogies between whites' treatment of blacks and men's treatment of women."

A small group of these women prepared the paper in secret and presented it anonymously. They had reason to fear derision. In King's words, the "reaction to the anonymous position paper was one of crushing criticism. . . . People quickly figured out who had written the memo. Some mocked and taunted us." Other women, including black women, didn't feel they had experienced any sex discrimination. Hayden later wrote, "Whether women held leadership positions didn't matter in actuality prior to this time, since the participatory, town-hall style, consensus-forming nature of SNCC's operation meant that being on the Executive Committee or a project director didn't carry much weight anyway." Still, the paper—with specific but relatively mild complaints—was a ringing indictment of movement men's insensitivity toward their female comrades.[32]

The most famous response to the position paper came from Stokely Carmichael, whose words—"The only position for women in SNCC is prone"—would become infamous, providing shocking evidence of men's disrespectful treatment of women within the movement. At first, Carmichael evidently meant it as an inside joke, a reference to all the sexual adventures that took place during Freedom Summer. After a day of exhausting confrontations and debates, a group of SNCC staffers had "gravitated toward the pier with a gallon of wine." (Casey Hayden remembered some marijuana as well.)

According to Mary King, "Under a bright, cloudless sky, we talked and laughed among ourselves as we walked to the bay seeking humor to salve the hurts of the day." Carmichael's monologues supplied some of the evening's entertainment. Born in Trinidad, educated at New York City's Bronx High School of Science and then at Howard University, the articulate, handsome, and gregarious Carmichael was gifted with a quick wit and "the ability to joke like a professional stand-up comedian." King remembered that

> he led slowly and then began to warm up. One humorous slap followed another. We became more and more relaxed. We stretched out on the pier, lying with our heads on each other's abdomens. We were absorbed by the flow of his humor and our laughter. He reveled in our attention as we were illuminated by the moon. Stokely got more and more carried away. He stood up, slender and muscular, jabbed to make his points, his thoughts racing. . . . He started joking about black Mississippians. He made fun of everything that crossed his agile mind.

Finally, he turned to the meeting under way and the position papers. He came to the no-longer-anonymous paper on women. Looking straight at me, he grinned broadly and shouted, "What is the position of women in SNCC?" Answering himself, he responded, "The position of women in SNCC is prone!" Stokely threw back his head and roared outrageously with laughter. We all collapsed with hilarity. His ribald comment was uproarious and wild. It drew us all close together, because, even in that moment, he was poking fun at his own attitudes.[33]

His joke offended neither King nor Hayden, who, at the time, regarded Stokely Carmichael as one of the men most sympathetic to their position paper. But one northern white woman, who had just had a brief sexual encounter with Carmichael during the conference, overheard him say that "he'd rather masturbate than go to bed with a white woman." To her, his joke did not seem humorous at all.[34]

What began as a joke soon entered Carmichael's repertoire of humor. Cynthia Washington heard Carmichael's one-liner at a district meeting in Mississippi:

I was standing next to Muriel Tillinghast, another project director, and we were not pleased. But our relative autonomy as project directors seemed to deny or only override his statement. We were proof that what he said wasn't true—or so we thought. In fact, I'm certain that our single-minded focus on the issue of racial discrimination and the black struggle for equality blinded us to other issues.

In England, Sheila Rowbotham, the British socialist-feminist and author, listened with shock as Carmichael spoke at a Dialectics of Liberation Congress in London in 1967. Asked about the role of women in the revolution, Carmichael uttered one word: "Prone." "As a socialist," Rowbotham recalled, "I obviously supported the black movement in America. Now here was the person I thought I was supporting sneering at [women]."[35]

But it was not just Carmichael's repetition of his crowd pleasing one-liner that amplified the impact of his words. Clearly, he had touched a very raw nerve. His joke captured the growing racial and sexual tensions within the movement, North as well as South. Raised to be "nice" girls, movement women generally welcomed sexual adventure, but as daughters of the fifties, they also feared sexual exploitation. They wanted respect—as political comrades *and* lovers. Carmichael's joke reinforced their fears, legitimizing the need for an autonomous women's movement.

By 1965, those in SNCC who favored a more centralized structure and black separatism had triumphed, and whites were asked to leave the group and to organize poor whites. The interracial movement was over; in its place was the demand for black power and self-determination.

A KIND OF MEMO

Many former SNCC members naturally turned to the Students for a Democratic Society (SDS). By 1965, both SDS and SNCC had cut loose from their parent organizations, severed their alliances with liberals, and embraced a generational politics that shut off input from elders. Like SNCC, early SDS had begun as a small community whose values and goals were cemented by personal friendships. But most of the group's original members—the Old Guard—had already graduated from college and now worked in SDS's Economic Research and Action Project (ERAP). A new generation of recruits, largely from the Midwest—dubbed "Prairie Power"—had taken over the leadership. Many younger recruits only knew the Old Guard men and women by reputation, if at all. As in SNCC, the older sense of community had vanished and it was unclear what would replace it.

Unlike SNCC, with its emphasis on direct action, early SDS had been best known for its intellectual discourse and position papers. Its founding statement, drafted by Tom Hayden and others in 1962 in Port Huron, had proposed the immodest goal of ending racism and war, questioned America's exploitative relations with the rest of the world, condemned the corporate control of economic life, denounced the materialism and anonymity of American life in general, and condemned the bureaucratic, profit-making, and dehumanizing aspects of American society. Through participatory democracy, people would make the decisions that affected their own lives. Rejecting the hierarchic, dogmatic, and centralized nature of the Old Left and the American Communist

Party, SDS created a national office loosely tied to autonomous local campus chapters. Fearful of the tyranny of leadership, the organization rotated its leadership positions.

In the spring of 1965, Casey Hayden went north to work with SDS's organizing project in Chicago. ERAP projects, seeded in a number of cities from Newark to Cleveland, reflected SDS's efforts to organize poor whites. To live with and organize the poor was meant to convey a powerful statement of revulsion with American materialism. The journalist Andrew Kopkind, who visited ERAP projects in various cities, thought its members lived in worse poverty than SNCC staffers in the South:

> They are part of the slums, a kind of lay-brotherhood, or worker-priests, except that they have no dogma to sell. They get no salary; they live on a subsistence allowance that the project as a whole uses for rent and food . . . they eat a spartan diet of one-and-a-half meals a day, consisting mainly of powdered milk and large quantities of peanut butter and jelly, which seems to be the SDS staple.

In Chicago Casey Hayden watched SDS men try, but fail, to organize young men, some recently arrived from Appalachia, whose violent and retrograde attitudes toward women they accepted—and even imitated. Marilyn Webb, an early SDS activist, recalled that in the unsuccessful Chicago project to organize former hillbillies, "The [SDS] men seemed fascinated by the violence; they even tried to imitate the men's swaggering and violent postures. Worst of all, some of the men tried to pressure SDS women into sleeping with community men."[36]

As it turned out, the major successes in urban organizing came thanks to women organizers. "Much of ERAP was a dismal failure," one former SDSer now concedes, "but what *we* did in Cleveland and Boston later turned into a national welfare rights movement." With pride, former SDS member Sharon Jeffrey recalls what she and Carol McEldowney accomplished in Cleveland. "We quickly realized that the most promising strategy was to organize women at the food stamp redemption center. The men tried to organize—and even imitate—ghetto men, but it never worked. While they hung around pool halls, trying to speak and act tough, we organized women on the food stamp lines."

"That's where we learned that women really knit together a community," observed a former ERAP organizer. "Standing up at city council meetings against landlords and welfare bureaucrats taught us to value our abilities and skills." According to another, "Community women really taught us a great deal about solidarity and strength—something we would need later on in the women's movement." One woman, who worked in the Newark ERAP project, proudly recalled that some SDS women remained there long after SDS abandoned the project, and opened the first women's center in the city.

Women welfare recipients, like their black counterparts in the South, were the glue that held together the poor white community. Casey Hayden's experience now taught her that organizing women was the key to social change. In the fall, feeling at loose ends, she headed for Mary King's family cottage in the remote woods in Spotsylvania County, Virginia. Together they holed up in the remote rural area, and Hayden wrote a manifesto about women's position that would ignite the women's liberation movement. "There, in the quiet isolation of a forest," wrote King,

> and with wood smoke from the cottage fire scenting our walks, on November 18, 1965, Casey wrote the first draft and then together we polished our challenge to women who were involved across the spectrum of progressive organizing. This call would go out to [forty] women in Students for a Democratic Society, the National Student Association, the Northern Student Movement, and the Student Peace Union as well as SNCC.[37]

Hayden's paper summed up what they had learned during their years in SNCC. King, for example, attributed many of her ideas to Ella Baker, who had taught young activists "that a fundamental purpose of the civil rights movement was to teach people to make their own decisions, to take responsibility for themselves, and to be ready to accept the consequences . . . you must let the oppressed themselves define their own freedom." Reflecting on the origins of the women's memo, King wrote, "Wasn't that in fact what we were seeking to do, to define our own freedom?"[38]

For Hayden—cut off from the movement that had sustained her for half a decade and recently divorced from Tom Hayden—the writing also represented an effort to create a new community. Blacks had decided that whites could no longer organize blacks. Men had begun organizing men against the Vietnam War. In part, the manifesto represented her effort to re-create SNCC's beloved community: "It was a search for a home, a sisterhood, an attempt to create real discussion. The means and ends were one. . . . The paper was not a rebellion; it was an attempt to sustain."[39]

Hayden and King called the manifesto "A Kind of Memo," a title whose modesty masked their actual ambition to mobilize women in the movement. In order to analyze women's relations to men, they once again drew upon the language and world they knew best—that of race relations. Unlike the 1964 list of grievances, the "Memo" focused on the larger problems women were experiencing in the movement. Searching for a way to situate women as a group, Hayden settled on the concept of a "caste." Unable to imagine a separatist women's movement, she predicted that women would not withdraw from the situation "à la black nationalism." "Objectively," Hayden wrote confidently, "the chances seem nil that we could start a movement based on anything as distant to general American thought as a sex-caste system. Therefore, most of us will probably want to work full time on problems such as war, poverty, race." That settled, Hayden went on to question woman's "natural" role in society, as well as a range of movement assumptions from "who cleans the freedom house, to who accepts a leadership position, to who does secretarial work, and to who acts as spokesman for groups."

In SNCC, women had enjoyed considerable freedom from hierarchy and learned to question the "natural order of things." It was only logical to apply these ideas to the most intimate aspects of their lives. "The reason we want to try to open up dialogue," the "Memo" explained, "is mostly subjective. Working in the movement often intensifies personal problems, especially if we start trying to apply things we're learning there to our personal lives." Years before feminists invoked the slogan "The personal is political," Hayden had defined the political dimensions of personal relations.

> We've talked in the movement about trying to build a society which would see basic human problems (which are now seen as personal troubles) as public problems and which would try to shape institutions to meet human needs rather than shaping people to meet the needs of those with power. . . . [We've learned] to think radically about the personal worth and abilities of people whose role in society had gone unchallenged before [and now] a lot of women in the movement had begun trying to apply those lessons to their own relations with men.

Already, in 1965, Hayden was articulating what women's liberationists would later call "consciousness-raising"—"trusting *our inner feelings,*" as she put it, "learning to see the world through women's own experiences." Hayden also realized that the ghost of the fifties haunted their highly politicized lives. Under the heading of institutions, Hayden underscored their growing rejection of the very institutions of traditional family life: "Nearly everyone has real questions about those institutions which shape the perspectives about men and women: marriage, child rearing patterns. . . . People are beginning to think about and even to experiment with new forms in these areas."[40]

Hayden and King sent their three-page document to forty women active in the civil rights, student, and peace movements sometime after November 18, 1965. It reached an even wider readership when the magazine *Liberation* reprinted it in April 1966. "From our black women friends," recalled King, "to whom we had sent the missive . . . we heard nothing. Not one responded." The problems Hayden had identified addressed the stereotype of white women's learned helplessness, not the racism that forced black women to support themselves, their families, and their communities. And as more black women embraced black separatist politics, they also viewed "women's issues" as divisive.[41]

White women activists responded with greater enthusiasm. "I was very turned on by the memo and wanted to do some kind of exposé on male leadership of the ILGWU [International Ladies' Garment Workers' Union]," the labor activist Jan Goodman wrote Hayden. A former editor of the *Nation*, Elizabeth Sutherland, offered to rewrite the memo to submit to mainstream magazines. Years later, Barbara Raskin, an activist attached to the leftist Institute for Policy Studies (IPS), told Mary King that she would never forget the day the letter arrived in the mail:

> It was stunning in its effect on me. I read it and reread it, and shared it with all my friends. Eventually we started a group in Washington and met on a regular basis to discuss the issues you and Casey raised. From reading and rereading it, the letter became creased and dirtied. Finally, I could hardly read it anymore but by then I knew it by heart.[42]

INSIDE SDS

Like Betty Friedan's discovery of housewives' nameless problems, "A Kind of Memo" captured the unarticulated simmering resentments of young activist women and sparked serious soul-searching among them. The "women's issue" surfaced just as SDS's fragile unity faced dramatic expansion in the face of growing protests against the war in Vietnam and increasing political divisions.

The small, face-to-face community of SDS had been overwhelmed by the growing student and antiwar movements. Inspired by the Free Speech Movement that erupted in 1964 at the University of California at Berkeley, students across the country had begun to question the relevance of their education and the authority of their professors. In August 1964, Congress had passed the Gulf of Tonkin Resolution at the behest of President Lyndon Johnson, confirming the fact that the United States was embroiled in a major war in Vietnam. When the president ordered the bombing of North Vietnam in February 1965, SDS, a visible dissident student organization, found itself cast as the leadership responsible for organizing an antiwar movement.

Across the country, students organized "teach-ins," marathon events in which educators and experts taught a generation of students, many of whom would have been hard-pressed to find Vietnam on a map, the history of America's ongoing intervention in Southeast Asia. In April 1965, SDS drew some twenty-five thousand people to the nation's capital for the first national demonstration against the Vietnam War. By the spring of 1965, in response to the accelerating war in Vietnam, SDS had ballooned into a national organization of some forty chapters with over two thousand paid members.

Many women participated in SDS, as well as in the student and antiwar movements. What historian Sara Evans has described as SDS's "competitive intellectual mode" intimidated many female (as well as male) members. Early SDS attracted an exceptional core of young men who "were diligent readers, active thinkers and talkers, and as the later literature lists of SDS will show, prodigious writers."[43] If they had wanted, these young men could have achieved early success—and economic security—in any number of careers. Instead, they rebelled against conventional definitions of male success.

As the organization grew, alienation escalated. Among the alienated were SDS women who were at least as remarkable as their male counterparts, arguably more so. A number of them had mothers who viewed themselves as feminists; a few had parents who, as Communists or former Communists, had taught their daughters about the "woman question." Others came to an understanding of women's oppression through their own personal and political experience.

Vivian Rothstein was typical of the women who became part of the SDS inner circle. Raised in Los Angeles, Rothstein went to Berkeley as an undergraduate in 1963 and soon joined the Congress of Racial Equality (CORE) demonstrations against the discriminatory employment practices of Lucky Foods and the Sheraton Plaza Hotel. Along with five hundred other demonstrators, she was arrested for civil disobedience in an action against auto dealerships that refused to hire black salespeople, and spent the summer of 1964 in group trials in San Francisco. She participated in the Berkeley Free Speech movement, and in the summer of 1965 went to Jackson, Mississippi, as part of the second Mississippi Freedom Summer project. In Jackson, police arrested her in a mass action challenging local restrictions on political demonstrations. After ten days in a Jackson jail, she was assigned to a rural Mississippi county to work on voter registration, school integration, and the development of a local Freedom School.

Rothstein took seriously blacks' admonition to organize other whites. She returned to Berkeley, where she joined a fledgling SDS ERAP project in Oakland, California. When that project failed, she moved East to join the SDS JOIN project, which was organizing poor white southern Appalachian migrants in Chicago. It was in Chicago that she became involved with the leadership core of SDS. Like many women in that initial group, Vivian's admission to the inner circle was facilitated by her subsequent marriage to an early SDS leader.

Many women in the New Left—not only in SDS—felt intimidated by the movement world in which they lived but rarely starred. In contrast, early male SDS leaders boldly expressed a sense of entitlement that had been part of their upbringing. They expected to be heard, even in Washington. During the Cuban missile crisis, Elinor Langer, married to the founder of the Institute for Policy Studies, remembered that "the women, come to think of it, were making coffee and setting the table while the men were trying to figure out by what chain of who-knows-who they could reach the higher authorities with their proposals and demands." Looking back, Sue Thrasher, the first executive secretary of the Southern Student Organizing Committee, recalled, "The officers in

SSOC were all men except me. It became clear to me that I was doing all the shit work, holding the office together, keeping the mailing and stuff like that going on." But like many young women in such situations, she repressed any sense of resentment. She simply loved being in the movement. "A lot of my anger about the position of women came later."[44]

Unlike the Old Left, which at least recognized "the woman question," SDS did not even address the issue. Barbara Epstein, whose activism spanned both the Old and New Left, found SDS astonishingly ignorant of what the Communist Party had called "male chauvinism." In "the Old Left," she noted, "one could at least bring up the issue, even if Communists regarded it as a 'bourgeois matter' to be solved 'after the revolution.' " . . . "Inside SDS," explained Epstein, "you see, it was laughed at. I tried to bring this up in SDS and it was impossible."

Power came and went depending on a woman's relationship to men in the inner circle. Barbara Haber, one of the founding members of SDS, recognized that as the wife of the group's first president, she had special status, but not necessarily more credibility. "I was the wife of a 'heavy' [movement shorthand for an important leader who wielded influence]. It was a double-edged status. It certainly did not mean that I was seen as a person in my own right and treated with respect."

Such daughters of the fifties, well educated and brimming with intellectual curiosity, had little inclination to write theoretical papers on the nature of the university or the military-industrial complex. Casey Hayden felt that "SDS shaped my politics, but SNCC had my heart."[45] They were accustomed to using their intelligence for organizing and solving concrete problems. Little in their background or education had encouraged them to theorize about corporate America or to analyze the nation's foreign policy with a voice of authority—in fact, to do anything with the kind of authority that seemed to come so naturally to their male peers. Raised to be polite, some waited patiently for men to stop speaking, but as one former SDS woman complained, "The men, they never finished."

At large national council meetings women felt especially intimidated by the long speeches and the intellectual competition among male leaders. And when they did speak, they were often ignored. Nanci Hollander, an SDS activist then married to Todd Gitlin, president of SDS in 1963, noticed that whenever a woman began to speak, "the men suddenly stretched, and chattered among themselves." Women got the message: what they had to say was, by definition, of *so* little importance that it could be ignored. The issues women most wanted to discuss—how to organize more effectively, how to improve the group process, or how to address the problems of community women—were discredited as "soft subjects," certainly less important than an analysis of corporate liberalism or American foreign policy.

It was the same wherever the New Left met. Anne Weills, then married to Robert Scheer, the editor of the leftist magazine *Ramparts*, also felt invisible at Bay Area movement meetings. "Even if you said it well," she recalled,

> half the time people would ignore you. I'd think, "I'm not saying it well. I'm not saying it loud enough." Finally, I'd get to say something. Complete Silence. A few minutes later, a man would get up and say the same thing. Suddenly the room became electrified. Invisibility. That's what was so painful.

Parliamentary rules, wielded as weapons by men on a podium, made Marilyn Webb, an SDS activist, "afraid to say anything. . . . There was no feeling women were encouraged, and parliamentary rules, often byzantine, seemed so alienating."[46]

"The SDS Old Guard," Todd Gitlin later conceded, "was essentially a young boys' network. . . . Men sought [women] out, recruited them, took them seriously, honored their intelligence—then subtly demoted them to girlfriends, wives, note-takers, coffee makers. . . . Ambition, expected in a man, looked suspiciously like ball-busting to the male eye. An aggressive style, which might pass as acceptably virile in a man, sounded 'bitchy' in a woman."[47]

The historian Maurice Isserman has suggested that life at the national office—"with its pressure-cooker atmosphere and the premium placed within it on forceful public speaking as the mark of leadership"—may have been less hospitable than in SDS local chapters. But at the national level, women felt overshadowed and often suffered from debilitating self-doubt. Carol McEldowney, a respected and talented organizer who had helped turn Cleveland's ERAP project into a welfare rights movement, confided her own disabling insecurity in a private letter to a trusted SDS friend in 1964: "You know, or maybe you don't, that I've endured many feelings of insecurity and inferiority lately in the intellectual realm, and for a long time I've felt dwarfed being around the intellectual elite."

McEldowney was well aware that most SDS male leaders valued

intellectual theory more than organizing skills. "I often find myself frustrated and hamstrung by my own inadequacy, which is not a happy situation. The most obvious manifestation of this is the fact that I often . . . lose my tongue when in a conversational situation with those of that superior ilk."[48] Such paralyzing self-doubt prevented McEldowney from accepting the reins of national leadership. During the summer of 1965, a group of SDS friends tried to persuade her to become the national secretary of the organization. Overwhelmed, she wrote to friends, "Me. Nat'l Sec'y. A joke." She refused, explaining that the very idea terrified her. After a recent meeting, she had left feeling "like crawling into a hole. My lack of information of American foreign policy, coupled with my shyness in such a situation and fear of saying something that would be rebuffed. . . . I have trouble saying this to people because the standard response is, 'oh, stop being silly,' which does nothing, absolutely nothing, to reassure me. . . . The damn thing of it is that I'm sure many other people in SDS feel as I do."[49]

They did, but at the time, each woman assumed that her alienation and lack of confidence was her own private problem. At an SDS reunion in New York in August 1988, the women decided to reconsider their own history in SDS. By 1969, when SDS had splintered into warring factions, these women no longer lived in the same community. They told other women their stories, but not the women with whom they had worked and shared their lives in SDS in the early sixties.

Now they told each other how they felt in SDS. Several women described the terror of talking at national meetings. "But I thought you were so strong and articulate," own woman commented to another. "I thought I was the only one who felt that way." "Every time I spoke, I trembled," said another former member. Another woman added almost in a whisper, "Many of us left meetings and quietly cried alone."[50] "Why did we feel so devalued?" someone then asked. Betty Garman, a member of the first SDS Executive Council, suggested one answer. "What seemed important to men never seemed all that important to me. I wanted to organize, not engage in verbal debate." Sharon Jeffrey added that "SDS revered the mind, but ignored feelings. Perception, not intuition, was honored."

Each story tapped into some wellspring of sadness. Tears flowed—for doubting their intellectual talents, for accepting men's definition of the world. Sala Steinbach said softly, "SDS was the center of my life." Another woman added, "And we have to admit that SDS was extraordinary precisely because of those brilliant men. Many of us were seduced by their great minds and ambitious visions. And yet that very same talent was what intimidated us." A brief period of silence followed. "We are angry at ourselves," one former SDSer said quietly. "How could those men be so smart and still so sexist?" wondered another woman, half-laughing and half-crying.

Dorothy Burlage, one of the Old Guard, highlighted the difference between her generation and the younger women who followed: "The opportunity for exploitation grew because the institution of marriage was breaking down within the movement, many of us were getting divorced, and women were becoming more vulnerable and alone." Another woman added that "the high drama of personal relations became part of political culture." "We began to live as though we had already created a new society, but we certainly weren't ready for it!" "And nothing was ever wholly private," Dorothy Burlage added. When Tom and Casey Hayden divorced, an SDS memo documented the split.

One of the women who entered SDS after 1965 pointed out that by then, the change in sexual mores and lifestyles had transformed the culture of SDS. "To men, especially the Old Guard, the story is one of political decline and disintegration." But women, she argued, experienced more continuity:

> All of us, one way or another, achieved our status through our connection to a man. No matter what year you entered SDS, that was the truth. The big difference—for us—is that as the movement grew, and the sexual revolution and drugs changed our lives, we no longer gained status as wives, but as lovers of important men. So we became more vulnerable to sexual exploitation.

She hit a raw nerve. A number of women nodded in agreement. "The only way to gain any authority," as one woman put it, "was to be with a man in the Old Guard." Sometimes, added Marilyn Webb, "men used younger women to threaten and control older women." To which a former SDSer added, "Yes, and women rose or fell depending on a man's sexual interests. When an affair ended, we could be thrown out of the inner circle. We didn't want—or have—the marriages that would have offered some security." Sarah Murphy, who first joined SDS at fourteen, described how she avoided sexual liaisons by allowing herself to be cast as a "mascot." "I think it was a strategy that worked, but at a very high cost to me personally."[51]

In December 1965, one month after "A Kind of Memo" reached movement women, Students for a Democratic Society convened what organizers dubbed a "rethinking" conference in Champaign-Urbana. As with SNCC at Waveland, the conference represented the group's attempt, in a period of enormous growth in membership, to recapture the soul of its original vision. At the conference, many SDS women experienced the kind of intimidation or exploitation they later described in 1988, but they didn't know how to talk about it. Men set the political agenda because, well, they knew about politics. Women did the mimeographing and coffee-making because, well, women always did such things. "We just didn't think it could be different at that time," one former activist remembered. "In many ways, the movement was so much better than ordinary life, who would have thought of complaining?" The movement, after all, gave them great freedom to explore their ideas and values. They also learned how to organize, write press releases, run mimeograph machines, and mediate conflicts. Intimidating, not to say tedious, as the verbal debates and position papers might have been, they were teaching a critical mass of young women how to think strategically and theoretically.

Still, feelings of status deprivation ran deep. Gaining skills and confidence, but not recognition, provided some of the fuel for women's dissatisfaction.[52] As Barbara Haber pointed out, "It is precisely because the early years so closely matched my ideal of a dream life that the disappointments felt so enormous." Ambitions ran high. They were going to overthrow the world of their parents. They were in the process of redefining "obscenity" as war, racism, and poverty. They wanted to be viewed as serious people, not simply as the playmates or housewives of movement men. The difficulty men had in recognizing this budding sense of self-confidence set the stage for a painful collision.

In the wake of the conference, most SDS activists agreed that the "rethinking" had been a dismal failure. The organization had neither recaptured its earlier spirit nor discovered a new vision. While some men would view that failure as the beginning of the end of the New Left, some women would later regard it as the beginning of the women's movement.

Hayden's "Memo" dominated the conference. Discussions trailed into the early hours of the morning. Some remember an all-men's group forming briefly. Just who was where, and who met with whom, is now impossible to reconstruct. When someone finally announced a workshop to discuss women's problems in the movement, most of the Old Guard men and women immediately joined right in.[53]

At first, the discussion turned on whether or not women constituted an oppressed group within SDS. Most women said they did; many of the men denied it. The fact that the debate began—and foundered—at such an elementary level so angered some of the women that they decided to meet by themselves in another room. In the mixed group that met outdoors, the members began to debate whether there was any problem at all and whether "sex roles" were natural or not.

Martha Zweig, an SDS activist, shocked Barbara Haber by insisting that the sexual division of labor—in society as well as in SDS—was both natural and essential to maintain, rooted as it was in women's sexual and emotional passivity. Haber, who had avoided joining the all-women's group—out of loyalty to her husband, Al—became indignant. She argued with Zweig, saying that she didn't experience herself as a passive sexual being. As her irritation grew, Haber found herself regretting that she had not joined the women's group. In front of the approximately twenty or so men and remaining women, she heard herself defending women's right to equality with men. "At that moment," she recalled, "I knew I had become a feminist."[54]

As the evening grew chilly, Haber suggested that the group move inside. No one noticed; no one moved. She made the same suggestion several more times; no one paid any attention. "Watch this," her husband Al Haber sympathetically whispered. He repeated her suggestion. Everyone picked up their chairs and withdrew from the nippy night air.[55]

Meanwhile, the all-women's group listened as someone read the "Memo" out loud. When a few men asked to join, the women made a historic decision to meet alone. They began by asking questions. What were legitimate "women's" issues as opposed to individual problems? What aspects of sex roles were, in fact, natural? Where was the vocabulary to discuss any of this? The word "sexism" did not yet exist. If some daughters of the Old Left were familiar with the terms "male supremacy" and the "woman question" in the winter of 1965, there were still precious few ways to talk about and explore such matters.

Shortly afterward, Sharon Jeffrey and Carol McEldowney mailed out typewritten notes based on the workshop. In a preface, they expressed their anxiety that "their notes might not capture the excitement and emotion, and real seriousness with which these questions were pursued at the conference."[56] What made the moment historic, Heather Booth later recalled, was not that women discussed their grievances with men's behavior and attitudes in their absence, but that they also explored their own dreams and aspirations.

In those brief few hours alone for the first time, they addressed many of the issues that feminists would debate for the next three decades. Are women essentially different from men or socially constructed as different creatures? What, if any, male qualities should women seek to embrace? Is there a female way of knowing and doing? Who would care for the children if women entered the labor force? How can a woman be a sexual person and still be treated as a serious person? What kind of equality would also recognize and honor the differences between men and women?

The issue of "identity" surfaced again and again. Men, they pointed out, gained their identity through work, income, and public activity. How could women achieve their own independent identities and still maintain love for and a connection with men and children? As a start, suggested these activists, "We should develop our own personal identity and accept our limitations, abilities and needs, as WE define them, and not as men define them. . . . When a woman tries to prove herself, it should be to herself and not to a man, or men, or society." Like Betty Friedan, they also advocated work as the solution to women's inequality, but as radical activists, they favored work that fostered social change.

These women felt little desire to imitate men. Even in 1965, the group already recognized that they needed to transcend conventional male and female social identities and career paths. How to do that, they could not yet imagine. Although few SDS women had children, most realized that childbearing complicated any discussion of changing the future for the benefit of women. Given the organization of society, children were bound to deepen the inequality between movement men and women. The most striking statement—years ahead of its time—came from Nanci Hollander, who said, "Instead of the women assuming the major responsibility for raising the children, the man and woman should assume and share in the task equally. In order for this to work, however, society would first have to re-arrange work and make it more flexible."[57]

Responses to the workshop varied considerably. Some men viewed the women's criticism as a way to restore community and civility in SDS.

Some of the married women felt apprehensive about recognizing the subordinate nature of their situations. They feared the struggles and ruptures that lay ahead. But everyone agreed that what had seemed like personal dilemmas suddenly had taken on a new significance when amplified by a group of women. Some women felt the full weight of the moment. Nanci Hollander remembered thinking, "We've just started a women's movement."[58]

AS THE WORLD TURNED

It would take another two years before significant numbers of New Left women began leaving what many would call "the mixed Left" or the "the male Left." Meanwhile, activists were swept up in a dizzying swirl of events. The emergence of black power had ended an era in which white women could participate in an interracial civil rights movement. Students demonstrated against the draft, held gigantic antiwar marches, and when neither ended what seemed like an interminable war in Vietnam, some activists moved from protest to what they called "resistance" in a militant effort to "shut down" the system.

In 1968, history seemed to speed up. Many American activists, as well as ordinary citizens, began to wonder whether the nation, if not the world, was unraveling. The assassinations of Martin Luther King, Jr., and Robert F. Kennedy, the election of Richard Nixon, and the collapse of international youth activism and rebellions from Mexico to France moved New Leftists from hope to despair. During the month of August 1968 alone, police beat activists outside the Democratic National Convention and Soviet tanks rolled into Czechoslovakia to stop the democratic flowering of "Prague Spring."

In the midst of these tumultuous events arose another kind of dissidence—a new hippie culture or "counterculture," strongly linked to the Beats, that encouraged the young to "drop out" of schools and jobs, "to do your own thing," and to live as if the revolution had already happened. Appearing just as the women's movement took off, the hippie counterculture also challenged conventional ideas of appropriate gender roles. Both men and women grew their hair long, dressed in loose, flowing garments, and adorned themselves with jewelry from various folk and Indian traditions. "Be-ins" and "happenings" created cultural solidarity among these alienated youths. Dancers, high on psychedelic drugs, freed of clothes, let their bodies and minds float toward an altered state of consciousness. Excess became common as a new language reflected that things were "far out," "out of sight," beyond normal comprehension.

In the spring of 1965, at the first antiwar march in Washington, D.C., young men had dressed in suits and ties and worn their hair short. Their female companions had worn neat shirtwaists, nylons, and flats. Only a scattering of demonstrators had long hair and wore sandals—even though they were the ones who always appeared on the evening news. Two years later, in 1967, San Francisco's burgeoning hippie counterculture had completely transformed the look of demonstrations. The immense antiwar marches in San Francisco combined political protest with celebrations of love. People danced in the street to rock bands perched on flatbed trucks. Stoned on marijuana or psychedelic drugs, young marchers protested not only the war, but also the "straight" society that "made war, not love."

At first, "politicos" and hippies seemed to have nothing in common. As one hippie admitted, "We weren't interested in taking over administration buildings. We were interested in blowing people's minds, basically. Making them confront the idea that there was an alternative to the straight way of life."[59] And a few staunch politicos never touched any drugs or danced all night to psychedelic music. But between 1965 and 1967, these worlds began to overlap. "There was a continuum between politics and culture at every school," explained former student activist Paul Buhle.

> At one end there were these tight-assed people whom you suspected of being close to the Communist Party. At the other end you had a lot of burn-outs. Radical political publications soon appeared at "head shops" along with underground comics—or comix as they were relabelled—incense, posters and drug paraphernalia. At a hippie grocery store you could see a poster with the headline "Fight Imperialism! Eat Organic Food!" It was something you couldn't believe in unless you were nineteen years old.[60]

The blurring of the radical political and countercultural worlds also accelerated all sorts of social relationships. "You became intimate with people very easily," recalled Devra Weber, then a Los Angeles student.

You were with large groups of people your own age, mostly single, who were all involved in intellectual work, and that was exciting all by itself. The attempt to be direct, where politeness was not the big issue, really getting at the truth behind the matter, this basically made people close. And there was the music. The nights staying up and playing Bob Dylan, smoking pot, red lights on the lamps, and lots of people over talking, everyone sitting comfortably on a mattress because that's the one piece of furniture in the room except for a chair.[61]

From such cultural and political gatherings did new friendships and sexual relationships flow.

But the counterculture also left an ambiguous legacy for young feminists. On the one hand, it legitimized all kinds of informal and unconventional behavior. It offered young women a sense of liberation, much of which revolved around drugs and sex. At the same time, the hippie culture tended to glorify women as barefoot and pregnant; many young women rejected suburban materialism, grew and prepared their own food, sewed their own clothes, and lived off the land. Hippie women were not concerned about discrimination; they didn't want jobs. But to politically engaged women, who were just carving out a new identity, what did it mean to "turn on, tune in, drop out"? They had just begun to drop in and take themselves seriously. They had little inclination to drop out.

Although it seemed like "women's issues" had been left to simmer on the back burner, young women, in fits and starts, were creating the momentum to build a new women's movement. Cathy Barrett, Cathy Cade, and Peggy Dobbins, for instance, initiated a groundbreaking course on the sociology of women in the summer of 1966 at a "free school" in New Orleans. In 1966, Heather Booth tried to organize a "women's" workshop at an antiwar "We Won't Go" conference at the University of Chicago, but many women activists thought the draft was more urgent. The 1966 SDS National Convention managed to ignore women's issues, but for the first time provided child care.

In 1967 SDS women once again brought up their grievances, this time issuing a resolution calling for "the liberation of women." Given the Third World–oriented revolutionary rhetoric of the time, they described themselves as having a "colonial" relationship to men. They called for the creation of a new society that protected women's repro-

REFUGEES AND REBELS

Betty Friedan, an early labor journalist, with one of her three children in the 1950s. *Courtesy of the Schlesinger Library, Radcliffe College*

Among the founding members of NOW were Betty Friedan, co–vice presidents Aileen Hernandez and Richard Graham, Sister Joel Read, attorney and activist Pauli Murray, Caroline Davis of the United Auto Workers, and Kay Clarenbach, a former professor. *Courtesy of the Schlesinger Library, Radcliffe College*

Laura Murra, who renamed herself Laura X, started the world's first women's history archive in her Berkeley home in 1969. *Photo by Ruth Rosen*

Many women continued their antiwar work, even as they began to publicize their growing awareness of their subordinate role in New left movements. (Berkeley, California, 1971) *Photo by Richard Sammons*

When the University of California at Berkeley refused to provide equal gym facilities for women students in 1969, members of women's liberation protested by invading a locker room filled with stunned, half-dressed men. *Photo by Ruth Rosen*

When the Berkeley Public Library refused a request for just *one* shelf of books about women, activists staged a sit-in, supported by the indomitable civil rights activist Flo Kennedy. Fourteen were arrested and convicted of trespassing and disturbing the peace. (Berkeley, California, 1973) *Photo by Cathy Cade*

The growing awareness of male violence motivated many activists to learn martial arts. The media repeatedly used such images as evidence of the militance and hostility they attributed to feminists. (San Francisco, 1974) *Photo by Cathy Cade*

From the earliest days of the movement, feminists condemned corporate exploitation of women, men, and children. Here they blocked the entrance and exits of the stock exchange as they denounced corporate lack of responsibility. (New York, October 1984) *Photo by Joan E. Biren (JEB)*

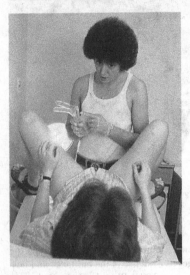

During the early 1970s, activists began teaching each other about their bodies, often through self-help vaginal exams. (Washington, D.C., Women's Health Clinic, 1979) *Photo by JEB*

Few Americans had any idea how many women had died of botched abortions before the Supreme Court's 1973 *Roe v. Wade* decision made abortion legal. (San Francisco, 1989) *Photo by Cathy Cade*

Growing rage at how much rape curtailed women's mobility turned into annual "Take Back the Night" marches held in cities across the country. (Washington, D. C., 1981) *Photo by JEB*

Having taken DES to prevent a miscarriage, Pat Cody raised questions about the potential health problems faced by the sons and daughters of mothers like herself. Her kitchen-table activism rapidly turned into an international movement. *Photo courtesy of Pat Cody*

DES.
The wonder drug women should wonder about.

DES (diethylstilbestrol) has been linked with medical problems in the children of women who took it.

Find out if you were given DES. Ask your doctor or local health department.

N.Y.S. Health Department
Office of Health Promotion

Posters educated mothers and their children about the need for constant monitoring of DES daughters and sons for certain kinds of cancers.

The struggle to keep abortion available, safe, and legal never seemed to end. In 1989, this young woman joined thousands of activists in nonviolent protests against judicial decisions and legislative efforts to chip away at a woman's right to abortion. (Washington, D. C.) *Photo by JEB*

As the women's health movement grew, different populations of women began demanding access to health care for themselves and their communities. (San Francisco, 1989) *Photo by Cathy Cade*

By the late 1980s, feminist health activists had created grassroots groups to provide services and information for women patients, and national organizations to lobby for greater breast cancer research. (San Francisco Freedom Day Parade, 1993) *Photo by Cathy Cade*

WORK

When the Bank of America suddenly stopped paying taxi fares for women whose shift ended in the early morning hours, Union Wage, a socialist feminist group in Oakland, California, supported women workers' demand for employer protection. (San Francisco, 1972) *Photo by Cathy Cade*

Contrary to popular belief, quite a few feminists believed that mothers should be paid a substantial stipend for caring for their families and homes. (Graffiti found on wall in Berkeley, California, 1973) *Photo by Cathy Cade*

Union and feminist activists began organizing nurses, clerical workers, and stewardesses. These stewardesses, supported by male cable-car drivers, went on strike for their right to pensions and employment based on competence, rather than age or appearance. (San Francisco, 1973) *Photo by Cathy Cade*

As opportunities began to expand, many women took up such formerly "male" occupations as carpentry, masonry, plumbing, and other skilled work. (A woman building a house in rural Albion, California, 1973) *Photo by Lynda Koolish*

ductive rights, supported communal child care centers staffed by men and women, and required housework to be shared until "technology and automation would eliminate work which is necessary for the maintenance of the home." The resolution also called for all SDS chapters to cultivate female leadership, solicit articles written by women, and create bibliographies and pamphlets on women's issues. It ended with what was probably the last conciliatory and loving statement New Left women would make to their male compatriots:

> We seek the liberation of all human beings. The struggle for liberation of women must be part of the larger fight for human freedom. We recognize the difficulty our brothers will have in dealing with male chauvinism and we will assume our full responsibility in helping to resolve the contradiction. Freedom now! We love you!

New Left Notes published the resolution, but its accompanying illustration carried a different message: a cartoon of a young girl, wearing long earrings and matching polka-dot minidress and panties, carrying a placard that read: "We Want Our Rights and We Want Them Now." The ridicule incited indignation. As Sara Evans later observed, "SDS had blown its last chance."[62]

In 1967, during the Vietnam Summer Project, Marilyn Webb and Sue Thrasher found themselves talking about women's roles as they worked to end the war. Naomi Weisstein and Heather Booth convened a summer course on women at the Center for Radical Research in Chicago. "We spent a long time," recalled Weisstein, "trying to consider alternatives to wife and mother [and asking] why women were not in positions of power."[63] At the national SDS office, Jane Adams, a prominent SDS activist, called together women for a similar discussion. Jo Freeman, a veteran of the civil rights and Free Speech movements, began to recruit women in Chicago to use an upcoming meeting, the National Conference for New Politics (NCNP) in late August 1967, as a way of raising women's issues. She convened a meeting of women, largely composed of SDS women, but not all of them supported the idea. In fact, few agreed how to proceed.

LAST STRAWS

The NCNP proved to be a last-ditch effort to unify the New Left. The ostensible purpose was to nominate a presidential ticket for 1968 that would be headed by Martin Luther King, Jr., and Benjamin Spock, the famed pediatrician and antiwar activist. Clearly, the impulse to heal movement wounds was widespread, for some two thousand activists from over two hundred organizations poured into Chicago that Labor Day weekend. But the search for unity failed. Angry black activists from northern cities lashed out at white hypocrisy, while middle-class whites seemed desperate to gain legitimacy from them. Some black delegates screamed, "Kill Whitey"; others demanded that they should receive half the votes at the conference and 50 percent of all committee slots, though they made up only one-sixth of the conference participants.

When a women's caucus met, they hammered out a resolution. But on learning of it, the chairman of the conference warned, "We don't have time for a resolution about women." Drawing on her years of experience in the Democratic Party, Jo Freeman threatened to use parliamentary delaying tactics to tie up the proceedings for hours. The chairman backed down, partway, agreeing to bring up their resolution, but only after the conference had voted upon ten other resolutions.

Working through the night, Jo Freeman and Shulamith Firestone, another longtime activist, wrote a new version of the resolution, demanding that women receive 51 percent of the convention votes and committee slots. It was a move designed to appeal to white men's guilt. The problem was, they had misjudged their audience; most of these men did not feel any guilt about white women.

The next day, they patiently waited while the conference debated the first ten resolutions. When the time came for the women's resolution, a man simply read it aloud in a monotone, the audience greeted their ideas with derision and ridicule, and a voice vote quickly approved it. This was hardly what Freeman and Firestone had in mind. They had wanted to discuss the problems behind the resolution, not to be dismissed out of hand by a "positive" vote.[64] In response, the women threatened to seize the microphones.

Jo Freeman never forgot how the affair ended: "Suddenly, a rather short and younger man rushed in front of me to the microphone, raised his hand, was recognized and began speaking: 'Ladies and gentlemen, I'd like to speak to you today about the most forgotten American group in America.' " Before he finished his sentence, Freeman felt a sudden moment of elation, certain he was about to support their resolution. Instead, he finished his sentence with "the American Indian." A number of women, including Shulie Firestone, "were ready to pull the place apart." Then, according to Jo Freeman, "William Pepper patted Shulie on the head and said, 'Move on little girl; we have more important issues to talk about here than women's liberation.' That was the genesis. We had a meeting the next week with women in Chicago."[65]

This first Chicago group decided to draft a letter titled, "To the Women of the Left," to be published in New Left media, as well as in mimeographed form. Separatism and self-determination would now saturate movement culture and women would accelerate that process. Influenced by black successes at the conference, they declared their independence from the male Left.

AN EPIDEMIC OF ENTHUSIASM

A good epidemiologist could have traced the rapid transmission of the infectious enthusiasm for women's liberation that swept the country. Networks of New Left women, accustomed to traveling to national conferences and organizing local and national meetings, became the carriers of that enthusiasm. Pam Allen, a former SNCC organizer, for example, heard about women's liberation from Sue Munaker, already active in Chicago Women's Liberation. Pam Allen then moved to New York, where she and Shulamith Firestone began organizing the first women's liberation groups in New York. Allen then moved to San Francisco, where she wrote her famous pamphlet about the "free space" that women needed to rethink their lives, and helped organize *Sudsafloppen*, a San Francisco group. Kathie Sarachild, already active in New York, visited Boston and persuaded Nancy Hawley to join the movement. Hawley, an early SDS member, then began an informal women's group, which later became part of the collective that wrote the famous women's self-help health manual, *Our Bodies, Ourselves*. Roxanne Dunbar, who had been active on the West Coast, moved to Boston in the summer of 1968 and recruited women through an ad in an underground newspaper and started Cell 16. Carol Hanisch, who had worked in the South, now moved to New York and became a central organizer and writer in the new women's liberation movement.[66] And this was just the beginning.

Through the civil rights, SDS, and antiwar movements, these highly mobile women had developed friendships and networks that now disseminated ideas of women's liberation like grass seed blown by the wind. The movement had taught women how to organize, and this they now did with a vengeance. Between the fall of 1967 and the end of 1968, personal friendships, organized media events, and word of mouth, or some combination of all of them, led to the creation of women's liberation groups in nearly every major American city. As one woman said, "I had never known anything as easy as organizing a women's group—as easy and as exciting and as dramatic."[67]

Consider what happened when Marilyn Webb, married to SDS leader Lee Webb, visited Anne Scheer, wife of Robert Scheer, in Berkeley in 1967. According to Webb, "Anne had a small son and while the men talked politics downstairs, we discussed our grievances as women upstairs." Anne had not yet wanted to become a mother, but her husband, approaching thirty, profoundly wanted a child. In 1967, Anne and he made a solemn agreement. She would get pregnant if he agreed to share the child care.

Scheer did, in fact, take his parental responsibilities seriously. But as editor of *Ramparts*, he needed to travel, attend conferences, and launch fund-raising campaigns. Anne became filled with despair.

> At one point I complained about how hard it was to take care of another human being 24 hours a day, and he told me "to get a nurse." I went into a rage, cried for days, and realized that it was over. I felt that he had broken a solemn contract. It was a real betrayal that went so deep I just knew it was the end.

It was at this point that Marilyn Webb visited them, and then went home enlightened by Anne's story.[68]

One of the national events that helped bring all these women together was the Jeanette Rankin Brigade, an all-women antiwar demonstration that took place in January 1968. During the preceding year, Anne Scheer had been meeting with a group of younger women who were helping the Women Strike for Peace organize the event. "It was in that group," Anne Weills (who had taken back her name) remembered, "that we began to discuss how much we felt like second-class citizens in the movement. We were sick and tired of playing an auxiliary role. We were never taken seriously." Although Anne could not attend the Washington, D.C., event, she soon learned how many younger women—like herself and Marilyn Webb—came together and realized that they were indeed creating a women's movement.[69]

The angrier New Left women became, the greater their expectations. The higher their expectations, the more New Left men failed them.[70] Rayna Rapp, who had joined SDS in 1964, later explained that once she "let feminism in, it reorganized everything [she] understood about the world."

> That was my conversion experience—it was natural and it stuck. Afterwards, I was so angry about the number of mimeograph machines I had turned and the number of phone calls I had made, and the number of cups of coffee I had brought for other people. They had all this empathy for the Vietnamese, and for black Americans, but they didn't have much empathy for the women in their lives; not the women they slept with, not the women they shared office space with, not the women they fought at demonstrations with. So our first anger and anguish and fury was directed against the men of the Left. [The men] should have known better, as far as we were concerned. And we should have known better, too. A lot of it was self-anger, that we had allowed ourselves to be put in such a secondary role.[71]

Men in the New Left also helped spread word of women's liberation, if only through repeated derision and ridicule. In February 1968, *Ramparts* magazine decided to "cover" the "sexy" story of the newly emerging movement. The resulting article, titled "Woman Power," proved to be a condescending, snide appraisal of the new women's movement.[72] On the magazine's cover appeared a voluptuous female torso with a button saying "Jeanette Rankin for President," referring to the congresswoman who had voted against both world wars. Inside the magazine, photographs of Anne Scheer and Marilyn Webb, in miniskirts, with long, gleaming hair, accompanied the text. The article ridiculed radical women as the "miniskirt caucus," and fell back on the cliché of the Old Left that women would be liberated after the revolution.

Ramparts's cheeky coverage enraged many movement women, who denounced it as "a movement fashion report." Some activists wondered why Anne and Marilyn, both well-respected activists, had posed in such sexy and provocative poses. Looking back, Anne Weills reflected:

It was a really transitional period. We were still wearing mini-skirts, we looked like these little chicks and we still sought male approval. At the same time, we felt exploited and ironi-cally, we were a party to our own exploitation. The truth is, Marilyn and I were having fun. We didn't resist or say, hey, let's put on jeans and sweatshirts. We even considered wear-ing false eyelashes. We were enjoying being glamorous.[73]

At the same time, women who worked at *Ramparts*, like Susan Grif-fin, later to become a well-known feminist writer, began to rebel against their subordinate status. "I went to work at *Ramparts* magazine," re-called Griffin,

and I loved working there and learned a great deal, but I learned something else besides journalism and muckraking and all about the nasty stuff the CIA does, and that was the nasty stuff my buddies, my brothers on the left were doing. They were getting twice my salary, they would ask me to rewrite their pieces and fully acknowledge that I wrote better than they did but no editorship, not a single woman was a full staff writer.[74]

As anger at both the leftist and the countercultural press grew, the mushrooming women's liberation movement began creating its own net-work of publications. In the first issue of *The Voice of Women's Libera-tion*, in March 1968, Jo Freeman wrote, "It is time Movement men realized"

they cannot speak the language of freedom while treating women in the same dehumanizing manner as their establish-ment peers. It is time Movement women realized this is a so-cial problem of national significance not at all confined to our struggle for personal liberation within the Movement and that, as such, must be approached politically.[75]

Meanwhile, Laura Murra, a longtime activist in Berkeley, began to publish *SPASZM*, a newsletter that reported activities of women's lib-eration groups all over the country. Within a year, Murra had changed her name to Laura X and Jo Freeman called herself Joreen. The black leader Malcolm X had argued that all surnames had been given by slave owners. In a similar spirit, Laura and Jo decided to erase the patriarchal legacy of their last names. Some feminists adopted their mother's maiden name; Kathie Amatniek chose to reinvent herself as the daughter of her mother, Kathie Sarachild. Still others decided to go by a first name only, like the poet Alta.

Laura X had the foresight to collect every document that came out of the movement. The Women's Herstory Library, which took over her home, became a repository of all the tracts, publications, speeches, minutes, and newspapers of the second wave of feminism.[76] Pamphlets and newspapers crisscrossed the country rapidly, read by women in distant cities, invariably ending up somewhere in Laura X's home. With names like *Off Our Backs* (Washington, D.C.), *It Ain't Me Babe* (Berkeley), *Mother Lode* (San Francisco), *No More Fun and Games* (Boston), *Notes from the First Year* (New York), *Women: A Journal of Liberation* (Washington), and *Up from Under*, and *Big Mama Rag*, women's liberationists began declaring their independence, publicizing their actions, exploring new ideas, and offering referral services to women in need.

BURNING HUMILIATIONS

By 1968, some New Left women lived a schizophrenic life. Once a week, they went to their women's group, where their understanding of their lives and the world around them kept shifting. At night, they slept with men whom they had just criticized in front of other women. In the morning, they worked with New Left men they had condemned the evening before.

Meanwhile, insults seemed to pile up on top of ridicule and humiliation. During an occupation of Columbia University, the audience booed and jeered when a woman gave her first political speech, one that protested that institution's racist housing policies and war involvement. At the Chicago Democratic Convention in 1968, the Yippies, a self-proclaimed group of countercultural revolutionists, suggested that *their* women pose as prostitutes and spike the delegates' drinks with LSD. In 1969, the Black Panthers (an Oakland black power group that advocated the use of arms to defend their community) sponsored the Revolutionary People's Constitutional Convention. Huey P. Newton, a cofounder of the Black Panther Party, broke his promise to permit women's caucuses. Afterward, the women accused the Panthers of sexism and said, "The Black Panther Party, supposedly our brothers in revolution, oppresses us." In another incident, the leaders of a "Venceremos Brigade" to cut sugarcane in Cuba denied a woman's application because of her political naïveté, which was how they characterized her feminism.[77]

Some insults, because they took place in public, caused irreparable harm. One day before Richard Nixon's inauguration in January 1969, a group called the National Mobilization Committee sponsored a "counter-inauguration" and rally against the Vietnam War in Washington, D.C. As was the custom, the male organizers chose speakers from various groups, including SDS veteran Marilyn Salzman Webb and the New York radical feminist Shulamith Firestone, to represent two perspectives on the fledgling women's liberation movement.

Webb, who had remained within the Left, began her speech by declaring, "We as women are oppressed. We, as women [who] are supposedly the most privileged in this society, are mutilated as human beings so that we will learn to function within the capitalist system." Suddenly, pandemonium broke out below the stage. Webb plunged on, denouncing a system that treated women as objects and property. To her horror, she watched as "fist fights broke out. Men yelled things like 'Fuck her! Take her off the stage! Rape her in a back alley!'" Shouts followed, like "Take it off!"

Webb was speechless. "It was absolutely astonishing, and this was the Left," the movement she was defending to Firestone. Shaken, Webb finished and Firestone, who had already given up on the Left, strode on the stage to condemn men as well as capitalism. "Let's start talking about where *we live, baby,*" she shouted. "Because we women often have to wonder if you mean what you say about revolution or whether you just want more power for yourselves." The largely male crowd booed and shouted obscenities.

Among the crowd was Irene Peslikis, also a New York feminist, who felt shell-shocked. "They were disgusting. The violence from the audience was just phenomenal." Sitting on the stage was the journalist and radical feminist Ellen Willis, who wondered why none of the male leaders tried to subdue the crowd. Furious at Dave Dellinger, a well-respected veteran pacifist and an "indefatigably even-tempered man in his mid-fifties," she asked, "Why isn't he telling *them* to shut up?" Later, she wrote, "If radical men can be so easily provoked into acting like rednecks, what can we expect from others?" Standing in the crowd, the unflappable dissident journalist I. F. Stone found himself astonished by the antics of the entire New Left. "Their speakers," he wrote in his newsletter, "sounded as if they had been invented by Art Buchwald with

assistance from Aristophanes. Their accusation that men were only calling for revolution to get power for themselves was met by obscene jeers
from the male audience in an uproarious climax of self-satire."[78]

Later, Webb, Firestone, and other women held a postmortem at
Webb's apartment. The New York radical feminists, who had given up
on movement men, in effect said, "I told you so." For Webb, married to
a veteran SDS activist, trashing movement men had previously been unthinkable. But the event had traumatized her. "We stared at each other
in disbelief. These were my brothers. We were very depressed afterward. I mean the Washington women had not expected it. They were not
man haters."[79]

Then the phone rang. She picked up the receiver and heard giggling
on the line. Then a woman's voice warned her, "If you or anybody like
you ever gives a speech like that again, we're going to beat the shit out
of you. SDS has a line on women's liberation, and that is *the line*." (To
this day, no one is sure who made the call—perhaps a woman in SDS,
an FBI agent, or some other person.) The SDS line on women was, of
course, that women's struggles were "secondary" to the fight against
capitalism and imperialism.

That was the last straw. Webb felt convinced that "we had to make a
break from SDS and become an autonomous movement." Firestone
summed up the moment: "Worse than our worst suspicions were confirmed and for some of us, in a traumatic way. . . . We're starting our own
movement."[80] In her description of the day's events, Ellen Willis wrote:

> A genuine alliance with male radicals will not be possible
> until sexism sickens them as much as racism. This will not be
> accomplished through persuasion, conciliation, or love, but
> through independence and solidarity; radical men will stop
> oppressing us and make our fight their own when they can't
> get us to join them on any other terms.

A less-publicized repudiation came from Carol Hanisch, who worked
for the Southern Conference Educational Fund, a civil rights organization. She decided then and there that working for women's liberation
within a mixed movement was a waste of time.[81]

At first, few people noticed that growing numbers of women were
leaving the male Left. By 1969, the New Left had splintered into competitive sects, each worshiping a different vanguard group—peasants,
workers, or Third World liberation fighters. Some of these factions spoke

in revolutionary jargon that further alienated women who were accustomed to exploring their experiences in plain and accessible language. No longer a beloved community, the Left seemed more like a series of violent eruptions, with young men pelting police with stones and hurling tear gas canisters back at armed officers. Some women silently wondered if these activists were simply trying to earn the manhood they had forfeited through their avoidance of the draft. In response to violent antiwar protests by the Weather Underground, an offshoot of SDS committed to armed revolution, the Boston Bread and Roses women's liberation group held up signs that condemned the violence of the male Left.

In the spring of 1969, students and community people in Berkeley turned a muddy, vacant, urban lot into a "People's Park," complete with whimsical landscaping, newly planted sod, trees, and shrubs, nightly collective soup dinners, swings and slides for children, and endless dancing and celebration. When the University of California, which owned the land, circled it with a high wire fence, students and community marched "to take back the park." Police riots resulted in the National Guard occupying the city for several weeks. For many women's liberationists, it was the final straw; they loathed gratuitous violence and refused to become street fighters. Susan Griffin said, "I hated the romanticization of violence associated with the male Left and the Black Panthers. This is when I could no longer be part of the male Left." As the clenched fist (of black power groups and the Weathermen) replaced the V sign for peace, growing numbers of women—and men—withdrew from what seemed like futile and dangerous fights with the police.[82]

Although many women continued to work in the antiwar and black liberation movements, some had begun to concentrate on women's liberation, which infuriated some movement men. Robin Morgan remembered having "huge arguments in 1968 with [Tom] Hayden, with [Jerry] Rubin, with Abbie [Hoffman] . . . they simply could not believe that I was going to go with these 'dumb broads' to protest against the Miss America Pageant when the revolution was going to be happening in Chicago."[83] Soon the men would learn that the only revolution about to happen in the United States would *not* take place in Chicago, but in their homes.

From minority women, who viewed feminism as a white woman's issue, or as a divisive threat to "liberation movements," and discredited women's issues as a "secondary form of oppression," white feminists encountered little interest and considerable anger. Some young black and

Chicana activists early recognized the "double jeopardy" they faced as minority women.[84] But for most African-American, Chicana, American-Indian, and other minority women activists, the freedom to discuss sexism within their own movements would occur slightly later, and lead to the creation of autonomous organizations and independent feminist agendas.

Rejected as racists or as irrelevant by minority women and fed up with the male Left, some white women tried to combine their left and feminist convictions by forging ties with the women of Vietnam. On International Women's Day in 1970, the Berkeley Women's Liberation Front, for instance, circulated a pamphlet titled *Vietnamese Women: Three Portraits*, which told of their heroism and suffering as women. "What does the Vietnamese war have to do with women's liberation?" the pamphlet asked.

> Everything! Women in the movement here are talking about the essential right of people to live full and meaningful lives, demanding an end to the way women, throughout history, have been objectified and dehumanized. How then can we not recognize these same claims that are being made not only by the oppressed in our own country, but by those who are oppressed *by this country abroad?*

Vietnamese women and their heroic struggle became a symbol of both American imperialism *and* the revolutionary potential of women. One of the most popular posters in the early women's liberation movement, regularly seen on the walls of bedrooms and makeshift offices, featured a Vietnamese woman with a baby on her back and a gun in her hand. On the ABC evening news, Marya Mannes, a critic, writer, and editor, even offered a commentary in the early seventies in which she celebrated the high status that Third World liberation movements offered women. In particular, she cited Nguyen Thi Binh, the National Liberation Front's representative at the Paris peace talks, where Americans and Vietnamese were attempting to negotiate an end to the war. Mannes then asked, "When will half the population of this country be given a proportionate voice?"[85]

Through their attempted solidarity with women of Vietnam and women of color more generally, New Left women hoped to link their commitments to both the antiwar effort and the new women's movement. In the middle of a shooting war, a few New Left women traveled to

Canada, Hanoi, and Budapest to meet with Vietnamese women who were fighting U.S. involvement in their country. In 1967, for example, Vivian Rothstein attended a conference in Bratislava, Czechoslovakia, between American antiwar organizers and North and South Vietnamese political activists. From there, she traveled to North Vietnam, where she spent nineteen days with a delegation of seven Americans visiting bombing sites, learning about Vietnamese history, studying American weaponry, and meeting women from the Women's Union of North Vietnam. "It was there," Rothstein later recalled, "that I was introduced to the idea of a women's union and the possibility of organizing women independently of men. When I returned to Chicago, I helped found the Chicago Women's Liberation Union, served as its first staff director, and started the Chicago Liberation School for Women."[86]

The effort to stay in the Left proved costly to some women. Margaret Randall, who spent decades studying and writing about women revolutionaries, later concluded that "a fundamental error of twentieth-century revolutions has been their inability—or unwillingness—to develop a feminist agenda." Roxanne Dunbar, an early and influential radical feminist, abandoned her initial focus on women. Later, she wrote, "I had been tamed by Leftist arguments and was dedicated to bringing the women's liberation movement 'inside' the revolution movement. In the worst mistake of my life, next to marriage, I had backstepped to that servile leftist-woman position."[87]

ANGRY FAREWELLS

Women exited the male Left in their own ways, at different times. Some simply stopped going to meetings. In Berkeley, a woman in the campus Radical Student Union stood up and spoke about the need for a women's anti-imperialist contingent for an upcoming antiwar demonstration. The membership burst into laughter. She stormed out, precipitating an exodus by all the women. Afterward, when the organization collapsed, Wendel Brunner, then its president, explained the reason for its demise. "What men would keep coming to meetings without women?"[88]

By 1970, many New Left women knew that they were speaking to a new constituency. In her powerful essay, "The Grand Coolie Damn," Marge Piercy, a novelist and poet, wrote, "My anger is because they have created in the movement a microcosm of that oppression and are proud of it. Manipulation and careerism and competition will not evaporate of themselves. Sisters, what we do, we have to do together and we will see about them."

In a widely reprinted essay, Ellen Willis declared her independence from the Left and argued that to "work within the movement is to perpetuate the idea that our struggle is secondary." Fed up with countercultural ridicule, feminists bristled at articles on "Pussy Power," or headlines like "Clit Flit Big Hit" (for a story on clitoral orgasm), and classifieds that advertised the selling of female flesh. In New York, a coalition of women (including radical feminists, self-proclaimed Witches, and Weatherwomen) led a coup at the underground paper *Rat* and produced an all-women's issue (February 9, 1970), the centerpiece of which was Robin Morgan's unforgettable farewell, "Goodbye to All That."[89] "It is the job of the revolutionary feminist," Morgan exhorted,

> to build an even stronger independent Women's Liberation
> movement, so that sisters in their counterfeit Left captivity
> will have somewhere to turn, to use their power and rage and
> beauty and coolness in their own behalf for once, on their own
> terms, on their own issues in their own style—whatever that
> may be.

Morgan's splenetic diatribe against the male Left reminded some of Allen Ginsberg's famous poem *Howl*. Like Ginsberg, Morgan's words shrieked with pain and outrage. "Goodbye, goodbye, forever, counterfeit Left, counter-Left, male-dominated cracked-glass-mirror reflection of the Amerikan nightmare. Women are the real Left." After blasting the hypocrisy, sexual exploitation, and discrimination of the male Left, Morgan concluded:

> We are rising, powerful in our unclean bodies; bright glowing,
> mad in our inferior brains; wild hair flying wild eyes staring,
> wild voice keening; undaunted by blood we who hemorrhage
> every twenty-eight days; laughing at our beauty we who have
> lost our sense of humor; mourning for all each precious one of
> us might have been in this life in this time-place had she not
> been born a woman; stuffing fingers into our mouths to stop
> the scream of fear and hate and pity for men we have loved
> and love still; tears in our eyes and bitterness in our mouths

for children we couldn't have or couldn't *not* have, or didn't
want, didn't want *yet,* or wanted and had in this place this
time of horror. We are rising with a fury older and potentially
greater than any force in history, and this time we will be free
or no one will survive. *Power to all the people or to none.* All
the way down, this time.[90]

Could it have ended differently? Probably not. Even had New Left
men never ridiculed their female comrades, black separatism and identity politics were in the air. The "movement," which had begun to romanticize violence and to believe that a revolution was imminent, no
longer appealed to many women. The people who were now identified as
the vanguard of the "New Left" seemed to have lost their grip on reality.
In 1969, Naomi Weisstein concluded that some of its members had
"dropped off the edge of the world." For many men, whose entire adult
lives had been lived in the movement, that movement ended in 1969,
leaving behind a powerful sense of loss and disorientation. "Sisterhood
was powerful partly because movement brotherhood was not," wrote
Todd Gitlin. In contrast, the women's movement had not only re-created
a new sense of community, but also provided the exhilarating opportunity to start all over again, to rethink priorities, and to view the world for
the first time through the eyes of women.[91]

Still, however crazy and violent the New Left had become, it was
family, where you'd grown up, where you'd learned equality and justice.
Like an ambivalent wife who seeks a divorce, New Left women required
rage to fuel their departure. Just as Britain's North American colonists
listed their grievances against King George in order to declare their independence, so, too, did these women need to repeat every insult and
etch every humiliation into memory—men's treatment of women at SDS
conventions, at the New Politics Conference, at *Ramparts,* in underground newspapers, at the 1969 "counter-inauguration," and in the
counterculture.

Endlessly repeated, Stokely Carmichael's joke about the desirable
position of movement women resonated in ways he never intended or
imagined. With these few words, he expressed the subterranean sexual
and racial tensions that had always threatened to shatter the movement.
For what drove white women out of the New Left, aside from searing humiliations and rising expectations, was their unarticulated anger at the
hidden injuries of sex.

Part Three

THROUGH THE EYES
OF WOMEN

Chapter Five

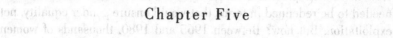

HIDDEN INJURIES OF SEX

Soon after I arrived at college in 1963, campus officials invited all the women who lived in the "girls' dorm" to an important meeting. The university asked us whether we wanted to abolish all curfews and to enjoy the same freedom granted to male undergraduates. The alternative was to sign out, sign in, and when we missed curfew, get hauled up before a judicial council—all to protect us from ourselves. I barely listened; of course we would vote to eliminate such a demeaning rule. But to my astonishment, a majority of the women voted to retain it.[1]

What I didn't grasp then was just how ambivalent my generation of young women felt about the new sexual freedoms then looming on the horizon. Armed with contraceptives but lacking access to legal abortions, the elders of the baby boom generation were beginning to live what the American media would dub in 1965 "the sexual revolution."[2] Suddenly, peer pressure to say yes replaced the old obligation to say no, threatening to eliminate a young woman's sexual veto. No longer could young women trade sex for love and a future commitment. The students who voted to keep the curfew intuitively understood that new freedoms brought new dangers as well. With one foot firmly rooted in the fifties— and the other sliding into the sixties—many of them were uncertain whether to embrace new freedoms or to protect themselves from the possibility of sexual exploitation. The historic connection between sex and reproduction had finally been ruptured, but what replaced it was the dangerous idea of casual sex. Curfews offered a perfect compromise; they created limits, while still providing enough opportunity for sexual experimentation.

As the sexual revolution accelerated, some young women began to view these new pressures as part of a "male" sexual revolution that needed to be redefined in terms that would ensure gender equality, not exploitation. But how? Between 1965 and 1980, thousands of women participated in an enormous archaeological dig, excavating crimes and secrets that used to be called, with a shrug, "life." Without any training, these amateur archaeologists unearthed one taboo subject after another. Typically, a major book or article by a feminist writer would redefine or "name" one of these hidden injuries. National magazines would rapidly turn the subject into a cover story. Soon, the general public would learn that sometimes a custom is actually a crime.

The cumulative impact was breathtaking. Like the "hidden injuries of class" described by authors Richard Sennett and Jonathan Cobb, feminists discovered far more than they had expected. Having empha- sized the similarity of men and women in the wake of the fifties, this ex- cavation would remind them of the significance of their biological difference from men. Once they had named so many specific injuries, mere "equality" with men would no longer be sufficient. Rather, they would insist upon a society that valued women's contributions, honored women's biological difference, and supported women's childbearing and sexual experiences.[3]

THE MALE SEXUAL REVOLUTION

In the avalanche of sixties' literature that condemned the men of the Left, Marge Piercy's devastating critique, "The Grand Coolie Damn" (1969), was perhaps the most widely publicized. Tellingly, she observed how much changing sexual mores had altered movement culture. Piercy excoriated men for turning sex into movement currency.

> Fucking a staff into existence is only the extreme form of what passes for common practice in many places. A man can bring a woman into an organization by sleeping with her and re- move her by ceasing to do so. A man can purge a woman for no other reason than that he has tired of her, knocked her up, or is after someone else; and that purge is accepted without a ripple. There are cases of a woman excluded from a group for no other reason than one of its leaders proved impotent with her.

Some movement men treated women's new sexual availability as if they had been let loose in a candy shop—and many women didn't like being treated as free goodies to be tasted. Looking back, Tom Hayden admitted that the "new sexual freedom only tended to legitimize promiscuity. Women could freely take multiple boyfriends, but not as freely escape their image as passive objects. For male students like myself, the new climate simply meant that more women were openly 'available,' but it told us nothing about the souls and needs of those women."[4]

As SDS mushroomed between 1965 and 1967, the sexual revolution intersected with a movement increasingly made up of strangers, rather than old friends. All too many men began to treat movement women with a disrespect that had been previously unthinkable. The libertine counterculture, which elevated freedom over equality, intensified such sexual exploitation. In 1968, recalled Todd Gitlin,

> the druggy White Panther Party manifesto urged men to "Fuck your woman so hard till she can't stand up. . . ." Five years earlier, the violence of the fantasy would have been unthinkable anywhere in the movement's orbit.

Searching for an explanation, he wrote, "At the heart of the matter were the befuddlements of sex. To be at once the comrades and bedmates of power in an egalitarian climate was unsettling. What was a woman supposed to make of her lover's remark that 'The movement hangs together on the head of a penis'?"[5]

But sexual exploitation wasn't entirely new. Even before drugs and casual sex altered the movement, recalled Barbara Haber, some men had thrust women into a specific role. "Women were meant to put up a traveling SNCC leader, and what put up meant was to 'put out.' "[6] By 1965, things had gone too far. In such a sexually charged atmosphere, some women began to feel like Kleenex, rather than cherished lovers. This, above all, explains the splenetic rage that women directed against their movement "brothers." In addition to the factionalism, violence, vanguardism, and hallucinogenic expectations of "revolution" that help explain the demise of the New Left should be added the fact that the sexual revolution arrived on men's terms.[7] For women, the price of sexual freedom seemed so much more costly than for men, especially with abortion still illegal.

Karen Lindsey, an SDS activist, witnessed these cultural changes in the movement. "I'm not sure when the revolution began to hurt," she wrote in her essay "Sexual Revolution Is No Joke for Women." As part of an SDS couple, she had been privy to men's discussions that ridiculed other women:

> I listened to the putdown of one of the other woman members who wasn't sleeping with anybody. "The girl with the cast-iron clit," they called her and I refused to acknowledge the queasy feeling in my stomach as I joined in their laughter and closed my ears to what I didn't want to hear. . . . I'd been pushing myself into "freedom"—into sleeping with men I didn't give a damn about and sometimes wasn't even attracted to, because I'd gotten dependent on the notion of sex as fulfillment and (status). . . . One night, I lay there, suddenly aware that my body was having a great time while my mind was sitting back waiting for the whole thing to be over. The next morning we woke up . . . and I jumped up, chirped, "Well, how about some coffee?" kept up a merry stream of chatter all through breakfast, kissed him good by, and didn't fuck for a year.

It took Lindsey a year to understand her anger.

> I realized that the sexual revolution, like the structures it purported to overthrow, was based on myth. Part of the myth was that male sexuality, unlike female romanticism, was based on real, honest, animal lust, and women would have to learn to be as free as men and everything would be fine. But what I had seen in men was . . . the necessity for conquest, for challenge. . . . Male mythology has demanded of men that their sexuality be a function of their control over women, and they have to struggle over that component of their sexuality. God help them. And God help those of us who still have some need for them. It's going to be a hard struggle. But until men change, the sexual revolution is just another ugly, dirty joke, and the women aren't laughing.

The similarities between "establishment" and movement men gradually became less and less clear. A cartoon distributed by the Liberation News Service, a leftist wire service, captured this comparison perfectly:

Two men discuss their lives. The "straight" man, dressed in a suit and tie, gloats, "I come home from the office, rest, my wife gives me something good to eat. She takes good care of my kids all day and to be frank she's a terrific lay." The counterculture man, wrapped in a long robe, hair flowing to his shoulders, boasts, "My old lady's outta sight, made me beans and fish last night. She's soft and quiet, good for my head. Her sign is Virgo and she's great in bed." Below the cartoon, two women, one "straight" and one countercultural, both on their knees. The caption beneath them reads, "The Sexual Revolution Is Yet to Come."[8]

The new problems created by the availability of the Pill and changing sexual mores didn't affect only movement women. All over the country, women encountered similar experiences. The difference was that movement women, disappointed by the behavior of their male comrades, talked about it, wrote about it, and tried to find some way to challenge what they came to see as a male sexual revolution. Some movement women, for instance, began to realize that the popular slogan "Make Love, Not War" had reinforced movement pressure to say yes. Another slogan promised that "Girls Say Yes to Men Who Say No." What right, young women began to ask, did men have to offer them as rewards for men who refused the draft? One woman worked in one of the GI coffeehouses that had been established at military bases in order to encourage active-duty military personnel to engage in antiwar organizing. Later, she confided, "I felt like a hooker for the anti-war movement."[9]

Black women activists also spoke out, condemning black male leaders' insistence that women should not use contraception or have abortions. Black people, these men argued, needed more black warriors for the coming revolution. In response, one black women's group in Mount Vernon, New York, insisted, "Poor black sisters [will] decide for themselves whether to have a baby." Although they agreed that "whitey" had genocidal motives, they also insisted that the birth control pill gave them "freedom to fight the genocide of black women and children. . . . Having too many babies stops us from supporting our children, teaching them the truth . . . and fighting black men who still want to use and exploit us." Birth control, they decided, was necessary for them to care for their children, and to ensure they became educated adults. "When Whitey put out the Pill, and poor black sisters spread the word, we saw how simple it was not to be a fool for men any more. . . . That was the first step in our waking up!"[10]

When black male revolutionaries insisted that women should bear many "warriors" and never even consider having an abortion, many black women offered strong resistance. "Breeding revolutionaries," Florynce Kennedy responded, "is not too far removed from a cultural past where Black women were encouraged to be breeding machines for their slave masters." Congresswoman Shirley Chisholm also denounced such demands as "male rhetoric, for male ears." "Don't these men know how many women of color die because of illegal abortions?" she wondered.[11]

THE FAKED ORGASM

In the small groups that young women's liberationists created, they began to share, first with hesitation and then with urgency, their sexual disappointments and delights. In hundreds of "consciousness-raising groups," women described how often they failed to reach orgasm during sexual intercourse. Robin Morgan remembered when she first admitted to "the faked orgasm":

> I made this absolutely stunning confession and I was convinced that I was the only woman on the planet who had ever been sick enough to do this, but I finally did confess that I actually faked an orgasm with my husband, at which point every woman in the room leaned forward, grinning, and said, "oh you too."[12]

In the future, people may wonder why the "faked orgasm" became such an important topic in women's liberation groups. Many young movement men, products of the fifties, had only the vaguest ideas about female sexuality. And daughters of the fifties often knew even less. Initially, sexual experimentation seemed exhilarating, but it didn't take long for young women to realize that *more* sex did not necessarily result in *better* sex. Ignorant of their own bodies, embarrassed to discuss sexual matters, many young women faked orgasm for fear of being labeled with that terrifying accusatory term of the fifties, "frigid."

Discussions of sex saturated the women's liberation movement. Women constantly revealed secret embarrassments that they had hidden all their adult lives. In Alix Kates Shulman's 1972 novel *Memoirs of an Ex-Prom Queen*, the main character realizes that she has been preparing for men's sexual approval since she was a child: "By third grade . . . I came to realize there was only one thing worth bothering about . . . becoming beautiful." Shulman, an early member of the group New York Radical Feminists, recalled that the subject of sex "produced a great emotional outpouring of feelings against the way women had been used sexually and revelations of sexual shames and terrors." In *Loose Change*, Sara Davidson's popular 1977 novel that explored the lives of three Berkeley women in the 1960s, the wife of a movement leader routinely fakes orgasm, but keeps this terrible secret to herself. Afraid that LSD might act as a truth serum, she avoids hallucinogenic drugs. After one druggy dinner on marijuana, she begins cleaning up the kitchen, but her husband says, " 'Leave all that to sit. Let's ball.' " In a scene all too familiar to many young women, Davidson described what followed: "He pushed inside her and it hurt, it burned. When it was over, she stood up and walked to the kitchen."[13]

In 1966, psychiatrist Mary Sherfey published an article about female sexuality that challenged the Freudian belief in two kinds of orgasms. Drawing on Albert Kinsey and the research of Masters and Johnson, Sherfey argued that it was the suppression of female sexuality that created civilization's "discontents." In the same year, Berkeley feminist Susan Lydon wrote "The Politics of Orgasm," an article that captured the essence of the sexual predicament of many women, not just those in political movements.

> Rather than being revolutionary, the present sexual situation is tragic. Appearances notwithstanding, the age-old taboos against conversation about personal sexual experience still haven't broken down. . . . With their men, they often fake orgasm to appear "good in bed" and thus place an intolerable physical burden on themselves and a psychological burden on the men unlucky enough to see through the ruse.[14]

By the sixties, these women expected to be full and equal partners in the new sexual revolution. One of the earliest activists in a women's liberation group described this process, as well as her own confusion and isolation, in an anonymous essay:

> I had been faking orgasm for four years when I encountered the women's liberation movement, and I had not mentioned it to A SINGLE OTHER WOMAN. I carried my sexual inferiority as a dark secret. When the subject of sex initially came up in women's liberation—or should I say when the subject of

sex got liberated—everyone admitted to faking orgasms. . . .
What I did . . . was stop faking orgasms after that. I was now
permitted—or was it liberated—to have a genuine sexual
response—whatever it was.[15]

In 1968, Shulamith Firestone and then Anne Koedt helped end that
silence for good. Firestone's "Women Rap About Sex," which appeared
in *Notes from the First Year*, a thirty-page typed journal written and distributed by the group New York Radical Women, revealed some of the
disappointment that had remained hidden behind satisfied smiles. In
the same issue appeared Anne Koedt's widely read essay, "The Myth of
the Vaginal Orgasm," which would become an instant feminist classic.

Koedt denounced Freud's version of the vaginal orgasm and condemned the doctors who freely dispensed a psychiatric diagnosis of
frigidity to women who only had "clitoral" orgasms. "The myth of the
vaginal orgasm," Koedt wrote, "was a conspiracy by which men controlled women's highly passionate sexuality." How, she asked, could a
profession whose method was based on scientific observation construct
two kinds of orgasms, describing one, the vaginal, as "mature," and the
other, the clitoral, as "infantile," and then label any woman frigid simply because she failed to reach the "more desirable" kind? In her view,
men had prevented women from realizing that the clitoris was the key to
female orgasmic stimulation. And if the clitoris were the key to orgasmic stimulation, her argument implied that women could replace men
with masturbation, other women, and sex toys.[16]

"The faked orgasm" soon became a metaphor for sexual exploitation.
Koedt's essay provoked countless debates, discussions, and disagreements among feminists. Some years later, for instance, Laura X denounced the sexual revolution as a "hoax" and argued that all the
"hullabaloo over the female clitorally stimulated orgasm" had done
nothing to improve women's lives. "Men are heard gloating . . . 'I can
make my girl go off like a machine gun'—this decade's version of scalp
and bedpost notches." Some women would disagree with Koedt's conspiratorial view of the origins of the problem. Some would argue that
they did, in fact, experience two different kinds of orgasms. Still, no one
disputed Koedt's skepticism about male sexual experts or denied the
ubiquity of the faked orgasm.[17] Attacks against Freudian thought grew
fierce. By 1972, Ellen Frankfort would argue in *Vaginal Politics* that
Freud had been a product of his repressed Victorian culture and that he
had nothing to say to midcentury feminists.

The ubiquity of the faked orgasm also revealed how overwhelming a young woman's need was to please a man, even when she herself was not being satisfied. Stimulation through penetration wasn't always enough. Yet most women feared asking for what they wanted; many didn't know what they needed. After all, women learned from popular and pornographic literature that an aroused woman reached orgasm seconds after penetration. This clearly was not a universal experience. Initially, some groups focused on new sexual positions that might increase women's pleasure. But as one woman asked, "What kind of a 'revolution' makes women compete in the race for multiple orgasms?" In a "Letter to Dear Sisters," Micaela Griffo, an early activist, urged women to start defining themselves "sexually because most sex on male terms seems like rape." Still others urged masturbation as a legitimate way of gaining self-knowledge and sexual independence from men.[18]

In the midst of so much pressure, some women decided to withdraw entirely from what seemed like an insane sexual competition. In an essay, "On Celibacy," Dana Densmore declared in 1969 that "sexual freedom is the first freedom a woman is awarded and she thinks it is very important because it's all she has; compared to the dullness and restrictiveness of the rest of her life, it glows very brightly." Densmore urged women to call time-out. "This is a call not for celibacy," she wrote, "but for an acceptance of celibacy as an honorable alternative, one preferable to the degradation of most male-female sexual relationships."[19]

A few groups even began to adopt a "no sex" position. Members of the Boston radical feminist group Cell 16, led by Roxanne Dunbar, called for long-term celibacy as a precondition for women's liberation. Ti-Grace Atkinson, the leader of The Feminists in New York, similarly decided that "women should neither marry nor engage in sex with men." Although such groups made up a tiny part of the burgeoning women's movement, they were disproportionately influential because their charismatic leaders wrote striking, often shocking, articles that provoked a great deal of the debate within the movement. Without the complications of sex, they suggested, women could enjoy the platonic love of "sisterhood" and channel all their passion into the movement.[20]

Sexual repression, in the midst of a so-called sexual revolution, created all kinds of unanswered questions. If sex was free, where did you draw the line? In one Washington, D.C., group, a member complained that "the sexual revolution is making me miserable because my husband is fucking everything in sight, and I'm not supposed to be jealous." Rosalyn Baxandall recalled that in her group, they talked "in absolute detail, on how you lost your virginity, interracial sex, what sex was like, techniques, different men, what people did in bed, and even masturbation." One woman, whose group had "these graphic, screaming yak sessions about this stuff," later admitted, "One of the things I remember is that I began to feel permanently guilty and I had nightmares about people like Ti-Grace Atkinson who were so draconian about sex."[21]

Older women sometimes found themselves bewildered by young women's obsessive discussions about sexuality. Betty Friedan thought that such attention to sex distracted feminists from the more important subjects of employment and poverty. Cindy Cisler, a major activist for the legalization of abortion, who was just a few years older than most members of the movement, admitted, "I never heard of a faked orgasm until I got into women's liberation. . . . I realized that this so-called sexual revolution had created this need for fakery, the sudden flip of 'don't do it' to 'you damn well better do it you frigid deviant' . . . and I had escaped that." Pat Cody, a veteran activist who, with her husband, Fred, had created and sustained Cody's Bookstore in Berkeley, joined a small group of women who, like herself, were married and in their thirties or early forties. "We never got into really intimate sex problems [we had] with our husbands. That was never brought out . . . or 'what do you like to do in bed?' " Instead, they focused on the careers they had given up as wives and mothers, how to resume active intellectual lives and the obstacles they faced. One of the longest-lived women's groups, it continued meeting for three decades.[22]

But for young women, sex seemed like the stuff of high drama. In 1970, many groups read and debated Shulamith Firestone's original and controversial book *The Dialectics of Sex*, a dense theoretical work that tried to explain why sex, not class, lay at the root of all oppression. Firestone championed a "cybernetic socialism" . . . "the freeing of women from the tyranny of their biology by any means available, and the diffusion of the childbearing and child-rearing role to the society as a whole, to men and other children as well as women."[23] In short, if babies could be conceived in test tubes and mature outside the female body, women would be freed from the tyranny of their biological fate. Reaction to Firestone's book was mixed. Some women thought she had found *the* solution. Other feminists were furious that Firestone seemed to accept men as the normative human being, rather than demanding that society accommodate—and honor—women's important biological contribution as the bearers and rearers of children.

In the same year, Kate Millett dissected the male sexual revolution in her book *Sexual Politics*. Many young women had previously welcomed court rulings that banned the censorship of literature, magazines, and films. They had supported and defended the right to publish D. H. Lawrence's *Lady Chatterley's Lover*, Henry Miller's *Sexus*, and William Burroughs's *Naked Lunch*, and argued that far from being obscene or pornographic, such highly praised novels told the truth about sex. But few young budding feminists realized before Millett that it wasn't *their* truth, but a sadistic view of men abusing women.

Kate Millett grasped this with uncanny clarity. Through a close reading of their texts, Millett demonstrated how much cruelty and hatred these misogynist authors had directed at women. Her book, originally a doctoral thesis, jump-started the field of feminist literary criticism and altered millions of women's views of "sexual emancipation." As one woman wrote nearly thirty years after the publication of *Sexual Politics*, "Reading Millett was the 20th century equivalent of picking up Darwin a hundred years before and realizing that the whole internalized structure of the human place at the pinnacle of the Great Chain of Being was simply wrong."[24]

Millett quickly became a media celebrity, praised (and condemned) by people in academic life and mainstream literary criticism. When she declared her bisexuality, the media tried to discredit her literary criticism by portraying her as a "man-hating dyke." But those efforts failed. Her book had changed the terms of debate. Heterosexual women proved quite as capable as lesbians of recognizing the misogyny and sexism in these novels, once Millett had shown the way. The female characters never seemed to mind male acts of rape, violence, or mutilation. The moment a man penetrated a woman, she invariably experienced sublime heights of orgasmic bliss. In fact, the crueler a male character was, the greater her sexual satisfaction seemed to be. Consider this scene from Henry Miller's *Sexus* in which a woman desires sex, but then protests that it "hurts." Since she has already consented, the "hero" assumes she has waived all rights:

> Shut up, you bitch! You said "It hurts does it? You wanted it, didn't you?" I held her tightly, raised myself a little higher to get it into the hilt, and pushed until I thought her womb would give way. Then I came—right into that snail-like mouth which was wide open. She went into a convulsion, delirious with joy and pain. Then her legs slid off my shoul-

ders and fell to the floor with a thud. She lay there like a dead one, completely fucked out.[25]

For women who viewed themselves as already "emancipated," *Sexual Politics* sparked some serious soul-searching.

In 1971, Germaine Greer, author of *The Female Eunuch*, swooped into the United States advocating sexual liberation as the precondition for women's liberation. A tall, svelte Australian, Greer had earned a Ph.D. in literature, and edited the European pornographic journal *Suck*. Promoted by slick full-page ads that hailed *The Female Eunuch* as "the women's liberation book of the year," Greer quickly became the feminist du jour, a media star who appeared on many TV talk shows. After Norman Mailer published *Prisoner of Sex* in 1973, an attack on the women's movement, Greer agreed to a live debate with him in New York's Town Hall, an event that received considerable publicity.

Greer argued that mothers and wives were cut off from sexual pleasure. In her view, women's liberation meant that all women should become sexually liberated, as she defined it. "The castration of women," she argued, "had reduced all heterosexual contact to a sadomasochistic pattern." Unimpressed by reform movements, Greer claimed she sought "revolution" and "liberation," rather than equality for women. She even advocated the use of the "weapon" most honored among the proletariat—the strike, which in her case meant the withdrawal of sexual labor.[26]

Greer's aura of aggressive sexuality made her especially appealing to men. Unlike many American feminists, she seemed to be conflating the sexual revolution with feminism. Her book, in fact, advocated using men for women's own pleasure. Rejecting the moral self-righteousness for which American reform movements are famous, Greer emphasized joy, spontaneity, and the pleasure principle. She didn't want women to be men, but she did hope women could gain the same sexual freedom, unrestrained by family or marriage, that was then available to men.[27]

Greer flirted and flaunted her way through a media circus, even as she made serious arguments for the sexual liberation of women. As one annoyed American feminist wrote, "Here was a libber a man could like." What especially irritated some American feminists was that Greer had never been attached to any women's group in England. Some viewed her as an exotic opportunist who wanted to replace the "grim institution of marriage" with "the dehumanizing, anonymous and spiritually debilitating thrusting that men call sex." Greer seemed to accept the male sexual revolution on its own terms, as long as women received as much pleasure as they gave. "The difficulty," as one American feminist writer wrote, "is that many feminists have been to that movie before. . . . They still remembered when, in order to qualify as a hip, emancipated female, their alternate-culture brothers insisted they perform as sexual gymnasts. Resentment at this treatment is one powerful motive for the current women's movement."[28]

Erica Jong offered a far more complicated portrayal of the problematic relationship between sex and independence for women in her best-selling 1972 book, *Fear of Flying*. The media hyped Jong's work as an erotic novel that admitted, yes, women want "it" too. But that was a narrow and perhaps willful misreading of her novel. Jong deeply understood that sexual emancipation did not necessarily confer on women any independence.[29]

Isabel White Wing, the heroine of the novel, is afraid of flying, a metaphor for her even greater fear of independence. Accompanying her husband to a scholarly conference in Europe, Isabel fantasizes about the "zipless fuck," a passionate sexual act in which there is no conversation, no sense of past or future, in which passion rules and all inhibitions disappear. Bored and restless at the conference, Isabel meets Adrian Goodlove, with whom she starts a passionate affair. Unlike her husband, Adrian turns out to be a poor and unimaginative lover; nor does the affair even remotely resemble a "zipless fuck." Isabel, who compulsively tells him (and the reader) every neurotic turn in the dramatic plot of her life, soon begins to fantasize about Adrian and realizes that she has once again yoked sex to commitment. "All my fantasies included marriage. No sooner did I imagine myself running away from one man than I envisioned myself tying up with another. . . . I simply couldn't imagine myself without a man. Without one, I felt lost as a dog without a master: rootless, faceless, undefined."[30] When Adrian announces that he will neither leave nor hurt his wife and children, Isabel is plunged into an existential crisis.

On a train home, Isabel also realizes that she never really wanted a zipless fuck after all. What she wanted was a man to complete her. "But perhaps that was the most delusional of all my delusions. People don't complete us. We complete ourselves. The search for love becomes a search for self-annihilation; and then we try to convince ourselves that self-annihilation is love."[31] When a train conductor suddenly proposes a quick "zipless fuck," Isabel panics and flees. "My zipless fuck! My stranger on a train! Here I'd been offered my very own fantasy. The fantasy that had riveted me to the vibrating seat of the train for three years . . . and instead of turning me on, it had revolted me."[32] By novel's end, Isabel's existential terror has diminished. "Whatever happened, I knew I would survive it. I knew, above all, that I'd go on working. Surviving meant being born over and over. It wasn't easy, and it was always painful. But there wasn't any other choice except death."

Jong appealed to a broad audience. The very *idea* of the "zipless fuck" challenged almost everything most Americans had learned to value about the connection between sex and commitment. But Isabel, unable to shake herself loose from the fifties, instead resorts to an old-fashioned affair, dreams of a future with her lover, and, when rejected, returns to her husband.

Fear of Flying, as most readers realized, was about a woman attempting to take off and define herself. How to do this was not at all self-evident. Isabel had few ideas about what she—or any other woman—really enjoyed. "I learned about women from men," Isabel muses, echoing Millett's argument in *Sexual Politics*:

> Naturally, I trusted everything they said, even when it implied my own inferiority. I learned what an orgasm was from D. H. Lawrence. . . . I learned from him that all women worship "the Phallus"—as he so quaintly spelled it. I learned from Shaw that women never can be artistic; I learned from Dostoevski that they have no religious feeling; I learned from Swift and Pope that they have too much religious *feeling*. . . . I learned from Faulkner that they are earth mothers and at one with the moon and the tides and the crops; I learned from Freud that they have deficient superegos and are "incomplete" because they lack the one thing in this world worth having: a penis.

Through Isabel's musings, Jong captured an entire generation's confusion about its sexuality. As Isabel says to herself, "Until women started writing books there was only one side of the story. . . . Until I was twenty-one, I measured my orgasms against Lady Chatterley's and wondered what was *wrong* with me. Did it ever occur to me that Lady Chatterley was really a man? That she was really D. H. Lawrence?"[33]

In 1979, *Playgirl* magazine—that odd mixture of hedonism and feminism—published an article titled "Sex in the '70s: A Wrap-Up of the Decadent Decade." The article rightly emphasized the commercialization of what passed for sexual liberation in the larger society, including sex toys, lingerie, and endless shelves of self-help books—such as Alex Comfort's *The Joy of Sex* (1972) or Xaviera Hollander's *The Happy Hooker* (1972). *Playgirl* also emphasized the significance of *The Hite Report* (1976), the first survey of American women's sexual experience since Kinsey's studies in the 1950s. Ten years after women liberationists first exposed the ubiquity of "the faked orgasm," Shere Hite's survey of three thousand women revealed that 95 percent of them claimed to always reach orgasm through masturbation, while only 30 percent claimed to do so exclusively through intercourse. One woman, who answered a Hite question about the faked orgasm, replied, "I never need to fake—no man noticed I didn't come." But perhaps Deirdre English and Barbara Ehrenreich, two well-known feminist intellectuals and activists, gave the decade its definitive feminist spin with the title of an essay they jointly wrote: "Sexual Liberation: The Shortest Revolution."[34]

WHEN ABORTION WAS A CRIME[35]

One reason that the sexual revolution proved to be so short was that without access to legal abortion, this revolution had caused more, not fewer, illegal abortions. Despite the presence of the Pill, many women had to use—for all kinds of medical reasons—other contraceptive devices that were not nearly as effective.

The movement for abortion reform actually began long before the women's movement. Abortion had been illegal for nearly a century when, in 1959, the American Law Institute recommended that abortion should be available when either the mother or child might suffer from continuation of the pregnancy. Throughout the sixties, a variety of activists—including many male doctors who sacrificed their medical careers, population control advocates, welfare rights groups, and lawyers—joined the reform movement.[36]

Despite their persistence, abortion activists made very little progress until the women's movement added its voice to the call for abortion reform. During the sixties, hospitals still admitted thousands of women whose wombs were forever scarred by botched abortions. The real question was not whether women would have abortions, but if they would be safe and affordable. Cindy Cisler, a tireless advocate for legalized abortion, along with the determined Bill Baird, spoke for many when she argued that "without the full capacity to limit her own reproduction, a woman's other 'freedoms' are tantalizing mockeries that cannot be exercised."[37]

By the early seventies, eleven states, including New York and California, had liberalized their abortion laws, allowing the procedure under particular conditions. But feminists soon complained that liberalized laws simply put them at the mercy of the medical establishment instead of the legislature. In California, a woman had to undergo the humiliation of two psychiatric evaluations that testified to her mental incapacity to bear a child. In New York, where the availability of abortion drew women from all over the country, prices for abortion skyrocketed.[38]

When the women's liberation movement joined the abortion rights campaign in the late sixties, feminists rejected the more politically acceptable call for the "reform" of abortion laws and insisted upon the "repeal" of *all* laws that limited a woman's right to abortion. All over the country, the growing women's movement intensified the struggle to repeal laws that prohibited or limited abortion. In New York, feminists testified before the legislature and passed out copies of their model abortion law—a blank piece of paper. Through public "speak-outs," feminists admitted to illegal abortions and explained why they had made this choice. "The speak-out," explained one New York activist, was "unbelievably successful and it turned out to be an incredible organizing tool. It brought abortion out of the closet where it had been hidden in secrecy and shame. It informed the public that most women were having abortions anyway. People spoke from their hearts. It was heart-rending."[39]

On January 22, 1973, a day women of a certain age will never forget, the Supreme Court handed down the *Roe v. Wade* decision. "We recognize the right of the individual, married or single, to be free from unwanted governmental intrusion into matters so fundamentally affecting a person as the right of a woman to decide whether or not to terminate her pregnancy." With those few words, the controversial decision struck down state laws that prohibited abortion and permitted a woman and her doctor to make all decisions about reproduction during the first six months of a pregnancy.[40]

Many sighed with relief, hoping that not one more woman would ever have to go through the nightmare of an illegal abortion. But no real national consensus had been reached. Congress had not legislated a woman's right to abortion. What the Court gave, Congress could take away. Without the extended national debate that usually preceded legislation, the right to a legal abortion was fragile and precarious.

Almost as soon as abortion became legal in 1973, a variety of religious and antiabortion groups began building what would become a powerful movement to repeal *Roe v. Wade*. At first, feminists did not recognize its growing strength and commitment. Yet, by 1977, the antiabortion movement had lobbied Congress successfully to pass the Hyde Amendment, which prevented government funding of abortions for poor women.[41] During the 1980 presidential campaign, abortion would become a litmus test for those seeking local as well as national office. By then, the country would be deeply polarized by "pro-life" activists who wanted to abolish abortion and "pro-choice" partisans who were equally committed to preserving a woman's right to make her own choice.

THERE SHE IS, MISS AMERICA

Young women sometimes ask, "Why were feminists in 1968 so angry at beauty pageants?" The Miss America Pageant seemed to sum up everything these women rejected: woman as spectacle, woman as object, woman as consumer, woman as artificial image. What they wanted was to be taken seriously, not to be judged by their appearance. Why, they asked, couldn't women look just ordinary and why couldn't a woman be a subject, instead of an object?

In the days preceding the pageant, members of the group New York Radical Women publicized their intention to "protest . . . an image that has oppressed women," the ideal of the svelte beauty queen. Most of the organizers had been activists in the civil rights, student, or New Left movements, but according to Robin Morgan, "none of us had ever organized a demonstration on her own before." "I can still remember," she wrote,

the feverish excitement I felt: dickering with the company that chartered buses, wrangling a permit from the mayor of Atlantic City, sleeping about three hours a night for days

preceding the demonstration, borrowing a bullhorn for our
marshals to use. The acid taste of coffee from paper contain-
ers and the cigarettes from crumpled packs was in my mouth;
my eyes were bloodshot and my glasses kept slipping down
my nose; my feet hurt and neck ached and my voice had gone
hoarse—and I was deliriously happy.[42]

On September 7, 1968, the protest began. Inside the hall at Atlantic
City, as the winner paraded onstage, a group of activists stood up and
unfurled a women's liberation banner and chanted a few slogans. Their
protest barely made a ripple within the hall, but network television did
broadcast the protest to viewers all across the country. Outside, some
two hundred women were picketing the pageant. One group trotted out a
sheep, which they then crowned as Miss America in their own mock
minipageant. In a pamphlet, protesters denounced the fact that "women
in our society find themselves forced daily to compete for male approval, enslaved by ludicrous 'beauty' standards we ourselves are con-
ditioned to take seriously." Into a large "Freedom Trash Can," they
threw "instruments of torture"—girdles, curlers, false eyelashes, cosmetics of all kinds, wigs, issues of both *Cosmopolitan* and *Playboy*, and,
yes, bras. Although the plan was to light a fire in the can, they decided
to comply with the Atlantic City police's request not to endanger the
wooden boardwalk. Asked by a reporter why the city had objected to the
protest, Robin Morgan replied that the mayor had been concerned about
fire safety. Perhaps trying to provoke some media interest, she added,
"We told him we wouldn't do anything dangerous—just a symbolic bra-
burning." The *New York Times* correctly reported that no fire had been
lit that day. But by September 28, the *Times* referred to "bra-burnings"
as though they had actually happened. By then, the media, all by itself,
had ignited what would prove to be the most tenacious media myth
about the women's movement—that women "libbers" burned their bras
as a way of protesting their status in American society.[43]

Actually, at that moment, bras held little symbolic meaning for feminists. Many had stopped wearing them years before. Aprons were a
much more powerful symbol to these young women. But bras seemed to
mean a great deal to those journalists who couldn't tell the difference
between the sexual revolution and women's liberation. And so the myth
spread that women's liberationists burned bras as an act of defiance. A
sexy trope, the media used it to sell papers. In a breast-obsessed soci-

ety, "bra-burning" became a symbolic way of sexualizing—and thereby trivializing—women's struggle for emancipation.[44]

After the Miss America Pageant, some of the organizers criticized themselves for their lack of sensitivity. Carol Hanisch observed that the action appeared to be against the contestants, instead of against the pageant itself. "Miss America and all beautiful women came off as our enemy instead of as our sisters who suffer with us." Although organizers had banned antiwoman signs, some women waved them anyway, proclaiming, "Up Against the Wall, Miss America," "Miss America Sells It," and "Miss America Is a Big Falsie." "Ironically enough," Hanisch observed, "what the Left/Underground press seemed to like best about our action was what we realized was our worst mistake—our antiwoman signs."[45]

Those who had left the Left had brought heavy cultural baggage to the new movement. New rituals and new language would take time to develop. Hanisch, in particular, worried about the "revolutionary language" that might repel otherwise potentially sympathetic women. "Stop using the 'in-talk' of the New Left/Hippie movement (Yes, even the work FUCK!!)," she warned. "We can use simple *(real)* language that everyone from Queens to Iowa will understand and not misunderstand." Robin Morgan also criticized herself for her use of movement language. "I pepper my language with -isms and -ations . . . this is still the style coming out of the New Left. I began to realize . . . I'm not reaching these women, these women are reaching me, and that's wonderful, these women in their little Iowa dresses. . . . And I cleaned up my act, my language."[46] But Morgan, like many other New Left women, had not yet recognized her unexamined contempt for those women in their "little Iowa dresses."

The political culture of the New Left/hippie movement clung to the women's movement like barnacles to a ship's bottom. The early women's liberation movement appropriated "zap actions," in-your-face street guerrilla theater tactics, and posters like "FUCK HOUSEWORK" that were meant to be aggressively offensive without realizing that they might alienate rather than reach ordinary women. Some of the protesters at the Miss America Pageant, for instance, sang a "Miss America song," to the tune of "Ain't She Sweet": "Ain't she cute, standing in her bathing suit, selling products for the corporations, now ain't she cute."[47]

Feminist attacks on consumer culture proliferated. The advertising industry had already used images of female bodies to sell cars, hacksaws, and even electric drills. Some activists retaliated by plastering stickers that declared, "This is only one example of the many ways in which society uses and degrades women" all over such ads and billboards. After 1972, when journalist Gloria Steinem founded *Ms.* magazine, the editors institutionalized a page called "No Comment." Readers simply sent in advertisements that degraded women. The magazine reprinted them without comment. The ads, in the context of a national feminist magazine, spoke for themselves and the language they spoke was a new and startling one.

Within a year of the first Miss America protest, activists began targeting other "sex crimes." On September 21, 1969, five members of a group called Bay Area Women's Militia discovered that the men who were starting *Dock of the Bay*, a new alternative newspaper, planned to finance their project by publishing a pornographic magazine titled *The San Francisco Review of Sex*. After they gained the support of the *Dock's* women staffers, the Militia sabotaged the plates from which the *Review* was to be printed. Proudly, they reported their success in a local women's liberation paper, *Tooth and Nail. The Dock of the Bay* soon folded. Financing "the revolution" on the backs of half of the population would no longer be possible. One year later, in April 1970, the Bread and Roses collective in Boston protested the showing of a "skin flick" at the Orson Welles art film cinema in Cambridge, Massachusetts. A few months later, San Francisco liberationists claimed responsibility for an act of sabotage against the offices of the *Berkeley Barb*, an underground newspaper that partially financed itself with pornographic ads.

Feminists also began targeting Hugh Hefner, publisher of *Playboy* magazine. On April 15, 1970, Hefner hosted a benefit party at his Chicago mansion for the local antiwar movement. As one feminist explained, "[We] were anxious to expose the hypocrisy of Hefner's opposition to the Vietnam War while profiting from his own exploitation of women at home. . . . The *Playboy* Empire is built on the concept that a woman is a mindless big-boobed cunt; another accessory to a playboy's total wardrobe." But since these women also supported the antiwar movement, they asked that guests sign their checks outside the mansion, but not attend the party inside.[48]

At Grinnell College in Iowa, women's liberationists gave Bruce Draper, a recruiter of "beautiful babes for *Playboy*," an unforgettable welcome. Ten members of the local women's liberation movement met him stark naked to protest *Playboy's* exploitation of the female body.

"*Playboy* magazine," their leaflet declared, "is a money-changer in the temple of the body." In a speech delivered on the spot, one woman explained,

> Pretending to appreciate and respect the beauty of the naked human form, *Playboy* is actually stereotyping the body and commercializes it. *Playboy* substitutes fetishism for honest appreciation of the endless variety of human forms. We protest *Playboy*'s images of lapdog female playthings with idealized proportions. . . . The *Playboy* bunnies are an affront to human sexual dignity.[49]

Soon protesters began to picket Playboy Clubs around the country. In Chicago, the Women's Liberation Union decided to wage war on Hefner. "Our first action," recalled Naomi Weisstein, "was gluing together *Playboy* magazines. . . . We had code names and wore sunglasses and disguises. What we did was to go into every magazine store and deface and pour glue on *Playboys*."[50]

Despite such protests, which only multiplied, most young feminists never felt they had gained the right to look "ordinary." True, some women cut their long hair, stopped shaving hair off their bodies, ceased to use makeup, gave up high heels, and began wearing comfortable clothes. But this was a luxury of the young or the independently wealthy who did not have to keep jobs. As young feminists entered male-dominated professions and occupations, they experienced great pressure to conform to strict corporate and professional dress codes that implicitly stated what it meant to be a woman. In the late seventies, a New York City judge, for instance, ordered a female attorney, dressed in a tailored, designer pants suit and silk blouse, to leave his courtroom and not to return until she wore a skirted suit that demonstrated proper respect for the court. Dressing for success sometimes meant survival in a career or job, which feminists had no power to change.[51]

In the midst of their battle against artificial female beauty, few young feminists seemed to realize that many of their sisters—both in and out of the movement—had never viewed themselves as anything but "ordinary." Older women experienced themselves as invisible. No one whistled at them on the street; no one insisted they smile to keep their jobs.[52] Embarrassed to talk about their invisibility as aging women, they tended to keep their sense of humiliation to themselves. While attractive budding feminists worried whether movement men took their ideas seriously and denounced the exploitation of the female body they saw everywhere, other movement women, wishing they were more attractive to men, found it difficult to relate to the "problem" of being treated as a sex object. Later, some of them spoke of the resentment they felt when movement men listened to their ideas, but never approached them as desirable lovers. One woman, who had long felt excluded as a possible lover, confided, "[The men] had all the power. They could affirm your beauty and choose you as a lover and ignore your ideas. Or they could turn you into an asexual comrade, who by definition, did not qualify to be a lover."[53]

In a culture that idealized blond, blue-eyed, slim white women, African-American, Mexican-American, Filipina, Native American, and other minority women knew that being a sex object was certainly not their greatest problem. Their color was too dark, their hair was the wrong texture, and their bodies didn't conform to the Anglo-Saxon societal ideal. In the view of black activist Frances Beale, a black woman was the "slave of a slave." Not only had she been raped and beaten by white slave owners, but her beauty had been ignored by black men who viewed her through the lens of a white-dominated culture. When "they told us that we were black, ugly, evil bitches and whores," complained a group of black women, these men demonstrated their preference for the white cultural ideal. The black nationalist slogan "Black is Beautiful" attempted to reinstate black features, bodies, hair, and movements as attractive, sexy, and desirable. But it would take several more years until most minority women gained the freedom to see their beauty through their own eyes.[54]

COMPULSORY HETEROSEXUALITY

The women's movement helped liberate two generations of women from the loneliness and isolation they suffered as they hid in closets or cruised bars. To older lesbians, the movement offered an opportunity to embrace the identity of lesbian with pride and, if possible, to "come out" to friends and family. For younger women, feminism and the sexual revolution provided a safe space in which to explore a different sexual preference.

Born before World War II, Julia Penelope Stanley already "felt different" at an early age. "My first conscious expression of my Lesbianism," she recalled, occurred when there was a song about "the girl that I marry." I was standing on our front porch, singing the song to myself when I turned to my mother and said, "I want to marry a girl just like you." She said, "You can't marry a girl. Girls can't marry girls. Only boys can marry girls. You'll have to marry a boy." I decided never to marry because I had no intention of marrying a boy. If I couldn't have what I wanted, I would have nothing.

By the sixth grade her "crushes" began. "I mooned, courted, wrote poems and followed numerous girls around." By 1957, she had begun to discover the gay bars that flourished in Miami.

I had a new word for myself, "gay." I wasn't "homosexual" or "queer," I was "gay." It's hard to explain now the tremendous freedom that word bestowed in those years. More than anything, I now knew for sure I was not alone, that I wasn't the only "one" in the world.[55]

According to another woman, named Merill, Miami Beach was a gay paradise during the fifties. "Countless gay bars entertained suntanned, white-ducked Lesbians and homosexuals all year round. Always there were parties, cliquey, of course, but there were so many lesbians that it didn't matter." Like many other lesbians of the time, Merill and her friends chose either butch or femme roles.

In general butches looked and acted more-or-less like men, wore ducktail haircuts and men's clothing, were aggressive, drank, swore, led when a couple danced, held the door open for the femme, lit the femme's cigaret etc. . . . There was a great deal of public embarrassment and ridicule of a butch who "went femme," and often the derision was enough to prevent many butches from allowing their lovers to touch their bodies in lovemaking.

"I practiced developing masculine movements," Merill remembered, "aping and emulating the men we professed to despise. To be a man meant to be strong and to have power. The best we could do as wimmin was to be like men, since we had not yet learned of wimminstrength and wimmin power."[56]

Before the movement, such women had few models for any other kind of relationship. Elana had spent many years trying to go "straight," even while she enjoyed lesbian relationships with women. "The only knowledge I had about Lesbians came from Radclyffe Hall's *The Well of Loneliness*, which my mother gave me when I was 14 and in the throes of a serious crush on a girl in high school."[57]

The women's movement would have a tremendous impact on this earlier generation. It encouraged them to come out; it named their desires. But it also rejected the butch/femme roles, that is, one woman dressing and acting manly and the other dressing and behaving in a traditional feminine manner. Instead, new feminists promoted loving relationships between two strong, independent women.

Still, the political and cultural upheavals of the sixties freed some of these women from self-hatred. "I first realized I was a Lesbian in 1968," wrote one twenty-six-year-old woman. "I had always known that I loved, was attracted to, was comfortable with women, but before the Women's Movement I didn't have a word for someone who felt those feelings."[58]

But lesbians still had no visible movement and no refuge. In 1969, gay men successfully fought off police raids at New York's Stonewall bar, igniting the gay liberation movement. Some lesbians joined them, hoping they would fight together for social acceptance and civil rights. But to their disappointment, many lesbians discovered that gay men could be just as blind to the needs of women as straight men. By 1970, Del Martin, a prominent lesbian activist, was already writing her "farewell" to the male gay movement, much as Robin Morgan had done to the New Left. She called her missive "If That's All There Is."[59]

At the same time, lesbians who had joined NOW felt outraged by Betty Friedan's characterization of them as a "lavender menace" that would provide enemies with the ammunition to dismiss the women's movement as a bunch of man-hating dykes. Homophobia had injured countless women, confining them to the closet, condemning them to psychiatric wards, and taking away their children. Purging lesbians from movement was a morally indefensible solution and, in the view of many, would have discredited the movement even more. The real menace would have been a feminist movement that stigmatized and excluded other women. Some lesbians now fled the Gay Liberation Front and NOW for the women's liberation movement, where they found a somewhat more open and hospitable atmosphere.

For younger women who had never identified themselves as lesbians, the women's liberation movement provided a political and highly sexualized context in which to explore their sexuality. Between 1967 and 1970, relatively few women felt secure enough to come out in the women's groups they had joined. The feminist writer Susan Griffin, whom I met in our small group, never discussed her attraction for women at any of the meetings that spanned two years. Later, she told me, "I certainly didn't feel it was safe in this group either. But it wasn't as if it were a characteristic of this group as opposed to other groups; this group was safer than anything else. It's just that the topic seemed so completely *verboten*."[60]

"In the early days," explained Cindy Cisler, "we were boy-crazy. There was practically no discussion of lesbianism." Rosalyn Baxandall remembered Robin Morgan asking her group to discuss their attraction to one another, but the group decided "we don't want to talk about that."[61] In 1969, Martha Shelley began to articulate the political importance of lesbian feminism in an essay titled, "Notes of a Radical Lesbian." "Lesbianism," she wrote, "is one road to freedom—freedom from oppression by men. . . . The woman who is totally independent of men—who obtains love, sex, and self-esteem from other women—is a terrible threat to male supremacy. She doesn't need them, and they have less power over her."[62]

In New York City, a group of young women who called themselves "Radicalesbians" started recasting lesbianism as a political choice in 1970. These lesbian-feminists declared themselves the "new vanguard" of the women's movement and denounced sleeping with men as "reactionary" political behavior. Only with women, they insisted, could feminists integrate their emotional, political, and sexual lives. Only with women could feminists discover emotional freedom and sexual satisfaction.

"Vanguardism" had long poisoned the movements of the Left, most recently in the sixties. Casting yourself as the "vanguard" meant that you were morally superior because you had suffered the most and had therefore gained the right to lead the much-awaited "revolution." During the sixties, the "vanguard" kept changing—from students to black nationalists to the working class. In the end, it also fragmented movements, leading to separatist politics rather than to political coalitions rooted in inclusiveness.[63]

Political lines began to be firmly drawn. At the Second Congress to Unite Women in 1970, Radicalesbians wearing T-shirts that read "Lavender Menace" grabbed an open microphone to promote the politics of lesbianism, and passed out copies of an essay called "Woman-Identified

Woman," a position paper that quickly swept through the nation's women's liberation groups. "What is a lesbian?" the paper asked.

> A lesbian is the rage of all women condensed to the point of explosion. She is the woman who, often beginning at an extremely early age, acts in accordance with her inner compulsion to be a more complete and freer human being than her society . . . allows. . . . On some level she has not been able to accept the limitation and oppression laid on her by the most basic role of her society—the female role.[64]

But who qualified to be a woman-identified woman? Did a woman have to support lesbians or sleep with them in order to be labeled a woman-identified woman? Some heterosexuals (wishfully) concluded that a "woman-identified woman" simply had to swear allegiance to lesbians as the vanguard. Yet others interpreted the "woman-identified woman" as a lesbian litmus test that decided each woman's political credibility.[65]

Invited by a friend in NOW to the Congress to Unite Women, one feminist began to realize how scared some feminists were of lesbians. "I went to the Conference with much curiosity. I had high hopes of seeing a Lesbian. And I did . . . and they didn't look very different from anyone else except that they seemed stronger, more articulate, more attractive, more powerful, and funnier than the other women."

> Rita Mae Brown was the first up-front lesbian I ever saw. She was marvelous. Small, beautiful, strong, wearing a "Super-Dyke" T-shirt which she had dyed Lavender. . . . When she asked for women in the audience to join their Lesbian sisters at the front of the auditorium, I jumped up, eager to be counted as a sister traveler. A friend sitting with me, who I knew to be a Lesbian, would not join us. When I asked her why, she said it was too dangerous. That made me want to be a Lesbian even more. After all if Kate Millett and Anselma Del'Olio were not afraid to be lesbian-identified, why should I be? Besides, I thought the Lavender Menace take-over of the conference was done delightfully and humorously. . . . They had seized the time and created a Lavender Happening.[66]

Between 1970 and 1975, countless women's liberationists made the "political choice" to live life as lesbians. By describing lesbianism as a political choice, these activists reframed female homosexuality as something other than sexually deviant behavior. The American Psychiatric Association's 1973 decision to remove homosexuality from its list of disorders provided legitimacy for such a position. But to women who already considered themselves lesbians, these "political lesbians" seemed strange. One young feminist "decided" that she was going to have sex with a woman.

> Even though I had not yet had sex with a woman, I was sure that it would be far superior to sex with men. Politically, I wanted my energy to be going to support wimmin and to building a feminist revolution together, not to struggling with individual men.

When she met an older lesbian, she was scared to tell her that

> I had never slept with a woman, afraid she would not be interested in me because I was so inexperienced. She was very surprised and taken aback by my hesitant admission of Lesbian virginity. A dyke of ten years, out long before there was any such thing as feminism, she could not understand how I could be so militantly Lesbian before I had even made love with a woman![67]

In 1972, Robin Morgan found herself caught in the crossfire between lesbian and heterosexual feminists. The First Lesbian Feminist Conference in Los Angeles had invited her to give its keynote address. Criticized and questioned by lesbian feminists as to why she—a wife and a mother of a son—was going to address the fifteen hundred lesbians at the conference, she responded that she was an engaged activist in the movement who supported lesbians. In New York, Radicalesbians had recently warned her, "Don't you dare call yourself a lesbian—you live with a man and you have a child." Like other women, Morgan was discovering that in such an environment, you could not, after all, simply identify yourself as a "political lesbian."

Tired of what she called "vanguarditis," Morgan later described the absurd fragmentation of the movement:

There were lesbians, lesbian-feminists, dykes, dyke-feminists,
dyke-separatists, "old dykes," butch dykes, bar dykes, and
killer dykes. . . . There were divisions between Political
Lesbians and Real Lesbians and Nouveau Lesbians. Heaven
help a woman who is unaware of these fine political distinctions and who wanders into a meeting, for the first time,
thinking she maybe has a right to be there because she likes
women.[68]

Many heterosexual and lesbian feminists shared Morgan's sentiments, but just as many felt intimidated by some lesbians' moral self-
righteousness. In 1974, a member of a Kansas City women's liberation
movement wrote that "she and other heterosexuals felt uncomfortable
with lesbians—not because they were deviant, but because they felt
their entire lives judged to be as inadequate, inferior, backsliding, not
feminist enough." She still felt like a novice, she explained, and had
"not come far enough along for a lesbian love relationship right now."[69]

But it was not just political pressure that turned some feminists' attention to other women. Nor did all lesbians feel a need to politicize
their sexual orientation. "Nouveau Lesbians," a term used to describe
the newly converted by those who had been lesbians before the women's
movement, made their exodus from heterosexuality seem immensely appealing. More than one feminist discovered that life as a lesbian quickly
resolved the painful conflicts between her feminist convictions and heterosexual relationships. "I think that part of it was dealing with issues
like pornography," the novelist Valerie Miner explained. "It was very
hard to go from [these kinds of revelations and discussions] to home to a
man at the end of the day. . . . I felt that I would be able to have more
time for women and feminist activities if I were involved with a
woman."[70]

In personal conversations, in testimonies, in feminist fiction, and at
meetings, new lesbians gushed euphorically, thrilled by their newfound
sexual passion. Women, they said, were better lovers. They took their
time, they snuggled, they teased, they wove sexual and emotional intimacy into a seamless passionate experience. And, better yet, they didn't
need a guided tour of women's anatomy. Given the self-evident superiority of such relationships, they asked, how could women still sleep
with men?

Women who had married early, doubtful of their attraction for men,
sometimes discovered that they were actually attracted to women. "I

really had no identity of my own," wrote one married woman. "I was somebody's wife, mother, lover, friend, daughter and so on, ad infinitum. I blended. I accommodated. My theme song was, 'tell me what it is you want me to be and I'll be that.' " The woman's movement freed her to see "her sexual preference" no longer as a handicap, or a "crippling disease." "My life changed dramatically in a relatively short time from Mrs. Straight White Suburbia to Ms. Alternative Lifestyle."[71]

As a result of the women's movement, wrote Sara Lucia Hoagland,

> forgotten dreams became possibilities as my first feminist perceptions, having snatched my attention two years earlier, now settled solidly in my gut. I had never quite buried my childhood rage at grown women acting like two-year-olds around men.

At the time, Hoagland didn't think she was physically attracted to women but had begun to argue that "political Lesbianism was a legitimate alternative." Soon she experienced sex with a woman. "It was the most natural thing in the world. I wondered where I had been all my life, yet I did not regret one moment spent in arriving. To this day I wonder why it is not called, 'coming home.' For the first time I was at ease with being a woman, body and soul were united—healed—or was it completed?"[72]

Beverly Toll could hardly believe the love and passion she now experienced with another woman. "The best way I can describe it," she wrote, "is to say that this is the only time in my life when making love was completely spontaneous. I didn't think about it; if I had I would probably have pulled away from this kind, gentle womyn that was touching me. It didn't occur to me to question what was happening. There were no decisions to be made. I thought of nothing, experienced for the first time in my life, the tender, satisfying love of a womyn."[73]

The difference seemed astounding to women who had rarely enjoyed sex with men. "Suddenly you aren't alone anymore. This closeness, this sharing with another womon amazes you. This could be a womon you've known all your life, you know each other so well. You can't believe that all this happiness has descended upon you in the form of this blue-jeaned thick-shoed womon."[74]

Some lesbians feared straight women's disapproval. And many straight women feared lesbians' condemnation. In such an atmosphere, fear turned into self-righteousness, and by 1972, a "gay-straight" split affected nearly every women's liberation group. Only in small cities or less-urban settings did gay and straight feminists continue to cling together, given the common enmity they faced. By the end of the decade, some heterosexual women clearly felt defensive. As one straight woman quipped, "The women's movement is the only place in the world where women have to come out of the closet as a heterosexual."[75]

Not surprisingly, idealizing lesbian relationships created its own problems. Some feminists ended their relationships with men only to discover the predictable reality that all intimate relationships are laced with emotional land mines. Between lesbian feminists, who were students or middle-class, and "bar lesbians," who were predominantly working-class, lay even deeper cultural and political differences. In Columbus, Ohio, for example, lesbian feminists at first criticized bar lesbians "for mimicking heterosexuality" by adopting butch-femme roles. These new lesbians, committed to equality between themselves, argued that the butch-femme relationship replicated heterosexual power relations, turned women into sex objects, and they criticized the bar lesbians for not participating in feminist activities. Over time, these differences diminished. By the late seventies, a local lesbian bar hosted feminist fund-raisers. Lesbian feminists, for their part, began to recognize how bar culture had allowed prefeminist lesbians to survive and began to mute their critiques of butch-femme subculture.[76]

In some regions, at particular moments, the pressure to identify as a lesbian grew fierce. Naomi Weisstein, in Chicago, recalled, "Everybody I knew experimented with lesbian relationships—the openness to lesbianism was really very strong." One day, she went to a meeting and found two women colleagues naked on the sofa. "In those days, it was really uncool to go 'hey, you're naked and I'm coming for a meeting.' There was an acknowledged social protocol, which was 'congratulations, how are you?' "[77] Barbara Haber remembers moving to Boston in the early seventies as lesbian feminism was just emerging as the political choice du jour. Two of her close friends were having their first lesbian love affair with each other while most of her other friends and acquaintances had already become lesbians. "Many of them," she observed,

> have returned to heterosexuality since that time; others have not. But at that moment it was impossible to be heterosexual. Even if you didn't become a lesbian, you couldn't be a hetero-

sexual. There was definitely a recoil from heterosexual relationships. If you want to talk about the roots of the women's movement, you have to talk about the roots of that "recoil."[78]

Pressure for separation grew increasingly strong. Jill Johnston's book *Lesbian Nation: The Feminist Solution* (1973) gained a surge of media publicity unavailable to most lesbian feminist writers. Based on a series of articles in the *Village Voice*, New York's alternative newspaper, Johnston's book reported on living at the edge of New York's avant-garde art scene and rejected the idea that lesbians were simply women attracted to other women. Such a sexual definition, in her view, was too narrow, even in its focus essentially pornographic, because lesbians were revolutionaries and subversives. "Many feminists," she argued, "are now stranded between their personal needs and their political persuasions. The lesbian is the woman who unites the personal and the political in the struggle to free ourselves from the oppressive institution [marriage]. . . . By this definition lesbians are in the vanguard of the resistance." By sleeping with the enemy, heterosexual feminists were, she believed, undermining the revolution against patriarchy.[79]

The urge to separate not only from men, but also from the nonlesbian women's movement sometimes seemed irresistible. Small groups of lesbian feminists began to found separatist communes, urban as well as rural, some of which even excluded male infants or male children. The Furies, a Washington, D.C., group, became one of the most influential lesbian separatist groups in the country, partly due to the power of their writings, first published in *Off Our Backs* and then in *Quest*, a new magazine they founded.

Before she joined The Furies, Charlotte Bunch, already a veteran activist in the civil rights and antiwar movements, had been married. After sleeping with a woman, she chose complete separatism from heterosexual women as well as men. Later, she explained why the Furies had separated from the women's movement:

> It [was] because it has been made clear to us that there was no space to develop a lesbian feminist politics and life-style without constant and nonproductive conflict with heterosexual fears, antagonism and insensitivity. . . . The Furies was not just an "alternative community," but a commitment to women as a political group.[80]

In 1973, Bunch reemerged from this separatist period. The Furies had made important breakthroughs, but after a year, she reported, "the positive intensity of our interaction threatened to deteriorate into destructive cannibalism." Still, she wanted heterosexual women to understand that "our time as lesbian feminist separatists . . . allowed us to develop both political insights and concrete projects that now aid women's survival and strengths." An original thinker with a strong flair for organizing, Bunch would emerge in the 1980s and 1990s as a leading organizer of the international movement to redefine women's rights as "human rights."[81]

The gay-straight split fragmented "the sisterhood," creating various kinds of hierarchies that excluded many women. The emphasis on sexual orientation scared away some women fearful of unfamiliar and unconventional relationships, as well as an alien alternative culture. On the other hand, the rise of lesbian feminism infused the movement with new ideas and theories that helped feminists—and later scholars—to consider the social and cultural construction of gender, as well as the biological nature of sex.[82] Lesbian feminists also contributed a disproportionate amount of dedication and energy to the movement. They were the women who worked in the trenches, the women responsible for staffing the growing network of self-help institutions that crisscrossed the country. All over the country, lesbians sustained shelters for battered women, rape crisis hot lines, and health clinics used by women who wouldn't have known the difference between NOW and The Furies, but welcomed the refuge and services that they received. Heterosexual women frequently found it difficult to integrate this mushrooming women's culture into their jobs and families.

During the 1980s, the role of lesbians became even more important, as they nurtured and sustained a growing women's culture, which expanded to include a dizzying array of local bookstores, coffeehouses, musical festivals, summer camps, peace encampments, child care centers, women's health centers, and centers for women's studies. This women's culture, which may have seemed apolitical to some feminists, in fact provided a much-needed political refuge for women who had previously hidden in closets, completely isolated from one another. Unlike ethnic or racial minorities, lesbian feminists began with no historically shared culture, except that of the bar. Through music, dance, art—as well as thousands of centers and institutes—lesbian feminists invented traditions and rituals that created a warm and hospitable environment for the many women just "coming out," searching for support for themselves and often for their children.[83]

The excavation of lesbian sexuality also unearthed one of this society's best-kept secrets—what poet Adrienne Rich called in an influential essay the "compulsory heterosexuality" of American culture, the unquestioned assumption that everyone is heterosexual or should be. What if this "compulsory" pressure were removed? Rich thought that many more women would choose to love and live with other women. Most important, lesbians encouraged women to explore their own passion rather than to act out male-authored sexual scripts. By legitimizing sexual intimacy between women, they challenged the male sexual revolution and its simplistic vision of heterosexual promiscuity and offered an ideal of same-sex love among women.

WOMEN'S BODIES AND THE REDISCOVERY OF DIFFERENCE

Although the American women's movement began by emphasizing women's "sameness," exposing the hidden injuries of sex refocused attention on those female experiences that made women unique. The women's health movement, arguably one of the most important and successful accomplishments of second-wave feminism, emphasized the specific health concerns of women, and in the process helped feminists rediscover their "difference."

Generally treated as ignorant or hysterical patients, women had long suffered the medical establishment's arrogant attitude toward their ailments. The experience could be humiliating, enraging, and, in the context of a developing women's movement, induce visceral understanding of women's secondary status. The journalist Barbara Ehrenreich, who had a Ph.D. in biology, recalled how her first pregnancy had altered her consciousness.

> I began to realize how much women had experienced humiliation or even injury in the medical system. I had a bad time with the doctor during my first pregnancy and that's when I really became a feminist. . . . I became really furious dealing with sexism and the fact that I could not escape these bloody issues.[84]

Even the new hippie "free clinics" that sprang up in the late 1960s treated women without the dignity they deserved. Would women doctors have thoughtlessly shoved a cold metallic speculum into another woman? Would feminist doctors have blithely told patients that the dilation of the cervix wouldn't hurt? The woeful ignorance of the female biological experience sparked a campaign to train more women doctors, to reeducate male physicians, and to create a women-oriented health movement.

That movement started rather modestly. In the spring of 1969, several women—most of whom had no medical training—participated in a small workshop on "women and their bodies" at a conference held in Boston. It didn't take long for them to begin venting their anger toward "condescending, paternalistic, judgmental and non-informative physicians." Rather than just rant and rave, they decided to enhance their own knowledge of the female body. Together, over that summer, they studied anatomy, physiology, sexuality, venereal disease, birth control, abortion, pregnancy, and childbirth. They analyzed medical institutions and the health care system as it then existed within the context of a capitalist economy. Armed with this knowledge, they began giving courses on women's bodies in homes, day schools, nursery schools, and churches.

By 1971, a group of these activists—now named the Boston Women's Health Collective—had collected and published several versions of their notes and lectures, eventually called *Women and Our Bodies*, which quickly made its way across the country. In March of that year, some eight hundred women gathered in New York for the first Women's Health Conference. Two years later, in 1973, when a much-expanded *Our Bodies, Ourselves* appeared as a book, feminists realized that they had created a full-blown health movement.[85]

Health activists not only disseminated biological knowledge, they also questioned why doctors controlled women's reproductive decisions. Only doctors could dispense the Pill or other contraception; only doctors could verify the need for a therapeutic abortion to save a woman's life. Why did doctors, rather than women, have this power? Couldn't women take back some control over their bodies? To teach women about their bodies, some activists began practicing "self-help gynecology." On April 7, 1971, at Every Woman's Bookstore in Los Angeles, Carol Downer inserted a speculum into her vagina and invited other women to observe her cervix. Five months later, a similar demonstration took place at a national meeting of NOW in Los Angeles. Within a year of

Downer's first self-exam, over two thousand women had attended such self-help women's clinics.[86]

On September 20, 1972, Los Angeles police arrested Downer for practicing medicine without a license. She had helped a woman insert a speculum and had suggested yogurt for a yeast infection. Although a jury acquitted her of all charges two months later, the incident outraged local feminists. One wrote:

> WHAT MAN WOULD BE PUT UNDER POLICE SURVEIL-
> LANCE FOR SIX MONTHS FOR LOOKING AT HIS PE-
> NIS? What man would have to spend $20,000 and two
> months in court for looking at the penis of his brother? This
> case is a clear cut version of the position of women in
> America—the lengths to which we must go and the obstacles
> which must be overcome to be FREE.[87]

Downer had become a police target in part because she had challenged physicians' control over women's reproductive lives. She and other women had popularized a procedure called "menstrual extraction," in which blood and any fertilized egg were withdrawn from a woman's body before menstruation began, in order to prevent pregnancy. Since abortion was still illegal, authorities viewed her work as illegal as well as subversive.

Some doctors bristled simply at the prospect of dealing with women who became *active* patients. A woman who told her doctor that she had learned to examine herself with a speculum and a mirror and wished to watch his examination of her, described his reaction this way: "He looked at me as if I were a rare species of caterpillar. Like a little boy whose toy had been taken away, he said, 'You had no business doing that!' It really was scary to see what happened when his 'omnipotence' was threatened."[88]

Activists responded to such hostile attitudes by bringing note-taking "patient advocates" to medical appointments. For women just learning to stand up to male authority, having a friend take notes felt reassuring. But some doctors resisted. "On my next visit, Deb came with me," ran a typical account. "When I introduced her and told the doctor that she wanted to watch the examination, he said that it was against his ethics. When we questioned him further as to what he meant, he said, 'Look, dear, I just won't do it.' I was stunned."[89]

Challenging medical authority proved a brilliant strategy when it came to undermining the health profession's control of childbirth and reproductive technology. Male doctors became proxy figures for all male authority. Rejecting the role of passive patient, women learned to be assertive, to ask tough questions, to do their own research, to insist on certain tests, to refuse others, and to demand that doctors take their ailments seriously. As a result, the women's health movement sometimes turned women into feminists.

The women's health movement taught many Americans—not only feminists—to view themselves as medical consumers, rather than as passive patients. Decades later, journalist Sheryl Gay Stolberg wrote in the *New York Times*, "It was feminism, most experts agree, that changed . . . medical paternalism. The 1973 publication of *Our Bodies, Ourselves* by the Boston Women's Health Collective was the turning point. This book taught women to distrust male doctors' authority."[90]

The women's health movement also helped introduce Americans to alternative medicine. In 1969, Joshua Horn, an English doctor enamored with the Chinese medical system, published a book titled *Away with All Pests* that compared the difference between Western and Eastern medicine. Inspired by Horn, as well as the "barefoot doctors" of Mao's Cultural Revolution, some activists began to promote acupuncture, herbalism, and traditional Chinese medicine as treatments that they favorably compared with aggressive and interventionist Western methods.[91] They also contrasted the dedication of China's "barefoot doctors," who treated poor peasants in an egalitarian fashion, with American doctors, who treated patients with the arrogant condescension of mandarins toward peasants.

Perhaps most important of all, the authors of the 1973 edition of *Our Bodies, Ourselves* expressed no disdain for motherhood, and portrayed pregnancy and childbirth as "important feminist life-events" that need not be medicalized. Women, they argued, should be aware and alert, not drugged, while they were giving birth to their children. They described breast-feeding, discredited by the medical profession in the fifties, as "satisfying, sensual and fulfilling . . . a pleasant and relaxing way for both mother and baby to enjoy feeding and . . . an affirmation of our bodies."[92]

By the middle of the seventies, an important ideological shift had occurred within the movement. "Rather than considering women's difference from men as a form of inadequacy and a source of inferiority," the historian Hester Eisenstein has observed, "this view considered difference to be a source of pride and confidence." The reasons for this dramatic shift, according to Eisenstein, were the development of women's studies programs, consciousness-raising groups, and lesbian feminist theory, which took as the starting point women's experience on their own terms. To these, I would add the women's health movement, which, by emphasizing biological difference, greatly contributed to the celebration of motherhood and women's distinct experiences.[93] But valuing women's difference only underscored a central paradox of feminism, namely, how to pursue equality while still honoring women's difference from men.

Feminists also began to question the safety and rationale for particular medical practices and procedures. Already in 1969, Barbara Seaman began questioning the routine use of the Pill in *The Doctors' Case Against the Pill*. In her 1972 book *Women and Madness*, Phyllis Chesler questioned the psychiatric treatment of angry or depressed women and attacked the practice of prescribing tranquilizers to such women, but not to men in similar conditions. In 1975, in *Breast Cancer: A Personal History and Investigative Report*, Rose Kushner challenged doctors' routine recommendation for radical mastectomies whenever breast cancer was detected. Others began to challenge the suspiciously high incidence of cesarean deliveries and of hysterectomies.[94]

In the early seventies, Pat Cody, an economist by training and a longtime activist in Berkeley, began to question the long-term effects of a drug called diethylstilbestrol (DES), which doctors had given her and many other women in the postwar period to prevent miscarriages. One of the many unsung heroines of the movement, Pat Cody convened a group of women around the proverbial kitchen table, where most women's movements have begun, to figure out what to do. After careful research and organizing, Cody created a grassroots organization called the DES Information Group, which, based on its suspicions that DES had created a cohort of children particularly susceptible to a variety of cancers, began to lobby the government for research and to raise funds to educate the public. By 1975, Cody's group published a pamphlet titled *Women Under Thirty, Read This!* And, by 1979, they created DES Action, an international organization that publicized the need for medical monitoring of all children born to DES mothers.[95] In such small ways did many American feminists take a personal concern, research, study, and name it, and create an international awareness of some injury, in this case a drug that could harm the sons and daughters of DES mothers.

By the end of the 1970s, a loosely connected women's health network stretched from Boston to Los Angeles, with local, national, and even international organizations that monitored health policies aimed at women. In addition to challenging mainstream medicine, introducing the public to alternative medicine, and demanding women's right to their own bodies, the women's health movement created a relatively rare opportunity for cross-class and interracial activism.

Most of the original health advocates were college-educated, middle-class, and white: women's liberation activists, nurses, a few women doctors, and research scientists, all of whom saw their greatest problem as a lack of information rather than access to medical care, which was the barrier faced by poor women. In the seventies, for the first time, poor and minority women—supported by government training programs—began entering these programs as aides to work in women's health clinics. Together these women from different worlds created community-based local women's health clinics.[96]

Instead of focusing narrowly on the right of women to have abortions, these women tried to educate the public about the broader issue of "reproductive rights." At a socialist-feminist conference in Yellow Springs, Ohio, in 1975, Helen Rodriguez-Trias, a health activist, addressed the sterilization abuse of poor women, which inspired the formation of the Committee to End Sterilization Abuse, the Committee for Abortion Rights and Against Sterilization Abuse, the Reproductive Rights National Network, and other groups around the country.

Together, these activists helped make visible what an indifferent white middle-class population refused to see—the fact that poor women on welfare were often pressured to be sterilized if they wanted government-paid abortions. Reproductive rights meant that women not only had the right to abortion, but also the right to have children. The pioneering work of these groups eventually created a constituency for and shaped the agenda of the National Women's Health Network, formed in 1975, a national organization dedicated to advancing the health of women of all classes and races. The Health Network flourished and, by the nineties, became a highly respected and authoritative watchdog organization, evaluating treatments, research trials, and government health policies.

The impact of the women's health movement is hard to exaggerate. Two examples will perhaps offer some idea of its global reach. In 1986, I met with a small group of women in a barrio located on the outskirts of Managua in Nicaragua. With great pride, they showed me their single tattered copy of *Our Bodies, Ourselves*, translated into Spanish. I asked how the book had affected their lives. "We know what to ask from our doctors and our husbands," one woman responded with a mischievous grin. Another woman said she now understood her own anatomy, as well as what to expect during childbirth and lactation. Eventually, *Our Bodies, Ourselves* appeared in dozens of languages, providing reproductive, contraceptive, sexual, and medical information to women all over the globe.[97]

That same year, American women health activists began creating advocacy groups for women with breast cancer. Besides forming support groups, they also offered patients social services and research information on new treatments. By the early 1990s, they successfully lobbied Congress to provide more funds for breast cancer research.

Unsurprisingly, the women who politicized breast cancer were middle-aged women, veteran feminists of the women's movement who had embraced, two decades earlier, the political dimensions of "private" health matters. They showed how few resources were spent on breast cancer research; they lobbied for preventive care, as well as new treatments, and, in the process, turned a shameful taboo into a highly politicized disease. In 1988, I discovered this just-emerging movement when I had a biopsy for a suspicious breast lump. In a journal, I recorded my experience:

> As I slowly climb out of the fog of anesthesia, I see my surgeon's face, grief-stricken and sorrowful. He grips my hand tightly, tells me he's sorry, it is malignant. Everything goes out of focus. Through a fog of confusion, I feel the firm grip of a nurse's hand. She gently whispers, "You'll get through this, but make sure you join a women's support group." She has no idea who I am. She doesn't know how central feminism is to my life. She doesn't know that I have spent two decades active in the women's movement. She doesn't know that I have devoted my career to writing and teaching women's history. What I helped create now returns to comfort me in my moment of greatest need. The circle remains unbroken. Amazingly, a surge of pleasure softens my anguish.[98]

WHEN IS A CUSTOM A CRIME?

Before the women's movement, rape—like breast cancer—had been a shameful secret. Conventional wisdom held that a raped woman had invariably "asked for it." In "Rape: The All-American Crime," a groundbreaking essay published in *Ramparts* magazine in 1971, Susan Griffin argued that rape was not an act of lust but an assaultive act of power in which a man attempted to gain complete control over a woman. Rape, she pointed out, not only occurred all the time but targeted females of all ages, from small girls to women in their nineties. Griffin was the first person to make clear how "just one rapist" could keep all women off the street at night, keep women from taking night classes, prevent women from taking night jobs. The streets and the night belonged to men, even to men who wished it weren't so.[99]

At the time, rape was dealt with as a rare occurrence—partly because so few women dared report it. To publicize the high incidence of rape, the New York Radical Feminists held a public "speak-out" on rape in January 1971. Soon, feminists began to criticize the treatment of rape victims. Why did police and hospital personnel treat rape victims like perpetrators or sinners? Why did New York require two witnesses for a woman to be credible? Why did a woman have to prove that she resisted in order to be believed? Why could a defense attorney use a woman's sexual history to discredit her accusation? Who, they asked, was on trial, the raped woman or her assailant?

In 1975, Susan Brownmiller's groundbreaking book *Against Our Will* revealed the universality of rape—of women, children, and prisoners in war, in peace, at home, on the streets, in the country, in the city, in every part of the world, in all periods of history. Brownmiller's exhaustive book put rape onto the political agenda. During the next few years, networks of rape-crisis centers and antirape advocacy organizations sprang up across the country. Prodded by feminists, police departments began to teach officers to treat traumatized raped women with greater sensitivity. Hospitals began to teach doctors and nurses to regard raped women as traumatized patients, not female sinners. Many states altered their rules of evidence, making a rape victim's sexual past inadmissible in court. All of these changes, which took less than two decades to accomplish, encouraged more women to report rape to the police.[100]

As is often the case in modern American culture, a criminal trial helped publicize the seriousness of rape. In 1974, two men raped thirty-year-old Inez Garcia. Married at fifteen, she had lived in Miami until authorities sent her husband to a California prison. With her eleven-year-old son, Garcia moved to California in order to work in the fruit fields near the prison. After being raped, she took a rifle and went out looking for her two assailants. When she found the men, one drew a knife. She fired the gun several times, killing the man who had held her down during the rape. Charged with homicide, Inez Garcia found herself a cause célèbre among feminists and radical sympathizers. Defended by Charles Garry, an attorney for the Black Panthers and other movement groups, Garcia argued that she had "a right to protect her integrity when violated." While out on bail, she briefly joined a feminist commune that had supported her, but felt manipulated and used by feminists, radical groups, and the media. In the end, the jury found her guilty. Two years later, however, she was acquitted and released. The case caused considerable debate among feminists and the public in general. Did a woman have the right to self-defense hours after she was raped?[101]

One year later, in 1975, the nation witnessed yet another rape-murder trial. Joanne Little, an African-American prisoner in a North Carolina jail, stabbed to death Clarence Alligood, a white county guard who attempted to rape her. The trial of Little became another cause célèbre. Both feminists and black activists argued that white men would always be acquitted for raping a black woman. William Kunstler, another well-known movement lawyer, defended Little and reframed the case as a trial of "the Southern justice system." A jury of six blacks and six whites took exactly seventy-eight minutes to acquit Little of second-degree murder. Like the Inez Garcia case, the Little acquittal ignited fierce public debate. Widely covered by the national media, these two cases not only helped publicize the ubiquity of rape, especially among minority women, but also raised the question whether a woman had a right to kill her assailant after she was raped, in some cases, hours or days after the event took place.[102]

Inevitably, feminists discovered that sexual violence did not occur only between strangers. Husbands raped their wives, but the law, as well as conventional wisdom, held that a man could rape neither a wife nor a prostitute—in essence, they belonged to him.[103] As Bob Wilson, then chair of the Judiciary Committee of the California Senate, joked, "If you can't rape your wife, then who can you rape?"[104]

Diana Russell, whose pioneering book *The Politics of Rape* reached a wide audience in 1975, should be credited as the major archaeologist who unearthed the secret of marital rape. Russell was a friend of Laura X, the founder of the Berkeley Women's History Library. After learning from Russell that several foreign countries had outlawed marital rape, Laura X launched a campaign to redefine marital rape as a sexual crime. In 1979, she organized the National Clearinghouse on

Marital Rape in Berkeley and then spent the next two decades speaking at college campuses and at professional associations, and lobbying state legislatures to reclassify marital rape as a crime.

Once again, an important trial helped publicize the crime of marital rape. In 1978, a jury in Salem, Oregon, acquitted John Rideout of beating and raping his wife. At the time, Oregon was one of three states that actually classified marital rape as a crime. During the trial, the national media parachuted into tiny Salem, riveting the nation's attention with the details of the legal proceedings. For the first time, many Americans heard about "marital rape" in a context that criminalized it, and people began to debate whether such a crime actually existed.

By "naming" such hidden crimes, feminists generated the kind of debate that could turn a "custom" into a crime. Less than two decades after Laura X launched her campaign, the Beijing World Conference on Women in 1995 passed a resolution recognizing marital rape as a violation of women's rights. By 1997, all fifty states in the United States had criminalized marital rape. Laura X could look back at a campaign that had successfully provided married women with greater protection from male violence.

Whenever Laura X lectured at colleges, she immediately noticed that women students naturally showed far more interest in rape on campus than in marital rape. Rape by a date, like that by a husband, proved difficult to corroborate. The "his" and "her" versions never matched and there were rarely witnesses. A college woman went out, got drunk, landed in a bedroom, perhaps with the desire to engage in some sexual activity, but not intercourse. If she suddenly refused, the young man often interpreted her refusal as a tease or as an "old-fashioned" way of saying yes. No one was sure how to describe, let alone prove, the existence of what was then called "stranger rape." But these men were not, in fact, strangers. In her 1987 book *Real Rape*, law professor Susan Estrich created quite a stir when she introduced the phrases "date rape" and "acquaintance rape." During the late 1980s and throughout the 1990s, campuses all over the country held debates on date rape, teaching young women to be clear about their intentions and instructing young men to seek consent.[105]

To publicize violence against women, feminists also invented new rituals. "Take Back the Night," for instance, became an annual symbolic march, held after dark, to protest women's fear of male violence at night. In March 1982, three hundred undergraduates at the University of California, Davis, participated in the annual "Take Back the Night" march.

When they passed "fraternity row," they encountered a shocking display
of gross hostility. While one young man backed a car straight into the
crowd, another urinated on the marchers; several "mooned" the women;
some men threatened to rape them later; still others hung out of windows
shouting obscenities. Though the university disciplined them, such incidents reminded women that even at a liberal research university, a
peaceful march for a rape-free society still threatened some men.[106]

For black women, the subject of rape brought up similar, but also different, injuries. White planters had raped black women for their own
pleasure, as well as to reproduce a slave class. White men had lynched
black men, ostensibly for their violation of white women's purity, but actually for sport and to prop up white supremacy. During the last century,
more black women had experienced rape—by relatives, white masters,
and black men—than white women could ever imagine. For black
women, rape was not only a sexual violation, it was also a symbol of
white power and their double subordination as black women.[107] Yet, the
rape of black women remained invisible to an indifferent white majority.
What stayed in the American imagination was black male attacks
against white women, the exact opposite of historical reality.

Nor did most white—or black—Americans ever discuss the incest
that had scarred the lives of so many young girls. Sandra Butler, the author of *The Conspiracy of Silence: The Trauma of Incest* (1978), helped
end the silence that surrounded the subject of incest. Behind the doors
of both affluent and impoverished homes, fathers, brothers, and other
relatives sexually abused young girls with remarkable frequency. Sworn
to silence, many of these victims of incest grew up guilty, confused,
traumatized, fearing men or compulsively searching for sex as a sign of
love. Many women functioned only by repressing their memories of
these incidents. Later, as adults, some recovered these painful memories and faced the ordeal of integrating them into their adult lives.[108]

What had been unspeakable, unthinkable, and unimaginable became,
by the nineties, the subject of popular memoirs and a staple on talk
shows. Before the women's movement, few Americans had realized how
many relatives sexually violated young girls. Afterward, it would become the stuff of controversy as the public questioned whether memories were, in fact, recalled or "induced" by overly eager therapists.

Like incest, wife-beating was another secret carefully hidden behind
the charade of a happy marriage. It turned out that women had no particular proclivity for walking into doors, falling down stairs, or smashing
their faces on the ground. Men from all classes and races slugged their

wives—when they drank too much, when their dinner arrived late, when they felt jealous, when they became impotent, when high on drugs, when in withdrawal, when the boss laid them off, when their job frustrated them. Typically, a man would later beg for forgiveness, but forgiveness seldom ended such domestic violence. Studies showed that violent men tended not to blame themselves but the women they lived with for provoking their rage and violence.[109]

Before the seventies, few women ever dared to admit that they had been beaten. The police, who regarded domestic violence as a private matter, rarely interfered. During the 1970s feminists renamed wife-beating—which sounded more like a traditional custom than a crime—"battering." As the plight of battered women received growing attention, law enforcement officials—prodded by feminist activists—helped reframe domestic violence as a crime.[110]

Most Americans had a hard time grasping the reality of battered women. Why did they remain with abusive men? Why did they refuse to testify against them in court? Wasn't it their fault that the situation continued? Why didn't they just leave? No one had ever heard of "battered women's syndrome." They didn't understand that violent husbands or boyfriends regularly stalked or hunted down women who fled their grasp and killed them and their children. They did not know that battered women generally had no safe refuge and no money with which to restart their lives.

Between 1974 and 1980, feminists created battered women's shelters all over the country. Brandishing the motto "We will not be beaten," thousands of women activists, joined by social workers, created grassroots organizations that lobbied for social and legal reforms. By 1977, the phrase "battered woman" had entered public discourse. By 1982, feminists had established three hundred shelters and forty-eight state coalitions of service providers for battered women, while offering countless women refuge from violent men. In the process, they helped to redefine wife-beating as neither a custom nor a private matter, but as a felony.[111]

If homes were not always safe havens for women, neither was the workplace, where a boss might hold absolute power over a woman's livelihood. The idea that a man's sexual predatory habits on the job should be illegal had simply never occurred to most women. That's the way it was. When harassed, women tended to feel guilty, blame themselves, and wonder what they had done to deserve such attention. At first, no one even knew what to call this abuse of power, except perhaps sexual blackmail. In 1975, a group of women at Cornell University banded together to expose the sexual behavior of a male professor and coined the term "sexual harassment." Almost immediately, Nadine Taub and other feminist lawyers began to file suits using the term as well. In 1979, law professor Catharine MacKinnon's groundbreaking book *The Sexual Harassment of Working Women* publicized both the term and the way in which such male behavior prevented women from achieving true economic independence. As Susan Griffin had once argued that rape was a matter of power and control, so MacKinnon now argued that sexual harassment was also about power and control and constituted sex discrimination at work.[112]

Once named, sexual harassment seemed to be everywhere. Hollywood's faded casting couch was not the only site where sexual harassment occurred. At colleges and universities, male faculty sometimes demanded sexual favors from students in return for high grades or letters of recommendation. In business, men often made promotions contingent on a woman's willingness "to put out." In factories, foremen gave special favors to women who treated them "right."

In 1980, the Equal Employment Opportunity Commission added sexual harassment to its "Guidelines on Discrimination." Once unwelcome sexual advances were redefined as a violation of a woman's rights, working women could file grievances against their employers. As a result, men discovered that certain kinds of behavior were illegal, as well as unacceptable.

But change did not occur overnight. The good old days when men could abuse or harass women with impunity were fast disappearing. But a new national consensus had not been reached. When does "no" really mean "no"? Can and should a society legislate affairs of the heart? Men were confused and no longer knew how to behave around women. Women were baffled as well. And feminists vehemently disagreed whether new policies should *protect* women or *defend* their newfound sexual freedom.[113]

During the 1990s, the subject of appropriate sexual conduct suddenly burst into public consciousness in the form of national hearings, trials, and scandals. It wasn't until 1991, when Judge Clarence Thomas was nominated for a Supreme Court vacancy, that his former aide Anita Hill accused him of all kinds of sexual harassment. How was it possible to distinguish friendly flirtation on the job from a sexually hostile work environment? What evidence was necessary to prove sexual harassment?

When the Senate confirmed Clarence Thomas, most Americans disbelieved Anita Hill's testimony. Yet, just one year later, a majority of citizens had changed their minds and believed her. Why? Because the hearings spurred countless personal and formal debates about the nature of sexual harassment. Afterward, many women, both black and white, privately remembered and publicly recounted their own experiences of being sexually harassed.[114] As a result, more men and women began to appreciate why a genuinely hostile work environment interfered with a woman's ability to support herself. Just four years later, the Senate forced Bob Packwood, one of its members accused of compulsive sexual harassment, to resign from office. Some of his colleagues, who now viewed him as an embarrassment, seemed downright eager, even desperate, to prove that yes, they had finally "gotten it."

Through these widely publicized political soap operas, Americans began to learn about some of the "gender crimes" feminists had identified during the 1970s. In addition to the Clarence Thomas hearings (1991), the public followed the Navy's Tailhook sex scandal (1991), the William Kennedy Smith and Mike Tyson date rape trials (1992), the Spur Posse sexual athleticism in Lakewood, California (1993), the trial that publicized the gang rape of a retarded girl in Glen Ridge, New Jersey in 1993, the furious debate over homosexuals in the military (1992–1996), the O. J. Simpson trial and verdict (1994–1995), and the Army's and Navy's scandalous sexual harassment incidents (1996–1997), all of which informed millions of Americans that some kinds of behavior were no longer socially acceptable. These media circuses gradually had a cumulative impact on American political culture. Although many of the accused were acquitted, the nation became immersed in debates over date rape, battering, and sexual harassment. Once hidden, these "sex crimes" now became part of common discourse, so common that they began to enter mainstream culture and politics.[115]

SEX WORKERS—PROSTITUTION AND PORNOGRAPHY

It took a while, but a majority of feminists eventually agreed that rape, incest, battering, and sexual harassment violated women's rights. But no such consensus existed about whether misconduct in the sex industry violated the rights of the women who worked as prostitutes or in the pornography industry. On the issue of prostitution, American feminists found it difficult if not impossible to agree whether they should protect the rights of sex workers or simply abolish the industries that employed them.

In 1971, feminists convened a conference on prostitution in New York City. Kate Millett, who chronicled the conference in *The Prostitution Papers* (1971), described how "all hell broke loose—between the prostitutes and the movement." Although skeptical, the prostitutes had come to the conference as working women, "in the life," looking for support in a difficult and dangerous trade. They were not simply movement women who had once turned a trick or two. "They had a great deal to say," reported Millett, "about the presumption of straight women who fancied they could debate, decide, or even discuss what was their situation and not ours. The first thing they could tell us—the message coming through a burst of understandable indignation—was that we were judgmental, meddlesome, and ignorant." For some feminists, prostitution seemed like the quintessential exploitation of women. In the eyes of the disgusted prostitutes, the movement women reminded them of the middle-class wives and mothers who tried to drive them out of their neighborhoods.[116]

The gulf between prostitutes and movement women proved impassable. Both groups agreed that prostitution should be decriminalized, but for radically different reasons. Prostitutes demanded safer working conditions for an ongoing trade; feminists wanted to abolish prostitution altogether. Alix Kates Shulman recalled that after several prostitutes described the working conditions they wanted, "one feminist jumped onto the stage, and said, well, why are you prostitutes? Why aren't you making a living some other way? Like, as a file clerk."[117] Millett wrote:

> In the interminable "just let me finish my point" vs. "Baby you don't know where it's at" that prolonged itself in doorways and staircases . . . we were at last becoming persons to each other. There was a gulf . . . but it was closing.

Or so Millett hoped. But the next day, the conference spiraled out of control. The prostitutes bristled at the day's program, titled "Towards the Elimination of Prostitution." To add insult to injury, the panel of "experts" included not one prostitute. Millett reported that "a few prostitutes arrived late and after some hesitation, were allowed to sit on the platform. The panel then fell into 'tedious bickering.' The audience, outraged by the growing chaos, began forming long lines to speak into microphones." Millett watched the conference disintegrate into accusations and recriminations:

> Everyone talked. No one made any sense. Things rapidly degenerated into chaos. . . . Beyond the absurdly hypothetical threat posed by the term "elimination" . . . was the greater threat of adverse judgment by other women. For if large numbers of "straight" women congregate to agree that there is an absolute benefit in the elimination of prostitution—what does this convey to the prostitute? . . . that she is despised and rejected by her sister women. Never mind if this makes no sense—it was there like an edict upon the heart.

The more feminists argued, the more prostitutes viewed them as ignorant moralists. In the heat of the moment, some feminists revealed their real feelings of revulsion toward prostitution and then were shocked when pandemonium broke out. The shrillness of the organizers was matched by the even shriller shouts of the prostitutes.

> The accusation so long buried in liberal good will or radical rhetoric—"You're selling it, I could too, but I won't"—was finally heard. Said out loud at last. The rejection and disapproval which the prostitutes have sensed from the beginning . . . is now present before us, a palpable force in the air. There is fighting now in earnest. Someone is struck, the act obscene, irreparable. Attempts at reconciliation are futile. . . . The afternoon is in shambles.

"It was simply too early," Millett sadly concluded. Perhaps, but American feminists have a long history of lacking genuine empathy with prostitutes. During the first two decades of the century, feminists played a decisive role in ensuring that prostitution became illegal. Now, during the second wave of feminism, many feminists again found the idea of women selling sex unacceptable. The "whore stigma" scared many of them away. The sexual revolution had not erased memories of good and bad girls, especially for white middle-class women. But Flo Kennedy, one of the movement's sassiest, most outspoken veterans of the civil rights and women's movements, pointed out that "feminists always talk about prostitutes getting beaten up by the pimps, but statistically women get beaten up even more by their husbands."[118]

In contrast to American feminists, Dutch and French activists created encounter groups with prostitutes, and in some European cities, feminists and prostitutes worked together in coalitions to improve the working conditions of sex workers. In America, the legacy of American Victorian values, as well as feminists' ambivalent attitudes toward the sexual revolution, combined to push prostitution to the bottom of the feminist agenda, a subject rarely raised except as an issue of "sexual slavery."

Deeply disappointed, Millett wrote, "It may be that the West Coast will get it together before we do in the East." She was right. In San Francisco, the flamboyant and politically astute Margo St. James, herself a former prostitute, organized a union of prostitutes in 1973 called COYOTE, an acronym that stood for "Call Off Your Old Tired Ethics." COYOTE successfully provided prostitutes with adequate counsel and persuaded public defenders to prosecute crimes that had actual victims. COYOTE also convinced some municipal judges to release prostitutes arrested on routine street sweeps on their own recognizance. In Seattle, Jennifer James, another former prostitute and advocate, pulled together a similar union. Over the decade, unions of prostitutes that sought decriminalization began appearing in major cities in Europe as well. Not surprisingly, only a few American feminists actively became involved in lending their support.

The subject of pornography polarized the women's movement much more than prostitution, turning friends into enemies, and persuading some outsiders that a feminist was just another name for a prude who wore sensible shoes. In the earliest years of the movement, feminists had felt queasy about denouncing pornography for fear of appearing "straight" and prudish. Robin Morgan recalled that "there was a time when rape and pornography were embarrassing issues even in the Women's Movement . . . such things were deplorable . . . but they had to be explored with a sophisticated snicker—not with outspoken fury." Morgan's famous statement, "Pornography is the theory, and rape the practice," captured an idea that would only grow in the movement— that the cultural dehumanization of the female body was a precondition for and invitation to commit violence against women.[119]

In 1976, the release of *Snuff*, a pornographic film that sexualized the torture and evisceration of women, sparked the organization of the first feminist antipornography organization. That same year, feminists in the San Francisco Bay Area created Women Against Violence in Pornography and the Media, sponsored a national conference, "Feminist Perspectives on Pornography," and organized the first "Take Back the Night" march. In New York City, another group, Women Against Pornography, organized biweekly "tours" of the prostitution and pornography trade in Times Square.[120]

Catharine MacKinnon and Andrea Dworkin, two leaders whose names became closely associated with the movement, reframed pornography as a violation of women's civil rights. To those who remained unconvinced, they explained that the objectification and dehumanization of women reduced them to "things and objects," which made it much easier for men to batter, exploit, and rape them. According to MacKinnon, pornography inspired violent fantasies that men might then act out on women they knew or even on strangers. In Minneapolis, MacKinnon and Dworkin tried to secure an antipornography municipal ordinance that would have allowed women to take action against pornographers for the injuries they sustained if raped. MacKinnon, an imaginative and original thinker, eventually pushed the argument against pornography even further.[121] In a controversial work, *Only Words*, she made the argument that the representation of violence against women was as dangerous as actual violence itself.

An example cited by Andrea Dworkin was the pornographic film *Deep Throat*, which glorified a woman's ability to open up her throat to give her lover maximum pleasure. "We see an increase since the release of *Deep Throat* in throat rape—where women show up in the emergency room because men believe they can penetrate, deep-thrust, to the bottom of a woman's throat." Linda Lovelace, the woman who had starred in the film, later wrote of her pimp's brutality and the near-suffocation she suffered while pretending to enjoy herself. According to Dworkin, that film alone increased the popularity of throat rape in pornographic literature. An example:

> He could kill me with [his cock], she thought. He didn't need
> a gun in his hand. . . . She swallowed and swallowed at each
> of his forward thrusts, but her throat wouldn't stretch large
> enough to accommodate him. It wasn't until he grabbed her
> hair with his left fist and held her head against the force of his
> tool that she was able to relax her throat muscles enough that
> his cock raped its way over her tongue and buried itself in the

passage to her stomach. Pain seared through her throat like she had swallowed a hot branding iron as her throat stretched to its maximum capacity.... She nursed greedily at his body.[122]

The antipornography movement grew at a furious pace in the early 1980s. Meanwhile, a group of feminist intellectuals and activists, who did not necessarily approve of or like pornography, began to argue that feminists ought to mobilize to protect the rights and working conditions of sexual workers in the industry. They accused MacKinnon and Dworkin of attempting to protect women by thoroughly desexualizing them, by embracing Victorian ideals of women's passionlessness, encouraging censorship, and exaggerating the sexual slavery that held women who worked in the pornographic film industry in bondage. Fearing censorship, these activists worried that any attempt to weaken the First Amendment—such as banning pornography—would likely be used against feminists, Marxists, and gays and lesbians. They also worried that their opponents had recast sex as an exclusively dangerous and frightening activity.

The "anti-anti-pornography movement" drew a variety of activists into its orbit. In 1981, Gayle Rubin, Amber Hollibaugh, and Deirdre English published an article titled "Talking Sex," in which they attacked the antiporn movement for equating sex with abuse and humiliation. Ellen Willis argued that like many other women, she enjoyed pornography (even if that meant enjoying a rape fantasy) and that it intensified her life as a rebel. Ann Snitow thought that feminists' excavations of male violence had "frightened themselves." "Visibility," she wrote, "had created a new consciousness, but also new fear—and new forms of old sexual terror: It was almost as if, by naming sexual crimes, by ending female denial, we frightened ourselves more than anyone else."[123]

At times, the pornography wars seemed to deepen the gulf between straight women and lesbians. An unforgettable scene at a conference on pornography typified the passion and anger that the topic seemed to arouse. As Susan Brownmiller remembered it, "There was one [lesbian] sitting in front who started to bait me. Finally, she got up and took the microphone and said, 'We do all the work in this movement and you go home and suck cock.' And I said 'If you hate men so much, why are you dressed in men's clothes?' "[124]

But lesbians didn't always agree about sex either. While many supported the antipornography movement, others demanded an acceptance of a broad repertoire of sexual practices. The invention of the "political lesbian," these women argued, had created an unrealistic cuddly and snuggly view of lesbian sex. They thought it was time for lesbians to "get real" and openly accept the world of down-and-dirty sex, including sadomasochism, with its whips and other sexual toys. These "sex radicals," as they called themselves, came to champion any kind of consensual sex. Pat Califia, Joan Nestle, Gayle Rubin, and Amber Hollibaugh, among other advocates, argued that the antiporn movement discriminated against sexual minorities. In "Pornography and Pleasure," Paula Webster described her impatience with the antiporn movement for condemning "voyeurism, bondage, s/m, fetishism, pornography, promiscuity, and intergenerational sex as incomprehensible."[125]

The pornography wars fought by feminists invariably trivialized and simplified the ideas of both sides. Each group, riding high on self-righteousness, accused the other of condescending attitudes toward sexual workers. Many misconceptions swirled around the antipornography movement. Most of its activists were neither "prudes" nor advocates of censorship. Andrea Dworkin and Catharine MacKinnon hardly spoke for all feminists on the issue of pornography. Some feminists argued that poverty, not pornography, should be the movement's greatest priority. But the antipornography movement also exposed the dangers that many sex workers did face, including torture and slavery, and highlighted the impact of hard-core pornographic films that sexualized the subjugation, degradation, and even the death of women.[126]

IT SEEMED LIKE NOTHING HAPPENED

At the end of the 1970s, feminists were deeply divided about sexual matters. Was sex mainly a dangerous or a pleasurable activity? Had the sexual revolution brought liberation or exploitation?[127] Feminists didn't agree, but neither did the rest of the nation. With the election of Ronald Reagan in 1980 and the rising political power of the New Right, the feminist "sex wars" merged into the larger cultural wars.

Oddly enough, pundits and journalists didn't seem to notice that feminists had unearthed so many hidden injuries or that they had spent the decade trying to find some kind of equality within the sexual revolution. Instead, journalists and pundits happily buried the decade as though nothing of significance had occurred. The seventies, they said with a sigh of relief, were finally over. They were tired of Americans indulging in narcissistic psychological explorations or soaking in hot tubs.

Perhaps this was an accurate depiction of a small, elite group of journalists and others who had the wealth to own, and the time to sit in, hot tubs. But those years, arguably the most intellectually vital and exciting ones in the history of American women, also witnessed an amazing array of revelations and changes in social, political, and public thought and policy.

Paradoxically, the exposure of so many crimes and secrets did little to cast feminists as agents of change. Although activists challenged all kinds of received wisdom, including the language permitted by men on the street, in the bedroom, in the office, and in political office, the cumulative impact of all these revelations also helped implant an image of women as passive victims of villainous men. By the 1990s, for example, many young women possessed an awareness of date rape and sexual harassment inconceivable to their mothers, but they also viewed sex (exacerbated by the fear of AIDS) largely as a dangerous activity. In a culture increasingly titillated by victimology, the image of woman as victim received far more publicity than stories that recounted feminists' courageous determination to challenge the norms and customs of American culture and society.[128]

Most women, of course, suffered not from pornography, but from poverty and unemployment. But rape, incest, battering, homophobia, prostitution, pornography, and sexual harassment had also ruined the lives of countless women of all classes. The excavation of the hidden injuries of sex underscored the inadequacies of the male sexual revolution, redefined certain customs as crimes, and ultimately redrew the political and social agenda of American political culture.

The disillusioned liberal and New Left women who began the women's movement had come a long way in little more than a decade. They had gained a new sense of political entitlement. They newly recognized that genuine emancipation required that the state protect women's rights—as wives and mothers, as workers and lovers, as students and dreamers, and, of course, as citizens. Nothing less would do. As taboo subjects turned into talk show topics, American women began to view their lives through new eyes. Rage replaced shame. Entitlement supplanted despair. Activism led to pride. Nothing would ever seem quite the same again.

Chapter Six

PASSION AND POLITICS

Sixteen years ago, the young woman emigrated from Vietnam, a toddler in a boat filled with refugees and rats. Now she is a university under-graduate, eager to understand the alien political culture of her adopted country. One day, after class, she asks the simplest of all questions, to which no simple answers are available: "What was the women's move-ment like?"

No matter what I say, she looks increasingly bewildered. From her, I learn that the only way to convey a sense of the women's movement is to evoke the passions that made the movement the stuff of high drama—euphoric exhilaration, murderous rage, romantic rejection, apocalyptic expectation, squandered opportunity, unexpected possibility.

CONSCIOUSNESS-RAISING

Much of this drama resulted from seeing the world through new eyes. In 1968, Carol Hanisch, a civil rights worker in Mississippi in 1964–1965, a member of Gainesville Women's Liberation and then New York Radical Women, coined the slogan "The personal is politi-cal." By this, she meant to convey the then-shocking idea that there were political dimensions to private life, that power relations shaped life in marriage, in the kitchen, the bedroom, the nursery, and at work. Politics existed beyond Congress, beyond global affairs. Kathie Sara-child (formerly Amatniek), a peace activist at Harvard and a civil rights organizer in Mississippi, became a member of the New York Radical Women, and then the Redstockings. It was Sarachild who coined the term "consciousness-raising," the process by which women in small groups could explore the political aspects of personal life. Building on SNCC's tradition of "speaking truth to power," Sarachild understood that women would see the reality of their lives only when they grasped that their problems were not theirs alone. By sharing life stories and questioning the "natural order of things," women could begin to see their condition through their own eyes. In a number of articles, she suggested topics for small groups to explore, including family life, work, sex, health, and education. Why, for example, did men enjoy more leisure time? Why were women's nimble fingers considered perfectly suited for making small widgets on an assembly line, but not for neurosurgery? Why did women clean the toilet while men cut the grass? Why did employers pay women less than men for the same work? Why did schools routinely steer girls toward teaching and nursing?[1]

Invariably, consciousness-raising dredged up personal revelations. Suddenly, "one got it." This isn't just my problem; millions of other women have shared this experience. What had until that moment seemed so "normal" suddenly appeared artificial, not to say coercive. This is what consciousness-raising meant—looking at your life through your own eyes, reflecting on the choices you had made, realizing who had encouraged and discouraged your decisions, and recognizing the many obstacles and constraints that had little to do with individual temperament or talent.

When enough women had told their stories, enough such meetings had taken place, the "personal" no longer seemed a purely individual problem, but the result of deep cultural, social, and economic forces and assumptions. Having learned to see the world through men's eyes, one suddenly began to view life through the eyes of a woman, and that woman was you.

Consciousness-raising took place everywhere, not only in small groups. Novels, position papers, essays, and new forms of artistic expression also raised a woman's consciousness. Anyone who read Naomi Weisstein's essay "Psychology Constructs the Female" would never forget how society created the compliant woman. Anyone who read Pat Mainardi's "The Politics of Housework" would forever recognize the socially acceptable excuses men used to avoid doing housework. Anyone who read Anne Koedt's "The Myth of the Vaginal Orgasm" would never again trust male sexual experts. Anyone who read *Our Bodies, Ourselves* would never again feel so alienated from her body.[2]

Not surprisingly, consciousness-raising ended up fueling a good deal of anger. Foreigners frequently have asked why American feminists seemed so much angrier than their European counterparts. American women had believed they were among the most emancipated women in the world. But now they realized that most European countries had already instituted nationwide systems of child care and paid maternity leave. Now they understood that the hyperindividualism of American political culture framed juggling work and family life as an individual problem. Discovering their subordinate status suddenly threw everything in doubt.

It was a time of discovery, and insults stoked simmering fires. The more feminists learned, the more sinister the world seemed. Everything sounded and looked different. Advertisements that used women's bodies to sell things now seemed like public insults. Media jokes about "women's libbers" felt like chalk squeaking on a blackboard. Men who belittled feminism suddenly took on the appearance of "pigs" groveling in their hovels. It didn't last that long, this initial period of rage, but it did make life quite miserable for feminists and for those around them.

Every woman had a story to tell. In 1969, for instance, sociologist Pauline Bart, then a visiting assistant professor at Berkeley, introduced a new course on women. A prominent male leftist sociologist warned her, "There simply isn't enough to teach." Laura X, whose home was fast turning into a national archive, mobilized her friends to help Bart. A few weeks later, the sociologist arrived at his office and there, tacked onto his door, was a list of one thousand women's names, culled from various historical documents.[3]

"For the first time we were talking pain," recalled Naomi Weisstein. "We were discovering our own righteous anger, and for the first time we had become truly authentic actors in a movement with real revolutionary implications." The writer Karen Durbin later realized that she always said "everything was fine" out of fear that her anger might turn into a flood she could not control. "I felt that if I tapped the anger in me, I would up and destroy the world. And I was so mad, I couldn't see straight."[4]

In the suburbs, as well as in large cities, the small group often turned depression into anger. In the first years of the movement, the writer Vivian Gornick visited a consciousness-raising group in suburban Westchester County in which most of the members were housewives. "They were talking about marriage . . . we went around the room twice and not once was the word love mentioned. They were all really in a rage by then." Observing the mounting anger, Gornick pointed out that "many women are acting ugly now because they feel ugly."

> For a long time these women acted sweet when they didn't
> necessarily feel sweet. They did so because deep in their be-
> ing, in a place they believed their lives depended upon their
> being sweet. Now, when they think of that time, of all that life
> spent on their knees, they feel green bile spreading through
> them and they feel that their lives *now* depend upon calling
> men "male chauvinist pigs."[5]

At the same time, an unexpected sense of exhilaration sent many feminists into a drugless euphoria. Suddenly, you knew that other women shared your grievances, that cultural and institutional discrimi-nation could explain what had previously seemed like personal inade-quacy. This intoxication reminded some women of falling in love. They felt deeply seen and understood. Vivian Gornick even compared such intoxication to the experience of religious or intellectual conversion.[6]

> For the feminist it is exactly the same. . . . The excitement,
> the energy, the sheer voluptuous sweep of the feminist ide-
> ology is almost erotic in its power to sway me. Feminism has
> within it the seed of a genuine world view. Like every real
> system of thought it is able to refer itself to everything in our
> lives.

Intoxication took many forms. For women who had been activists in the New Left, the women's movement offered a renewed sense of com-munity. "What I was impressed with," reported Ellen Willis, "was that people were talking about substantive things; it wasn't like the usual political meeting. And I also felt immediately accepted. If I made a comment, people listened to it, as if I were really in the group, which I wasn't used to in New Left groups. I was used to feeling like an out-sider."[7] Once you stopped viewing women through male eyes, they often became interesting, even fascinating people. Susan Griffin recalled that before the women's movement, at parties hosted by the Left maga-zine *Ramparts*, where she then worked, "Various women associated with the movement would be there, but they were people's wives. And I was not interested in them. I talked to the men. I made the assumption, particularly if they came as somebody's wife, that they were going to be boring."[8] The sheer intellectual excitement of reexamining all received wisdom created an ongoing euphoric expectation. In Susan Brownmiller's memory, "It was intellectually the most stimulating experience of my life. I miss that more than anything." Becoming an agent of historical change inspired great personal commitment. Irene Peslikis, a New York feminist and artist who had written about women's resistance to consciousness-raising, described those early days as "totally electric. . . . I knew I was a part of making history. . . . It gave you a real high, because you knew real things could come out of it." At the first National Women in Print Conference, recalled Charlotte Bunch, "We argued over how to relate to the mainstream media . . . debates were fierce, but the energy of over one hundred women engaged in feminist publishing was intoxicating."

Within small groups, women learned they could reinvent themselves. At her very first meeting, historian Carol Groneman, then a graduate student, watched herself take back her own name. "As people went around the room introducing themselves, I was thinking to myself, 'What am I going to say? My husband's name? I don't want to have whatever I do here identified with my husband. I don't want to taint him.' But I really think there was something else going on. Groneman was my name and I decided I was taking it back."[9]

Pat Cody, in a small group of middle-aged Berkeley mothers, recalled how each of them gradually rediscovered the value of her experience, energy, and talent.

> I'll never forget one night, this marvelous woman. She was very blunt, very outspoken; she was talking about how while she grew up, she wasn't the stereotypical feminine type, and how this caused her a lot of grief. Then she said, "I realized that it was ok to be a strong woman." Suddenly there was complete silence, followed by shouts of agreement. It was a very exciting moment. People were getting it, right there, in that meeting.

Vivian Gornick was right; sometimes it felt like falling in love. Flo Kennedy, an activist and lawyer who had dedicated her life to social change, particularly in the civil rights movement, viewed the women's movement as the apex of her political life. Suddenly, she understood what had been incomprehensible. "Everything that happened was exciting. It's just like when you're in love."[10] Ann Snitow recalled that her first meeting permanently ended her hatred of being a woman. "I felt the passion. It was like paradise. It was so exciting, you could die for this. I had waited for this moment all my life."[11]

TAKING TO THE STREETS

Actions *do* speak louder than words. Political actions, in particular, not only reveal the passions felt by protesters, but also those targets they view as symbolic of their inequality. It didn't take long for feminists to move from living rooms to the streets. Within a few months, a small group might begin thinking about how to raise the consciousness of the public. The protests, "zap actions," "invasions," marches, and "guerrilla actions" organized by the women's movement ranged from the zany to the sublime. Cumulatively, they brought consciousness-raising out of the living room and into the public arena.

One of the most important but least-remembered demonstrations took place on January 15, 1968, six months before the protest against the Miss America Pageant. Women Strike for Peace (WSP), which had long protested nuclear testing and development, organized an all-women antiwar protest against the Vietnam War. In honor of the congresswoman who had voted against America's entry into both world wars, they called themselves the Jeanette Rankin Brigade. Their goal was to recruit huge numbers of American women to protest the war in Vietnam. To Congress, they brought a petition that demanded an immediate withdrawal of all American troops from Vietnam.

Meanwhile, the younger New York Radical Feminists decided to join in and, quite predictably, gave the protest a generational spin. They would protest the war, they announced, *not* as peaceful mothers, but as active feminists. As they later explained in the *Voices of the Women's Liberation Movement*, the early Chicago newsletter, their goal was to "prevent the kind of ineffective protest the Jeanette Rankin Brigade represented." Clearly, the female generation gap still haunted them, shaping their words as well as their acts.[12]

To publicize their views and gain media attention, they planned a purposefully outrageous bit of guerrilla theater, the sort of gesture that would announce a new style of activism no longer based on their potential motherhood, but on their rights as citizens. For weeks, they threw themselves into building a larger-than-life dummy installed on top of a bier, "complete with feminine getup, blank face, blonde curls, and candles. Hanging from the bier were such disposable items as S&H Green Stamps, curlers, garters, and hair spray. They carried large banners that declared 'DON'T CRY; RESIST!' "[13]

They planned an elaborate farewell to Traditional Womanhood. The funeral entourage sang songs especially composed for the occasion, accompanied by a drum corps and a kazoo. A long funeral dirge, written by Peggy Dobbins, lamented "woman's traditional role which encourages men to develop aggression and militarism to prove their masculinity." Kathie Amatniek wrote and planned to deliver a "Funeral Oration for the Burial of Traditional Womanhood" at Arlington Cemetery. It began with a critique of the feminine mystique, and ended with a plea for a new woman: "And that is why we must bury this lady in Arlington Cemetery tonight, why we must bury Submission alongside Aggression. And that is why we ask you to join us. It is only a symbolic happening, of course, and we have a lot of real work to do. We have new men as well as a new society to build."[14]

To the rest of the Jeanette Rankin Brigade, the young women issued black-bordered invitations, "joyfully" urging them to join a torchlight Burial of Traditional Womanhood, "who passed with a sigh to her Great Reward this year of the Lord, 1968, after 3000 years of bolstering the ego of War makers and aiding the cause of war." Many of the older activists, mothers and veterans of decades of political work, snubbed their invitation. They felt insulted and outraged by these radical young feminists who seemed like so many undisciplined hippies. In the middle of a shooting war, how dare they promote their trivial feminist complaints? Who were these young women to condemn my life as a mother and activist? Wait till they have children![15]

Interestingly, none of the Jeanette Rankin Brigade speeches at the Washington rally contained even the slightest whiff of such maternal language, although Women Strike for Peace activists had often used such rhetoric to condemn war and to reach other mothers. Nonetheless, this formidable and effective political group remained a "straw woman" for young women trying to find an identity beyond that of a mother and wife. As a result, at the congress that the Jeanette Rankin Brigade convened in Washington, the young women insisted on carrying the dummy across the stage and announcing that their Burial of Traditional Womanhood would take place that evening at Arlington Cemetery. They then issued a call for a counter-congress for "all radical women."

Amy Swerdlow, a WSP activist (and historian of the organization), decided to go, assuming she would hear "more radical and militant strategies for ending the war." Instead, she listened to what struck her as an incoherent rant against WSP and, more generally, women of her generation. "We had come as mourners and supplicants," she reported them as saying. "We had failed to challenge the power of men and the seeming weakness of women, and, if we didn't change our ways, women would remain powerless and wars would go on forever." According to Swerdlow, other WSP women who attended the counter-congress, many of whom "had always thought of themselves as radical in terms of left-right politics, came away more confused than enlightened, but definitely shaken." What they had heard seemed bizarre, insulting, threatening, and strangely unsettling.

Although many WSP members seemed to have paid little attention to this generational collision, the young women nonetheless ended up having an impact on some of the older women. According to Swerdlow, "It left many of us with a great deal to think about."

> The trains and buses returning the JRB women to New York hummed, not with the usual reports from the congressmen visited, but with heated debates about traditional sex roles, the meaning of woman power and women's liberation, and whether or not affluent young radical women had the right to push their demands forward when our sisters were dying in Vietnam.[16]

The media, for its part, either trivialized or ignored the Jeanette Rankin Brigade protest. Still, the impact on the women's liberation movement was even more momentous. It was there that many young activists realized how broadly their movement had spread. It was there that a new generation of female peace activists refused to use the moral rhetoric of traditional motherhood and instead demanded to protest as citizens. (Significantly, by the early 1980s, during a resurrected antinuclear peace movement, when many of these young women had become mothers, they once again celebrated women's traditional peacefulness.)[17]

In January 1968, the Burial of Traditional Womanhood protest had rejected the feminine mystique; in September, the Miss America Pageant protest condemned society's evaluation of women by their appearance. In the years that followed, inventive feminist protests proliferated with stunning speed. For instance, a group of feminists who called themselves "BITCH" held an "Ogle-In" on June 9, 1970. The purpose of the street protest, as one newspaper put it, "was to make men understand how degrading their flattery is." The women whistled at men's "tight buns," loudly admired young men's bulging arm muscles, and heckled construction workers with shouts and whistles.[18]

Corporations quickly became a popular feminist target. At an annual meeting of CBS shareholders in San Francisco, ten women suddenly appeared at the front of the small auditorium, shouting, "We won't be slaves." They then denounced CBS for its "mindless-coddling and dull programming," including its characterization of women, and for its excessive profits. In New York City, a group called Women's International Terrorist Conspiracy from Hell (WITCH) decided to deploy their magical powers by hexing Wall Street. The stock market inexplicably declined.[19]

A distaste for the institution of marriage showed up in a variety of protests. Ti-Grace Atkinson and her group, The Feminists, plastered the New York subway system with "Fuck Marriage, Not Men" stickers. In one of her most widely publicized actions, Atkinson also led a protest at the Marriage License Bureau. "We wanted to raise women's consciousness about marriage and a state contract," Atkinson explained. "So we drafted something like 'legal charges against the Marriage License Bureau of New York City,' accusing them of committing fraud with malicious intent on the women of New York."

Bridal fairs, which literally "sold marriage"—or at least the products and services that went with it—became a favorite target of the women's movement. In Columbus, Ohio, feminists argued that bridal fairs "add to the sales itch for crystal and furniture and the bride, herself, becomes a commodity." In San Diego, the Women's Liberation Front and the San Diego State Guerrilla Theater invaded a bridal fair and handed out leaflets condemning consumerism, and denounced the profits that manufacturers of household goods accumulated from the "selling" of marriage.

On February 15, 1969, women's liberation groups on both coasts disrupted gigantic bridal fairs. Targeting the marketers of gowns, wedding pictures, caterers, furniture, appliances, and honeymoon trips, the protesters condemned "consumer culture" for turning marriage into an excuse for conspicuous consumption. Did a new bride really need to have "sixteen appliances and a matching bedroom set"? In San Francisco, feminist activists picketed a bridal fair, handing out leaflets to new brides-to-be that denounced the "mass media [for its] images of the pretty, sexy, passive, childlike vacuous woman."[20]

In New York, on the same day, members of WITCH, after plastering the city with ten thousand stickers urging other women to join them, led a protest against a bridal fair held at Madison Square Garden. They chanted, "Confront the Whoremakers," cast a "hex" on the "manipulator-exhibitors," sang "Here Comes the Slave, Off to Her Grave," and distributed free "shop-lifting bags" (which the prospective brides evidently eagerly grabbed up). Their signs declared, "Always a Bride, Never a Person," "Here Comes the Bribe," and "Ask Not for Whom the Wedding Bell Tolls." In response to the fact that feminists had just disrupted bridal fairs on each coast on the same day, Robin Morgan quipped, "Yes, Betty Crocker, a conspiracy (or at least synchronicity) *does exist*."[21]

Anything that seemed degrading to women, especially advertising, became a target for feminist protesters. In Indiana, NOW launched a national boycott against Canada Dry for its ad "A Good Club Soda Is Like a Good Woman; It Won't Quit on You." In both San Francisco and Boston, women liberationists invaded radio stations for playing rock music they felt degraded women. NOW also picketed National Airlines' headquarters in New York City for an outrageous campaign that used photos of come-hither smiling flight attendants, who urged businessmen to "Fly me."[22]

The San Francisco Bay Area—ground zero of the student movement— quite naturally became a hub of university and community feminist activism. It didn't take long, for instance, for women students at U.C. Berkeley to protest the "patriarchal" nature of their educations and the fact that they had learned nothing about women's history, literature, or work. All over the country, students and faculty began demanding and creating new courses. In 1969, for instance, a group of U.C. Berkeley undergraduate students held a rally at which they issued a leaflet declaring, "We've been burned. We thought we were free human beings." Now they viewed themselves as brainwashed victims, trapped in an educational institution that refused to allow them to challenge the basis of knowledge. They then demanded that the ROTC building be converted into a space for women's studies, that the university provide child care, and that funds used for "war-related and counter-insurgency research" be converted into stipends to support women's education. As the television cameras whirred, a group of women graduate students and young assistant professors gathered in a circle and burned their master's and doctorate degrees.[23]

Some protests and marches grew out of a passion for discovering the previously hidden history of women. Laura X, Phyllis Mandel, and other members of Berkeley Women's Liberation, for instance, resurrected International Women's Day, a holiday that actually had its roots in American labor history, but was only celebrated in Communist countries. On March 8, 1911, American working women had celebrated the First International Women's Day with parades and demonstrations. The ritual quickly spread to other countries. Due to its radical and socialist origins, Americans had long ago stopped commemorating the event. On International Women's Day, in 1969, about fifty women, dressed in turn-of-the-century costumes, marched through the city of Berkeley. The following year, thirty other American towns and cities celebrated the day. By the end of the seventies, nearly all schools and cities commemorated it.

Furious that the University of California refused to provide women with facilities for weight-training and courses in self-defense, members of the Women's Liberation Front invaded the men's gym. Banging pots and pans, chanting "Self-defense for women now," about fifty women charged into the men's locker room, surprising a group of half-dressed men. Afterward, they marched to the chancellor's house, where they presented demands for free child care for all students and employees, new courses in the history of women, the hiring of more women professors, the granting of maternity and paternity leave for both students and employees, an end to all-women dormitories, the distribution of free birth control devices, and the availability of abortion at the campus hospital.[24]

Feminists also targeted media organizations all over the country. Tired of being trivialized or ignored by the *San Francisco Chronicle*, seventy-five members of Berkeley Women's Liberation crossed the Bay Bridge and invaded its editorial offices in 1969. When the phone rang, one activist simply picked it up, declared "The paper's closed down," and slammed down the receiver. The group demanded 50 percent women employees in all departments, a revision of its women's pages, and an end to the acceptance of any advertising that exploited women.[25]

After months of negotiation, KPFA, the local listener-sponsored radio station in Berkeley, continued to stonewall requests for programs by and about women. One warm evening in the summer of 1970, five women in

my small group decided to invade its offices. Here is a peek behind a
feminist guerrilla action. Sitting in Susan Griffin's living room, members
of our small group strategized about how to influence the radio station.
At about 11:00 P.M., we concocted a plan. Susan Griffin called the
KPFA office, which was always locked at night, and said she had left
her purse there earlier that day. The night manager said, "Come on by
and I'll unlock the door." We piled into a car and drove to KPFA. Susan
announced herself on the security phone, the door automatically un-
locked, and we charged in. After an unsuccessful effort to grab the microphone, we identified ourselves to the startled skeletal night staff as
Radio Free Women dedicated "to giving women at home, isolated from
society, knowledge and contact with their sisters." We left a list of our
"demands" and signed them with our noms de guerre: Rosa Luxemburg,
Sarah Grimké, Susan B. Anthony and Emma Goldman, all well-known
activists from the past. The media picked up the story the next day.
Shortly afterward, KPFA began producing programs on women's history,
poetry, literature, music, news, and public affairs. The name "Radio
Free Women" never appeared again. In the spirit of guerrilla actions, we
simply melted back into polite and respectable womanhood. No one
knew who had invaded the radio station.[26]

Everywhere, the media proved terrific targets for women intent on
publicizing the movement (and changing the world). During the first
media blitz about the women's liberation movement in 1970, feminists
all over the country, but especially in New York City, launched sustained campaigns against the various media. Forty-six women employees of *Newsweek* magazine, for example, filed a complaint charging the
magazine with systematic discrimination against women. In Hollywood,
women members of the Screen Actors Guild charged that the television
and movie industries discriminated against women; women in the
American Newspaper Guild insisted that female writers be permitted
to report on any subject, not just—as was so often the case—society
news.[27]

There were thousands of protests, rallies, and marches. All over the
country, feminists invaded and "occupied" all-male bars and clubs.
There was, for instance, "Lysistrata Day" on March 14, 1970. To protest
men's control over abortion laws, the National Association for the Repeal of Abortion Laws asked women to abstain for a day "from the joys
of love." There is no way of knowing how many women withheld sex that
day, but as "Count Marco," the nom de plume of a contemptuous San
Francisco male columnist, pointed out, "With 27 million unattached

women in this country, NO MAN is likely to go more than a few hours without finding some other woman breathing heavily into his ear with her offerings. Most of them have never heard of Lysistrata, and if they had, they figured she was some kind of a nut."[28]

Sadly, he was right. One dilemma for heterosexual feminists was that if a woman demanded too much, acted too uppity, or became too independent, a man could simply replace her with another woman, a younger wife, or, in the feminist language of the time, a "scab." With so many single young women, scabs would inevitably cross the invisible feminist picket line. In the rhetoric of the day, "A man could always find another slave."

One of the least dramatic but persistent protests was the constant demand for child care. Hundreds of activists, like myself, sat for years on committees that never seemed to convince universities that women students, staff, and faculty required child care. So many women fought for child care, but most of these failed efforts are simply too boring to recount. But I will never forget when one of my closest friends, Mary Felstiner, received her Ph.D. degree at Stanford University in June 1972. With her husband out of town and no available baby-sitter, she had no choice but to hold her infant child while she waited to receive her degree. To calm her daughter's cries, she fed her small pieces of chocolate, which, under a hot California sky, soon melted all over the baby's body and clothes. Then, she heard her name called, and she climbed up to the podium, carrying her baby in her arms. On her daughter's back hung a sign, "Why Doesn't Stanford Have Child Care?" The crowd roared its approval. Somehow, she managed to shake hands and receive her degree. But as she descended the stairs, she left the president wondering about the nature of the gooey brown stuff that stuck to his hands.[29]

CLICK! *MS.* PUBLICIZES THE PERSONAL

Not all feminists experienced their conversion in small groups. Women like Gloria Steinem, who were older and already in the work world, also experienced a sense of conversion, but without a small group to fall back on. During the 1960s, Steinem worked as a journalist, protested against the Vietnam War, and supported "La Causa" (The Struggle) of Cesar Chavez to organize a union of farmworkers in California. Like many female journalists, Steinem's first experience of the women's movement occurred when she was assigned to cover a feminist event. For Steinem, it was a New York abortion speak-out organized by Redstockings in 1969. The New York group Redstockings had tried to speak at a February 1969 legislative hearing on abortion law reform. But the fourteen men and one nun on the panel had hastily adjourned the hearing.

One month later, the Redstockings held a speak-out at which twelve women testified about their abortions before an audience of some three hundred persons. As she listened to the women speakers—movingly, with grief and pain, relating tales of their illegal abortions—Steinem suddenly felt as though a "great blinding lightbulb" had just been turned on. In that instant, she knew she was a feminist. "It wasn't until I went to cover a local abortion hearing for *New York* that the politics of my own life began to explain my interests. . . . Suddenly, I was no longer learning intellectually what was wrong. I knew." As her biographer Carolyn Heilbrun has noted, "All the humiliation of being a woman, from political assignments lost to less-experienced male writers to a lifetime of journalists' jokes about frigid wives, dumb blonds and farmers' daughters" suddenly made sense to Steinem. She, who had kept her own abortion a secret, now realized she was not alone.[30]

Like many other feminists, Steinem was furious with herself, for her "capitulation to the small humiliations, and my own refusal to trust an emotional understanding of what was going on, or even to trust my own experience. For instance, I had believed that women couldn't get along with one another, even while my own most trusted friends were women."

> I had agreed that women were more "conservative" even while I identified emotionally with every discriminated-against group. I had assumed that women were sexually "masochistic" even though I knew that trust and kindness were indispensable parts of my sexual attraction to any man. It is truly amazing how long we can go on accepting myths that oppose our own lives, assuming instead that we are the odd exceptions. But once the light began to dawn, I couldn't understand why I hadn't figured out any of this before.[31]

Steinem's conversion in 1969 irreversibly altered the direction of her life. She spent the next three decades traveling, lecturing, writing, editing, publishing, and campaigning for women's liberation. In 1971, she began to think about publishing a mainstream magazine that might reach women who didn't—and perhaps never would—read movement newsletters and newspapers. Clay Felker, editor of *New York* magazine, offered to finance a special one-time preview issue of *Ms.* The cover of the December 20, 1971, issue of *New York* showed two hands holding the new preview issue. The cover of *Ms.* featured a surreal image of a woman with eight arms, grasping a frying pan, a clock, a feather duster, a typewriter, a steering wheel, an iron, a telephone, and a mirror. Exhausted, the woman is weeping and visibly pregnant. The cover advertised such stories as "The Housewife's Moment of Truth" by Jane O'Reilly, "Sisterhood" by Gloria Steinem, "Raising Kids without Sex Roles" by Letty Pogrebin, and "Women Tell the Truth about Their Abortions" by Barbaralee Diamonstein. Inside was Johnnie Tilman's consciousness-raising article "Welfare Is a Woman's Issue," which asked readers, "Stop for a minute and think what would happen to you and your kids if you suddenly had no husband and no savings." Another essay, Judy Syfers's "Why I Want a Wife," would soon become a feminist classic. With wry wit, Syfers reminded readers what wives did, what they made possible, and the fact that a wife permitted all kinds of options that most women didn't have. As Carolyn Heilbrun would later comment, "That subjects such as these, still viable and debated today, appeared in this new feminist magazine is certainly astonishing."

> For women throughout the country, it was mind-blowing. Here was, written down, what they had not yet admitted they felt, had always feared to say out loud, and could not believe was now before their eyes, in public, for all to read.[32]

The preview issue sold out so quickly that Steinem was able to publish another issue three months later. Though discouraged by other publishers and journalists, she took the plunge. The July 1972 issue sold out as soon as it hit the stands. That night, *Ms.* held a celebratory party at the New York Public Library. According to Cathy Black, an early member of the magazine's staff, the event seemed like a microcosm of the many constituencies *Ms.* would have to please.

> I can honestly remember walking into the party thinking Oh my God, what have I gotten myself into. . . . There was a traditional group of women who looked like I did . . . blond hair and a ready smile. There was certainly a much more radical looking group of feminists that night. There was a wild all-

women's band, and there were some advertisers who looked
like they had wandered from Mars into this group.[33]

Like the sociologist who had warned there was not enough to teach
about women, the late journalist Harry Reasoner predicted, "I'll give
[Ms.] six months before they run out of things to say." (Years later, he
graciously took it back.) But Ms. never ran out of things to say. All the
first issues sold out and the magazine became one of the most important
sources of consciousness-raising in the country.[34]

From the beginning, Ms. faced the double task of speaking to the converted *and* recruiting new readers. Ms. covered grassroots organizing
activities of feminist activists as well as the different problems faced by
minority and poor women. But more often the magazine focused on the
problems encountered by its largely middle-class audience of white
women.

Still, the magazine had an astonishing reach. Many ordinary housewives and working women seemed to find in its pages a reflection of
their own lives and problems. Thousands of women wrote passionate
letters to the magazine. When read together, they constitute a rare
archive of the difficult, brave, and sometimes clumsy efforts of women to
embrace the new opportunities and shoulder the new burdens that the
movement had created.

Like an early electronic bulletin board, the letters section of Ms.
functioned as a national consciousness-raising group. Here was the
high drama of personal life; here was where women learned they were
not alone; here was where a reader learned that however much feminism
had raised expectations, daily life had a way of dampening them; here
were stories of women creating new lives, only to watch them fall apart
under the weight of too much responsibility, coupled with too little support from their families.

Many of the letters were filled with gratitude expressed by women
whose previous idea of a women's group had been the local PTA. Such
women read every issue, wrote letters to the editors, and passed Ms. on
to friends and to daughters, with a proselytizing zeal. Their voluminous
letters to the editors, whether furious or grateful, document the tremendous impact Ms. had on the lives of its readers.[35]

Hardly a topic went undiscussed. Women wrote about their dissatisfaction with their husbands and the traditional marriages they had
entered years ago. They wrote about their fantasies of a future egalitarian family. They wrote about problems at work and with their health.

They wrote of the newly discovered pleasure of other women's company. They wrote about mistakes they made, about dreams lost and found, of opportunities squandered and possibilities lost. Often, they described the famous "click" that *Ms.* had popularized, the exact moment when a woman realizes her problem is not hers alone, but the result of living in a patriarchal society in which many assumptions remained unquestioned.

Conventional wisdom held that housewives didn't care about feminism, but letters poured into *Ms.* from homemakers who were beginning to view their lives through different eyes. One woman, for example, liked the feminist proposition that child-rearing and housework constituted a full-time job for which women should receive financial compensation and which should be included in the GNP. Of her "job," she wrote:

> I thought that most of my clicks were behind me, but tonight, as I cleared the table, I had a new one. I was complimenting myself (since no one else had) on a meal I'd gone to some trouble to prepare. I began to wonder why so many of us wait trembling for "the verdict" at every meal; why my mother and so many others risk antagonizing their families by having the gall to ask outright if everything is okay.
>
> I decided it's not just neurosis. We really know they're judging even when they don't say so. House wifing is an occupation in which every single waking act is judged by the persons who mean the most to you in the world. Is the house clean? Is the food good? Was it too expensive? Are the children well behaved?
>
> A thousand times a day our contracts come up for renewal. No wonder our nerves are shot.[36]

Readers proudly reported every new step they took, which, in turn, inspired other readers. "Thanks to Ms. Magazine's reporting women's accomplishments, I decided to try a man's task myself," wrote Pat Luiz in 1974 from Oakland, California. "I and two friends broke up a sidewalk to make room for an . . . above-ground swimming pool we are assembling." As growing numbers of women entered the labor force, readers began to share the changes they were making in their families. From Jane Wright, in Dover, Delaware, came this missive.

The day our twelve-year-old son stomped up the stairs—
leaving behind the mud that had collected on his sneakers—
took a shower, came back downstairs barefoot, and complained
about the dirt on the stairs, was the day Mom and Dad decided we were going to raise the consciousness of our nine-,
ten-, and twelve-year-olds. A family conference resulted in a
family cleaning night on Friday night.

Ms. magazine also covered every injury and injustice that feminists
excavated during the 1970s, usually with a cover story. In this way, the
magazine educated women about the hidden injuries of sex. Readers
wrote revealing letters, in which they described, often for the first time,
the devastating experiences that they had undergone in the recent or
distant past. An anonymous writer wrote in 1975:

Last year I was terrorized and raped and the Philadelphia
Center for Rape conducted several interviews with me to see
how my personality, attitudes, sex life, and relationships had
changed. The major change was in my response to street insults. I, too, had ignored them, "like a good girl," but I found
myself seething at them. I started to hurl my own choice comments and give the insulter the finger in retaliation. The top-
per came the day when a straight-looking man in a business
suit and attache case walked up next to me while I was going
to work and asked me if I wanted to fuck. I was carrying a
hardback copy of the *The Gulag Archipelago* in my handbag
at the time and I belted him with it. The look of fear and surprise on his face was delicious. I felt wonderful.

A story on street harassment drew numerous responses from women
who resented men invading their space and demanding that they smile.
Mary Louise Ho, from York, England, complained, "Men find unsmiling
women threatening because we don't fit their image of the subordinate,
placating, feminine female."

They are compelled to bully us into that role because it
makes them feel more secure and powerful. No doubt, to
the individual man, he thinks he is being friendly and that
we should appreciate his attention. It's time he learned

otherwise. The next time a man says, "I hate to see a lady so
serious," tell him, "That's your problem."

To which Naomi Weisstein, in New York City, offered another possible
retort: "How about (preferably snarling), 'Say something funny.' "

Readers didn't hesitate to celebrate—or criticize—anything that appeared in "their" magazine. In response to a *Ms.* cover on "The Truth
About Battered Wives," in 1976, Nancy King from Baltimore, Maryland,
wrote, "*Ms.*, I congratulate you on your August cover, a new low in
judgment. The battered wife as fashion model—bruised, maybe, but
ever young and lovely, and with her eye makeup still intact. Click,
indeed!" In response to another cover that featured Lillian Carter, President Jimmy Carter's mother, Ruth Schissler from Jamaica Plain, Massachusetts, applauded. "I give *Ms.* a lot of credit for putting a sweet,
wrinkled old woman on the cover. It was good to see a real person for a
change, instead of perfect, youthful-looking models. Keep up the good
work in breaking precedents." But another woman wrote a scathing letter in which she denounced the *Ms.* editors. "I am not sure that I shall
ever forgive you for the picture of Lillian Carter on the October cover. It
is one of the most unkind photographs I have seen. If *Ms.* is Lillian
Carter's friend, she certainly does not need enemies."

The magazine couldn't win. When *Ms.* presented a special issue in
1976, "Why Women Don't Like Their Bodies," Robin McKiel from
Alexandria, Virginia, protested:

> I was shocked that you would publish an issue probing into
> the reasons women don't like their bodies and then feature a
> skinny white woman on the cover. *That's* why women don't
> like their bodies—because we've been told we *should* look
> like the woman on the cover when most of us don't!

The editor later explained the challenge they faced. "We first tried a
heavier woman . . . but that conveyed a different, old-fashioned idea:
that only fat women have a body-image problem. We also tried a darker-
skinned woman, but that conveyed a limited or racist message for the
same reason."

Some letters came from young women who had just had some experience that had resulted in a "click." In 1977, an anonymous writer
wrote:

After talking with my man friend and housemate of six months about my doing most of the housework, I finally presented him with a bill today for "domestic services," approximately four hours a week at three dollars and fifty cents an hour. This so-called liberated male (he talks a good line) thought about this for two minutes, then drew up his own bill. "Sexual services": approximately four hours a week at five dollars an hour. He even thinks his sexual services are worth more than mine! Click.[37]

But many more letters were written by women who had just divorced and found themselves without resources or employment. In their letters, they described the exhaustion and self-doubt they experienced as they tried to cobble together new lives for themselves. One mother of five, for example, began college at age thirty-nine and was trying to finish her dissertation in a state of poverty. Her former husband gave her small amounts of child support; her father pitched in with modest help "because it's not right." After describing the enormous stress of her new life, she conceded, "I find myself so *angry* now. It has been so *hard.* I've been on welfare and food stamps; I've run up twenty-eight thousand dollars in student loans and cannot borrow any more because I'm over the limit."

Ms. also spurred one of the most dramatic changes in the English language: the use of Ms. to replace Mrs. or Miss. Language usually changes rather slowly. Yet, by mid-decade, Ms. had already begun to appear on most business mail and applications. Like the title Mr., Ms. covered all possibilities, and included all women, regardless of their marital status.

Ms. never pleased everyone and, as the premier, best-known feminist magazine, found itself under constant attack. Radical and socialist feminists distrusted the slick mainstream magazine, denounced its acceptance of advertisements that depicted thin, rich women, and dismissed the *Ms.* staff as sellouts; Carol Hanisch, Ellen Willis, and many other radical activists wrote articles condemning "The Liberal Takeover of Women's Liberation" and "The Conservatism of *Ms.*" The growing New Right, for its part, would condemn the magazine as an antifamily publication that contributed to the destruction of American traditional values.[38]

For some readers, the magazine focused too much on lesbians; others felt it concentrated too little on the lives of minority and poor women.

Some feminists enjoyed the inspirational stories of women who had faced enormous obstacles and attained great recognition and success. But others thought the magazine subtly contributed to the idea that women could have it all, if they just willed it, and did it all. The fact is, the magazine broadcast more than one message. While it urged women to turn their world upside down, *Ms.* also tried to teach women how to cope with the world they had inherited.[39]

What the magazine did contribute, however, was incalculable. After 1972, women who had begun questioning their lives found in *Ms.* a guide for understanding women's subordination, stories of reinvented lives, and articles and letters that reassured them that they definitely were not alone. The cumulative and visible impact of the women's movement thrilled many readers. At the end of the seventies, Jill Wood, from Toronto, Canada, wrote:

> One day last week, I pulled up to a four-way stop in my taxi. At one of the stop signs sat a police officer in a chase cruiser, and at the third, a telephone installer in a van. What made the occasion memorable was the fact that all three of us were women. We celebrated with much joyful laughter.

One year later, Dr. Martha Hurley wrote from Kansas City, Missouri:

> In the middle of an operation today, I looked around the room—to the first assistant, my scrub nurse, and circulating nurse, the anesthesia doctor, nurse anesthetist, and the patient—and suddenly realized that we were performing major surgery and there was not a man in the room![40]

Steinem's bold move to create a new magazine catapulted her to celebrity status in the media, even as it created distrust and jealousy among other women activists. Some younger feminists wondered about her "belated" conversion (in 1969) from a high-powered journalist into a media-anointed, telegenic leader of the movement. They resented her beauty and glamour, and distrusted her ability to represent them when she took feminist campaigns to editors, politicians, even to the White House. Some members of Redstockings even regarded Steinem and various lesbians as "co-conspirators in a plot to eliminate radical feminism."

Betty Friedan, who viewed her as a rival, testily compared Steinem's role as a "missionary, a public relations person," with her own role as "the founder." Friedan was partly right. Steinem did make a perfect movement public-relations representative to a nation already primed by all sorts of media images to fear the very idea of a feminist. For this, Steinem was an unmitigated asset. A beautiful and intelligent woman, she reassured the unconverted that feminists were not, after all, hairy, ugly, man-hating shrews. Having enjoyed a series of serious relationships with men, or "little marriages," as she called them, she was an advertisement for the fact that feminism did not require a loveless or a manless life. A good journalist as well as an engaging speaker who remained calm and collected under fire, Steinem countered the media's stereotype of shrill "libbers" and proved that feminists came in many sizes, enjoyed different styles of life, and embraced a wide range of political views.

Attacked from so many sides, it is amazing that Steinem never responded in kind. The product of a working-class home, she made special efforts to enlist the privileged to assist poor and minority women. She defended lesbians and worked to create coalitions with women of color. She traveled the country with Flo Kennedy, the irreverent African-American who made bigoted white men tremble, speaking to all kinds of groups about the need for a new women's movement. For decades, she dedicated herself to a movement that did not always appreciate her generosity of spirit or her ecumenical inclusiveness. But by creating *Ms.*, Steinem left a legacy for which she would be rightfully remembered: she helped educate millions of women to see the world through their own eyes.

CREATING CULTURE

One of the ways the movement spread was through the creation of a vibrant women's culture, which invented new traditions and constructed a usable history that would help activists bring the past to bear on the present. This women's culture offered feminists a safe refuge from which to express new artistic visions, compose new styles of music, explore new literary themes, and develop a feminist sense of humor. At its worst, it sometimes became an end in itself that led toward a hermetically sealed separatism that nurtured converts and excluded ordinary women from participation.[41]

During the first heady years of the movement, cultural events were often electrifying experiences. Imagine the following scene. It's 1970 in

Berkeley, California. Several hundred women have squeezed into a sti-
fling room for a feminist poetry reading. The poets take off their shirts,
some to cool off, some to protest a law that prohibits breast-feeding in
public, and some because it feels deliciously sexual. "Baring your
breast," recalled Susan Griffin, "was like saying this is not something
evil, I claim this. This is me, and that was enormously powerful."

Griffin never forgot "those amazing poetry readings. Each person
would go up and read and the audience would go wild, laugh, and
scream and yell." Provocative, sensual, thoughtful, serious, angry,
snide, funny, a new poetic sensibility was emerging. Susan Griffin re-
memberered moving to a podium, bare-breasted, to read, "An Answer to
a Man's Question, 'What Can I Do About Women's Liberation?' " The
crowd greeted the title with howls of laughter and the poem itself
brought down the house.[42]

An Answer to a Man's Question, "What Can I Do About Women's Liberation?"

Wear a dress.
*Wear a dress that you made yourself, or bought in a dress
        store.*
*Wear a dress and underneath the dress wear elastic, around
        your hips, and underneath your nipples.*
*Wear a dress and underneath the dress wear a sanitary
        napkin.*
Wear a dress and wear sling-back, high-heeled shoes.
*Wear a dress, with elastic and a sanitary napkin underneath,
and sling-back shoes on your feet, and walk down Telegraph
        Avenue.*
*Wear a dress, with elastic and a sanitary napkin and sling-
        back shoes on Telegraph Avenue and try to run.*

Find a man.
Find a nice man who you would like to ask you for a date.
Find a nice man who will ask you for a date.
Keep your dress on.
Ask the nice man who asks you for a date to come to dinner.
*Cook the nice man a nice dinner so the dinner is ready before
        he comes and your dress is nice and clean and wear a
        smile.*

> *Tell the nice man you're a virgin, or you don't have birth*
>   *control, or you would like to get to know him better.*
> *Keep your dress on.*
> *Go to the movies by yourself.*
>
> *Find a job.*
> *Iron your dress.*
> *Wear your ironed dress and promise the boss you won't get*
>   *pregnant (which in your case is predictable) and that you*
>   *like to type, and be sincere and wear your smile.*
> *Find a job or get on welfare.*
> *Borrow a child and get on welfare.*
> *Borrow a child and stay in the house all day with the child,*
>   *or go to the public park with the child, and take the child*
>   *to the welfare office and cry and say your man left you and*
>   *be humble and wear your dress and your smile and don't*
>   *talk back, keep your dress on, cook more nice dinners, stay*
>   *away from Telegraph Avenue and still, you won't know the*
>   *half of it, not in a million years.*[43]

In "that chick is SO REVOLUTIONARY," the Berkeley poet Alta, who also founded the Shameless Hussy Press in order to publish women's poetry, satirized middle-class feminists who could not begin to grasp the realities of her life as a mother alone caring for two children, in a working-class suburban tract home:

> *Poem*
> *that chick is SO REVOLUTIONARY*
> *she dresses poor on purpose.*
> *She eschews the boozhwa comforts like*
> *washing machines, male lovers, &*
> *flush toilets. I mean she is*
> *EVERY KIND of revolutionary!*
> *She'd bum off her friends before she'd work*
> *in a counter-revolutionary government job!*
> *(How come she can afford to be so revolutionary?)*
> *I mean, this chick is SO REVOLUTIONARY,*
> *she laughs at housewives, agrees that*
> *we're an inferior breed.*
> *She would never have a kid if she could have*

an abortion instead. Get it? This chick is
SELF FULFILLED!
super chick ta daa!
Even her period glows in the dark.[44]

Admittedly, feminists were not known for their humor. Although the media invariably depicted them as dour and humorless women, I am hardly alone in my memories of meetings filled with uproarious laughter and aching belly laughs. The reason for the discrepancy is that American feminists *were* rather humorless—in public. Fighting for institutional and cultural change required determination; excavating sexual crimes called for convincing debate; ignoring gratuitous insults required the patience of a saint. Rape and domestic violence weren't funny, nor was sexual harassment. Male jokes about feminist goals only deepened activists' anger.

Within the movement, though, feminists were refreshingly goofy, silly, witty, and sarcastic, reframing the normal as bizarre, playing with role reversal, satire, and parody. As the poet Maya Angelou quipped, "There are those moments when the 'new woman' confronts the 'old man' and the result can be as comic as Charlie Chaplin on the run or Lucille Ball on the loose."[45] In fact, much of humor appeared as sardonic commentary and functioned as consciousness-raising.[46]

Parody was often the humor of choice. For the August 26, 1970, national "strike," the New York chapter of NOW published a mock version of the *New York Times*. On the first page appeared a new feminist motto: "All the News That Would Give the Times Fits." A front-page article described a protest led by 500,000 radical masculinists protesting "female chauvinism" in the nation's capital. The piece lampooned the male lament that they, too, were oppressed by sex roles. "While we almost monopolize the top employment levels and earn far more money as a group than women," one masculinist complained, "we control less than a third of the nation's buying power. We are the castrated consumers of America."

The parody issue also included an outlandish fashion satire, "Men in a Tizzy over Cuff Length," and a wicked spoof on the *Times*'s typical marriage announcement, "Sec'y of State Weds James R. Buckingham." "Mr. and Mrs. Theresa Buckingham," it began,

announce the marriage of their son, James Leslie, to Anne Strongen Sharpe, the Secretary of State. Mr. Sharpe's mother is the well-known heart surgeon and his grandmother, Della Buckingham, ran for the Presidency in 1920, but did not live to see the election. Mr. Sharpe, a graduate of the Deadbriar Finishing School, made his debut in 1965 at the Honeysuckle Cotillion. He attended Yale, Harvard, Radcliffe, and participated in the Junior Year Aboard program in Liechtenstein, where he learned to make dumplings.

The announcement ended with a description of the bridegroom's attire—"a simple black Cardin suit with an Edwardian shirt of Alençon lace dotted with seed pearls"—followed by the statement that "it was Ms. Sharpe's draft of the Vietnam Peace Treaty that was finally accepted." A picture of a smiling, somewhat daft bridegroom, identified as "Mr. Anne Strongen Sharpe, the former James Leslie Buckingham," accompanied the announcement.

Other articles in the issue described feminist successes in redrawing society's priorities, a kind of feminist wish list: The Senate had just passed a National Priorities Bill, providing $300 billion for U.S. domestic programs; city "unplanners" won the struggle to redesign the skyline and create a more beautiful environment; a court ruling had just decriminalized prostitution; the new universal day care centers produced happier and healthier children; the Supreme Court, led by Chief Justice Diana Ross, had crucified the KKK; and, finally, the chiefs of state (all women) of various nations meeting in Paris had settled, in one hour, the terms of the peace treaties for the Vietnam and the Arab-Israeli conflicts.[47]

Similarly, the first issue of *Ms.* magazine featured Judy Syfers's "Why I Want a Wife," which began with this plea:

I want a wife who will take care of *my* physical needs. I want a wife who will keep my house clean. A wife who will pick up after me. I want a wife who will keep my clothes clean, ironed, mended, and who will see to it that my personal things are kept in their proper place so that I can find what I need the minute I need it. I want a wife who cooks the meals, a wife who is a good cook. I want a wife who will plan the menus, does the necessary grocery shopping, prepares the meals, serves them pleasantly, and then does the cleaning up while I do my studying . . .

and ended with these words: "My God, who *wouldn't* want a wife?"[48] An instant classic, "Why I Want a Wife," created a sensation when first published; it encouraged women to grasp the injustice of anyone working as an unpaid servant for another person.

In "The Politics of Housework," Pat Mainardi used humor to analyze one of the most private forms of exploitation, the excuses men habitually used to avoid housework. Mainardi offered translations for some of these familiar excuses. For example, when a man said, *"I don't mind sharing the work, but you'll have to show me how to do it,"* Mainardi offered this translation: *"I ask a lot of questions and you'll have to show me everything I do because I don't remember so good. Also don't try to sit down and read while I'm doing my jobs because I'm going to annoy the hell out of you until it's easier to do them yourself."*[49]

In her well-known essay "If Men Could Menstruate," Gloria Steinem offered a send-up of men's sense of entitlement and privilege. "What would happen," she coyly asked, "if suddenly, magically, men could menstruate and women could not?"

> Clearly, menstruation would become an enviable, boast-worthy, masculine event:
>
> Men would brag about how long and how much.
>
> Young boys would talk about it as the envied beginning of manhood. Gifts, religious ceremonies, family dinners, and stag parties would mark the day.
>
> To prevent monthly work loss among the powerful, Congress would fund a National Institute of Dysmenorrhea. Doctors would research little about heart attacks, from which men were hormonally protected, but everything about cramps.
>
> Sanitary supplies would be federally funded and free. . . .
>
> Generals, right-wing politicians, and religious fundamentalists would cite menstruation ("*men*-struation") as proof that only men could serve God and country in combat ("You have to give blood to take blood"). . . .
>
> Street guys would invent slang ("He's a three-pad man") and "give fives" on the corner with some exchange like, "Man, you looking *good!*" "Yea, man, I'm on the rag!" . . .

Menopause would be celebrated as a positive event, the symbol that men had accumulated enough years of cyclical
wisdom.

Men would convince women that it was *More* pleasurable at
"that time of the month.". . . .[50]

Not surprisingly, given that rock 'n' roll had set a generation in motion (even when written, played, and sung largely by men), and that folk
and gospel had given expression to every aspect of the civil rights and
antiwar movements, music also drew feminists together. At first, some
women simply wrote new lyrics to old movement and folk melodies.
Laura X even published an early *Women's Songbook*. But soon women
were dancing, marching, relaxing to music, bands, lyrics that were
purely from women.

In Chicago, for instance, Naomi Weisstein decided to start a Women's
Liberation rock band:

I was lying on the sofa listening to the radio—a rare bit of
free time in those early hectic days of the women's movement. . . . Mick Jagger crowed that his once feisty girlfriend
was now "under his thumb." Then Janis Joplin moaned with
the thrilled resignation that love was like "a ball and chain."
I somersaulted off the sofa, leapt into the air, and came down
howling at the radio. Rock is considered the insurgent culture
of the era. How criminal to make the subjugation and slug-
ging of women so sexy! We've got to do something about this!
We'll organize our own rock band.[51]

Whenever the Women's Liberation Rock and Roll Band played, as
Weisstein recalled, "women's response to the music was to take off their
shirts and dance bare-breasted. . . . One of the things that it made me
realize is the restraint of our bodies and repression of our sexuality—
the rebellion against this was a very deep aspect of our movement."[52]

By the mid-seventies, Holly Near, Chris Williams, Margie Adams,
Sweet Honey in the Rock, and dozens of other talented singers and musical groups had created a new genre of "women's music" that accompanied every women's dance, rally, and party. In the privacy of living
rooms, groups of women—sometimes gay and straight together—

swayed or rocked to this music. The words mattered. At large concerts, when Holly Near performed, thousands of women would sing along, the lyrics second nature to them. Near, an activist with the kind of powerful, clear voice often heard in American musicals, initially wrote songs that protested the Vietnam War, the torture of Latin American activists, or celebrated her childhood in rural Northern California. In the late seventies, she "came out" with an album whose title, *Imagine My Surprise*, expressed her astonishment at falling in love with a woman. Sweet Honey in the Rock, a group started by Bernice Johnson Reagon, a former civil rights activist in SNCC, combined the magisterial power of gospel with the edgy beat of rock. It didn't take long before they became the most popular and successful group on the women's music scene.

No aspect of culture remained untouched by feminist perspectives and challenges. By the 1970s, feminist fine artists began to knock on the doors of museums that had previously excluded them and guerrilla arts groups launched imaginative acts of protest against the male art scene. At the same time, feminist art historians began to discover talented painters and sculptors who had long been ignored or forgotten. Not surprisingly, feminists disagreed over what constituted "women's art." Should women artists struggle to be integrated into the mainstream culture or ought they to have their own shows? Did something called "women's art" really exist? In the end, it probably didn't matter. The energy lay in the arguments, not in the answers.[53]

Imagine, if you can, a Sunday-morning brunch held in the living room of a modest home in Berkeley in 1971. The featured guests are Judy Chicago, the auteur of the *Dinner Party* (an elaborate artistic installation that featured a long dinner table, exquisitely hand-sewn linens, and handcrafted sexualized ceramic dinner settings that honored individual women from the past), and Anaïs Nin (the writer whose intimate diaries about her bohemian life in the 1920s captured the imagination of a generation of women). Chicago proudly shows her newest work, a print of a woman pulling a used Tampax out of her vagina. Nin is appalled. Wrapped in an elegant black cape and dress, she recoils from what she describes as "vulgar art." Soon they retreat to the kitchen, shouting and arguing, while the guests take up the debate in the living room. Do women, should women, choose different themes than men? Not surprisingly—and to the relief of many—the assembled group can reach no consensus. The truth is, none of them wants a minister of culture who will dictate the acceptable parameters of women's art.[54]

If women were finally breaking the high arts barriers, no area of graphic expression proved livelier than poster art. Though white middle-class writers filled their novels with the travail of women like themselves, poster artists, many of whom were from the same background, seemed unwilling to portray themselves at all. A famed exception was the "Fuck Housework" poster, in which a white woman, dressed like a witch, breaking a broom in half, stared out at the viewer with a sly Mona Lisa smile.

What then did feminist poster art convey? Emerging from poster collectives in the late 1960s, feminist poster art initially focused almost exclusively on the oppression of minority women or working-class women. Much of the initial burst of poster art in the women's movement grew out of poster collectives that supported campus strikes for black or Third World studies departments or Third World liberation movements. Eager to combine their Left and feminist commitments, women graphic artists rarely if ever depicted white women. In this way, they could maintain their political credibility and legitimacy as leftists, while publicizing the particular problems faced by women.[55] As Jane Norling, a talented muralist and poster artist, later explained:

> We wanted to identify as women, but not as white women, and
> were drawn to create images of women in Vietnam, Africa,
> Latin America. I was moved by images of working-class
> women such as textile workers, women of mining families, or
> agricultural workers. Middle- and upper-middle-class women
> didn't look like they needed "change." Who wanted to iden-
> tify oneself with that? We were thrilled at the images of Viet-
> namese women fighting in the trenches. The images of third
> world women were more glamorous in their "otherness." . . .
> Art for social change MEANT picturing nonwhite people.[56]

The movement needed heroines and a usable history and posters could provide both, *and* depict white women, as long as they belonged safely to the past. One early poster simply declared, "Our History has been Stolen from US." The past conferred legitimacy on the present. Posters of bold and courageous women—Amelia Earhart, Susan B. Anthony, Elizabeth Cady Stanton, Sojourner Truth, the Pankhurst sisters, Mary Wollstonecraft, Rosa Luxemburg, Lucy Stone, Harriet Tubman, Emma Goldman, Agnes Smedley, and Eleanor Roosevelt—introduced feminists to forgotten activists and rebels. One of the more popular posters featured a portrait of the suffragist Lucy Stone, along with her famous words: "In education, in marriage, in religion, in everything, disappointment is the lot of women. It shall be the business of my life to deepen this disappointment in every woman's heart until she bows down to it no longer" (1855).[57]

Feminist poster artists routinely recycled images from the past in order to inspire action in the present. On one poster, an image from 1907 showed an exhausted woman worker bent over a sewing machine, her baby at her breast. Next to it was a picture of a modern poor and harried mother in 1976. Underneath, the caption read: "$acred Motherhood." Another poster reproduced a picture of striking women at the textile mills in Lawrence, Massachusetts, in 1912. Underneath this image were the words "8 hours a day, abolish child labor." Next to it was a photograph of working women in 1972, with the caption "Free Abortion, child care, equal pay." The message couldn't be clearer; if they could win their goals, so could we.

From the late seventies on, some feminist poster artists began replacing figurative or photographic images of heroines and Third World women with a new celebratory style that drew on mythic images to promote the developing world of feminist cultural activities—art shows, music festivals, dances, and summer camps. Posters still promoted the needs of women of color, and advertised social services like rape or battered women's hot lines. But the trend was not to dwell on obstacles, but rather to celebrate female strength and spirituality. In one poster, "Woman is Rising," a stylized female figure typically emerged from the luminous edge of a moon. In another, women's bodies merged with ancient Celtic designs from an era when, it was believed, women had greater influence in society.

By the end of the 1980s, you couldn't go into a college, to a health clinic, or to a federal building without seeing posters that educated, cajoled, and challenged women's unexamined assumptions about what they deserved. Posters advertised International Women's Day; taught women that sexual harassment was illegal; helped legitimize lesbian relationships; and publicized the courage and strength of women from the past. Posters could be didactic, rageful, hilarious, zany, sarcastic, or celebratory. But like the women's movement itself, they revealed rather than obscured, and honored rather than ridiculed, the reality and diversity of women's lives.

Chapter Seven

❧

THE POLITICS OF PARANOIA

In 1976, Jean Curtis wrote a provocative article in the *New York Times Magazine*, titled "When Sisterhood Turns Sour." Curtis admitted that she felt great *Schadenfreude*—joy at another person's unhappiness—when other women fell on their faces. "When a woman has written a bad book and gotten panned for it, I'm delighted. I'm almost as pleased when a woman has written a stupid review and is certain to be criticized for it." For her, she admitted, the early camaraderie of the women's movement was gone and older feelings of competition were returning.[1]

Beneath the proclamation of sisterhood, women injured one another deeply. In movement circles, some called it "trashing" or even "psychological terrorism." No one has ever described or explained this destructive behavior better than Jo Freeman, who during the first years of the movement wrote under the name Joreen. In a classic essay, "The Tyranny of Structurelessness," Freeman observed how the movement's unwillingness to elect officials, and its tendency to reject emerging talented writers and orators, gave the media complete freedom to anoint their own "leaders." It also created a vacuum in which any woman could promote herself as a leader. Such women were accountable to no one except themselves. Fearful of structure and formal officials, the movement ended up with "leaders" who had the loudest voice, the flashiest public style, or the most time to stay at meetings. "Contrary to what we would like to believe," she wrote,

> there is no such thing as a structureless group. . . . For everyone to have the opportunity to be involved in a given group

and to participate in its activities the structure must be explicit, not implicit. The rules of decision-making must be open and available to everyone, and this can happen only if they are formalized.[2]

Freeman described "trashing" as

a particularly vicious form of character assassination. It is manipulative, dishonest, and excessive. It is occasionally distinguished by the rhetoric of honest conflict, or covered up by denying that any disapproval exists at all. But it is not done to expose disagreement or to resolve differences. It is done to disparage and destroy.

Feminists used trashing to punish women who seemed too concerned with individual achievement, or too eager to grab the spotlight. The punishment was heavy criticism, even ostracism. Accusations and rejection might be based on political differences or personality clashes. But some activists felt such intense jealousy and competition that these feelings could only be assuaged by tearing apart another woman's credibility. As Vivian Rothstein, an early founder of Chicago Women's Liberation Union, put it, "Many of us were damaged people. How could we not have created a damaged movement?"[3]

Whenever I asked former activists about their darkest moments in the women's movement, tears often preceded words. The wounds had never healed; the scars had never disappeared. Only through the language of romance is it possible to describe how trashing devastated feminists. Talented women fell in love with a movement that seemed to grant them a legitimacy they had never felt, gave them a voice, and welcomed their presence. Then, as one feminist put it, "like a lover who abruptly walks out on you and never tells you why, the movement rejected your talents, ordered you to cease speaking, told you to stop writing and to become invisible again."[4] The women who experienced such rejection often compared it to the searing pain of unrequited love.

Trashing emerged within a particular historical context. For sixties activists, the idea of elections or of hierarchies of any kind smacked of "reformist" organizations, not a movement set on turning society upside down and inside out. Having roundly criticized the elitist leadership of New Left men, these women had vowed to act differently. They were going to create a truly democratic, egalitarian, and participatory movement. Distrust of expertise and talent—a central tenet of the Chinese Cultural Revolution, then little understood but much admired by some young feminist activists—deepened an existing rejection of authority and leadership. If Chinese professors could clean university toilets (widely publicized at the time), then feminist leaders, too, could do their share of what was commonly called "the shit work."

Fear of leadership and of hierarchy—that is, fear of domination and subjugation—sometimes produced political paralysis. Meredith Tax recalled that when her Boston group began mushrooming into Bread and Roses, "All we did was argue about whether or not we should have an organization. People were so frightened of taking any leadership role and of being trashed for being elitist." Some of the women felt, to her surprise, that the group should not be open to new women. They feared that "we would become leaders and we would be bound to oppress other women. And I said, 'How would we be oppressing women if we decided to have a women's movement?' "

> We had no strategy. Our feminist political culture got us into a box we couldn't think ourselves out of. . . . We said revolution meant the transfer of power . . . but we were terrified of power. To us power meant oppression; we knew what it felt like to be the object of other people's power and we couldn't stand the thought of acting like bosses or fathers and being hated. . . . Our organizations lasted five minutes. We didn't know how to keep them going, partly because no one would take long-term responsibility to keep things together. People fought to avoid power, not to get it. They didn't have the time or money to be leaders, or the social support. Or maybe the guts. It's not easy to be a leader in a movement that hates leaders.[5]

The personal often became *too* political. Some activists began to scrutinize women's private lives, bedmates, and career choices. Some feminists felt threatened by women who did not act, look, or think like themselves. The belief that activists should "live" their politics, as though a feminist revolution had already taken place, created some of the darkest moments the movement would ever experience. Barbara Haber watched as empathy turned into judgmentalism in her group. "I remember at one point there was this very aggressive conversation going on about why anyone would get married and I said, very naïvely, that I wanted emotional security, and I got really trashed." Accustomed as she was to questioning received wisdom, Haber felt "when it came to the core of my life and my desire to be a married woman, I didn't want that touched."[6]

Along with rage and exhilaration came the guilt of never being sufficiently radical. "Guilt-tripping" was the means by which trashing took place. Women made other activists feel guilty for having married, borne children, or prepared for a professional career. Some women grew fearful of wearing fashionable clothing, using makeup, or shaving their body hair. As one feminist quipped two decades later, "In 1970, it was less shameful to have venereal disease than to wear eye shadow." Some heterosexual women, fearing such criticism, refrained from cuddling their men or children in public. Responding to lesbian-feminist vanguardism in the movement, some married women became almost apologetic for their lives as mothers and wives. Some movement activists, for instance, trashed Robin Morgan for being a wife and a mother. "I had a male child and had kept him. I couldn't figure out whether I was supposed to put him in a garbage can or what I was supposed to do, but I felt guilty about that, too."[7]

Class-baiting was another popular form of attacking other women. Many members of women's liberation, who had grown up in middle-class homes or gained middle-class status through their educations, felt perfectly free to trash anyone who had grown up in a more privileged family or who dressed in conventional middle-class outfits. At one of the earliest women's liberation conferences, Cindy Cisler, who had worked tirelessly for abortion rights throughout the sixties, felt embarrassed to admit that she had gone to the best universities. Half a decade older than most liberationists, she also felt harshly judged for her "grown-up lady" clothes. "I didn't have Mississippi Summer blue denim jumpers or anything like that. I didn't get a pair of slacks until 1971." People also "criticized the indomitable Flo Kennedy for wearing eight-foot eyelashes. The truth is, people were slightly obsessed with the correct cultural politics."[8]

Cindy Cisler felt unfairly attacked. "I was the perfect target because I had the effrontery to work with a man, the effrontery to be straight, to work on these tiresome, tedious women's issues." Cisler received letters from women who didn't even know her, accusing her of having too much money. "There was a tremendous effort expended to trash me and destroy and crush me, and it basically worked."[9]

Some women hurled the accusation of "elitism" at other feminists. To be an elitist meant you thought yourself superior to others—which quickly destroyed your reputation. Marilyn Webb, who had gained experience as a journalist and speaker before she helped organize the women's movement, was dogged by accusations of elitism whatever she did. "Somebody from a Washington paper called me up and asked me for a quote, and I ended up on television . . . and people were furious, because we had been having this whole thing about stars and they kicked me out of the Magic Quilt [a Washington, D.C., group]. They said I had to leave women's liberation. I was really shocked . . . they went around the room and it was like a witch hunt."[10]

Trashing occurred in part because many feminists had unrealistic expectations of the movement's capacity to fulfill their deepest needs. "From saying men are my best friends," confided one woman,

> it flipped to the opposite, which is "all women are wonderful" and I remember being badly hurt by a woman I thought was marvelous and I thought was my best friend. . . . Lots of us had tremendously deep bonds, because we had done so much work together. But that was not necessarily the basis for long-term friendships. Sisterhood was not all that it was cracked up to be.

Phyllis Chesler, the author of *Women and Madness*, later wrote, "I expected so much of other feminists—we all did—that the most ordinary disappointments were often experienced as major betrayals. We expected less of men and forgave them, more than once, when they failed us. We expected far more of other women, who paradoxically had less (power) to share than men did. We held grudges against women in ways we dared not do against men."[11]

Some feminists trashed other women for committing themselves to an intellectual life. Too many young movement activists viewed writing and thinking as "male-identified" behavior. Using one's mind, no less preparing for a life of the mind, turned you into an instant "sellout," even if your goal was to excavate women's history, create a women's health clinic, or support women prisoners. Barbara Haber encountered such an anti-intellectual atmosphere in Boston. "Having [an academic career] was just plain individualistic—not properly collective," she recalled. "There was a lot that said it's not okay to strive for the rewards that society gives you. It's definitely not okay to be academic. I bought into that and it took me a long time to undo the damage."[12]

To stand out in any way was to risk being attacked. Fear of feminist "stars" shadowed the movement for years. Looking back, Naomi Weisstein felt that "the kind of radical egalitarianism which doesn't let each member of a group use her gift in the service of the movement is simply destructive. The implications of that distrust of stars was very damaging." Weisstein, a charismatic speaker who had helped create a speakers' bureau, agreed that different women should speak in public. But, over time, some members of Chicago Women's Liberation Union asked her not to speak so often, to which she agreed. Later, with much sadness, she realized that "the movement gave me my voice. Now please let me use it. Well, the decision was no."[13]

Not surprisingly, talented writers, artists, speakers, and professionals suffered the worst attacks, the most painful rejections. Weisstein, who was already a young scientist, had been an active New Leftist and had started a Women's Liberation Rock and Roll Band. At one point, she needed to leave the band for two months to write a grant application for her scientific research. The band members felt betrayed.

> And after that there was very heavy trashing of my motives and my politics and my heterosexuality. By that time the band had gone gay. So here was my movement telling me to get out of pig science; here was my band telling me to go gay; and here was the Left telling me I was a bourgeois feminist; and here were the feminists telling me that I was a Left serpent.[14]

"My feminist generation ate our leaders," wrote Phyllis Chesler. "Beheading of leaders was the name of the game in those days," recalled Ann Snitow. Trashing had "happened in the black movement and it had happened in the peace movement," recalled Susan Brownmiller, "but they didn't destroy their leaders quite the way we did." At the 1970 Congress to Unite Women, fear of stars grew so strong that "a resolution was read on the floor that Lucy Comisar and Susan Brownmiller [both writers] were seeking to rise to fame on the backs of the women's movement." "I yelled out," said Brownmiller, " 'that's my name you're saying there,' and kind of exploded a bit." When asked why feminists had attacked her so fiercely, Brownmiller suggested that her accusers saw "her as a media-anointed star and they felt that the media divides, that certain people are going to become successful. I think they were so shut out of success and had no idea of some normal ways that one might actually get to do what one wanted to do in life." On one occasion, some women from The Feminists demanded an explanation for her journalistic success: "They asked me if I slept with my editors." On another occasion, Brownmiller helped to organize a conference and invited Gloria Steinem and Bella Abzug in order to gain greater media coverage. When photographers asked for pictures, "Gloria and Bella pushed me in the middle of them and the *Times* took a lovely picture of the three of us, which was in the paper the next day." Then movement activists screamed at her, "You had no right to be there."[15]

Phyllis Chesler, whose contribution to the psychology of women had influenced the movement a great deal, also encountered the dark side of the women's movement. "Behind closed doors," she wrote, "we behaved toward women the way most women did: we envied, competed with, feared, and were ambivalent about other women; we also loved and needed them. . . ."

> I saw feminists steal each other's work, money, job, spouses, physically hit each other, padlock doors, turn other feminists into the police. I saw feminists either refuse to pay or grossly underpay their female employees, or "groupies," whom they sometimes also treated as if they were stupid, slaves or servants. . . . I saw feminists instigate whisper-and-smear campaigns to wreck each other's reputations, both socially and professionally.

Chesler also watched some feminists dropped from guest lists, even from the movement itself.

> Perhaps some thought she was too pretty, too angry, not the right color, or class, too outspoken, unpredictable, perhaps she slept with the wrong people, refused to sleep with the right person, or had chosen the wrong side. . . . As much as we longed for sisterhood, we only started the process and we failed at the task.[16]

One of the strangest consequences of such anti-elitism was that activists pressured one another to write without bylines. Writing anonymously had been required of modest ladies of the nineteenth century. Now, in the name of solidarity, some women's liberationists asked that no woman take credit for her words. In 1970, a fed-up Robin Morgan decided to leave the *Rat* alternative newspaper collective. "I had been told that I wrote too well and that people were buying the newspaper to read me and that all I could do was to take my name off the piece. So, of course, dutifully, I took my name off my writing."[17]

The novelist Alix Kates Shulman also feared being silenced by the movement. "The worst thing for me was what happened to writers. I had started writing half a year before I met the movement, and so I felt I had to write." She thought she might be accused of "ripping off" the movement, which in those years meant using the movement for one's own career goals. Even more, she worried about the "snide remarks" she received about her writing

> because it was literary [rather than polemical]. That was elit-
> ist. That was even worse than ripping off the movement. I
> didn't want to be elitist, but I was going to write. That was for
> me the worst. I always felt as if at any moment I could be
> kicked out. I know this is extraordinary because I couldn't
> have been. And yet, whenever the question of spies came up,
> I would think they must mean me because I was married and
> had children.[18]

Erica Jong, having written a novel about a woman's passion for sex and independence, found herself described by some feminists as an opportunist. Looking back at how she suffered in those years, she wrote:

> You got the feeling that unless you had the trappings of radi-
> cal lesbianism about you, you would be shunned. And trap-
> pings there were. There was a style prevalent then in which
> you were expected to *look* like you'd stepped right off the
> commune. Lipstick and eyeshadow were not only counter-
> revolutionary, they would be mentioned in reviews of your
> books.

At one festival, women "hooted and booed" as Erica Jong read poems about motherhood, "though many of them had children in their arms. At the time, I was devastated. The criticism by women hurt far more than criticism by men."[19] Later, Jong wrote about her sympathy for the many mothers and wives who wanted to be involved with organized feminism but had encountered "the same kind of painful rejection I had experienced."

She understood this punitive attitude in generational terms and referred to second-wave feminists as the "whiplash generation."

> Brought up in the fifties, they whipped into the sixties with little preparation. How could our generation suddenly forswear the values with which it had been raised? It couldn't. So some of us became extremist, as all frightened people do. As usual in revolutions, the zealots drove out the moderates. And the haters of feminism exploited the split for their own end. Thus, a whole generation of daughters grew up turned off by the word "feminist."[20]

Perhaps no one suffered greater public trashing than Gloria Steinem. In May 1975, a newly constituted Redstockings in New York City, led by such early and important leaders as Carol Hanisch and Kathie Sarachild, issued a statement in which they publicly accused Steinem of having worked for the CIA—in the past, as well as in the present. They wrote that she was, in fact, a government spy or informer in their midst who had redirected the course of the movement toward moderation and capitulation.

The truth was quite a bit more complicated. During the late fifties and early sixties, Steinem helped found the Independent Research Service, a foundation set up in Cambridge, Massachusetts, which recruited American students to attend Communist-sponsored international youth festivals in order to proselytize the superior American way of life. Sponsored by the World Federation of Democratic Youth, the hope was to cultivate personal relationships with the youth of all nations. The CIA both funded and recruited many of the delegates. Steinem attended two International Communist Youth Festivals in 1959 and 1962.

Like many liberal young women of her generation, Steinem viewed the effort of "building bridges, deepening understanding, and identifying similar concerns among the world's youth" as important work. In the absence of organizations like SNCC or SDS, liberal students viewed these activities as an opportunity to enhance world peace. At the time, Steinem knew that the Independent Research Service was at least partly funded through the CIA and their various conduits. She perhaps believed that the CIA did so to help prevent wars, not as part of a systematic effort to contain and subvert Communism. In fact, still in the waning penumbra of McCarthyism, she at first worried more that the funding might secretly be coming from Communist-front organizations.

This, of course, was the fifties, when the CIA was still honored for protecting Americans from Communism. Few liberal students at that time knew about funding by the CIA. By the seventies, the very letters CIA dredged up images of assassinations, coups d'états, dirty tricks abroad, infiltration of radical organizations and surveillance of ordinary citizens at home. When the Redstockings issued their accusations, they also charged Steinem with using *Ms.* magazine to collect information on feminist activities in her ongoing work for the CIA. In fact, the magazine had resisted all such attempts, including an FBI request to use its subscriber list in a search for female fugitives.[21]

Steinem wasn't sure how to respond to these charges, though they were hardly new. In 1967, *Ramparts* magazine had exposed how the CIA had funneled its money secretly through foundations to the National Student Association. At the time, Steinem said she approved of the CIA effort in this operation because it was the work of liberals "who were far-sighted and cared enough to get Americans of all political views to the Festival." But that hardly meant that she had infiltrated the women's movement for the CIA a decade later. Since the mainstream press had not yet picked up the Redstocking story, friends advised her in 1975 not to dignify their accusations and just to let the matter drop. But that turned out to be impossible, in part because Betty Friedan seized upon these accusations, discussing them with reporters from New York City's *Daily News* and the wire service United Press International at the UN International Women's Year World Conference in Mexico City in 1975. Linked to Friedan's name, the story now spread swiftly though the mainstream media. Friedan compounded Steinem's difficulties by demanding that she "react" to the charges and by implying that a "paralysis of leadership" in the women's movement "could be due to the CIA."[22]

For both the Redstockings and Friedan to accuse Steinem was a profoundly disturbing matter. Still, Steinem didn't respond, fearing that people would only remember the charges and not her answers. All summer, Steinem brooded and agonized. After three months, she wrote a six-page letter and released it exclusively to feminist publications. But the mainstream press, excited by a feminist scandal, now picked it up, as she had feared, and amplified the accusation as it flew though the nation's news services and newspapers. In her letter, Steinem pointed out that the Redstockings had made no new discoveries, that she had revealed years before that her work in youth groups was partly funded by the CIA. She also systematically refuted the charge that she had ever been a full-time employee who worked for the CIA or any other government security agency. "I will repeat the facts one more time," Steinem wrote. "I worked on two of the World Festivals of Youth and Students for Peace and Freedom (to give them their proper name), held sixteen and thirteen years ago in Vienna and Helsinki, at which some of the American participation was partially funded by foundations that were in turn funded by the CIA. . . . I naively thought then that the ultimate money source didn't matter, since in my own experience, no control or orders came with it. (It's painfully clear with hindsight that even indirect, control-free funding was a mistake if it couldn't be published, but I didn't realize that then.)"[23]

There the story would perhaps have ended had not Betty Friedan seemed determined to keep it alive. On television programs, she would announce that she refused to discuss Steinem and the CIA connection and then proceeded to do so, even if just by implication. She never directly charged Steinem with anything, but clearly she did not want the American public to forget the accusation. In *It Changed My Life*, her next book published in 1976, Friedan again raised the CIA issue. Perhaps unwilling to share the feminist stage with any other leader, Friedan blamed the defeat of the Equal Rights Amendment by various state legislatures on "extremist groups," like *Ms.* magazine. She also used innuendo to tarnish the reputations of both Bella Abzug and Gloria Steinem. In a review of Friedan's book on July 4, 1976, in the *New York Times Book Review*, Stephanie Harrington wrote, "This is heady stuff. . . . Is she saying Steinem and/or Abzug have CIA and FBI connections? If so, why doesn't she say so plainly?"[24]

Why did both Friedan and the Redstockings—embracing such different politics—attack Steinem? One answer is that the relationship between the CIA and youth organizations still remained very murky. They could confidently smear Steinem precisely because so little was known. In the aftermath of the *Ramparts* exposé, there was, according to political scientist Karen Paget, "a 'deal' made between the National Student Association leaders and the CIA. Knowledgeable NSA officials and the agency agreed to confirm the relationship but to provide no details." Both Friedan and the Redstockings also seemed motivated by their ardent belief that FBI-paid lesbians and *Ms.* magazine, even if evidence was not at hand, had somehow conspired to take over *their* movement.

In Friedan's case, her obsession with Steinem also seemed driven by rivalry. She undoubtedly felt upstaged. She had ignited the American women's movement. She had named resentments that had been invisible. It must have pained her to watch the media cast her rival as a leader. Like Cinderella's older sister, Friedan had to watch as the media lavished attention on the telegenic Steinem. And she may have found it more than she could bear. "I was no match for [Steinem]," she wrote with some bitterness, "not only because of the matter of looks—which somehow paralyzed me—but because I don't know how to manipulate, or deal with manipulation myself"—an assertion that many feminists found odd and without much credibility.[25]

The Redstockings, for their part, believed that a CIA-funded conspiracy of lesbians and liberals had taken over *their* radical movement. Kathie Sarachild had long accused *Ms.* magazine (along with *Newsweek*, the *Washington Post*, Katharine Graham, and several well-known authors) of working to eliminate the real voice of radical feminism. Steinem, using the slick magazine she founded, had turned herself into a star. Sarachild and Hanisch felt that they had never received proper appreciation and recognition for their work. And they were right. Hanisch had coined the slogan "The personal is political," and Sarachild had "invented" the idea of "consciousness-raising," and promoted the idea of the small group as a way to create a new kind of movement. Yet they were not household names. In addition, Sarachild was perhaps miffed that *Ms.* had offered her an advance to write a book on consciousness-raising and then had decided to publish its own anthology on the subject. Although *Ms.* allowed her to keep the advance, Sarachild may have felt betrayed.

In the view of Sarachild, Hanisch, and Friedan, distinctive if very different leaders whose originality shaped the first decade of the movement, Steinem didn't deserve to be viewed as a leader. Yet, with her good looks, intelligent journalism, and successful magazine, she seemed suspiciously effective in mobilizing women around feminist causes. Nonetheless, to call Steinem a tool of the CIA, as biographer Carolyn Heilbrun has pointed out, was a "terrible accusation indeed. The Redstockings made a very clever move against a woman they perceived as having usurped their movement and the celebrity owed them." After years of careful research on Steinem's life, Heilbrun found the accusations to be "without substance and often ridiculous" and concluded that "there is simply no evidence to substantiate the Redstockings' reckless charges." Heilbrun eloquently summed up both what happened to Steinem and the more general phenomenon of trashing in the women's movement: "Just as men victimize the weak member of their group, women victimize the strong one. Why this is so is not entirely clear, but let us hope it disappears before the next wave of feminism crashes into women's lives."[26]

The movement only became more contentious as time went on. At a national women's studies meeting in the late 1970s, I sat stunned as every group created a caucus, and every caucus demanded to be heard. I saw Jewish, Islamic, Christian, Chicana, African-American, disabled, fat, and anorexic women, along with white lesbian feminists and Third World lesbian feminists, fight each other for visibility. As the day went on, I grew increasingly despondent. True, most of these women had recently discovered how much other women and men had silenced them. True, they desired legitimacy and acceptance—for their color, their sexual preference, their religion, their disabilities, or some combination of several of these. But victims were turning into heroines, while the idea of difference was becoming more seductive than solidarity. In the process, in one guise or another, women rather than men were becoming the new enemy.

All the makings of a paranoid movement, in which every group was dedicated to advancing a particular aspect of women's lives—religion, race, ethnicity, disability, appearance, and sexual orientation—were now in place. One could easily imagine that there were enemies out there, ready to take you down. All that was needed was a basis for that paranoia and that, in part, was provided by the FBI, along with other surveillance agencies. Soon, it became difficult to sort out paranoia from reality, imaginary enemies from perfectly real ones. And, to the best of our knowledge, the government did conspire, quite consciously, to heighten that atmosphere of fear.

THE FBI

Both feminists and the FBI suffered from legitimate fears as well as paranoia. Activists often imagined that agents were everywhere and that the FBI viewed the women's movement as a serious threat to "national security." But the truth, as always, was far more complicated. The women's movement *was* dangerous, but not in the way the FBI assumed, and FBI informants *were* everywhere, but they were not usually the most visible or obvious women.

Sometimes research ends up confirming your worst fears. The extent of FBI infiltration of movements of the sixties is by now well documented. Younger women in the New Left had firsthand acquaintance with the FBI's infiltration of civil rights groups, SDS, the Black Panther Party, the Native American Movement, the Yippies, and many other protest groups. They knew the Bureau's methods: create division and dissension. Spread false rumors about members. Plant bogus evidence to discredit leaders. Utilize agent provocateurs. Send false letters to intensify fear of infiltration. In an internal memo dated July 5, 1968, the FBI listed twelve suggestions for destroying the New Left. One was to take "advantage of personal conflicts or animosities existing between New Left leaders." Another suggestion was that agents should create "the impression that certain New Left leaders are informants for the Bureau or other law enforcement agencies." The memo also suggested that agents "consider the use of cartoons, photographs and anonymous letters which will have the effect of ridiculing the New Left. Ridicule is one of the most potent weapons which we can use against it." Above all, "whenever possible, agents and informers were to expose, disrupt, misdirect, discredit or otherwise neutralize specific individuals and groups."[27]

Through close coordination with local police—sometimes called Red Squads—as well as the press, universities, businesses, churches, and trade union officials, the FBI successfully cast suspicion on leaders and helped destroy their leadership and credibility. These young women also knew how FBI informers had pushed activists in the black power movement toward sectarian divisions and, in the case of the Black Panthers and other black nationalist groups, into deadly rivalries.

Older female activists—those who had been targeted as Communists or identified as labor organizers or members of Women Strike for Peace—were not at all surprised that the FBI would scrutinize their actions. During the fifties, the FBI had hounded these women, followed their children to school, interrogated their neighbors and coworkers, and often constituted nearly half the membership of some organizations.

Still, in my wildest flights of paranoia I never imagined the extent to which the FBI spied on feminists or how many women did the spying. We may never know the full extent of this infiltration, what damage it caused, or how it affected the trajectory of American feminism. Surprisingly, no significant examination of this secret has yet taken place.

Surveillance of the women's movement began as part of the Cointelpro program, an FBI domestic surveillance program begun in 1956. In 1968, J. Edgar Hoover redefined the Cointelpro mission: "It was to 'neutralize' the effectiveness of civil rights, New Left, antiwar and black liberation groups." Between 1968 and 1971, Cointelpro infiltrated both the New Left and the women's movement. Although the FBI did not *officially* employ women agents until after Hoover's death in 1972, its regional offices paid dozens—more likely hundreds—of female informants to infiltrate the women's movement. FBI director Hoover remained adamant that constant surveillance of the women's movement be maintained, in his words, for the "internal security of the nation." Some New Left activists, women as well as men, assumed that the FBI had decided to create a feminist movement as a wedge that would splinter the antiwar movement. Although the FBI certainly worked to exacerbate differences between existing movements and between factions within those movements, there is not much evidence—at least, not yet—that the Bureau spearheaded a campaign to create an autonomous women's movement.[28]

But that doesn't mean no one in the Bureau thought about this possibility. In a memo to the director in 1969, a special FBI agent in San Francisco wrote to Hoover, "The women's movement could be viewed as subversive to the entire younger New Left and revolutionary movement as they have proven to be a divisive and factionalizing factor. . . . It could well be recommended as a job for a counter-intelligence movement to weaken the revolutionary movement."[29] What Hoover did with this suggestion is not yet known.

Americans first heard about the Cointelpro program and learned something of its scope when a "Citizens Committee to Investigate the FBI" broke into the FBI office in Media, Pennsylvania, in March 1971, removed secret files, and subsequently leaked them to the press. Soon after Cointelpro was exposed, several agents resigned and blew the whistle on the agency's crimes against ordinary citizens. After Hoover's death in 1972, the agency issued a public apology and vowed to reform itself. In 1975, Senator Frank Church held congressional hearings that further exposed the program and confirmed some of the New Left's and women's movement's worst nightmares.[30]

The Church Committee interviewed FBI officials and agents who had orchestrated the infiltration of the women's movement—not only in Chicago, New York, and Berkeley, but in Kansas City, Columbus, Lawrence, Cleveland, Seattle, Gainesville, Florida, and dozens of other small towns and cities all over the country. Here is an excerpt of Senator Church's interrogation of James B. Adams, associate director of the FBI Intelligence Division, about the infiltration of the women's movement.

The Chairman: Now, the last few questions I would like to put to you, Mr. Adams, have to do with some confusion in my mind concerning the purpose of the FBI in monitoring the Women's Liberation Movement. What was the purpose of that surveillance? Why were you involved in monitoring that movement?

Mr. Adams: It was basically, as I recall, I have not reviewed the files, but from the information that I have acquired, it would indicate there were groups that were believed to be infiltrating and attempting to exert control over it.

The Chairman: But you never did find, did you, that the Women's Liberation Movement was seriously infiltrated, influenced or controlled by Communists?

Mr. Adams: No . . . It was a very independent group.

The Chairman: Well, we are trying to keep the country that way.

Mr. Adams: That's right. . . .

The Chairman: I call your attention to this ["Origins, Aims and Purposes," a description of the women's liberation movement in Baltimore, Maryland] because it seems to typify the whole problem of this generalized kind of surveillance over the activities of American citizens. Here is the report. If you read with me this paragraph:

The women's liberation movement in Baltimore Md. began during the summer of 1968. There was no structure or parent organization. There were no rules or plan to go by. It started out as a group therapy session with young women who were either lonely or confined to the home with small children, getting together to talk out their problems. Along with this they wanted a purpose and that was to be free women from the humdrum existence of being only a wife and mother. They wanted equal opportunities that men have in work and in society. They wanted their husbands to share in the housework and in raising their children. They also wanted to go out and work in what kind of jobs they wanted and not be discriminated [against] as women.

Now, can you find anything in that report that in any way suggests that these women were engaged in improper or unlawful
activity? . . . I think you would agree with me that women do have
the right to get together to talk about humdrum existence and
equal opportunities with men and equal opportunities for work in
society, don't they? That is not a subversive activity.

Mr. Adams: Well, but . . . interwoven with the Women's Liberation Movement goal for equal rights for women, there was an advocacy certainly of militancy and violence in achieving their goals.

The Chairman: I am told by the staff that . . . the only other
thing . . . was that those women had affiliation with an organization
that had protested the war in Baltimore.

Mr. Adams: I think there were some other items.

Mr. Chairman: That is the only other association that we have
been able to determine. Apparently the Women's Liberation Movement is no longer under suspicion by the FBI and the case
has been closed. What happens when the case is closed? Are
those women's names still left in the files? Are they forevermore
contained?

Mr. Adams: Yes.

The Chairman: In the system?

Mr. Adams: Yes.[31]

The FBI's view of the women's movement is summarized in a 1973 report listing the national women's newspaper *Off Our Backs* as "ARMED
AND DANGEROUS—EXTREME."[32]

Why did the FBI spend so many years infiltrating the women's movement? In the middle of the Cold War, Hoover never stopped looking for
Communists. The FBI believed, as did many activists, that the Socialist
Workers' Party was trying to infiltrate and influence the movement.
They therefore decided to infiltrate the infiltrator. Some of these women,
activists in the Left and antiwar movements, held support rallies for
black power groups, and even met with leaders and peace activists from
North Vietnam. Hoover also believed that any new movement, in the
midst of this explosive period, needed to be followed, understood, and
contained.

Who were the women who spied on other women? Their names are blackened out in the Bureau's files. But the Church Committee's documents and exhibits, while clearly sanitized, still provide a glimpse into the bizarre culture in which female informers reported to (male) field agents and to Hoover. From the New York regional office came this report to the director:

> On DELETED [19]69, informant DELETED who has furnished reliable information in the past, advised that a WLM meeting was held on DELETED at DELETED in New York City. Each woman at this meeting stated why she had come to the meeting and how she felt oppressed, sexually or otherwise. According to this informant, these women are mostly concerned with liberating women from this "oppressive society." They are mostly against marriage, children and other states of oppression caused by men. Few of them, according to the informant, have had political backgrounds. The informant states that a mailing list was passed around at the meeting. . . . On DELETED [19]69, informant advised that the WLM is only interested in changing abortion laws and birth control. They advocate free abortions for everyone and widespread information on birth control. According to the informant, women at the meeting on DELETED [19]69 state they are not revolutionaries and would not help anyone in a revolution until the oppression of women was solved first and completely.[33]

You'd think that such a tepid report would have ended further activity. But despite repeated reports that the women's movement posed no threat to national security, the FBI spent considerable resources to infiltrate feminist organizations. Regional offices recruited "volunteer" female informers, infiltrators, and observers. These informants sent back reports about radio interviews with local feminists, clipped stories that mentioned the names of feminists or protest activities in the mainstream and alternative press, joined feminist reading groups, and even sat through consciousness-raising groups. They collected flyers, the agendas and minutes of meetings, position papers, and conference programs. The FBI also targeted any "collective" that lived in a commune, created a community child care center, or helped set up or run a health clinic, all of which seemed suspiciously like Communist institutions.

A surprising number of regional field agents thought the FBI's scrutiny of the women's movement was unwarranted. In May 1969, the San Francisco Regional Office reported to the Bureau in Washington, D.C., that the women's liberation movement "was mainly concerned with male chauvinism and didn't seem to require any investigation." In April 1970, that office again reported that "the Women's Liberation Movement in the San Francisco area is a broad socio-political movement without any central direction or control from any organized group. It does not appear appropriate to conduct an investigation." The WLM appeared to have legitimate grievances and didn't seem to be involved in subversive activities. A few months later, the San Francisco office added, "In the view of this regional office, such surveillance was not warranted."[34]

FBI director Hoover snapped back:

> The Bureau does not concur with your recommendation that a report on WLM activities within your division is not warranted. ... Interwoven with its goals for equal rights for women is the advocation of violence to achieve these goals. The WLM has also demonstrated its readiness to support or accept support from other extremists or revolutionary-type organizations. ... SDS, BPP, SWP [Students for a Democratic Society, the Black Panther Party, the Socialist Workers' Party] ... WLM members have also established ties with their Canadian counterparts.
>
> In view of the above, it is absolutely essential that we conduct sufficient investigation to clearly establish the subversive ramifications of the WLM and to determine the potential for violence presented by the various groups connected with this movement as well as any possible threat they represent to the internal security of the United States.[35]

By 1972, the San Francisco office still had not uncovered any subversive activity. The field office reported that "Women's lib, as its partisans sometimes call it [actually, a derogatory term coined by the media] is an amoeba-like organism that reproduces by simple break-away." When the New York and Chicago offices also asked to be relieved of their surveillance of the women's movement, Hoover reminded all regional directors that members of the women's movement "should be viewed as part of the enemy, a challenge to American values." And so surveillance continued. From 1968 on, the New York office kept close tabs on the activities of women's groups, down to attendance at potluck dinners and the hiring of the buses that transported antiwar protesters to the Pentagon.[36]

Stuck with their assignments, FBI agents and their informers weren't sure how to infiltrate, let alone understand, the women's movement. In June 1969, Hoover sent the San Francisco field office this terse order: "San Francisco is instructed to identify the officers and the aims and objectives of this organization."[37] But they couldn't. As a Detroit informant explained, "This movement has no leaders, dues or organizations," which left FBI agents mystified. Nor could they make sense out of the names and references that were an everyday aspect of movement life. What did WITCH, Mother Jones, Molly Maguires, Anna Louise Strong, Keep on Truckin', Uppity Women, BITCH, and Redstockings stand for? Which ones were dangerous? How could any male agent—or female informant—begin to grasp the fine distinctions between radical lesbians, radicalesbians, lesbian feminists, political lesbians, liberal feminists, radical feminists, dykes, social feminists, feminist socialists, Marxist feminists and feminist Marxists? The politics of the women's movement flummoxed even the most experienced agents.

Trained to infiltrate highly structured and disciplined political organizations like the Communist Party, agents filed bizarre reports with Washington, sometimes filled with comic confusion. They spoke of "a reactionary group of women fighting for equal rights" or "a radical women's group which advocates complete equality for women." Since they didn't know the players, they wrote about "Case" Millett, not Kate Millett, discussed such "current" activists as the long-dead suffragist theorist Elizabeth "Katy" (actually Cady) Stanton, even the dead abolitionists "Grimshke sisters" (actually Grimké), reported on women's "roll" of submissiveness and activists' objection to "sexiest" practices, and worried about the influence of the Union of Soviet "Social" (actually Socialist) Republics and the activists who were "communistrically" inclined. Despite the search for Communists, none were discovered. One agent relayed an informant's matter-of-fact conclusion that "there is no information indicating that the National Organization of [for] Women (NOW) or the Women's International Terrorist Conspiracy from Hell (WITCH), a New York group, are Communist front organizations."[38]

Since they knew no women's history, FBI informers and agents sometimes searched for leaders who had died long ago, thinking them dangerous fugitives. An FBI informer described a women's liberation support rally for African-American Communist Party member Angela Davis, then fighting kidnapping and murder charges. The informer wrote that "no black women were present and the statement supporting Miss Davis was read by a quartet of members headed by Emma Willard" (a nineteenth-century educational reformer whose seminary was the first to include African-American students). We can only wonder how long the search for Emma Willard lasted.[39]

FBI reports almost always identified activists by marital status, class, race, and sexual preference. But they could never make sense of such a baffling and odd assortment of women. As *Ms.* editor Letty Pogrebin wrote, "The Panther women showed up with the housewives. Revolutionary firebrands appeared to be comfortably middle-class. High school hippies marched beside established professional women. . . . While women were worried about FBI informants tearing the Movement apart, the FBI was worried about radicals and mainstream women joining together."[40]

Women's appearance, predictably, interested FBI agents, partly because they were men, but also because they were searching for female fugitives. Informers, almost all of whom were women, dutifully padded their reports with endless descriptions of activists' attire:

> The women in general appeared to be hippies, lesbians, or from other far-out groups. Most of them were very colorfully dressed, but the majority wore faded blue jeans. Most seemed to be making a real attempt to be unattractive. . . . One of the interesting aspects about other delegates' dress was the extreme fuzzy appearance of their hair. . . . Some said this . . . was gotten by braiding and leaving it that way while it was wet until it dried. Then they would take out the braid. From the looks of their hair, they apparently really didn't bother to try and comb it out afterward.[41]

Since they had to submit regular reports, informers filled their dispatches with information on where members met, what they did, and when protests would take place. In New York, for instance, an informant reported on a group's grievances against men, as well as their discussions about lesbianism, child care, and abortion. In Baltimore, an

informer "exposed" the fact that the women's liberation movement had
held a dance. In Cleveland, an informant "revealed" that the women's
main issues seemed to be child care, abortion, and birth control. From
Nashville and Memphis came an informant's "exposure" of how Maoist
thought influenced women's communes; from New Orleans came the
"revelation" of what a study group, composed of mostly straight women,
had recently read.[42]

Informers also stuffed their reports with women's conversations. An
informant who infiltrated a small consciousness-raising group in Palo
Alto, California, reported on many of the group's discussions. A mother
of two boys, for instance, "feared she would lose her job if her connection with women's lib were revealed." Another member disclosed that
the group had enabled her to "see myself as part of a larger population
of women. My circumstances are not unique, but are due to the conditions of nuclear family life. I see that my frustration and self-doubts can
be traced to the social structure."[43] Yet another member, a thirty-four-
year-old mother of four children, who worked as a librarian at Stanford's
Linear Accelerator, reportedly said, "I was born a feminist and I've
been waiting thirty-four years for society to catch up." A twenty-seven-
year-old writer and editor with an educational firm confided, "I'd always
felt sympathy with the basic premises of Women's Liberation. But I felt
alone. I felt it must be a problem of adjustment within myself. In the
group, you're taken outside of yourself. Woman's main problem is not
legislation, but discovering mental attitudes that cripple her." A twenty-
four-year-old secretary added, "It's a place where I'm able to express
myself as an individual, something I'm not always able to do. The fact
that women get together for their own reasons and benefit is part of liberation. It's a place where you can get honest feedback."[44]

The FBI ordered especially close surveillance of those women's
groups that tried to organize women workers. When a women's group
held a rally in New York on March 8, 1971, protesting the firing of
maids, the local office filed a detailed report. On the West Coast, the Bureau closely watched Union WAGE (Women's Alliance to Gain Equality), a group of socialist feminists dedicated to helping gain equality for
union women, and to organizing nonunion women.[45]

The FBI was especially interested in locating female fugitives who
had taken part in bombings or other violent acts carried out by the
Weather Underground, a group of revolutionaries who had split from
SDS in 1969 and dedicated themselves to armed revolution. A number
of women—Susan Saxe and Jane Alpert among them—were wanted by

the FBI for their alleged role in violent acts. Sometimes, the effort to locate female fugitives generated endless descriptions of women's outfits
and hair. On one occasion, an informer who claimed to have spotted a
fugitive in a women's group wrote, "The weatherman is wearing a short
leather jacket, dark brown, multicolored dress over blue dungarees with
a red slash at bottom. DELETED has short blond hair and [is] wearing
large earrings."[46]

The FBI also infiltrated women's communes suspected of "revolutionary tendencies," or harboring fugitives from the Weather Underground. In New Haven and Oakland, where women's liberation
members had organized support rallies for the Black Panthers, the FBI
suspected local feminists of harboring women of the Weather Underground or others dedicated to what the Bureau called "strategic sabotage." The Washington, D.C., women's liberation newspaper *Off Our
Backs* described the FBI's search for Jane Alpert, who allegedly had
been involved in several bombings of military and war-related corporate
buildings in New York City in 1969. Between 1970 and 1974, Alpert
went underground with other fugitives. The Bureau suspected that she
and other female fugitives had simply melted into a network of women's
communes. The FBI struck back with a series of grand juries that forced
members of women's communes to answer endless questions about
these women's whereabouts. As Brian Glick later pointed out:

> These criminal investigations provided a convenient pretext
> for escalated attacks. . . . In purported pursuit of anti-war
> fugitives . . . FBI agents flooded the women's communities of
> Boston, Philadelphia, Lexington, Hartford and New Haven.
> Their conspicuous interrogation of hundreds of politically ac-
> tive women, followed by highly publicized grand jury subpoe-
> nas and jailing, wreaked havoc in health collectives and other
> vital projects.[47]

Hoover also targeted women actively involved in the anti–Vietnam
War movement. He even worried about mothers' objections to war,
which could be distinctly persuasive. After all, if the soldiers were their
sons, mothers who protested carried a moral authority that could not be
dismissed as unpatriotic. So the Bureau kept track of every women's
group that attended antiwar rallies, including where buses would be
parked, and at what hour they would depart. The Bureau also paid careful attention to young feminists who remained antiwar activists. In

1969, a Washington, D.C., regional agent warned that women who now called themselves "the Anti-Imperialist Women of the Women's Movement" were still linked with SDS activities. In 1971, the Washington field office warned that women who attended "The Women's National March on the Pentagon" should be closely watched.

Even more suspect was a group of activists who had written Madame Binh, the head of North Vietnam's National Liberation Front's delegation to the Paris peace talks. To most Americans, the NLF was still the nation's enemy. The women's letter, instead, offered solidarity as women "to turn toward each other and fight for our freedom." Concerned about such political support for the enemy, the Bureau tracked several dozen New Left women who met with North Vietnamese women in Budapest, Toronto, Montreal, and even in Hanoi. An FBI clipping of a story published by the *San Francisco Chronicle* reported "that Anne Scheer, wife of *Ramparts* Editor Robert Scheer, was one of a three member American Anti-War Committee who visited North Vietnam in July 1968 and to whom the North Vietnamese released three U.S. pilots being held captive as prisoners of war." This Left-feminist effort to make peace with the women of "the enemy" was regarded, in the middle of a shooting war, as treason.[48]

On a lighter note, the FBI also moved to protect the Nixon administration from feminist-inspired disruptions. In 1972, the New York office discovered that ten women from New York, "who have participated in the New Left in the past," had purchased tickets to a National Women's Republican Club luncheon with mayhem in mind. According to the informer, the women intended to disguise themselves—as Republican ladies—and sit at different tables. After lunch, "one of the women will stand up and deliver a short diatribe about Governor Rockefeller's [brutal] handling of the Attica [prison] rebellion. A few minutes later someone else will stand up and denounce the U.S. presence in Vietnam. As soon as the last woman denounces the U.S. Government's failure to move on housing and child care issues, the five women carrying live rats [in their handbags] will turn them loose."

Armed with this information from an informer, the New York Police Department and the FBI jointly foiled the protest. They refunded tickets to the suspected women and tightened their security at the luncheon. No disruption occurred, but FBI agents did report that guests complained of rats seen scurrying around the hallways and trapped in the telephone booths of the hotel.[49]

The FBI collected thousands of pages of memos, reports, teletypes, tape transcripts, press clippings, and leaflets published between 1969 and 1973, under the heading "Women's Liberation Movement." The Church hearings officially ended Cointelpro, but that didn't mean that infiltration and surveillance of the women's movement stopped. According to Brian Glick, whose book *War at Home* recounts the FBI's post-Church surveillance, "the Bureau continued to infiltrate and disrupt feminist organizations, publications, and projects." After the Church hearings were published in 1976, the *Los Angeles Times* broke the news that the FBI had been infiltrating the women's movement all across the country. A few months later, Letty Cottin Pogrebin of *Ms.* magazine spent six weeks analyzing FBI files on the women's movement. With "reactions ranging from shock to fascination to ennui," Pogrebin wondered why "the FBI's extensive file—the largest amassed since the Communist Party and the entire anti-war effort, according to one lawyer—received so little press and public attention."

As I discovered later, even the most passionate and respectable researchers of the Cointelpro program and FBI and CIA surveillance have barely looked into the government's infiltration of the women's movement. Ironically, the FBI deemed women activists more important than did the researchers who have exposed the agency's violations of other citizens' civil rights. The Freedom of Information Act, passed by Congress in 1974, additionally led to the release of a complicated paper trail left by regional agents and informants. The documents, carefully vetted by the FBI, now show that from San Diego to Vermont, from Seattle to Florida, women spied on other women's thoughts, feelings, and actions. Who those informants and informers were we still don't know.[50]

It was not until I read FBI files on Berkeley that I realized that informers had infiltrated—and reported on—many activities in which I had participated. FBI informants noted my activities, right down to a talk I had given at a political conference (sponsored by the Socialist Workers' Party, a group about which I knew nothing at the time). The FBI informer reported that "the speaker for this lecture ["Women in Revolt"] was listed as Ruth Rosen, Teaching Assistant, member of the Women's Caucus of the History Dept. at the Univ. of Cal."[51] (There was no such caucus.)

The accuracy of informers' reports was haphazard at best. If a woman's name were Elizabeth, the FBI might list her "aliases" as Beth and Liz. Informers rarely understood that a person mentioned in two different contexts was the same individual. In a subsequent document appeared my name, address, and phone number—here I was no longer a teaching assistant, but "a photographer who will do pictures for the women's movement only." (Ironically, I spent most of my graduate career taking pictures of famous men—Ronald Reagan, Bobby Seale, Huey Newton, various New Left leaders, as well as police who might be guilty of excessive force—for the campus newspaper and alternative newspapers, but not for women's publications.)[52]

Long after the Church report came out, the FBI continued to monitor the women's movement. When Margo St. James, the leader of the San Francisco union of prostitutes, sent for her FBI file in 1976, the Bureau replied that no file existed on either her or her organization, COYOTE (Call Off Your Old Tired Ethics). And when she checked with the San Francisco regional office, the agent replied with a grin, "We never considered COYOTE part of the women's movement." Later, the same agent "found" her files, brought them to her, and tried to convince her to be an informer.[53]

THE SMELL OF FEAR

Clearly, the FBI's infiltration intensified paranoia and provided one explanation for unresolvable differences. In 1973, Robin Morgan spoke of the "new smell of fear in the Women's Movement":

> It is in the air when groups calling themselves kill-dyke separatists trash lesbian-feminists who work with that anathema, straight women, and trash these lesbian-feminists as "pawns, dupes and suckerups to the enemy." . . . It was in the air when I trembled to wrench the Stones record from a phonograph at a women's dance, and when I was accused of being a uptight, puritanical, drag. And of course a hung-up man-hating "straight" for doing that. The words are familiar, but the voice used to be male. And the smell of fear was in my gut, writing this talk, and is in my nostril now, risking the saying of these things.[54]

But how can we distinguish paranoia from reasonable fear? We can't. As the saying goes, "Even paranoids have real enemies." What we *can* ask is how much the *belief* in FBI infiltration affected the thought and behavior of movement activists.

Given her years in and around the Left labor movement, Betty Friedan never doubted that the FBI would eventually infiltrate any women's movement. At the 1971 national NOW convention, she announced, "It should be recognized that because of NOW's size and strength, that NOW is going to be 'infiltrated.' We shouldn't worry, because we're too big to be co-opted."[55]

Later, Friedan would conclude that the FBI had likely infiltrated the Congress to Unite Women (in both 1969 and 1970), as well as various NOW national conventions. She was also convinced that the FBI had somehow manipulated the gay/straight split. "I think it is possible that the CIA or FBI manipulated some of the lesbians. . . . The agents deepened the divisions and I think that agents used ambitions and other issues like the lesbian thing and so on." As an example, Friedan pointed to a talk she had given in Seattle. The organizers asked if she would share the platform with a lesbian. When Friedan refused, women picketed and "that night the people that were picketing came in, occupied the first rows, and made it impossible for me to speak. . . . I think the Seattle thing was [the result of] agents." When asked about the impact of such infiltration, Friedan quickly responded, "It prevented the passage of the ERA."[56] Friedan's assessment is just one example of how some feminists attributed the divisions within the movement—or the backlash against the movement—to intelligence activities.

Younger feminists also blamed the FBI for what they saw as a change in the political direction of the women's movement. Porous and inviting, the movement permitted easy access and infiltration. For feminists, it was next to impossible to distinguish between informers and ordinary women who behaved oddly, suggested weird actions, held rigid positions, had poor judgment, or created dissension every time they opened their mouths. They also assumed informers were the same as "agents." Journalist Marilyn Webb, for instance, felt certain that agents had infiltrated the Washington, D.C., feminist newspaper *Off Our Backs*, which was then "taken politically from a centrist position to a radical lesbian fringe newspaper. I was absolutely devastated . . . and I knew one of those people was an FBI agent." Over time, Webb said, she noticed a pattern in which a small number of women used "innate disagreements that people had anyway and put a certain spin to them so that it destroyed the group . . . it was very skillful, these people were not fooling

around and were highly trained." Later, Webb discovered that a man
whom she had met in Cuba who had been her lover was a paid FBI
informer.[57]

The story of Sagaris, an ambitious, would-be feminist institute and
think tank, provides a snapshot of how fear could turn into paranoia and
help destroy a feminist institution. In 1974, a group of faculty and students at Goddard College in Vermont decided to create a feminist summer institute. According to Joan Peters, one of the founding members of
the collective, Sagaris would be for women of "all backgrounds and all
persuasions of feminism," and the women who applied to the school did
indeed range from "welfare mothers to college presidents." The dream
was ambitious. At the two initial five-week summer sessions in 1975,
ideas were to shape future activism, activist experience would inform
theory, and egalitarianism—rather than hierarchy and elitism—would
be the norm. As Susan Sherman, who taught poetry at the second session, later reflected:

> It was almost too perfect. And perhaps a more experienced
> and less enthusiastic observer might have predicted from the
> beginning that isolating over one hundred women of all ages,
> interests, and levels of emotional stability along with some of
> the strongest, most diverse and opinionated voices in the
> feminist community on an isolated hilltop for a period of five
> weeks would itself be a dangerous thing to do.

In the end, the dream met a nasty death, unraveling amid fierce political and cultural conflicts, crushed by a collision between purists and
pragmatists that would have seemed familiar to political activists in all
periods of history.[58]

The first session, though not exactly "harmonious," appeared to be
quite successful. Mary Daly, a major feminist spiritualist thinker, Rita
Mae Brown, a well-known lesbian novelist, Candace Falk, a socialist-
feminist, and Charlotte Bunch, a former civil rights, antiwar, and
lesbian rights activist, were among the teachers. Candace Falk remembered meeting women from small towns, who confirmed her sense that
"women's liberation was a truly grassroots organization." She felt that
her course on socialism and feminism, even though filled with angry
women who had "left the Left," turned into a stimulating and sustained
debate on feminism and socialism and on the directions women and

their movement should take. Although some women "resented her remaining on the Left, *and* living with a man," Falk never felt trashed. Banter, good will, and humor seemed to contain differences.

Like most good teachers, Falk learned as much as she taught. A token socialist at Sagaris, Falk was also one of a handful of heterosexuals. "Living among women who lived without men was a new and powerful experience," she recalled. She learned "how oppressed lesbian women must feel in a straight culture," and she learned to

> grasp the solidarity and integration that lesbians enjoyed in the core of their intimate as well as their public life. . . . I had the deepest gut sense that women always have a choice to go on with their lives and not deal with men at all . . . and I think that affected my relationships with men.[59]

During the first session, Charlotte Bunch taught a course on political strategies in organizing.

> I was talking about building feminist institutions, about women's centers, about the whole controversy over women's businesses, class and feminism. . . . It was very creative and exciting, and the women were from all over the country . . . and eager to have a place for five weeks to discuss feminist strategies. I think at least half of the people in the first session said afterwards how it had changed their lives. . . . It was one of those real catalysts for people.

Later, Falk received letters from students who told her how much her course had changed their lives, something "too threatening" to acknowledge in the intense radical feminist environment of Sagaris.[60]

In late July, Sagaris succumbed to splits and squabbles. The event that sparked the conflict involved funding. The *Ms.* Foundation, the nonprofit educational foundation supported by the magazine, had already given Sagaris $5,000 for seed money for the first session and now responded to a request for additional funding by offering the leadership $10,000 for the second session.

Only three months earlier, the Redstockings had issued their press release on Gloria Steinem and the CIA. The faculty who taught during the second session were angry that Gloria Steinem still had not responded to charges that she was guilty of political treason. To the leadership, Ti-Grace Atkinson argued, "You can't take that money. The Redstockings have just accused Gloria Steinem of being a CIA agent. The money is tainted, that money is suspect, and you're going to pollute Sagaris with it."[61]

For six hours, Ti-Grace Atkinson and Joan Peters publicly debated whether or not to accept the money from the *Ms.* Foundation, but they failed to reach an agreement. Afterward, a majority of the community voted to accept the financial support. Still, Atkinson disagreed so strongly that she began conducting classes off-campus, where she was soon joined by other faculty—Marilyn Webb, Susan Sherman, Alix Kates Shulman—who formed an alternative institute. According to Joan Peters, Atkinson and her student followers "rented a place in town and lived in our dormitories and ate in our dining hall, but had nothing more to do with the school."

While Sagaris waited for Steinem's response, the scene turned ever uglier. "There were fist fights in the courtyard," recalled Peters. "We were at war. It became more fashionable to go with the people who saw themselves as revolting against the institution. . . . We had become, in the course of six weeks, 'the establishment.' " As tempers flared, women began to accuse one another of the serious crime of "reformism," or not being sufficiently radical. Students criticized the Sagaris leadership collective for charging tuition, even though they did so on a sliding scale based on financial need and also provided scholarships. Other students accused those who had created an alternative institute of "elitism." "I guess that's the worst thing you could have called anybody in those days and so everybody was calling everybody elitist," Shulman recalled. Students who were mothers complained that Sagaris discriminated against them because it only provided six hours of child care each day (even though everyone at Sagaris had to take her turn as a child care provider).

As Sagaris unraveled, its culture of celebration turned into one of suspicion. Before the split, according to Alix Kates Shulman,

> every night there were dances. Women would dance after meals. Even the meals were highly charged. We would start with announcements and the announcements got wilder and wilder. And after that there would be dances and it was erotic. And I don't just mean people making love, I mean, the

air was charged with rebirth, which I guess I associate with eroticism.[62]

Now women circled one another warily. As Candace Falk noted, the students, many of whom came from smaller cities and towns, resented those leaders "who were more New York sophisticated." On the other hand, hero worship, which had begun earlier when Rita Mae Brown auctioned off her socks, became increasingly common during the second session. Some students picked particular "stars" and followed their decisions like so many disciples practicing the gospel. A newsletter issued by the "alternative school" condemned Sagaris for its lack of purity and described the think tank as "the McDonald's of the women's movement." In hindsight, Alix Kates Shulman deeply regretted her behavior and wished the dissident faculty had accepted the money. In her view, "Sagaris was a study in paranoia." She, like others, had been swept up by the atmosphere of fear and suspicion. Marilyn Webb, who was inclined to think that the accusation against Steinem might be true, wanted the leaders to wait for a statement from Steinem, but by the time she published her open letter, it was too late.[63]

The demise of Sagaris cannot be blamed exclusively on ideological differences. True, "revolutionaries" attacked "reformists," "purists" condemned "pragmatists," and everyone accused everyone else of "elitism." But Joan Peters offered a simpler explanation that spoke volumes about American political culture. "The women's movement entailed a lot of sacrifice and a lot of collectivity and a communal sense of 'we women together' and I think it was too much of a strain on people who were essentially individualists."[64]

Fueling these tensions was a national controversy surrounding Jane Alpert, a former secret member of a freelance bombing collective who had gone underground in 1970, after her alleged role in a bombing incident. After surrendering to the FBI in November 1974, Alpert was reportedly giving agents information about her former female and male compatriots who were still underground. Her conversion from armed revolutionary to radical feminist, she explained, had been provoked by her disgust with the Weathermen's sexism. Her statements and her decision to turn informer for the FBI sparked a heated debate among American feminists, which had not died down by the following summer. Some leftist women circulated petitions, attacking Alpert as a collaborationist. But many feminists, including Gloria Steinem, supported and defended her. Steinem even wrote an introduction to "A Letter from the Underground," a controversial article penned by Alpert that was widely reprinted. Many leftist feminists criticized Alpert's theory of "Mother Right," published in *Ms.* magazine, which based a woman's authority on her innate maternal nature. (Years later, Alpert also rejected this theory.)

Alpert's transformation from underground revolutionary to mother nurturer polarized feminists at Sagaris as well as elsewhere. Fearful of FBI infiltration, some women viewed Alpert as the enemy; others welcomed her as a convert who had come to grasp the significance of feminism—or, in some cases, women's moral superiority.

The tensions between the Left and feminism revisited earlier splits and resurrected old resentments. Journalist Judy Coburn wrote that "in a year's time, the net of the Alpert affair has been cast wide enough to include questions about the relationships between feminism and the Left and the infiltration of the women's movement by police, the FBI and the CIA. Scores of local and national feminist groups and institutions have been affected by the theoretical and practical questions, including *Ms.* magazine and the new Vermont-based feminist institute Sagaris."[65]

Fanning these brushfires at Sagaris was a widespread belief that FBI agents had infiltrated Sagaris and that spies, not feminists, had destroyed the second session. Living in close quarters made nearly any kind of behavior seem suspicious. Here is a case in which the belief in FBI infiltration, whether true or not, cast suspicion in every direction. Joan Peters suspected a few women "whose behavior we found very provocative . . . no one knew them beforehand, they knew each other, but they didn't have any group allegiances." But she thought that spies, if they were present, had catalyzed—not ignited—the political tensions and personality conflicts that afflicted the Sagaris community. In her view, the FBI amplified the differences, but did not cause them. Marilyn Webb suspected spies, rather than feminists, of dirty tricks, like stuffing apples up car tailpipes and painting obscenities on her door. Candace Falk thought that the level of anger was too high to be explained in any normal way. "It didn't fit, it didn't make sense. In the second session, [infiltrators] were even more sophisticated on how to bring it down." Falk suspected "certain women who looked like they had just gotten release time from prison. . . . They were very tough and very obstreperous." Alix Shulman distrusted a few women "who lived in this Swiss chalet. They had taken a house somewhat at a distance, much more bland. Everybody else lived on campus in the dorms. Everything about them was incongruous with everything else." Shulman, a wonderful novelist and highly intelligent woman, even pointed to the fact that "the spies had copies of the *New York Review of Books* in the chalet." Paranoia had spiraled out of control.[66]

The dream was over. Joan Peters concluded that "the factions, the schisms, were finally what tore everything apart. . . . I could not believe women could treat women so brutally . . . and behave in ways that were certainly no better than what I was accusing men of doing to me." Much later, she said, "What happened during the two sessions was that you watched the complete potential of the women's movement, everything that could happen perfectly, happen in the first session. In the second session, every disaster in the women's movement emerged. So that Sagaris ended in fist fights, animosity and division. In this way, Sagaris for me epitomized the larger movement."[67]

Did the FBI's infiltration decisively alter the trajectory of the women's movement? Probably not. Although it intensified paranoia, the FBI did not really change the movement's course. Without infiltration, women's liberationists still would have trashed their leaders, censored group members for having the wrong appearance, the wrong partner, or the wrong job. Without informants, Betty Friedan still would have blamed lesbians for causing the gay/straight split. Without informants, Sagaris would just have likely witnessed attacks on leaders, political divisions, and clashing egos. This was hardly the first time in history that social activists became increasingly dogmatic as a movement grew larger and more diverse.

Still, we should not diminish the significance of a government agency infiltrating a social movement. The FBI committed a flagrant violation of what Americans rightfully cherish as their civil rights. As Letty Pogrebin wrote in 1977:

> The important fact is that they tailed us and invaded our privacy, both psychic and physical. They snooped. They pressed their candid camera against a one-way mirror to our private lives. It seems impossible not to feel outrage at these flagrant violations of the rights of free speech, association and assembly. The FBI conducted a criminal investigation against women who were not accused of any crimes. This activity is unthinkable in a democracy.[68]

The FBI's impact, in my view, was that it exacerbated the movement's growing tendency to judge other women by examining the smallest details of their personal lives. Fear of provocateurs paralyzed some protestors. Fear of agents and informers eroded trust. Given the widespread assumption of infiltration, feminists sometimes found it easier to accuse one another of being informers than to accept the inevitable differences among them that, even without the FBI, would naturally result in different feminist perspectives and different ideas of sisterhood.

Ironically, the FBI searched for signs of subversion in the women's movement but couldn't recognize what was truly dangerous. While they looked for Communists and bombs, the women's movement was shattering traditional ideas about work, customs, education, sexuality, and the family. Ultimately, this movement would prove far more revolutionary than the FBI could ever imagine. Feminism would leave a legacy of disorientation, debate, and disagreement, create cultural chaos and social change for millions of women and men, and, in the process, help ignite the culture wars that would polarize American society. But at the time, these ideas were not what the FBI considered subversive.

Part Four

No End in Sight

Chapter Eight

THE PROLIFERATION OF FEMINISM

"I have seen some of the best minds of *my feminist* generation go mad with impatience and despair," wrote Robin Morgan in 1975. By then, many feminists sensed a change in the *Zeitgeist*. Like a swollen river, the women's movement had spilled over its banks, creating hundreds, then thousands of new tributaries, as it flooded the nation. All over the country, women were discovering feminist perspectives on race, ethnicity, labor, spirituality, education, ecology, and peace. "Feminism" and "sexism," language not widely used even in the late sixties, had now become commonplace household words. The distinction between women's liberation and women's rights had blurred into what was now simply called "the women's movement." But that movement had splintered, and fragmented; it was everywhere and nowhere.

The media had repeatedly announced the death of the movement, and now even some activists worried about its health. Naomi Weisstein and Heather Booth, two experienced movement organizers, decided to take stock of feminism in an article titled "Will the Women's Movement Survive?" As longtime activists, they knew that movements change, even die. Now they worried about the growing belief that a "changed consciousness" was all that women required to change economic and political structures in American society.[1]

Others, too, sensed the change. In 1975, *Harper's Bazaar* asked seven prominent feminists to assess the status of the movement. Susan Braudy, an editor and writer, replied, "We're in a period of transition." Erica Jong responded that the question itself was a predictable media trope: "First we discover a fad, then we say that it has run out of steam."

Congresswoman Elizabeth Holtzman noted that the ERA was in trouble. Betty Friedan replied that "goals get higher with greater success." Cynthia Glacken, a member of the board of directors of Stewardesses for Women's Rights, answered, "As each group of women organize, they will see how the movement applies to them and it won't be a theory anymore."[2]

Time seemed to have taken a toll, noted Charlotte Bunch, commenting on the striking numbers of burned-out women "among long-time activists who had been involved in building feminist institutions." The initial euphoria was long gone; consciousness-raising groups had all but disappeared; feminists felt more isolated; and many movement institutions and collectives had collapsed. Differences, not solidarity, now seemed more compelling to some activists; straight, white women had, in some cases, replaced men as the new enemy. At the same time, a growing anti-abortion movement had launched a fierce campaign to repeal legalized abortion and the ERA had stalled at the state level. By 1982, it would be dead.

CHALLENGING RELIGION AND EDUCATION

Fragmented and wounded, the movement remained immensely alive. In religion, for instance, women scholars in theological schools and seminaries challenged orthodoxy, reexamined translations, and reinterpreted religious texts. Some women in established religions began designing their own services, writing their own prayers, and inventing rituals that honored women and their experiences. The first time one feminist heard a woman cantor's voice soar through a Jewish synagogue, she wept. "Why haven't women been singing Hebrew for the last five thousand years?" she asked. Upon hearing a sermon given by an ordained female Methodist minister, another feminist felt, for the very first time, that she had come home, that she belonged.[3]

Catholic women and nuns faced a more complicated dilemma. Although the Catholic Church's attitudes toward contraception and abortion remained unchanged, when Pope John XXIII convened the Second Vatican Council in 1962 (the first was held in 1869), calling for radical reforms and a renewal of the Church, he opened the cloistered world of silence, shaved heads, and self-flagellation of nuns. In *No Turning Back*, a memoir written in 1990 by two former nuns, Barbara Ferraro

and Patricia Hussey recounted the electrifying experience of those
years and the impact of Vatican II's new liberalism on their religious order and their lives. As both women became increasingly involved in the
struggle for women's right to choose to have an abortion, Ferraro,
Hussey, and other activist nuns waged a war with the Vatican that they
could not win. Soon they left the Catholic Church to set up their own lay
communities. Though it was not their intention, their story made a
strong case for the early emergence of a feminist sensibility among
Catholic nuns.[4]

Meanwhile, feminists challenged all kinds of religious orthodoxy.
The scholar Mary Daly, a member of NOW's task force on women and
religion, launched what would soon become a widespread assault on the
identity of God "as an old man with a beard." Merlin Stone imagined
life "When God Was a Woman"; Rosemary Radford Ruether, a longtime
activist and well-respected theological scholar, critiqued the Judeo-
Christian duality between mind and body and its ecological impact on
humans and the planet; and Judith Plaskow resurrected the feisty
Lilith, whose insubordinate behavior had resulted in God's creation of
the more deferential Eve. Carol Christ extolled the psychic importance
of rediscovering prehistoric female goddesses, and Marija Gimbutas excavated goddess cultures of the ancient world. Charlene Spretnak analyzed the politics of women's spirituality, Paula Gunn Allen explored
the place of the spiritual in Native American cultures, Delores S.
Williams, Audre Lorde, and Alice Walker explored what kind of "womanist theology" would nourish African-American women; and Gloria
Anzaldua examined the impact of Catholicism on the lives of Chicanas.

Together, these scholars, intellectuals, and activists began to envi-
sion a different relationship to divinity, spirituality, and the religious experience. Many feminists, spiritually starved by patriarchal religions
and rituals, eagerly explored new ways of living a spiritual life. Such
women chose many different paths, including paganism, goddess worship, Buddhism, and witchcraft. As a result of this feminist assault on
patriarchal religions, women in some Christian and Jewish congregations became ordained rabbis and ministers, some of whom carried on
the feminist tradition of searching for a new language and new rituals
that would integrate women into the religious experience.[5]

At the same time, in the field of education, feminists fundamentally
altered the curricula of America's schools, colleges, and universities, so
that from first grade on, no child would ever again imagine that women

had not worked, raised families, written, loved, fought, protested, and organized in the past. Between 1970 and 1990, a revolution in knowledge occurred in American institutions of higher learning. Once the category of gender entered a discipline, the questions changed, as did the answers. Feminist scholars began challenging the established lists—"canons"—of literature, art, and music, while publishers like the Feminist Press played a vital role in reprinting neglected—or even lost—books, written by women in the past.

Soon feminist scholarship challenged the very assumptions of every discipline. How do we know what we think we know? they asked. Feminist scholars found bias wherever they looked. No field of research, they discovered, had integrated women into its basic assumptions about the human condition. Even clinical medical research, it turned out, had only used men in trials and then extrapolated those findings to women. Science now found itself assaulted by feminist scholars who questioned what assumptions were embedded in the questions scientists and medical researchers asked.

The cumulative impact of this body of scholarship was breathtaking. Together, this new army of feminist scholars not only questioned the content of modern knowledge, but also the assumptions on which that knowledge was based. "When women asked the questions," as historian Marilyn Boxer noted, "their answers were not only different, but downright threatening, even subversive, and they and their work became lightning rods in the academic cultural wars of the 1980s and 1990s." But to feminists, their influence seemed like the natural fruition of thousands of women working in the academic fields, dedicated to asking new questions, revisiting old ones, and turning a critical eye toward all claims of truth.[6]

Consider the field of women's history, which profoundly challenged the writing of the past. Historians of women, who were already well organized by the early seventies, questioned the conventional wisdom that professional historians taught and that textbooks repeated. Most women did not even know very much about the first wave of feminism, which had lasted for seventy years. Ellen DuBois retrieved that important history, as thousands of other historians, almost all feminist activists, began the painstaking work of making women's work, movements, families, and loves visible to an indifferent present.

By the end of the 1980s, all schoolchildren would honor National Women's History Month. How this came about is a good example of the confluence between various feminist institutions. Molly MacGregor worked on the Sonoma County Commission on the Status of Women, a local California organization that grew out of the 1961 Kennedy Commission on the Status of Women. Neither a professional historian nor an academic, MacGregor had been pondering how to promote a week that honored women's history. Three thousand miles away, professors Gerda Lerner and Joan Kelly, two of the earliest pioneers in the field of women's history, had created a graduate program in women's history at Sarah Lawrence College in 1972. Five years later, Gerda Lerner organized a Summer Institute on Women's History for Leaders of Women's Organizations. A consummate activist and educator, Lerner brought together "forty-five women representing the leadership of thirty-seven national women's organizations. They lived and worked together for seventeen days at Sarah Lawrence College." Molly MacGregor who had already initiated the celebration of Women's History Week in Sonoma Country for the last two years, arrived at the Institute hoping to persuade other attendees to embrace the idea as well. According to Lerner, the students "adopted as their class project the idea of turning Women's History Week into an annual national event." President Carter had already proclaimed the event, but only for one year. To turn it into an annual event, they would need a joint resolution passed by both houses of Congress and signed by the president.[7]

And they got it. Inspired by Gerda Lerner, MacGregor returned to California, where she and other activists formed the National Women's History Project (NWHP). By 1981, the national women's history network successfully lobbied Congress to recognize National Women's History Week. By 1987, they had pressured Congress into expanding the week into a month. Eventually, the NWHP circulated women's history curricula to millions of children, from kindergarten through grade twelve. Supported by scores of activist scholars, these determined women created a real revolution in the American history curriculum.[8]

MEANWHILE, IN THE HEARTLAND

As ideas from the women's movement began spreading into mainstream culture, making it a part of the everyday lives of American readers, viewers, listeners, and even couch potatoes, so the movement itself was spreading through the country. A Fort Wayne, Indiana, feminist recalled how her community became engrossed in the hectic activism of the 1970s:

We organized Take Back the Night marches, and Rape Crisis
Hotlines; we lobbied for a battered women's shelter and
a displaced homemaker program, and began two family
businesses—a bookstore and a coffeehouse. Spontaneous
task forces were created as needed. There was the Unity
Coalition to lobby for the ERA, and the Justice Coalition
campaign to impeach a sexist judge. And when the Women's
Health Organization was being harassed by city officials, local newspapers received letters signed by Catholic Grandmothers for Abortion.[9]

And her description might easily have held for many small cities and
towns across the American heartland where women staked out new
agendas alongside those that had originated in the biggest cities.

Take Dayton, Ohio, a city often compared to Muncie, Indiana, as the
archetypal "average" American city. It witnessed a similar explosion of
feminist activities. Feminists first formed three small consciousness-
raising groups in 1969. The members tended to be white, liberal Democrats who were college-educated, married, and middle-class. As in
other cities, these small groups eventually began to create institutions
and reach out to the wider community. By the mid-1970s, the movement
flourished under the umbrella of Dayton Women's Liberation, which
now boasted a phone bank, a speakers' bureau, a city-funded Women's
Center that offered self-help classes, a walk-in informational center, a
meeting place, an advocacy and referral service, political and personal
counseling, a lending library, an extensive education program, and
child care facilities.

During the second half of the decade, a critical mass of Dayton's
feminists began to focus their attention on the problems of working
women. Some of these activists, self-described socialist-feminists, had
met in 1975, when over two thousand socialist-feminists attended a national conference in Yellow Springs, Ohio. Despite all the usual factions
and splits, the conference had brought together feminists who discovered how many of them were working with trade union women or clerical workers. As early as 1971, for instance, a group of San Francisco
Bay Area feminists and trade union women founded Union WAGE
(Women's Alliance to Gain Equality), an organization dedicated to
creating union democracy, organizing women workers into unions,
and ensuring that both unions and employers took women workers'

needs—maternity, health care, and child care—seriously. By 1975, the Coalition of Labor Union Women (CLUW) had begun to recast feminist demands as the end of sexual discrimination in hiring and promotion, the abolition of sexual harassment, the training of women for skilled work, on-site child care, and flexible hours and work schedules. In Boston, a group called Nine to Five, founded by Karen Nussbaum, tried to improve the status of women office workers. Among their "Bill of Rights for Women Office Workers" was the right to respect as a woman, the right to maternity benefits, and the right to equal access to promotion opportunities and on-the-job training programs. Though the work was slow and difficult, Nussbaum watched as one woman worker after another changed before her eyes:

> Traudi says that she used to cry at her desk when her boss would yell at her. Now she is a leader of her union group, and when her boss tried to harass her out of her job, she said, "No!" Her boss brought her in to have a personal meeting in which he intended to get rid of her, and she said, "I insist on having a witness." She did not lose her job; she got promoted.

What groups like Union WAGE and Nine to Five set out to do was to transform working women's view of themselves and to learn, with them, how to organize other workers. "It's partly a question of skills," Nussbaum explained. "Nobody ever taught us how to hold a meeting or to plan a series of actions that would win your demands from your boss."

> And then, through being in a group you can see things happen around you. You can see yourself be part of an organization that has an impact—that can eventually make big changes for working women. It's really seeing yourself as part of history.[10]

Dayton activists soon took an even more active role in that history. The typical worker in Dayton was not a unionized male autoworker, but a female bank teller. Frustrated by male leftists who trivialized the significance of organizing clerical women, one activist, Sherrie Holmes, established the first NOW chapter in Dayton, out of which emerged Dayton Women Working (DWW), an organization dedicated to improving women's working conditions, and which linked up with the National

Women's Employment Project (NWEP), a consortium of six working women's organizations. The NWEP launched a national investigation of the working conditions of bank clerical workers. Dayton's local "banking study" exposed the industry's widespread discrimination against minorities and women. Forced to investigate, the federal government fined one bank for a pattern of discrimination and assessed nearly $1 million in back pay for 110 employees.[11]

The banking study was perhaps Dayton's greatest success. Like hundreds of other communities, Dayton's women's movement found itself factionalized and underfunded at the end of the decade. None of its major feminist organizations lasted past the 1970s. The Women's Center, led by a rotating leadership, split between women closely connected to the Left, and those activists who insisted upon an autonomous women's movement. By the mid-seventies, Dayton's feminist organizations, like their counterparts around the country, had come to depend on funds provided by the federal government or by private philanthropies. By the end of the decade, these funds began drying up.[12]

By the late 1970s, Dayton, like so many other cities and small towns, began to suffer from a growing backlash against feminism. Many feminists had burned out. Those who had created or staffed feminist institutions now had additional responsibilities, jobs, and/or families. Still, as feminist-created institutions collapsed, they often resurfaced as "mainstream" services. After the 1970s, for instance, the city of Dayton, the YWCA, churches, and universities began to fund and staff a rape crisis hotline, a battered women's shelter, a women's health clinic, and a women's studies program.[13]

In Fort Wayne, Indiana, and Columbus, Ohio (as well as in larger cities like San Francisco, Los Angeles, New York, and Boston), local women's movements took a similar trajectory. The initial movement fragmented; burnout was rampant; but self-help services founded and staffed by activists eventually turned into mainstream services funded by cities, universities, and religious organizations. Some feminists grieved that they had lost "their" institutions to the social service system. But other activists made careers out of directing and funding them. Karen Nussbaum, for example, became the head of the Women's Labor Bureau under the Clinton administration. Elaine Zimmerman, who had helped found the women's center in Berkeley, California, became a national expert on family and child care policy. Ruth Bader Ginsburg, a feminist attorney who had challenged the patriarchal bias of the law, became the second woman on the Supreme Court. Barbara Ehrenreich, an early socialist-feminist activist in health care, became a widely respected writer and public intellectual. These were women who had merged their commitment to other women, as well as to economic and social justice, with their passion for a particular field of interest. In some cases, that also resulted in a satisfying career.

DISPLACED HOMEMAKERS AND POSTFEMINISTS

Older women, younger women, minority women, trade union women, women in the heartland—groups previously considered beyond the reach of the women's movement—were also busy reinventing feminism for themselves. But the diffusion of feminism did not mean that a single movement, led by middle-class white women, spread to other groups who then added or subtracted particular issues. On the contrary, different groups of women spread completely new conceptions of "women's issues" throughout the country. In a space of time so short as to be stunning—a few years at the most—and in areas of the country where feminism had been unknown, then a joke, then a danger, new kinds of feminist sensibilities began to appear. Fragmentation, as troubling and confusing as it was, also made feminism accessible to new groups of women. Despite her concerns about the splintering of the women's movement, Robin Morgan optimistically observed that, with all its factions, the movement had expanded in all kinds of positive directions by 1975. "There are," she wrote,

> alternate feminist institutions all over the country, from Feminist Credit Unions to Women's Law Centers, from feminist presses to Women's Health Centers. [There is the] birth of a genuine feminist metaphysics, Mary Daly, Goddess spirituality. Today the National Black Feminist Organization—to name only one group—has chapters all over the country; Native American feminist groups are forming in the southwest, Chicana, Puerto Rican and Asian women are publicly affirming the feminist consciousness they had all along. Grandmothers and grammar school feminists are organizing, in every town from OWL [Older Women's League] to Little League. . . . The Coalition of Labor Union Women [CLUW]

is making waves within the male-controlled labor movement; and domestic workers, secretaries, hospital employees,
welfare mothers, waitresses and hundreds of thousands of
others . . . are fighting for their/our rights.[14]

Morgan's snapshot of the movement captured the dizzying diffusion
of feminism during the 1970s. In 1973, at age fifty-seven, Tish Sommers, a longtime civil rights activist, and for twenty-three years a
mother and housewife, ended her marriage. Newly won no-fault divorce
law reforms left many a long-married but suddenly divorced homemaker like Sommers without any means of support. Her response was to
found a NOW Task Force called Older Women's Liberation (OWL), then
defined, tellingly, as women over thirty. Without the existence of a
women's movement, Sommers might not have acted, but with its support, she became the first activist to link issues of aging with feminism.
Sommers also coined the term "displaced homemakers" to dignify the
lives of women who unexpectedly found themselves on their own, with
few marketable skills, and little self-confidence. In 1975, activist
lawyer Barbara Dudley drafted a bill to provide displaced homemakers
with job training and counseling in California. When the governor opposed the proposed legislation, Sommers threatened to stage a sit-in
with hundreds of elderly feminists. The state legislature passed the bill,
providing funds for a pilot project, housed at Mills College in Oakland.
Other colleges and universities soon created their own centers, welcoming these displaced homemakers because they were mature, experienced, and brought much-needed revenue to educational institutions.

In many ways, OWL could be viewed as a quintessential American
feminist organization. Like other feminists, Sommers considered her
own experience, judged it to be unfair, grasped the politics of the problem, found a way for people to discuss it, and began to challenge the
public policies that affected older women. Fueled by grassroots activists, the movement rapidly swept across the nation. By 1977, twelve
states had passed legislation to help displaced homemakers. In 1980,
Sommers founded the Older Women's League (also called OWL), which
by 1982 had its national headquarters in Washington, D.C.

Sommers's friendship with Laurie Shields, a recent widow, speeded
up this process. They became the closest of partners and together put
OWL's issues on the national agenda. As Sommers's health began to fail,
Laurie Shields, her partner, companion, housemate, and caregiver, criss-

crossed the country publicizing the problems faced by older women. By the mid-1980s, over one thousand centers had joined the Displaced Homemaker Network that Sommers and Shields had founded. Within a decade, the discrimination and invisibility faced by abandoned older wives, their need for support, job training, education, and for planning for "a good death," had all been redefined as feminist issues.

The extraordinary friendship that grew up between Sommers and Shields reminded some feminists of the energetic partnership that had fueled the suffragists Susan B. Anthony, the tireless organizer and orator, and Elizabeth Cady Stanton, the homebound visionary, writer, and theorist in the nineteenth century. Sommers, a tall, slim, and graceful woman, was the visionary who came up with ideas for job training, counseling, older women's co-housing, living wills, and hospice care. Her fierce sense of injustice struck a resonant chord. Her motto, inspired by the labor activist Joe Hill's famous last words, "Don't Mourn, Organize," was "Don't Agonize, Organize." Sommers knew how to change older women's consciousness. A typical OWL poster announced, "For men, they created retirement plans, medical benefits, profit sharing and gold watches. For women, they created Mother's Day."

Shields, shorter and stouter, was an exceptional organizer, blessed with an ability to reach out to people, and with the endless energy to travel and speak all over the country. Some people wondered if they were lovers. But one friend of Shields commented that "Laurie was so homophobic it was amazing," and pointed out that "Laurie Shields had always worried that others would think they were more than partners and companions." Sommers perhaps had a more tolerant view of the same-sex world in which she lived her later years. In a letter written to a close friend, she confided, "I have always felt closer to women. Despite close relationships with men, there is always a seventh (and maybe a sixth) veil. But you and I had a type of intimacy that went deeper. . . . Is that homo-sexuality? I don't think so—I think it is closer akin to soul— a shared 'oppression.' "[15]

Whatever the nature of their relationship, it was, by all accounts, emotionally intimate and mutually supportive. Together, they reached women who would never have imagined themselves participating in the women's movement. In 1976, for instance, I received an extraordinary letter from my mother, who had steadily voiced her strong objections to my activism in the civil rights, antiwar, and women's movements. The divorce she now faced in her early sixties had left her shaken and depressed; she realized that even those marketable skills she had, left over from working as an executive secretary during the 1930s, had become outdated. "I have just gone to an OWL meeting," she wrote me. "I have to admit, if I were your age, I think I would be an activist in the women's movement too. I'm just beginning to see how older women are treated in the courts, by lawyers, by everyone. We're dispensable. We're invisible. It's terribly shocking."[16]

In the late 1970s, younger women, for their part, felt conflicted and ambivalent about feminism. The young women of the postsuffrage generation had similarly harbored reservations about former suffragists, whom they viewed as dowdy women who wore sensible shoes. Instead of creating settlement houses or fighting for protective legislation, the most privileged of these young women spent the 1920s flouting Victorian propriety by dancing wildly, driving recklessly, and smoking heavily. Freedom meant shortening your hair and your skirts and enjoying premarital sex. They didn't *demand* anything; they simply *did* what they wanted; and their eagerness to embrace personal freedom changed the social and sexual mores of American women.[17]

The young women who grew up in the wake of the Second Wave of feminism also took much for granted. They would become the first generation, without the support of a movement, who tried to have it all— sexual freedom, career, marriage, and motherhood—without realizing that feminists had never wanted women to do it all. Increasingly reluctant to call themselves "feminists," they nonetheless embraced many of the movement's goals. By the early 1980s, the media labeled them the "Post-Feminist Generation." Had feminism been so successful that it was no longer needed? Many older and experienced feminists, then in their thirties and forties, didn't think so. Suddenly, postcards that announced "I'll be post-feminist in post-patriarchy" began sprouting on bulletin boards and refrigerators. In a signed editorial in the *New York Times*, Geneva Overholser spoke for many experienced activists when she denounced "post-feminism" as a way to "give sexism a subtler name."[18]

Here, in a nutshell, was another paradox of feminism. As the movement split into hundreds of causes and organizations, gender consciousness increased, but growing numbers of young women rejected the label "feminist." Yet, their own attitudes toward work were irreversible, in part because women's participation in the labor force grew year by year. The so-called postfeminist generation, in fact, embraced the movement's goal of equal pay for equal work. They simply took for granted their equal competence with men, their place in the workforce, and their right to a livelihood.[19]

But, for many, "feminism" had already turned into a dirty word. For some daughters of feminists, the women's movement triggered painful childhood memories. They had watched their mothers disintegrate after divorce, stumble into new jobs, or burn out from reinventing themselves over and over again. No great surprise; we had done the same. We had fled the domesticity of our mothers' lives, mistakenly concluded that it offered no satisfaction, just relentless misery, without realizing how many of our mothers' hopes and secret dreams we took with us.[20]

Most Americans first encountered the term "post-feminist generation" in an article written by Susan Bolotin for the *New York Times Magazine* in 1982. Titled "Voices of the Post-Feminist Generation," Bolotin reported what she had learned from interviewing women in their twenties. Although most of the women declined to identify themselves as feminists, they believed in gender equality and aspired to combine a career with a family life. But their images of feminists left a lot to be desired. Feminists were "icy monsters who have let themselves go physically." The F word conjured up images of exhausted superwomen, or unkempt, hairy, man-hating lesbians. Some of the women Bolotin interviewed rejected the bitterness they had witnessed in their mothers' lives. "My feelings about feminism," explained one young woman,

> are at least partially a reaction to my mother. . . . My abandonment of feminism was a process of intellect. It was also a process of observation. Look around and you'll see some happy women; and then you'll see these bitter, bitter, women. The unhappy women are all feminists. You'll find very few happy, enthusiastic, relaxed people who are ardent supporters of feminism. Feminists are really tortured people.

Some of the young women argued that the language of feminism was irrelevant to their lives. A 1982 graduate of the University of Vermont explained that "for most people, feminism means having a strong sense of yourself as an individual, independent female." Since she believed that women could achieve this confidence as individuals, she saw no need for a movement.

A few of the women in Bolotin's article did, in fact, embrace some aspects of the women's movement. Among them was Mindy Werner, a twenty-four-year-old assistant editor at a publishing company. Unlike most of the other young women, Werner described herself as a feminist who was wary of the tyrannical scrutiny with which feminists judged other women. She had been "around too many feminists for whom going to the bathroom is a political issue."[21]

The first "postfeminist" generation also included its share of committed young feminists, some of whom were daughters of well-known movement activists. Rebecca Walker (Alice Walker), Rosa Ehrenreich (Barbara Ehrenreich), Chloe Levy (Susan Griffin), and Abigail Pogrebin (Letty Pogrebin), to name just a few, proudly carried their mothers' torches and fought for or wrote about feminist causes. Nor were they alone. On most college campuses throughout the 1980s, small groups of young feminists organized "Take Back the Night Marches" and held symposia on date rape, pornography, and sexual harassment.[22]

These young activists helped sustain the movement by reinventing feminism for themselves. In 1983, Naomi Wolf, a writer of that younger generation, explained, "Like any real heirloom, feminism is not of our making and needs reconstruction to serve our time; and like any real treasure, it will last us forever." As a result of their writing and activities, they intensified the public's awareness of gender injustice. The Women's Action Coalition in New York (WAC), for instance, engaged in all kinds of inventive zap actions and guerrilla theater, and helped raise the public's consciousness about the backlash against feminism. In 1993, Rebecca Walker founded The Third Wave, a multi-issue activist group whose average age was twenty-five. They circulated a position paper titled, "Continuing the Women's Movement: The Third Wave." Four years later, young women born between 1963 and 1974 published a collection of essays called *The Third Wave Agenda*. To distinguish themselves from Second Wave feminists, one author explained that the strength of "third wave feminism is in its emphasis on making room for contradictions." For her, it was the instability of identity, as well as the search for contradictions, that created her generation's distinctive perspective.[23]

REINVENTING FEMINISM

One of the more pernicious consequences of the term "postfeminism" was that it completely ignored the vibrant feminist sensibility that had emerged and was still growing among racial minorities in the United States. Although the second wave of feminism initially grew out of problems encountered and addressed mainly by white women who had achieved middle-class status, it didn't take long for women of different ethnic and racial backgrounds to reinvent feminism for themselves. Nor did it take them long to realize that *their* historical burden and *their* culture had created different problems, obligations, and needs that partly overlapped with those of white women, but mostly did not.

The awakening consciousnesses of minority women, at least on the surface, appeared to have much in common. Women in nearly every racial group—including African-Americans, Chicanas, Filipinas, Asian Americans, American and Alaskan indigenous tribes, and Puerto Ricans—first discovered, much as had white women, that their status in New Left or liberation or independence movements was one of subordination. Since the men in these groups already felt emasculated by the economic discrimination they encountered in a white-dominated culture, the women hesitated to further threaten their sense of manhood. But they were also not willing to turn themselves into mere followers. Creating and sustaining egalitarian relationships in these movements proved extremely difficult. Wanting to support their men, but unwilling to defer to them, the women faced a dilemma. Their most common solution was to work with poor women and children among their people and to publicize what they most needed. In this way, they could combine their loyalty to their movement, directly help other women, and still retain their independence as organizers and leaders.

But first they needed to know their history, so they could understand how they came to be in these situations. Ever since slavery, for instance, black women had borne the burden of working to support their families, often with husbands who could not find jobs or training in white America. Black women often dreamed of spending more time, not less, with their families. Learned helplessness was *not* the problem of women who had spent the last century holding together families, churches, and communities. And the work for which they received wages—taking in laundry or cleaning white women's homes—was hardly glamorous or self-fulfilling. To black women, as historian Paula Giddings put it, Friedan's advice to find a meaningful career "seemed to come from another planet." The novelist Toni Morrison succinctly summarized the differences separating the lives of white and black women.

> Aggression is not as new to black women as it is to white women. Black women seem able to combine the nest and the adventure. They don't see conflict in certain areas as do white women. They are both safe harbor and ship, they are both inn

and trail. We, black women, do both. We don't find these places, these roles, mutually exclusive. That's one of the differences. White women often find if they leave their husband and go out into the world, it's an extraordinary event. If they've settled for the benefits of housewifery that precludes a career, then it's marriage or a career for them, not both, not *And*.[24]

As early as 1970, quite a few African-American activists were already considering whether feminism had anything to contribute to their lives. The poet and writer Nikki Giovanni was typical in rejecting the women's movement, saying that she didn't want to get involved in the "white family quarrel." Other writers and activists—like Frances Beale, Linda La Rue, Eleanor Holmes Norton, Celestine Ware, Angela Davis, Toni Cade (later Bambara), Charlayne Hunter, Toni Morrison, and Maxine Williams, among many others—took up the challenge of exploring and articulating the "double jeopardy" of black women's lives. In their view, pervasive racism was their greatest problem. This is what kept them and their men from learning the skills, joining unions, and earning the salaries that could improve the lives of their families and communities.

In 1970, the black lawyer and civil rights activist Eleanor Holmes Norton argued that

> Black women cannot—must not—avoid the truth about their special subservience. They are women with all that implies. If some have been forced into roles as providers or, out of insecurity associated with being a black woman alone, have dared not develop independence, the result is not that black women are today liberated women. For they have been "liberated" only from love, from family life, from meaningful work, and just as often from the basic comforts and necessities of an ordinary existence. There is neither power nor satisfaction in such a "matriarchy." There is only the bitter knowledge that one is a victim.

She also urged African-Americans to "remake the family unity, not imitate it. Indeed, this task is central to black liberation." But many African-American women were still outraged at the government's publication of Daniel Patrick Moynihan's 1965 report, "The Negro Family:

The Case for National Action." Concerned about rising unemployment
and crime among blacks, Moynihan located the problems of African-
American life *not* in racism or in discrimination, but inside the black
family, and blamed black matriarchs for dominating their families ever
since the end of slavery: "The Negro family has been forced into a
matriarchal structure which, because it is so out of line with the rest of
American society, seriously retards the progress of the group as a
whole." In response, angry black women refuted the accusation that
they had "castrated" black men and exposed what they called "the myth
of black matriarchy." As the writer and activist Maxine Williams wrote,
black women "had gotten authority in the family by default," because
black men could rarely find jobs in white America. But this hardly constituted real power. When some black men also blamed them for their
domination of the family, women activists grew even angrier. In 1970,
the writer Linda La Rue argued that to confront racism and capitalism,
black men would have to cease stereotyping black women as either "a
matriarchal villain or a step stool baby-maker."[25]

In the same year, the African-American writer Celestine Ware published *Woman Power: The Movement for Women's Liberation*. In a chapter called "The Relationship of Black Women to the Women's Liberation
Movement," she noted how long African-Americans had tried to imitate
whites, and how they had internalized the belief that lighter-skinned
blacks were more attractive and more talented. "Joining the Women's
Liberation Movement," Ware wrote, "may seem at this time like a re-
entry into the old farce of pretending to be white." Ware also raised the
objection that "poor black women are too occupied struggling for
essentials—shelter, food and clothing—to organize themselves around
the issue of women's rights." To white feminists, she explained that
"black feminism would be another attempt by the power structure to divide black men and women. Feminist goals, like abortion on demand
and easily obtainable birth control, are viewed with paranoid suspicion
by some black militants at a time when they are literally fighting for
their lives and looking everywhere to increase their numbers."

Still, Ware tellingly revealed the ways in which black women felt devalued and degraded in their own culture, called "black bitches" by
black men who sought out white women. "Black men," she wrote,

> pursue white women not simply as the most beautiful women
> and easy, but also as the symbols of the white man's privi-
> leges. White women and black women have been accepting

this without criticism, but now black women are becoming increasingly vocal in their anger at this manipulation. Most
white women still are not aware of the nature of black man's
desire for them.

Ware also criticized black men's unwillingness to share leadership.
Ware learned, for instance, "that whenever a black girl becomes too articulate and aggressive at our meetings, a boy from the group is assigned to seduce her and then, as his conquest, keep her in a more
traditional position within the organization." In short, black women—
whether as domestics, heads of households, welfare mothers, or militant
activists—found themselves facing many problems that had not been
addressed by white feminists. "Black and white women can work together for women's liberation," Ware wrote, "but only if the movement
changes its priorities to work on issues that affect the lives of minority-
group women."[26]

Though few black feminist consciousness-raising groups existed during these years, those that did were already debating the issues Ware
had outlined. When the Black Unity Party, a black nationalist organization in Peekskill, New York, decided that "none of the sisters should
take the pill" (so that they could produce more black warriors), a group
of black women in a Mount Vernon group—including Patricia Haden
and Rita Van Lew, both welfare recipients, Sue Rudolph, a housewife,
Joyce Hoyt, a domestic worker, Catherine Hoyt, a grandmother, and Patricia Robinson, a housewife and psychotherapist—denounced the
party's demand. The women took a strong stand against black men's insistence that they avoid birth control or abortion.

> If we practice birth control, it's because of poor black
> men . . . who won't support their families, won't stick by their
> women. . . . Poor black women would be fools to sit up in the
> house with a whole lot of children and eventually go crazy,
> sick, heartbroken, no place to go, no sign of affection—
> nothing.[27]

At the same time, La-neeta Harris, a thirteen-year-old Mount Vernon
schoolgirl, wrote a manifesto demanding sex education in junior high
school so that black girls would be able to continue their educations.
"Some people say," she wrote, "what you don't know won't hurt you but

it will and affect many other girls. . . . We have got to move on schools before they [boys] move on us. Sex education should be taught in school."[28]

Disappointed by male militants blinded by their sexism, and by white feminists ignorant of their racism, a number of black women activists took up the challenge of defining and describing their own reality as black and female. Which was more oppressive, being black—or being a woman? And why on earth should black women have to choose?

For white feminists, Maxine Williams pointed out, "marriage and the family are the roots of women's oppression, while to black women of the middle class that thought is abhorrent and to black lower-class women their oppression is completely racial." Black women, Williams continued, had always found themselves "fighting the beauty standard of white western society." The slogan "Black Is Beautiful" had provided them with a new ideal of black beauty, natural hair and all. "But there is a catch!" Williams insisted. "She is still being told to step back and let the Black man come forward and lead."[29]

In a widely reprinted essay, "Double Jeopardy: Black and Female," Frances Beale analyzed the double oppression that black women faced. As a former nonviolent civil rights activist, Beale could hardly ignore the fact that the rise of black power groups had resulted in a decline in black female leadership. "There seems to be some confusion in the movement today as to who has been oppressing whom," she wrote. "Since the advent of black power, the black male has exerted a more prominent leadership role in our struggle for justice in this country. He sees the system for what it really is for the most part. But where he rejects its values and mores on many issues, when it comes to women, he seems to take his guidelines from the pages of the *Ladies' Home Journal*." Beale warned that "those who are exerting their 'manhood' by telling black women to step back into a domestic, submissive role are assuming a counterrevolutionary position." Like Williams, Beale also sought some way to communicate with white feminists. In her view, white middle-class women didn't seem to grasp that male chauvinism was not the main enemy.

> The economic and social realities of the black woman's life are
> the most crucial for us. It is not an intellectual persecution
> alone; the movement is not a psychological outburst for us; it
> is tangible; we can taste it in all our endeavors. We as black

women have got to deal with the problems that the black
masses deal with, for our problems in reality are the same.[30]

But the writer Pamela Newman had a slightly different perspective.
"Ask yourself, have you ever been told, this is a man's conversation, so
be quiet or keep out because woman's work is only dishwashing, sewing
or laundry? This, my sister, is male chauvinism, not by the system but
by the brothers. . . . The exploitation of black women goes deeper than
that of white women."

African-American women soon found a way of employing their double jeopardy on behalf of themselves and other women. Some of these
women worked for the National Welfare Rights Organization (NWRO),
which had begun in the mid-1960s. As growing numbers of African-
American mothers assumed full responsibility for their children, they
faced a hostile, intrusive, and recalcitrant bureaucracy. The NWRO
tried to help poor women fight red tape that denied eligible mothers assistance, challenge unlawful exemptions, and restore some sense of dignity to them. For a variety of reasons, the NWRO began to collapse
during the early 1970s, leaving welfare recipients at the mercy of an
even less tolerant atmosphere toward welfare.

In addition to welfare activism, black women targeted child care, police repression, and medical care.[31] They also took an active part in
shaping feminism in national organizations. In 1970, NOW members
elected Aileen Hernandez as their president. Flo Kennedy maintained
a high-profile and influential presence in the women's movement, as
did Pauli Murray, Addie Wyatt, Eleanor Holmes Norton, and Shirley
Chisholm, a black politician who in 1972 became the first African-
American woman to run for president. By their presence, these women
ensured that black women's problems would not disappear from the political agenda.

With the collapse of the black nationalist movement, African-
American women felt freer to take a second look at the sexism within
their own community. In 1973, activists founded the National Black
Feminist Organization (NBFO), which, within a year, had spawned ten
local chapters and had held a national conference. A few years later, the
writer and activist Michelle Wallace candidly described some of the
conflicts that this national organization was never able to resolve. Some
of its members wanted the organization to have mass appeal, attracting
new members from the ranks of black women. They were quite dis-
mayed when Margaret Sloan, an editor at *Ms.* magazine, known for

singing a love song to her white female lover on local television, was elected president. Some of the members, according to Wallace, also had competing loyalties—to *Ms.* magazine, Radical Lesbians, the Socialist Workers' Party, or NOW, "in that order." Wallace also observed that the NBFO was like "a lot of feminist groups in that the . . . non-lesbians spent most of their time being intimidated or feeling guilty for fear of some deeply buried anti-lesbian feeling." Just as early feminists had felt the ghost of New Left activists in their midst, many NBFO members felt "white feminists peering over our shoulders every time we talked. 'That wouldn't be right for our white sisters,' was a frequent cry. Each proposal had to withstand the following test: had white women done it and would white women like it?"[32]

In 1974, a breakaway group of black lesbians from NBFO formed the Combahee River Collective and began organizing and writing against racism, sexism, heterosexism, and class oppression. Though they never developed into a large group, they became widely known for their radical critique of American culture and society. In their initial "Collective Statement," they declared their independence from all other groups, but refused to embrace any kind of separatism: "The most general statement of our politics at the present time," they wrote,

> would be that we are actively committed to struggling against racial, sexual, heterosexual, and class oppression and see as our particular task the development of integrated analysis and practice based upon the fact that the major systems of oppression are interlocking. The synthesis of these oppressions creates the conditions of our lives. As Black women we see Black feminism as the logical political movement to combat the manifold and simultaneous oppression that all women of color face.[33]

African-American women soon became engaged in what was now called "the black family quarrel." When Elaine Brown assumed the leadership of the Black Panther Party in 1975, some men labeled her a lesbian because she appointed women to leadership roles. She then began to reassess her earlier denunciations of feminism.

> I had joined the majority of black women in America in denouncing feminism. It was an idea reserved for white women, I said, assailing the women's movement, wholesale, as either

> racist or inconsequential. . . . Now I trembled with fury long
> buried. . . . The feminists were right. The value of my life had
> been obliterated as much by being female as being black and
> poor.

Michelle Wallace, the author of *Black Macho and the Myth of Super-woman* (1978), attributed the failure of the black nationalist movement to the tough, militant attitude of black men and their compulsion to bed white women. When she first wrote the book, Wallace argued that "there is a profound distrust, if not hatred, between black men and black women that has been nursed along largely by white racism but also by an almost deliberate ignorance on the part of blacks about the sexual politics of their experience in this country." Later, she reconsidered her analysis, concluded that black self-hatred had harmed the movement, and offered a far more nuanced explanation of what writer Ralph Ellison had described as the "invisibility of the American Negro."[34]

The search to integrate race and gender issues took a giant step forward when in 1983 Alice Walker described women of color as "woman-ists," rather than feminists. To Walker, the very word "feminism" conjured up an image of a white movement with different priorities. But the word "womanist," she explained, grew out of the black folk expression that mothers often used with their female children. "You acting womanish," a mother would say to her daughter, which meant that the youngster was engaging in outrageous, audacious, or *willful* behavior.

Who was this African-American woman, so invisible to white women and black men? This was the question at the heart of so many of the novels, poetry, essays, and criticism written by African-American women during the seventies, eighties, and nineties. The title of a well-known anthology expressed it best: *All the Women Are White, All the Blacks Are Men, and Some of Us Are Brave*, edited by Gloria Hull, Patricia Bell Scott, and Barbara Smith. Viewed collectively, this stunning literary renaissance, which included writers like Toni Morrison, Audre Lorde, Toni Cade, Alice Walker, Gloria Naylor, and Maya Angelou, to name but a few of the most famous writers, revealed new aspects of African-American women's history, experiences, relationships, families, and communities. Coupled with the powerful social, literary and historical criticism written by bell hooks, Patricia Williams, Barbara Christian, Bonnie Thornton Dill, Marsha Houston, Johnnetta Cole, Elizabeth Higginbotham, Sarah Watts, Mary Berry, Darline Hine, Angela Davis, Patricia Hill Collins, Paula Giddings, Nell Painter, and many other scholars, black women substantively created a new feminist scholarly agenda.[35]

As one might expect, the work of artists and scholars would excavate all kinds of hidden injuries that black women had faced. They publicized, for instance, the forced sterilization of poor welfare women, the hideous treatment of welfare mothers, the unspoken widespread incest in rural and urban communities, the impoverishment of black women and their children, and the violence committed by male activists against the "sisters." Alice Walker's Pulitzer Prize–winning novel and the film *The Color Purple* enraged many black men for exposing the internal oppression and abuse that existed within some families. Toni Morrison received the Pulitzer Prize for all her work, including *Beloved* (1987), which was a brilliant literary evocation of African-American history, as experienced by and understood through the travail of a slave mother.

Although some early black women activists, under pressure from nationalist groups, had argued that the women's movement was wholly irrelevant to their lives, that wasn't the opinion of ordinary community-based African-American women who expanded the concept of "women's issues" to include environmental justice, antigun legislation, and community struggles for decent shelter, adequate nutrition, safe schools and neighborhoods. Black women, as it turned out, consistently supported feminist goals with greater enthusiasm than white women. Year after year, black women demonstrated more support for women's issues than any other group of women in the United States. As women who had almost always worked, they viscerally understood the bitter experience of economic exploitation, the nightmare of finding child care, the humiliation of caring for white women's children when their own children cried out for them. They *lived* the double jeopardy that Frances Beale had described.[36]

DIVIDED LOYALTIES

Questioning women's position was in the air and few women who lived in the country could avoid it, especially if they were engaged in movements committed to social change. Young Mexican-American female antiwar activists began to address "women's issues" as early as 1967, questioning their role as cooks, caretakers, "busy bees," and secretaries within the newly organized Chicano movement. "We don't want to lead, but we won't follow," was the way one woman put it. Meeting separately, some of these young women decided that they didn't want to split the unity of the growing Chicano movement by joining the "white" women's movement. But nor were they willing to be treated as second-class citizens.[37]

Decades earlier, the term "Chicano" had been a racial slur. Now, young Mexican-American activists embraced with pride words that had been used to insult them. *Chicanismo* emphasized cultural pride as a source of political unity and crystallized the essence of a nationalist ideology that viewed Chicanos as an internal colony under the domination of, and exploited by, the United States. To be Chicano meant to engage in active resistance, not to be resigned to one's fate.

The issues Chicanas addressed overlapped with, but also differed from those of African-Americans. While black women lived with the brutal legacy of slavery, Chicanas felt the burden of a different history, that of a colonized people whose land had been stolen, and that of an immigrant group who had faced fierce racial discrimination. While black women sought to strengthen weakened families, Chicanas viewed the strong Mexican-American family as the backbone of their resistance against white America. At the same time, they also viewed the Chicano family as the bulwark of a Catholic and male-dominated culture that prevented them from using contraception, having abortions, and carving out more independent lives. Still, many Chicanas viewed the survival of La Raza, the Mexican-American people, as their highest priority. Maria Varela, an activist in the Chicano movement in the Southwest, put it this way:

> When your race is fighting for survival—to eat, to be clothed, to be housed, to be left in peace—as a woman, you know who you are. You are the principle of life, of survival and endurance. . . . for the Chicano woman battling for her people, the family—the big family—is a fortress against the genocidal forces in the outside world. It is the source of strength for a people whose identity is constantly being whittled away. The mother is the center of that fortress.[38]

As they fought for better schools and against the Vietnam War, Chicanas became increasingly politicized. Tanya Luna Mount, one high-school activist, expressed her outrage at the number of Mexican-

American men who were being killed in Vietnam, rather than educated. "Do you know why they [the Board of Education] have no money for us? Because of a war in Vietnam 10,000 miles away, that is killing Mexican-American boys—and for WHAT? We can't read, but we can die! Why?"[39]

On August 29, 1969, the Chicano Moratorium, which called for the immediate end of the war, held a peaceful antiwar protest rally in Laguna Park in East Los Angeles. Police rioted, fired on women and children, shot tear gas canisters into nearby bars, and ended up wounding sixty people and killing three Chicanos. Activists in the Chicano movement felt sickened and outraged. The pivotal Moratorium offered painful proof that Chicanos did not even enjoy the freedom of assembly. Out of such disillusionments, especially in Texas, grew La Raza Unida, a third political party that fielded candidates in southwestern and western states, in order that Mexican-Americans might govern themselves.

Meanwhile, many young Chicanos joined Cesar Chavez's La Causa, the United Farm Workers' (UFW) campaign to organize farm workers in the agricultural fields of Delano, California. By the late sixties, the movement was gaining considerable momentum. Together, Cesar Chavez and Dolores Huerta had organized strikes and boycotts, and achieved some victories against the state's powerful agribusiness interests; a few growers had finally realized that they would have to employ unionized farm workers. Within the UFW were strong and effective women organizers, most famously Dolores Huerta, the vice president of the UFW. Huerta informed the men in the UFW that she had no intention of taking over, but would not simply follow male leaders: "We will lead together." Huerta also understood that women were key to organizing the farmworkers; they not only worked in the fields, but also desperately wanted a different future for their children.

As the growing student Chicano movement embraced a stronger cultural nationalism, Chicanas sometimes found themselves cast as women of a mythical Aztec homeland who were supposed to follow the strong male warriors. Some Chicanas already suspected that *Chicanismo* could be oppressive to women activists. The activist Enriqueta Longauex y Vasquez described what happened when a group of women met at the First National Chicano Youth Conference in Denver in 1969, an event that, in the view of some, gave birth to cultural nationalism. When women emerged from the Chicana Workshop, they simply stated, "It was the consensus of the group that the Chicana woman does not want to be liberated." "I felt this as quite a blow," Longauex y Vasquez wrote. "I could have cried. Surely we could at least have come up with something to add to that statement." But as she puzzled over the announcement, she realized that "liberation" to these women meant isolating themselves from the men of the larger Chicano movement. It also symbolized alienation and rupture from community, family, and tradition, and this they would not accept.[40]

That didn't mean that Chicanas were willing to be led or dominated. By 1970, Chicanas had organized the Comisión Femenil Mexicana (Mexican Women's Commission), a platform "for women to use for thinking out their problems, to deal with issues not customarily taken up in regular organizations, and to develop programs around home and family needs." Soon the Comisión became a catalyst for a growing movement of Chicana feminists.[41]

Like African-American women, Chicanas often felt torn between their own needs and ambitions as women and their loyalty to their community. Some young women resented what they viewed as a culturally sanctioned male domination of women. As activist Nancy Nieto explained, in an article titled "Macho Attitudes,"

> When a freshman male comes to MECHA [a national Chicano student organization], he is approached and welcomed. He is taught by observation that the Chicanas are only useful in areas of clerical and sexual activities. When something must be done there is always a Chicana there to do the work. "It is her place and duty to stand behind and back up her Macho!" . . . . Another aspect of the macho attitude is their lack of respect for Chicanas. They play their games, plotting girl against girl for their own benefit. They use the movement and Chicanismo to take her to bed. And when she refuses, she is a *vendida* [sellout] because she is not looking after the welfare of her men.[42]

Nevertheless, as historian Vicki Ruiz has written, "at times biting their lips, most Chicana feminists chose to remain involved in the movimiento."[43]

In May 1971, six hundred Chicanas met in Houston, Texas, to hold the First National Conference of Chicanas. Just two years after the Denver conference, Chicanas now met alone to define their own lives as women *and* Chicanas. Some of the workshops—"Sex and the Chicanas" and "Marriage, Chicana Style"—reflected a new view of themselves as more than future mothers or activists in the Chicano movement. Risking condemnation from their families, their men, and their community, the women called for free, legal abortion and birth control, controlled by Chicanas. "We have a right to control our own bodies," their resolution read. They also called for "24 hour child-care centers in Chicano communities" and announced that "Chicana motherhood should not preclude educational, political, social and economic advancement." At the Texas conference, Elma Barrera, a Chicana activist, addressed the thorny issue of Chicano unity versus women's liberation:

> I have been told that the Chicana's struggle is not the same as the white women's struggle. I've been told that our problems are different and that . . . the Chicana's energies are needed in the barrio and that being a feminist and fighting for our rights as women and as humans is being anti-Chicano and anti-male. But let me tell you what being Chicana means in Houston, Texas. It means learning how to please the men in the church, and the men at home, not in that order.[44]

Of the many controversial resolutions passed at that conference—including recognizing the Catholic Church as an oppressive institution—the women also declared that "the Chicana should not be a scapegoat for the man's frustration" and that "with involvement in the movement, marriage must change. Traditional roles for Chicanas are not acceptable or applicable."[45] So radical were these resolutions that half of the participants walked out of the conference.

Some of their male comrades, to put it mildly, were not pleased. But Chicanas fully embraced the credo of the Chicano movement—"Go back to the community with your education"—and concentrated on Mexican-American women's needs. They defended the rights of welfare mothers and lobbied for job training for women. The Chicana Action Service Center in Los Angeles, as Vicki Ruiz has noted, "helped thousands of women secure jobs and pioneered the development of placement mentors with corporations and nonprofit agencies." Chicana activists also established health care centers and helped community organizing, including providing contraception and abortions. In the 1970s, Communities Organized for Public Service (COPS) became central to organizing the Mexican-American community in San Antonio. Later, the Mothers of East Los Angeles (1984) would take up the battle to fight for decent housing, create community patrols, and fight for gun control and safe neighborhoods. By the 1980s and 1990s, Mexican-American female community activists, drawing on decades of community activism, would be instrumental in organizing the growing environmental justice movement, which refused to allow either the government or corporations to dump toxic wastes in their communities.[46]

No matter where they directed their activism, some Chicanas still felt the pain of their invisibility—to both their Chicano *compañeros* and to white middle-class feminists. In the anthology *This Bridge Called My Back*, edited by Cherrie Moraga and Gloria Anzaldua, Chicana activists voiced the frustration and anger they experienced as they tried to navigate through both the feminist and Chicano movements. Chicana lesbian feminists, including the writers Cherrie Moraga, Emma Perez, Ana Castillo, Carla Trujillo, Alicia Gaspar de Alba, and Gloria Anzaldua, experienced even greater alienation. Often, as Gloria Anzaldua wrote, they felt that they belonged nowhere: "As a mestiza I have no country, my homeland cast me out; yet all countries are mine because I am every woman's sister or potential lover. ('As a lesbian I have no race, my own people disclaim me; but I am all races because there is the queer of me in all races.')"[47]

Mexican-American women also formed their own national organization. In 1974, the Mexican-American Women's National Association (MANA) embraced many feminist goals, but also emphasized the need to protect the family. By 1990, MANA had chapters in sixteen states. Although most members were Catholic, MANA nevertheless embraced a pro-choice position, along with a program to protect women from forced sterilization. Concerned about providing leadership for the Mexican-American community, MANA launched an impressive project called Hermanitas, through which members became mentors to young girls.

Women from Asia and the Pacific islands, from the Philippines, from Puerto Rico, and from indigenous Indian and Alaskan tribes, similarly organized at both the local and national levels during the seventies. Women in Indian and Native Alaskan tribes, who constituted a very small minority—1 percent of the U.S. population in 1980—and spoke hundreds of different languages in hundreds of different tribes, participated in the Native American liberation movement that took great pride in indigenous culture, but also ignored many of women's needs. The women felt the heavy burden of the past, which, in this case, included the history of genocide and the intentional destruction of tribal cultures. To preserve tradition was to resist the dominant culture. But tradition also limited women's opportunities to live more independent lives. Yet, at stake was not only a culture, but also the very physical survival of a people.[48]

Since half of their constituency remained on reservations, many American Indian women activists chose to organize at the local level. For them, "women's issues" translated into getting much-needed social services from the government, dealing with domestic violence, alcoholism, and child abuse, providing for health care and employment needs of tribal members, and the nonnegotiable demand that their children be educated in their own language, with their own traditions.

Each group of minority women tried to explode negative stereotypes of its women. Native American feminists sought to counter cinematic images of themselves as dirty squaws (a word that originally meant, simply, "woman"), nubile naked savages, and, as the activist and writer Shirley Hill Witt put it, "a brown lump of a drudge, chewing buffalo hide, putting that tipi up and down again and again, carrying heavy burdens along with dogs while the tribe moves ever onward, away from the pursuing cavalry."[49] Asian women fought against images of themselves as dragon ladies, deferential brides, and seductive geisha entertainers.

Each group linked women's issues to larger political issues—the survival of indigenous peoples, the independence of Puerto Rico, and racism toward Asian Americans. Each group also understood that different histories had created a unique women's agenda. Though many refused to call themselves feminists, the very existence of a women's movement ignited great activity among women of racial minorities, who began to identify, name, publicize, and fight for what they decided needed to be changed.

THE GLORY THAT WAS HOUSTON

In the middle of this extraordinary explosion of feminist activity, the United Nations declared 1975 International Women's Year (IWY). Congresswomen Bella Abzug, Patsy Mink, and Margaret Heckler seized the opportunity to introduce legislation to honor IWY by funding a national women's conference, to "promote equality between men and women." Congress passed the bill, allocating $5 million to fund a conference in Houston, Texas, in 1977.

The process of selecting state delegations to the conference turned out to be a competitive, brutal, but invigorating experiment in American democracy. More than two thousand women, elected at special community meetings, represented various constituencies at the conference. Members of racial and ethnic groups ended up attending in proportions greater than their percentage in the general population. Every profession, every occupation, every age, and every racial and ethnic group were represented. The result was a cross-section of American women, including a number of antifeminists who controlled several state delegations.

Some skeptical feminists had greeted the announcement of a congressionally-sponsored conference with a yawn. Who needed one more conference, more data on discrimination, more useless guidelines that no one would consult, more co-optation by a government that seemed increasingly less concerned with women's lives?[50] But to almost everyone's surprise, the conference turned out to be an historic moment for American women. As one skeptical feminist later admitted:

> Little did we realize that what we saw, at best, as a well-intentioned, moderate, outreach program would ultimately be seized on by the right-wing as the first serious offensive in what they perceived as the cleverly plotted Amazon attack on God, home, and the American family—or that their attempts to stop the Women's Movement cold would provide us with one of the best testing grounds for grassroots feminism that we've had in many years. . . . What angered the Right was that tax dollars were being used for a national representative meeting with a legislatively stated feminist purpose: to promote equality.[51]

A highly publicized torch relay, which became a national media event, led up to the upcoming conference. Two thousand women and girls each carried a lighted torch part of the way—twenty-six hundred miles in all—from Seneca Falls, New York (the site of the first women's rights convention in 1848), to Houston, Texas. The national news tracked the progress of the runners and local television stations featured the women as they waved at onlookers along the way. Cheered by supporters, jeered by hecklers, the women ran on, braving rain, hail, and fog.

Fifty-one days later, the last relay runners reached Houston. For the very last mile, one thousand women accompanied three young athletes who carried the torch through a steady rain. When a waiting crowd of delegates first glimpsed the torch's arrival, they roared their delight and began chanting for the passage of the ERA. The poet Maya Angelou read a stirring rendition of a new "Declaration of Sentiments" (named after the document passed at Seneca Falls in 1848), which she had written for the occasion, called, ". . . To Form a More Perfect Union." Included in the poem was the solemn recognition that "we recognize that no nation can boast of balance until each member of that nation is equally employed and equally rewarded" and the promise that "Because we are women, we make these promises."[52]

The torch was then passed to Billie Jean King, the great athlete who had successfully turned women's tennis into a much-watched and highly paid sport. She then handed it to Susan B. Anthony, the grandniece of the famous suffragist. When Anthony repeated her great-aunt's famous phrase, "Failure is impossible," the crowd thundered its approval. The next morning, organizers presented the torch and Maya Angelou's new "Declaration of Sentiments"—signed by members of the conference—to the three First Ladies, Rosalyn Carter, Betty Ford, and Lady Bird Johnson, who presided over the opening ceremonies.

Sensing an early battle in what would later be called the culture wars, the media had predicted that a "cat fight" would break out between the representatives to the National Women's Conference and the fifteen thousand right-wing women who had announced a rival gathering across town. As the conference drew nearer, suspense began to build. Would feminists and right-wing women really end up fighting in the streets? Although the followers of Phyllis Schlafly, the leader of Stop ERA, encamped across town and denounced the IWY conference and the ERA as "sick," "immoral," "ungodly," "unpatriotic," and "antifamily," no fight ever materialized.

Few right-wing women (with the exception of the Utah delegation) had been elected to the National Conference. But that didn't mean that no conflicts erupted at the conference. Still, what impressed most participants was how well these delegates managed to forge "The National Plan of Action," the document that addressed the overlapping yet different needs of such diverse women. This twenty-six-plank agenda affirmed support for the ERA, and addressed the needs of battered, disabled, minority, rural, poor, young, and older women. Women of color mostly felt relieved by their unusually strong representation, but also realized that their marginalization in the women's movement had not ended.[53]

But it was the plank that affirmed lesbian rights that created the greatest drama. To everyone's surprise, Betty Friedan unexpectedly lent her support to the resolution to eliminate discrimination based on sexual orientation and preference. When the plank passed, lesbian activists shouted, "Thank you, sisters," and released hundreds of pink and yellow balloons into the air. On the balloons were printed the words, "We Are Everywhere." As ecstatic supporters snake-danced across the front of the arena, delegates from Mississippi turned their backs, bent their heads in prayer, and hoisted signs that begged, "Keep them in the closet."[54]

Soon after the conference, President Carter sent legislative recommendations to Congress and issued an executive order to establish a standing National Advisory Committee for women. But the recommendations were never implemented. By then, the New Right had created cultural and political gridlock. With the election of Ronald Reagan in 1980, memories of Houston would quickly come to seem like a dream from a distant past.

Chapter Nine

SISTERHOOD TO SUPERWOMAN

"There are no individual solutions," feminists had chanted in the late sixties. Steeped in the rhetoric and worldview of liberals and the Left, members of the movement sang the praises of a mythical, deeply desired sisterhood. If feminism were to succeed as a radical vision, the movement had to advance the interests of all women: "None of us are free until we are all free."

Yet, by 1980, most Americans imagined a feminist as a Superwoman, hair flying as she rushed around, an attaché case in one arm, a baby in the other. In the words of a popular song recycled into a perfume advertisement, she could "bring home the bacon, fry it up in the pan, and never, ever let you forget you're a man." The Superwoman could "have it all," but only if she "did it all."[1] How did this change come about in just a decade?

Despite the widespread media coverage of the National Women's Conference, most Americans were neither activists nor protesters and had little personal acquaintance with rank-and-file feminists. Newspapers and television mainly reported on stars or on the bizarre, and so the public image of the women's movement invariably came from the way in which popular and political culture translated it to its American audience.

Alongside the feminist movement described in earlier chapters grew another kind of feminism, one that existed largely in the kingdom of images, shaped by the media and by the consumerist and therapeutic self-help movements that sprang up in the 1970s. The media produced two basic stereotypes of feminists. One was the hairy, man-hating dyke, dressed in overalls and stomping boots, an image mostly confined to college campuses and to the youthful women's culture. The second and far more ubiquitous image was that of a selfish "superwoman"—who would come to stand for all women in the movement. For the vast majority of Americans who had not participated in the movement, here was the hateful woman who came to represent the feminist in the American imagination. A selfish and demonic individualist, the superwoman threatened the very fabric of American society. And, by 1980, she had become both a symbol *and* a scapegoat for other intractable problems and irreversible changes in American society.

THE MEDIA BLITZ OF 1969–1970

The sudden appearance of a new women's movement took the American media by surprise. The new feminist movement made for great copy and the media soon responded with a mixture of glee, derision, and condescension. The resulting blitz of media attention spotlighted activists in ways that proved distinctly awkward and uncomfortable. It was a shock to go home, turn on your television set or read your morning newspaper and discover that everything you cared about was summed up in the image of a zany hysteric who sought, through flamboyance, what she was unable to achieve through physical attraction. Not surprisingly, many in the new movement soon grew wary of media attention. For feminists, the question was how to use the media without being used. And, as they were to discover, in the battle for popular culture, feminists didn't have a chance.

Few feminists could forget, for example, how the media had covered the 1970 Women's Strike for Equality in New York City. Television news and newspapers used that march to sensationalize *and* discredit the women's movement, which became a typical trope of the great media blitz of 1969–1970. Television news coverage, in particular, infuriated many feminist activists. At ABC, Howard K. Smith began his report on the 1970 August march in New York with this snide introduction: "Three things have been difficult to tame. The ocean, fools, and women. We may soon be able to tame the ocean, but fools and women will take a little longer." Smith gave the last word to West Virginia senator Jennings Randolph, who described the women's movement as "a small band of bra-less bubble heads." At CBS, Eric Sevareid began his coverage with the condescending observation that "no husband ever won an argument with a wife, and the secret of a happy marriage is for the man to repeat those three little words, 'I was wrong.' " He then proclaimed, "The plain truth is, most American men are startled by the idea that American women generally are oppressed, and they read with relief the Gallup poll that two-thirds of women don't think they're oppressed either."[2]

Much of the subsequent news coverage, especially on the network news shows, assumed the same patronizing and bemused tone of these early news reports. As media critic Susan Douglas has noted, this coverage was "typical of how the news media framed what was and continued to be, by almost any measure, one of the most consequential social movements of the twentieth century."[3]

Editors and producers began scrambling for ways to capture and cover this sudden revolt of women. In 1968, editors had seized upon the image of bra-burning to symbolize feminist rebellion. But since feminists had neither focused on—nor burned—their bras, no visuals existed to support this enduring myth. Instead, by 1969, editors chose, as their image of choice, photos of "women's libbers" practicing karate. With arms and legs punched outward, these self-defense novices seemed threatening and militant. Conspicuously absent were pictures of women sitting in one another's living rooms and kitchens, where the real revolution was going on. But editors had no access to these meetings and probably would have viewed them as insufficiently dramatic. The hidden injuries of sex remained just that—invisible. There were no photographs of aggressive men, rapists, or scenes of domestic violence. Nor were there pictures of men excluding women from conversation, demanding that dinner be served on time, or denying women promotions. These stories would finally make it on screen, in film, in made-for-TV movies, and on television talk shows only in the 1980s and afterward.

In 1970, journalists and editors simply didn't know how to write about women as political or social actors, as opposed to zealous transgressors or passive victims. Confused and perhaps threatened, editors quickly adopted the word "strident" to describe any angry spokeswoman. Unconvinced reporters placed quotation marks around "women's oppression" and "male chauvinism" to indicate the questionable nature of feminists' claims. Television newscasters routinely trivialized feminist grievances by cutting away to "ordinary women" in supermarkets who were sure to ridicule feminists as social or sexual misfits.

The relationship between feminists and journalists became immensely complicated. Feminists sought to publicize the seriousness of their grievances, but were extremely fearful of creating permanent media spokeswomen. One strategy, which some feminists adopted, perhaps from Eleanor Roosevelt's example, was to speak only with female reporters.[4]

The media, for their part, regarded the movement as a provocative but passing fad, and happily sought to expand their audience with what was arguably the moment's sexiest story, filled with attractive women (despite the fact that opponents always described them as ugly and man-hating) instigating all kinds of newsworthy events. The media also tried to identify the movement's leaders and to distinguish "legitimate" activists from those they labeled "fringe" elements. Organizations such as WITCH, Redstockings, The Feminists, or Cell 16, which participated in zap action and guerrilla theater, therefore received a disproportionate amount of coverage. Ti-Grace Atkinson, who had denounced NOW and formed The Feminists, became a media star not only because of her tall, svelte Brahmin looks, but also because she predictably provided reporters with such provocative sound bites as "Marriage means rape" and "Love has to be destroyed." Interviewed on Walter Cronkite's *CBS Evening News*, she compared marriage to the institution of slavery: "People say, well, couldn't we get rid of the bad things about marriage? Could you have gotten rid of the bad things about slavery and still have slavery?"[5]

Some editors or producers decided to send female journalists to report on the new women's liberation movement, hoping they would be received with less hostility. Many of these women, already experienced journalists, didn't assume that they needed their consciousnesses raised, but were thrilled to get such an interesting assignment. Often obliged to participate in the groups they wrote about, some of them discovered that they were not as emancipated as they had imagined. The conversion of so many women journalists to feminism is one reason that the early media blitz of 1969–1970, particularly in newspapers and magazines, resulted in as much accurate and sympathetic reportage as it did.[6]

As it happened, female journalists often recognized in feminists' grievances problems they had run up against in their own professional lives. Consider what happened when *Newsweek* decided to run a cover story ("Women in Revolt") on the women's movement in 1970. The editors decided that their own reporter was insufficiently objective. So they hired Helen Dudar, a freelance writer who was also the wife of one of the editors, to produce a piece more to their liking. They patronizingly described her as "a topflight journalist who is also a woman."

Helen Dudar admitted that she had spent "years rejecting feminists without bothering to look too closely at their charges." When assigned the story, she acknowledged her distinct ambivalence toward feminism. In the published story, she dutifully described all the different trends and groups in the movement. But then she ended her report with this remarkable personal disclosure:

> Superiority is precisely what I had felt and enjoyed, and it was going to be hard to give it up. That was an important discovery. One of the rare and real rewards of reporting is learning about yourself. Grateful though I am for the education, it hasn't done much for the mental stress. Women's lib questions everything; and while intellectually I approve of that, emotionally I am unstrung by a lot of it. Never mind. The ambivalence is gone; the distance is gone. What is left is a sense of pride and kinship with all those women who have been asking all the hard questions. I thank them and so, I think, will a lot of other women.[7]

When Marlene Sanders, a veteran news journalist, reported on the women's movement for a special CBS television documentary, she, too, treated the movement sympathetically. Sanders, who had already covered student riots and the presidential campaign of Robert F. Kennedy, had done her homework. She knew how easy it would have been to elicit bizarre and threatening statements from the usual suspects in New York City. Instead, she interviewed women's groups at Duke University, and in North Carolina. In the lively documentary that CBS eventually broadcast, Sanders revealed in passing that most of the new women's liberationists she interviewed were married and had children. Instead of expressing the bemusement of so many male journalists, she provided in-depth coverage of women's desires, needs, and issues. She ended her televised report with these prescient words:

> The Women's Liberation Movement will not disappear after the singing, marching and shouting have died down. Man himself may not be the enemy, but his practices are under attack, whether they are motivated by prejudice, profit or habit. This is a search for equality of opportunity, not the wish to be just like men. It is the desire for more options, for choice, for shattering of stereotypes, for women to choose more freely the

kinds of lives they want to live, and if we choose to work, to
be paid in full. The status quo is being challenged by the
Women's Liberation Movement. Today it's still a man's world.
And just look at it. Move over, gentlemen. Maybe you can use
some help. This is Marlene Sanders.[8]

Viewers wrote appreciative letters to Sanders, some asking how they
could join "the cause." A typical note came from a grateful woman from
Muncie, Indiana: "I must say, as a fairly young mother, busy housewife
and soon to be working woman, I'm in dire need of some kind of liberation. Your help would be greatly appreciated and thanks again for an en-
lightening program."[9]

Wary as they were of the media, women's liberationists nevertheless
sought widespread media attention by planning well-publicized demonstrations. Consider the dramatic sit-in staged in May 1970 at *Ladies'
Home Journal*, one of the most popular general women's magazines,
whose slogan "Never underestimate the power of a woman" suddenly
took on new meaning. Nearly two hundred women, including some employees, sat in at the office of the *LHJ* to protest a "women's magazine"
whose advertisements routinely exploited women. They also demanded
a day care center for the children of employees. A group of radical feminists also insisted that *LHJ* include a special section on the women's
liberation movement. In an open letter to other feminists, the activists
explained, "We seek to raise questions, analyze the condition of wom-
ankind, and to search for new answers."[10]

To the feminists' surprise, *Ladies' Home Journal* responded quickly.
By August 1970, the magazine published a special eight-page insert titled "The Power of a Woman" on "the New Feminism," written by "the
women's liberation movement." To their readership, the editors explained the sudden appearance of this insert:

> We had been following this movement with great interest,
> of course. But it wasn't until 200 of these new feminists
> marched into the Journal's office and stayed for 11 hours that
> we were literally confronted with the intensity and reality of
> this brand of women's rights thinking.

The insert included critiques of work, sex, love, marriage, poetry, and
long lists of women's groups across the country. It profiled causes like

the Equal Rights Amendment and even described meetings held between the delegations of American socialist-feminists and North Vietnamese women.[11]

Curious about their readers' responses to their bold move, *LHJ* took a
readers' survey, the results of which they published in November 1970.
Asked their opinions about the women's movement, 46 percent of readers described themselves as "con," 34 percent as "pro," and 20 percent
expressed mixed feelings, cheering women's support of equal pay for
equal work, but expressing distaste for "stridency."[12] But the most important vote was the one held by magazine readers. Circulation rose
dramatically. Other women's magazines quickly followed *LHJ*'s example. *McCall's*, for example, produced an insert called "Right Now," a digest of feminist causes and news.

In less than a year, the media realized that the women's movement
was not only an exciting story, but a profitable one as well. Feminists
gained also, attracting more national attention than they had ever expected. Monitoring the media became one of the movement's consuming
passions. Throughout the decade, various chapters of NOW and other
local groups put tremendous pressure on magazines, television stations,
and newspapers to stop portraying women in stereotypical ways.[13]

Still, the stubborn images of the "bra burner" as well as "the women's
libber" left many women feeling that they wanted to distance themselves from such a movement. The media also legitimated some "players," like the lovely Gloria Steinem, while demonizing other activists,
like the openly bisexual Kate Millett. They largely discredited the anger
of young feminists toward marriage, motherhood, the commercial exploitation of women's bodies, and the inequalities that the sexual revolution had brought with it, even as they promoted women's demands
for equal pay for equal work, for legal abortion, and for child care
facilities.[14]

News of the movement also spread because of several media-
generated spectacles. On September 20, 1973, Billie Jean King, a
twenty-nine-year-old feminist tennis star who had campaigned for equal
prize money for women athletes, beat Bobby Riggs, a fifty-nine-year-old
former tennis champion, in what was hyped as the "Battle of the Sexes."
A wave of pregame publicity sparked widespread national interest.
Riggs entered in a ricksha drawn by his famed "bosoms," the two
women who brought him onto the court. Billie Jean King arrived on an
Egyptian litter carried by a troupe of bare-chested musclemen. They

even exchanged gifts. Riggs gave King a huge Sugar Daddy. She gave him a live baby pig. King won.[15]

Among the many events that publicized feminist ideas was Norman Mailer's publication of "Prisoner of Sex," a fifty-five-thousand-word article published in *Harper's* magazine in 1971. Having been crowned Chief Male Chauvinist by Kate Millett and others, Mailer now responded with a robust, even self-mocking, tongue-lashing polemic that spread feminists' ideas to an even greater audience. Some feminists were more interested in demonizing Mailer than in reading "Prisoner of Sex," which actually revealed personal ambivalence and vulnerability, as well as fear and anxiety.

Describing himself as the Prisoner of Sex, Mailer poked, jabbed, ridiculed, and essentially used the subject of women's liberation as an opportunity to explore his own need for women, his contempt for political cant, and his horror of the technological fix. Still smarting from Kate Millett's attack on his novels' negative images of women, he now fought back, describing Millett's writing style as "suggestive of a night-school lawyer who sips Metrecal to keep his figure,* and thereby is so full of isolated proteins, factory vitamins, reconstituted cyclamates, and artificial flavors that one has to pore over the passages like a business contract." Mailer's notorious 1973 debate with Australian feminist Germaine Greer, author of *The Female Eunuch*, created yet another explosion of media hype, and helped vault the debate about sex and sexism to the top of the cultural agenda.[16]

By the end of 1971, few literate Americans could ignore the emergence of the women's movement. *Time, Newsweek*, the *Atlantic Monthly, Saturday Review, Look, Life*, the *New York Times Magazine*, had all run cover stories on the new movement. Television, moreover, had begun broadcasting a long list of documentaries on the new female rebellion. In the process, the media turned the phrase "women's lib"—as they so chummily dubbed it—into a household phrase.[17]

THE "FIRST WOMAN" STORY

Pressured by feminists, a wave of newspapers began to replace their "women's pages" with newly redesigned sections called View, Style,

*Metrecal was a widely used diet drink.

A MOVING BODY

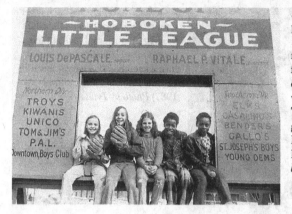

After Congress passed Title IX in 1972, all schools receiving federal funds had to provide equal resources for women's sports. These were the first girls to play in Little League. (Hoboken, New Jersey) *Photo by Bettye Lane*

In the aftermath of Title IX, girls and women began training for and winning Olympic medals. In 1999, the U. S. women's soccer team mesmerized the nation when they captured the World Cup. (Relay Hand Off, Hayward, California, 1973) *Photo by Cathy Cade*

Billie Jean King was indefatigable in her successful campaign to transform women's tennis into a highly paid and popular sport by creating a separate women's tennis tour. (Wimbledon, 1975) *Corbis*

WOMEN'S CULTURE

As women started to see each other through their own eyes, rather than through the distorted lens of their culture, they began to respect and love each other. (Country Women's Festival, Mendocino, California, 1987) *Photo by Lynda Koolish*

The Michigan Womyn's Music Festival turned into an annual celebration of the growing women's culture and featured some of the movement's most talented musicians and singers. (1977) *Photo by JEB*

Margie Adams, along with Holly Near, Chris Williams, and Sweet Honey and the Rock, were among some of the most talented new musicians who played at women's concerts and dances during the 1970s. (Los Angeles, 1973) *Photo by Lynda Koolish*

POLITICS AND PROLIFERATION

At a Forum for the Future held in New York City to create a feminist agenda for the 1980s, four of the movement's prominent early leaders posed for photographers: Ti-Grace Atkinson, Flo Kennedy, Gloria Steinem, and Kate Millet. *Photo by Bettye Lane*

The National Conference on Women in 1977 featured a torch relay from Seneca Falls, New York (site of the first women's rights conference), to Houston. Bella Abzug, Billie Jean King and Betty Friedan—pioneers who had dramatically changed the lives of American women—accompanied young runners through a euphoric crowd. *Photo by Diana Mara Henry*

When delegates at Houston finally voted for the first far-reaching National Plan of Action, activists cheered and snake-danced across the hall. *Photo by Diana Mara Henry*

Feminists joined United Farm Workers in their campaign to improve the labor conditions of agricultural workers. Dolores Huerta and Gloria Steinem with Bella Abzug, congresswoman, Chair of the 1977 Houston Conference. *Photo by Bettye Lane*

In 1978, Gerda Lerner, who had co-founded the first program in women's history at Sarah Lawrence College with Joan Kelly, brought together leaders of women's organizations for a summer institute in women's history. They took on the project of creating women's history week, which later turned into a month. From left to right: Professors Gerda Lerner, Amy Swerdlow (with her fist raised) and Alice Kessler-Harris. *Courtesy of Gerda Lerner*

Every January 23rd, on the anniversary of the 1973 *Roe v. Wade* Supreme Court decision that legalized abortion, activists against abortion demonstrated in Washington, D. C. In 1987, feminists satirized the opposition, but the media couldn't tell the difference. *Photo by JEB*

On October 11, 1987, 500,000 lesbians, gay men, and their supporters assembled in Washington, D. C., to demand an end to discrimination against lesbians and gay men. A few days later, Congress passed amendments restricting funds for AIDS research. *Photo by JEB*

When the UN declared 1975 International Women's year, delegates immediately expanded it to a decade. Conferences in Mexico (1975), Copenhagen (1980), Nairobi (1985), and Beijing (1995) brought together thousands of the world's women, who created vast networks, redefined women's rights as human rights, and began to build a global feminist movement. (Beijing, 1995) *Photo by Jo Freeman*

With the publication of *I Know Why the Caged Bird Sings* (1970), poet and novelist Maya Angelou transported readers through the searing and exhilarating experiences of African-American women. (Berkeley Community Theatre, 1994) *Photo by Lynda Koolish*

Poet and essayist Susan Griffin's pioneering essay, "Rape: The All-American Crime," (Ramparts, 1970) was followed by such critically acclaimed works as *Woman and Nature* (1978) and *A Chorus of Stones* (1992). (Author's home, Berkeley, California, 1975) *Photo by Lynda Koolish*

Toni Morrison, the author of *The Bluest Eye* (1970), *Sula* (1974), *Song of Solomon* (1977), and *Beloved* (1987), was awarded the Pulitzer Prize for her entire literary work. (Black Oak Books, Berkeley, California, 1987) *Photo by Lynda Koolish*

A novelist, short fiction writer, essayist, and activist-at-large, Tillie Olsen taught a new generation of women about their lives in *Tell Me a Riddle* (1961) and *Silences* (1978). (Virginia Woolf Conference, Santa Cruz, California, 1973) *Photo by Lynda Koolish*

Novelist Maxine Hong Kingston was the author, most famously, of *The Woman Warrior* (1976) and *China Men* (1980). An activist, she helped Vietnamese veterans heal themselves through their writings. (Oakland, California, circa 1988) *Photo by Lynda Koolish*

The author of many critically acclaimed collections of poetry and essays, Adrienne Rich inspired her readers to hear the magic of words and to stand up for their convictions in *Diving into the Wreck* (1973), *Of Woman Born* (1976), and *On Lies, Secrets and Silences* (1979). (San Francisco, 1978) *Photo by Lynda Koolish*

Poet and essayist Audre Lorde taught her readers about being African-American, a lesbian, and a woman—but never a victim—in *Sister Outsider* (1984) and *The Cancer Journals* (1980). (Full Moon Coffeehouse, San Francisco, 1972) *Photo by Linda Koolish*

Canadian author Margaret Atwood's chilling dystopian novel *The Handmaid's Tale* (1986) raised the specter of how an elected totalitarian, right-wing, American government might treat its female citizens. (San Francisco Bay Area, private reading, 1979) *Photo by Lynda Koolish*

Novelist, poet, and essayist, Alice Walker received the Pulitzer Prize for *The Color Purple* (1982). Walker proposed "womanism," rather than feminism, as more appropriate for African-American and other minority women. (San Francisco, KQED Radio Station, 1988) *Photo by Lynda Koolish*

Lifestyle, or, in the case of the *New York Times*, "the family, food, fashions and furnishings" section. By shrinking the number of inches allotted to the former "club-wedding-parties format," editors created more room for feature stories, particularly about women entering male professions and occupations.[18] Such stories also appeared in special issues of news magazines. The March 1972 issue of *Time* magazine, for instance, profiled an airport attendant, a radio disk jockey, a computer engineer, a telephone installer, a stockbroker, and an auto mechanic, all of whom were identified as the "first woman" to be employed in these occupations.

But it was the daily newspaper that developed the particular formulaic conventions that characterized "first woman" stories. These tales of individual success began to appear during the early 1970s, peaked around 1976, and practically vanished by the end of the decade. Caught off guard, fumbling headline editors frequently employed Cold War imagery—like "invasion"—to describe women's entry into a new profession. Patronizing language often accompanied the news of a woman's accomplishments. When San Francisco appointed the first woman to the position of port director, the local paper headlined the story, "New Port Director Is a Lady Lawyer." When a famous female conductor replaced Seiji Ozawa as a guest conductor in San Francisco, the headline read, "Symphony Guest Gets to Do a Man's Job."[19]

At first, reporters didn't do much better. Some journalists wrote their stories as if they had just learned of a deep, dark secret: "A gun-toting woman correction officer has been working inside the walls of San Quentin Prison for the past week, it was learned yesterday."[20] The "first woman" narrative almost always noted a woman's appearance, often through words, frequently with a photograph, and predictably described her marital and parental status. Invariably, the reporter asked the first woman whether she considered herself a "libber," whether feminism had helped her secure her new position, and if she had encountered resentment from male coworkers or subordinates. The first women learned the right answers to these questions: No, being a woman had never harmed them, nor had it helped them. No, they had no connection with "women's libbers." When asked how they "juggled" their domestic and work responsibilities, they rarely admitted to any difficulties. When asked whether men had expressed any hostility to their arrival in the workplace, they diplomatically described themselves as "good sports" and "one of the guys."

Strangely, the term "affirmative action" never seemed to appear in these stories, and yet this policy and its guidelines had opened up all kinds of doors for women. The phrase "affirmative action" originated in a 1965 Executive Order issued by President Johnson and amended in October 1967 to include a ban on sexual discrimination. The newly renumbered Executive Order 11375 required that all institutions that did business with or received grants from the federal government should not only refrain from racial or sexual discrimination, but should also "take affirmative action to ensure that applicants are employed, and employees are treated during their employment without regard to their race, color, religion, sex, or national origin." During the early seventies, the government, universities, and even the private corporate sector made great efforts to find such qualified candidates. Instead of just relying on the old boys' network, employers now advertised jobs all over the country. Equally qualified women and minorities were supposed to be considered to make up for past discrimination.

Middle-class educated women, as it turned out, were undoubtedly best positioned to pounce on these new opportunities. As a result, women found many formerly all-male jobs and careers open to them for the first time. Yet none of the reporters or the interviewed first women seemed to know—or wished to publicize—that affirmative action had helped them. Perhaps this is one reason why so few women later understood that they owed their jobs to affirmative action.[21]

I still remember a feature story that made a great impression on me in this period. It profiled a "lady neurosurgeon" who rose at dawn to train for marathons, made breakfast for her children, operated on six or seven brains, returned home for a few "quality hours" with her children, cooked a gourmet dinner for her husband, and then, with her children asleep, enjoyed a few hours of intimacy with him.

The story contained all the first-woman elements I have since reread in newspapers from that decade. I remember the sinking feeling I had afterward. I knew I was not—and could not be—such a superwoman. Of course, there was no way to know whether this superwoman eventually succumbed to exhaustion, or how her marriage and children survived the stress of such a driven life. Nor did anyone know about any obstacles she had encountered during medical training or, later, in the operating room. It all seemed so simple. The "can do" American spirit, grafted onto a first female professional, had given birth to a somewhat unbelievable typecast character, the Superwoman, who, with her inexhaustible energy and talent, would be the dominant media image of the feminist in the 1980s. From helpless housewife to bionic woman in one decade.

Consider the tale of Marion McAllister. In February 1973, the *New York Times* profiled McAllister, an African-American woman who had just entered a training program that promised to make her the first Transit Authority "motorwoman" in New York City's subway system. Alongside her photograph, the story described her as married and the mother of a fifteen-year-old daughter. The fact that affirmative action had created these new training opportunities was, as usual, ignored. Instead, the article cast McAllister as a female Horatio Alger, a hardworking, ambitious young woman who had begun her career as a counter girl in a restaurant and was heading ever upward toward her dreams. McAllister publicly credited her husband, a subway yardmaster, with encouraging her to apply for the position. To the reporter, she confided her long-range ambition to become a dispatcher, a position in which she would have matched her husband's salary.

Unlike the typical "first woman" narrative, this story revealed how McAllister had encountered sexual discrimination in her earlier attempt to enter an all-male occupation. Three years before, McAllister had applied to take a civil service exam to become an assistant dispatcher. To hide the fact that she was a woman, she had signed up under the name M. McAllister. When she arrived for the exam, the Transit Authority refused to permit her to take the exam, simply because she was a woman. They even called the police. Since no rules—simply custom—prevented a woman from taking the exam, McAllister—shaken and stunned—took it and failed. Now, having passed the exam, she was finally on the fast track to becoming a "motorman," a short step to her real goal as a dispatcher.

Or so the reader assumed. Unlike most first women quoted in the press, McAllister openly admitted to some apprehension about entering the program. "Today in class," she said, "I was just 'one of the boys,' but I think quite a few train conductors will have a feeling about being 'co-pilot' to a woman motorman." Just three months later, in a tiny paragraph squeezed under "Metropolitan Briefs," the *Times* reported that "citing 'personal reasons,' Marion McAllister resigned from the Transit Authority motorman training program that would have made her the city's first subway 'motorwoman.' " The newspaper now described her as the thirty-six-year-old mother of *two* children.[22]

What had happened? Had her coworkers hassled or harassed her with racist or sexist comments? Had her home life become intolerable?

Had she given birth to or adopted another child? Had she or one of her family members become ill? Readers had no way to know; most of those who read the initial article probably never even noticed the news of her resignation.

First women learned that they should be good sports, attribute their success to family or to meritocracy, and always show more interest in becoming one of the boys than in advancing other women's careers. When a woman became San Francisco's first "lady bartender," she joked about the ribbing she received from male customers, adding, "I'm just one of the fellows—36-24-36." When voters in Hayward, California, elected a woman as mayor, she quickly pointed out that "it was not a women's lib thing. I asked voters to judge me as a person, not as a woman." When Bonnie Tiburzi became the first woman to pilot a commercial passenger plane, she attributed her success to her "strong father and two brothers." "I guess," she said, "I just considered myself one of the boys." When Sally Ride, then a graduate student, was chosen to be one of the first American women astronauts, she emphatically stated at a press conference that it "was not a feminist breakthrough. . . . I don't think I was hired because I'm a woman, but because I'm a scientist."[23]

First women rarely mentioned the women's movement. When they did, they took special pains to distance themselves from the "women's libbers" the media had so successfully created. One twenty-seven-year-old, who became the first woman to hold a high office in the FBI, broke with tradition when she announced that she intended to use Ms. rather than Miss or Mrs. When asked about women's liberation, she said that she didn't support that "part of the movement that says men are bad, who say that we should have a completely different society." Equal pay for equal work. With these words, women could nod to feminism even as they distanced themselves from the media's hardly recognizable version of the movement itself.[24]

Men were the good guys in these narratives—not because of their willingness to embrace affirmative action and to search out female talent, but because they so warmly welcomed women into new occupations. The first woman story compulsively described male coworkers as generous and welcoming people. When San Francisco began assigning female officers to book prisoners at San Francisco City Prison, one of the female officers said, "When I first came here, I was a bit wary of how the men would treat me, but I've found them to be the nicest people I've ever worked with." When Marjorie Downing became the first woman president of Sonoma State College in California, she swore she never had difficulty with men. "I've been dealing with largely male faculties all my life and I've never had any trouble. I don't foresee any major problems, do you?" In marked contrast, the friends and families of these first women almost always mentioned how tough-minded they were and how capable they would be of handling whatever the " 'diehards' will dish out"—an implicit acknowledgment of the reality of resistance and resentment that these women undoubtedly did encounter.[25]

If affirmative action didn't help, and men didn't harm, good looks, of course, were irrelevant. In a *New York Times* feature about Stella Wilson, a woman who became the first female "salesman" for Xerox, the reporter wrote that "the blue-eyed, dark-haired former British model [had] marched into her boss's office two years ago and announced she wanted to become a salesman." Given a two-week trial, she proved herself and finally wound up as the top "salesman" at Xerox's New York office. The former model assured her interviewer, "I don't think my looks helped." Women, she explained, were simply "more intuitive" and "could evaluate the situation better." Quick to disagree that she was a pioneer libber, she repeated the required mantra, "I'm all for equal pay for equal work," adding, of course, "but I think a lot of the aspects of women's lib are rather bizarre. Like bra burning. I went to one women's lib meeting and all the women looked rather strange. Besides, I have all the liberation I can handle. And I think that a woman can get almost any job she wants—if she really *wants* it." When asked if she ever encountered male resentment, she replied, "You get a few snide remarks," but quickly added that "Men were charmed to be confronted by a woman sales representative."

Unmarried Stella Wilson had embraced the narcissism of the age with a vengeance. When she said that she had all the liberation she could handle, she meant that she already led a life wholly devoted to herself. She lived alone in an expensive rented apartment, shared a summer house in wealthy Southampton, and spent her leisure time sky diving, skiing, swimming, and painting portraits of old people. "They have so much character," she said. Wilson hoped to marry eventually but thought that children would limit her freedom. "The world is such an incredibly exciting place. There is so much to do and so many other ways in which I can use my energies. Motherhood is like childhood revisited. I've already had one childhood, and I don't want to go through another." Many young feminists also harbored reservations and apprehensions about marriage and motherhood, but for quite a different reason: they feared the feminine mystique's emphasis on exclusive domesticity. For Wilson, "liberation" meant the permission to consume whatever gave her greater "freedom." Like other first women, she made no mention of trying to help other women or even of liking other women. Asked about supervising men and women, she ended the interview predictably: "Oh, I much prefer to work with men. I can't stand the pettiness of women."[26]

Stella Wilson's story is a good example of the way that feminism came to be associated in the public mind with career women, single or married, who chose self-advancement and self-indulgence over hearth and home. Her avoidance of marriage and motherhood had little in common with the kinds of criticism feminists had raised about unequal power relations in traditional marriages and families. But such distinctions easily blurred in the minds of people whose only exposure to the women's movement was through media portrayals of the cool, manipulative, upwardly mobile woman, who chose career and consumption over family and children, which became the paradigmatic image of the feminist.

Although first woman narratives hid many truths about women's lives, they did help millions of women readers imagine themselves in new occupations and professions. The stories and photographs also provided female readers with a growing repertoire of images of blue, pink [clerical], and white collar workers.[27] No longer just brides or mothers in the "family, food, fashion, and furnishings" section of the New York Times, or in the features section of the San Francisco Chronicle, as well as other papers nationwide, women now appeared as gas station attendants, traveling salesmen, doormen, welders, truck drivers, steelworkers, members of a road gang, and pest exterminators. Photographs captured them hanging from ropes as they washed windows, receiving badges as California Highway Patrolmen, being sworn in as the first women police officers, hauling heavy weights as "roustabouts" on an off-shore drilling rig in the Gulf of Mexico, and descending into Kentucky coal mines as the first women miners.[28]

CONSUMER FEMINISM

While newspapers created new "lifestyle" sections to appeal to women readers, women's magazines helped translate and transform American feminism into a universe of goods and services that promised liberation.

The traditional magazines—*Harper's Bazaar*, *McCall's*, *Ladies' Home Journal*, and *Redbook*—maintained their usual staple of articles on diets, recipes, catching and holding men, sex and health.

But by creating sections devoted to the movement and by profiling feminists, mainstream magazines began to educate the nation's women (for men did not read these magazines) about what must have seemed to many of them like a sudden eruption of female rebellion. Many of these magazines also hired feminist writers to be columnists. In 1972, Letty Pogrebin began a regular column for *LHJ*, focusing on working women's issues. The column lasted until 1980 and publicized nearly every major feminist topic of the decade. In 1977, Mary Cantwell, the features editor of *Mademoiselle*, asked Judith Coburn to take over a regular column from Karen Durbin, another radical feminist. Cantwell insisted that the column keep its title, "The Intelligent Woman's Guide to Sex," but allowed Coburn to write on any subject that addressed women's lives. For four years, Coburn wrote freely about such feminist issues as abortion, women and the draft, wages for housework, the coming of the superwoman, and critiques of the birth control pill.[29]

But the traditional magazines didn't only advertise feminism. During the seventies, they also tried to find a balance between femininity and feminism. They idealized domesticity even as they romanticized careerism. In 1979, *LHJ* began a new section called, "It's not easy to be a woman today!" which, over the course of a year, included such features as "How I Went from Ruffles to Hard Hat," "I Learned to Love Myself after He Stopped Loving Me," "I Won't Apologize for Being a Housewife," "Can a [single] Woman Live Without a Man?," "It Took Me a Long Time to Grow Up," and "Will I Ever Find a Liberated Man?" In one short story a woman who had been analyzing cancer-producing environmental pollutants is forced by a mysterious dizziness to stay at home with her children. She discovers, much to her amazement, that she knows very little about their habits or abilities. In the end, she decides to stay at home, explaining:

> I was right when I said Women's Liberation wasn't titles on the door or salary raises, but I was wrong when I said it didn't exist. It does exist, and I've just been liberated from leading two fragmented lives, liberated from doing a juggling act on a tight rope—keeping sitters, children, husband, employer and myself, almost, but not quite satisfied. I was confusing liberation with freedom, because of course I am not free ... I am

liberated, but I am not free. With luck I will never be free, but
bound forever.[30]

In short, the traditional women's magazines—filled with stories, editori-
als, ads, and columns that frequently contradicted one another—
accurately captured the kaleidoscopic chaos of women's lives during the
seventies.

As growing numbers of women entered the labor force, these magazines began refocusing their traditional self-help features on the problems faced by working women. They taught newly divorced women how
to cope and instructed women on how to replace deferential behavior
with a more assertive stance that would gain them raises and respect.
They reassured working women that their children would survive their
absence, and that they could keep their husbands by setting time aside
for special "dates" and playing an active part in revitalizing their sex
life.[31]

Millions of nonmovement women first learned about feminism, as
well as the new occupations and opportunities that had opened up to
women during the seventies, within the familiar pages of women's magazines. They also read articles that encouraged them to find themselves,
to return to school, and to stand up to bullying husbands.[32] "Barbara
Shields," a graduate of a northeastern college, married in 1964 at the
age of twenty-two, and worked for three years as a high-school teacher
to support her husband's study of law. Afterward, she quit her job, bore
two sons, and spent the next sixteen years caring for her family in a
Connecticut suburb. When asked in the late 1980s how she had learned
about the women's movement, she pointed at the clutter of women's
magazines that littered her bathroom floor.

It was the women's magazines. You know, they had all these
articles about learning how to dress for work, how to ask for a
raise, how to juggle your family's needs and your work. I began to realize that I had followed my mother's life without
even questioning it. I wasn't sorry that I stayed home with my
boys. But when they reached high school, I went back to
graduate school.

During the late eighties, she began teaching at a local community
college and confided, "I never understood how working outside the

house could really change your sense of self-esteem. But it really did. I get dressed everyday, people need me and appreciate me in a different way." The women's movement, said this former housewife, had transformed her life, largely because she had read and heard about it so much in the magazines she had read.

> I felt that I wanted to be more assertive. I know that my marriage is in some sense different than it was in the beginning because I felt that I wanted to be more central in it, instead of always following someone else all the time. I'm sure the women's movement was the influence. I read magazines and books; I heard people speak and I felt more important as an individual.[33]

When her husband of some three decades suddenly left her, she wondered whether her growing independence—or the simple fact of her aging—contributed to his abandonment.

The advertising industry scarcely missed a beat as they geared up to sell "liberation" as early as 1970. In addressing the Association of Industrial Advertisers in 1971, one NOW leader tried to convince her listeners to use advertising as a constructive vehicle for social change. They ignored her advice. In fact, some of the most popular pseudo-feminist ads appropriated the language of emancipation in order to sell women products that could harm their health. "The Virginia Slims Campaign," launched in 1970, advertised a new cigarette that glamorized anorexic women as emancipated, rich, role models. Under the slogan, "You've Come a Long Way, Baby," the ads offered parables of women's historic subordination and tried to persuade them that smoking a Virginia Slims cigarette had a contribution to make to their personal freedom. Similarly, Massengill's feminine hygiene spray reinforced the belief that women's bodies were dirty and that a new (and quite unnecessary) product was necessary to establish "freshness." For its campaign slogan, the advertisers appropriated "Freedom Now," trivializing language that had been chanted by activists in the civil rights movement of the sixties. A Dewars' Scotch campaign, designed to persuade women to drink hard liquor, previously considered unladylike, profiled mothers who had careers, yet still drank, a sure sign of their emancipation from traditional womanhood.[34]

It didn't take long for the business and advertising industry to repackage feminism and try and sell it back to women. Appealing to the rejection of girdles and bras by the young, lingerie manufacturers came up with the "no bra" look, which allowed breasts to poke through sheer material and give a woman a "bra-less" look. Feminists had denounced artifice and cosmetics. Now, the cosmetics industry began to advertise all kinds of powder, lipstick, and eyeliner that promised "a natural look."[35]

A flurry of new magazines—*New York Woman, Self, Working Woman,* to name just a few—appeared during the 1970s, aimed at selling to young working women. Such magazines repackaged feminism into products and services and targeted the working woman, who supposedly needed these things to prosper. This new consumer feminism tended to equate liberation with the purchase of things—liquor, tobacco, vacations, stereos, cameras, and clothes. *New York Woman,* for example, laced its traditional articles on shopping, theater, and fashion with "liberation articles" like "Sex Equality: The Secret Storm" (a piece on the Equal Rights Amendment) and an article about Representative Bella Abzug. But the real intention of the magazine was to instruct readers on chic ways to spend their money.[36]

These magazines, which Stella Wilson (Xerox's new female wunderkind) might have devoured, had little to do with the 90 percent of women who worked in low-paid clerical service and sales jobs. Bernice Howe, a $4-an-hour clerical worker from Denver, picked up a copy of *Working Woman* the first time she saw it on the newsstand. "But the first article I turned to was on how to pick out an outfit for less than $200. They have to be kidding." Many housewives also felt that this upscale consumer feminism excluded them. When asked what she thought of the feminist movement, Lucille Schlecting, a fifty-year-old housewife in Lindenhurst, New York, said, "I see it as important for the professional women, especially the young ones. It helps them get into administrative positions. But for someone like me, well, I guess I'm over the hill as far as getting ahead." For such women, feminism came to be synonymous with professional women who could afford "liberation."[37]

Still, for the growing numbers of "entry-level" managerial or professional women—or for those who dreamed of such a future—"Dressing for Success" (the title of a best-seller of the time) was actually important. Dresses, blouses, and skirts—the traditional attire of secretaries—simply didn't establish the authority that men's suits commanded. The new magazines chided women for wearing "inappropriate" outfits, even as they instructed them how to buy a new wardrobe. As *New Woman* magazine editorialized, "although most women can put together great outfits for leisure, sport or an evening on the town, they do not know how to dress for success in their careers. And that is part of what is keeping them down."[38]

Magazines had always scolded women about their appearance. (How else to find and keep a man?) Cast as an individual problem, a working woman's appearance now became as important as dressing for men's approval had once been. The magazines warned women to give off no "sexual innuendos during working hours" and to avoid such feminine accouterments as "noticeable perfume, bouffant hairdos, tinted glasses, enormous shoulder bags, clanging or ornate jewelry or any kind of clothing without a jacket." Instead, managerial women were to wear their hair simply styled (no longer than shoulder length), and "clear glasses with frames that matched their hair color and skirt suits."

In other words, women were to adopt a pared-down and tailored male look, wear the same suit (but with a skirt) that had long conferred on men white collar status and distinguished managers from their employees. Such suits, which draped and hid men's bodies, especially their sexual organs, signaled authority and power. Just in case women still didn't get it, *New Woman* featured photographs of twins, side by side, one dressed in a skirt suit and one in a casual sweater and slacks. Beneath the photographs, the caption asked readers: "Which twin is the executive? Which twin is the secretary? Look at the executive (left) and see for yourself the power of clothing—how well she fits behind the desk of authority."[39]

Women at work began to don what had formerly been men's clothing. Unisex dressing also reflected the decade's trendy fascination with the androgynous personality as a new indicator of psychological health. Responding to an onslaught of new women workers, designers pushed the "power" business suit with padded shoulders, worn over a silk blouse, matching skirt, and high heels. Until the 1990s, this remained the new business uniform for women. By then, some women, more confident of their positions, began to seek comfort, alongside their authority, in their everyday appearance.[40]

The emphasis on appearance reinforced the very nonfeminist idea that each woman was responsible for her own failure or success. Feminism was fast being turned into an individual project. What a woman purchased decided her fate. Only with the right clothes could she signal, through appearance and behavior, that she was not the secretary, but the lawyer or the corporate executive. It was up to her. When a woman dressed properly, she could establish her authority. But learning how to exercise that authority in the corporate male world was quite another matter: that was a psychological issue each woman had to address alone.

THERAPEUTIC FEMINISM

It was one thing to march for equality, but quite another to implement it at home or at the workplace. Across the nation, men and women struggled with a shrinking economy that, in the wake of the OPEC oil crisis in 1973, would make two-income families increasingly necessary to sustain a middle-class standard of living. With two parents at work, the perennial question, Who will take care of the children?, became more urgent. Attempts to share household work and child care threw frantic parents into a battle for leisure time, a scarce and precious resource in a two-income family.[41]

Marriage—already battered by growing divorce rates, the values of the counterculture, and new ideas about sexual freedom—began to seem like just one of many lifestyles that men and women might choose. Never before in American history had such ambivalent attitudes toward fidelity and commitment entered mainstream culture. To be sure, small groups of free love advocates had challenged marriage and family in nineteenth-century communes and in the bohemian enclaves of New York City's Greenwich Village early in the twentieth century. But the sexual behavior of those communards and bohemians had never been regarded as a "lifestyle choice" by those in mainstream culture.

In contrast, the media of the seventies successfully popularized the new "human potential movement" and publicized sensational stories about sex-swapping couples, swinging singles, and sexual freedom parties. Aimed at an upscale elite, some of the media misled its audience into imagining that large numbers of adults had dropped out, or divorced, in order to spend time mingling with strangers at sexual orgies. Although the media vastly exaggerated adult behavior, bewildered older Americans could hardly ignore the frequency of divorce, the changing nature of gender relations and of sexual mores. The generation that came of age during the Great Depression and World War II had rarely divorced. During the sixties, however, divorce rates among this cohort began to rise sharply. By the end of the seventies, the human potential movement had redefined divorce as a "creative" act and some adults began to adopt the open marriage that became the title of another best-seller.[42]

Enough adults seemed bewildered and confused that John Silber, president of Boston University, felt compelled to tell the parents of three thousand incoming freshmen in the fall of 1977, "Every one of our students deserves a parent who is not going through an identity crisis. It is time that America faces up to the implication of having too many people aged forty and aged fifty asking questions that they should have answered when they were seventeen to twenty-five, 'Who am I and what ought I to do?' "[43]

The human potential movement, inspired by Aldous Huxley's use of the phrase during a lecture in 1960, grew out of the work of Abraham Maslow, Fritz Perls, and William Schutz, all psychological theorists who emphasized the realization of the self. The human potential movement presumed that individuals could best realize their true nature by engaging in a thorough psychological examination of the self. The implicit assumption was that mainstream culture kept people from realizing their deepest dreams and their greatest potential. Within the human potential movement, psychologists thought of potential not in terms of careers, but as the discovery of emotional, sexual, and spiritual parts of the self. What Tom Wolfe would dub the "Me Decade" (the seventies) included not only widespread narcissism and consumerism, but also hundreds of spiritual and therapeutic practices that promised such self-invention and self-realization.[44]

Soon, feminism intersected with the human potential movement. The feminist challenge to the psychotherapeutic profession had contested nearly all former definitions of women's mental health popularized by psychoanalytic theory. During the 1970s, feminist writers and therapists began creating a new kind of therapy, one that included a serious consideration of women's subordinate status. But it was not feminist thought or therapy, in the short run, that attracted the public's attention. The therapeutic books that would become best-sellers in the seventies—
The Managerial Woman, The Assertive Woman, When I Say No I Feel Guilty—helped promote what I call "therapeutic feminism," programs of self-help that ignored the economic or sociological obstacles women faced, and instead emphasized the way in which each individual woman,

if only she thought positively about herself, could achieve some form of self-realization and emancipation.[45]

Naturally, the editors of women's magazines quickly latched onto the human potential movement. Self-help in its various forms was nothing new to them. For nearly a century, they had instructed women how to improve their domestic skills, enhance their appearance, beautify their homes, and, most importantly, how to catch and keep their men. But the human potential movement added the necessity for a new kind of therapeutic intervention. Society had changed and it was up to women to embrace the power of positive thinking.[46]

What were women supposed to change, then? Basically, themselves; women could never be perfect enough. In 1976, one typical magazine article urged women to write daily affirmations "to erase old thought patterns." Like children kept after school, readers were to write—dozens of times—how much they loved themselves or how much they forgave their husbands.[47]

The human potential movement probably affected women even more through the popular books that crowded bookstore shelves. In *Super Self: A Woman's Guide to Self-Management*, Dorothy Tennov identified "time" as women's worst enemy. To overcome the burden of housework, child care, and jobs, women needed to discipline themselves and learn to manage their time. The author rightly assumed that working women would feel responsible for dinner, child care, and dirty floors at home. The idea that men might help or that the government might assist through child care facilities, flexible hours, and shared jobs had largely vanished. The path to individual success was not to share any of this, or to act in concert with others to change it, but to manage one's time well. Still others instructed women how to change their "scripts" and what therapeutic skills they needed to learn.[48]

The allure of "assertiveness training" was that it spoke directly to the learned passiveness that feminists had already identified as one of the most serious handicaps of (white) middle-class women. As one feel-good writer declared in the typical psychobabble of the day:

> The question of identity is an important one: whether you identify yourself as a mother, a feminist, a student, a lover, an executive, a rebel girl, a socialist or a divorcee—if you can put the word assertive before any of those identities, you will feel and convey strength no matter who you are or what you are trying to accomplish.[49]

An entire industry of "assertiveness training" workshops began to sprout nationwide, devoted to teaching women how to assert themselves in a straightforward manner, rather than through deferential behavior or aggressive demands. In *How to Be an Assertive Woman*, author Jean Baer argued that the major reason women don't get what they want is that "they haven't yet learned how to communicate what they want." When they learned new communication skills, they would see "the change in their self-esteem." The fact that most workplaces allowed little or no assertiveness of any kind from their female employees was simply ignored. Asked about the new assertiveness-training workshops, a New York practical nurse replied sarcastically, "I don't know about assertiveness. Where I work it's called 'insubordination.' "[50]

Arguably the most famous self-help (and antifeminist) book of the decade was Marabel Morgan's *Total Woman*, published in 1973. Morgan's title quickly entered the popular lexicon and in 1974 topped the nonfiction best-seller list, right above Carl Bernstein's and Bob Woodward's exposé of the Watergate scandal, *All the President's Men*.[51]

Morgan spoke directly to the reader, in a chatty personal style. She addressed a topic that had been a staple of women's magazines—"How to Save Your Marriage." The popularity of her book revealed how much women preferred to repair rather than forsake their marriages—and yet here was a book that could not have been written had the women's movement not existed. Morgan used her own life as an example. After a thrilling courtship and honeymoon with her husband, Charlie, Morgan had watched helplessly as communication began to break down. She became a nag; he withdrew behind the newspaper. Like the women interviewed by Betty Friedan, Morgan began to "feel trapped—work, the house, two little children, a husband who wouldn't talk to me. When I told him he was becoming a stranger to his children, he just pulled the paper higher."

Her solution was not to seek a career, or enter a consciousness-raising group, but to defer to her husband, who regularly described women's liberation as "organized selfishness." After all, it was all her fault. She had pushed him away by stating her opinions, asking for help, and demanding his attention. So Morgan studied the Bible, took self-improvement courses, read psychology books, and soon realized that the solution was embarrassingly obvious: give a man everything he wants and let him make all the decisions. The change in her marriage, Morgan gushed, was immediate and dramatic. As soon as she accepted her subordinate position in the marriage, Charlie began bringing her presents and "allowed" her to redecorate the house. The goal of her book, as she put it, was for "any wife to have her husband absolutely adore her in just a few weeks' time." The book itself was an odd hodgepodge of advice on time management, domestic tips, and the sort of positive thinking that would help people change their attitudes rather than the condition of their lives.[52]

Unlike feminists, Morgan encouraged her reader to accept her husband as he was, "without nagging or trying to change him." In a chapter titled "Admire Him," Morgan urged her reader to "listen attentively to her husband, to admire his every trait, to pander to his every whim." Ignoring the craze for assertiveness training, Morgan instead instructed women to learn age-old, tried-and-true methods of manipulating men. "Let your husband be President of the family business," Morgan exhorted.

> A Total Woman is not a slave. She graciously chooses to adapt
> to her husband's way, even though at times she desperately
> may not want to. . . . It is only when a woman surrenders her
> life to her husband, reveres and worships him and is will-
> ing to serve him, that she becomes really beautiful to him.
> She becomes a priceless jewel, the glory of femininity, his
> queen.[53]

Total Woman struck a nerve with many married (and unmarried) women. But it was not simply female surrender that catapulted Morgan into national celebrity. Morgan also offered titillating tales of domestic sexual encounters right out of the sexual revolution as the media had described it. Quoting Dr. David Reuben, the author of the 1970 bestseller *Any Woman Can!*, Morgan argued that "the inability of having an orgasm is simply the unconscious refusal to have one in order to get revenge on the husband." In one of the most widely quoted—and remembered—passages of her book, Morgan urged wives to meet their husbands at the door, nude, draped only in Saran Wrap. Here was the feminine mystique in the wake of the women's movement, updated through the highly sexualized and therapeutic culture of the seventies.[54]

Morgan soon created a full-time career telling other women to stay at home, a long and dishonorable tradition in the history of American women. As her fame grew, her life became a series of interviews and appearances on television talk shows. Skeptical reporters asked her how working women—strained for leisure time—had any energy left to meet their husbands in little nighties and high heels, or in Saran Wrap. Morgan reluctantly conceded that she was just now learning about these problems. "I wouldn't change one word in the book," she insisted, "but if you have a career you have to scramble to be Total. You really have to hustle so you don't let things slip in your marriage."

Most working women already knew that. But Morgan's promotion of the Total Woman—a sexier and snazzier version of the housewife who dutifully devoted her life to home and hearth—highlighted a growing debate over whether it was possible or desirable for women to "have it all." Probably no one better summed up the individualistic ethos of consumer and therapeutic feminism than Helen Gurley Brown. In *Sex and the Single Girl* (1962), Brown, the glamorous editor of *Cosmopolitan* magazine, had encouraged single women to enjoy sex before marriage. Twenty years later, in 1982, Brown now informed women that *Having It All*, as her new book was called, was within any woman's reach.

Brown's recipe for success blended a traditional work ethic with ideas from the human potential movement and redefined feminism as a program for self-advancement. Reflecting on her youth, the fifty-nine-year-old Brown described the strict discipline she had employed to gain fame and fortune. Anyone, she claimed, could get it all. In her chatty and breezy style, Brown recounted how far she had come from her "hillbilly" origins. "From a problem youth spent in Little Rock, Osage and Green Forest . . . through seventeen secretarial jobs in Los Angeles, to my present job at *Cosmo* in New York, I have applied myself almost *daily*." Women not born into wealth no longer needed to marry a rich man or an upwardly mobile Horatio Alger. Any woman, she insisted, could pull herself up by her pumps and "have it all." All it took was discipline, determination, and desire.[55]

What did "it" mean to Brown? "Deep love, true friends, money, fame, satisfying days and nights—anything you *want* when you apply yourself *seriously*." But notice that "it" did not include children. Although Brown offered an entire chapter on how to catch and keep a husband, she wrote only three and a half pages about children. Under "Children—Part of Having It All," she portrayed them as more of a nuisance than a blessing. For those who had the poor taste to want children anyway, she supplied this advice: "Never waste time feeling guilt, never agonize too much, and have a lot of paid help at home, and never, ever, let them interfere with the long climb to the top." Husbands, by definition, could not be counted on. "Although they probably wouldn't do much housework," Brown wrote, "they usually do something to make up for household imbecility—like love you and pay a lot of bills."[56]

Brown's version of "having it all" was a far cry from the early vision of women's liberation. In their passion to free themselves from exclusive domesticity, sixties feminists had argued that they could both work and have a family. But they had also insisted that men share family responsibilities and that the government provide child care services and other assistance to working parents. In contrast, Brown regarded having-it-all as the result of a thousand small individual choices. What were women without wealth to do? Poor women didn't appear on Brown's radar screen. If they were poor, after all, it was because they had not "applied themselves." Like Marabel Morgan, Brown glamorized sex. But unlike Morgan, she forfeited family life. Neither woman really had it all. Nor could most women, unless they had abundant wealth or an inexhaustible amount of energy, two preconditions for living life as a superwoman.

THE QUEST FOR IDENTITY

The film and television industries took more time absorbing the domestic turmoil and workplace confusion that feminism had brought into American life. But once both went into gear, they, too, began to recast "feminism" as a quest for individual identity, which indeed it was, for many middle- or upper-middle-class women.

On television, as the cultural critic Ella Taylor has observed, viewers watched the "perfect family" comedies of the fifties and sixties replaced by new series that dramatized the ambiguities and tensions afflicting family and work life. Searching for "relevance," the producers of these comedies hoped to explore the impact of women's growing independence and men's relative loss of authority in the family—without alienating those viewers who might resent such changes.[57]

All in the Family, the classic example of such sitcoms, pitted a white, working-class, middle-aged couple, Archie and Edith Bunker, against their feminist daughter, Gloria, and her Polish-American liberal husband, Michael (or as Archie called him, "Meathead"). A bewildered but lovable bigot, Archie argued through every show with his daughter, son-in-law, and even finally his wife, Edith, who eventually got a job and began to defend her right to an independent opinion.

Seeking a broad audience, the producers of *All in the Family* ridiculed feminist and antifeminist positions. Gloria spouted crude dogmatic feminism, while Archie regularly launched malapropistic tirades against minorities and women. Later studies showed that "although Archie may have lost the arguments, viewers took away whatever attitudes they brought to the show; racists felt confirmed in their racism, liberals in their broad-mindedness and sense of superiority." In this way, the program provided comic relief, even as it seemingly confirmed all points of view.[58]

Still, for all its conflicts, the Bunker family remained intact. The real change on television in the seventies was the appearance of new kinds of families. What Ella Taylor has dubbed "Prime Time Feminism" showcased newly formed families and dramatized the "domestic distress" of families fractured by divorce, two working parents, and changing sexual mores.[59] In comedies like *The Mary Tyler Moore Show* (1970) or *Maude* (1972), television also began to reflect some of the bewilderment and burdens created by a changing economy and by the growing numbers of women working outside the home. These were comedies, as Taylor noted, whose premise turned on the painful art of "learning to live without men. And the men, for their part, are either macho buffoons or effeminate wimps. It is the women who learn to create a new *ad hoc* family."[60]

Maude, a spin-off of *All in the Family*, starred a loud-mouthed, opinionated, middle-class New York suburbanite, an outspoken feminist who had been divorced three times, whose daughter had been divorced, and whose best friend, Vivian, had also been divorced. When Maude decided to have an abortion in middle-age, she plunged the nation into a heated debate. Under pressure from pro-lifers, sponsors of *Maude* began pulling their ads. Feminist organizations responded by launching a consumer boycott against those sponsors. Three hundred "Right to Life" activists circled CBS's New York headquarters to protest Maude's abortion; thirty-nine affiliates refused to show the episodes that dealt with it. The American Civil Liberties Union, the National Council of Churches, the Union of American Hebrew Congregations, the Young Women's Christian Association, and the Freedom to Read Committee of the Association of American Publishers joined together to charge the network with censorship of pro-choice perspectives.[61]

To resurrect *any* believably intact family, television producers began creating "surrogate families" that supported women and men at the workplace, rather than at home. Most of the new "work-family" dramas

and comedies of the seventies, in fact, featured women who were searching for familial support and feminist respect at the workplace. Work-
families also reinforced the association of feminism with an identity
based on something outside of home and hearth.[62]

The Mary Tyler Moore Show, one of the most popular situation
comedies of the seventies, revolved around a "work-family" that repeatedly demonstrated that the stability of *Father Knows Best* had been
replaced—outside of work, at least—by precarious and transient relationships. In the blink of an eye, life could change and only the folks at
work offered the kinds of connection and continuity that people once
expected from their families at home. Mary Richards, the lead character, was a single career-minded woman in her early thirties. When a
four-year relationship with a man dissolved, she moved to Minneapolis
and took a job as assistant producer of a local television news show. Her
behavior outside of work alternated between that expected of an old-
fashioned spinster and that of a newly divorced working woman. Like
other work-family comedies, *The Mary Tyler Moore Show* managed to offer glimpses of the country's new feminist-influenced world while still
endorsing traditional values. The show offered compassion for those
who were blindsided by changing social and sexual mores—like Mary's
boss, Lou, who in the show's fourth year found himself abandoned by his
wife of twenty-six years so that she "could find herself." In other famous
"work-families" of the seventies, single women—though rarely the
main characters—secured their identity within surrogate families. Margaret "Hotlips" Houlihan in *M*A*S*H*, or Billie in *Lou Grant*, forged
their ties with the men of their work family. We, the audience, never
knew very much of Margaret's or Billie's "home" life. Their life at work,
not at home, is what defined them.

Week after week, these prime-time working women faced uncharted
territory as they tried to command respect from coworkers, learn how to
date after thirty, or raise children without fathers. Unlike the "first
woman" narratives in newspapers or the self-help therapeutic literature,
television series offered a much more complicated picture of both the
new opportunities and barriers women faced. Driven by plot, these television sitcoms sometimes confirmed women's worst fear that they, too,
might have to do it all, without a man. Tempered by comedy, these
series often reminded viewers of just how precarious were the lives
they led.

Films also began to explore the domestic dislocations of the era. In

1977, the columnist Ellen Goodman wryly observed that in the love story of the seventies, "it's gotten so that what passes for a happy ending is a no-fault divorce." Goodman was right. Romance and marriage no longer fared well on the screen. Ingmar Bergman's *Scenes from a Marriage* (1973, viewed by a large American audience) offered an excruciating dissection of a disintegrating marriage. In *The Way We Were* (1973), we learned that love did not, in fact, triumph over political differences. *Annie Hall* (1977) offered viewers a grim (if hilarious) view of romance and love. As Ellen Goodman quipped, "They are movies about the people who survive romance, rather than romances that survive. . . . In the seventies, when one basket case meets another, you figure it will never work out."[63]

If romance didn't "work out" in the seventies, women's friendships found new life on the big screen. Alongside the predictable male buddy films appeared a new genre of film, dubbed by Goodman, the "Female Friendship" film.[64] Feminism had encouraged women to seek support from and solidarity with other women. Now, filmmakers began to explore the complex nature of such relationships. In *The Turning Point*, *Julia*, and *Girlfriends*, the filmmakers dramatized the competition between women who had chosen different paths, the difficulty of ever having it all, and the connections that sustained and nurtured women's love for each other.

The more films focused on feminist issues, the more film critics noticed how little the film industry had ever explored the real experiences—or, for that matter, the fantasies—of women. Now, a new crop of films began to track the confusion feminism had injected into lives shaped by the fifties. *Kramer vs. Kramer* and *An Unmarried Woman*, two box office hits released at the end of the decade, captured some of the fallout from the diffusion of feminism. Both films ignited fiery criticism—from feminists who thought the films trivialized and distorted feminism and from traditionalists who believed they condoned a selfish feminist quest for an independent identity.

Kramer vs. Kramer, based on a novel by Avery Corman, was about what happens when an unhappy wife walks out on her husband and their six-year-old child, only to return eighteen months later to claim custody of their child. But the film was also an exploration of feminism's impact on unsuspecting adults.

The film opens with a tight close-up of a very depressed woman. As the frame widens, we watch Joanna (Meryl Streep) putting her son to sleep. "See you in the morning," he says. Hesitantly, she replies, "I love you." The viewer already senses that she is about to leave her child. Her husband, Ted (Dustin Hoffman), is an assistant art director who is married to his work. He arrives home late that night, ecstatic that he has just received a promotion, just as Joanna announces that she is about to leave. Completely bewildered, Ted defends his neglect of his family: "I was busy making a living. Tell me what I did wrong." Her reply, which mystifies him, is simply "I can't take it anymore." Fleeing suicidal impulses, Joanna adds, "And I don't love you anymore." She leaves no address, she simply vanishes.

Initially, Ted blames her disappearance on feminism. "Sisterhood," he growls to Joanna's best friend (Jane Alexander). But her friend reminds him of Joanna's deepening depression and insists that "it took a lot of courage" for her to leave. Ted angrily snaps, "How much courage does it take to leave your kid?"

Ted has been the proverbial breadwinner and absentee father, and knows nothing about his son, not even what grade he's in at school. His first attempt to make breakfast is a comic farce. But he's determined to learn, a nod perhaps to the feminist insistence that men were also capable of raising and nurturing children. "Life can go on without Mommy," Ted tries to convince himself. "Daddy can bring home the bacon and cook it up too."

Immersed in his career, driven by ambition, Ted never realized how much time it takes to create an intimate relationship with a child. As he and his son grow closer, his work suffers. His boss reminds him that he "needs him seven days a week and twenty-five hours a day," another nod to the women's movement and its advocacy of a flexible and family-friendly workplace. At home, he can no longer work in the evenings without interruption. Nor can he stay late at work to socialize with promising new clients. His son, he gradually realizes, comes first.

By the end of the film, the audience understands why the Kramer family disintegrated. Children of the fifties, Joanna and Ted automatically embraced the breadwinner and housewife roles of that era. The script could have been lifted straight out of Friedan's *Feminine Mystique*. A graduate of Smith College, Joanna worked briefly for *Mademoiselle* magazine and then married. After the birth of her son, she quit her job to take care of her family. Although she wanted to discuss her unhappiness with her husband, he seemed too distracted by his career to care about her deepening sense of despair.

Ted now understands the ludicrousness of his attempt to turn his well-educated wife into a homemaker. Trying to explain his failures to his son, he admits, "I tried to make her be a certain kind of wife that I thought she was supposed to be." When Joanna unexpectedly returns, she explains why she left: "I didn't know who I was." Always someone's daughter, wife, or mother, she had no independent identity. "And that's why I had to go away." "Away" turns out to be California, the heartland of therapeutic America, where Joanna finds a job and a "good" therapist. A newly reinvented Joanna now seeks custody, but Ted feels too close to his son to simply let him go.

And so begins a courtroom drama—*Kramer vs. Kramer*—in which estranged husband and wife fight for possession of their child. Appealing to traditional values, Ted's attorney forces Joanna to admit that her husband was a faithful, gentle provider. With scathing sarcasm, turning his back to her, the lawyer adds, "I can see why you left him."

What the judge must decide is whether a mother who abandons her small child still has a right to custody. Ted challenges this implicit legal assumption. When questioned by Joanna's attorney, he concedes that he had been a poor parent. But he insists that he has now become a loving and responsible father. What law, he asks, says that women make better parents? If women have the right to men's work, why don't men have the right to custody?

Predictably, the court awards custody to the mother, leaving the audience with a sour taste and the sense that feminists seem to want "it" both ways. Though devastated, Ted tenderly prepares his traumatized son for another major transition. Now a devoted father, his only concern is for his son's happiness. Then, a humbled Joanna suddenly arrives, realizes that her son *is* already home, and allows him to stay with his father.

By film's end, both parents have rededicated their lives to the best interests of their child. Traditional values have been upheld, even though the father has gained primary custody. Both have been chastised for "abandoning" their child. The story ends on an ambiguous note, leaving the impression that it's just possible these two parents might reconcile, on new terms, with new ground rules, united by the recognition that what really matters is not career, ambition, or self-invention, but the well-being of their son.

A number of feminist critics viewed the film as antifeminist because it implied that the "best Moms are Dads," a theme that surfaced with alarming frequency in films and TV sitcoms of the seventies and eighties. They also objected to the mother's mysterious abandonment of her

child. By associating individual whim with feminism, some argued, the
film trivialized the actual feminist goal of making family and work available to both men and women. Some feminists also chided the film because, as they accurately noted, in the real world, it is fathers, not
mothers, who generally abandon their children.[65]

An Unmarried Woman opens with scenes from a perfect family: Erica
(Jill Clayburgh) is blessed with a nearly perfect stockbroker husband, a
charming and witty daughter, a part-time job in an art gallery, and a circle of women friends (dubbed "the club") who meet weekly at restaurants
for mutual support. We soon learn that appearances, as always, deceive.
The daughter suddenly announces that she will never marry. Then Erica's
husband tearfully admits that he's in love with a younger woman.

Erica must now live as "an unmarried woman." In her search for a
new life, she beds a number of men, and reassesses her marriage. "I was
a hooker," she says, reinterpreting her former economic and emotional
dependence. Now she is determined to support herself. By the end of
the film, she meets Mr. Right (Alan Bates), a handsome and lovable
artist who wants to whisk her away to his Vermont retreat. It is an entic-
ing invitation; he offers a new home, and the promise of a new life.

To his astonishment, Erica declines, explaining that she might return
to school, and that what she seeks is greater challenge in her work and
the opportunity to be more independent. But Erica is not all that convincing. "Independent?" he asks. "Trying to be," she admits. Mr. Right
departs for Vermont, leaving open the possibility that, if and when Erica
finds her cherished independence, they may get back together again.
Here, too, the ending is ambiguous. We don't know the answer and neither do they.

Both *Kramer vs. Kramer* and *An Unmarried Woman* appeared just before the backlash against feminism began to demonize independent
women. Both captured the culture's anxieties about feminism without
turning its women characters into psychopathic killers (as would happen in films like *Fatal Attraction* in the eighties). At the same time, both
films contributed to the image of feminism as a matter of upper-middle-
class women searching for identities beyond that of mother and wife.

Significantly, the films encouraged the audience to judge men by
feminist values. We admire Ted only after he finds a balance between
family and work. In *An Unmarried Woman*, the "club" members explicitly describe their ideal (feminist) man. "A 'good man' is tender, gives
long massages, never rushes lovemaking, and craves intimacy. He
doesn't pounce; he cuddles." For these women, the achingly sensitive

Alan Bates or Alan Alda has replaced the silent and rugged machismo of a John Wayne.

THE NEW SUPERWOMAN

By 1980, the supermom of the fifties had been replaced by a new and improved Superwoman. Ellen Goodman, dubbing the new ideal "Supermom II," satirized an entire decade's advice on how easily a woman could "juggle" her life with ease and grace.

> The all-around Supermom rises, dresses in her vivid pants suit, oversees breakfast and the search for the sneakers and then goes off to her glamorous high-paying job at an advertising agency, where she seeks Personal Fulfillment and the kids' college tuition. She has, of course, previously found a Mary Poppins figure to take care of the kids after school. Mary Poppins loves them as if they were her own, works for a mere pittance and is utterly reliable.
> Supermom II comes home from work at 5:30, just as fresh as a daisy, and then spends a truly creative hour with her children. After all, it's not the quantity of the time, but the quality. She catches up on their day, soothes their disputes and helps with their homework while creating something imaginative in her Cuisinart (with her left hand tied behind her back). After dinner—during which she teaches them about the checks and balances of our system of government—she bathes and reads to them, and puts the clothes in the dryer. She then turns to her husband and eagerly suggests that they explore some vaguely kinky sexual fantasy.[66]

The American woman, Goodman decided in a moment of despair, had not won all that much. "The only equality she's won after a decade of personal and social upheaval is with the working mothers of Russia."[67]

Barbara Ehrenreich similarly worried about the new Superwoman. What bothered Goodman, Ehrenreich, and other feminist critics was that the feminist had turned into a mythic figure who bore little resemblance to ordinary women and the problems they daily faced. She was as remote from their lives as the anorexic models who advertised the cigarettes and liquor that promised women new freedoms. Only the well-to-do could afford to be that thin or that well dressed or hire full-time nannies or housekeepers. As Ehrenreich noted, "For the millions of women who suffer from embarrassing handicaps like poverty, dead-end jobs, small children or even excess pounds, the New Woman is a constant reminder that they, in all probability, are still 'losers.'" Feminism had become unrecognizable. Consumer and therapeutic feminism emphasized individual problems and proposed individual solutions. Where had the collective effort to advance all women gone?[68]

Even as feminists puzzled over that question, economic necessity continued to push even more women—and even more mothers of very young children—into the labor force. These women found themselves worn down by frantic schedules and numbing exhaustion. When viewed up close, the lives of these women often seemed like a Sisyphean effort to fulfill endless responsibilities. Absent a full-time housekeeper, many a working mother, teetering precariously at the edge of a cliff, had to learn to become an expert "juggler." With muscles tensed, the super-woman threw all her balls into the air, caught them, breathed a sigh of relief, threw them up once more, and caught them, again and again. But when the baby-sitter called in sick or the school declared an unscheduled holiday, the balls came crashing down and she wept and blamed herself for her failure.

Susan Douglas has shown how popular culture created a grotesque vision of feminism that trivialized and ridiculed rebellious women. To this I would add that the media also helped depict the feminist as an eager participant in America's wildly accelerating consumer and therapeutic society, joining prosperous men in the creation of a life dedicated to consumption and self-absorption.[69]

The historic rupture between home and work, which began for many men in the nineteenth century, affected most women a century later. For the male entrepreneurs and workers of that time, commuting between the home with its religious and neighborly values and the competitive nature of the market proved confusing, sometimes even disabling. Sooner or later, men became accustomed to the schizophrenic nature of work and home life. At work, they learned to bluff and fight for the dollar. At home, they could assume a titular patriarchal role and enter what social critic Christopher Lasch called a "haven in a heartless world."[70]

Meanwhile, middle-class white women took on the cultural burden of guarding the home from market values, which conferred upon them a mantle of moral superiority. They launched reform movements—

asylums for the mentally ill, shelters for wayward girls, charities for the poor, and the immediate abolition of slavery—to care for the casualties of early American capitalism. They became the ones who patrolled society and culture for transgressions against the purity of the home and family.

Early-twentieth-century Americans witnessed—with considerable ambivalence—the gradual transformation of their society from a nation that extolled character, a work ethic, and a producer mentality into a consumer culture that celebrated leisure, consumption, and "personality." The hedonistic values of that new culture directly challenged those traits publicly cherished by the nineteenth-century middle class—self-control, restraint, and delayed gratification. Advertising made honesty seem quaint. Consumerism celebrated vanity and leisure rather than hard work. The cultivation of "personality" and of celebrity, rather than old-fashioned character, made sincerity seem downright eccentric.

In the years after World War II, a Depression-scarred generation justified their new enthusiasm for consumer goods by purchasing products mainly for home and family, not for the individual self. But in the sixties, sensing a change, advertisers began to target the individual consumer rather than the family. Consider the change in the promotion of bed linens. In the 1950s, a typical magazine ad for linens used the image of the dainty housewife, dressed in a modest shirtwaist and apron, putting nicely folded, well-ironed sheets into a linen closet. By the mid-sixties, the same linen manufacturer advertised the same product with an image of a woman in a see-through negligee, provocatively stretched upon those same sheets, implicitly announcing her sexual availability. Nothing, one might say, remained in the closet.[71]

The baby boomers, the children of the Great Depression generation, came of age just as the sexualization of consumer culture began to crest. Raised in relative affluence and accustomed to few sacrifices, they came into conflict with parents whose values reflected the ordeals of the Depression and the war. But members of both generations, in fact, felt bewildered by what was, by any measure, a profound societal transformation, one that challenged a past that valued work, delayed gratification, and commitment to families.

In hindsight, the emergence of something like the human potential movement in the seventies now seems inevitable. The therapeutic culture was not merely a fad. It offered secular guidance to modern men and women, at a time when the self was becoming increasingly unmoored from family and community. The human potential movement, in its many guises, tried to reassure the confused men and women from two generations, in a world where all values seemed up for grabs, that individual happiness should be one's highest priority. And this, of course, fueled a consumer culture that was now targeting and producing for the individual, rather than the family.

The second wave of feminism did not create this individualistic culture, but it emerged at a time when a majority of Americans were already worried, however inchoately, that the celebration of the individual was eroding the cohesion of family and community life.

Middle-class women had long provided moral cover for the spiritual loss and soulless greed that created a society governed by the profit motive and market values. Now such mothers and wives worked outside the home, producing and promoting that very culture. Without women as moral guardians, Americans had to face the threat of a society-wide sense of moral bankruptcy. Who would preserve communal and religious values? Who would counsel compassion rather than competition? Who would care for the nation's children, families, and communities?

The feminist, as remade by the media and popular culture, emerged as a superwoman, who then turned into a scapegoat for America's irreversible decline into a nation of individual consumers. For this, the women's movement was blamed, even though this selfish superwoman would have seemed bizarre, not to say repellent, to most of its early members. Ironically, the women's liberation movement, which had attacked both consumerism and the commodification of women's bodies, ended up being consumed—and condemned—for promoting the very materialism its early members had attacked.

The backlash against feminism, directed as it was against the women's movement, reflected a profound moral revulsion against the shallow self-absorption of that consumer and therapeutic culture. Nonetheless, the growing New Right and social critics like Christopher Lasch blamed feminism—not consumer culture—for the loss of "traditional values" and the unraveling of the family.[72] And when Americans took a good, hard look at this narcissistic superwoman who embraced the values of the dominant culture, they grew anxious and frightened, for they no longer saw loyal mothers and wives who would care for the human community, but a dangerous individual, unplugged from home and hearth, in other words, a female version of America's ambitious but lonely organization man.

Chapter 10

∽◆∾

BEYOND BACKLASH

"If you're on the right track, you can expect some pretty savage criticism," veteran feminist Phyllis Chesler warned young women at the close of the twentieth century. "Trust it. Revel in it. It is the truest measure of your success." Words of wisdom from one of the pioneer activists who understood the meaning of a fierce backlash.

No movement could have challenged so many ideas and customs without threatening vast numbers of women and men. Some activists viewed the backlash as either a political conspiracy or a media plot hatched to discredit feminists. But the backlash, in fact, reflected a society deeply divided and disturbed by rapid changes in men's and women's lives, at home and at work.

Abortion genuinely polarized American women. Working women, as sociologist Kristin Luker discovered, tended to support abortion rights, while homemakers, who depended on a breadwinner's income, were more likely to regard children as a means of keeping husbands yoked to their families and so opposed it.[1] The backlash, which had grown alongside the women's movement, gained strength in 1973 after the Supreme Court, in its *Roe v. Wade* decision, made abortion legal. The Catholic Church—and later the evangelical Christian Right—quickly mobilized to reverse that decision. By 1977, Congress had passed the Hyde Amendment, which banned the use of taxpayers' money to fund abortions for poor women. By 1980, the New Right had successfully turned abortion into a litmus test for political candidates, Cabinet officials, and Supreme Court justices. By 1989, the Supreme Court's *William L. Webster v. Reproductive Health Services* decision began the process of chipping away at women's right to abortion.

A long, drawn-out struggle over the Equal Rights Amendment also helped consolidate opposition to the women's movement. Passed quickly by Congress in a burst of optimism in 1972, the ERA needed to be ratified by thirty-eight state legislatures in order to become a part of the Constitution. Within a year, the ERA received swift ratification or support from thirty states, but then it stalled, and in 1978, proponents extracted a reluctant extension from Congress. By 1982, the ERA, unable to gain more state ratifications, had been buried, a victim of the rising symbolic politics of a triumphant political movement of the Right.

The ten-year battle over the ERA and the escalating struggle over abortion helped mobilize conservative women. Ironically, women of the Right learned from the women's movement, even if in opposition to it. In a kind of mirror-image politicking, they began to form their own all-female organizations, including Happiness of Motherhood Eternal (HOME), Women Who Want to Be Women (WWWW), American Women against the Ratification of the ERA (AWARE), Females Opposed to Equality (FOE), and the Eagle Forum. Soon, they engaged in their own kinds of local and national consciousness-raising activities. Their tactics, like those of the women's movement, included polite protest and lobbying in Washington, as well as more militant rallies and protests. But unlike the women's movement, the fringes engaged in actual terrorism at abortion clinics.

The political struggle also catapulted several conservative women to national prominence. Among them was Phyllis Schlafly, a shrewd attorney who nonetheless—like Betty Friedan almost two decades earlier—described herself as "just a housewife," and founded Stop ERA, which she credited with defeating the ERA. An influential if little-known member of the conservative Right, Schlafly had written a book, *The Power of the Positive Woman* (1977), which attacked feminists for their negative assessments of women's condition in the United States. Schlafly also blamed "limousine liberals," "the cosmopolitan elite," and "chic fellow travelers" for living in a rarefied world that cared little about the traditional family and its values. Schlafly used her antifeminism as a vehicle for reinventing herself as a national celebrity. Thanks to the media, her name soon became a household word.[2]

The growing engagement of women in the religious and secular New Right legitimated an increasing fusillade of attacks on feminism by right-wing male religious and political leaders. In *The New Right: We're Ready to Lead*, Richard Viguerie, one of those leaders, announced that the New Right had to fight "anti-family organizations like the National Organization for Women and to resist laws like the Equal Rights Amendment that attack families and individuals." Schlafly, Viguerie, and other leaders of the New Right blamed the hedonistic values of American culture on feminists. For them, an independent woman was by definition a selfish, self-absorbed creature who threatened the nation's "traditional values."[3]

Support for the growing backlash came from many directions, including many women who were not members of any New Right organization. Some of those disgruntled women now felt overwhelmed by the double responsibilities they bore at home and at work; they blamed feminism for their plight. The media took its cue from such women. A new formulaic narrative appeared in the print media, that of the repentant career woman who finally realizes that feminism had very nearly ruined her life. Editors began to dispatch reporters in search of professional women who had quit their high-status jobs and returned home with great sighs of relief to care for their husbands and children.

Like the "first woman" stories of the 1970s, these cautionary tales of the 1980s obscured the actual lives of the vast majority of women in the labor force, for whom there was no choice but to get up every morning and go to work. Most working mothers labored at low-paid jobs, and husbands generally avoided even a reasonable share of the housework from their now-employed spouses. So women daily returned home to what sociologist Arlie Hochschild dubbed the "second shift."[4] Even successful professional women were discovering that they, too, had no choice but to enter careers on men's terms. Their new employers expected them to be available "25 hours a day, seven days a week" and their husbands, too, expected the same services they would have received from an unemployed wife. To secure promotions, career women—but not men—felt compelled to choose whether to dedicate their prime childbearing years to their careers and remain childless, or to face the daunting prospect of trying to do it all.

Despite the difficulties women and men experienced as they tried to adjust to this newly configured home life, it's important to recognize that the women's movement did not invariably pit men against women. This was not a battle between the sexes; it was part of the highly gendered and racialized cultural wars that polarized Americans in the wake of the 1960s. Men and women fought *together* on both sides of the divide, for this was a struggle between social and cultural ideals.

Across the great cultural divide of the post-1960s era, one group of men and women, whom we might call neo-traditionalists, resisted any change that altered familiar gender relations. For them, feminism symbolized the decadence of the 1960s and the loss of women's moral guardianship of the family. Fearful of an uncertain future, they yearned for a mythic past in which men earned a family wage and ruled a patriarchal family, when women bore many children and stayed at home to care for them, when homosexuals prayed for conversion or absolution and stayed out of sight, when African-Americans didn't ask for special reparations, and when schools and universities taught the superiority of Western European culture.[5]

Peering across that cultural divide were their adversaries, men and women whom we might call "progressives," who knew that the past was far more complicated, and could not be resurrected. But they also lacked a detailed blueprint for creating a different kind of future. Unlike their opposition, these men and women regarded feminists' demands as legitimate claims that expanded American democracy. They also realized, however reluctantly, that irreversible economic and social changes had transformed the nation into a society of individuals, alongside families and communities. Their goal was to protect those individuals from the centrifugal forces of a global economy. Like sailors without a map, they stumbled into uncharted waters, braved storms of protest and waves of resistance, and if they were honest with themselves, they knew that a blurry image of the future faced stiff competition from a finely etched picture of an idealized but somewhat familiar past.[6]

What both groups viscerally understood was that women had sustained America's families and communities. What to do when women worked was a serious dilemma. Neo-traditionalists decried the materialism, selfishness, and greed that undermined "traditional values." Progressives blamed consumer and corporate capitalism for the exploitation of workers, the destruction of families, and the fragmentation of communities.[7]

Meanwhile, resentment against feminism only grew fiercer. In her groundbreaking book *Backlash: The Undeclared War Against American Women* (1991), journalist Susan Faludi exposed the many media-generated stories that frightened feminists and women otherwise attracted to the goals of a women's movement. Media-fueled panics about an infamous "man shortage" or "an infertility epidemic" spooked women who had postponed marriage and motherhood. Now some wondered if they had lost what the media claimed were their infinitesimal chances to meet mates and have children. A popular T-shirt of the time reflected the fears of this generation. Drawn in the melodramatic style of a comic book romance, a weeping woman cries, "Oh dear, I forgot to have children!" Never mind that the man shortage was due to the peculiar demographics of the baby boom generation or that women over thirty-five kept on having children. Even when the authors of these academic studies repeatedly protested the media's distortion of their research, the damage had already been done.[8]

What really shocked and demoralized many veteran feminists was Betty Friedan's critique of the women's movement in her book *The Second Stage*, published in 1981. Worried that the movement might be undermined by the power of the right-wing assault, Friedan tried to promote a new agenda that would, in her eyes, isolate radicals and bring the women's movement into the mainstream of American life. The feminine mystique, Friedan insisted, no longer oppressed women. What women now suffered from was a "feminist mystique" that prevented them from spending sufficient time with their families. Rather than lambasting men or the government for failing to support working women, or analyzing how consumerism or therapeutic culture had transformed feminism, Friedan blamed the movement itself for the assault upon it.

Her book generated sharp criticism and fierce controversy. In the midst of the Reagan Revolution, some feminists viewed Friedan's new emphasis on family life as "a reactionary retreat." *The Second Stage* also infuriated those feminists who felt that Friedan had never grasped how sexual politics had rescued thousands of women from assaultive husbands and boyfriends, sexual harassment from bosses and co-workers, or homophobic violence from strangers. And more than a few feminists argued that she was in too much of a hurry; that the first stage of feminism was hardly finished.[9]

The backlash also sparked a round of soul-searching among veteran feminists who began to feel demoralized, even defeated. In a 1989 reflective essay, Carol Hanisch, an early and influential radical feminist writer and activist, wondered if "giving up a normal life" for the women's movement had been a waste. "Did I blow my life?" she asked herself.

> I had a serious consciousness-raising session with myself and asked myself if I would have wanted to live the next 20+ years under the conditions for women of pre-1968.

Then, lifting her own spirits, she remembered

> the ways my life would have been circumscribed. . . . I began
> to feel a real panic welling up. It wasn't the "sacrifices" that I
> had made that were bothering me so much as that we hadn't
> been able to go further—far enough to really solve the prob-
> lems we raised and were now facing—and we were sort of
> caught out on the proverbial limb.[10]

What really disturbed her was the fact that women had gained the right
to work, but that men had not taken over much of the responsibility for
family life.

The feminist writer and activist Jane O'Reilly came to a similar conclusion in her engrossing memoir, *The Girl I Left Behind* (1980). At the
book's end, O'Reilly imagined a conversation with a future granddaugh-
ter, a curious little girl who plies her with endless questions about the
early women's movement. O'Reilly conceded that the women's movement caused great suffering, that it initially created an impassable gulf
between male and female activists, and often left feminists feeling
isolated, alone, and afraid. She recalled summers when every one of
her friends questioned the wisdom of pursuing professional careers.
But then, in a moving ending, O'Reilly described the legacy of the
movement:

> That night at dinner the girl I will leave behind me, the girl
> we have given a start, will look at me and say: "But granny,
> were you happy being a feminist?" Of course I was happy be-
> ing a feminist. After all, consider the alternatives.[11]

Feminist responses to the backlash began to appear in literature as
well. During the heady years of the 1970s, feminist utopian novels had
become the *genre du jour*. Some of the most prominent novels—Marge
Piercy's *Woman on the Edge of Time* or Ursula Le Guinn's *The Left Hand
of Darkness*—had played with gender and sexual identity and optimistically imagined new ways of achieving gender equality. In the wake of
the backlash, the Canadian novelist Margaret Atwood published a bleak
dystopian novel, *The Handmaid's Tale* (1986), which quickly became a
best-seller. This chilling novel took the destructive potential of the religious backlash seriously and offered a scary answer to the question:
"What if the religious Right actually gained political power?"[12]

Despite the sense of gloom and defeat that many feminists experienced at the time, American women were, in fact, increasingly embracing the goals of the women's movement. Reasons were not hard to fathom. Growing numbers of women were falling into poverty. Diana Pearce's 1978 phrase "the feminization of poverty" caught a startling and unexpected reality of American life. Divorce rates, which had doubled since 1965, had created a new cohort of women who joined the poor when their marriages ended. By 1984, working women began to outnumber women who worked at home and the glamorization of the superwoman and her career choice had eroded the prestige of homemaking. The growing tendency of middle-class women to postpone marriage and motherhood, combined with an increase in single mothers and divorced mothers, created a critical mass of women who now wondered how they were going to support themselves and their children.[13] Polls steadily revealed what the much-publicized backlash obscured, that a majority of women now looked favorably upon the goals of the women's movement.[14]

Women's attitudes had, in fact, changed rapidly. In a 1970 Virginia Slims opinion poll, 53 percent of women cited being a wife and mother as "one of the best parts of being a woman." By 1983, that figure had dropped to 26 percent.[15] In 1970, very few women expressed concern over discrimination. By 1983, one-third of women agreed that "male chauvinism, discrimination, and sexual stereotypes ranked as their biggest problem"; while 80 percent agreed that "to get ahead a woman has to be better at what she does than a man." Nor did women still believe they lived privileged lives, as they had in 1975, when one-third of Americans viewed men's lives as far more difficult. By 1990, nearly half of all adults assumed that men had the easier life.[16]

At the height of the backlash, in short, more American women, not fewer, grasped the importance of the goals of the women's movement. In 1986, a Gallup poll asked women, "Do you consider yourself a feminist?" At a time when identifying yourself as a feminist felt like a risky admission, 56 percent of American women were willing to do so (at least privately to Gallup's pollsters). Women of all classes were also becoming aware of the ways in which gender shaped their lives. Sixty-seven percent of all women, including those who earned under $12,500 *and* those who made more than $50,000, favored a strong women's movement. Pollsters consistently found that more African-American women approved of the goals of the women's movement than did white women. A 1989 poll found that 51 percent of all men, 64 percent of white women, 72 percent of Hispanic women, and 85 percent of African-American women agreed with the statement: "The United States continues to need a strong women's movement to push for changes that benefit women."[17]

In 1989, *Time* magazine ushered in a new decade with yet one more pronouncement of the death of feminism. Its cover story, "Women Face the '90s," bore the subtitle "During the '80s, they tried to have it all. Now they've just plain had it. Is there a future for feminism?" But, inside, the reader discovered quite a different story. Feminism was endangered, *Time* magazine suggested, not because it had failed, but precisely because it had been so successful. "In many ways," the article declared,

> feminism is a victim of its own resounding achievements. Its triumphs—in getting women into the workplace, in elevating their status in society and in shattering "the feminine mystique" that defined female success only in terms of being a wife and a mother—have rendered it obsolete, at least in its original form and rhetoric.[18]

The growth of gender consciousness had, in fact, altered society and culture in countless ways.[19] In August 1980, a *New York Times* editorial declared that the women's movement, once viewed as a group of "extremists and troublemakers," had turned into an "effective political force." The editorial concluded that "the battle for women's rights is no longer lonely or peripheral. It has moved where it belongs; to the center of American politics."[20] In 1984, commenting on legislation that would grant child support for all families and give wives access to their husbands' pensions, the *Times* editorialized that " 'Women's Issues' have already become everyone's." And so they had. Perhaps the important legacy was precisely that "women's issues" had entered mainstream national politics, where they had changed the terms of political debate.[21]

Everyday life had changed in small but significant ways. Strangers addressed a woman as Ms.; meteorologists named hurricanes after *both* men and women; schoolchildren learned about sexism before they became teenagers; language became more gender-neutral; popular culture saturated society with comedies, thrillers, and mysteries that turned on changing gender roles; and two decades after the movement's first years, the number of women politicians doubled.[22] Even more significantly, millions of women had entered jobs that had once been reserved for men.

Although women had not gained the power to change institutions in fundamental ways, they had joined men in colleges and universities in unprecedented numbers. In the 1950s, women had constituted only 20 percent of college undergraduates, and their two most common aspirations, according to polls of the time, were to become the wife of a prominent man and the mother of several accomplished children. By 1990, women constituted 54 percent of undergraduates and they wanted to do anything and everything. Women had also joined men in both blue collar and professional jobs in startling numbers. In 1960, 35 percent of women had worked outside the home; by 1990, that figure had jumped to 58 percent. During the same period, the number of female lawyers and judges leaped from 7,500 to 108,200; and female doctors from 15,672 to 174,000.

The cumulative impact of decades of revelations, education, debates, scandals, controversies, and high-profile trials raised women's gender consciousness, which in turn eventually showed up in a long-awaited political "gender gap." In 1871, Susan B. Anthony had prematurely predicted that once women got the right to vote, they would vote as a bloc. A gender gap did not appear until 1980, when more men than women voted for Ronald Reagan, whose opposition to the Equal Rights Amendment and abortion may have moved some women into the Democratic column. More important was Reagan's pledge to dismantle the welfare state, which nudged even more women toward the Democrats, the party more likely (theoretically) to preserve the safety net. Eventually, the gender gap would cause at least a temporary realignment of national politics. In 1996, 16 percent more women than men voted for Bill Clinton for president. Some political analysts now believed that women were voting their interests as workers, family caregivers, or as single or divorced mothers.[23]

Gender gap or not, the rightward tilt of American politics led to the demonization of poor women and their children. As some middle-class women captured meaningful and well-paid work, ever more women slid into poverty and homelessness, which, on balance, the women's movement did too little, too late, to change. On the other hand, the lives of many ordinary working women, who had not become impoverished, improved in dramatic ways. In 1992, a *Newsweek* article described how twenty years of the women's movement had changed Appleton,

Wisconsin (the hometown of Joseph McCarthy and the headquarters since 1989 of the John Birch Society). Women, the magazine reported, had taken on significant roles in local politics. In addition, the article observed,

> There are women cops and women firefighters, and there are women in managerial jobs in local business and government. There is firm community consensus, and generous funding with local tax dollars, for Harbor House, a shelter for battered women. And there is an active effort, in the Appleton public schools, to eliminate the invidious stereotyping that keeps young women in the velvet straitjacket of traditional gender roles.[24]

GLOBAL FEMINISM

As ideas from the Western women's movement traveled across the Atlantic, American feminists learned more than they taught. On October 25, 1985, President Vigdis Finnbogadottir of Iceland joined tens of thousands of women who had walked off the job in a twenty-four-hour protest against male privilege on the island. She also refused to sign a bill that would have ordered striking flight attendants back to work. Iceland's telephone system collapsed, travel came to a halt, and groups of men crowded into hotels for the breakfast their wives refused to cook for them.[25]

As feminism began spreading beyond industrialized nations, American feminists also encountered new definitions of "women's issues." Sometimes "freedom" meant better access to fuel and water, toppling a ruthless dictator, or ending a genocidal civil war. The gradual emergence of global women's networks made such encounters and confrontations inevitable.

Many of these networks grew out of the United Nation's 1975 International Women's Year. At the first World Conference on Women in Mexico, delegates urged the UN to proclaim the years between 1975 and 1985 "The Decade for Women." At each subsequent UN conference, there were two parallel meetings—one for delegates who represented their governments and another for women who participated in the nongovernmental organization (NGO) meetings. The numbers of NGO participants mushroomed. Six thousand women participated in the second conference, held in 1980 at Copenhagen; fourteen thousand attended the third in 1985 in Nairobi; and a startling thirty thousand arrived in Huairou, China, for the fourth in 1995.

What President Kennedy's Commission on the Status of Women had done for American women activists, the UN's World Conferences now did at a global level. Proximity bred intimacy and spread knowledge. The thousands of women rubbing shoulders or debating in Mexico, Denmark, Kenya, or China were learning from and teaching each other about their lives. Aside from their differences, they were also discovering the ubiquity of certain kinds of shared oppression—violence and poverty that had once seemed local, rather than global. And, in the process, they were nurturing and legitimating a global feminism, which was quite literally being born at UN conferences as they watched.

That didn't mean that women everywhere interpreted the information newly available to them in the same way. From the start, the NGO forum meetings witnessed serious clashes between "First" and "Third" World women, and between women whose nations were at war. Over time, the atmosphere began to improve. Western feminists began to *listen,* rather than *lecture,* and women from developing countries, who had formerly viewed Western concerns over clitoridectomies, dowry deaths, wifebeatings, and arranged marriages as so many instances of cultural imperialism—the urge of developed countries to impose their values and customs on underdeveloped nations—began the painful process of redefining their own customs as crimes.

Here was the essence of global feminism—addressing the world's problems *as if women mattered.* Human rights organizations, for instance, had traditionally focused exclusively on state-sanctioned violence against political activists. But most women encountered violence not in prison or at protests, but in their homes and communities. Viewed as customs rather than crimes, wife-beating, rape, genital excision, dowry deaths, and arranged marriages had never been certified as violations of women's human rights.

At a 1993 UN World Conference on Human Rights in Vienna, women from all over the globe movingly testified to the various forms of violence that had devastated their lives. Feminists successfully made their case; the conference passed a resolution that recognized violence against women and girls as a violation of their human rights. One immediate consequence of this historic redefinition of human rights was that Western nations could now grant *political* asylum to women fleeing certain violence or death from husbands or other relatives.[26]

Two years later, at a 1995 UN Conference on Development and

Population in Cairo, feminists criticized accepted development policies that promoted massive industrial or hydroelectric projects as *the* way to improve the standard of living of developing nations. Such projects, they argued, irreversibly damaged the human and natural ecology, provided work for indigenous men, but not for women, and undermined women's traditional economic role and social authority. Instead, they advocated small-scale cottage industries, through which women could earn money for their education.[27] They also attacked those population experts who took it, as an article of faith, that population growth automatically declined when industrial development lifted people out of poverty. Citing the failure of such policies, feminists countered that educating women and giving them control over their reproductive decisions was a far more effective way of controlling population growth. As one reporter wrote, "The deceptively simple idea of a woman making a decision about her future is one of the cornerstones of the emerging debate on global population policy."[28]

The "Platform for Action," the document that emerged from the Bejing conference in 1995, asked the nations of the world to see social and economic development through the eyes of women. Although the "Platform" recognized the differences that separated women, it also emphasized the universal poverty and violence that crippled the lives of so many of the world's women. In addition to affirming women's rights as human rights, the conference also declared three preconditions for women's advancement: equality, development, and peace. To many participants, the event seemed like a miracle, a moment existing out of time, when the world's women imagined a different kind of future, even if they had little power to implement it.

By publicizing even more gender consciousness, the 1995 Fourth World Conference on Women probably encouraged greater numbers of the world's women to challenge traditional forms of patriarchal authority. In the years following the conference, feminist activists and scholars began the process of redefining rape (when it occurred during a military conflict) as a war crime, publicizing the particular plight of refugees (most of whom were women), and rethinking the role women might play in reconstructing societies ravaged by war.[29]

At the same time, women in both developed and developing nations began debating the impact of feminism itself on global culture and economics. Was feminism yoked only to concepts of individual rights? Was it simply an inevitable by-product of Western consumer capitalism, whose effects would rupture the ties that bound families and communities together—and to the land? Or could feminism help protect the rights of women as they left family and land behind and entered the global wage economy? Could women's rights, redefined as human rights, provide a powerful new stance from which to oppose totalitarian societies of both the Right and the Left? Many theories proliferated, heated debates took place, but the answers—even many of the questions—lay in the future.[30]

There is no end to this story. Over a hundred years ago, the suffragist Matilda Gage turned her gaze toward the future. The work of her generation of activists, she wrote, was not for them alone,

> nor alone for the present generation, but for all women of all
> time. The hopes of posterity were in their hands, and they
> were determined to place on record for the daughters of 1976,
> the fact that their mothers of 1876 had thus asserted their
> equality of rights, and thus impeached the government of to-
> day for its injustice towards women.[31]

Nearly a century later, veteran feminist Robin Morgan, along with thousands of other twentieth-century "daughters," took up the unfinished agenda left by the suffrage movement. Morgan, too, realized that she struggled for future daughters and worried that her generation might squander precious opportunities.

> I fear for the women's movement falling into precisely the
> same trap as did our foremothers, the suffragists: creating a
> bourgeois feminist movement that never quite dared enough,
> never questioned enough, never really reached out beyond its
> own class and race.[32]

As women in developing countries become educated and enter the marketplace as wage-earners, they will invariably intensify existing cultural conflicts between religious and secular groups, and between those sectors of society living under preindustrial conditions and those who connect through cyberspace in a postmodern global society. Like small brushfires, these cultural wars may circle the globe, igniting a wild and frightening firestorm. Inevitably, some women will feel defeated as they encounter wave after wave of backlash. But in the darkness of their despair, they should remember that resistance is not a sign of defeat, but rather evidence that women are challenging a worldview that now belongs to an earlier era of human history.

Each generation of women activists leaves an unfinished agenda for the next generation. First Wave suffragists fought for women's citizenship, created international organizations dedicated to universal disarmament, but left many customs and beliefs unchallenged. Second Wave feminists questioned nearly everything, transformed much of American culture, expanded the idea of democracy by insisting that equality had to include the realities of its women citizens, and catapulted women's issues onto a global stage. Their greatest accomplishment was to change the terms of debate, so that women mattered. But they left much unfinished as well. They were unable to change most institutions, to gain greater economic justice for poor women, or to convince society that child care is the responsibility of the whole society. As a result, American women won the right to "have it all," but only if they "did it all."

It is for a new generation to identify what they need in order to achieve greater equality. It may even be their solemn duty. In the words of nineteenth-century suffragist Abigail Scott Duniway:

> The young women of today, free to study, to speak, to write, to choose their occupation, should remember that every inch of this freedom was bought for them at a great price. It is for them to show their gratitude by helping onward the reforms of their own times, by spreading the light of freedom and truth still wider. The debt that each generation owes to the past it must pay to the future.[33]

The struggle for women's human rights has just begun. As each generation shares its secrets, women learn to see the world through their own eyes, and discover, much to their surprise, that they are not the first, and that they are not alone. The poet Muriel Rukeyser once asked, "What would happen if one woman told the truth about her life?" Her answer: "The world would split open." And so it has. A revolution is under way, and there is no end in sight.

EPILOGUE TO THE 2007 EDITION:
GENDER MATTERS IN THE NEW CENTURY
∽∾

Sometimes history seems to speed up. So much happens, we lose perspective about how our lives have been shaped and affected. When that happens, I try to imagine how a historian in 2075 might view the present. As she pores over electronically preserved archives, I see her face frozen in a frown. "How do I make sense of the tumultuous early years of the twenty-first century?" she asks herself. "I see endless stories about military conflicts, political campaigns, and environmental crises. But what about all the battles over gender matters? How did the cultural and economic tensions of the era affect women's lives? And how did they shape this period of history?"

Our future historian might first remind her readers that rapid economic globalization, like industrialization a century earlier, disoriented millions of people. Bewildered by new prosperity or deepening poverty, traumatized by unexpected transnational migrations, and suddenly assaulted by unfamiliar cultural ideas, social customs, and religious beliefs, they felt anxious, uncertain about the future, and resistant to changes that affected family life. At the same time, she would note that global communications spread ideas about equality and human rights across the planet, giving the exploited and dispossessed a powerful language in which to express their grievances.

Even now, without the benefit of a future historian, we are already familiar with the dizzying effects of unimaginable rapid change. In a world made smaller by satellite television, the Internet, e-mail, and a global market in music, film, and pornography, many people have understandably resisted such cultural and social intrusions, resented their economic insecurity, and sought the comfort and continuity provided by ethnic loyalties, national identities, and religious fundamentalisms.

Some people, of course, have enthusiastically welcomed global free trade because it improves their standard of living or enhances the profits of multinational corporations. Still others, aware that globalization is irreversible but creates great inequities, have seized upon the opportunity to promote "fair trade," greater economic and social justice, environmental protections, and to expand workers' and women's human rights.

By the start of the new century, growing numbers of women across the globe had joined the paid labor force and gained access to some education. In many developing nations, human rights advocates also launched campaigns to prevent violence against women, to achieve greater female economic and political participation, and to provide women with choices about their own reproduction and marriages.

Not surprisingly, such challenges threatened the traditional hierarchical power once reserved for male religious leaders, as well as for fathers and husbands. Cultural battles erupted all over the planet as people fought bitterly over many economic, religious, and social issues. But one question—"*What is the appropriate role of women in contemporary society?*"—nearly always divided traditionalists, who included many religious fundamentalists, from modernists, who often embraced a more secular and pluralist view of society. Whatever their response to the sweeping changes brought about by globalization, nearly everyone agreed that women's historic role has been to preserve and reproduce the traditional customs and values of their culture. Working for wages outside the home challenged centuries of tradition.

To defend cherished values and customs, many men *and* women, within the United States as well as elsewhere, mobilized to prevent *their* women from turning into the iconic image of the emancipated Western woman—a sexually and economically independent person, seemingly unprotected by her family and unmoored from her community.

This cultural storm—in which women, gender relations, and sexuality became lightning rods in both national and global politics—profoundly shaped the early years of the twenty-first century.

THE GENDER WARS IN THE UNITED STATES

The backlash against the women's movement reached a high point in the 1980s. By 2000, it had gained even greater momentum. Feminists had been stereotyped, scapegoated, and vilified as man-hating, hairy, anti-family misfits for so long that young women, with good reason, wanted to distance themselves from the "F" word. The televangelist and political power broker Reverend Pat Robertson, for example, called feminism a "socialist, anti-family political movement that encourages women to leave their husbands, kill their children, practice witchcraft, destroy capitalism, and become lesbians."[1]

Although candidate George W. Bush ran as a "compassionate conservative" in 2000, the extreme Religious Right, long hostile to the women's movement, formed a significant part of his political base. After the Supreme Court halted a recount of votes in Florida, Bush lost the popular vote but won the election. The new president cast this controversial victory as a mandate for radical change. Fueled by a zealous faith in Market Fundamentalism—the belief that unregulated free markets solve all problems—and by his own religious fundamentalism, Bush sought to shrink the federal government, to enact huge tax cuts that mostly benefited the wealthiest Americans, to eliminate or privatize as many government services as possible, to transfer the costs of health care, retirement, and higher education onto families, and to repeal much of the legacy of the 1960s, including women's rights.

Efforts to regulate sexuality, ban abortion, and limit the rights of gays and lesbians quickly vaulted to the top of the national political agenda. Conservative women's groups played an increasingly powerful role in discrediting the achievements of the women's movement. The extremely religious members of Concerned Women of America, for example, crusaded to outlaw abortion and to restore "Christian values" and women's traditional domestic role in the family. Serrin Foster of Feminists for Choice tried to persuade young women that feminism had robbed them of the "choice" to have children, but she offered no means for supporting the offspring of these young single mothers. The Independent Women's Forum (IWF) and The Women's Freedom Network (WFN), both secular organizations of professional women, dubbed themselves "equality feminists," by which they meant that self-made women needed no assistance from the government. They based their antifeminism on their hostility to liberalism and on their belief that an unregulated economy would provide prosperity for women. The IWF derided modern feminists as "Dependency Divas"—women who sought government assistance for working families and the poor. These equality feminists also insisted that each woman, as a self-made individual, should pull herself up by the straps of her stiletto heels.[2]

The right-wing Republican war against women's reproductive and sexual choices began on the first day the president took office. Bush restored the Reagan-era global gag rule, which prohibited any international agency from receiving U.S. funds if it performed abortions, lobbied to make abortion legal, or even provided counseling about the procedure. The result was disastrous: women in developing countries had less access to contraception and reproductive health care, which inevitably resulted in hundreds of thousands of unwanted pregnancies and abortions.[3]

After the September 11, 2001, attacks on the World Trade Center and the Pentagon, President Bush declared a "war on terror" and pursued a domestic agenda that had less to do with protecting the nation from terrorism than with manipulating fear, expanding executive power, eroding civil rights and civil liberties, and governing in an atmosphere of unprecedented secrecy. The declaration of an endless war provided him with the political opportunity to advance the Religious Right's political agenda, which had immediate consequences on women's lives.

The Bush administration, for example, repeatedly tried to ban abortion by conferring "personhood" on the fetus. "In as many areas as we can, we want to put on the books that the embryo is a person," boasted Samuel B. Casey, executive director of the Christian Legal Society.[4] In 2003, Congress passed the so-called Partial-Birth Act, which restricted late-term abortions; in 2004, it passed the Unborn Victims of Violence Act, conferring legal personhood on the fetus of an injured pregnant woman. During these years, at least twenty states passed laws designed to restrict access to abortion, by requiring women to submit to advanced counseling, "cooling off" periods, parental notification, and by limiting funds for reproductive health services.[5]

Battles over Bush's nominees for the Supreme Court inevitably turned on whether the candidate would vote to overturn *Roe v. Wade*, the 1973 Supreme Court ruling that had given American women the constitutional right to choose an abortion. In short, former President Bill Clinton's famous declaration that abortion should be "safe, legal, and rare" was replaced by an all-out effort to outlaw abortion within the United States.

The relentless campaign to impose legal personhood on the fetus soon rippled outward to other areas of American life, including attempts to make emergency contraception inaccessible, to intervene in end-of-life decisions, to halt stem-cell research, and to place restrictions on assisted reproduction.[6]

In its efforts to regulate sexual and reproductive choices, the Bush administration politicized science in an unprecedented way. In 2002, for example, the administration appointed physicians opposed to contraception, reproductive rights, and mifepristone (used for medical abortions) to the Reproduction Health Drugs Advisory Committee of the Food and Drug Administration. When vetting scientists for some 250 advisory boards, Bush officials stunned scientists when they asked such inappropriate political questions as "Do you support abortion rights?" "The death penalty for drug kingpins?" "Did you vote for Bush?" Worried about the politicization of science, Donald Kennedy, former president of Stanford University and editor of the prestigious journal *Science*, wrote, "If you start picking people by their ideology instead of their scientific credentials, you are inevitably reducing the quality of the advisory group."[7]

Ignoring criticism from the scientific community, the Bush administration nevertheless staffed scientific advisory panels with right-wing religious ideologues who disregarded scientific evidence and even posted inaccurate information on government Web sites. In 2002, for example, the National Cancer Institute's Web site inaccurately described abortion as a possible cause of breast cancer. In the same year, the Centers for Disease Control scrubbed information from its Web site about how condoms can protect teens from HIV infection, pregnancy, and sexually transmitted diseases. Its new version declared that "more research is needed" and omitted a passage on how to avoid unwanted pregnancies. Ignoring recommendations from its own scientific experts, the Food and Drug Administration repeatedly postponed a decision to permit over-the-counter emergency contraception, known as Plan B. After the Religious Right organized the Pharmacists for Life movement, *The Economist* magazine reported that "A rising number of pharmacists are refusing to dispense prescriptions [in the United States] for birth control and morning-after pills, saying it is against their beliefs."[8]

Determined to defend "traditional family" values, the Bush administration budgeted millions of dollars to promote marriage for poor women and to teach "abstinence only" courses to teenagers. Teen pregnancy had actually declined to record lows—a drop of 20 percent between 1987 and 1994 and another 27 percent decline between 1994 and 2000. Still, as the nonpartisan Alan Guttmacher Institute reported, "the U.S. teen birthrate is one of the highest in the developed world."[9]

The president's response to that serious problem was to withdraw funds from any state that offered sex education classes that actually taught about contraception and how to avoid unwanted pregnancies. "Abstinence only" courses, by contrast, only instructed young people to avoid sex until they married. In 2004, a congressional report concluded that two-thirds of these federally funded "abstinence only" courses contained "false, misleading, or distorted information about reproductive health."[10]

Both the president and the Religious Right also sought to prop up the heterosexual "traditional family," which, by the turn of the twenty-first century, included only 25 percent of American households. Divorce, single parenthood, same-sex parenting, economic distress, and cohabitation had transformed American family life. Even Bush's born-again religious constituency was just as likely to divorce as traditional Christians, and the divorce rate of both was only 2 percent below that of atheists and agnostics.[11]

Gay marriage quite naturally became a symbol of the dramatic changes that had altered American families. Bush not only called for a constitutional ban against same-sex marriage (which failed) but also denounced the growing judicial acceptance of legal civil unions. Critics of the Bush administration argued that social conservatives seemed to care more about containing sexuality within heterosexual marriage than preventing unwanted pregnancies or sanctifying relationships between loving partners, or matching needy children with same-sex adoptive parents.

GENDER RESISTANCE AND RIGHTS

But the conservative campaign to regulate sexuality and reproduction and to promote marriage is only part of a far more complicated story. During these very same years, the nation also witnessed major campaigns—by women, gays and lesbians, and transgendered people— to expand reproductive, marital, and sexual rights.

In April 2004, for example, a million people of all ages and from many ethnic and racial backgrounds marched in the nation's capitol to defend a woman's right to reproductive health care and abortion. Organized by a broad coalition of women's and civil rights groups, "The March for Women's Lives"—thought to be the largest demonstration in the nation's history—proved that American women were not willing to concede defeat in the abortion wars.

This rearguard action to protect women's reproductive choice and health was accompanied by aggressive movements to expand the right to express any sexual orientation or embrace any gender identity without fear of violence or discrimination.

After decades of coming out of the closet and fighting for their civil rights, gays and lesbians were hardly strangers to most Americans. Popular culture, including television series and sitcoms, regularly featured at least one gay or lesbian character. When *Queer Eye for the Straight Guy* debuted on cable television, the five gay men who gave advice on fashion and home decorating to clueless heterosexual men turned the program into a smash hit. In 2005, the feature film *Brokeback Mountain*, which won an Oscar nomination for best picture, challenged America's iconic image of masculinity when it explored—with great sensitivity and tenderness—the love and passion that endured between two ranch hands throughout their marriages and adult lives.

In rapid succession, gays and lesbians also won expanded rights from American courts. In 2003, the Supreme Court reversed itself and ruled that a Texas law against sodomy was unconstitutional, and in 2004, the Massachusetts Supreme Court decided that same-sex couples are entitled to the "protection, benefits, and obligations of civil marriage." Just days later, Gavin Newsom, San Francisco's newly elected handsome and heterosexual mayor, stunned the nation when he announced that the city would issue marriage licenses to same-sex couples. Newsom honored Del Martin, 83, and Phyllis Lyon, 79, pioneering feminists and gay rights activists who had shared their lives for fifty-one years, by having them become the first same-sex couple declared "spouses for life."

During the next month, same-sex couples braved the rain and lined up around San Francisco's City Hall, even sleeping on the sidewalk, hoping to get married before a court injunction closed this historic window of opportunity. It was an unforgettable sight. Beaming faces spread an infectious sense of joy throughout City Hall. Women dressed in stunning white gowns juggled babies and bouquets. Men outfitted in elegant tuxedos, sporting carnations in their lapels, cradled infants, while friends held their paperwork. As couples looked into each other's eyes, arms wrapped around each other, their friends took snapshots and the national media documented the occasion for the evening news. One burly veteran cameraman was so overwhelmed by the scene that he found himself blinking back tears.

"What difference will marriage make in your lives?" reporters asked these exuberant couples. Most had already shared their lives for many years and had held commitment ceremonies. Still, they were ecstatic about getting married. One woman said, "I won't have to call her my partner or girlfriend at a doctor's office or a hospital. She's now my spouse." Another replied, "We want to have children. Someday I can call a child-care center or a school and say that my spouse will be picking up our child. We'll be viewed as a valid family." Two men who had lived together for sixteen years rejoiced at the idea of their newfound legitimacy. One said he simply "wanted the respectability accorded married couples." Even though they rightly suspected that the California courts would later invalidate their licenses, those who married during those days radiated a contagious sense of joy. "It's a historic milestone," said one recently married man. "We're part of history and we know it." So did the rest of world, as television broadcast images of these couples around the planet.[12]

A few months later, in May 2004, Massachusetts became the first state to legally permit same-sex marriage. By the end of 2005, five nations—Belgium, The Netherlands, Canada, Spain, and South Africa—had legalized same-sex marriage, and England and New Zealand had made civil unions legal.

A backlash was predictable. Same-sex marriage, presumably between two equal partners, challenged the idea of a dominant husband and a submissive wife. Gay marriage quickly turned into a wedge issue during the 2004 presidential election. Although Bush's call for a constitutional amendment banning gay marriage failed in Congress, voters in eleven states passed all referenda banning same-sex marriage—placed by the Conservative and Religious Right—in the 2004 election.

But the attack against gay marriage paradoxically also changed the terms of debate. A growing number of moderate politicians, who once shied away from the subject, now began to embrace "civil unions" as a compromise position that conferred all civil rights, except the legal status of marriage, upon same-sex couples.

Still beneath the political radar was the rapidly growing transgender movement in the United States, which traced its roots back to large urban communities in the 1990s. The women's movement had challenged rigid gender roles. Now people who felt trapped inside their bodies began to seek freedom from discrimination and violence. Gradually, the movement gained a few of its goals. By 2005, more than half the states had passed legal protection for transgendered people.

Still, the transgender movement remained unfamiliar to most Americans until films, literature, and television began to publicize the anguish of those men and women who desperately wanted to change their gender identity, if not necessarily their bodies. In the 1999 film *Boys Don't Cry*, actress Hillary Swank played a teenage girl who began living as a young man, with lethal consequences. The highly acclaimed 2002 novel *Middlesex*, by Jeffrey Eugenides, publicized the not-so-rare lives of those born with ambiguous genitalia, known as intersexed. In 2003, the feature film *Normal* focused on a middle-aged, married man in a conservative western Illinois town, who, after twenty-five years of marriage, stuns his wife, grown children, and church by announcing that he's always felt trapped inside a male body and now wants to live as a woman. In 2005, the Sundance Channel featured an eight-part documentary series, *Transgeneration*, which followed four college-aged students for a year as they confronted their desires to dress and live as the opposite sex. The year ended with a riveting feature film, *TransAmerica*, in which a rather prim transsexual, about to undergo surgery to become a physical woman, discovers that she once fathered a child who is now a teenaged male plying the streets as a prostitute.

THE NEXT GENERATIONS

The lesbian, gay, bisexual, and transgender movements were hardly alone in challenging conventional ideas about sexuality or gender. While the Bush administration eagerly promoted abstinence, chastity oaths, and new marriage covenants, some young people were busy celebrating the historic rupture between sexuality and reproduction that had taken place long before they were born. Most visible on liberal college campuses, and in nightclubs or raves, some of these young men and women flaunted their sexuality, paraded their pierced and tattooed bodies, and played with their gender identity through cross-dressing.

Among this group were some young women, born between 1965 and 1975, who called themselves the Third Wave. They knew that nineteenth-century First Wave feminists had fought for the vote and that 1960s and 1970s Second Wave feminists had tried to transform public and private life. Now, these young Third Wave feminists acknowledged their continuity with those who came before them.

Third Wave feminism had its roots in *both* academic life and the punk/grunge rock scene. In the mid-1980s, a group of feminist activists and academics concerned about racism in the women's movement collaborated

on an anthology titled *The Third Wave: Feminist Perspectives on Racism*.[13]
Although some young African American feminist activists described
themselves as "hip-hop feminists," their white counterparts committed
themselves to building an inclusive, multi-cultural, multi-issue movement,
with a focus on women's multiple racial, class, and sexual identities.

Third Wave feminism also came out of young women's collective
protests in the alternative rock scene, most notably sparked by the band
the Riot Grrrls. "Whereas some second wave feminists fought for equal
access to the workplace," explained essayist Melissa Klein, "some third
wave feminists fought for equal access to the punk stage."[14] Feminist
punk rock musicians inspired a "riot grrrl" movement that rejected the
idea of "good" and "bad" girls, and promoted a defiant, sexual female
stance on stage, as well as in their own lives. Many of these musicians
dressed in gender-bending clothes—short skirts with heavy boots—and
wore thick makeup and bleached hair—"for the pleasure of other
women, not men," they said. One fan of the punk rock band Bikini Kill
described an unforgettable moment when its founder, Kathleen Hanna,
"climbed on-stage in a mini-skirt, lipstick smeared, and sang/screamed
about incest or rape or girl-girl desire."[15]

The Clarence Thomas hearings in 1991, at which Anita Hill accused the
Supreme Court nominee of sexual harassment, also galvanized some
members of this generation. The next year, Rebecca Walker, daughter of
the well-known feminist writer Alice Walker, defiantly responded to the
New York Times' seemingly endless campaign to pronounce an era of
postfeminism. In *Ms.* Magazine, she wrote, "I am not a postfeminist feminist. I am the third wave." With Amy Richards, she cofounded the Third
Wave Foundation which, among other activities, mobilized young women
to vote. That same year, the youthful Women's Action Coalition began
organizing a series of consciousness-raising public events. On Mother's
Day in 1992, they draped a Grand Central Station board with a pink
banner that read, "It's Mother's Day: $30 Billion owed in child support."[16]

On television and radio talk shows, Americans mostly heard the conservative voices of such authors as Christina Hoff Sommers (*Who Stole
Feminism?* and *The War Against Boys*), and Katie Roiphe (*The Morning
After: Sex, Fear and Feminism*), who were regularly called upon to discredit feminists by denouncing them as too ideological or too caught up
in their own victimhood.

The Third Wave grassroots movement was far less audible and visible, but it gradually swept up many young Generation X artists, arti-

sans, writers, and performers interested in exploring women's power and identity. Feminist magazines like San Francisco's *Bitch: Feminist Response to Pop Culture* and the New York-based *Bust*, which billed itself as "the Voice of the New Girl Order," spoke to a generation eager to take up the feminist torch, but on their own terms. The turn of the millennium also witnessed an explosion of feminist "zines" and influential books, including Rebecca Walker's anthology *To Be Real* (1995), which used autobiographical stories to explore women's lives, Leslie Heywood and Jennifer Drake's *Third Wave Agenda: Being Feminist, Doing Feminism* (1997), and Jennifer Baumgardner and Amy Richards's *Manifesta: Young Women, Feminism, and the Future* (2000), which described the next generation's direction and goals.

Third Wave feminists clearly valued, even honored, the legacy of older feminists who had opened up public life for them. "For anyone born after the early 1960s," wrote the authors of *Manifesta*, "the presence of feminism in our lives is taken for granted. For our generation, feminism is like Fluoride. We scarcely notice that we have it—it's simply in the water." But, wrote the editors of the 3rdWWWAve Web site, "This is not the second wave warmed over. We are building on what they accomplished and taking it in new directions appropriate for the twenty-first century."[17]

One important difference lay in their distinctive sensibility, which dramatically contrasted with the women who had forged the women's movement in the late 1960s. Younger women were ironic, cool, outrageous, and self-consciously politically incorrect. Baumgardner and Richards rejected ideology in favor of accepting the "lived messiness" of feminism. To some younger feminists, Second Wavers seemed like dogmatic, humorless, prudish women who demanded that men call them women, rather than girls or chicks and even worse, wore sensible shoes.

Inevitably, tensions arose between Second Wave feminists, who had emphasized collective action, and younger feminists, who often focused on individual self expression. Some older feminists argued that equating appearance and sexual adventures with empowerment, however playful or ironic, skirted feminism's still unachieved goals of social and economic equality. By itself, they argued, personal expression offered no real threat to discrimination or injustice, failed to free women from the home, and ignored the limitations on women's real choices.[18]

What some older critics failed to grasp, though, was that this generation felt burdened by the pervasive stereotype of a feminist as a bra-burning, hairy-legged, ugly, shrewish, man-hating lesbian misfit. For younger heterosexual women, a major issue was how to reconcile their feminism with their desire to embrace their sexuality and femininity. Liz Funk, a young NOW member in upstate New York, explained, "Just because a young woman feels inclined to argue in a class debate for pro-choice abortion rights, equal pay or having a woman president doesn't mean she cannot do so in Tiffany jewelry, a pink dress, and sequined sandals. . . . People are surprised," she added, "that a 16-year-old high school junior doesn't 'look like a feminist.'"[19] To counter the media's negative image of feminists, some young college women sported tight pink-and-black T-shirts with the words "This is What a Feminist Looks Like" written across their chests. "People have said to me you can't be a feminist, you are too sexy to be a feminist," said Lisa Covington, a senior at Clarion University of Pennsylvania. "The T-shirt is a way to reconcile this. . . . I am a feminine feminist." "The shirts are hot," said Amy Littlefield, a freshman at Brown University in Providence, R.I. "Maybe they help us send the message that you can be sexy and proud of your appearance and still be a feminist."[20]

Some Third Wave feminists also embraced what Baumgardner and Richards labeled as "Girlie feminism"—the color pink, glitzy fashion, Barbie dolls, cheerleading for causes, knitting, and cooking—traditional feminine activities or styles that Second Wave feminists had discarded in their effort to enter male-dominated institutions.[21] Some even fetishized fashion and consumerism, flaunted their sexuality, and argued for a "do-your-own-thing" feminism in which they emphasized individual choice and self expression. In the mid-1990s, Marcelle Karp, editor of *Bust*, wrote, "We've entered an era of DIY feminism—sistah, do it yourself. . . . Your feminism is what you want it to be and what you make of it." The authors of *Manifesta* agreed: "Feminism isn't about what choice you make, but the freedom to make that choice."[22]

An important contribution of this generation was to make feminism appealing and attractive. For them, reclaiming sexual power and a feminine appearance was vital. With a certain gleeful political incorrectness, Third Wave feminists reappropriated the words *cunt* and *bitch*. Some women even urged using their sexuality to wield power over men. *Bust* tested sex toys. In an essay titled "Lusting for Freedom," Rebecca Walker expressed her generation's conviction that there was nothing incompatible with sexuality and feminism: "When I think back," she wrote, "it is that impulse I am most proud of. . . . I deserve to live free of shame, that my body is not my enemy, and that pleasure is my friend and my right."[23]

But Third Wave feminists did not always agree about sexual behavior, which has often divided feminists. Second Wave feminists had split over the emergence of lesbian feminists. Now, noted Lisa Jarvis, editor of *Bitch* magazine, "genderqueers"—young activists in the transgender movement—"were occupying the place that lesbian issues did in the last generation."[24] Genderqueers rejected all gender categories and promoted the ideal of a gender-blind culture. Speaking to NOW's National Board on Transgender Inclusion, Ricki Wilchins, an architect of the genderqueer movement, said, "Consider for a moment that men with vaginas are what gender looks like when it's deregulated."[25]

Not surprisingly, *Sex and the City*, an HBO television series that celebrated female friendship, glamorized consumerism, and unabashedly explored all kinds of sexual preferences and exploits, became a phenomenal hit among this cohort of women. So did Eve Ensler's play, *The Vagina Monologues*, a one-woman performance that premiered in 1996 and, like *Sex and the City*, explored women's sexual desires. It also condemned rape as a war crime, riffed on women's body image, and celebrated what women couldn't see—their vaginas. In 1997, Ensler created V-Day, a grassroots nonprofit campaign to end violence against women. By 2006, the play, often performed on Valentine's Day, had been staged in fifty-four countries and on hundreds of campuses across the United States.

The Third Wave's emphasis on individualism naturally concerned some young feminists. Some worried that the political had become *too* personal—detached from a larger vision of economic and social equality. Leslie Heywood and Jennifer Drake, editors of *Being Feminist, Doing Feminism*, wrote "Despite our knowing better, despite our knowing its emptiness, the ideology of individualism is still a major motivating force in many third wave lives."[26] Carter-Ann Mahdavi, the editor of *World Feminism*, an international feminist online magazine, argued that such individualism "is a very laissez-faire form of politics that makes me nervous. What I find disconcerting is how the 'personal is political' slogan is being interpreted. The focus on individualism can be interpreted as the freedom not to worry about issues that do not personally affect you."[27]

Unlike Second Wave feminists, who had met in consciousness-raising groups in women's living rooms, Third Wave feminists mostly shared their revelations, desires, and dilemmas in magazines and on blogs and feminist Web sites. One sixteen-year-old from Nebraska wrote Lisa Jervis, publisher of *Bitch*:

My view of my whole life, from boys to bodies and from TV
to tampons, has changed drastically since I read my first
Bitch. . . . Thank you for teaching me how to think for myself.
Thank you for letting me know it's okay to voice my opinion,
no matter how cynical or harsh it may be, no matter how
much the world around me doesn't seem to care. Thank you,
Bitch: I am a 16-year-old feminist and for once in my life I
feel comfortable saying so.[28]

Cyberspace also helped create a sense of a feminist community. On
feminist Web sites, young girls discovered each other and most important, found that they were not the only ones who felt outrage and indignation. One young high school student posted this note: "I had no idea
there were any other girls my age who identified as feminists the way I
did—angry, sluttily rageful girls who took no shit." Another young high
school student, who had discovered feminism, contributed this revelation: "There is this whole other world simmering below the surface, and,
like Alice, I just tumbled down into it."[29]

The group of young women writers and activists that identified with
Third Wave feminism was extremely articulate, highly prolific, but actually quite small. Far greater were the numbers of young female activists
(including the elders of Generation Y, born after 1976) who took their
feminism for granted, integrated it into their personal lives, and carried
it into their work as activists against the war in Iraq, advocates for
reproductive and transgender rights, the homeless and the poor, female
immigrants, and as organizers and activists in the labor, environmental,
anti-sweatshop, and human rights movements. Also high on their agenda
were the problems of HIV/AIDS awareness, prison reform, child sexual
abuse, self-mutilation, eating disorders, mandatory drug sentencing, domestic workers' rights, as well as gaining equal access to the Internet.[30]

Many of these activists also joined the interminable battle to defend
women's reproductive rights. One-third of the participants in the 2004
March for Women's Lives were young women who had not yet celebrated
their thirtieth birthdays. Kystal Lander, campus program director of the
Feminist Majority, observed that "Bush's relentless attempts to confer
personhood on the fetus and to choose judges who are opposed to abortion have galvanized young women all over the nation. They get it now;
it's real. Bush is educating a whole new wave of women, more than anyone could have imagined."[31]

Although a majority of young women favored the goals of the women's movement, many still uttered the famous phrase, "I'm not a feminist, but . . ." In their next book, titled *Grassroots: A Field Guide for Feminist Activism*, Baumgardner and Richards urged their generation to change these words to "I'm a feminist *and* . . ." and encouraged them to engage in "Everyday Activism," which might include supporting socially responsible companies, starting campus organizations, or letter writing campaigns.[32]

Everyday activism surfaced with particular creativity during the 2004 presidential election. One group of young friends in Berkeley, California, for example, decided to find some edgy but effective way of mobilizing women to register and vote. The group christened itself 1,000 Flowers and sent beauty salons in swing states nail files, postcards, and posters that urged, "Nail the election," "Shape the oval office," "File your complaint," and "Don't let this election be a nail biter."[33]

Young activists often deployed their generation's sense of irony to mobilize other women. Heidi Sick, a thirty-two-year-old technology analyst, organized twenty of her friends to march in D.C. as "San Francisco Choice Chicks." Medea Benjamin of Global Exchange, who founded CodePink as a women's antiwar organization, gave pink slips (the kind worn under dresses) as dismissal notices to President Bush and Vice President Dick Cheney. Such playful theatrics attracted young women, who, unlike their mothers' generation, happily dressed from head to toe in pink at antiwar demonstrations.

One issue, however, that did not appear on the Third Wave feminist agenda was child care. Though many young women agonized—sometimes alone, often with friends—and obsessively tried to plan a future that combined a career and children, they tended to view child care as an individual problem. *Manifesta*, for example, contained a thoughtful thirteen-point agenda that never mentioned child care. The authors explained that they had not yet had children when they authored this important book.[34] In a similar vein, Jessica Valenti edited feministing.com with all the cool, ironic outrage typical of her generation; her Web site featured a defiant image of a mudflat figure with its finger raised in the air. But when I asked her and dozens of other young editors, reporters, activists, and writers about their highest priorities, many cited abortion rights, racism, health care, poverty, and violence against women. None mentioned child care.

Born into a political era dominated by rampant individualism rather than by large social movements, some young women clearly could not imagine child care as anything but their own responsibility. They also

expressed considerable skepticism about government-subsidized child
care, which they envisioned as some grubby Department of Motor Vehi-
cles center, not the clean and educational Scandinavian child care centers that had inspired an earlier generation.[35]

Here was a serious disconnect. Young women privately anguished
over an issue they could not imagine turning into a public and political
debate. Even sadder, more than a few young women said that the lack of
affordable or available child care made them reconsider their plans to
have children.[36] One young feminist put it this way: "I feel terrified of
the patchwork situation women are forced to rely upon. I think many
young women are deciding not to have children or waiting until they are
well established in their careers—and that this has become an individual solution for many." In short, they had no language for what they
viewed as the most important dilemma they faced in their immediate
futures.[37]

THE CARE CRISIS: THE PROBLEM THAT HAS NO NAME

A baby is born. A child is stricken with a serious illness. A spouse has a
stroke. A parent falls ill. These are the kind of events that throw a working woman's delicate balance between work and family into uncon-
trolled chaos.

For four decades, American women had entered the paid work force,
but American society had done precious little to restructure the
workplace or family life. Women still bore most of the burdens of family
life. The country was stuck in what sociologist Arlie Hochschild has
called a "Stalled Revolution" and suffered from what she described as a
"Care Deficit." An inadequate and hopelessly broken health care system,
which left more than forty million Americans without health coverage,
often meant that this care deficit, which has turned into a full-blown
Care Crisis, became a matter of life and death. To imagine erasing that
deficit, wrote political scientist Joan Tronto, Americans would have to
embrace an "ethic of care," by which she meant that the highest "goal of
society should be to protect and care for its citizens."[38]

By 2000, the Care Crisis, in a very real sense, had replaced The
Feminine Mystique as the new "problem that has no name." It was the
800 pound elephant at home, at business, and in national politics—

gigantic, but ignored. The Second Wave movement had succeeded at turning many personal and private experiences into public and political issues. But neither they nor Third Wave feminists had so far been able to get Americans to grasp the danger of the mounting care crisis.

More than three decades after Congress had passed—and President Richard Nixon had vetoed—comprehensive child care legislation in 1971, child care had dropped off the national political agenda. Small wonder, then, that so many young women viewed the care of their children as their own problem, to which they needed to find an individual solution.

As a result, most American women suffered privately, without realizing that the care crisis was a pandemic problem among working- and middle-class families. And, with each passing year, the care crisis only grew larger, burdening the lives of working mothers. But it never became part of a national conversation or central to the nation's political agenda. One of America's dirty little secrets was that the government and business—as well as many men—found it both profitable and convenient for women to do the unpaid work of housework and caregiving.

It was as though Americans were trapped in a time warp in the 1950s, still convinced that women *should* and *would* care for children and the elderly. But of course they couldn't. In 1950, less than one-fifth of mothers with children under the age of six worked in the labor force. By 2000, two-thirds of these mothers worked in the paid labor market.[39]

Antifeminists naturally blamed the women's movement for creating the impossible ideal of "having it all." But it was journalists and popular writers, not feminists, who had created the myth of the "Superwoman." Second Wavers had known that women couldn't do it alone. In fact, they had insisted that men share the housework and child raising and that government and business provide and subsidize child care.

The good news was that men in dual-income couples *were* steadily increasing their participation in household chores and child care. But women still managed and organized much of family life.[40] By 2000, moreover, the political atmosphere had grown positively hostile to using federal funds for subsidizing working families.

The truth is, Market Fundamentalism had failed to provide a much-needed answer to the question, "Who will care for America's children and elderly?" As a result, most working women returned home after work to what Hochschild called a "Second Shift"—housework, child care, and sustaining the social networks of their extended families and communities. Looming ahead, in a rapidly aging society, was even a "Third Shift," caring for aging parents.[41]

Although America's working women felt burdened and exhausted, desperate for sleep and leisure time, they made few collective protests for child care or for family friendly workplace policies. Globalization created stiff competition and both men and women tried to hold on to their jobs; American businesses and corporations sought higher profits through layoffs; and cell phones and e-mail accelerated life and blurred work and family time. Single mothers naturally suffered the most from the care crisis. But even when two parents worked forty or more hours a week, there was simply no time for a balanced life. Parents became overwhelmed, children often felt cranky, spouses felt neglected, workers quietly seethed and gulped antacids and sleeping pills, and extensive volunteering in community life began to vanish.

Overworked American families, whose time spent at work had increased three extra weeks between 1986 and 1997, suffered from what Hochschild called a "Time Bind" and a few people even started movements "to take back their time." But neither the secular nor the Religious Right, who glorified "family values," supported any national effort to help working families regain a sense of stability and balance.[42]

The wealthy solved their own care crisis by hiring full-time nannies or attendants, often from developing countries, to care for their children or parents. Middle-class families tried to patch together care for their children with relatives and babysitters. The very poor sometimes gained access to subsidized child care or elder care, but more often, women who worked in the low-waged service sector lost their jobs when children or parents required urgent care.[43]

True, some businesses had adopted some family friendly policies. Every year, *Working Mother* magazine published the 100 most "family friendly" companies. In 2000, the magazine reported that companies that were making "significant improvements in 'quality of life' benefits such as telecommuting, on-site child care, career training, and flextime," were, as a result, "saving hundreds of thousands of dollars in recruitment in the long run."[44] Although some progressive universities, law firms, and hospitals had made career adjustments for working mothers, the basic clockwork of the male career had remained largely unchanged. Career demands almost always collided with women's most intensive childrearing years. Many women quite reasonably couldn't or wouldn't handle such a burden. And, sadly, without the support of a vibrant women's movement, too many working mothers felt they had failed, rather than realizing that the organization of work made it nearly impossible to earn a living, advance in a career, and still enjoy a family life.[45]

The truth is, the feminist agenda remained woefully unfinished. Women had entered the paid labor force on men's terms, not their own. It was not until 2006, for example, that the nation's largest public institution of higher education, The University of California, adopted a serious family friendly initiative for parents. Although women now made up at least half of all college, law, and medical students, and appeared on television as lawyers, surgeons, police officials, and even briefly as the Commander in Chief, most American employers and men had not done all that much to alter the conventional structure of the workplace or family life.

Since most people viewed the care crisis as an individual problem, books, magazines, and newspapers offered American women an endless stream of advice about how to become better organized and more efficient, or how to meditate, exercise, and pamper themselves. Many of these articles were useful and even empathic, but only addressed the individual woman. Missing in all this advice was the very pragmatic proposal that American society still needed to rethink and reorganize both the workplace and the family for the twenty-first century.

But conventional wisdom reinforced the widespread myth that American women had gained equality, solved all problems, entered a post-feminist era, and that it was time for disgruntled feminists "to move on." Such advice was hardly new. Ever since 1970, the mainstream media had been pronouncing the death of feminism and reporting how career women had returned home to care for their children. In 2000, Ellen Galinksy, president of the Families and Work Institute in New York, wearily responded, "I still meet people all the time who believe that the trend has turned, that more women are staying home with their kids, that there are going to be fewer dual-income families, but it's just not true."[46]

The early twenty-first century version of this journalistic narrative now described how feminism had duped women, forcing them to choose between family and career. With a certain celebratory tone, such stories described how elite, wealthy, and predominantly white women were "choosing" to ditch their educational credentials and "opting out" in favor of home and children.

Some of these highly educated women who did leave their careers channeled all their energetic perfectionism into producing perfect babies, a pattern Judith Warner described in a book appropriately titled

Perfect Madness. A growing industry offered affluent and anxious mothers an array of expensive toys designed to create a "Baby Einstein."

When some of these mothers began to experience isolation and loneliness, they joined a growing number of virtual or actual mothers' support groups. Three so-called "opt out" moms even started a new magazine, *Total 180!*, which targeted stay-at-home moms with the slogan "From briefcase to diaper bag." One feminist reporter described the world she found inside the magazine to be "a dark, dark place." She was particularly appalled by an editor's description of "pizza joints where groups of stay-at-home moms 'let out' by their husbands huddle 'for a once-weekly session of lamenting, venting, laughing, and girding for the next week of chaos.'"[47]

Stories that celebrated what some called "choice feminism"—the belief that any choice is as good as any another—conveniently obscured the fact that an absence of quality, affordable, and accessible child care and flexible working hours, among other family friendly policies, greatly contributed to a woman's so-called "choice" to stay at home. Such articles, moreover, hardly represented the lives of most working women. The seemingly endless parade of articles about "opt out" career women relied on sloppy outdated social science research that focused largely on wealthy women who had married even wealthier men. More recent surveys had in fact showed that highly educated women intended to pursue careers, and that most women, in any event, had to work, regardless of their preference.[48]

Anecdotal evidence, in short, substituted for a statistical or analytic assessment of the limited choices women faced. In 2005, for example, the media began describing "the daughter track," or the exit of women (mostly the leading-edge of baby boomers) from well-established careers in order to be full-time caregivers for an elderly parent. Such stories grabbed the public's attention, described women as "opting out," but failed to describe the incredible anguish, lack of part-time alternatives, and inadequate social services that forced women to give up careers to take care of their parents.[49]

In short, the media mostly ignored the growing care crisis. Instead, they published sensational stories that pitted stay-at-home mothers against "working women" in what they coyly called the "Mommy Wars." When the *New York Times* ran a story about why some feminists rejected the concept of "choice feminism," one woman wrote the *New York Times* editor:

The word "choice has been used in the context of women working at home versus working outside the home, as a euphemism for unpaid labor, with no job security, no health or vacation benefits and no retirement plans. No wonder men are not clamoring for this "choice." Many jobs in the workplace also involve drudgery, but do not leave one financially dependent on another person.[50]

Despite such protests, the Mommy Wars raged on. In 2006, writer Caitlin Flanghan published *To Hell with All That: Loving and Loathing Our Inner Housewife* and gained considerable celebrity and professional attention by urging other women to honor "their inner housewife." Flanaghan had just joined a long and dishonorable American tradition in which women made careers out of telling other women to stay home with their families.[51]

The Mommy Wars, however, *did* reflect the fact that many women felt they had to choose between work and children. Scholars have long noted that in Scandinavian countries, where laws provide for generous parental leave and subsidized child care, women participate in the labor force at far greater rates than in this country.[52] Many American women who left their jobs, moreover, were lulled by the widely held belief that they could easily reenter the labor force. In many European countries, such reentry was even mandated. Not so in the United States.

As it turned out, returning to work was not that simple. One woman who had left her six figure position as a CEO to stay at home offered this advice to other women: "Don't quit your job. Definitely don't stop. You will not be able to pull yourself back."[53] According to one study, those who held advanced degrees in law, medicine, or education, often faced a "frosty reception" and found themselves shut out of their careers.[54] In her 2005 book *Bait and Switch*, social critic Barbara Ehrenreich described how difficult it was to find employment as a mid-level manager, despite waving an excellent résumé at potential employers. Summing up the plight of the back-to-work mom, Ehrenreich issued this caveat: "The prohibition on résumé gaps is pretty great. . . . You have to be getting an education or making money for somebody all along, every minute."[55]

POVERTY? WHAT POVERTY?

For poor women, for whom there never was much "choice," the care crisis was even more acute. But poverty, like the care crisis, remained invisible to mainstream America and largely outside the national political discourse. During a 2004 vice presidential debate, Gwen Ifill, an African American anchor on PBS, asked both Senator John Edwards and Vice President Dick Cheney how they would address the needs of HIV-infected African American women, the most rapidly growing infected part of the American population. Both men looked stunned and ignored the specific question. Cheney blathered about AIDS in Africa. John Edwards filled his time by discussing the need for greater health care coverage in the United States. It was a shameful moment in American politics.

When Hurricane Katrina tore into New Orleans in 2005, the American public—including many veteran mainstream journalists—seemed genuinely shocked that poor people lived from hand to mouth, owned no cars, and were unable to escape the torrential flooding that destroyed their homes and communities.

During the presidential tenure of George W. Bush, Americans fought cultural wars over sex education, stem-cell research, same-sex marriage, abortion, university curriculum, and intelligent design, but they avoided the plight of the poor. Meanwhile, poverty soared and the middle class shrank. In 2004, the U.S. Census Bureau announced that poverty rates in United States had increased for the fourth straight year and had jumped from 31.6 million people in 2000 to 37 million, including 13 million children.[56] Federal data revealed that 14.3 million women lived below the poverty line, which underscored the feminization of poverty. Blue-collar men also suffered a catastrophic downward mobility as their union jobs were outsourced and they moved to the low-wage sector of the economy. Full-time working women experienced a "wage gap," earning 76.5 percent of men's salaries.[57] As working mothers, moreover, they also suffered from a "mother gap" that cost them hundreds of thousands of dollars in lost income, lower pensions, and less social security over their lifetimes.[58]

Upper-class tax cuts also widened the gap between the wealthy and the poor. In 2004, the editors of The Economist, one of the world's most pro-capitalist publications, described the damage that growing income disparities was causing the United States. Thirty years earlier, they noted, the average annual compensation of the top 100 chief executives was thirty times the pay of the average worker. By 2000, it had jumped to 1,000 times the pay of the average employee. They also described the American educational system as "increasingly stratified by social class," because poor children "attend schools with fewer resources than those of their richer contemporaries." America's celebrated universities, they noted, were increasingly "reinforcing rather than reducing" these educational inequalities, largely because of rising tuition. They also blamed American corporations for failing to be agents of upward mobility.[59]

Another cause for rising poverty was linked to the fallout from the 1996 Welfare Reform Act (The Personal Responsibility and Work Opportunity Reconciliation Act), which had eliminated guaranteed welfare and replaced it with Temporary Assistance to Needy Families (TANF). Administered by the states, TANF's actual goal was to reduce the number of mothers on welfare rolls, not to reduce poverty. TANF also created a five-year lifetime limit for single poor mothers receiving assistance.

Ironically, TANF was supposed to provide self-sufficiency to poor women. But most states forced them into unskilled low-wage work, where they joined the working poor. In her best-selling book, *Nickel and Dimed*, Barbara Ehrenreich wittily exposed how subsistence wages with unaffordable health care benefits made it impossible for low-waged women to support themselves, not to mention their children. By 2002, one of ten former welfare recipients in seven Midwestern states had joined the homeless, despite the fact they were working.[60]

TANF also disallowed higher education as a work-related activity, which robbed many poor women of an opportunity for upward mobility. "Our demands are quite simple," said one welfare mother. "Give us a real chance towards self-sufficiency." TANF also emphasized abstinence and marriage formation, to which one welfare mother responded, "We want caps and gowns, not wedding gowns." Some children also suffered from welfare reform. Instead of utilizing a highly respected public program like Head Start, TANF issued vouchers that mostly resulted in inadequate child care. Many women who didn't receive child care assistance reluctantly left their children with irresponsible relatives or babysitters they had good reasons not to trust.[61]

Although the media celebrated the highly educated career woman who quit her job to become a stay-at-home mom, the federal government required TANF single mothers to leave their children somewhere, anywhere, so that they could fulfill their requirement to work and get off welfare. Repeated attempts by a group of Senators to allocate more child care to recipients of welfare fell on deaf ears.

TANF, however, was merely a symptom of this country's failure to address poverty. All American welfare efforts have tried to modify or regulate the behavior of individual poor women, rather than address the education, health care, child care, mass transit, affordable housing, and progressive tax structure that could eliminate the catastrophic poverty that has persisted in such a wealthy nation.

WOMEN AND GLOBALIZATION

For women, globalization proved a mixed blessing, creating many casualties, as well as opportunities. The care crisis and poverty, for example, were certainly not limited to the United States. Forty-nine percent of all international migrants around the globe were women, many of whom left their children with husbands or other relatives, which created yet another care crisis in their own countries. While Americans worried about unemployment and focused on the outsourcing of technical and customer service jobs, they tended to ignore the huge numbers of women immigrants from developing countries who entered the country and worked as low-paid nannies, cleaning women, or nursing attendants. Many of these women felt like indentured servants. But their jobs also made it possible for them to feed their families back home. Coincidentally, their caregiving work also made it easier for well-off and middle-class Americans to ignore the nation's growing Care Crisis.[62]

Factory work also proved a mixed blessing. The worldwide gender revolution pulled countless girls and women into the manufacturing paid labor force. The conditions of some factories made many young women feel like slaves.[63] At the same time, paid work fed their families, gave them access to urban life, and provided young women with new opportunities to achieve a little economic independence, which they increasingly used to avoid arranged marriages and to resist customs that maimed or killed them.[64]

The spread of global media and the Internet around the world also had both positive and negative consequences. Some television series or films, which portrayed women as leaders of nations, lawyers, soldiers, doctors, or teachers, inspired young women. But these same images often offended their more traditional elders. Those films, television series, and Web sites that broadcast sexualized or pornographic images of Western women scandalized traditional communities. Consumer capitalism—accustomed to using sex to sell nearly everything—outraged religious fundamentalists and cultural traditionalists who viewed scantily clad or nude women as an insult to female modesty and a threat to male control over women.

In many ways, globalization revealed that women still remained second-class citizens in most parts of the globe. As the world grew smaller, human trafficking for prostitution or labor became pervasive. Promised an education or a job in a foreign city, untold young women—particularly from rural Asia, Russia, and East and Central European nations—found themselves sold as sex slaves or as workers in foreign sweatshops. A few scandals even discovered immigrant maids imprisoned in American suburban homes. International marriage brokers also exploited the hopes and dreams of many young women, who found themselves imprisoned in countries where they could not speak the native language.[65]

Women and their children, moreover, still made up most of the world's refugees, as well as a majority of the poor, who lived on less than a dollar a day. And for all the discussion of women's rights, girls and women continued to suffer unspeakable violence. In 2004, the Geneva Center for the Democratic Control of the Armed Forces found that every year 1.5 million to 3 million girls lost their lives from gender-based violence—honor killings, domestic violence, dowry deaths, human trafficking—and from the neglect they suffered in their families.[66] In 2005, the Geneva-based World Health Organization studied 24,000 women in ten countries and found that violence against women was pandemic, but "preventable."[67] In 2006, the first comprehensive report on domestic violence in Syria found that one in four married women had been beaten.[68] One of the most chilling examples of indifference and neglect was that neither the Bush administration nor the European Union stopped the genocide of whole villages and the rape of women in the Darfur region of Sudan.

But globalization didn't just cause casualties. It also created global feminist networks that helped spread the idea that "women's rights are human rights," words formally articulated and embraced at the U.N. Conference on Women at the 1995 meeting at Beijing.

Since the 1990s, growing numbers of women and human rights activists around the globe had used the language of human rights to fight against all forms of violence against women and girls, to improve their labor conditions, and to win greater participation in the economic and political world in which they lived. In 2001, an international court—for the first time in history—indicted soldiers for war crimes because they had raped women. In 2005, women in Colombia used the language of women's rights when they fought to make abortion legal. In the same year, fifteen African nations agreed upon a comprehensive protocol on women as part of their African human rights charter. True, such conventions, protocols, and treaties were often ignored. But they did create a moral compass by which behavior toward women could be evaluated.

A shrinking planet also promoted ideas about women's right to health care and reproductive choice. As satellite television broadcast images of small and prosperous Western families, growing numbers of educated and working women began to seek out and use contraception. As the infant mortality rate fell, they became more confident that their babies would survive. In 2002, demographic experts began to notice that both rural and urban women in many developing countries, including Brazil, Egypt, India, and Mexico, were having fewer babies. "Whether they live in villages or high-rises," explained Cythnia Steel, at the International Women's Health Coalition in New York, "women have always known what's best for them and their families. Now we're seeing the result of their own choice to have fewer children." As it turned out, there was no great mystery about how to control the world's population. The problem was that the solution—ensuring women's access to education and reproductive choice—was rejected not only by the United States, but by many local communities as well.[69]

For three decades, American feminism had greatly influenced global women's rights movements. Challenging and transforming women's health care had arguably been one of the most significant achievements of the American movement. In 2005, the National Women's Health Network celebrated its thirtieth anniversary. For three decades, it had acted as women's domestic and global watchdog, cautiously warning women to take control of their own health and carefully scrutinizing drugs that might harm their bodies or babies. One of the American movement's classic books, *Our Bodies, Ourselves*, published by Boston health activists in the 1970s, had long educated American women about reproduction, contraception, exercise, nutrition, and sexuality. By 2005, it was published in eighteen nations, in seventeen languages, and in Braille, and had become a basic health text across the globe, addressing the specific health problems of women in different societies.

The United States, however, was no longer in the forefront of improving women's lives. In 2004, Harvard University's "Project on Global Working Families," found that the United States's family policies lagged behind most developed and developing nations. As early as 1983, Australia had required a "gender budget statement" or "gender audit" that analyzed mainstream public policy—including legislation that dealt with regulations, allocations, taxation, and social projects—in order to increase gender equality. By 2006, both Chile and England floated proposals for giving those who cared for families credit toward future pensions. In the same year, more than fifty nations conducted some kind of "gender audit," sometimes with the help of nongovernmental organizations (NGOs). The United States was not among them.[70]

Growing numbers of countries also began to recruit women into the political process. Some African nations, for example, not only used affirmative action, but even mandated quotas to ensure greater female political participation. By 2006, the Rwandan parliament was 49 percent female and one-third of the parliament members in Mozambique, South Africa, Burundi, and Tanzania were women.[71] In 2005 and 2006, countries on three continents—Germany, Liberia, and Chile—elected their first female heads of states.

Most important, nearly all industrialized nations offered the kind of universal health and child care and paid parental leaves that American feminists had dreamed about for more than thirty years, but never achieved. Eighty-four other nations capped the working week, so that parents could care for their children. Thirty-seven other nations guaranteed parents some kind of paid leave for when their children were ill. The United States, by contrast, did not limit mandatory overtime; nor did it offer lengthy paid leave to parents.[72]

Around the world, women activists increasingly viewed the American government's rightward political turn as a major obstacle to the advancement of women's rights. At the 2005 U.N. Beijing Plus Ten conference, members once again reaffirmed the expansive 1995 Beijing Platform of Action, but they also argued that President Bush's conservative global policies prevented them from improving women's education and reproductive health. They nevertheless vowed to insert and mainstream gender into all global policies, including those that affected development, trade, macroeconomics, and environmentalism.

Although the Bush administration attacked women's rights at home, the president opportunistically deployed the rhetoric of women's rights to advance his foreign policy goals. After the 9/11 attacks, the language of women's human rights suddenly slipped into the lexicon of American foreign diplomacy. The Taliban's brutal treatment of women became one of the justifications for toppling the government in Afghanistan. "The rights of women of Afghanistan will not be negotiable," said Secretary of State Colin Powell. First Lady Laura Bush then used the weekly presidential radio address to promote the rights of Afghan women in shaping a post-Taliban society. A few days later, the president's advisors pressured the Afghan delegation to include women in the councils that would create a new government.

Distracted by the Iraq war, Bush never provided sufficient funds for women's education or health or for the reconstruction of Afghanistan. Still, the language of women's human rights had entered American foreign policy discourse. Once such words are uttered, they can take on a life of their own. "Consider it a window of opportunity," said Kavita Ramdas, the CEO of the Global Fund for Women, a San Francisco nonprofit grant-making foundation that seeds small women's organizations ultimate groups all over the world.[73]

At the 2005 U.N. International Day for the Elimination of Violence Against Women, Secretary-General Kofi Annan felt compelled to declare, in words that pleased many human rights activists:

> Violence against women remains pervasive worldwide. It is the most atrocious manifestation of the systemic discrimination and inequality women continue to face—in law and in their everyday lives—around the world. It occurs in every region, country, and culture, regardless of income, class, race, or ethnicity. Gender-based violence is also damaging to society as a whole. It can prevent women from engaging in productive employment, and girls from attending school. It makes women more vulnerable to forced and unprotected sex, which plays a key role in the spread of HIV/AIDS. It takes a deep and enduring toll on the entire family, including and especially the next generation.[74]

Violence against women, of course, did not stop because the Secretary General condemned its practice. Yet he did publicize how violence threatened women's health, even their survival, and helped change the terms of global debate about the obstacles that kept women from attaining gender equality.

DARING TO DREAM, IF WOMEN
REALLY MATTERED . . .

Even as American feminists struggled to defend the accomplishments they had achieved during the last three decades, they also dared to dream of a different future.

Decades earlier, at the highly publicized 1970 Women's Strike for Equality march down New York's Fifth Avenue, an event that turned women's liberation into a household word, women activists had settled on three core goals to improve their lives: the right to abortion, equal pay for equal work, and universal child care.

A generation later, women activists knew how far they were from achieving these goals. The stalled revolution had not transformed the workplace or the family. Abortion was under serious attack; one-third of American women no longer had access to an abortion provider in the county in which they lived. Equal pay for equal work did not address the fact that women still worked in different sectors of the economy; a female college graduate employed as an elementary school teacher, for example, earned half as much as a male high school graduate who labored in a unionized construction job. Even women who did the same full-time work earned less than men.[75] And child care, for all practical purposes, had largely disappeared from the national political agenda.

Goals proposed in 1970, in any event, were no longer sufficient for the new century. And so, even during these bleak, politically conservative years, many women activists were already plotting and planning for a brighter future.

If women really mattered, they asked, how would we change public policy and our society? Or, as the author of one "stay-at-home mom" article put it, "So what would the brave new world look like if women could press reboot and rewrite all the rules?"[76]

First, American women would have to vote in their own interest. Ironically, President Bush's conservative policies had, in fact, mobilized several generations of women to protect their reproductive rights—a feat not matched by feminists for more than thirty years.[77] But he had not changed their electoral choices. Although more women than men voted for John Kerry in 2004, they did not repeat their astonishing role in helping to elect Bill Clinton in 1996. The gender gap shrank to only 7 percent, partly because of widespread fears of terrorism and concern for national security and partly as a result of a "marriage gap." Seventy-one percent of married women, whom Republican political analyst Kellyanne Conway described as concerned with "marriage, munchkins, mortgages, and mutual funds," went to the polls and tended to vote Republican. In contrast, only 59 percent of "women on their own"—those who were unmarried, divorced, and widowed—bothered to vote at all. Yet these women, because of their economic insecurity, traditionally tended to vote for Democratic candidates.[78]

Some activists and scholars argued that all political candidates should be pressured to describe the policies they would promote in order to achieve greater gender equality. Charlotte Bunch, president of the Center for Women's Global Leadership at Rutgers University, went further and argued that a feminist redefinition of "national security" would have to address the health and welfare of all Americans.[79]

In 2006, Joan Blades, cofounder of the online progressive organization MoveOn.org and her coauthor Kristin Rowe-Finkbeiner, published *The Motherhood Manifesto*, with the goal of vaulting family policies to the top of the political agenda. Many other activists and scholars described a similar wish list and argued that universal health care, paid parental leaves, high-quality, subsidized, and accessible child care, a higher minimum wage, as well as a real living wage, job training and education, flexible work hours, greater part-time work opportunities, investment in affordable housing and mass transit, and the reinstatement of a progressive tax structure, would go a long way to help support working mothers and their families.[80]

And how would this wish list be funded? Activists still dreamed of a time when the United States would use its military only for defensive or humanitarian ends, reduce military expenditures for unnecessary space-based weapons and the vast network of American military bases that circled the globe, end resource wars for oil, and instead invest heavily in new sustainable energy sources. They also dreamed of a government that would eliminate tax cuts for the wealthiest Americans, reinstate the estate tax and the progressive tax structure that had created a broad and prosperous middle class in the middle of the twentieth century. Together, these savings could fund a great deal of their wish list.

On March 8, 2006, International Women's Day, two Democratic members of the Progressive Caucus—Representatives Barbara Lee (D-Oakland), and Lynn Woolsey (D-Petaluma), even proposed legislation to transfer $60 billion allocated for outdated Cold War-era weapons from the Pentagon's bloated budget of $439 billion to schools, health-

care, and humanitarian aid. "It's time we invest more in our people and
less in our defense contracts," said Woolsey at a press conference. They
called their bill the Common Sense Budget Act.[81]

Was this really so ridiculous? Not if the United States did a "gender
audit"of its budget. Not if the American government, like other industrial societies, provided for the health and welfare of its citizens.

Although Americans have famously rooted for the underdog and
believed in "fairness," they no longer seemed to feel compassion or
empathy with the poor and the vulnerable or even with the struggling
middle class. The conservative right wing had successfully persuaded
many people that an activist government was the problem, rather than
the solution, and that people should rely entirely on themselves. Americans had forgotten that taxes paid for what an individual cannot create
or maintain: sewers, highways, public schools and hospitals, emergency
preparedness, public health, social services for the aged, disabled, and
unemployed, and the nation's vast infrastructure they use every single day.

Nor had the country embraced what sociologist Fred Block has called
a Moral Economy, an economic system whose guiding principles—
justice and fairness—have long been taught in kindergarten.[82] This is
where most Americans have been taught to share with others, to obey
rules, to learn not to waste materials, to care for the kid who gets hurt,
and to wait and take their turn. This is where they learned cooperation,
reciprocity, sustainability, and the democratic regulation of greed.[83]

Instead, at the beginning of the new century, growing numbers of
American adults seemed absolutely besotted with the right to accumu-
late wealth and to avoid taxes as the dues they owed their society. Greed
no longer seemed shameful; the idea of a common good seemed almost
quaint.

Ever since the early 1980s, right-wing social conservatives had persuaded Americans that they—and not liberals—were the ones who em-
bodied and embraced morality and traditional values. But those who
dared to dream knew that America's most deeply cherished values
had inspired progressive activists when they ended slavery, fought for
women's suffrage, passed social security for the aged and insurance for
the unemployed, marched to end segregation, fought for the rights of
women and gays and lesbians, and launched a campaign for environmental health and justice. This great progressive American tradition
had expanded the nation's democracy and reinforced the belief in
a public good. But it failed to gain traction at a time when rampant

individualism and the celebration of greed triumphed over movements for social and economic justice.

Yet, as everyone knows, change is inevitable. Would the pendulum swing in a different direction? Would Americans once again root for the underdog and demand fairness from their government? Would the nation engage in endless cultural wars or try to close the widening gulf between the rich and the poor? Could activists renew a sense of a common good, publicize the care crisis, and change the family and workplace for the twenty-first century?

No one knew.

One thing was clear: globalization would certainly accelerate the worldwide gender revolution. The result? As growing numbers of the world's women enter the paid labor force, they will inevitably challenge—and change—women's place in traditional cultures and fundamentalist religions, igniting even more cultural wars, as well as a fiery backlash.

They will also contribute to a global care crisis. Who will care for the world's children, the disabled, and the elderly? Despite feminists' best efforts, the United States certainly has not provided a solution to its own catastrophic Care Crisis. On the contrary, the modern women's movement set in motion thirty years of cultural wars about women's place in modern society.

Observing the social and cultural backlash that accompanied this unfinished gender revolution, Vera Rubin, an astronomer celebrated for her early battles for women in science, sadly concluded, "Thirty years ago we thought the battle would be over soon, but equality is as elusive as dark matter."[84]

True, the world split open when women spoke the truth about their lives. Their revelations contributed to an irreversible but unfinished gender revolution that has upended millions of lives. Fortunately, there are still countless men and women everywhere struggling to put our world back together—this time, with equality and respect for women.

NOTES

❧

See Archival Collections, page 401, for meaning of the abbreviations in these Notes.

Chapter One: Dawn of Discontent

1. Linda Gray Sexton and Lois Ames, eds. *Anne Sexton, A Self-Portrait in Letters*, (Boston: Houghton Mifflin, 1977), 339–400.
2. Barbara Berg, *The Crisis of the Working Mother: Resolving the Conflict between Family and Work* (New York: Summit, 1986), 38.
3. *Tikkun* (January/February 1988), 25.
4. Betty Friedan, *The Feminine Mystique* (New York: Norton, 1963), 25. The term "popular front feminist" was coined by Daniel Horowitz to describe a woman of the Old Left who had always been interested in the problems working women faced.
5. Gerda Lerner to Betty Friedan, February 6, 1963, Box 201, Folder 715, Betty Friedan Papers, SL; cited and quoted with permission by Daniel Horowitz, "Rethinking Betty Friedan," *American Quarterly* (March 1996): 1–31. I thank Daniel Horowitz, author of *Betty Friedan and the Making of Women's Liberation* (Amherst: University of Massachusetts, 1998), for giving me early drafts of his meticulous research on Friedan's life and for drawing to my attention the changes in the ten drafts of her work.
6. Reviews of *The Feminine Mystique*, Box 18, Folder 676, Betty Friedan Papers. Letter in response to *The Feminine Mystique*, Box 21, Folder 739, Betty Friedan Papers; *McCall's*, 1963, 38.
7. Folder 617, *Feminine Mystique* Letters, Friedan Papers.
8. Box 21, Folder 739; Box 19, Folder 683; Box 19, Folder 683; *Feminine Mystique* Letters, Friedan Papers.
9. The contributions of Joanne Meyerowitz, ed., and the other authors to *Not June Cleaver: Women and Gender in Postwar America, 1945–1960* (Philadelphia: Temple University Press, 1994) are an important corrective to the view that the feminine mystique ruled every woman and permitted no exit. As much as I respect the contribution made by Meyerowitz and the other authors, I believe the power of the feminine mystique was stronger than the undertow that was pulling it down.

10. Some of the best sources that reveal the making of lesbian and gay subcultures are John D'Emilio, *Sexual Politics, Sexual Communities: The Making of a Homosexual Minority in the United States, 1940–1970* (Chicago: University of Chicago Press, 1983); Donna Penn, "The Meanings of Lesbianism in Post-War America," *Gender and History* (Summer 1991): 190–203; Kate Weigand, "The Red Menace, the Feminine Mystique, and the Ohio University American Activities Commission: Gender and Anti-Communism in Ohio, 1951–1954," *Journal of Women's History* (Winter 1992): 70–94; Lillian Faderman, *Odd Girls and Twilight Lovers: A History of Lesbian Life in Twentieth-Century America* (New York: Columbia University Press, 1991), 130–87. One of the best ethnographies is Elizabeth Lapovsky Kennedy and Madeline D. Davis, *Boots of Leather, Slippers of Gold: The History of a Lesbian Community* (New York: Routledge, 1993).

11. Warren Susman, *Culture As History* (New York: Pantheon, 1984); William Whyte, *The Organization Man* (New York: Simon and Schuster, 1956); C. Wright Mills, *White Collar: The American Middle Class* (New York: Oxford, 1956). See Glen Elder, *Children of the Great Depression* (Chicago: University of Chicago Press, 1974).

12. Dr. Paul Pepenoe, who had been a biologist and founder of the social hygiene movement, became the best-known publicist through the column "Can This Marriage Be Saved?"; Benita Eisler, *Private Lives: Men and Women of the Fifties* (New York: Franklin Watts, 1986), 278.

13. William Chafe, *The Unfinished Journey* (New York: Oxford, 1995), 119; Landon Y. Jones, *Great Expectations: America and the Baby Boom Generation* (New York: Ballantine, 1980), 43; Kenneth Jackson, *Crabgrass Frontier* (New York: Oxford, 1985); Sylvia Hewlett, *A Lesser Life: The Myth of Women's Liberation in America* (New York: William Morrow, 1986), 38.

14. Douglas T. Miller and Marion Nowak, *The Fifties: The Way We Really Were* (New York: Doubleday, 1977), 8.

15. Marc Richards, "Recruiting in the Nursery," dissertation, U.C. Davis, 1998; Donna Alvah, "Unofficial Ambassadors: American Military Families Overseas and Cold War International Relations, 1945–1961," dissertation in progress, U.C. Davis.

16. Elaine May, *Homeward Bound* (New York: Basic Books, 1988), 25.

17. "The Two Worlds: A Day Long Debate," *New York Times*, July 25, 1959, 1,3; "Setting Russia Straight on Facts about the U.S.," *U.S. News and World Report*, vol. 47, August 3, 1959, 36–39, 70–72; "Encounter," *Newsweek*, August 3, 1959, 15–19.

18. J. Warren Kinsman, "The Responsibility of Women in Today's World," an address before the Wilmington City Federation of Women's Clubs and Allied Organizations, in E. I. Du Pont de Nemours Inc., Papers, Hagley Museum and Library, Wilmington, Delaware.

19. Anita Colby, "Ideas from a Woman's Viewpoint," prepared for the 1955 Du Pont Advertising Clinic, in the E. I. Du Pont de Nemours, Inc. Papers, series II, part 2, Box 18, Hagley Museum and Library.

20. Miller, 116; Chafe, *The Unfinished Journey*, 112; Miller, 107; *New York Times*, February 14, 1956, 20; September 3, 1956, 14.

21. For a lengthy discussion of the full impact of McCarthyism on American culture and society, see Ellen Schrecker, *Many Are the Crimes: McCarthyism in America* (Boston: Little, Brown, 1988).

22. Joseph Veroff, Elizabeth Douvan, Richard A. Kulko, *The Inner American: A Self-Portrait from 1957 to 1976* (New York: Basic Books, 1981), 147–149. Ninety-five percent of Americans of marriageable age made the trip to the altar, 5 percent more than their parents. Jones, p. 15; Susan Hartman, *The Home Front and Beyond*, 165ff.; U.S. Department of Commerce, Bureau of the Census, *Historical Statistics of the United States, Colonial Times to 1970* (Washington, D.C.: 1975), part 1, 49, 54, 64; John Modell, Frank F. Furstenberg, and Douglas Strong, "The Times of Marriage in the Transition to Adulthood, Continuity and Change," in *Turning Points: Historical and Sociological Essays on the Family, American Journal of Sociology* 84 (supplement, Chicago, 1978:s120–s150); Paul C. Glick, "A Demographer Looks at American Families," *Journal of Marriage and the Family* 37: 1 (February 1975), 15–26; Andrew Cherlin, *Marriage, Divorce, Remarriage* (Cambridge, Mass.: Harvard University Press, 1981), 22–23. J. Edgar Hoover, "The Twin Enemies of Freedom: Crime and Communism," address before the 28th Annual Convocation of the National Council of Catholic Women, Chicago, Illinois, November 9, 1956, in *Vital Speeches* 23:4 (December 1, 1956), 104–107, quote on p. 104.

23. Such large families were, in fact, the exception, not the norm. Between 1955 and 1959, the average American woman bore 3.7 children during her lifetime. What accounted for the high fertility rate was the fact that two overlapping generations married after the war, creating *medium-sized* families, and that the postwar years witnessed so few childless couples and single women.

24. Miller, 238. Adrienne Rich, *Of Woman Born* (New York: Norton, 1976), 35.

25. Lois Banner, *American Beauty* (New York: Knopf, 1983), chapter 13; Hartman, *The Home Front*, 203; Brett Harvey, *The Fifties: A Women's Oral History* (New York: Harper, 1994), xi.

26. Friedan, *The Feminine Mystique*, 52–53. Deborah Rhode, *Justice and Gender* (Cambridge: Harvard University Press, 1989), chapter 4; Ruth Schwartz Cohen and Joanne Vanek, "Time Spent in Housework," *Scientific American* 231 (November 1974): 116–20; Helen Zopata, *Occupation Housewife* (New York: Oxford, 1971), 47–53.

27. May, 307; Friedan, *The Feminine Mystique*, 206; Eisler, 291.

28. Eisler, *Private Lives*, 10.

29. Benjamin Spock, *The Common Sense Book of Baby Care* (New York: Pocket Books, 1946), 63–64.

30. Albert Kinsey, et al., *Sexual Behavior in the Human Female* (New York: Pocket Books, 1953), 292. May makes the same argument in *Homeward Bound*, in chapter 5.

31. Eisler, 158; May, 208, 233; Eisler, 124, 129.

32. Kinsey, 292; Barbara Ehrenreich, *Remaking Love: The Feminization of Sex* (New York: Doubleday, 1986), 47; Theodoor H. Van de Velde, *Ideal Marriage* (New York: Random House, 1961); Eustace Chesser, *Love Without Fear* (New York: Roy Publishing, 1947).

33. One reason is that when Masters and Johnson announced in 1966 that clitoral stimulation was the basis for all orgasms, their findings produced a flood of recognition and rage from women of all ages.

34. Also see May, 226; Case 223, in May, Kellogg Longitudinal Study; May, 220. Also see chapter 8, "Hanging Together," in May. For a more detailed discussion, see chapter 5, "Hidden Injuries of Sex," in this book.

35. May, 226. In May, see Kellogg Longitudinal Study (KLS) in Appendices. KLS respondents.

36. Eisler, quoting interview, 306; Barbara Ehrenreich, *The Hearts of Men: American Dreams and the Flight from Commitment* (Garden City, N.Y.: Doubleday, 1983); George Gallup, *The Gallup Poll: Public Opinion 1935–1971*, vol. 1–3 (New York: Random House, 1972); for 1972–1978 data, see National Opinion Research Center, General Social Survey; Abbott L. Ferris, *Indicators of Trends in the Status of Women* (N.Y.: Russell Sage Foundation, 1971), 85–86, 99, 104; U.S. Department of Commerce, Bureau of the Census, *Statistical Abstracts of the United States 1975* (Washington, D.C., GPO, 1975), 346–347; also see Valerie Kincade Oppenheimer, *The Female Labor Force in the United States: Demographic and Economic Factors Governing Its Growth and Changing Composition* (Westport, Conn.: Greenwood, 1971).

37. Chafe, *Unfinished Journey*, 84–85; Peter Filene, *Him/Her/Self: Sex Roles in Modern America* (New York: Harcourt Brace Jovanovich, 1975), 167–68; Bureau of Labor Standards, *Perspectives on Working Women: A Datebook* (Washington, D.C., 1980), Bulletin 2080, 10, 52; Miller, 163; *Part Time Employment for Women*, Women's Bureau Bulletin No. 275 (Washington, D.C., GPO), 40.

38. William Chafe, *The American Woman: Her Changing Social, Economic and Political Roles, 1920–1970* (New York: Oxford, 1972), 18.

39. For important work on women and World War II, see the Bibliography. Also, see poll by United Automobile, Aircraft and Agricultural Workers of America—Congress of Industrial Organizations, that showed 85 percent of UAW women planned on working after the war. Women's Bureau studies found that 80 percent of women in Detroit and Erie Country, New York, wanted to keep their jobs. *CIO News* 30 (July 1945), quoted in Cynthia Harrison, *On Account of Sex: The Politics of Women's Issues, 1945–1968* (Berkeley: University of California Press, 1988), 242.

40. Interview with Charlicia Neuman by Sherna Gluck in *Rosie the Riveter Revisited: Women, The War and Social Change*, Sherna Berger Gluck, ed., 169.

41. Ethel Klein, *Gender Politics* (Cambridge: Harvard University Press, 1984), 40; Chafe, *Unfinished Journey*, 84–85; Filene, *Him/Her/Self*, 167–68; Bureau of Labor Standards, *Perspective on Working Women*, 10, 52; Miller, 163; *Part-*

Time Employment for Women, Women's Bureau Bulletin No. 273 (Washington, D.C., 1960), 3; and *1960 Handbook on Women Workers*, 40.

42. U.S. Bureau of the Census, *Statistical Abstracts of the United States 1975*, 347; Chafe, *The American Woman*, 218.

43. Cherlin, *Marriage*, 51; Klein, 43; Hazel Erskine, "The Polls: Women's Roles," *Public Opinion Quarterly* 35 (Summer 1971): 282–87; and Barbara McGowan, "Postwar Attitudes toward Women and Work," in Dorothy McGuigan, ed., *New Research on Women and Sex Roles* (Ann Arbor, Mich.: University of Michigan Press, 1976); Leila Rupp, *Surviving in the Doldrums* (New York: Oxford, 1987), 36.

44. Letter dated August 4, 1964, from Glen Ridge, Letters, Betty Friedan Papers.

45. Harvey, 134.

46. Harvey, 135.

47. See Pauline Bart, *Depression in Middle-Aged Women*, unpublished dissertation, UCLA, 1967. Public Health Service, National Center for Health Statistics, *Vital Statistics of the United States, 1968*, vol. II, part A, and unpublished data, quoted in *Social Indicators*, 26; Dorothy Barclay, "After the Children Leave Home," *New York Times Magazine*, September 19, 1951; "What Women Want," *Newsweek*, May 21, 1956.

48. Author's interview with Doris Earnshaw, March 11, 1998, Berkeley, California.

49. Harvey, 145.

50. May, quoting one of Kellogg respondents, 226.

51. *Life*, January 4, 1954, 42–45. Sidonie M. Gruenberg and Hilda S. Krech, *The Modern Mothers' Dilemma*, (New York: Public Affairs Committee, 1957), pamphlet No. 247, 18–20. Joanne Vanek, "Household Work, Wage Work and Sexual Equality," in Sarah Berk, ed., *Women and Household Labor* (Beverly Hills: Sage, 1980); Heidi Hartmann, "The Family as the Locus of Gender, Class and Political Struggle," *Signs* (Spring 1981): 366–94; Nadine Brozan, "Men and Housework: Do They or Don't They?" *New York Times*, April 4, 1980, 52.

52. This happened to my own mother, Ida G. Rosen, without whose earnings I could not have bought books or clothes during college. Author's interview with IGR in New York, 1973.

53. Ferdinand Lundberg and Marya Farnham, *The Modern Woman: The Lost Sex* (New York: Harper and Brothers, 1947), 370–71.

54. Quoted in *Esquire*, July 1962; author's interview with Alice Quaytman, 1987, Oakland, California; author's interview with Wendel and Alice Brunner, 1996, Berkeley, California.

55. Margaret Mead, *Male and Female: A Study of the Sexes in a Changing World* (New York: Dell, 1949), 35.

56. Jennifer Levine, "A Study of the Changing Influence of Societal Attitudes Upon Three Cohorts of Women Veterinary Students," unpublished senior thesis, U.C. Davis, June 1985. Rhode, *Justice and Gender*, chapter 4; Lundberg and Farnham, 771; Chafe, *The American Woman*, 106.

57. Rupp, *Surviving*.
58. Leila Rupp, *Worlds of Women: The Making of an International Women's Movement* (Princeton, N.J.: Princeton University Press, 1997); Nancy Cott, *The Grounding of Modern Feminism* (New Haven: Yale, 1987).
59. Ellen Carol DuBois used the term "left feminists" in her article, "Eleanor Flexner and the History of American Feminism," *Gender and History* 3 (Spring 1991): 84. All my information on CAW comes from Amy Swerdlow's pioneering essay, "The Congress of American Women: Left-Feminist Peace Politics in the Cold War," in Linda Kerber, Kathryn Sklar, and Alice Kessler-Harris, eds., *U.S. History As Women's History* (Chapel Hill: University of North Carolina Press, 1996). The contributions of the Old Left to the women's movement of the 1960s can be found in the Bibliography.
60. Harvey, 209–11.
61. The New York neighborhood was Knickerbocker Village, the California town was El Cerrito, and the preschool was in the San Francisco Bay Area. During the early sixties, some former Communists joined city and state commissions on the status of women in order to focus attention on the problem of women workers and women in minority groups. By then, most were no longer in the party, but were still activists. Author's interviews with three women in Northern California, former members of the Communist Party, in "The Radical Elders Oral Project," who do not wish to be identified.
62. Stella Novicki, "Back of the Yards," in *Rank and File: Personal Histories by Working-Class Organizers*, Alice and Staughton Lynd, eds., (Princeton: Princeton University Press, 1973; 1981 edition), 83–84.
63. Betty Millard, "Woman Against Myth," *New Masses*, December 30, 1947.
64. Author's interviews with Alice Quaytman, April 1985, 1987, and 1997, in Oakland and Hayward, California.
65. Harvey, 223.
66. Eleanor Flexner, quoted by Fitzpatrick, xiv. Gerda Lerner, "The Lady and the Mill Girl," first appeared in *Midcontinent American Studies* 10:1 (1969).
67. Klein, 44; "The Girls," *Life*, August 1949, 39–40; "An Introduction by Mrs. Peter Marshall," *Life*, December 24, 1956, 2–3; Friedan, *The Feminine Mystique*, 44. This included *New York Times, Newsweek, Harper's Bazaar, Redbook, Time,* and CBS Television, which are cited in Sara Evans, *Born for Liberty* (New York: Free Press, 1997), 265.
68. National Manpower Council, *Womanpower in Today's World: A Statement with Chapters by the Council Staff* (New York: Columbia University Press, 1957); National Manpower Council, *Work in the Lives of Married Women* (New York: Columbia University Press, 1958).
69. Interview with Susan Ikenberry, Washington, D.C., March 8, 1998, the daughter of this mother. The city in which this took place was White Plains, New York, where one young woman was not permitted to visit this home in 1959. Author's interview with "Barbara Shields," (not her actual name) July 18, 1998.
70. Dorothy Thompson, "It's All the Fault of Women," *Ladies' Home Journal*, May 1960, 11.

Chapter Two: Female Generation Gap

A version of this chapter originally appeared in the collection *U.S. History As Women's History*, Linda Kerber, Kathryn Sklar, and Alice Kessler-Harris, eds., (Chapel Hill: University of North Carolina Press, 1996), which was collectively dedicated to Gerda Lerner.

1. Anna Quindlen, "Mother's Choice," *Ms.*, February 1988, 55.
2. Letter to Betty Friedan, July 23, 1970, from Kansas City, Missouri, Friedan Papers.
3. Paula Weideger, "Womb Worship," *Ms.*, February 1988, 54.
4. For demographic data, see Andrew J. Cherlin, *Marriage*. For an overview of the baby boom generation and its impact on American culture, see Landon Y. Jones, *Great Expectations* (New York: Coward, McCann & Geoghegan, 1980).
5. "The Generation Gap," *Life*, May 17, 1968; "TV: Poignant Study of Generation Gap, Fathers and Sons in CBS Documentary," *New York Times*, August 13, 1969.
6. See Richard Flacks, "The Liberated Generation: An Explanation of the Roots of Student Protest," in *Conformity, Resistance and Self-Determination*, Richard Flacks, ed., (Boston: Little, Brown, 1973). See, for example, the classic study by Kenneth Keniston, *Young Radicals: Notes on Committed Youth* (New York: Harcourt Brace, 1968), especially the appendix. Both Flacks and Keniston included young women among the activists they studied, but they based their analyses and conclusions on the male experience.
7. Susan Griffin, panel discussion on the women's movement, Berkeley, California, October 1988. For scholarly perspectives on the different ways daughters and sons individuate from their mothers, see Nancy Chodorow, *The Reproduction of Mothering: The Psychoanalysis and the Sociology of Gender* (Berkeley: University of California Press, 1978), and Jean Baker Miller, ed., *Psychoanalysis and Women* (New York: Vintage, 1978).
8. Phyllis Chesler, *Letter to a Young Feminist* (New York: Four Walls, Eight Windows, 1997), 55. Phyllis Schlafly, "The Right to Be a Woman," *The Phyllis Schlafly Report* 6 (November 1972): 4.
9. Lauri Umansky, *Motherhood Reconceived: Feminism and the Legacies of the Sixties* (New York: New York University Press, 1996).
10. Barbara Berg, *The Crisis of the Working Mother* (New York: Summit, 1986), 40.
11. Dorothy Thompson, "It's All the Fault of Women," *Ladies' Home Journal*, May 1960, 11.
12. Lynn White, *Educating Our Daughters* (New York: Harper and Brothers, 1950), 77–78, 82, 85, 91. Mary Bunting, "The Radcliffe Institute for Independent Study," in American Council on Education, *The Educational Record*, October 1961, 19; Adlai Stevenson, "Commencement Address," reprinted in *Woman's Home Companion*, September 1955, 29–31; Robert Coughlan, "Changing Roles in Modern Marriage," *Life*, December 24, 1956, 110–12.
13. *New York Times*, June 7, 1945, 1. Quoted in Eugenia Kaledin, *Mothers and More: American Women in the 1950s* (Boston: Twayne, 1984), 44; Friedan, *The Feminine Mystique*, 145.

14. Letter to Betty Friedan from Ruth Kelso from Guilford, Connecticut, March 4, 1963, Friedan Papers; Letter to Betty Friedan, September 19, 1964, Friedan Papers; Kaledin, 58; *Social Indicators*, 90.
15. Kaledin, 34. See Elizabeth Stone, "Mothers and Daughters," *New York Times Magazine*, May 13, 1979, 91.
16. George Gallup and Evan Hill, "The American Woman," *Saturday Evening Post*, December 22, 1962. Letters dated May 17, 1963, from Irvine, Texas, and March 13, 1963, from Ridgewood, New Jersey, Betty Friedan Papers, SL.
17. Wini Breines's study of girls in the fifties also documents this profound undercurrent of ambivalence, especially through fiction and popular culture. Wini Breines, *Young, White, and Miserable: Growing Up Female in the Fifties* (Boston: Beacon Press, 1991). Here I draw upon interviews with women who became leaders of the younger branch of the women's movement. Also see Kathleen Gerson, *Hard Choices: How Women Decide About Work, Career and Motherhood* (Berkeley: University of California Press, 1985), 55.
18. Assata Shakur, *Assata* (Chicago: Lawrence Hill Books, 1987), 37.
19. Alix Kates Shulman, *Burning Questions* (New York: Bantam, 1978), 3.
20. These observations are made by Wini Breines in *Young*, p. 79, who quotes from Barbara Raskin, *Hot Flashes*, Lynn Lauber, *White Girls*, and Annie Dillard, 237.
21. See Robyn Rowland, *Women Who Do and Women Who Don't Join the Women's Movement* (London: Routledge, 1984). The author is an Australian who sought to find differences and commonality between feminists and antifeminists in five countries.
22. See David McClelland, *Follow-up Patterns of Childrearing Subjects*, 1978, of thirty-eight middle-class daughters of mothers interviewed in 1951 and 1952. These mothers' interviews appeared in Robert Sears, Eleanor Maccoby, and Harry Levin, *Patterns of Child Rearing* (New York: Harper and Row, 1957). Also see Diane Franklin, "Correlates of Participation and Nonparticipation in the Women's Liberation Movement" (Ph.D. diss., University of Chicago, 1975). For a scholarly discussion of these studies, see Breines, 71, 225. For a variety of different explanations, see Robyn Rowland. This part of the study is based particularly on interviews with Naomi Weisstein, Alix Kates Shulman, Barbara Ehrenreich, Vivian Gornick, Ellen Willis, Charlotte Bunch, Susan Griffin, Ti-Grace Atkinson, Barbara Haber, Valerie Miner, and Irene Peslikis.
23. Author's interview with Barbara Ehrenreich, New York City, April 6, 1987.
24. Phyllis Chesler, *Letters*, 22; author's interview with Irene Peslikis in New York City, April 4, 1987.
25. More than half of the women in my consciousness-raising group in 1967, for example, came from working-class homes, but through university experiences, seemed middle-class in appearance and in speech. Author's interview with Anne Scholfield, Berkeley, California, April 1986; also Mary Waters, Valerie Miner, Pat Cody. Author's interviews with Ellen Willis and Ti-Grace Atkinson, in New York City, April 16, 1987. Writings by Molly Haskell and several dozen other interviews confirm this fear of replicating one's mother's life.

26. This is revealed in the memoirs of at least two major New Left leaders, but it is also evident in the position papers of SDS writers in general. See Todd Gitlin, *The Sixties: Years of Hope, Days of Rage* (New York: Bantam, 1987), and Tom Hayden, *Reunion: A Memoir* (New York: Random House, 1988). In the field of history, for example, "consensus" was celebrated and "conflict" was diminished; in sociology, functionalism helped rationalize the status quo.

27. Marilyn Coffey, "Those Beats," in *Sixties Without Apology*, Sonya Sayres, Anders Stephenson, Stanley Aronowitz, and Frederic Jameson, eds. (Minneapolis: University of Minnesota Press, 1984), 238–40.

28. Author's interviews with Barbara Ehrenreich and Susan Griffin. For a description of young women's forays into bohemian culture as part of their search for something "real," see Breines; also Ellen Maslow, "Storybook Lives," in *Liberation Now*, Deborah Babcox and Madeleine Belkin, eds. (New York: Dell, 1971), 175.

29. Joyce Johnson, *Minor Characters* (Boston: Houghton Mifflin, 1983), 56.

30. Johnson, 151, 171, 207, 260.

31. Barbara Ehrenreich, Elizabeth Hess, and Gloria Jacobs, *Re-Making Love*.

32. Helen Gurley Brown, *Sex and the Single Girl* (New York: Pocket Books, 1962), 206.

33. Cynthia Gorney, *Article of Faith: A Frontline History of the Abortion Wars* (New York: Simon and Schuster, 1998), 23. Also see Leslie Reagan, *When Abortion Was a Crime* (Berkeley: University of California Press, 1997); Carol Joffe, *Doctor of Conscience: The Struggle to Provide Abortion Before and After Roe v. Wade* (Boston: Beacon, 1995); and Rickie Solinger, *The Abortionist: A Woman Against the Law* (New York: Free Press, 1994).

34. These stories are from women whom I have interviewed but who did not want their names made public, even now. For a scholarly treatment of the long century in which abortion was illegal, see Reagan, 225.

35. Gorney, 31–32.

36. Part of this line of reasoning is persuasively argued in Ehrenreich, Hess, and Jacobs, *Re-Making Love*; Harvey, *The Fifties*, 15.

37. For an analysis of how different generations of women responded to de Beauvoir's classic work, see Judith Okely, *Simone de Beauvoir* (New York: Pantheon, 1986). Simone de Beauvoir, *The Second Sex* (New York: Harmondsworth, 1953), 295.

38. Alice Schwarzer, *After the Second Sex: Conversations with Simone de Beauvoir* (New York: Pantheon, 1984), 13, quoted in Okely, *Simone de Beauvoir*, 2. See also the description by Judith Okely, a British biographer of de Beauvoir, of her fascination with this bohemian life and critique of family and motherhood. Rachel Brownstein, an American literary critic, was similarly influenced by de Beauvoir. See Brownstein, *Becoming a Heroine* (New York: Harmondsworth, 1984), 18. King, *Freedom Song*, 76.

39. Susan Griffin, "Eco-Feminism," talk at a panel on feminism and ecology, San Francisco, April 10, 1988.

40. It is worth noting that the translation that was published in the United States omitted her discussion of women in history, but her view of woman as "other" still did not provide a way of grasping women's agency in history.

41. One recent work that provides a good overview of her life is Deirdre Bair's *Simone de Beauvoir: A Biography* (New York: Summit, 1990). A film titled *Daughters of de Beauvoir*, directed by Imogen Sutton, explores her influence on the women's movement. A brilliant essay by Mary Felstiner early assessed Second Wave feminism's relationship to de Beauvoir. See Felstiner, "Seeing the Second Sex through the Second Wave," *Feminist Studies* 6 (Winter 1986): 247–76.

42. For a detailed discussion of the male version of generational divide, see Gitlin, *The Sixties*, 230.

43. See Amy Swerdlow, "Ladies' Day at the Capitol: Women Strike for Peace versus HUAC," *Feminist Studies* 2 (Fall 1987): 493–521; and "Pure Milk, Not Poison: Women Strike for Peace and the Test Ban Treaty of 1963," paper presented at the Berkshire Conference on Women's History, Wellesley College, Massachusetts, June 1988.

Chapter Three: Limits of Liberalism

1. Robert Arthur, "No!," *Esquire*, July 1962, 32 ff.

2. *Washington Post*, "JFK Seeks Equal Job Status for Women," December 15, 1961, C1; *New York Times*, "President Names Panel on Women," December 15, 1961, 15.

3. Sidney Shalett, "Is There a Woman's Vote?" *Saturday Evening Post*, September 1960, 31, 79, 80.

4. Shalett, 31, 80.

5. Shalett, 80.

6. *New York Post*, December 1960, clipping in Folder "1960," Box 1, of India Edwards Papers, Lyndon Baines Johnson Library, Texas. Cited in Cynthia Harrison, *On Account of Sex: The Politics of Women's Issues, 1945–1968* (Berkeley: University of Calif. Press, 1988), 261. Other than my own interviews and archival research, I have relied heavily on Cynthia Harrison's splendid political history here.

7. Letter from Emma Guffey Miller to John F. Kennedy, February 1961, quoted in Harrison, 76.

8. Harrison, 79.

9. Pauli Murray Papers, "Speech about President's Commission," SL.

10. Betty Friedan, *The Feminine Mystique*, "Epilogue," 368.

11. U.S. President's Commission on the Status of Women, *American Women* (Washington, D.C., 1963), 70.

12. Loreta Korns, "Treatment by Seven Newspapers of the Report of the President's Commission on the Status of Women," December 9, 1963, in General Correspondence folder, PCSW, January 1964, PCSW Papers, Washington, D.C.

13. Abbott L. Ferriss, *Indicators of Trends in the Status of American Women* (New York: Russell Sage Foundation, 1971), 21, 63, 85, 209ff.

14. Klein, *Gender Politics*, 22. These cases are known as *Griswold v. State of Connecticut* in 1965 and *White v. Crook* in 1966. Klein, 23. See Jo Freeman, *The Politics of Women's Liberation* (New York: McKay, 1975), 177. In addition to Harrison, I have also heavily relied on Freeman's early and insightful work as well as one of the first histories of the movement, Judith Hole and Ellen Levine, *Rebirth of Feminism* (New York: Quadrangle, 1971), 29; also see U.S. Congress, Senate Committee on Labor and Public Welfare, *Equal Pay Act of 1963, Hearing Before a Subcommittee of the Committee on Labor and Public Welfare* in S. 882 and S. 910, 88th Congress, 1st sess., 1963.

15. See Daniel Horowitz, "Rethinking Betty Friedan," and the "The Feminine Mystique: Labor Union Radicalism and Feminism in Cold War America," *American Quarterly* (March 1996): 1–31. There is now an extensive literature that details the continuities between labor union and Left activists of the forties and fifties and the origins of American feminism in the 1960s. See, for example, Kathleen A. Weigand, "Vanguards," and Gerda Lerner, "Midwestern Leaders of the Modern Women's Movement: An Oral History Project," *Wisconsin Academy Review* (Winter 1994–95): 11–15; Nancy Gabin, *Feminism in the Labor Movement: Women and the United Auto Workers, 1925–1975* (Ithaca: Cornell, 1990); Susan Lynn, *Progressive Women in Conservative Times: Racial Justice, Peace and Feminism, 1945–1960's* (New Brunswick: Rutgers University Press, 1992). Most of the articles collected for *Not June Cleaver: Women and Gender in Postwar America, 1945–1960*, Joanne Meyerowitz, ed. (Philadelphia: Temple University Press, 1994), also point to the continuities between radical movements of the 1940s and 1950s and 1960s feminism. Also see Joyce Antler, "Between Culture and Politics: The Emma Lazarus Federation of Jewish Women's Clubs and the Promulgation of Women's History, 1944–1989," and Amy Swerdlow, "The Congress of American Women," in *U.S. History As Women's History*.

16. Pauli Murray Papers, speech, SL.

17. Gabin, *Women and the United Auto Workers*, links feminism to labor; of the twenty-two women interviewed for this Midwest leaders oral history project at the WHS, seven were trade unionists and workers, and four were African Americans.

18. Author's interview with Kay Clarenbach, Mildred Jeffrey, and a circle of other women at a postconference group interview, November 22, 1992. "Documents of the Midwestern Origins of the Twentieth Century Women's Movement." Tapes and transcripts, State Historical Society of Wisconsin, Madison, Wisconsin.

19. Clarenbach Papers, WHS, Box 2, Folder 11.

20. See "Resolution Adopted Unanimously by the National Council of the National Woman's Party—Regarding the Proposed Civil Rights Bill (H.R. 7152)," December 16, 1963, Reel 108, National Woman's Party papers, on microfilm.

21. Harrison, 178. Much of my discussion on the PCSW is grounded in Harrison's meticulous work.

22. Probably the best account of the history behind this so-called "fluke" is Jo Freeman's "How 'Sex' Got into Title VII: Persistent Opportunism as a Maker of Public Policy," *Law and Inequality: A Journal of Theory and Practice* 9 (March 1991): 163–84, reprinted on the H-Net for Women's History. Freeman demonstrates how a small group of women took advantage of a long-standing desire to legislate against sex discrimination. The debate on Smith's amendment can be found in the *Congressional Record*, 88th Congress, 2nd sess., February 8, 1964, 2577–84; EEOC, *Legislative History of Titles VII and XI of Civil Rights Act of 1964*, Washington, D.C., Government Printing Office, n.d., 3312–28; Caroline Bird, *Born Female* (New York: Pocket Books, 1971), chapter 1; Harrison, chapter 9.

23. Martha Griffiths' speech, U.S. Congress, House, 89th Congress, June 20, 1966, *Congressional Record* 112: 13689–94. *Washington Post*, November 23, 1965, in Folder "Title VII Civil Rights Act of 1963, Legislation 1964–65." National Business and Professional Women's Clubs (BPW) Archives cited in Harrison, 187. *New York Times*, July 3, 1964.

24. *New York Times* editorial, August 21, 1965, 37.

25. *New Republic*, September 4, 1965, 3; *Wall Street Journal*, June 22, 1965.

26. A good source for Title VII is Donald Allen Robinson, *Signs* 4 (Spring 1979): 411–34, and "Development in the Law: Employment Discrimination and Title VII of the Civil Rights Act of 1964," *Harvard Law Review* 84 (March 1971).

27. Martha Griffiths, statement on floor of Congress, June 20, 1966, *Congressional Record*, 13054.

28. Betty Friedan, *It Changed My Life: Writings on the Women's Movement* (New York: Random House, 1976), 80.

29. Friedan, *It Changed My Life*, 80.

30. Friedan, 80, 82.

31. Friedan, 83.

32. Kay Clarenbach Papers, Box 2, Folder 9, WHS.

33. Friedan, *It Changed My Life*, 83.

34. Marya Mannes, "Female Intelligence: Who Wants It?" *New York Times Magazine*, January 3, 1960; Mary Freeman, "The Marginal Sex: America's Alienated Woman," *Commonweal* 75:19 (February 2, 1962); "The American Female: A Special Supplement," *Harper's*, October 1963, 225. The best description of these representations can be found in Cynthia Harrison, "Women and the New Frontier," master's thesis, Columbia University, 1975.

35. Alice Rossi, "Equality Between the Sexes," *Daedalus* (1964): 608. Later, she changed her position: Alice Rossi, "A Biosocial Perspective on Parenting," *Daedalus* (Spring 1977): 1–31. Also see the following critique of Rossi's new views in Wini Breines, Margaret Cerullo, and Judith Stacy, "Social Biology, Family Studies, and Antifeminist Backlash," *Feminist Studies* 4 (February 1978): 43–67.

36. Friedan, *It Changed My Life*, 84.

37. Friedan, *It Changed My Life*, 87, "Statement of Purpose." For much of the

history of NOW, I have used the late Frances Kolb's uncompleted manuscript, "The National Organization for Women: A History of the First Ten Years," which she generously shared with me before her death. Unpublished ms., chapter 1, APA.

38. U.S. Department of the Census: "Money Income of Families and Persons in the United States," *Current Population Reports, 1957 to 1975,* U.S. Department of Labor, Bureau of Labor Statistics: *Handbook of Labor Statistics,* 1975, cited in *The Earnings Gap Between Women and Men,* U.S. Department of Labor Employment Standards Administration, Women's Bureau, 1976; and U.S. Department of Labor, Women's Bureau, "Background Facts on Women Workers in the United States," January 1962, Document VI-39, PCSW papers, Washington, D.C., cited in Harrison, 90; Women's Bureau, "Fact Sheet on the Earnings Gap" (Washington, D.C., 1970); Friedan, *It Changed My Life,* 89.

39. Friedan, 90, 89.

40. Friedan, "Statement," 89ff.

41. *New York Times,* November 22, 1966, 44:1; *Washington Post,* November 23, 1966, n.p.

42. NOW mimeographed pamphlet, *Special Edition #2: NOW vs. Segregated Help-Wanted Ads.* Unpaginated. 1965, APA. See Hole and Levine, *Rebirth,* for a full description.

43. Friedan, *It Changed My Life,* 94.

44. Freeman, 83.

45. Friedan, *It Changed My Life,* 105.

46. Interview, February 1971; Hole and Levine, 96, 97.

46. Freeman, 99.

48. Friedan, *It Changed My Life,* 108.

49. Friedan, 108.

50. Author's interview with Meredith Tax, December 1983, New York City.

51. *New York Times Magazine,* March 10, 1968, 24.

52. Hole and Levine, 91.

53. *Report,* Congress to Unite Women, New York City, November 21–23, 1970, 3, Women's Liberation Vertical File, SL; Friedan, *It Changed My Life,* 387.

54. *It Changed My Life,* 138. Among many topics I pursued when I interviewed Betty Friedan in Southern California, May 1986, was this generational split. At that time, she still harbored many antipathies toward the women's liberation movement, in part because her more recent book *The Second Stage,* which called for feminists to value families and to create goals that supported them, was being attacked by some young radical feminists.

55. Clarenbach interview, WHS, Tape 57.

56. Joseph Rheingold, *The Fear of Being a Woman* (New York: Grune and Stratton, 1964), 714.

57. Friedan, *It Changed My Life,* 258.

58. Harrison, ix.

59. See Flora Davis, *Moving the Mountain* (New York: Simon and Schuster, 1991), 282 ff. for a fuller description of child care legislation.

60. See Toni Carabillo, Judith Meuli, and June Bundy Csida, eds., *Feminist Chronicles*, 1953–1992, (Los Angeles: Women's Graphics, 1993) for these simultaneous events and movements.

61. To be sure, these three demands excluded a much longer list of demands made by both branches of the movement. But they also implicitly acknowledged NOW's acceptance of the bases of political liberalism, for they embraced equality of opportunity, not equality of result.

62. Clipping, *Chicago Daily News*, August 20, 1970, 5. Vertical File Clippings on March, SL. Clipping, *Evening Star*, Washington, D.C., August 20, 1970, Women's Liberation Papers, Folder Four, SL. As with all movement marches, figures differed greatly. The *New York Times* described the march as having ten thousand in the parade, but organizers argued that fifty thousand women were present at the rally. Whatever the actual number, most observers seemed to think the numbers were staggering. The marchers spilled off the sidewalks into the streets. See *New York Times* coverage, August 27, 1970, 30.

63. "Women March Down Fifth in Equality Drive," *New York Times*, August 27, 1970, 1, 23. For other media accounts, some of which were very balanced, some of which ridiculed everything, see *Newsweek*, "Women Rally to Publicize Grievances," August 5, 1970; Myra MacPherson, "Battle of the Sexes Becomes a Word War," *New York Times* Style section, C1; "Women's Lib Asks Boycott of 4 Products," *Washington Post*, August 27, 1970; "For Most Women, 'Strike Day' Was Just a Topic of Conversation," *New York Times*, August 27, 1970, 1—which is right next to the article "Newsweek Agrees to Speed Promotion of Women"; "The Feminine Protest," *New York Times*, August 28, 1970, 20; " 'Equal Rights Now,' Exhort Women Protesters," *Washington Post*, August 27, 1970, 1. Hole and Levine, 269. The poll was conducted September 4–5, 1970.

64. Friedan, *It Changed My Life*, 154.

Chapter Four: Leaving the Left

1. *The Daily Californian*, May 14, 1964; January 5, 1970.

2. There is now an enormous bibliography on histories and memoirs from the New Left. Some of the important works that trace the development of the New Left and its formative ideas are in the Bibliography.

3. As Belinda Robnett has argued in her book, *How Long? How Long? African American Women and the Struggle for Freedom and Justice* (New York: Oxford University Press, 1997), historians have focused too much on white activists at the expense of black activists, and especially black civil rights grassroots activists in the South. And yet I can't ignore the fact that the story of white women's liberation begins in the integration movement of SNCC, in which black influences gave rise to the consciousness and ideas that would affect every movement that came after it. See Bibliography for other important works.

4. King, *Freedom Song*, 37.

5. Author's interview with Dorothy Burlage, May 11, 1989, Boston, Massachusetts.

6. King, 40.
7. Casey Hayden, "Women's Consciousness and the Nonviolent Movement Against Segregation, 1960–1965: A Personal History," 1989, 2, 3. Given to author, APA.
8. Author's interview with Dorothy Burlage, October 12, 1990, Boston, Massachusetts.
9. King, 5.
10. King, 9.
11. King, 8.
12. King, 116; Casey Hayden, "A Nurturing Movement: Nonviolence, SNCC, and Feminism," *Southern Exposure* (Summer 1988): 51.
13. King, 141. Kay Mills, *This Little Light of Mine* (New York: Dutton, 1993), which is a biography of Fannie Lou Hamer, has greater detail.
14. Author's notes, 1988 SDS reunion at Poughkeepsie, New York. Evans, *Personal Politics*, 53.
15. King, 404; Casey Hayden, quoting Stembridge in "Women's Consciousness," 9.
16. Author's interview with Dorothy Burlage, 1990. See Clayborne Carson, *In Struggle*, for a fuller description of the trajectory of SNCC.
17. Author's interviews with Casey Hayden, Dorothy Burlage, Betty Garman, Elaine Delott Bakers, Leni Wildflower, Honey Williams, Dorothy Burlage, Mickey Flacks, Helen Garvey, and others at the SDS reunion in 1988, including the former Weatherwomen Bernadine Dohrn, Cathy Wilkerson, and others. Interviews also with Rennie Davis and Dick Flacks.
18. Author's interviews with Casey Hayden and Dorothy Burlage.
19. King, 404.
20. Evans, 79; author's interview with "Anonymous," May 8, 1989, a white northern woman who participated in SNCC's Freedom Summer, 1964.
21. King, 464.
22. Doug McAdam, *Freedom Summer* (New York: Oxford University Press, 1988), 108, 106. On sexual exploitation of white volunteers by black men during Mississippi Freedom Summer, see Mary Aiken Rothschild, "White Women Volunteers in the Freedom Summers, Their Life and Work in a Movement for Social Change," *Feminist Studies*, 5:3 (Fall 1979), 466–95; and Mary Rothschild, *A Case of Black and White: Northern Volunteers and the Southern Freedom Summers, 1964–1965* (Westport, Conn.: Greenwood Press, 1982).
23. McAdam, 109.
24. McAdam, 107.
25. McAdam, 107, 110.
26. Author's interview with Dorothy Burlage, 1990; McAdam, 106; King, 465.
27. King, 15.
28. Cynthia Washington, "We Started from Different Ends of the Spectrum," *Southern Exposure*, 4:4 (1977), 14.
29. Doug McAdam, "Freedom Summer," paper presented at Stanford Conference, April 1990.

30. Hayden, "Women's Consciousness," 12.
31. Author's telephone interview with Casey Hayden, May 6, 1989.
32. King, 443, 445, 569. For a long time, many white female liberationists thought that the paper was written by a black woman, Ruby Doris Smith, because Robin Morgan erroneously described her as the author in her introduction to *Sisterhood is Powerful*. Ruby Doris Smith died of cancer in 1967. Hayden, "Women's Consciousness," 14.
33. King, 450; author's interview with Casey Hayden at SDS reunion, and telephone, May 6, 1989.
34. King, 451–52; author's telephone interview with "Anonymous," August 9, 1995, and again, on November 24, 1997.
35. Evans, 239; Fraser et al., *1968*, 342.
36. See Evans, 129, for a good history of money and support of ERAP projects; Kopkind quoted in Evans, 130; author's 1988 SDS reunion notes.
37. King, 456.
38. King, 456.
39. Author's telephone interview, Casey Hayden, 1989; Hayden, "Women's Consciousness," 18.
40. Burlage 1990 interview.
41. Michael Honey, "The Legacy of SNCC," in *OAH (Organization of American Historians) Newsletter*, February 1989, and Joanne Grant, "Sexual Politics and Civil Rights," *New Directions for Women*, January/February 1989, 4.
42. King, 466, 467. Also see Clay Carson's attribution, *In Struggle*.
43. Evans, 110. As former students or political leaders, they had already demonstrated formidable intellectual and organizing talents. Tom Hayden had edited the *Michigan Daily* and founded the VOICE political party; Robb Burlage edited the *Daily Texan*; Paul Potter was vice president of the National Student Association (NSA); and Todd Gitlin had been president of Tocsin, a campus peace group at Harvard University. At the University of Michigan, Al Haber, the first president of SDS, was a student leader. Dick Flacks, already a young professor, had been a political activist and strategist since adolescence.
44. *New Left Notes*, 1967, 59; Fraser, 340.
45. Evans, 119; author's interviews with Casey Hayden, Arizona.
46. Author's interview with Susan Griffin, Marilyn Webb; Anne Weills at a panel on women's liberation at FSM reunion, 1984, U.C. Berkeley.
47. Todd Gitlin, *The Sixties*, 357, 367 (paperback ed.). Also see Todd Gitlin, "Notes on the Pathology of the N.C.," *New Left Notes*, 1:3 (February 4, 1966), 4, for an insightful description of the politics of the National Council.
48. Letter from Carol McEldowney to Todd Gitlin, November 18, 1964, TGPA.
49. Letter from Carol McEldowney to Todd Gitlin and Nanci Hollander, August 31, 1965, TGPA.
50. Author's interviews with Sharon Jeffrey and Betty Garman, SDS reunion, 1988.
51. Author's interview with Casey Hayden, Betty Garman, Dorothy Burlage,

Sharon Jeffrey, and about ten other women at 1988 SDS reunion in Pough-keepsie, New York. Author's telephone interview with Betty Garman, July 13, 1989.

52. The concept of status deprivation was used by U.S. historians like Richard Hofstadter to explain why a group feels resentment when they have been de-prived of the status they believe they should have. It also appears in some his-tories of the movement. Maren Carden, *The New Feminist Movement* (New York: Russell Sage Foundation, 1974), and Jo Freeman in all her various works on the women's movement: See *The Politics of Women's Liberation: A Case Study of an Emerging Social Movement and Its Relation to Policy* (New York: McKay, 1975); *The Women's Liberation Movement: Its Aims, Structures, and Ideas* (Pittsburgh: KNOW, 1971); and *Women, A Feminist Perspective*, Jo Freeman, ed. (Palo Alto: Mayfield Publishing, 1975).

53. Author's interview with Vivian Rothstein, June 26, 1989, Santa Monica, California; author's notes from Sharon Jeffrey interview, SDS 1988 reunion.

54. Author's interview with Barbara Haber, at SDS 1988 reunion.

55. Author's interview with Barbara Haber, June 27, 1989, Berkeley, California.

56. Sharon Jeffrey and Carol McEldowney, typewritten notes mailed out to mem-bership. 1965. VRPA.

57. Evans, 167; author's telephone interview with Nanci Hollander, August 24, 1989, Texas.

58. Some men responded favorably to the women's workshop in 1965. Jonathan Steinberg, "Comments," *New Left Notes*, 1:9 (March 18, 1966); *New Left Notes*, vol. 1, no. 4. Author's telephone interview with Nanci Hollander, Au-gust 24, 1989; author's interview with Burlage, 1990.

59. Fraser, *1968*, 116.

60. Fraser, 117.

61. Fraser, 118.

62. "Liberation of Women," in *New Left Notes* (July 10, 1967). Evans, 191–92.

63. Author's interview with Naomi Weisstein, October 9, 1997, New York.

64. Author's interview with Jo Freeman, August 28, 1990, in Berkeley, California.

65. Evans, 199.

66. All this information comes from Evans, chapter 8, "The Dam Breaks."

67. Author's interview with Marilyn Webb; Evans, 210, quoting letter from Mari-lyn Webb to Heather Booth, November 21, 1968, in author's file.

68. Author's interview with Anne Weills, August 1, 1998, Berkeley, California.

69. Weills interview.

70. There are now a number of local studies available. See the Bibliography.

71. Evans, 301.

72. Warren Hinkle and Marianne Hinkle, "Woman Power," 22–43, *Ramparts*, February 1968.

73. Author's interview with Anne Weills.

74. "Woman Power," *Ramparts* (February 1968): 22–43. Responses to the issue came from Lynn Flartyney, "A Letter to the Editor of *Ramparts* Magazine,"

Notes from the First Year, and Anne Koedt, "Women and the Radical Movement," *No More Fun and Games*, 1968. APA. Author's interview with Susan Griffin; Kate Coleman, interviewed in *Berkeley Monthly*, April 1987; Author's interview with Judith Coburn.

75. In "Seize the Press Sister," *Off Our Backs*, 4 (1968). Marilyn Webb advocated that radical women should create communications for a new movement. Jo Freeman, "Editorial," *Voice of Women's Liberation* (VOWL), 1:1 (March 1968), 5.

76. For a longer list of periodicals available in 1970, see Leslie Tanner, *Voices of Women's Liberation* (New York: New American Library, 1970), 444.

77. See for example, VOWL, no. 5, Marilyn Webb, "We Are Victims," 1967; Clara Fraser, "Which Road Toward Women's Liberation?" in *Women: A Journal of Liberation*, 2:1, (1970); Sue Baker, interview, *Off Our Backs* (April 1970). Deirdre Baire, *Simone de Beauvoir: A Biography* (New York: Summit, 1990), 535; Gitlin, *The Sixties*, chapter 14; *Ain't I a Woman*, no. 7; unsigned "Panther Constitutional Convention," *Rat*, no. 1; Marlene Elkind, "On the Man's Convention," *Rat*, 14; Leslie Tanner, "Venceremos Brigade: An Elitist Authoritarian Organization," in *Rat*, 21, clippings, APA; and *The Fourth World Manifesto*.

78. Author's interview with Marilyn Webb in New York City, April 16, 1986; Gitlin, 273–74; author's interview with Irene Peslikis, New York; author's interview with Ellen Willis, New York, April 16, 1986. Also see Ellen Willis, "Up from Radicalism: A Feminist Journal," 1969, 114, for a more detailed account of the event, APA. Other accounts include Bobbie Spalter-Roth, "January 20: A Sad Celebration," *Off Our Backs* (March 1973): 14–16; and for consequences, "I Ain't Fighting in No Man's War," *Off Our Backs* (May 1970). *I. F. Stone's Weekly*, January 27, 1969, UWA.

79. Author's interviews with Judy Coburn, Ros Baxandall, Ellen Willis. Texts of speeches by Firestone and Webb in "Factionalism Lives," in *Voice of Women's Liberation Movement*, 6 (February 1969), author's files; and Ellen Willis, "Up from Radicalism: A Feminist Journal," 114. Other responses include "New Mobe" *Off Our Backs* 1:2 (March 19, 1970); "I Ain't Fightin in No Man's War" *Off Our Backs* 1:5 (May 16, 1970).

80. Author's interview with Marilyn Webb; author's interview with Ellen Willis; Gitlin, *The Sixties*, 372–375. Author's interview with Marilyn Webb; Shulamith Firestone, "Women," *Guardian*, February 1, 1960, UWA.

81. "A Declaration of Independence," in the *Voice of Women's Liberation Movement*, no. 6, UWA; Carol Hanisch, "Hard Knocks," *Notes from the Second Year*, UWA.

82. See Meredith Tax and Cynthia Michel, "An Open Letter to the Boston Movement," mimeo, quoted and cited in Ann Popkin, 191; also see Ellen Dubois and Suzanne Gordon, "The National Action: A Women's Perspective," in *Women: A Journal of Liberation*, vol. 1, no. 1; author's interview with Barbara Epstein, November 8, 1997, Berkeley, California.

83. Author's interview with Robin Morgan, April 17, 1986.

84. See their early articles in Robin Morgan, *Sisterhood Is Powerful* (New York: Vintage, 1970). The poet and novelist Ana Castillo called for Xicanisma (Chicanisma), a kind of Chicano womanism, which could bridge antiracist and antisexist struggles. Also see the wonderful collection that Toni Cade published in 1970, *The Black Woman: An Anthology* (New York: New American Library, 1970).

85. Canada Conference, April 6, 1971, cosponsored by Canada WLM and Women Strike for Peace; WLM FBI Files, Schlesinger Library, Radcliffe; Judith Ezekiel, "Une contribution à l'histoire du mouvement feministe americain," 154. I was one of the supervisors of this dissertation. "OPEN LETTER FROM WOMANPOWER TO YOU," April 1969, Oakland, California; also see Rita Mae Brown, "Commentary: Hanoi to Hoboken, a Round Trip Ticket," in *Off Our Backs* (March 25, 1971): 4–5, in which she argues that women should form their own anti-imperialist groups. For an example of the romanticization of the Vietnamese women, see Bernadine Dohrn, "The Liberation of Vietnamese Women," *Liberation News Service*, 115 (November 1, 1968), Social Protest Collection, Bancroft Library, U.C. Berkeley.

86. Three hundred women from the western United States and Canada and Vietnam met in Canada on July 11 and 12, 1969. They demanded complete U.S. withdrawal and self-determination for Vietnam. Social Protest Files, Bancroft Library, U.C. Berkeley. Also see "Projected Conference in North America with Indochinese Women," Position Papers Vertical File, SL; phone and e-mail interview with Vivian Rothstein, July 7, 1998.

87. Frances Beale, "Speaking Up When Others Can't"; Elizabeth Martinez, "A Call for Chicanisma"; and Roxanne Dunbar (Ortiz), "Back to My Roots in Radical Feminism," part of "Sisterhood Is Still Powerful" in *Crossroads* (March 1993): 4–9; Robin Morgan, *The Word of a Woman: Feminist Dispatches 1968–1992* (New York: W. W. Norton, 1992); Margaret Randall, *Gathering Rage: The Failure of 20th Century Revolutionaries to Develop a Feminist Agenda* (New York: Monthly Review Press, 1992); and Elaine Brown, *A Taste of Power: A Black Woman's Story* (New York: Pantheon, 1992).

88. Author's interview with Jane and Wendel Brunner, August 1988, Oakland, California. Also see leaflet, "Women Unite Against the War," announcing a women's contingent at the April 24, 1971, March against the War in San Francisco. Women's Liberation Files, Social Protest Collection, Bancroft Library, U.C. Berkeley. To gain a sense of the logic for a caucus, rather than creating a separate group, see "The Relationship of Women's Liberation to the Total Movement," two-page flyer, circa 1969, MWA.

89. Robin Morgan, "Goodbye to All That," in *Rat* (January 19, 1969). Also see "A Letter to the Editor of *Ramparts* Magazine," *Notes from the First Year: Women's Liberation*, June 1969, unpaginated, APA, and Rita Mae Brown, "Say It Isn't So," *Rat* (March 7–21, 1970): 18.

90. Marge Piercy, "Grand Coolie Damn," *Leviathan*, November 1969, reprinted as a pamphlet by New England Free Press, in APA. Also reprinted in Morgan, *Sisterhood*, 473–92. In *The Fourth World Manifesto*, which appeared in *Notes*

from the Third Year, the authors, veterans of the Left movement, argued that
the male Left was beyond redemption and proposed the controversial theory
that women, as a group, constituted a new Fourth World that could be organized on the basis of their sex. Also see *VOWL*, no. 5, and Marge Piercy,
"Grand Coolie Damn," in Morgan, ed., *Sisterhood Is Powerful*, 473–92, and
Ellen Willis, "Declaration of Independence," *VOWL*, 6, 1969. Robin Morgan,
"Goodbye to All That," in *Going Too Far: The Personal Chronicle of a Feminist* (New York: Vintage, 1978), 131, also reprinted in Tanner, *Voices*, 268–77.
91. Naomi Weisstein, self-interview for Peg Strobel, 21; Gitlin, *The Sixties*, 373.

Chapter Five: Hidden Injuries of Sex

1. This vote took place in the fall of 1963 at the University of Rochester, New
York.
2. Two of the earliest examples of these media pronouncements were the cover
stories, "Sex in the U.S.: Mores and Morality," *Time*, January 24, 1964, and
"Morals on Campus," *Newsweek*, April 6, 1964. The question whether the
sexual revolution was really that new has been asked by many scholars and
journalists. Suffice it to say, to the young women growing up in the fifties, the
loosening of sexual mores seemed quite different. See Richard L. Worsnop,
"Sexual Revolution: Myth or Reality," in *Editorial Research Reports*, 1 (1970):
241–57.
3. I have adapted the title of this chapter from Richard Sennett and Jonathan
Cobb's important study, *The Hidden Injuries of Class* (New York: Knopf, 1972).
4. Tom Hayden, *Reunion: A Memoir* (New York: Random House, 1988), 107.
5. Todd Gitlin, *The Sixties*, 373, 368.
6. See, for example, Marilyn Salzman Webb, "Woman as Secretary, Sex-
pot, Spender, Sow, Civic Actor, Sickie," *Liberation News Service* (May 10,
1969): 10; author's interview with Barbara Haber, Berkeley, California,
June 27, 1987.
7. Interviews with women of SNCC and SDS at a variety of places and times, but
especially with Dorothy Burlage, in Boston in 1990; Casey Hayden, Leni
Wildflower, Kathy Wilkerson at an SDS reunion in Poughkeepsie, New York,
in 1988; author's interview with Barbara Haber, and author's interview with
Mickey Flacks, Santa Barbara, 1985, 1987, 1988.
8. Karen Lindsey, "The Sexual Revolution Is No Joke for Women," three-page
essay, *Rainbow and Lightning Collection*, n.d., SL Women's Liberation Vertical Files; Fraser, 342; *Liberation News Service*, n.d., UWA.
9. Author's interview with Sarah Stage, February 4, 1991, at UCLA. She used
this term because she felt pressured by GIs to say "yes to men who say no."
10. Quotes are from Rivka Polatnick's "Diversity in Women's Liberation Ideology: How a Black and a White Group of the 1960s Viewed Motherhood,"
Signs 21 (Spring 1996): 679, and from Black Women's Liberation Group,
Mount Vernon, New York, *Statement on Birth Control*, in Morgan, *Sisterhood*,
404. For a variety of views, see "Birth Control Pill and Black Children, a
statement by the Black Unity Party," Peekskill, N.Y.; "A Response" by black

sisters, and "Poor Black Women," by Patricia Robinson, in the pamphlet *Poor Black Women*, published by New England Free Press, Boston, Massachusetts, circa 1968, MWA.

11. See Rivka Polatnick, "Strategies for Women's Liberation: A Study of a Black and a White Group of the 1960s," unpublished dissertation, Sociology Department, U.C. Berkeley, 1985. In this study, Rivka Polatnick compared a poor black group of women in Mount Vernon and New Rochelle, New York, with the New York Radical Women in New York City. Their concern to secure birth control was accompanied by a politics that favored an anticapitalist perspective. The New York Radical Women, in contrast, focused on sex roles and an independent women's movement. Frances Beale, "Double Jeopardy: To Be Black and Female," in Morgan, *Sisterhood*, 392. Kennedy quoted in Reagan, 232; Chisholm's sentiments in her autobiography, *Unbought and Unbossed* (Boston: Houghton Mifflin, 1970).

12. Robin Morgan, in *Going Too Far*.

13. Alix Kates Shulman, *Memoirs of an Ex-Prom Queen* (New York: Knopf, 1972), 20; Sara Davidson, *Loose Change* (New York: Doubleday, 1977), 86.

14. Susan Lydon, "The Politics of Orgasm," in Morgan, *Sisterhood*, 227–28; Barbara Ehrenreich, Elizabeth Hess, Gloria Jacobs, *Re-Making Love*. The best single study of feminism and its relationship to psychoanalytic thought is by Mari Jo Buhle, *Feminism and Its Discontents* (Cambridge: Harvard University Press, 1999). See her discussion of Sherfey on p. 224.

15. An anonymous early activist in a New York women's liberation group, "Sex and Women's Liberation," in Redstockings, *Feminist Revolution* (New York: Random House, 1975), 141.

16. Anne Koedt, "The Myth of the Vaginal Orgasm," *Notes from the First Year* (New York, 1968) and an expanded version in Shulamith Firestone and Anne Koedt, eds., *Notes from the Second Year* (New York: Ace, 1970), 36–41, APA. Reprinted in the widely read anthology edited by Anne Koedt, Ellen Levine, Anita Rapone, *Radical Feminism* (New York: Quadrangle, 1973), 198–207. For other critiques of the sexual revolution, see Dana Densmore, "Independence from the Sexual Revolution," reprinted in *Radical Feminism*, 107–18; Barbara Seaman, "The Liberated Orgasm," *Ms.*, August 1972; and Anselma Dell'Olio, "The Sexual Revolution Wasn't Our War," *Ms.*, Spring 1972, 104–09.

17. Laura X, "Our Sexual Revolution," *Velvet Glove*, circa 1969, 142.

18. Robin Morgan, "Lesbianism and Feminism, Synonyms or Contradistinctions," *The Second Wave*, 2:73 (1973), 14–23; Gayle Huelsman, "Open Letter to a Housewife," *Dayton Women's Liberation News*, November 5, 1970, 2–3. The collective that wrote the second chapter of *Our Bodies, Ourselves* (New York: Simon and Schuster, 1973) similarly worried about women learning to view sex in competitive ways, that is, the search for more and stronger orgasms; Alix Kates Shulman, "Sex and Power: Sexual Bases of Radical Feminism," *Signs* (1980): 592; Michaela Griffo, "Dear Sisters," *Rat* (March 21, 1970): 19.

19. Dana Densmore, "On Celibacy," in Tanner, *Voices from Women's Liberation*, first published in the feminist journal *No More Fun and Games*, 1 (1969); Kate, "What Is There to Say About Celibacy?" *Kansas City Women's Liberation Newsletter*, 4:1 (1974), 10; Leila, "Voices," *Country Women* (April 1975): 8–9. Celibacy was especially appealing when women needed a respite, felt confused after so much rapid change, and needed to sort things out. In short, for some women, celibacy represented a necessary cooling-off time, while they came to terms with their sexual orientation and sexual desires. Also see Dana Densmore, "Freedom from Sex," reprinted in Koedt, *Radical Feminism*, 107–19.

20. Cell 16's journal *No More Fun and Games*, 1968–1973, called for celibacy. Roxanne Dunbar, "Everything Is Necessary Is Realistic," *Pandora's Box*, 1:4. (1971), 1–3; "Celibacy," *Country Women* (June 1973): 22; Ti-Grace Atkinson, "Vaginal Orgasm as Mass Hysterical Survival Response," written speech, unpaginated, April 5, 1968, UWA.

21. Author's interview with Candace Falk, Berkeley, California, May 15, 1986; author's interview with Judith Coburn, Berkeley, California, March 10, 1985; author's interview with Rosalyn Baxandall, New York, December 4, 1985; Alice Echols's interview with Rosalyn Baxandall, 12; author's interview with Karin Durbin, New York, April 16, 1986.

22. Author's interview with Betty Friedan, Los Angeles, California, April 4, 1986; author's interview with Lucinda Cisler, New York, April 13, 1986; author's interview with Pat Cody, Berkeley, California, July 29, 1986.

23. Shulamith Firestone, *The Dialectics of Sex: The Case for Feminist Revolution* (New York: Bantam, 1970). See especially the first chapter, "The Dialectic of Sex," and p. 238. Linda Grant, "Feminist Who Lit the Torch," *Guardian* (July 30, 1998).

24. Kate Millett, *Sexual Politics* (New York: Doubleday, 1970).

25. Henry Miller, *Sexus* (New York: Grove Press, 1965), 384; quoted in Millett, *Sexual Politics*, 306.

26. Germaine Greer, *The Female Eunuch* (New York: McGraw Hill, 1971), 121, 6.

27. Greer, 322.

28. Claudia Dreifus, "The Selling of a Feminist," which first appeared in the *Nation*, and then in *Notes from the Third Year*, reprinted in Koedt, *Radical Feminism*, 358–60.

29. Erica Jong, *Fear of Flying* (New York: Signet, 1973). All citations are from this edition.

30. Jong, 80.

31. Jong, 299.

32. Jong, 302.

33. Jong, 154, 24.

34. Diana Newell, "Sex in the '70s: A Wrap-Up of the Decadent Decade," *Playgirl*, December 1979; Shere Hite, *The Hite Report* (New York: Dell, 1976), 263; Deirdre English and Barbara Ehrenreich, "Sexual Liberation: The

Shortest Revolution," in *The Women Say, The Men Say: Women's Liberation and Men's Consciousness*, Evelyn Shapiro and Barry Shapiro, eds. (New York: Delta, 1979), 120–27. This collection, which reprinted some of the most important documents of the movement, is difficult to find, but a very important anthology. APA.

35. This is the title of Leslie Reagan's fine book on the century between when abortion was made illegal and when it was again legalized.

36. The difference between reform and repeal is discussed in Sheryl Burt Ruzek, *The Women's Health Movement* (New York: Praeger, 1978), 19.

37. Author's interview with Lucinda Cisler, New York, April 13, 1986. The origins of the Webster decision can be found in Cynthia Gorney, *Articles of Faith* (New York: Simon and Schuster, 1998).

38. Ellen Frankfort, *Vaginal Politics* (New York: Quadrangle, 1972), 36.

39. For an excellent narrative and analysis of the struggle in Seattle against abortion, see Barbara Winslow, "The Struggle for Abortion Reform in Washington State, 1967–1970," paper given to author in 1993; author's interview with Irene Peslikis, New York, April 11, 1987; Carolyn Heilbrun, *The Education of a Woman: The Life of Gloria Steinem* (New York: Dial Press, 1995).

40. A good source for the complicated search for the right "Jane Doe" can be found in Marian Faux, *Roe v. Wade: The Untold Story of the Landmark Supreme Court Decision That Made Abortion Legal* (New York: New American Library, 1988).

41. Suzanne Stagenborg, "Can Feminist Organizations Be Effective?" in *Feminist Organizations: Harvest of the New Women's Movement*, Myra Ferree and Patricia Yancey Martin, eds. (Philadelphia: Temple University Press, 1995), 354.

42. Robin Morgan, "Women Disrupt the Miss America Pageant," in Morgan, *Going Too Far* (New York: Vintage, 1978), 62.

43. Both movement organizers and the FBI estimated that two hundred women picketed the pageant. "FBI Probed Women's Lib for LBJ White House," *Arizona Republic*, September 15, 1991; Charlotte Curtis, "Miss America Is Picketed by 100 Women," *New York Times*, September 9, 1968. For other accounts, see Lindsey Van Gelder, "The Truth about Bra-Burners," *Ms.*, September/October 1992, 89, and Echols, *Daring to Be Bad*, 95.

44. "The Great No-Bra Controversy Rages On," *San Francisco Chronicle*, August 21, 1969, n.p., UWA.

45. Carol Hanisch, "What Can Be Learned: A Critique of the Miss America Protest," in Tanner, *Voices from the Women's Liberation Movement*, 132–34.

46. Author's interview with Robin Morgan.

47. This song is from Susan Adelman and Miriam Boxer, "Up Against the Wall, Miss America." Newsreel footage compiled from the 1968 demonstration quoted in Samantha Barbas, "Miss America: The Making of a National Ideal," unpublished research paper, U.C. Berkeley, 1997.

48. "Plastic Sex Melts," in *San Francisco Express Times*, clipping, circa 1970, UWA.

49. Pamphlet, circa 1970, n.d., UWA.

50. Peg Strobel's interview with Naomi Weisstein, p. 54 of transcript.

51. In practice, this occurred long before feminist books began addressing fat as a "feminist issue." See Kim Chernin, *The Obsession* (New York: Harper and Row, 1981), and Marcia Millman, *Such a Pretty Face* (New York: W. W. Norton and Company, 1980). Interview with Herman S. Rosen, March 21, 1979, New York City.

52. This important insight was repeated to me by women I interviewed in New York, Seattle, Chicago, Boston, Dayton, Minneapolis, Bloomington, and Berkeley, California, who asked me to not make any attributions. The woman in Berkeley told me that she never could understand the fuss over being a sexual object. She *wanted* to be a sexual object.

53. This quote is from a woman who was an activist in the antiwar movement who wishes to preserve her anonymity. Several women who became leaders in the Free Speech Movement at U.C. Berkeley in 1964 described similar feelings at the thirtieth reunion of the FSM, Berkeley, California. Interviews by author at reunion in 1994.

54. Frances Beale, "Double Jeopardy: To Be Black and Female," in Morgan, *Sisterhood*, 1969, 382–96. Francis Beale was the New York coordinator of SNCC's Black Women's Liberation Committee; Black Women's Liberation Group, Mount Vernon, New York, *Statement on Birth Control*, in Morgan, *Sisterhood*, 404. This statement is written as a letter to "Brothers" in the movement.

55. Julia Penelope Stanley, "My Life As a Lesbian," in *The Coming Out Stories*, Julia Penelope Stanley and Susan J. Wolfe, eds. (Watertown, Mass.; Persephone Press, 1980), 195.

56. Merill, "Letter," *Coming Out*, 136.

57. Elana, "Confessions of Country Dyke," *Coming Out*, 156.

58. Miriam Keiff, "Coming In or Will the Real Lesbian Please Stand Up?" *Coming Out*, 207.

59. Del Martin, "If That's All There Is," n.d., UWA.

60. Author's interview with Susan Griffin.

61. Author's interviews with Cisler and Baxandall, respectively April 13, 1987, and December 1983.

62. Martha Shelley, "Notes of a Radical Lesbian," in Morgan, *Sisterhood*, 343–48. Sandra Bem developed a new psychological test that examined a personality for androgynous health, rather than adjustment to artificial expectations of masculinity or femininity. Carolyn Heilbrun's widely read book, *Toward a Recognition of Androgyny* (New York: Knopf, 1973), provoked much discussion, especially since so many lesbians viewed bisexuality and androgyny as still rooted to male characteristics.

63. For a good discussion of the political limits and contradictions of the "woman-identified woman" see Shane Phelan, *Identity Politics: Lesbianism and the Limits of Community*, (Philadelphia: Temple University Press, 1989). Also see Charlotte Bunch, "Learning from Lesbian Separatism," in *Passionate Politics* (New York: St. Martin's Press, 1987), 185. In *Passionate Politics*,

Bunch includes a number of essays that first justify and then explain what she learned from being a separatist. See the section titled "Lesbian Feminism" in *Passionate Politics*, 159–215; Beverly Jones and Judith Brown, "Analyses of the Movement," Tanner, 406–408; Gay Women's Liberation, Berkeley, "What It Means to Be a Lesbian," December 1969, APA, reprinted in *Lesbians Speak Out*; Gay Women's Liberation, "Lesbians As Women," November 1969, in *Lesbians Speak Out*.

64. Radicalesbians, "The Woman-Identified Woman," APA, also reprinted in Koedt, *Radical Feminism*, 240–46.

65. There is, of course, an enormous literature on the origins, impact, and consequences of lesbian feminism, separatism, and women's efforts to define what a "political" lesbian might be. See the Bibliography, as well as the bibliography in Phelan's book.

66. Keiffer, *Coming Out*, 207.

67. "Anonymous," *Coming Out*, 76.

68. Morgan, *Going Too Far*, 178.

69. Betty, "REFLECTIONS ON 'I TALK ... YOU LISTEN, OR DO YOU?'" *Kansas City Women's Liberation Newsletter* (October/November 1974): 5–7; also see Rachel, "Lesbian Separatism—A Straight View," *Goldflower* (January 1974): 4–5.

70. Author's interview with Valerie Miner, Berkeley, California, May 17, 1986; Adrienne Rich, "Compulsory Heterosexuality," from *Powers of Desire*, 105–22.

71. C. J. Martin, "Diary of a Queer Housewife," *Coming Out*, 62.

72. Sara Lucia Hoagland, "Coming Home," *Coming Out*, 147.

73. Beverly J. Toll, "Strong and Free: The Awakening," *Coming Out*, 28.

74. Martha Pillow, "Untitled Story," *Coming Out*, 8.

75. Nancy Whittier, *Feminist Generations*, 108. This study of Columbus, Ohio, reveals the tensions between lesbians and straights, but also the ways in which they came together.

76. Whittier, *Feminist Generations*, 108. Also see Elizabeth Kennedy and Madeleine Davis's important study of bar culture in the 1950s in Buffalo, New York, *Boots of Leather, Slippers of Gold: The History of a Lesbian Community* (New York: Routledge, 1993).

77. Author's interview with Ann Snitow, New York, April 16, 1986; Peg Strobel's interview with Naomi Weisstein.

78. Author's interview with Barbara Haber.

79. Jill Johnston, *Lesbian Nation: The Feminist Solution* (New York: Bantam, 1973), 25, 81, 276–77.

80. Charlotte Bunch, "Lesbians in Revolt," *The Furies* (January 1972); Charlotte Bunch, "Not for Lesbians Only," *Quest: A Feminist Quarterly* (Fall 1975), reprinted in *Passionate Politics*, 175.

81. Bunch, *Passionate Politics*, 7; Charlotte Bunch, "Learning from Lesbian Separatism," *Ms.*, November 1976; reprinted in *Passionate Politics*, 191.

82. Of all the magnificent writing published by Audre Lorde, perhaps her book

Sister Outsider: Essays and Speeches (Trumansburg, N.Y: The Crossing Press, 1984), and her article, "An Open Letter to Mary Daly," in *This Bridge Called My Back: Writings by Radical Women of Color*, Cherrie Moraga and Gloria Anzaldua, eds. (New York: Kitchen Table Press, 1983), offer the best examples of her ability to describe triple oppression, while not casting herself as a victim.

83. Whittier, *Feminist Generations*; see especially chapters 1 and 6, which describe the evolution and consequence of radical feminism in Columbus, Ohio.

84. Author's interview with Barbara Ehrenreich.

85. Boston Women's Health Collective, *Our Bodies, Ourselves* (New York: Simon and Schuster, 1973).

86. Collete Price, "The First Self-Help Clinic," *Feminist Revolution*.

87. Ruzek, *The Women's Health Movement*, 53–57.

88. Ruzek, 35.

89. Ruzek, 35.

90. Sheryl Gay Stolberg, "Now, Prescribing Just What the Patient Ordered," *New York Times Week in Review*, August 10, 1997, 3.

91. Joshua Horn, *Away with All Pests* (Monthly Review Press, 1969); editorial: "Chinese Health System," in *Health/Pac Bulletin*, 47 (1972). Also see Sheryl Burt Ruzek, "Medical Response to Women's Health Activities: Conflict, Accommodations and Co-optation," 336.

92. Ruzek, 12; *Our Bodies, Ourselves*, 157–225.

93. Ruzek, 12; Eisenstein, *Contemporary Feminist Thought*, 45.

94. Barbara Seaman, *The Doctors' Case Against the Pill* (New York: P. H. Wyden, 1969); Rose Kushner, *Breast Cancer: A Personal History and Investigative Report* (New York: Harcourt Brace Jovanovich, 1975); Phyllis Chesler, *Women and Madness* (New York: Doubleday, 1972).

95. Author's interview with Pat Cody in Berkeley, California, July 29, 1986, December 1998; Dorothy Bryant, "The DES Odyssey of Pat Cody," in *California Living*, San Francisco *Examiner/Chronicle Magazine*, March 18, 1997, 22.

96. On the East Coast, middle-class women formed CARASA to fight against the forced sterilization of women. On the West Coast, the Coalition to Defend Reproductive Rights (CDRR) worked for the same goals.

97. Raquel Scherr and Leonore Taboada were the women who translated the 1973 edition into Spanish. Author's interview with Raquel Scherr, August 19, 1997, Berkeley; author's interview with a group of neighborhood women who met weekly to study this torn and well-worn edition of *Our Bodies, Ourselves*, Managua, Nicaragua, June 1986.

98. Excerpt from Rosen, "A Life of One's Own," unpublished, written at Blue Mountain Lake and Ragdale, Fall 1990 and 1991, both residential communities for artists and writers.

99. Susan Griffin, "Rape: The All-American Crime," *Ramparts*, 10:3 (1971), 26–35. Other early critiques are Barbara Mehrhof and Pamela Kearon, "Rape: An Act of Terror," reprinted in Koedt, *Radical Feminism*, 228–33; Women Against Rape, *Stop Rape* (Detroit, 1971); "Anatomy of a Rape" and "Disarm Rapists" in *It Ain't Me, Babe*, July 23 and August 6 issues, 1970.

100. Susan Brownmiller, *Against Our Will: Men, Women and Rape* (New York, Bantam, 1975).

101. This trial is extremely complicated. For the full story, see the following coverage: *New York Times*, August, 1974, 321; *New York Times*, October 3, 1974, in Family, Food, Fashion, Furnishings, 21, and October 6, 1974, k10; *New York Times*, November 22, 1974, 29; Shana Alexander, "A Simple Question of Rape," *Newsweek*, October 28, 1974, 110.

102. This trial was covered by the *New York Times* throughout 1975. Her acquittal is described on August 15, 1975, 10: 1. See the *New York Times Index* for references to other developments in the case.

103. Some of the most influential works were Diana Russell's pioneering book, *The Politics of Rape: The Victim's Perspective* (New York: Stein and Day, 1975); Florence Rush, *The Best Kept Secret: Sexual Abuse of Children* (New York: McGraw-Hill, 1980); and Judith Herman, *Father-Daughter Incest* (Cambridge: Harvard University Press, 1981).

104. This was said by Bob Wilson, then chair of the Judiciary Committee of the California Senate, to the National Council of Jewish Women's meeting in L.A. in 1979, where he was the featured speaker.

105. For a good overview of twenty years of antirape activism, see Nancy A. Mathews, *Confronting Rape: The Feminist Anti-Rape Movement and the State* (New York: Routledge, 1994).

106. See Laura Lederer, ed., *Take Back the Night: Women on Pornography* (New York: William Morrow, 1980); *The Aggie*, March 10, 1982, 1; "UCD Hits Frat's Actions," *Daily Enterprise*, March 31, 1982, 1; "Women's March Saga Grows Angry," *Davis Enterprise*, March 11, 1982, 1; "Fraternity-Feminist Dispute Stirs Davis," *San Francisco Sunday Examiner and Chronicle*, B2; Letter from Vice Chancellor Thomas Dutton to Barry Boatman, presented to the Interdisciplinary Council, March 30, 1982, Women's Resource and Research Center Archives, University of California, Davis. I thank Joy Fergoda, librarian par excellence, for helping me find all the materials related to this case.

107. Rennie Simson, "The Afro-American Female: the Historical Context of the Construction of Sexual Identity" in *Powers of Desire*, 229–36.

108. One of the most interesting treatments of the politics of such memories is Judith Herman, *Trauma and Recovery: The Aftermath of Violence—From Domestic Abuse to Political Terror* (New York: Basic, 1992).

109. Interview with Professor Isabel Marcus, who worked in Buffalo, New York, for two years with a court-mandated counseling project for men who battered, Buffalo, November 1992. Also see Isabel Marcus, "Reframing 'Domestic Violence': Terrorism in the House," in M. Fineman and B. Mykitiuk, eds., *The Public Nature of Private Violence: The Discovery of Domestic Abuse* (New York: Routledge, 1994).

110. Some of the earliest books that helped redefine wife beating were William Ryan, *Blaming the Victim* (New York: Pantheon, 1971); Del Martin, *Battered Wives* (San Francisco: Glide Publications, 1976). For a good overview of the battered women's movement, an extensive bibliography on battered women

and battered women's syndrome, manuals and films and case studies of shelters, see Susan Schecter, *Women and Male Violence* (Boston: South End Press, 1982), and the Bibliography.

111. Susan Schecter points out in *Women and Male Violence* how much these feminist-inspired shelters changed when they were funded by local government. This question, whether an institution is part of a movement or simply a service, is discussed in detail in Schecter's work, 6.

112. Author's phone interview with Nadine Taub, September 8, 1997.

113. Carol Vance, ed., *Exploring Female Sexuality* (New York: Routledge, 1984), explores whether the sexual revolution was exploitative or emancipatory. Also see the bibliography in Nancy Wolloch, *Women and the American Experience, From 1860*, 2d ed. (New York: McGraw-Hill, 1997), 580.

114. See my article on sexual harassment: Ruth Rosen, "Sex, Lies, and Vulnerability." *Tikkun* 7:1 (January/February 1992), 22–25.

115. "Big Trouble in Glen Ridge," *New Directions for Women* (January/February 1993): 19. For a wide range of opinion and interpretation on the O. J. Simpson trial, see Toni Morrison and Claudia Brodsky Lacour, eds., *Birth of a Nation'hood* (New York: Random House, 1997). There is now a huge literature on this trial. For further articles and books, see Wolloch, *Women and the American Experience*, 580.

116. Kate Millett, *The Prostitution Papers* (New York: Avon, 1973), reprinted from first edition in 1971, published by Basic Books. The chronicle of this conference is described by Millett on pp. 17–27.

117. Author's interview with Alix Kates Shulman, New York, April 13, 1987.

118. Author's interview with Flo Kennedy, New York, April 14, 1986.

119. See Jan Fichtel et al., "Pussy Power Putdown," *Berkeley Tribe* (February 6, 1970); Bobby Goldstone, "The Politics of Pornography: The Pornography of Politics," *Off Our Backs* (December 14, 1970): 10; Women's Militia, Berkeley Chapter, "Tits 'n' Ass," *Berkeley Tribe* (August 1970): 14–21. For a broader overview of the underground paper world, see Abe Peck, *Uncovering the Sixties: The Life and Times of the Underground Press* (New York: Pantheon, 1984), especially 206–20. Peck is the author of the phrase "dildo journalism." Robin Morgan, "Theory and Practice: Pornography and Rape," *Going Too Far*, 163–70.

120. For informal accounts of the women's liberation protests against the film *Snuff*, see Beverly LaBelle, "*Snuff*: The Ultimate in Woman-Hating," and Martha Gever and Marge Hall, "Fighting Pornography," in Lederer, *Take Back the Night*, 272–85; Andrea Dworkin, *Letters from a War Zone* (London: Secker and Warburg, 1988; Women's Action Alliance, *Women's Action Almanac: A Complete Resource Guide*, Jane Williamson, Diane Winston, and Wanda Wooten, eds. (New York: William Morrow, 1979), 224–27. Lederer, *Take Back the Night*, 23–24; Dworkin, *Letters*, 312–14; Marcia Womongold, *Pornography: A License to Kill* (Somerville, Mass.: New England Free Press, 1979), 9–14.

121. See Andrea Dworkin, *Pornography and Civil Rights: A New Day for Women's*

Equality, and Andrea Dworkin and Catharine A. MacKinnon, *Organizing Against Pornography* (Minneapolis, 1988); Catharine MacKinnon, *Feminism Unmodified: Discourses on Life and Law* (Cambridge, Mass.: Harvard University Press, 1987); Catharine MacKinnon, *Toward a Feminist Theory of the State* (Cambridge, Mass.: Harvard University Press, 1989), and *Only Words* (Cambridge, Mass.: Harvard University Press, 1993).

122. Quoted by Sheila Jeffreys in *Anticlimax*, 255.

123. See Gayle Rubin et al., "Talking Sex," *Feminist Review*, 11 (June 1982): 40; Ellen Willis, "Feminism, Moralism and Pornography," in Ann Snitow et al., eds., *Desire: The Politics of Sexuality* (London: Virago, 1984), 85; Ann Snitow, "Retrenchment versus Transformation: The Politics of the Antipornography Movement," in Varda Burstyn, ed., *Women Against Censorship* (Toronto: Douglas and McIntyre, 1985), 111.

124. Author's interview with Susan Brownmiller, New York, April 14, 1986.

125. The debate over sadomasochism played a large role in the politics of sex. Some women viewed the practice as imitative of men's violence against women. But others felt that S&M was part of the range of appropriate sexual practices. See, for example, Robin Morgan, "Politics of Sado-Masochism," in *Going Too Far*, 227–41; Bat-Ami Bar, "Feminism and Sadomasochism: Self Critical Notes," in *Against Sadomasochism: A Radical Feminist Analysis*, Robin Ruth Linden and Darlene Pagano, eds.

126. See, for example, Susan Griffin, *Pornography and Silence* (New York: Harper & Row, 1981), and Robin Morgan, "Theory and Practice: Pornography and Rape," in *Take Back the Night*, 125–32, who were also very influential in linking violence to pornography. Alice Echols, in *Daring to Be Bad*, views the antipornography movement as part of the decline into cultural feminism. But I think it became several thousand movements, which pushed feminism even deeper within American culture. The antipornography movement was simply one of the most sexy and therefore visible parts of that splintering.

For those whose argued against porn, see Valerie Miner, "Fantasies and Nightmares: The Red-Blooded Media," in *Jump Cut*, December 1981. For information on the group FACT, created in 1984, which struggled against statutes against pornography, see "New Fact Group Battles Censorship Law," in *New Directions for Women* (January/February 1985): 1; Adrienne Rich, "We Don't Have to Come Apart over Pornography," *Off Our Backs*, July 1985.

127. See the introduction in *Powers of Desire*, which provides an excellent historical overview of this ambivalence and the sexual wars that resulted.

128. In 1985 and again in 1995, I did an anonymous survey of 250 undergraduate women at the University of California, Davis. Unlike former students, they were familiar with the concept of date rape and sexual harassment. But what had changed was that their overall view of sex was that it was dangerous. AIDS, of course, contributed to this view, but it wasn't their only reason for this perspective. APA.

Chapter Six: Passion and Politics

1. APA. These were later reprinted in 1975 in Redstockings, *Feminist Revolution* (New York: Random House, 1975). Also see Kathy Mulherin, "Consciousness Raising," *Dock of the Bay*, September 23, 1969, n.p., APA. Carol Hanisch, "The Personal Is Political," published in 1969, reprinted in *Feminist Revolution*, and Kathie Sarachild, "Program for Feminist Consciousness-Raising (1968), in *Notes from the First Year*, APA.
2. See Peggy White and Starr Goode, "Women's Liberation" and "The Small Group," in *Women: A Journal of Liberation* (Fall 1969): 56–57.
3. Author's interview with Laura X, September 5, 1997, Berkeley, California.
4. Author's interview with Naomi Weisstein, self-interview for Peg Strobel, 11; author's interview with Karen Durbin, April 18, 1986, New York City.
5. Author's interview with Vivian Gornick, April 6, 1987, New York City; Vivian Gornick, "The Light of Liberation Is Blinding," in *Village Voice*, December 10, 1970, 21.
6. Gornick, 22.
7. Author's interview with Ellen Willis.
8. Author's interview with Susan Griffin.
9. Author's interview with Carol Groneman, June 11, 1984, New York City.
10. Author's interview with Flo Kennedy, April 14, 1986, New York City.
11. Author's interview with Irene Peslikis; Charlotte Bunch, *Passionate Politics*, intro., 8; author's interview with Ann Snitow. Author's interview with Pat Cody, July 29, 1986, Berkeley, California.
12. For two different views, see Pam Allen, "Radical Women and the Rankin Brigade," New York; and Marilyn Webb, "Call for a Spring Conference," Washington, D.C., both in *Voices of Women's Liberation*, 1:1 (1968).
13. Shulamith Firestone, "The Jeanette Rankin Brigade: Woman Power?" New York Radical Women, *Notes from the First Year*, published pamphlet, New York, June 1968, 22.
14. Kathy Amatniek, "Funeral Oration for the Burial of Traditional Womanhood," reprinted in *Notes from the First Year*, 24.
15. Author's interviews with Gerda Lerner, Mickey Flacks, Pat Cody, and Amy Swerdlow between 1986 and 1996, University of North Carolina, Santa Barbara, Berkeley, Wisconsin.
16. Amy Swerdlow, *Women Strike for Peace: Traditional Motherhood and Radical Politics in the 1960s* (Chicago: University of Chicago Press, 1993), 140. All quotes from Swerdlow are from this source, 139–40.
17. Ruth Rosen, "The Day They Buried Traditional Womanhood," in *The Legacy: Vietnam in the American Imagination*, Peter Shafer, ed. (Boston: Beacon, 1990), 233–62.
18. Renee Blakkan, "New York Women 'Ogle' Construction Workers," *Guardian* (June 20, 1970): 3. Protest Files, Herstory, UWA.
19. "Women Disrupt CBS Annual Meeting," Liberation News Service Release, April 22, 1979, clipping, Protest Files, UWA.
20. "Bridal Protest—Position Paper," San Diego Women's Liberation Front, n.d.,

Protest Files, UWA; "Forum Bridal Fair Unfair," no date, no journal citation, signed by Columbus OSU Women's Liberation, Protest Files, UWA; "Fair Head Bristles As Women Unveil Shuck," *Berkeley Barb*, February 2, 1969, 3. Clipping from Protest Files, UWA.

21. "W.I.T.C.H. Hexes Bridal Fair," clipping, unidentified magazine, March 15, 1969, 26–27, Protest Files, UWA.

22. Position Paper, Bread and Roses, March 8, circa 1970, against WBCN; Berkeley Women's Liberation against KSAN in San Francisco. Clipping "ksan: hip/pg radio," *Berkeley Tribe*, March 31, 1971. Media Protest Files, UWA; "Sexist Sell," NOW Newsletter, Indianapolis, Indiana, December 20, 1972, Protest Files, UWA; clipping, Protest Files, UWA; clipping, *Berkeley Barb*, December 2, 1971, Protest Files, UWA.

23. Leaflet, "Women, We've Been Burned," Rally, June 2, 1971, Women's caucus of CPE. Protest Files, UWA.

24. FBI WLM Files. Letter dated August 11, 1969, SL.

25. FBI WLM Files, SL.

26. "Women Invade KPFA for Air Time," *Daily Californian*, July 24, 1970, 11, Protest Files, UWA. Among the women involved that evening were Mary Waters, Alta, Susan Griffin, and myself.

27. "Women Challenge Media Roles," *People's World* (June 20, 1970): 8, Media Protest Files, UWA; "Charge TV Movie Industries Discriminate Against Actresses," *Enquirer*, August 19, 1973, n.p., Media Protest Files, UWA.

28. "Women, It Is Insufferable," NARAL leaflet, March 14, 1970, Protest Files, UWA. In San Francisco, "Count Marco," "When Sex Is Too Much to Bear," *San Francisco Chronicle*, n.d., clipping, Protest Files, UWA.

29. Mary Felstiner, professor of history at San Francisco State University, from memoir in progress.

30. Carolyn Heilbrun, *The Education of a Woman*, 170, 171.

31. Gloria Steinem, *Outrageous Acts and Everyday Rebellions* (New York: Holt, Rinehart, and Winston, 1983), 19.

32. Heilbrun, 229.

33. Mary Thom, *Inside Ms.: 25 Years of the Magazine and the Feminist Movement* (New York: Holt, 1997), 43.

34. Thom, 43.

35. *Ms.* Letters Collection, SL. These letters are an important archive of the original letters. Most are sealed for ten years after they are written. More available for the general reader is the book, *Letters to Ms.: 1972–1987*, Mary Thom, ed. (New York: Holt and Company, 1987).

36. *Ms.* Letters Collection, Kathleen Phillips Satz, El Cerrito, California, November 1982 issue.

37. Thom, 79, 81, 87, 98, 200, 12, 106.

38. These articles appear in a section called "The Liberation Takeover of Women's Liberation," in *Feminist Revolution*.

39. Socialist and radical feminists didn't think the magazine dealt sufficiently with class. See the section "The Liberal Takeover of Women's Liberation" in

Redstockings, *Feminist Revolution*. My discussion of *Ms.* is based on reading ten years of the magazine when first published, and then again, for this book. Also see Amy Erdman Farrell, "Self-Help and Sisterhood: The Limits to Feminist Discourse in *Ms. Magazine*, 1972–1989," paper delivered at the Berkshire Conference on the History of Women, June 12, 1993.

40. Thom, 106.

41. See Alice Echols, *Daring to Be Bad* (Minneapolis: University of Minnesota Press, 1989).

42. Author's interview with Susan Griffin.

43. Susan Griffin, "An Answer to a Man's Question, 'What Can I Do About Women's Liberation?' " in *Let Them Be Said* (Berkeley: Shameless Hussy Press, 1971), APA.

44. Barry Shapiro, 214.

45. Maya Angelou, "Are Feminists Humorless?" *Playgirl*, November, 1975, 16.

46. Naomi Weisstein, "Why We Aren't Laughing . . . Any More," *Ms.*, November 1973, 49.

47. "*The New York Times*, August 27, 1970"—NOW parody of *New York Times*. UWA and APA.

48. Judy Syfers, "I Want a Wife," *Ms.*, Spring 1972, 56. Note that in 1997, Judy Brady wrote a new introduction that appeared at the top of her article (see Documents from the Women's Liberation Movement, Special Collections, Duke University On-Line Archives): "If you read this essay in 1972 in the first issue of 'Ms,' you thought it was written by Judy Syfers. Wrong: It was written by Judy Brady. The difference between now and then? Mr. Syfers went off to find a traditional wife, and Ms. Brady got herself back. Meanwhile, this Instant Classic has been reprinted over 200 times in at least 10 languages." HTTP://www.geocities.com/Wellesley/5175/wife/html. August 26, 1998.

49. Pat Mainardi, "The Politics of Housework," pamphlet, APA.

50. Gloria Steinem, "If Men Could Menstruate," *Outrageous Acts and Everyday Rebellions* (New York: Holt, Rinehart, 1983).

51. There is a trove of songs in the Schlesinger Library archives in Folder 31, in the Women's Liberation Collection. Many of these songs were written to other tunes, such as "Bella Ciao," or the "Battle Hymn of the Republic"; Naomi Weisstein, "Days of Celebration and Resistance; the Chicago Women's Liberation Rock Band, 1970–73," APA, in Feminist Memoir Project; Naomi Weisstein and Virginia Blasedell, "No More Balls and Chains," *Ms.*, 1972.

52. Naomi Weisstein self-interview for Peg Strobel, 35.

53. See, for example, *Framing Feminism: Art and the Women's Movement 1970–1985*, edited and introduced by Rozsika Parker and Griselda Pollock (London: Pandora Press, 1987).

54. *Women: A Journal of Liberation*, Fall 1970. See also Sandra Roos, "Women's Imagery/Women's Art," in Gayle Kimball, *Women's Culture* (New Jersey: Scarecrow Press, 1981), 42–60; and Judy Chicago in the same volume, "A Female Form of Language," 60–72; Linda Nochlin, *Women, Art and Power* (New York: Harper and Row, 1988); Linda Nochlin and Ann Harris, *Women*

Artists: 1550–1950 (Los Angeles: L.A. County Museum of Art, 1976); Moira Roth, ed., *The Amazing Decade: Women and Performance Art in America 1970–80* (Los Angeles: Astro Arts, 1983).

55. Michael Rossman, a Berkeley activist and writer, collected about four hundred posters from the women's movement. Michael Rossman, AOUON Archive (founded in 1977), 1741 Virginia Street, Berkeley, CA 94703. Collection, Berkeley, California. Michael Rossman, "Social Serigraphy in the Bay Area: 1966–1986," tabloid-sized brochure from exhibit at de Saisset Museum Gallery, Santa Clara University, January 17 to March 15, 1987. APA.

56. Author's interview with Jane Norling, November 2, 1997, Berkeley, California.

57. Ruth Rosen, "Posters of the Women's Movements: Imagine My Surprise," American Studies Association, New Orleans, 1988.

Chapter Seven: The Politics of Paranoia

1. Jean Curtis, "When Sisterhood Turns Sour," *New York Times Magazine*, May 30, 1976, 15–16. But it wasn't until 1987 that feminists began to acknowledge and explore their competition with each other—not for men, but for fame, leadership, and prestige. Valerie Miner and Helen Longino, eds., *Competition: A Feminist Taboo?* (New York: The Feminist Press, 1987).

2. There were endless flyers and position papers filled with arguments about what kinds of structures would work and which would oppress. See "Steering Committees Are Death," by Gina and Judy, in Social Protest Collection, Bancroft Library, U.C. Berkeley; "The Small Group in Women's Liberation," by Peggy White and Starr Goode, APA, circa 1968; Sheryl Kallaway, "Organization Structures of Retaliation within Women's Liberation," by the Thursday Night Co-op Group, circa 1970, Berkeley, APA; "Communication Structures from Berkeley Women's Liberation," by the Tuesday Night Co-op Group, APA; Becca, "Berkeley Women Organize," *Dock of the Bay*, September 25, 1969, 9.

3. Jo Freeman, author of "The Tyranny of Structurelessness," first wrote this article in 1970. It appeared without permission in "It Ain't Me, Babe" and was reprinted in *The Second Wave*, 2:1 (1972), 20, again with no permission. It gained even wider publicity when published in *Radical Feminism*.

4. Naomi Weisstein quotes these words by Chelsea Dreher in Naomi Weisstein, "Days of Celebration and Resistance: The Chicago Women's Liberation Rock and Roll Band, 1970–1973," 14.

5. Author's interview with Meredith Tax; Meredith Tax, "The Sound of One Hand Clapping: Women's Liberation and the Left," *Dissent* (1988): 457, 461.

6. Author's interview with Barbara Haber.

7. Carol Lynn Withers, "The High Cost of Being a Woman," *Village Voice*, March 24, 1987, 31; author's interview with Carol Groneman; author's interview with Robin Morgan, April 18, 1986, New York City.

8. Author's interview with Lucinda Cisler.

9. Cisler interview.

10. Author's interview with Marilyn Webb.

11. Phyllis Chesler, *Letters to a Young Feminist*, 54.
12. Author's interview with Barbara Haber.
13. Naomi Weisstein self-interview for Peg Strobel, 26; author's interview with Naomi Weisstein.
14. Naomi Weisstein self-interview for Peg Strobel, 37, 41.
15. Chesler, 56; author's interview with Ann Snitow, April 16, 1986, New York City; Chesler, 57. All of the above stories are from author's interview with Susan Brownmiller, April 14, 1986, New York City.
16. Chesler, 56–57.
17. Author's interview with Robin Morgan.
18. Author's interview with Alix Kates Shulman, April 13, 1987, New York City.
19. Erica Jong, "Men Are Not the Problem," in *Fear of Fifty* (New York: Harper-Collins, 1994), 327.
20. Jong, *Fear*, 328. Note that Jong points out that both Naomi Wolf and Katie Roiphe revealed their discomfort with women as victims, and women as passive sexual recipients.
21. Thom, *Inside Ms.*, 76.
22. For a view from the perspective of *Ms.* magazine, see Thom, 74–79; John Ranelagh, *The Agency: The Rise and Decline of the CIA* (New York: Simon and Schuster, 1997). Direct quote from *New York Times*, February 21, 1967.
23. Heilbrun, *Education*, 290.
24. Heilbrun, 290.
25. Friedan, *It Changed My Life*, 179.
26. Carolyn Heilbrun tells the story of this accusation in her biography of Gloria Steinem, *The Education of a Woman*, 284–95. All quotes, unless otherwise noted, are from this work; Heilbrun, 294.
27. Quoted from Counterintelligence Program Memo, "Concerning Disruption of the New Left" in Brian Glick, *The War at Home* (Boston: South End Press, 1989), 27, 80. FBI letter, August 25, 1970, excerpted in Glick, 77.
28. Although the FBI exacerbated this division, there is not sufficient evidence, as of yet, that they worked to create a separatist women's movement. I would not be surprised, however, to eventually discover that evidence. Still, a women's movement would have emerged without FBI infiltration.
29. FBI WLM Files, SL. Also reprinted in Pogrebin, 38.
30. Paul Cowan, Nick Eglesson, and Nat Hentoff, *State Secret: Police Surveillance in America* (Holt, Rinehart & Winston, 1974).
31. *Hearings Before the Select Committee to Study Governmental Operations with Respect to Intelligence Activities of the United States Senate*, 94th Congress, 1st sess., volume 6, November 18–19 and October 1, 3, 10, 11, 1975 (Washington, D.C.: U.S. Government Printing Office, 1976), 100.
32. Glick, 27.
33. May 23, 1968, Document Exhibit from Church Committee hearings.
34. Memo from S.F. Office to Director, FBI, May 13, 1969. Charlotte Bunch Papers, Schlesinger Library; Letty Cottin Pogrebin, "The FBI Was Watching You," *Ms.*, June 1977, along with all the excerpts she included in this issue, 75; FBI WLM Files, SL.

35. S.F. Agent to Director, FBI, May 1970, WLM FBI Files, SL.
36. S.F. Field Office to Director, February 24, 1971, Charlotte Bunch Papers, SL; Letter from Bureau to Chicago Regional Office, May 11, 1970, FBI WLM Files, SL; Memo from S.F. Field Office, re: Women's Liberation Movement, FBI Files, April 25, 1973, SL; Letty Pogrebin, "The FBI," *Ms.*, June 1977, 72.
37. Memo from Director, FBI, to S.F. Field Office, June 5, 1969, FBI WLM Files, SL.
38. Pogrebin, 38, 44.
39. Summary of story in October 19, 1970, *S.F. Examiner*, entitled "S.F. Women's Lib Support Angela Davis," FBI WLM Files, S.F. Region, SL.
40. Pogrebin, 44.
41. Letty Pogrebin, "The FBI Was Watching You," *Ms.*, June 1977, excerpt, 39.
42. FBI WLM Files, SL.
43. FBI WLM Files, SL.
44. "Who Joined Women's Lib and Why," Informant report, S.F. Section, FBI WLM Files, SL.
45. Pogrebin, *Ms.*, 75. For more information on these feminist groups that worked to improve the lives of working women, see, for example, "The Union Women's Alliance to Gain Equality (WAGE) Organizing Statement," 73; "The Bill of Rights for Women Office Workers," Nine to Five, 73; Union WAGE, "Purpose and Goals," 74; Al Lannon, ILGWU Local 6, "Antisexism at Work," 75; Karen Nussbaum, "We Have the Power of Women," 71, in Shapiro, *The Women Say . . .* ; WLM Berkeley FBI Files, 1970, SL.
46. Pogrebin, 37.
47. Memo from S.F. Office to Director, Re: Black Panther Party, Racial Matters, Women's Liberation Movement, FBI WLM Files. "Stormy Scene for Women's Liberation," *People's World*, July 26, 1969, Charlotte Bunch Papers, FBI clipping, SL; Grand juries assembled to ask women where the fugitives were. WLM Files, SL; Glick, *War at Home*, 27; *Off Our Backs* (April/May 1975): 1; also see article written by Jeanne Cordova, "FBI Hot on Underground Trail," n.d., unpaginated, in Charlotte Bunch Papers, SL.
48. Letter to Director, Domestic Intelligence Division, New York and Alexandria, from Washington Field Office on "Women's National March on the Pentagon, April 20th, 1971." Teletype, FBI Files, SL. Copy of letter with many deletions with the heading "Women's National March on the Pentagon, April 10, 1971." The letter to Madame Binh is dated March 25, 1971. Summary analysis of a variety of stories from the *S.F. Chronicle*. Titled "Anne Bitterfeld Scheer," July 19, 1968, FBI WLM files, SL.
49. Teletype from New York Office to Bureau, March 9, 1972. FBI WLM Files, SL.
50. Glick, in *The War at Home*, makes a persuasive case that surveillance of domestic groups continued during the seventies and eighties under new FBI programs and includes evidence of this continued surveillance; letter from Letty Cottin Pogrebin, April 1977, to subscribers of *Ms.*, FBI Files, SL.
51. WLM Files, section on Berkeley Activities, SL.

52. To protect the privacy of these activists, I have not used their actual names or any names. These files were obtained through the FOIA; FBI WLM Files, S.F. Bay Area Activities, SL.

53. Margo St. James, "FBI Expose," *COYOTE HOWLS: The Intermittent Journal of a Loose Woman's Organization* (August 1977): 4.

54. Robin Morgan, *Going Too Far*, 185.

55. See, for example, Angus Mackenzie, *Secrets*. Betty Friedan, FBI WLM Files, SL, reprinted in *Ms.* under "Excerpts from the Files," 42.

56. Author's interview with Betty Friedan, April 4, 1986, Santa Monica, California.

57. Author's interview with Marilyn Webb. Author's interview with Irene Peslikis.

58. Susan Sherman, *The Color of the Heart: Writing from Struggle and Change, 1959–1990* (Willlamantic, Conn: Curbstone Press, 1990), 105.

59. Author's interview with Candace Falk, May 15, 1986, Berkeley, California.

60. Author's interviews with Candace Falk and Charlotte Bunch, April 13, 1987, New York City.

61. Redstockings, "Press Release," May 9, 1975, APA; author's interview with Ti-Grace Atkinson, April 9, 1987, New York City, and Joan Peters, April 16, 1986, and September 26, 1997, New York City. For movement documents, see "Redstocking Challenge," in *Off Our Backs* (July 1975): 10ff. Much of the chronology, the charges, and the inquiries are in this issue.

62. Author's interview with Alix Kates Shulman.

63. This information comes from the following documents, some of which Alix Kates Shulman and Joan Peters gave me, for which I thank them once again. "An Analysis of Sagaris, Inc. by the August 7th Survival Community"; "Statement of the August 7th Committee"; "The August 7th Survival Community Newsletter," all in APA. Also see "Our New Community," "Budget of Sagaris," "Sagaris: Table of Contents, Description, Self Criticism," all in Charlotte Bunch Papers, SL.

64. Author's interview with Joan Peters, September 16, 1997, New York City.

65. Judith Coburn, "Sisterhood Is Not Magic," *Village Voice*, April 1975. A few weeks later, Coburn published a longer and more detailed inquiry in *The Real Paper*, Boston, circa April, 1975. Author's interview with Judy Coburn, September 29, 1997.

66. Author's interview with Alix Kates Shulman. Other information comes from Carolyn Heilbrun's account of the Sagaris in her biography of Gloria Steinem, *The Education*.

67. Author's interview with Joan Peters.

68. Pogrebin, 41.

Chapter Eight: The Proliferation of Feminism

1. Naomi Weisstein and Heather Booth, "Will the Women's Movement Survive?" Position paper published by Sister, Wynn, 250 Howard Avenue, New Haven. Women's Liberation Files, Tamiment Library, New York University.

2. "What Has Gone Wrong with the Women's Movement?" *Harper's Bazaar*, February 1976, 59, 60.

3. Both of these women prefer to retain their anonymity. The Jewish woman ex-

perienced this surprise at the Kehilla temple in Berkeley, California, in 1987. The Methodist woman found this change when she returned to Ohio in 1990.

4. Barbara Ferraro, Patricia Hussey, with Jane O'Reilly, *No Turning Back: Two Nuns' Battle with the Vatican over Women's Right to Choose* (New York: Poseidon, 1990), 76.

5. See the Bibliography.

6. The best and most recent study of this academic revolution is Marilyn Boxer, *When Women Asked the Questions: Creating Women's Studies in America* (Baltimore: Johns Hopkins University, 1999). Also see Ellen Dubois et al., eds., *Feminist Scholarship: Kindling in the Groves of Academe* (Chicago: University of Illinois Press, 1985), especially part 3, "The Response from the Disciplines," and Christie Farnham, *The Impact of Feminist Research in the Academy* (Bloomington, Indiana: Indiana University Press, 1987), for a good idea of how far feminist scholarship altered the disciplines by the mid-eighties.

7. Interview with Gerda Lerner by author, February 10, 1998, Berkeley, California.

8. Kris Montgomery, "The Story of Women's History Month: Reclaiming the Past, Rewriting the Future," in *Women Change America Gazette* (Sonoma: National Women's History Project, 1997), APA. Author's telephone interview with Molly MacGregor, November 3, 1997. Personal letter from Gerda Lerner to Ruth Rosen, October 21, 1997, in which she describes the founding of the institute.

9. Mary Kay Blakely, "Growing Girls and Grandmothers," *Ms.*, June 1987, 12.

10. In Shapiro and Shapiro, *The Women Say*, see Denise D'Anne, "Working Women on Welfare," 64; Lynn O'Connor, Fred Garner, and Par Mialocq, "Office Politics," 45–51; Union WAGE, "Organizing Statement," 73; Nine to Five, "The Bill of Rights for Women Office Workers," 73; Union WAGE, "Purpose and Goals," 74; Karen Nussbaum, "We Have the Power of Women!" 71; Jesusita Novarro, "I Am a Working Mother," 72.

11. The socialist feminists of Dayton received some support from NAM, the New American Movement, which tried to organize workers throughout the country.

12. Judith Sealander and Dorothy Smith, "The Rise and Fall of Feminist Organizations in the 1970s: Dayton as a Case Study," *Feminist Studies* 12:2 (Summer 1986), 221–339.

13. Nancy Whittier's study, *Feminist Generations*, of Columbus, Ohio, was extremely useful, as was Judy Ezekiel's "Une contribution à l'histoire du mouvement feministe americain: l'etude du cas de Dayton, Ohio (1969–1980)." Unpublished dissertation, Paris, 1987, APA.

14. Robin Morgan, "Rites of Passages," *Ms.*, September 1975, 76.

15. Patricia Huckle, *Tish Sommers, Activist and the Founding of the Older Women's League* (Knoxville, Tenn.: University of Tennessee Press, 1991), 211.

16. Letter from Ida G. Rosen to author, January 1976, APA.

17. For a fuller discussion of the postsuffrage and postfeminist eras, see Rayna Rapp and Ellen Ross, "It Seems We've Stood and Talked Like This Before," *Ms.*, April 1983, 54–56.

18. Geneva Overholser, "What 'Post-Feminism' Really Means," *New York Times*,

September 19, 1986, 30; for an analytic attempt to distinguish antifeminism from postfeminism, see Deborah Rosenfelt and Judith Stacey, "Second Thoughts on the Second Wave," *Feminist Studies* 13 (Summer 1987): 341–61.

19. A study conducted by Alexander W. Astin and Kenneth Green analyzed data involving almost six million students. Quoted in "College Freshmen Still Reveal Liberal Streak," *San Francisco Chronicle*, October 31, 1986, 1, 9. Tim Schreiner, "Demographic Change Is Reshaping Workforce," *San Francisco Chronicle*, October 28, 1986, 12.

20. Susan Bolotin, "Voices from the Post-Feminist Generation," *New York Times Magazine*, October 7, 1982, 28–31.

21. Bolotin, 31, 30.

22. Bolotin clearly touched a nerve. See letters she received in Susan Bolotin Collection, SL. In *Women in College: Shaping New Feminine Identities* (New York, 1985) 89–92, 225–300, Mirra Komarovsky showed that college women felt that finding one's place in the world of work had become essential to one's personal dignity in this generation, yet a career without marriage was the choice of only 2 percent of the sample. An intimate article by Abigail Pogrebin discloses her relationship to her mother's feminism in "Bridges: Divided Loyalties," *Glamour*, June 1996, 100.

23. Naomi Wolf quoted by Diane Salvatore, "Young Feminists Speak for Themselves," 89. Leslie Heywood and Jennifer Drake, eds. *Third Wave Agenda: Being Feminist, Doing Feminism* (Minneapolis: University of Minnesota, 1997), 124. See Paula Kamen, *Feminist Fatale: Voices from the "Twenty Something" Generation Explore the Future of the "Women's Movement"* (New York: Fine, 1991).

24. Toni Cade, *The Black Woman* (New York: New American Library, 1970); Celestine Ware, *Woman Power* (New York: Tower 1970); Linda LaRue "The Black Movement and Women's Liberation," in *The Black Scholar*, 1:7 (May 1970); Gloria Hull, "My Life," APA; Toni Morrison, "Interview with Claudia Tate," *Black Women Writers at Work*, Claudia Tate, ed. (New York: Continuum, 1983), 117–31, quote from p. 122.

25. See Linda La Rue, "The Black Movement and Women's Liberation," *Black Scholar*, 1 (1970), 42, from Third World Women's Alliance, "Black Women's Manifesto," n.d.; Linda La Rue, "Black Liberation and Women's Lib," *Transaction* (November–December 1970); Toni Morrison, "What the Black Woman Thinks About Women's Lib," *New York Times Magazine*, August 22, 1971; Charlayne Hunter, "Many Blacks Wary of 'Women's Liberation Movement,'" *New York Times*, November 17, 1970, 60; Angela Davis, *Angela Davis: An Autobiography* (New York: Random House, 1974); Lee Rainwater and William L. Yancey, *The Moynihan Report and the Politics of Controversy* (Cambridge, Mass.: MIT Press, 1967); and the account given by Paula Giddings, *When and Where I Enter: The Impact of Black Women on Race and Sex in America* (New York: Bantam, 1984).

26. Celestine Ware, *Woman Power*, 78, 91, 95, 99.

27. See Rivka Polatnick, "Diversity in Women's Liberation Ideology: How a

Black and White Group of the 1960's Views Motherhood," *Signs* (Spring, 1996), as well as her dissertation, "Strategies for Women's Liberation: A Study of Black and White Groups of the 1960s," La-neeta Harris, "Black Women in Junior High Schools," in Tanner, *Voices*, 216. "The Sisters Reply," September 11, 1968, Mt. Vernon, New York, responding to "Birth Control Pill and Black Children," a statement by the Black Unity Party in Peekskill, New York, n.d.; Patricia Robinson, "Poor Black Women," n.d., all in Nancy Gray Osterud Collection, SL.

28. La-neeta Harris, "Black Women in Junior High Schools," in Tanner, *Voices*, 215–16.

29. Mary Ann Weathers, "An Argument for Black Women's Liberation As a Revolutionary Force," *No More Fun and Games* (February 1969), APA. Also reprinted in Morgan, *Sisterhood*, 303–7.

30. Frances Beale, "The Double Jeopardy of Black Women," in "Documents from the Black Women's Liberation Movement," in Documents from the Women's Liberation Movement, An On-Line Archival Collection, Special Collections Library, Duke University (DU).

31. Pamela Newman, "Take a Good Look at Our Problems," DU.

32. Michelle Wallace, "On the National Black Feminist Organization," June 1975, reprinted in Redstockings, *Feminist Revolution*, 174.

33. The Combahee River Collective, *The Combahee River Collective Statement: Black Feminist Organizing in the Seventies and Eighties* (New York: Kitchen Table: Women of Color Press, 1985), pamphlet, APA.

34. Michelle Wallace, *Black Macho and the Myth of the Superwoman* (London: Verso, 1990). See her new introduction in which she explores why and how her mind has changed on a number of issues she first discussed.

35. Gloria Hull, Patricia Bell Scott, and Barbara Smith, eds., *All the Women Are White, All the Blacks Are Men, and Some of Us Are Brave* (New York: Feminist Press, 1982). Extensive bibliographies on minority women's history can be found in Ellen Carol DuBois and Vicki Ruiz, eds., *Unequal Sisters: A Multicultural Reader in U.S. Women's History* (New York: Routledge, 1997).

36. One of the best examples of this community work occurred in South Central Los Angeles, as well as in Oakland, California. The Women's Economic Agenda Project (WEAL) in Oakland, California, turned women's issues into economic struggles on behalf of minority women. For poll data, please see Epilogue.

37. From the PBS Documentary *Chicano! History of the Mexican American Fight for Civil Rights*, 1997.

38. Maria Varela, quoted in Morgan, *Sisterhood*, 424.

39. Vicki Ruiz, *Out of the Shadow: Mexican American Women in the Twentieth Century* (New York: Oxford, 1998), in chapter 5, La Nueva Chicana, 68. Also see Alma M. Garcia, *Chicana Feminist Thought: The Basic Historical Writings* (New York: Routledge, 1997).

40. Enriqueta Longauex y Vasquez, "The Mexican American Woman," in Morgan, *Sisterhood*, 378–79.

41. See editors, "Introduction to Encuentro Femenil," 113–17; Francisco Flores, "Comisión Femenil Mexicana," 150; Alicia Sandoval, "Chicana Liberation," 204, all in Garcia, *Chicana Feminist Thought*.

42. Nancy Nieto, "Macho Attitudes," *Hija de Cuauhtemoc*, vol. 1, no. 1, (1971). Also see Mirta Vidal, "Women: New Voice of La Raza," (New York: Pathfinder Press, 1971), reprinted in *Chicanas Speak Out*, DU.

43. Ruiz, 112.

44. "Statement by Elma Barrera," DU.

45. "Workshop Resolutions for the First National Chicana Conference," DU.

46. See Beatrice M. Pesquera and Denise A. Segura, "There Is No Going Back: Chicanas and Feminism," and Pesquera and Segura, "Talk on Chicana Feminism," April 30, 1990, Tape, U.C. Davis, 1990, APA; Segura and Pesquera, "Beyond Indifference and Antipathy: The Chicana Movement and Chicana Feminist Discourse," *Aztlan* (Fall 1988): 69–82. Also see Adalijiza Sosa Riddell, "Chicanas and El Movimiento," *Aztlan* 5:1 (1974), 155–65; Mary Pardo, *MELA* (Philadelphia: Temple University Press, 1998).

47. Gloria Anzaldua, *Borderland/La Frontera: The New Mestiza* (San Francisco: Spinster/Aunt Lute, 1987), 80.

48. Much of the writing on Native Americans is from the 1980s. But see Elsie Allen, *Pomo Basketmaking: A Supreme Art for the Weaver*, Vinson Brown, ed. (Happy Camp, California: Naturegraph Publishers, 1972), and the Bibliography.

49. Shirley Hill Witt, "Native Women Today: Sexism and the Indian Woman," *Civil Rights Digest* (Spring 1974).

50. *Ms.*, November 1977, 60.

51. *Ms.*, 60.

52. Maya Angelou, "To Form a More Perfect Union," reprinted in National Commission on the Observance of International Women's Year, *The Spirit of Houston: An Official Report to the President, the Congress and the People of the United States* (Washington, D.C., March 1978); *The Spirit of Houston*, 195.

53. *The Spirit of Houston*, 129; "The Torch Relay," 193; "Billie Jean King Statement," 202; "What the Press Said," 205; "Houston Day by Day," 119; "Feminism Now," *New York Times*, December 30, 1974, xii, 7; Also see the briefing paper prepared by the IWY Secretariat, "Women's Movement in the U.S. 1960–1975: Government's Role in the Women's Movement," Vertical File, "Women's Liberation," SL; National Commission on the Observation of International Women's Year, *Declaration of American Women* (Washington, D.C.: IWY Commission, 1977). Also see Cecelia P. Burciaga, "The 1977 National Women's Conference," 182–83, in Garcia, *Chicana Feminist Thought*.

54. *The Spirit of Houston*, 166; Also see Kay Clarenbach Oral History, Box 2, Folder 15, for more detailed stories about Houston, WHS.

Chapter Nine: Sisterhood to Superwoman

1. To the best of my knowledge, I have coined the terms "consumer feminism" and "therapeutic feminism" for this book. Others have described similar phenomena as "lifestyle feminism."

26. See chapter 2, "Female Generation Gap" for a discussion of young feminists' fears of turning into imprisoned housewives and mothers; *New York Times*, July 4, 1971, 41.

27. *New York Times*, May 14, 1974, 21.

28. *San Francisco Chronicle*, September 1971, 3; note that most of this coverage, though not all, appeared in the "family, fashions, food, and furnishings" section of the *New York Times*; *New York Times*, January 5, 1975, III, 1; *New York Times*, May 18, 1974, 6; *New York Times*, August 28, 1973, 74; *New York Times*, April 30, 1974, 37; *New York Times*, November 22, 1972, 1; *New York Times*, April 26, 1971, 44; *New York Times*, December 28, 1969, section 3, 1; *New York Times*, December 30, 1975; May 18, 1974, 6.

29. Author's interview with Judy Coburn in April 1987 and again in August 1996 in Berkeley.

30. *Ladies' Home Journal* issues from November 1979 to August 7, 1979; Marnie Ellingson, "Women's Lib, the Tooth Fairy, and other Myths," *Ladies' Home Journal*, March 1971, 116, 184–87.

31. These generalizations are from a decade of *Ladies' Home Journal*, *McCall's*, and *Redbook*, 1960–1970.

32. "Feminists vs. the Media," *New York Times*, March 14, 1972, Media Protest Files, UWA. This clipping describes a number of eventually aborted television magazine programs aimed at translating feminism to women.

33. Interview with Barbara Shields, whose name has been changed to protect her privacy. Interviewed by the author in a suburb in the state of Connecticut, in May 1988, and again in October 1998.

34. Lee Walker, "Can We Live with Women's Liberation?" speech to Association of Industrial Advertisers, June 22, 1971, Protest Files, UWA. Also see Elisabeth Cagan, "The Selling of the Women's Movement," *Social Policy* (May/June 1978); Scot Winoker, "Freud and Fashion; Tobacco Firms' Seduction of Women," *San Francisco Chronicle*, August 21, 1983, 6; "Brooke Shields Takes a Stand Against Smoking But the Government Didn't Want Her Message," *American Lung Association Bulletin* (June/July 1981); Lawrence Wallack, "Mass Media Campaigns in a Hostile Environment: Advertising as Anti-health Education," paper for Health Education and Media International Conference, March 24, 1981, Edinburgh, Scotland.

35. *New Woman*, May/June 1976, 76; Douglas, 12.

36. For a description of the new magazines, see Linda Charlton, "Feminist vs. the Me," *New York Times*, "family, food, fashion, and furnishings," section, March 14, 1972, 7, Media Protest Files, UWA.

37. Barbara Ehrenreich, "Combat in the Media Zone," *Seven Days*, 2 (March 10, 1978), 14.

38. "To Gain Power in the Office—Wear a Jacket," *New Woman*, May/June 1976, 93.

39. For a discussion of how suits created an abstract vision of male authority and attractiveness, see Anne Hollander, *Sex and Suits* (New York: Kodansha Books, 1994); *New Woman*, May/June 1976, 93.

40. See, for example, the well-know BEM scale that was developed during the

1970s. Sandra Bem, *Homogenizing the American Woman* (Pittsburgh: Know, 1972); also see Carolyn Heilbrun's classic text from that era, *Toward a Recognition of Androgyny* (New York: Knopf, 1973); "New Relationship with Fashion for Many Women," *New York Times*, August 5, 1996, 1, C9.

41. See, for example, Arlie Hochschild, *The Second Shift* (Berkeley: University of California Press, 1989).

42. See Peter Carroll, *It Seemed Like Nothing Happened*, which was prescient in its awareness of what had truly changed and what was media hype.

43. Quoted by Ellen Goodman, *Close to Home* (New York: Simon and Schuster, 1979), 32.

44. See *Monterey Peninsula Guide*, which describes Huxley's lecture to the University of California at San Francisco Medical Center in 1960 (Carmel, California: Somerset Publications, 1997).

45. See, for example, Phyllis Chesler, *Women and Madness* (New York: Doubleday, 1972); Jean Baker Miller, *Toward a New Psychology of Women* (New York: Brunner, 1973); Nancy Chodorow, *The Reproduction of Mothering* (Berkeley: University of California Press, 1978); Dorothy Dinnerstein, *Mermaids and Minotaurs: Sexual Arrangement and Human Malaise* (New York: Harper, 1977).

46. Carol Tavris, "Women and Man," *Psychology Today*, March 1972, 57, 58, 61. For a more detailed discussion of the print media and the women's movement, see Theresa Kaminski, "These Chicks Are Our Natural Enemy: Women's Liberation Rhetoric and the Print Media," unpublished chapter of dissertation, paper presented at 1993 Berkshire Conference on Women's History, Vassar; and Ellen Gruber Garvey, *The Adman in the Parlor: Magazines and the Gendering of Consumer Culture, 1880s–1910* (New York: Oxford University Press, 1996).

47. Sondra Ray, "Affirmations That Can Change Your Life," *New Woman*, January/February 1976, 75.

48. Dorothy Tennov, *Super Self: A Woman's Guide to Self-Management* (New York: Funk and Wagnalls, 1977). Dorothy Jongeward and Dru Scott, *Women as Winners: Transactional Analysis for Personal Growth* (Reading, Mass.; Addison-Wesley Publishing Company, 1976). Stanlee Phelps and Nancy Austin, *The Assertive Woman* (San Luis Obispo: Impact, 1975). See especially chapter 5, "From Apology to Power."

49. "Assertiveness—Learning a Kind of Honesty," *San Francisco Chronicle*, November 10, 1975. Phelps and Austin, *The Assertive Woman*, 3.

50. Jean Baer, *How to Be an Assertive (Not Aggressive) Woman in Life, in Love and on the Job: A Total Guide to Self-Assertiveness* (New York: Rawson Associates Publishers, 1976); Ehrenreich, 14.

51. Reprinted from *Publisher's Weekly*, February 3, 1975, in Reference and Directory Information, 417.

52. Claire Safran, "The Total Woman: Is She Happy?" *New Woman*, 1977, 40, reprinted from *Redbook*, February 1976. Marabel Morgan, *The Total Woman* (New York: Pocket Books, 1973), 45.

53. Morgan, 36, 61, 82, 97.

54. David Reuben, *Any Woman Can! Love and Sexual Fulfillment for the Single, Widowed, Divorced, and Married* (New York: D. McKay, 1971). For information on how bestsellers changed during the seventies, see *The Bowker Annual Book Trade Statistics*, based on actual sales reports of bookstores, p. 118 and p. 136.

55. Helen Gurley Brown, *Having It All* (New York, Pocket Books, 1982), 2.

56. Brown, 66.

57. Ella Taylor, *Prime Time Families: Television Culture in Postwar America* (Berkeley: University of California Press, 1989). See especially chapters 4 and 5. For a good analysis of the production of prime-time television during the seventies, see Todd Gitlin, *Inside Prime Time* (Berkeley: University of California Press, 1983), especially chapter 10, "The Turn Toward 'Relevance.'"

58. Chapter 10, Gitlin, *Inside*, explains how television producers tried to have it both ways, thus appealing to the largest possible audience during the 1970s, 213.

59. Gitlin, *Inside*, 158.

60. For a good appraisal of Moore's popularity see Tracy Johnston, "Why 30 Millions Are Mad about Mary," *New York Times Magazine*, April 7, 1974, 30; 100.

61. There is an enormous literature on this debate, in particular, Judy Stone, "She Gave Archie His First Comeuppance," *New York Times*, November 19, 1972, 17; "300 Anti-Abortionists March on CBS in Maude Protest," *New York Times*, August 22, 1973, 75; "5 Diverse Groups Urge Action to Counter Censorship of TV," August 30, 1973, 67; "Program Pressure," *New York Times Editorial*, August 24, 1973, 32; "TV: Pressure Tactics Testing Network's Mettle," *New York Times*, August 21, 1973, 67; "28 CBS Affiliates Won't Show Maude Episodes on Abortion," *New York Times*, August 14, 1973, 63; Aljean Harmetz, "Maude Didn't Leave 'em All Laughing," *New York Times*, December 10, 1972, II, 3; Albin Krebs, "Maude Sponsorship Decline Laid to Abortion Foes," *New York Times*, August 10, 1973, 61.

62. Ironically, these work families prefigured Arlie Hochschild's informants in *The Time Bind* who reported that they increasingly regarded work as a refuge and home as too much work. Arlie Hochschild, *The Time Bind* (New York: Viking, 1997).

63. Goodman, 137.

64. "Female Friendship films" is how columnist Ellen Goodman dubbed films that explored female friendship and the competition between women who chose a career and those who lived a domestic life. Goodman, 122, 139.

65. See Judith Maybe's discussion of *Kramer vs. Kramer* in "The Woman at the Keyhole: Women's Cinema and Feminist Film Criticism," in Mary Anne Doane et al., *Re-Vision: Essays in Feminist Film Criticism* (Frederick, Md.: University Publications of America, 1984), 61–62. For a popular view of how the film mirrored growing uncertainties about changing gender roles, see

Time, December 3, 1979, 74; Vincent Canby, "Screen: *Kramer vs. Kramer*," *New York Times*, December 19, 1979, C23; Barbara Grizzuti Harrison, "Seeing," *Ms.*, January 1980; "Custody: Kramer vs. Reality," *Time*, February 4, 1980, 77; Gene Lichtenstein, "*Kramer vs. Kramer*," *Atlantic*, March 1980.

66. *Atlantic*, May 1976, 180.

67. Goodman, 84.

68. Ehrenreich, 13; See note no. 1 about the terms "consumer feminism" and "therapeutic feminism."

69. See chapters 7 to 11 in Susan Douglas, *Where the Girls Are*. For a good description and analysis of the postmodern self, see Robert J. Lifton, *The Protean Self: Human Resilience in an Age of Fragmentation* (New York: Basic Books, 1993), and Kenneth Gergen, *The Saturated Self: Dilemmas of Identity in Contemporary Life* (New York, Basic Books, 1991). *The Rise of Selfishness in America* (New York: Oxford, 1991), by James Lincoln Collier, also argues that the 1970s witnessed an accelerated move into a hyperconsumer and therapeutic culture. Warren Susman in *Culture as History: The Transformation of American Society in the Twentieth Century* (New York: Pantheon, 1973) provides an historical framework.

70. This argument is made by Anthony Rotundo in *American Manhood: Transformations in Masculinity from the Revolution to the Modern Era* (New York: Basic Books, 1993).

71. Unpublished research paper by author, 1972, on what had and had not changed in the advertising promoted by women's magazines. I compared advertising in *Godey's Lady's Book* during the 1860s with *McCall's* and *Ladies' Home Journal* in the 1960s. APA.

72. A good example of radical feminists' attack against fashion and the "capitalist" commodification of bodies can be found in "Capitalists Discover Women's Liberation," Liberation News Service, undated, circa 1970, Media Protest Files, UWA; interview with Christopher Lasch, May 17, 1989, Berkeley, California.

Chapter Ten: Beyond Backlash

1. For more detailed discussions and different interpretations about why the ERA battle was lost and lasted until 1983, see Theodore S. Arrington and Patricia A. Kyle, "Equal Rights Amendment Activists in North Carolina," *Signs* (Spring 1978): 666–80; for profiles of anti-ERA opponents, see David W. Brady and Kent Tedin, "Ladies in Pink: Religion and Political Ideology in the Anti-ERA Movement," *Social Science Quarterly* 45 (March 1976): 564–75. Also see Jane De Hart Mathew and Donald Mathew, "The Cultural Politics of ERA's Defeat," *Organization of American Historians Newsletter* 10, 4 (November 1982): 13–15. See the Bibliography.

2. Midge Decter, *The New Chastity: And Other Arguments against Women's Liberation* (New York: Berkeley, 1972); Phyllis Schlafly, *The Power of the Positive Woman* (New York: Jove/HBJ, 1977); Lisa Cronin Wohl, "Phyllis Schlafly: The Sweetheart of the Silent Majority," *Ms.*, March 1974, 63, and

the longer biography by Carol Festenthal, *The Sweetheart of the Silent Majority* (New York: Doubleday, 1981).

3. Richard Viguerie, *The New Right: We're Ready to Lead* (Falls Church, Va.: The Viguerie Company, 1980), 196.

4. See Arlie Russell Hochschild, *The Second Shift* (New York: Viking, 1989).

5. See, for example, Pamela Johnston Conover and Virginia Gray, *Feminism and the New Right: Conflict over the American Family* (New York: Praeger, 1983); Andrea Dworkin, *Right-Wing Women* (New York: Perigee Books, 1983); Zillah Eisenstein, *Feminism and Sexual Equality: Crisis in Liberal America* (New York: Monthly Review Press, 1984). One of the best works that provides an historical context for the curricula battles is Lawrence Levine, *The Opening of the American Mind* (Boston: Beacon, 1996). Some of the best archival material on antifeminist sentiment can be found in a new collection called *Antifeminism in America: A Collection of Readings from the Literature of the Opponents to U.S. Feminism, 1948 to the Present*, edited with introductions by Angela Howard and Sasha Ranae Adams Tarrant (New York: Garland Press, 1997).

The literature on the cultural wars is vast. However, the majority of commentators have not recognized how deeply the gender wars have shaped the assumption of both sides in the cultural wars. See the Bibliography.

6. Those who might be included under such progressive views include Barbara Ehrenreich, Katha Pollitt, Ellen Goodman, Patricia Ireland, and Marian Wright Edelman. Hillary Rodham Clinton's controversial book *It Takes a Village: And Other Lessons Children Teach Us* (New York: Simon and Schuster, 1996), as well as Judith Stacey's *In the Name of the Family: Rethinking Family Values in the Postmodern Age* (Boston: Beacon Press, 1996), both acknowledge the atomization and fragmentation of postmodern society and try to find ways to sustain the nurture of children and families, even within these limits.

7. Christopher Lasch, *The Minimal Self: Psychic Survival in Troubled Times* (New York: W. W. Norton, 1984) and *The Culture of Narcissism: American Life in an Age of Diminishing Expectations* (New York: W. W. Norton, 1978), as well as Robert C. Bellah, et al., *Habits of the Heart: Individualism and Commitment in American Life* (Berkeley: University of California Press, 1985), all set the terms of debate on the lost sense of a common good in American culture.

8. During the baby boom (technically, 1946 to 1964), each year produced more babies. Since women tend to marry men older than themselves, they found a "shortage" of men who were older than they. Since men tend to marry younger women, men of the baby boom generation always had more women available. This peculiar demographic profile changed with the emergence of the baby bust generation in 1964, in which men found fewer young women, and women found more older available men.

9. *The Second Stage* (New York: Summit, 1981) created quite a flurry and much debate. For a sample of reviews and news about the book, see Pamela Marsh,

"Betty Friedan Calls for Less Abrasiveness, More Emphasis on the Family," *Christian Science Monitor*, October 28, 1981, 17; Susan Lee, "Just What Does She Want?" *Wall Street Journal*, December 4, 1981, 24; Bella Abzug, "Forming a Real Women's Bloc," *Nation*, November 28, 1981, 576; Ellen Willis, "Betty Friedan's 'Second Stage': A Step Backward," *Nation*, November 1, 1981, 494; Herma Hill Kay, "Do We Suffer from a Feminist Mystique?" *New York Times Book Review*, November 22, 1981, 3; Catherine Stimpson, "From Feminine to Feminist Mystique," *Ms.*, December 1981, 16; and "The Second Stage," *National Review*, February 5, 1982.

10. Carol Hanisch, "Paying the Piper: Did I Blow My Life?" *Meeting Ground: A Project of the Women's Liberation Project* (July 1989), 1–2.

11. Jane O'Reilly, *The Girl I Left Behind* (New York: Macmillan, 1980).

12. Some prominent examples of feminist utopian novels include: Suzy McKee Charnas, *Motherlines* (New York: Berkeley Books, 1978); Ursula Le Guinn, *The Left Hand of Darkness* (New York: Ace, 1969); Marge Piercy, *Woman on the Edge of Time* (New York: Fawett Crest Books, 1976); Joanna Russ, *The Female Male* (New York: Bantam Books, 1975).

13. See Lenore J. Weitzman, *The Marriage Contract, Lovers and the Law* (New York: The Free Press, 1981). For a critique of Weitzman's thesis, see Susan Faludi, *Backlash*, 19–25.

14. Arlie Hochschild quoted in Alison Cowan, "Poll Finds Women's Gains Have Taken Personal Toll," *New York Times*, August 21, 1989, 1. Also see Arlie Hochschild, *The Second Shift*.

15. Maureen Dowd, "Many Women in Polls Equate Values of Job and Family Life," *New York Times*, December 4, 1983, 1.

16. Linda Destafano and Dr. Diane Golasanto, "Most Americans Believe U.S. Men Have a Better Life," *Los Angeles Times Syndicate* and Gallup Organization, February 5, 1990, B5.

17. "Most Americans," 14, 36.

18. "Women Face the Nineties," *Time*, December 4, 1989. All stories and data described in this issue come from this cover story.

19. For other views on the gender gap, see Martha Burke and Heidi Hartmann, "Beyond the Gender Gap: A Recovery Program for the Women's Movement," *Nation*, June 10, 1996, 18–21; "Women Made the Difference," *San Francisco Chronicle*, November 7, 1996, A3; "Clinton Stresses the Concerns of Women," *New York Times*, October 28, 1996, A1; Hanna Rosin, "Sister Sledgehammer," *New Republic*, June 24, 1996, 6–49; Sidney Blumenthal, "A Doll's House," *New Yorker*, August 19, 1996, 30–33; and Pamela Guthrie O'Brian, "Women Voters: Fed Up and Furious: LHJ and the League of Women Voters Poll," *Ladies' Home Journal*, June 1996, 88ff. Also note how Bella Abzug regarded the *Gender Gap* (Boston: Houghton Mifflin, 1984).

20. "Storm over Women's Rights," *New York Times*, 1980, 20.

21. *New York Times*, 1980, 20; "Not Just 'Women's Issues,' " *New York Times*, October 25, 1984, editorial page.

22. During the 1970s, the number of women elected to state and local govern-

ment doubled. See Martin Gruberg, "From Nowhere to Where?" Women in State and Local Politics," *Social Science Journal* 21 (January 1984): 5–11.

23. The gender gap had already shown up in 1980. Women preferred Reagan to Carter by only 47 to 45 percent and men supported Reagan by a margin of 55 percent to 36 percent. Adam Clymer, "Women's Political Habits Show Sharp Change," *New York Times*, June 30, 1982, A1.

24. See, for example, Ruth Sidel, *On Her Own: Growing Up in the Shadow of the American Dream* (New York: Viking, 1990); Ruth Sidel, *Women and Children Last: The Plight of Poor Women in Affluent America* (New York: Viking, 1986); Mimi Abramovitz, *Regulating the Lives of Women: Social Welfare Policy from Colonial Times to the Present* (New York: South End Press, 1988); and Rochelle Lefkowitz and Ann Withorn, eds., *For Crying Out Loud: Women and Poverty in the United States* (New York: The Pilgrim Press, 1986). "A Quiet Revolution: How Life in One Wisconsin City Has Changed Since the Beginning of the Women's Movement," *Newsweek*, December 28, 1997, 29.

25. Oct. 25, 1985, *New York Times*, in Around the World section, clipping, APA, n.d.

26. Diana Russell and Nicole Van de Ven, eds., *The Proceedings of the International Tribunal on Crimes Against Women* (East Palo Alto: Frog in the Well, 1984). There are a number of publications and videos of the tribunal that reveal the masterful organization that preceded the conference and the impact of women's testimonies on human rights activists. See the Center for Women's Global Leadership, *Demanding Accountability: The Global Campaign and Vienna Tribunal on Violation of Women's Human Right*, Charlotte Bunch and Niamh Reilly, eds., 1996.

27. The Grameen Bank was founded by Muhamed Yunus. It began as an experimental project in 1976 and was turned into a formal financial institution in Bangladesh with seventy-five branches in 1983.

28. Kim Murphy, "U.N. Conference Tried New Tack," *San Francisco Examiner*, September 4, 1994, A5.

29. Some of the reference works that have since appeared, for example, presume the existence of global women's movements. Some valuable sources, distributed by Gale in Detroit, include: *Chronology of Women Worldwide; International Who's Who of Women; Statistical Record of Women Worldwide; Women's Information Directory; Encyclopedia of Women's Associations Worldwide; Women's Rights on Trial*, all published between 1993 and 1995. One of the single best reference works that contains an accessible evaluation of the trends affecting women's lives worldwide is *The World's Women: The Trends and Statistics 1970–1990* (New York: The United Nations, 1991), which covers economic life, population, health, childbearing, education, leadership and decision-making, and political involvement. Also see Birgitte Sorensen, *Women and Post-Conflict Reconstruction* (Geneva: The War Town Societies Project, 1998). Also see Bibliography.

30. Some of these debates took place, for example, at the Berkshire Conference on Women's History at the University of North Carolina in 1995 and at two

panels at the American Studies Association meetings in Washington, D.C., October 31–November 2, 1997. Women from nearly every continent discussed how their political culture had received or absorbed feminist ideas and how, in turn, feminist ideas were affecting their society and political culture.

31. Matilda Joslyn Gage, *History of Woman Suffrage*, vol. 3 (New York: Fowler and Wells, 1881), 1.

32. Robin Morgan, *Sisterhood Is Powerful* (New York: Bantam, 1970), xxv–xxvi.

33. Abigail Scott Duniway, *Path Breaking: An Autobiography of the Equal Suffrage Movement in Pacific Coast States* (New York: Schocken Books, 1971. Reprinted from the James, Kerns & Abbott edition of 1914), 297.

34. Muriel Rukeyser, from "Kathe Kollwitz," *The Speed of Darkness* (1968), xii.

Epilogue: Gender Matters in the New Century

1. Gloria Feldt, "Ban Those Pots and Keep This Movement Moving," *Women's eNews*, March 3, 2006, http://www.womensenews.org/.

2. Also see Jean Hardisty's *Mobilizing Resentment: Conservative Resurgence From the John Birch Society to the Promise Keepers* (New York: Beacon, 2000) about right-wing women's groups. Other important works on right-wing women's groups include Elinor Burkett, *The Right Women* (New York: Scribner, 1998); Brenda Brasher's *Godly Women* (New Brunswick: Rutgers University Press, 1998); Sylvia Bashevkin's *Women on the Defensive* (Chicago: University of Chicago Press, 1998); Rebecca Klatch, *Women of the New Right* (Philadelphia: Temple University Press, 1987) and Tanya Melich, *The Republican War Against Women* (New York: Bantam, 1996).

3. "Breaking the Silence: The Global Gag Rule's Impact on Unsafe Abortion," The Center for Reproductive Rights, October 22, 2003, http://www.crlp.org/pub_bo_ggr.html (accessed June 18, 2004).

4. Quoted in Ruth Rosen, "Abortion Rights, 30 Years Later," editorial, *San Francisco Chronicle*, January 22, 2003.

5. Study by New York–based Center for Reproductive Rights quoted in *Women's eNews*, December 31, 2005, http://www.womensenews.org/.

6. In a pamphlet published by the Heritage Foundation in 1980 titled "The Family, Feminism and the Therapeutic State," Onalee McGraw noted that the issue of child care was the first shot across the bow in the cultural wars, even before abortion. Quoted in Carole Joffe, *The Regulation of Sexuality: Experiences of Family Planning Workers* (Philadelphia: Temple University Press, 1986), 42. Joffe also describes the spread of abortion to other areas of life in "Abortion as Moral Panic," *American Sexuality*, Special Issue on "Sexual Rights and Moral Panics," June–July 2005.

7. Quoted in Ruth Rosen, "When Politics Trumps Science," editorial, *San Francisco Chronicle*, January 5, 2002.

8. "In search of Plan C: Pharmacists get caught in the debate over abortion," *The Economist*, April 7, 2005.

9. See their report at http://www.guttmacher.org/pubs/tgr/05/1/gr050107.html.

10. Waxman report: "Abstinence courses flawed," http://www.washingtonpost.com/wp-dyn/articles/A26623 (accessed December 1, 2004).

11. Stephanie Coontz, *Marriage, A History: From Obedience to Intimacy, Or How Love Conquered Marriage* (New York: Penguin, 2005) describes this decline and transformation of the American family.

12. All interviews, quotes, and observations by the author, who was then working as a columnist at the *San Francisco Chronicle*. From notes taken on February 17, 2004.

13. See Leslie Heywood, ed., *The Women's Movement Today, An Encyclopedia of Third Wave Feminism* (Two Volumes) (Westport, CT: Greenwood Press, 2005).

14. Melissa Klein, "Duality and Redefinition: Young Feminism and the Alternative Music Community," in Leslie Heywood and Jennifer Drake, eds., *Third Wave Agenda: Being Feminist, Doing Feminism* (Minneapolis: University of Minnesota Press, 1997), 215.

15. Griselda Pollack, "Tracing Figures of Presence, Naming Ciphers of Absence; Feminism, Imperialism and Postmodernity in the Work of Sutapa Biswas," in Lisa Bloom, ed., *With Other Eyes: Looking at Race and Gender in Visual Culture* (Minneapolis: University of Minnesota Press, 1999), 237.

16. This is described in Women's Action Coalition, http://www.lib.umb.edu/archives/wac.html.

17. Jennifer Baumgardner and Amy Richards, *Manifesta: Young Women, Feminism, and the Future* (New York: Farrar, Straus and Giroux, 2000), http://www.3rdwwwave.com/ (accessed Nov. 18, 2005).

18. See Astrid Henry, *Not My Mother's Sister: Generational Conflict and Third-Wave Feminism* (Bloomington: Indiana University Press, 2004) for a generational analysis.

19. "Feminism, Fashion Can Go Hand in Hand," *Chicago Tribune*, April 20, 2005.

20. Hannah Seligson, "Campus Women Wear Feminism on Their Chests," *Women's eNews*, February 24, 2006, http://www.womensenews.org/. These shirts were sold by the Feminist Majority after 2003.

21. Deb Stoller of *Bust* magazine enthusiastically helped revive a third wave knitting mania and wrote three books on knitting, including *Stitch and Bitch: The Knitter's Handbook* (New York: Workman Publishing Company, 2004).

22. Michelle Karp, "Herstory: Girl on Girls," in Karp and Stoller, *The Bust Guide to the New Girl Order* (New York: Penguin, 1999), 310.

23. Rebecca Walker, "Lusting For Freedom," in Barbara Findlen, ed., *Listen Up 2 Ed: Voices from the Next Feminist Generation* (Seattle: Seal Press, 2001), which first appeared in *Ms.* magazine, January 1992. For other work not already cited, see Naomi Wolf, *The Beauty Myth* (New York: Anchor, 1992); Rebecca Walker, *To Be Real: Telling the Truth and Changing the Face of Feminism* (New York: Anchor, 1995); Kristin Rowe-Finkbeiner, *The F Word: Feminism in Jeopardy: Women, Politics and the Future* (Seattle: Seal Press, 2004); Paula Kamen, *Her Way: Young Women Remake the Sexual Revolution* (New York: New York University Press, 2000); Daisy Hernandez and Bushra

Rehman, eds., *Colonize This! Young Women of Color on Today's Feminism*, (Seattle: Seal Press, 2002); Rory Dicker and Allison Peipmeier, eds., *Catching a Wave: Reclaiming Feminism for the 21ˢᵗ Century*, (Boston: Northeastern University Press, 2003); Vivien Labaton and Dawn Lundy Martin, eds., *The Fire This Time: Young Activists and the New Feminism* (New York: Anchor, 2004); Ophira Edut, ed., *Body Outlaws: Young Women Write About Body Image and Identity* (Seattle: Seal Press, 2003); Jo Regal, *Different Wavelengths: Studies of the Contemporary Women's Movement* (New York: Routledge, 2005). Important articles I've drawn upon include "Writing the Wave: A Dialogue on the Tools, Tactics and Tensions of Feminist Practices over Time and Place," *NWSA Journal* 17:1 (March 2005); Catherine Orr, "Charting the Currents of the Third Wave," *Hypatia* 12, no. 3 (1997); Kimberly Springer, "Third Wave Black Feminism?" *Signs* 27 (2002), 1059–82; Gayle Wald, "Just a Girl? Rock Music, Feminism, and the Cultural Construction of Female Youth," *Signs* 23 (1998), 585–610; Kathleen Hanna, "Riot Grrrl Manifesto" (1991) in Jessica Rosenberg and Gitana Garofalo, "Riot Grrrl: Revolutions from Within," *Signs* 23 (January 1998), 812–13; Susan Archer Mann and Douglas J. Huffman, "The Decentering of Second Wave Feminism and the Rise of the Third Wave" in *Science and Society*, Vol. 69, no. 1, Jan. 2005, 56–91.

24. E-mail from Lisa Jarvis to author, August 29, 2005.

25. Ricki Wilchins, "Women Rights are Human Rights," in Joan Nestle, Riki Wilchins, Clare Howell, eds., *Genderqueer: Voices from Beyond the Sexual Binary*," (Alyson Publications, 2002), 290.

26. Heywood and Drake, *Being Feminist, Doing Feminism*, 138.

27. E-mail from Carter Ann Mahdavi to author, February 2006. The URL is http://www.worldfeminism.com.

28. Lisa Jervis, letter from Emily, unpublished, sent by e-mail to author and which appeared in *Women's eNews*, December 12, 2005.

29. Quoted in Dawn Bates and Maureen C. McHugh, "Zines: Voices of Third Wave Feminists" in Regal, *Different Wavelengths*, 191.

30. *Manifesta*, 21. These goals were also articulated by young feminists at a meeting attended by the author with the Third Wave Foundation and Ms. Foundation, October 2004.

31. Ruth Rosen, "Bush Mobilizes Women," column, *San Francisco Chronicle*, April 19, 2004.

32. Jennifer Baumgardner, Amy Richards, and Winona LaDuke, *Grassroots: A Field Guide for Feminist Activism* (New York: Farrar, Strauss and Giroux, 2005).

33. Phone interview with Francesca Vietor, November 2004, Berkeley, California.

34. E-mail interview with the author, January 15, 2006. See also, "Plan A" by Claire Miller, a 2006 unpublished journalism masters thesis, University California, Berkeley, that vividly evokes the obsessive planning that has consumed the young women of her generation.

35. Interviews with the author, July 6, 2004. They asked that their names not be used.

36. Luchina Fisher, "Working Women Delay, Forego, Rethink Motherhood," *Women's eNews*, http://www.womensenews.org/article.cfm/dyn/aid/1592.

37. E-mail to author, December 2005, from Annie Tummino, a young feminist

working with the Social Wage Committee of Redstockings Allies and Veterans (www.redstockings.org).

38. Arlie Hochschild, The *Commercialization of Intimate Life* (Berkeley: University of California Press, 2003); Joan Tronto, *Moral Boundaries: A Political Argument for an Ethic of Care* (New York: Routledge, 1993), and Mona Harrington, *Care and Equality: Inventing a New Family Politics* (New York: Knopf, 1999), have all made arguments for an ethic of care.

39. Hochschild, *Commercialization*, 38.

40. Caryl Rivers and Rosalind Chait Barnett, "Housework Gap Closes for Dual-Earner Couples," citing 2003 study, "Housework Gap Closes for Dual-Earner Couples," conducted by the Families and Work Institute, *Women eNews*, February 2, 2006, http://www.womensenews.org/. See the Census Bureau "American Time Use Survey" (2004), http://www.bls.gov/news.release/atus.toc.htm, that showed that working men worked half as much as working women. However, in the case of dual-income couples, that had changed. See "Housework Gap Closes for Dual-Earner Couples," http://www.womensenews.org/article.cfm/dyn/aid/2082. A 2002 study done at the University of Michigan found that, on average, men do sixteen hours per week of housework to women's twenty-seven. It also found that men's household hours increased by four hours between 1965 and 1985, but have not increased since then. Also see the National Study of the Changing Workforce released by the Families and Work Institute in New York, 2002, http://www.familiesandwork.org/announce/2002NSCW.html.

41. Arlie Hochschild, *The Second Shift* (New York: Viking, 1989); Arlie Hochschild, "Who will care for the Elderly," op-ed, *The Los Angeles Times*, June 26, 2006.

42. Arlie Hochschild, *The Time Bind* (New York: Henry Holt, 1997); John de Graef, *Take Back Your Time* (Berret and Koehler, 2003), http://www.timeday.org; Juliet Shor, *The Overworked American: The Unexpected Decline of Leisure* (New York: Basic Books, 1993). Also see the Labor Project for Working Families, http://www.laborproject.org/.

43. Anju Mary Paul, "Work-Life Imbalance Acute for Hourly Wage Parents," *Women's eNews*, April 4, 2006, http://www.womensenews.org/.

44. "Family-Friendly Companies Reap Economic Rewards," *Working Mother*, September 7, 2000.

45. For the disadvantages experienced by academic women, for example, see Mason, M.A. & M. Goulden (2004), "Do Babies Matter (Part II)? Closing the Baby Gap," *Academe*, November–December 2004; Mason, M.A. & M. Goulden (2004), "Marriage and Baby Blues: Redefining Gender Equity in the Academy," *The Annals of the American Academy of Political and Social Science*, 596, no. 1, 86–103; and Mason, M.A., & M. Goulden, "Do Babies Matter: The Effect of Family Formation on the Lifelong Careers of Academic Men and Women," *Academe*, November–December 2002, Vol. 88, no. 6.

46. Ellen Galinsky, http://www.familiesandwork.org/announce/2002NSCW.html.

47. "The Stay-at-Home Mom Mystique," By Rebecca Traistor, *Salon.com*, December 6, 2005. http://dir.salon.com/story/mwt/feature/2005/12/06/total_180/index.

48. Such stories appeared in, for example, *The New York Times Magazine*, *The American Prospect*, *Time* magazine, the *Chicago-Sun Times*, the *Toronto Star*, *The Atlantic* magazine, the *San Francisco Chronicle*, and was broadcast by *60 Minutes*. For thoughtful critiques, see Susan J. Douglas, "The *Times* Disses Women," *In these Times*, November 23, 2005; Katha Pollitt, "Desperate Housewives of the Ivy League?" *The Nation*, October 15, 2005; Jack Shafer, "Weasel-Words Rip My Flesh! Spotting a Bogus Trend Story on Page One of Today's *New York Times*," *Slate*, September 20, 2005; Caryl Rivers and Rosalind C. Barnett, "Why Dowd Doesn't Know What Men Really Want," *Women's eNews*, November 11, 2005, www.womensenews.org/article.cfm/clyn/aid/2512.

49. Linda Hirschman credits herself with coining this term. Her essay "Homeward Bound" on the *American Prospect* Web site ignited a national discussion about "choice feminism." November 21, 2005, http://www.prospect.org/web/page.ww?section=root&name=ViewWeb&articleId=10659. Also see Linda Hirshman, *Get to Work: A Manifesto for Women of the World* (New York: Viking, 2006); Claudia Goldin, "Working It Out," *The New York Times*, March 15, 2006, A27; *Stephanie Coontz*, "Myth of the Opt-Out Mom," *The Christian Science Monitor*, posted on AlterNet.org, April 3, 2006; and Anju Mary Paul, "Work-Life Imbalance Acute for Hourly Wage Parents," *Women's eNews*, April 4, 2006, http://www.womensenews.org/, all argue that the media have selectively based their stories on relatively comfortable women, rather than ordinary working mothers. Joan C. William, a law professor, authored "One Sick Child Away from Being Fired: When Opting Out Is Not an Option," Center for Work Life Law, University of California-Hastings, March 14, 2006, which specifically focuses on women paid by the hour, rather than by salary, www.vchastings.edu/site_files/onesickchild.pdf. Also see The Project on Global Working Families, http://www.hsph.harvard.edu/globalworking families, Corporate Voice for Working Families, http://www.cvworking families.org/.

49. Jane Gross, "In a Word: The Daughter Track" *Week in Review*, *The New York Times*, December 26, 2005.

50. Barbara Cohn Schlachet, "Why Should It All Be Up to Women?" *The New York Times*, January 18, 2006, A22.

51. Caitlin Flanagan, *To Hell with All That* (New York: Little Brown, 2006). A whole slew of books about the Mommy Wars appeared in 2005–2006. See, in particular, *Mommy Wars*, Leslie Morgan Steiner, ed. (New York: Random House, 2006) and Miriam Peskowitz, *The Truth Behind the Mommy Wars: Who Decides What Makes a Good Mother?* (Emeryville, California: Seal Press, 2006).

52. "What Women Want: A Rebuttal to the Times" by Linda Basch, Ilene Lange, and Deborah Merrill-Sands, Alternet.org, http://alternet.org/mediaculture/26326/ctober 3, 2005.

53. Diana Kapp, "Trials of the New Stay-at-Home Supermoms—Parent Trap, Part II," *San Francisco Magazine*, 54. April 2006.

54. Sheryls Nance-Nash, "Those Who Step Out of Career Face Tough Re-entry," *Women's eNews*, December 18, 2005, http://www.womensenews.org/, based on

a study conducted by the Wharton Center for Leadership and Change Management, "Back in the Game: Women's Stories and Strategies for Returning To Business after a Hiatus," http://leadership.wharton.upenn.edu/digest/05-05.shtml.

55. Barbara Ehrenreich, *Bait and Switch: The (Futile) Pursuit of the American Dream* (New York: Metropolitan Books, 2005).

56. See Fred Bloch, Anna Korteweg, and Kerry Woodward, "The Compassion Gap in American Poverty Policy," *Contexts* 5:2, Spring 2006, 14–20.

57. Women's Policy Research Institute report quoted in *Women's eNews*, December 31, 2005, http://www.womensenews.org/.

58. See Ann Crittenden, *The High Price of Motherhood: Why the Most Important Job in the World Is Still the Least Valued* (New York: Owl, 2002); Nancy Folbre, *The Invisible Heart: Economics and Family Values* (New Press, 2001), and Claudia Goldin, *Understanding the Gender Gap: An Economic History of American Women* (New York: Oxford, 1990); Center For American Progress, August 30, 2005; and National Women's Law Center in Washington, D.C., quoted in *Women's eNews*, December 31, 2005.

59. "Meritocracy in America: Ever higher society, ever harder to ascend," *The Economist*, December 29, 2004.

60. Quoted in Ruth Rosen, "Helping the Working Poor," editorial, *San Francisco Chronicle*, April 26, 2002.

61. From Ellen Reese, *Backlash Against Welfare Mothers* (Berkeley: University of California Press, 2005), 198.

62. See the excellent essays in Barbara Ehrenreich and Arlie Hochschild, eds., *Global Woman: Nannies, Maids, and Sex Workers in the New Economy* (New York: Owl, 2003) from which some of this discussion derives, especially the international care deficit and the "feminization of migration."

63. Diane Wolf, *Factory Daughters: Gender, Household Dynamics, and Rural Industrialization in Java* (Berkeley: University of California Press, 1994) also discusses some of the benefits such workers have experienced.

64. Department of Economic and Social Affairs, Division for the Advancement of Women, *2002 World Survey on the Role of Women in Development and Women and International Migration* (U.N. New York, 2005).

65. Juliette Terzieff, "New Law Puts Brakes on International Bride Brokers," *Women's eNews*, March 5, 2006, http://www.womensenews.org/.

66. Ayaan Hirsi Ali, "Women Go 'Missing' by the Millions," *International Herald Tribune*, March 25, 2006.

67. Quoted in *Women's eNews*, December 31, 2005.

68. Katherine Zoepf, "U.N. Finds That 25% of Married Syrian Women Have Been Beaten," *New York Times*, April 11, 2006.

69. Quoted in Ruth Rosen, "When Women Decide," editorial, *San Francisco Chronicle*, March 18, 2002.

70. Barbara Swirski, "What is a Gender Audit," Center for Equality and Social Justice in Israel, August 2002, www.adva.org/genderbudgetsenglish.htm and www.adva.org/bender, European Parliament, Committee on Women's Rights

and Equal Opportunities, "Public Hearing 'Gender Budgeting,'" January 23, 2003, Harvard Study quoted in Anju Mary Paul, "Work-Life Imbalance," *Women's e-news*, March 4, 2006, http://www.womensenews.org/.

71. Anju Mary Paul, "More Women are MPs" *Women's eNews*, March 4, 2006, http://www.womensenews.org/.

72. Anju Mary Paul, "Work Life Imbalance," *Women's eNews*, April 4, 2006, http://www.womensenews.org/.

73. Kavita Ramdas, www.globalfundforwomen.org/press/news/2001/chronicle-window.html (accessed June 20, 2006).

74. The secretary-general in "Message on International Day, Says Violence Against Women Atrocious Manifestation of Continued Systematic Discrimination, Inequality," http://www.unis.unvienna.org/unis/pressrels/2005/sgsm 10225.html (accessed November 25, 2005).

75. Evelyn Murphy with E. J. Graff, *Getting Even: Why Women Don't Get Paid Like Men—and What to Do About It*. (New York: Touchstone, 2005).

76. Kapp, "Trials of the New Stay-at-Home Supermoms—Parent Trap, Part II," 58.

77. Rosen, "Bush Mobilizes Women."

78. Ellen Goodman: "Single and Not Voting," *The Boston Globe*, March 3, 2006. Also see appendix in Celinda Lake, Kellyanne Conway, and Catherine Whitney, *What Women Really Want: How American Women Are Quietly Erasing Political, Racial, Class, and Religious Lines to Change the Way We Live* (New York: Basic Books, 2005). For more information on *Women's Voice and Women's Vote*, a national project that tried to mobilize single female voters, see the PBS television program *NOW* by Bill Moyers available at http://www.pbs.org/now/politics/gendergap.html, aired November 10, 2004.

79. Charlotte Bunch, "Whose Security?" *The Nation*, September 23, 2002.

80. Joan Blades and Kirstin Rowe-Finkbeiner, *The Motherhood Manifesto: What America's Moms Want—and What to Do About It* (New York: Nation Books, 2006). Also see Marianne A. Ferber and Julie A. Nelson, eds., *Feminist Economics Today: Beyond Economic Man* (Chicago: University of Chicago Press, 2003); Martha Albertson Fineman and Terence Doughterty, eds., *Feminism Confronts Homo Economicus: Gender, Law, and Society* (Ithaca: Cornell University Press, 2005); Thomas A. Kochan, *Restoring the American Dream: A Working Family's Agenda in America* (Cambridge: MIT Press, 2005); Louis Uchitelle, *The Disposable American: Job Layoffs and Their Consequences* (New York: Knopf, 2006); Stanley Aronowitz, *Just Around the Corner: The Paradox of the Jobless Recovery* (Philadelphia: Temple University Press, 2005); David Shipley, *The Working Poor: Invisible in America* (New York: Knopf, 2004).

81. http://www.govtrack.us/congress/bill.xpd?bill=h109-4898, Edward Epstein, "Bay Area Liberals Lead House Panel's Defense-cut Plan," *San Francisco Chronicle*, March 9, 2006.

82. Fred Block, "A Moral Economy," *The Nation*, March 16, 2006, 16–19.

83. Robert Fulghum, *All I Really Need to Know I Learned in Kindergarten* (New York: Ballantine, 2004).

84. Vera Rubin, "How I Got There," *Newsweek*, October 24, 2005, 59.

ACKNOWLEDGMENTS

It takes a small army of colleagues, friends, and institutional supporters to bring a book like this to publication. When a book lives with you for an entire decade, how could it be otherwise?

Annual faculty research grants from the University of California, Davis, have allowed me to visit archives, interview participants, and attend conferences all over the world where new colleagues have sent me back to the drawing board. The Rockefeller Foundation generously supported this project with both its Humanities and Gender Roles fellowships. Residential fellowships at the U.C. Davis Humanities Institute, Blue Mountain Center in New York, and the Ragdale Foundation in Illinois provided the solitude and serenity that writing often required. The Institute for the Study of Social Change at U.C. Berkeley generously offered refuge and inspiration. The Institute for Global Conflict and Cooperation of the University of California and the William Joiner Center at Yale University both supported my exploration of women's role in peace movements with generous grants. The European Peace University at Stadtschlaining, Austria, and Dromahair, Ireland, gave me the privileged opportunity of teaching students from all over the world who greatly influenced this book. A visiting professorship at the Goldman School of Public Policy at U.C. Berkeley offered me the opportunity to finally understand what I really wanted to write. To all, I am very grateful.

I thank all the people who allowed me to enter their lives and generously shared their stories and memories with me. I am also in debt to two research assistants whose intellectual abilities and energetic engagement kept me from throwing up my hands in despair. Terri Strathman helped me organize my research during the early years of this project. Samantha Barbas helped me edit transcripts, copy endless materials, and proof many drafts of the manuscript. Without her, I would still be staring at piles of paper that might have become a book, but never did.

I especially want to thank Laura X, the founder of the Women's History Library in Berkeley, California, for having had the vision to create an archive in which our history would be preserved. In the future, historians will sing her praises for having understood the historical significance of the women's movement.

Certain individuals have given patience a new meaning. My agent, Sandra Dijkstra, and my initial editor, Mindy Werner, stood by me as I weathered all kinds of natural disasters that derailed the writing of this book. Tom Engelhardt, editor extraordinaire, coaxed me into writing a far more elegant book. It was my great fortune to inherit Wendy Wolf as my editor as my book neared completion. Another editor extraordinaire, her critical eye improved this book immeasurably, and her cheerful encouragement gave me the confidence and courage to finish it.

Friends and colleagues have supported this project with grace and honesty. Mary Felstiner read every word with her critical and loving eyes, supported me through illness and health, and stubbornly refused to let me give up this project. I am deeply grateful to Kira Brunner, Michael Ginsberg, Mike Kazin, Joan Levinson, Gerda Lerner, Vivian Rothstein, and Kitty Sklar, all of whom read the entire manuscript and offered the kind of criticisms one dare not ignore. Pat Cody, Barbara Epstein, Rachel Ginsberg, Todd Gitlin, Larry Levine, Karen Paget, Joan Peters, Vicki Ruiz, Jayne Walker, and Clarence Walker all read different parts of the book, discovered egregious errors, made important editorial contributions, and improved my evocation of particular events. Jayne Walker, my commuter partner, patiently shared her literary secrets with me. Photographer Lynda Koolish and poster archivist Michael Rossman generously helped me make decisions that concerned illustrations.

Certain friends contributed to my work in very specific ways. Ever since we were in graduate school, Isabel Marcus has romped with me on trails along the Pacific Coast. For more than a decade, she has patiently listened as I described yet another version of this book. My colleague and friend Sandra Gilbert, in addition to her intellectual contributions, nourished me through one very cold and wet winter with food and friendship. One day, Natalie Davis—in one of her characteristic flashes of brilliance—informed me that my book was probably completed . . . and she was right. Both Kitty Sklar and Gerda Lerner have offered the kind of collegial criticism that I count among my greatest blessings.

I am deeply grateful to other friends and colleagues who answered my endless queries, and who willingly engaged me in debates and conversations that sharpened my ideas and arguments. Some provoked me, some cheered me on; still others offered the steady support of friendship. I want to thank Charlotte Bunch, Judy Coburn, Claudia Coonz, Tom Dublin, Barbara Ehrenreich, Hester Eisenstein, Deirdre English, Dick Flacks, Mickey

Flacks, Carol Groneman, Carolyn Heilbrun, Joanne Landy, Jeremy Larner, Marge Lasky, Jesse Lemisch, Kristin Luker, Norman Mailer, Bob Martin, David Morse, Jane Norling, Alice Quaytman, Jerry Rosen, Vivian Rothstein, Jim Skelly, Blanche Walch, Ann Weills, Jean Weininger, Naomi Weisstein, the annual UCLA women's history teaching workshop, and the Berkeley women and work group, all of whom know what, when, how, and why they contributed to the completion of this book.

Some very special friends have helped sharpen my understanding of American political culture by teaching me about their own. I am especially grateful to my friend and colleague Professor Jirina Siklova of the Czech Republic, my friend and former student Dr. Wang Zheng of China, and Professor Ida Bloom of Norway.

Only now do I realize how much this book grew out of my undergraduate lectures at the University of California, Davis, and my op-ed pieces for the *Los Angeles Times*. I thank several generations of students for teaching me what I needed to learn. I am forever indebted to Bob Berger, op-ed editor of the *Los Angeles Times*, who, in his characteristically brilliant and blunt manner, taught me to write a convincing argument in 750 words.

As obvious as it may seem, I had to survive in order to write this book. I am profoundly grateful to Michael Lerner, intellectual and spiritual leader of Commonweal in Bolinas, California, for tutoring me in the art of healing and to doctors Paul Smith, Jan Kirsch, Lisa Bailey, and Paul Walton, for knowing that physicians must heal a patient's mind, body, and soul. And they did.

I also want to thank Jae-Jung McClure for her healing touch and Julie Cummings for maintaining domestic order, and Louise Bernikow, who early publicized Muriel Rukeyser's powerful words.

And then there is the next generation. Scott and Brian Rosen, my nephews, have been a great source of love. By word and by deed, Kevin Brunner has assured me that a new generation of boys has grown up to be strong men with soft hearts. Through her intellect, passion, and friendship, Kira Brunner has reassured me that the future of feminism is in sturdy hands. I am delighted to report that, while I wrote this book, my husband, Wendel Brunner, never gave up his own career as Director of Public Health, never quit struggling for a healthier and more just society, and never stopped sailing or backpacking. And, for the love and laughter he brought into my life, for his patience and generosity, for his irreverent humor and honest criticism, for his sublime sense of wonder, for his steady encouragement and loving presence, for all this, and more, I feel blessed and filled with gratitude.

Ruth Rosen
Berkeley, California, 2000

Interviews Not Cited in Notes

❦

Alta, 5/97, Berkeley, California
Bettina Aptheker (with Mark Kitchell), n.d., Berkeley, California
Elaine Baker, 6/19/89, Denver, Colorado (telephone)
Jill Benderly, 6/8/91, Dubrovnik, Yugoslavia
Kira Brunner, 10/98, Wellfleet, Massachusetts
Charlotte Bunch, 4/13/87, New York City
Rennie Davis, 1988 SDS Reunion
Bernadine Dohrn, 1988 SDS Reunion
Hester Eisenstein, 6/5/95, New York City
Dan Ellsberg, 10/98, Wellfleet, Massachusetts
Judy Ezekiel, 6/2/87, Paris, France
Anne Ferrar, 7/15/86, San Francisco, California
Dick Flacks, 1988 SDS Reunion
Mickey Flacks, 1/2/83, Santa Barbara, California
Ann Forer, 4/6/86, New York City
Betty Garman, 1988 SDS Reunion and by telephone 6/89
Helen Garvey, 1988 SDS Reunion
Sandra Gilbert, 4/93, Berkeley, California
Rachel Ginsberg, 7/24/91, Berkeley, California
Todd Gitlin, 1988 SDS Reunion
Vivian Gornick, 4/6/87, New York City
Tom Hayden, 2/93, Berkeley, California
Carolyn Heilbrun, 4/18/86, New York City
Nanci Hollander, 6/23/89, Austin, Texas (telephone)
Sharon Jeffrey, 6/24/89, California (telephone) at 1988 SDS Reunion
Flo Kennedy, 4/14/86, New York City
Amy Kessleman, 6/95, North Carolina
Pat Kovner, 4/15/86, Berkeley, California
Joan Levinson, 10/3/92, Berkeley, California
Kristin Luker, 5/6/97, Berkeley, California
Norman Mailer, 10/98, Wellfleet, Massachusetts
Erica Marcus, 2/5/86, Buffalo, New York
Isabel Marcus, 1/3/95, Buffalo, New York
Bob Martin, 10/98, Berkeley, California
Wendy Martin, 3/85, Berkeley, California
Valerie Miner, 5/17/86, Berkeley, California
Karen Paget, 10/5/98, Berkeley, California
Gail Pheterson, 6/92, Paris, France

Annie Popkin, 5/16/86, Berkeley, California
Vivian Rothstein, 6/24/89, 7/98, Los Angeles, California (telephone)
Vicki Ruiz, 10/98, Tempe, Arizona (e-mail)
Raquel Scherr, 7/96, Berkeley, California
Kitty Sklar, 5/97, Berkeley, California
Sala Steinbach, 1988 SDS Reunion
Mary Waters, 6/7/96, Seattle, Washington
Jean Weininger, 7/98, Berkeley, California
Leni Wildflower, 1988 SDS Reunion
Cathy Wilkerson, 1988 SDS Reunion
Honey Williams, 1988 SDS Reunion
Barbara Winslow, 6/95, North Carolina
Laura X, 8/28/97, Berkeley, California

ARCHIVAL COLLECTIONS

Bancroft Library, University of California at Berkeley (BL)
Social Protest Collection

Special Collections Library, Duke University (DU)
Women's Liberation Movement On-Line Archival Collection

Schlesinger Library, Radcliffe College, Harvard University (SL)
Susan Bolotin Papers
Charlotte Bunch Papers
Betty Friedan Papers
Ms. Letters Collection
Pauli Murray Papers
Nancy Gray Osterud Papers
Marlene Sanders Collection
Women's Liberation Files
Women's Liberation Movement FBI Files
NOW Papers

Wisconsin Historical Society (WHS)
Kay Clarenbach Papers
Oral Histories of Women Leaders of the Midwest
Pamphlet Collection, Women's History Archives, from Laura X's Women's
    History Library

New York University Tamiment Library (TL)
Women's Liberation Collection
New Left Collection

Women and Labor Collection
Social Movement Collection

University of Wyoming (UWA)
Protest Files
Media Protest Files from Women's History Health/Mental Health, Women
    and Law archives of Laura X's Women's History Library
Herstory Collection in Hard Copy

Northwestern University (NU)
The International Women's History Periodical Archives. The microfilm of
    this archive is called *Herstory.* Web site: http://ncmdr.org
This collection was begun in 1969 by Laura Murra (later Laura X), who
    created the major international archive of the modern women's
    movement.

Individual Collections
Todd Gitlin Personal Archives (TGPA)
Jo Freeman Personal Archives (JFPA)
Vivian Rothstein Personal Archives (VRPA)
Mary Waters Personal Archives (MWPA)
Author's Personal Archives (APA)

BIBLIOGRAPHY FOR FURTHER READING AND RESEARCH

These works have helped inform my ideas and offer further suggestions for reading and research for those interested in specific subjects. This is by no means a comprehensive bibliography of the works I have consulted, and does not include the many archival sources and articles on which this book is based. It is arranged by the chapters as they appear in the book.

GENERAL WORKS

Some of the most influential and earliest histories of the women's movement were Judith Hole and Ellen Levine, *Rebirth of Feminism* (New York: Quadrangle, 1971); Jo Freeman, *The Women's Liberation Movement: Its Aims, Structures, and Ideas* (Pittsburgh: Know, 1971); Jo Freeman, *The Politics of Women's Liberation* (New York: McKay, 1975); Maren Carden, *The New Feminist Movement* (New York: Russell Sage, 1974); and Leah Fritz, *Dreamers and Dealers: An Intimate Appraisal of the Women's Movement* (Boston: Beacon, 1979). General histories that cover parts or all of this period are Winifred Wandersee, *On the Move: American Women in the 1970's* (Boston: Twayne Publishers, 1988); William Chafe, *The Unfinished Journey* (New York: Oxford, 1995), *The American Woman: Her Changing Social, Economic and Political Roles, 1920–1970* (New York: Oxford, 1972), and *The Paradox of Change* (New York: Oxford, 1991). More recent studies of the women's movement include Alice Echols, *Daring to Be Bad: Radical Feminism in America, 1968–1975* (Minneapolis: University of Minnesota Press, 1988), which focuses on radical feminism; Flora Davis, *Moving the Mountain: The Women's Movement in America Since 1960* (New York: Simon and Schuster, 1991), which includes a broader emphasis on legislation; Sheila Tobias, *Faces of Feminism* (New York: Westview, 1996), which focuses on sexual politics, the politics of backlash, and includes biographical material; Cassandra Langer, *A Feminist Critique* (New York: HarperCollins, 1996), which offers analyses of images and popular culture; Susan Brownmiller, *In Our Time: Memoir of a Revolution* (New York: Dial, 1999); Susan Okin, *Is Multicultural Bad For Women?* (Princeton: Princeton University Press, 1999); Jo Freeman, *A Room at a Time: How Women Entered Party Politics* (New York: Rowman and Littlefield, 2000); and Harriot Woods, *Stepping Up to Power* (New York: Westview Press, 2000). Barbara Ryan, *Feminism and the Women's Movement: Dynamics of Change in Social Movement Ideology and Activism* (New York: Routledge, 1992), and Beth B. Hess, *Controversy and Coalition: The New Feminist Movement* (Boston: Twayne Publishers, 1985), both approach the movement from a more sociological perspective, emphasizing social movement theory. Lauri Umansky, *Motherhood Reconceived: Feminism and the Legacies of the 1960s* (New York: New York University Press, 1996), emphasizes the issue of motherhood; Deborah Rhode, *Justice and Gender* (Cambridge, Mass.: Harvard University Press, 1989), focuses on the law; Judith Grant, *Fundamental Feminism: Contesting the Core Concepts of Feminist Theory* (New York: Routledge, 1993), questions core concepts in feminism. Important books on political thought and feminism are Zillah Eisenstein, *The Radical Future of Liberal Feminism* (New York: Longman, 1981), and Susan Okin, *Women in Western Political Thought* (Princeton: Princeton University Press, 1979). Both Hester Eisenstein, *Contemporary Feminist Thought* (Boston: G. K. Hall & Co. 1983), and Linda Kauffman, ed., *American Feminist Thought at Century's End: A Reader* (Cambridge, Mass.: Blackwell, 1993), offer valuable intellectual histories.

Anthologies with primary documents, many of which are out of print, include Leslie Tanner, *Voices of Women's Liberation* (New York: New American Library, 1970); Toni Cade, *The Black Woman* (New York: New American Library, 1970); Alma Garcia, *Chicana Feminist Thought: The Basic Historical Writings* (New York: Routledge, 1997); Anne Koedt, Ellen Levine, and Anita Rapone, *Radical Feminism* (New York: Quadrangle, 1973); Robin Morgan, *Sisterhood Is Powerful* (New York: Vintage, 1970); Redstockings, *Feminist Revolution* (New York: Random House, 1975); Vivian Gornick and Barbara K. Moran, eds., *Woman in Sexist Society* (New York: Basic Books, 1971); Alice Rossi, ed., *The Feminist Papers* (New York: Columbia University Press, 1973); New York Radical Women, *Notes from the First Year* (New York: 1968); *Notes from the Second Year* (New York: Ace, 1970); *Notes from the Third Year* (New York: 1971); Evelyn Shapiro and Barry Shapiro, eds., *The Women Say, The Men Say: Women's Liberation and Men's Consciousness* (New York: Delta, 1979); Deborah Babcox and Madeline Belkin, eds., *Liberation NOW: Writings from the Women's Liberation Movement* (New York: Dell, 1971); Betty Roszak and Theodore Roszak, eds., *Masculine/Feminine* (New York:

Harper and Row, 1969); Mary Lou Thompson, ed., *Voices of the New Feminism* (Boston: Beacon, 1970); and Miriam Schneir, ed., *Feminism: The Essential Historical Writings* (New York: Vintage, 1972). Three recent collections are Bonnie Watkins and Nina Tothchild, eds., *In the Company of Women: Voices from the Women's Movement* (Minneapolis: University of Minnesota Press, 1997); Rachel Blau DuPlessix and Ann Snitow, eds., *The Feminist Memoir Project* (New York: Three Rivers Press, 1998); and Rosalyn Baxandall and Linda Gordon, eds., *Dear Sisters: Dispatches from the Women's Liberation Movement* (New York: Basic, 2000).

Classic works of the first years that were widely read and debated include Germaine Greer, *The Female Eunuch* (New York: McGraw-Hill, 1971); Jill Johnston, *Lesbian Nation: The Feminist Solution* (New York: Bantam, 1973); Kate Millett, *Sexual Politics* (New York: Doubleday, 1971); Shulamith Firestone, *The Dialectic of Sex: The Case for Feminist Revolution* (New York: Bantam, 1970); Adrienne Rich, *Of Woman Born* (New York: Norton, 1976); Susan Brownmiller, *Against Our Will* (New York: Simon and Schuster, 1975); Caroline Bird, *Born Female* (New York: Bantam Books, 1969); Jessie Bernard, *The Future of Marriage* (New York: Harcourt, Brace and World, 1968); Eva Figes, *Patriarchal Attitudes* (London: Faber, 1970); and Ti-Grace Atkinson, *Amazon Odyssey* (New York: Link, 1974). Celestine Ware's *Woman Power* (New York: Tower, 1970) was the earliest book to challenge the new feminist movement to address racism. Norman Mailer's *Prisoner of Sex* (New York: Primus, reprinted from 1971 edition) was probably the most important intellectual assault on the women's movement. Some of the most important early novels were Alix Kates Shulman, *Burning Questions* (New York: Bantam, 1978); *Memoirs of an Ex-Prom Queen* (New York: Knopf, 1972); Sara Davidson, *Loose Change* (New York: Doubleday, 1977); and Erica Jong, *Fear of Flying* (New York: Signet, 1973). For other literature, see Lisa Maria Hogeland, *Feminism and Its Fictions: The Consciousness-Raising Novel and the Women's Liberation Movement* (Philadelphia: University of Pennsylvania, 1998).

Important memoirs by women activists offer an insider's view of the movement. See Betty Friedan, *It Changed My Life: Writings on the Women's Movement* (New York: Random House, 1976); Betty Friedan, *Life So Far* (New York: Simon and Schuster, 2000); Daisy Bates, *The Long Shadow of Little Rock, A Memoir* (New York: McKay, 1962); Phyllis Chesler, *Letter to a Young Feminist* (New York: Four Walls, Eight Windows, 1997); Elaine Brown, *A Taste of Power* (New York: Pantheon, 1992); Anne Moody, *Coming of Age in Mississippi* (New York: Dial Press, 1968); Robin Morgan, *Going Too Far: The Personal Chronicle of a Feminist* (New York: Vintage, 1978); Angela Davis, *Angela Davis: An Autobiography* (New York: Random House, 1974); Assata Shakur, *Assata* (Chicago: Lawrence Hill

Books, 1987); Erica Jong, *Fear of Fifty* (New York: HarperCollins, 1994); Audre Lorde, *The Cancer Journals* (San Francisco: Spinsters, Ink, 1980); Gloria Steinem, *Outrageous Acts and Everyday Rebellions* (New York: Holt, Rinehart, and Winston, 1983); and *Revolution from Within* (Boston: Little, Brown, 1992); Shirley Chisholm, *Unbought and Unbossed* (Boston: Houghton, Mifflin, 1970).

CHAPTER ONE: DAWN OF DISCONTENT

For valuable literature on women's experiences during World War II, see Susan M. Hartman, *The Home Front and Beyond: American Women in the 1940's* (Boston: Twayne, 1982); Leila Rupp, *Mobilizing Women for War* (Princeton: Princeton University Press, 1976); D'Ann Campbell, *Women at War with America: Private Lives in a Patriotic Era* (Cambridge: Harvard University Press, 1984); Karen Anderson, *Wartime Women* (Westport, Conn.: Greenwood Press, 1981); Maureen Honey, *Creating Rosie the Riveter: Class, Gender and Propaganda During World War II* (Amherst: University of Massachusetts Press, 1984); Ruth Milkman, *Gender at Work: The Dynamics of Job Segregation by Sex During World War II* (Urbana: University of Illinois Press, 1987); John Costello, *Virtue Under Fire: How World War II Changed Our Social and Sexual Attitudes* (Boston: Little, Brown, 1991); Jack Goodman, *While You Were Gone: A Report on Wartime Life in the U.S.* (New York: Simon and Schuster, 1946); Judy Barrett Litoff and David C. Smith, *Since You Went Away: World War II Letters from American Women on the Homefront* (New York: Oxford University Press, 1991); Richard Lingeman, *Don't You Know There's a War On? The American Homefront 1941–1946* (New York: Putnam, 1970); Doris Weatherford, *American Women and World War II* (New York: Facts on File, Oxford, 1990).

For general overviews of the fifties, see David Halberstam, *The Fifties* (New York: Villard Press, 1993); Douglas Miller and Marion Nowak, *The Fifties: The Way We Really Were* (New York: Doubleday, 1977); Kenneth Jackson, *Crabgrass Frontier* (New York: Oxford, 1985); Eugenia Kaledin, *Mothers and More: American Women in the 1950s* (Boston: Twayne, 1984). Valuable works on adult women during the fifties include Elaine Tyler May, *Homeward Bound* (New York: Basic Books, 1988); Andrew Cherlin, *Marriage, Divorce, Remarriage* (Cambridge: Harvard University Press, 1981); Benita Eisler, *Private Lives: Men and Women of the Fifties* (New York: Franklin Watts, 1986); Brett Harvey, *The Fifties: A Women's Oral History* (New York: Harper, 1994); Albert Kinsey, *Sexual Behavior in the Human Female* (New York: Pocket Books, 1953); Ferdinand Lundberg and Marya Farnham, *The Modern Woman: The Lost Sex* (New York: Harper and Brothers, 1947); and Stephanie Coontz, *The Way We Never Were* (New York: Basic Books, 1992). Betty Friedan's image of *The Feminine Mystique* (New York: Norton, 1963) is challenged by essays in Joanne Meyerowitz, ed., *Not*

June Cleaver: Women and Gender in Postwar America, 1945–1960 (Philadelphia: Temple University Press, 1994). Useful works on McCarthyism are David Caute, *The Great Fear* (New York: Simon and Schuster, 1978), and Ellen Schrecker, *Many Are the Crimes* (Boston: Little, Brown, 1998). For women's political engagement, see Leila Rupp, *Surviving in the Doldrums* (New York: Oxford, 1987); Amy Swerdlow, *Women Strike for Peace: Traditional Motherhood and Radical Politics in the 1960s* (Chicago: University of Chicago Press, 1993) and her pathbreaking essay, "The Congress of American Women: Left-Feminist Peace Politics in the Cold War," in Linda Kerber, Kathryn Sklar, and Alice Kessler-Harris, eds., *U.S. History As Women's History* (Chapel Hill: University of North Carolina Press, 1996). The contributions of the Old Left to the women's movement of the 1960s can be found in Kate Weigand, *Vanguard of Women's Liberation*, dissertation, Ohio State University, 1995; in Daniel Horowitz, *Betty Friedan and the Making of the Feminine Mystique: The American Left, the Cold War, and Modern Feminism* (Amherst: University of Massachusetts Press, 1999); and in Judith Adler Hennessee, *Betty Friedan: Her Life* (New York: Random House, 1999).

CHAPTER TWO: FEMALE GENERATION GAP

Barbara Berg, *The Crisis of the Working Mother, Resolving the Conflict between Family and Work* (New York: Summit, 1986), is a study of this generation's attitudes toward domesticity, and Landon Y. Jones, *Great Expectations: America and the Baby Boom Generation* (New York: Ballantine, 1980), provides an overview of the baby boom and its influence on American society. For works on the specific experiences of young women, see Wini Breines, *Young and Miserable: Growing Up Female in the Fifties* (Boston: Beacon Press, 1992); Susan Douglas, *Where the Girls Are: Growing Up Female With the Mass Media* (New York: Random House, 1994); and Joyce Johnson, *Minor Characters* (Boston: Houghton Mifflin, 1983). On the influence of Simone de Beauvoir, see *The Second Sex* (New York: Harmondsworth, 1953); Judith Okeley, *Simone de Beauvoir* (New York: Pantheon, 1986); Alice Schwarzer, *After the Second Sex: Conversations with Simone de Beauvoir* (New York: Pantheon, 1984); and Deirdre Bair's *Simone de Beauvoir: A Biography* (New York: Summit, 1990). A film titled *Daughters of de Beauvoir*, directed by Imogen Sutton, explores her influence on the women's movement. An essay by Mary Felstiner early assessed feminism's second-wave relationship to de Beauvoir: "Seeing the Second Sex through the Second Wave," *Feminist Studies 6* (Winter 1986): 247–76.

On the roots of young people's rebellion, see Richard Flacks, "The Liberated Generation: An Explanation of the Roots of Student Protest," in Richard Flacks, ed., *Conformity, Resistance and Self-Determination* (Boston: Little, Brown, 1973), and Kenneth Keniston, *Young Radicals: Notes on*

Committed Youth (New York: Harcourt Brace, 1968), especially the appendix. Robyn Rowland, *Women Who Do and Women Who Don't Join the Women's Movement* (London: Routledge, 1984), is one study of the differences between those who joined the women's movement and those who did not.

For the creation of a singles culture, see Helen Gurley Brown, *Sex and the Single Girl* (New York: Pocket Books, 1962), and Barbara Ehrenreich, Elizabeth Hess, and Gloria Jacobs, *Remaking Love* (New York: Doubleday, 1986), which argues that it is women who made the sexual revolution during the twentieth century.

CHAPTER THREE: LIMITS OF LIBERALISM

The two best accounts of the women's movement and U.S. liberal politics during this period are Cynthia Harrison, *On Account of Sex: The Politics of Women's Issues 1945–1968* (Berkeley: University of California Press, 1988), and Ethel Klein, *Gender Politics* (Cambridge: Harvard University Press, 1984). Also see the U.S. President's Commission on the Status of Women, *American Women* (Washington, D.C., 1963); Gerda Lerner, "Midwestern Leaders of the Modern Women's Movement: An Oral History Project," *Wisconsin Academy Review* (Winter 1994–95): 11–15; Nancy Gabin, *Feminism in the Labor Movement: Women and the United Auto Workers, 1925–1975* (Ithaca: Cornell University Press, 1990); and Susan Lynn, *Progressive Women in Conservative Times: Racial Justice, Peace and Feminism, 1945–1960's* (New Brunswick, N.J.: Rutgers University Press, 1992). Most of the articles collected for *Not June Cleaver* also point to the continuities between radical movements of the 1940s and 1950s and 1960s feminism.

CHAPTER FOUR: LEAVING THE LEFT

For valuable sources on the history of the New Left, see George Vickers, *The Formation of the New Left* (Lexington, Mass.: Lexington Books, 1975); Maurice Isserman, *If I Had a Hammer . . . The Death of the Old Left and the Birth of the New Left* (New York: Basic Books, 1987); Paul Buhle, *History and the New Left: Madison, Wisconsin, 1950–1970* (Philadelphia: Temple University Press, 1990); Todd Gitlin, *The Whole World Is Watching: Mass Media in the Making and Unmaking of the New Left* (Berkeley: University of California Press, 1980), and *The Sixties: Years of Hope, Days of Rage* (New York: Bantam, 1986); Jim Miller, *Democracy in the Streets: From Port Huron to the Siege of Chicago* (New York: Simon and Schuster, 1987); Harvard Sitkoff, *The Struggle for Black Equality* (New York: Hill and Wang, 1981); Richard Flacks, *Making History: The American Left and the American Mind* (New York: Columbia University Press, 1988); Nancy Zaroulis and Gerald Sullivan, *Who Spoke Up? American Protest against the War in Vietnam, 1963–1975* (Garden City, N.Y.: Doubleday, 1975); David

Caute, *The Year of the Barricades: A Journey through 1968* (New York: Harper and Row, 1988); David Farber, *Chicago 68* (Chicago: University of Chicago Press, 1988); Ronald Fraser et al., *1968: Student Generation in Revolt* (New York: Pantheon, 1988); Dick Flacks, "What Happened to the New Left?" *Socialist Review* (January 1989): 91–110; and Wini Breines, *Community and Organization in the New Left, 1962–68* (New Brunswick, N.J.: Rutgers University Press, 1982).

The best sources on women in SNCC are Sara Evans, *Personal Politics* (New York: Knopf, 1979) and Belinda Robnett's critique of the emphasis on white women in *How Long? How Long? African-American Women and the Struggle for Freedom and Justice* (New York: Oxford University Press, 1997). Different perspectives are offered by Mary Rothschild, *A Case of Black and White: Northern Volunteers and the Southern Freedom Summers, 1964–1965* (Westport, Conn.: Greenwood Press, 1982); Cynthia Washington, "We Started from Different Ends of the Spectrum," *Southern Exposure* 4:4 (1977): 14; Michael Honey, "The Legacy of SNCC," in *OAH (Organization of American Historians) Newsletter* (February 1989), and Joanne Grant, "Sexual Politics and Civil Rights," *New Directions for Women* (January/ February 1989): 4. For further reading on SNCC, see Clayborne Carson, *In Struggle: SNCC and the Black Awakening of the 1960's* (Cambridge, Mass.: Harvard University Press, 1981); Mary King, *Freedom Song* (New York: Morrow, 1987); Doug McAdam, *Freedom Summer* (New York: Oxford University Press, 1988); David J. Garrow, ed., *The Montgomery Bus Boycott and the Women Who Started It: The Memoir of Jo Ann Gibson Robinson* (Knoxville: University of Tennessee Press, 1987); Vicki Crawford, Jacqueline Rouse, and Barbara Woods, eds., *Women in the Civil Rights Movement: Trailblazers and Torchbearers, 1941–1965* (New York: Carlson, 1990); Cheryl Greenberg, *A Circle of Trust: Remembering SNNC* (New Brunswick, Rutgers University Press, 1998); and *Deep in Our Hearts: Nine White Women in the Freedom Movement*, Constance Curry, Joan Browning, et al. (Athens, Georgia, University of Georgia Press, 2000). See especially Anne Standly's essay in this collection, "The Role of Black Women in the Civil Rights Movement," 183–203; Daisy Bates, *The Long Shadow of Little Rock* (New York: David McKay, 1962); Anne Moody, *Coming of Age in Mississippi* (New York: Dial Press, 1968); Bernice Reagan, who credited her confidence to the civil rights movement, in Dick Cluster, ed., *They Should Have Served That Cup of Coffee* (Boston: South End Press, 1979), 22–23, 29; Casey Hayden, "Women's Consciousness and the Nonviolent Movement Against Segregation, 1960–1965: A Personal History," 1989, APA; and "A Nurturing Movement: Nonviolence, SNCC, and Feminism," *Southern Exposure*, Summer 1988, p. 51.

For public farewells to the Left, see Robin Morgan, "Goodbye to All That," in *Rat* (January 19, 1969); "A Letter to the Editor of *Ramparts* Magazine," *Notes from the First Year: Women's Liberation*, June 1969; Rita

Mae Brown, "Say It Isn't So," *Rat* (March 7–21); Marge Piercy, "The Grand Coolie Damn," in Morgan, *Sisterhood is Powerful.*

For black women's struggle with black power advocates and nationalists, see Rivka Polonick's "Diversity in Women's Liberation Ideology: How a Black and a White Group of the 1960's Viewed Motherhood," *Signs* (Spring 1996): 679, and from Black Women's Liberation Group, Mount Vernon, New York, *Statement on Birth Control* in Morgan, *Sisterhood*, 404. For a variety of views, see "Birth Control Pill and Black Children, A Statement by the Black Unity Party" (Peekskill, N.Y.); "A Response," by black sisters, and "Poor Black Women," by Patricia Robinson, in the pamphlet *Poor Black Women* (Boston: New England Free Press, c. 1968).

CHAPTER FIVE: HIDDEN INJURIES OF SEX

Early critiques of the sexual revolution came fast and furiously. The best single work on the history of sexuality is Estelle Freedman and John D'Emilio, *Intimate Matters: A History of Sexuality in America* (New York: Harper & Row, 1988). Many young feminists argued that the sexual revolution had arrived on men's terms. See Roxanne Dunbar, "Sexual Liberation: More of the Same Thing," *No More Fun and Games: A Journal of Female Liberation 31* (November 1969): 49–56; Ti-Grace Atkinson, "The Institution of Sexual Intercourse," *Notes from the Second Year*, 42–48, APA; "Sex and Women's Liberation in Redstockings," *Feminist Revolution*; Nancy Hawley, "Dear Sisters," Xeroxed handout, October 8, 1970, APA; "Women Are Kept Apart," in Sooki Stambler, *Women's Liberation* (New York: Ace, 1970); "Did You Come," in *Notes from the First Year* (New York, 1968); "A Fat Woman's Journal," *Country Women* (October 1972): 7; Laura X, "Our Sexual Revolution," *Velvet Glove*, circa 1969. Anne Koedt, "The Myth of the Vaginal Orgasm," *Notes from the First Year*, and an expanded version in Shulamith Firestone and Anne Koedt, eds., *Notes from the Second Year*, 36–41, APA. For other critiques of the sexual revolution, see Dana Densmore, "Independence from the Sexual Revolution," reprinted in *Radical Feminism*, 107–118; Barbara Seaman, "The Liberated Orgasm," *Ms.*, August 1972; and Anselma Dell'Olio, "The Sexual Revolution Wasn't Our War," *Ms.*, Spring 1972; Dana Densmore, "On Celibacy," in Tanner, *Voices from Women's Liberation*, first published in the feminist journal *No More Fun and Games*, no. 1 (1969); Kate, "What Is There to Say About Celibacy?" *Kansas City Women's Liberation Newsletter* 4:1 (1974): 10; Leila, "Voices," *Country Women* (April 1975): 8–9. Celibacy was especially appealing when women needed a respite, felt confused after so much rapid change, and needed to sort things out. See Dana Densmore, "Freedom from Sex," reprinted in Koedt, *Radical Feminism*; Abby Rockefeller, "Sex: The Basis of Sexism," in *No More Fun and Games: A Journal of Female Liberation* (May 1973): 5–37; Ellen Willis, "Radical Feminism and

Feminist Radicalism," in Sonya Sayres, Stanley Aronowitz, and Ander Stephenson, eds., *The 60's Without Apology* (Minneapolis: University of Minnesota, 1984); "Women Rap About Sex," in *Notes from the First Year: Women's Liberation*, June 1968, unpaginated; Brenda Starr, "Beyond Orgasm," *Everywoman* (March 5, 1971): 12; Barbara Brenner Nizislek, "Liberating the Second Sex from the Heterosexual Norm," *Women: A Journal of Liberation* 3:1 (1972): 60; "Sex: An Open Letter from a Sister," *It Ain't Me Babe* (March 15, 1970). Masturbation as the route to sexual independence is discussed in "Very Pleasurable Politics," *Rat* (December 17, 1970): 12.

Sources for further research that may not be as widely known are "The Myth of the Liberated Female," Mary Ann Routledge, *Dayton Women's Liberation Newsletter* (September 27, 1972): 1–2; Ann Markin, *Letter to Women: A Journal of Liberation* (Fall 1969): 47, in which she argues that the freedom of the sexual revolution is simply to be a sex object; Claudia Dreifus, "The Selling of the Feminist: Who Is the Enemy?" in *It Ain't Me Babe* (February 1970).

Both the first edition of Boston Women's Health Collective's "Women and Their Bodies," printed by the New England Free Press in 1970, as well as the first commercial edition of *Our Bodies, Ourselves* (Simon and Schuster, 1973), included material on masturbation and described women's shame about the practice, as well as how they learned to do it.

Interpretative essays on the sexual revolution include: Diana Newell, "Sex in the '70s: A Wrap-up of the Decadent Decade," *Playgirl*, December 1979; Shere Hite, *The Hite Report* (New York: Dell, 1976), 263; Deirdre English and Barbara Ehrenreich, "Sexual Liberation: The Shortest Revolution," in Evelyn Shapiro and Barry Shapiro, eds., *The Women Say, The Men Say: Women's Liberation and Men's Consciousness* (New York: Delta, 1979), 120–27; Sheila Jeffreys, *Anticlimax: A Feminist Perspective of the Sexual Revolution* (New York: NYU Press, 1990); Ellen Willis, "Toward a Feminist Sexual Revolution" in *No More Nice Girls* (Hanover: University Press of New England, 1992), 19–51; Lynn Segal, *Straight Sex: Rethinking the Politics of Pleasure* (Berkeley: University of California Press, 1994); Susan Douglas, *Where the Girls Are: Growing up Female with the Mass Media* (New York: Anchor Press, 1987); Naomi Wolf, *Promiscuities* (New York: Random House, 1997); and David Allyn, *Make Love, Not War: The Sexual Revolution, an Unfettered History* (New York: Little Brown, 2000) offer different perspectives on the sexual revolution.

Abortion. For historical background, see Leslie Reagan, *When Abortion Was a Crime* (Berkeley: University of California Press, 1997); Cynthia Gorney, *Articles of Faith: A Frontline History of the Abortion Wars* (New York: Simon and Schuster, 1998); and Linda Gordon, *Woman's Body, Woman's Right* (New York: Grossman, 1976). The search for the right "Jane Doe" can be found in Marian Faux, *Roe v. Wade: The Untold Story of the Land-*

mark Supreme Court Decision That Made Abortion Legal (New York: New American Library, 1988).

The story of one illegal abortion underground service is in Laura Kaplan, *The Story of Jane: The Legendary Underground Feminist Abortion Service* (Chicago: University of Chicago Press, 1995); for feminist analysis and scholarship on abortion, also see Rosalind Pollack Petchesky, *Abortion and Women's Choice* (New York: Longman, 1984); Beverly Wildung Harrison, *Our Right to Choose: Toward a New Ethics of Abortion* (Boston: Beacon Press, 1983); Kristin Luker, *Abortion: The Politics of Motherhood* (Berkeley: University of California Press, 1985); Carole Joffe, *Doctors of Conscience: The Struggle to Provide Abortion Before and After Roe v. Wade* (Boston: Beacon, 1995) and *The Regulation of Sexuality: Experiences of Family Planning Workers* (Philadelphia: Temple University Press, 1986); Rickie Solinger, *The Abortionist: A Woman Against the Law* (New York: Free Press, 1994).

Androgyny. In the mid-seventies, the topic of androgyny became increasingly trendy. Some feminists took the idea seriously. See Paul Rust, *Bisexuality and the Challenge to Lesbian Politics: Sex, Loyalty and Revolution* (New York: New York University Press, 1995). The most important book was Carolyn Heilbrun's widely read book, *Toward a Recognition of Androgyny* (New York: Knopf, 1973), which was much debated.

Beauty. Some of the earliest writings in the women's movement addressed the artificial and narrow definition of beauty that the media promoted. See, for example, in Morgan, *Sisterhood*, Zoe Moss, "It Hurts to Be Alive and Obsolete: The Ageing Woman"; Alice Embree, "Media Images 1: Madison Avenue Brainwashing—The Facts"; Florika, "Media Images 2: Body Odor." Lois Banner, *American Beauty* (New York: Knopf, 1983); Kim Chernin, *The Obsession* (New York: Harper and Row, 1981), and Marcia Millman, *Such a Pretty Face* (New York: W. W. Norton and Company, 1980), were important early works that analyzed the influence of beauty culture.

Lesbian feminism. Two of the earliest pieces on lesbian feminism were Del Martin, "If That's All There Is," n.d., UWA, and Martha Shelley, "Notes of a Radical Lesbian," in Morgan, *Sisterhood*, 343–48. For powerful stories written by women who were hidden and eventually came out, see Julia Penelope Stanley and Susan J. Wolfe, eds., *The Coming Out Stories* (Watertown, Mass: Persephone Press, 1980). Two of the most widely debated essays were Radicalesbians, "The Woman-Identified Woman," APA, also reprinted in Koedt, *Radical Feminism* (New York: St. Martin's Press, 1987), 240–46, and Adrienne Rich, "Compulsory Heterosexuality and Lesbian Existence," *Signs* 5:4 (Summer 1980): 631–60; Nancy Whittier, *Feminist Generations: The Persistence of the Women's Movement* (Philadelphia: Temple University Press, 1995), emphasizes the importance of lesbians' role in sustaining the movement and its institutions. On the political limits and contradictions of the "woman-identified woman," see Shane Phelan, *Identity Politics: Lesbianism and the Limits of Community* (Philadelphia: Temple University Press, 1989), chapter 3. There is an enormous literature on the origins, impact, and consequences of lesbian feminism and separatism. See Nancy Myron and Charlotte Bunch, eds., *Lesbianism and the Women's Movement* (Baltimore: Diana Press, 1975); Dolores Klaich, *Woman + Woman: Attitudes Toward Lesbianism* (New York: William Morrow and Co., 1974); Alison M. Jagger, *Feminist Politics and Human Nature* (Totowa, N.J.: Rowman and Allanheld, 1983), 12; Lillian Faderman, *Surpassing the Love of Men* (New York: William Morrow, 1981); Toby Marotta, *The Politics of Homosexuality* (Boston: Houghton Mifflin, 1981); and Charlotte Bunch, *Passionate Politics* (New York: St. Martin's Press, 1987). Carol, Natalie, Ellen, and Pat, eds., *Lesbians Speak Out* (San Francisco: Free Women's Press, 1971), is an important essay collection. *Come Out! Selections from the Radical Gay Liberation Newspaper* (New York: Times Change Press, 1970); Gay Women's Liberation, Berkeley, "What It Means to Be a Lesbian," December 1969, APA, reprinted in *Lesbians Speak Out*; Gay Women's Liberation, "Lesbians As Women," November 1969. Audre Lorde, in her book *Sister Outsider: Essays and Speeches* (Trumansburg, N.Y.: The Crossing Press, 1984) and in her article "An Open Letter to Mary Daly," in Cherrie Moraga and Gloria Anzaldua, eds., *This Bridge Called My Back: Writings by Radical Women of Color* (New York: Kitchen Table Press, 1983), offers the best examples of her ability to describe triple oppression, while not casting herself as a victim.

Women's health movement. Sheryl Burt Ruzek, *The Women's Health Movement* (New York: Praeger, 1978), offers a good overview of the health movement. Barbara Seaman, *The Doctors' Case Against the Pill* (New York: P. H. Wyden, 1969), was a critique of the use of the Pill; Rose Kushner, *Breast Cancer: A Personal History and Investigative Report* (New York: Harcourt Brace Jovanovich, 1975), questioned radical mastectomies; Phyllis Chesler, *Women and Madness* (New York: Doubleday, 1972), examined gendered views of mental illness. Some of the most valuable criticisms of the medical establishment came from Ellen Frankfort, *Vaginal Politics* (New York: Quadrangle Books, 1972); Helen Marieskind and Barbara Ehrenreich, "Toward Socialist Medicine: The Women's Health Movement," *Social Policy* (May/June 1975); Colette Price, "The First Self-Help Clinic," *Feminist Revolution* (New York: Random House, 1978); "Off Our Backs," *Health Supplements* (Summer 1971); Ruzek, "Medical Response to Women's Health Activities: Conflict, Accommodation and Co-optation," *Research in the Sociology of Health Care* (Greenwich: Jai Press Inc., 1980); Paul Starr, *The Social Transformation of American Medicine* (New York: Basic Books, 1982). Health Policy Advisory Center, "Health PAC Bulletin"

(New York: 1970–72), offer different critiques of the medical profession's attitude toward and treatment of women. I am greatly indebted to Wang Zheng, whose unpublished master's thesis, "The Women's Health Movement in the United States," U.C. Davis, 1987, taught me a great deal. For critiques on how medicine abused women, see Lucinda Cisler, "Unfinished Business: Birth Control and Women's Liberation," in Morgan, *Sisterhood*, 274–320; Barbara Ehrenreich and Deirdre English, *Complaints and Disorders* and *For Her Own Good* (New York: Anchor, 1979); Helen Marieskind, "The Women's Health Movement," *International Journal of Health Service Research* 5:2 (1975); *Off Our Backs, Health Supplement* (Summer 1971); Gena Corea, *The Mother Machine* (New York: Harper and Row, 1985).

Rape. The most powerful and first critique of rape from a feminist activist came from Susan Griffin, "Rape: The All-American Crime," *Ramparts* 10:3 (1971): 26–35. Other early critiques are Barbara Mehrhof and Pamela Kearon, "Rape: An Act of Terror," reprinted in Koedt, *Radical Feminism*, 228–33; *Women Against Rape, Stop Rape* (Detroit, 1971); "Anatomy of a Rape" and "Disarm Rapists," in *It Ain't Me, Babe* (July 23 and August 6, 1970). In 1975, Susan Brownmiller's influential book *Against Our Will* appeared. Other important material on rape includes Dorothy L. Barnes, *Rape, A Bibliography 1965–1975* (New York: Winston Publishers, 1977); New York Radical Feminists, *Rape: The First Sourcebook for Women*, Noreen Connell and Casandra Wilson, eds. (New York: Plume, 1974); and Nancy Mathews, *Confronting Rape: The Feminist Anti-Rape Movement and the State* (London: Routledge, 1994); Kathleen Barry, "The Vagina on Trial: The Institution and Psychology of Rape," in *Women Against Rape, Stop Rape* (Detroit, 1971).

Date and marital rape. Some of the works that helped publicize rape include Diana Russell's pioneering book, *The Politics of Rape: The Victim's Perspective* (New York: Stein and Day, 1975); Robin Warshaw, *I Never Called It Rape* (New York: Harper and Row, 1988); and Peggy Sanday, *A Woman Scorned* (New York: Doubleday, 1996). An important film that made its way around women's centers and women's studies programs was the film *Rape Culture* (Margaret Lazarus and Renner Wunderlich, Cambridge Documentary Films, 1975). For further information, see Leslie Francis, ed., *Date Rape: Feminism, Philosophy, and the Law* (University Park: Pennsylvania State University Press, 1996); and Sally K. Ward, *Acquaintance and Date Rape: An Annotated Bibliography* (Westport, Conn.: Greenwood Press, 1994).

Incest. Sandra Butler, *Conspiracy of Silence: The Trauma of Incest* (New York: Bantam, 1979); Florence Rush, *The Best Kept Secret: Sexual Abuse of Children* (New York: McGraw-Hill, 1980); and Judith Herman, *Father-*

Daughter Incest (Cambridge: Harvard University Press, 1981), are three important books that exposed the widespread fact of child abuse and incest.

Battered women. For historical overviews of domestic violence, see Elizabeth Pleck, *Domestic Tyranny: The Making of American Social Policy Against Family Violence from Colonial Times to the Present* (New York: Oxford University Press, 1987). Del Martin, *Battered Wives* (San Francisco: Glide Publications, 1976), was the book that put the subject on the social service agenda. Suzanne Steinmetz and Murray Straus, eds., *Violence in the American Family* (New York: Dodd Mead, 1974); Judith Herman, *Trauma and Recovery: The Aftermath of Violence—From Domestic Abuse to Political Terror* (New York: Basic Books, 1992) and Isabel Marcus, "Reframing 'Domestic Violence': Terrorism in the House," in M. Fineman and B. Mykitiuk, eds., *The Public Nature of Private Violence: The Discovery of Domestic Abuse* (New York: Routledge, 1994), all offer valuable ways of understanding domestic violence. William Ryan, *Blaming the Victim* (New York: Pantheon, 1971), also contributed to the debate over battering and the battered-woman's syndrome. Susan Schecter's description of how battered women were treated before the women's movement can be found in her *Women and Male Violence: The Visions and Struggle of the Battered Women's Movement* (Boston: South End Press, 1982), which also offers a good overview of the movement. An innovative rehabilitative approach is described in Domestic Abuse Intervention Project, "Research Report" (Duluth, 1981), mimeographed; Anne Galey, *Court Mandated Counseling for Men Who Batter* (Tacoma: American Lake VA Medical Center, 1979); Mark Schulman, *A Survey of Spousal Violence Against Women in Kentucky* (U.S. Department of Justice: Law Enforcement Assistance Administration, Study No. 792701, July 1979). Other well-known studies of wife beating included Betsy Warrior, *Wifebeating* (Somerville, Mass.: New England Free Press, 1976); Lenore Walker, *The Battered Woman* (New York: Harper & Row, 1979); Terry Davison, *Conjugal Crime: Understanding and Changing the Battered Wife Pattern* (New York: Hawthorn, 1978); Frederique Delacoste and Felice Newman, eds., *Fight Back! Feminist Resistance to Male Violence* (Minneapolis: Cleis Press, 1981); R. Emerson Dobash and Russell Dobash, *Violence Against Wives: A Case Against the Patriarchy* (New York: The Free Press, 1979); and Letty Cottin Pogrebin, "Do Women Make Men Violent?" *Ms.*, November 1974.

Sexual Harassment. See Catharine MacKinnon, *Sexual Harassment of Working Women: A Case of Sex Discrimination* (New Haven: Yale University Press, 1979). MacKinnon's brilliant conceptualization of sexual harassment as discrimination provided the legal means by which the government could find such behavior illegal as well as how women could file grievances. For other work on sexual harassment, see Mark Gebicke, *DOD Service Academies: Further Efforts Needed to Eradicate Sexual Harassment* (Washington, D.C.: National Security and International Affairs, 1993); Terry Pattinson, *Sexual Harassment* (London: Future, 1991); Michael Rubenstein, *The Dignity of Women at Work: A Report on the Problem of Sexual Harassment in the Member States of the European Communities* (Luxembourg: Commission of the European Communities, 1988); G. La Marche, ed., *Speech and Equality: Do We Really Have to Choose?* (New York: New York University Press, 1996); Senate Committee on Labor and Human Resources, Ninety-seventh Congress, 1st sess., *Sex Discrimination in the Workplace* (Washington, D.C., 1981).

Prostitution. For historical overviews, see Ruth Rosen, *The Lost Sisterhood: Prostitution in America* (Baltimore: Johns Hopkins University Press, 1982); Barbara Hobson, *Uneasy Virtue: The Politics of Prostitution and the American Reform Tradition* (New York: Basic Books, 1987). The best analysis of contemporary prostitution is from Gail Pheterson, *The Prostitution Prism* (Amsterdam: University of Amsterdam Press, 1996). Kate Millett, *The Prostitution Papers* (New York: Avon, 1971), offers an unparalled account of a conference held for prostitutes and feminists. Kathy Barry, *Female Sexual Slavery* (Englewood Cliffs, N.J.: Prentice-Hall, 1979), offered strong documentation on the sale of women for prostitution.

Pornography. The debates over pornography produced a huge literature. For critique of the damage done by pornography, see Robin Morgan, "Theory and Practice: Pornography and Rape," *Going Too Far,* 163–70; Laura Lederer, ed., *Take Back the Night: Women on Pornography* (New York: William Morrow, 1980); Andrea Dworkin, *Pornography and Civil Rights: A New Day for Women's Equality*; Andrea Dworkin and Catharine A. MacKinnon, *Organizing Against Pornography* (Minneapolis, 1988); Catharine MacKinnon, *Feminism Unmodified: Discourses on Life and Law* (Cambridge, Mass.: Harvard University Press, 1987); Catharine MacKinnon, *Toward a Feminist Theory of the State* (Cambridge, Mass.: Harvard University Press, 1989), and *Only Words* (Cambridge, Mass.: Harvard University Press, 1993); and Susan Griffin, *Pornography and Silence* (New York: Harper & Row, 1981). For criticisms of the antipornography movement, see Ann Snitow, "Retrenchment Versus Transformation: The Politics of the Anti-Pornography Movement," in Varda Burstyn, ed., *Women Against Censorship* (Vancouver: Douglas & McIntyre, 1985).

Sex debates of the 1980s. Utlimately, the debates over pornography turned on whether sex represented more of a danger than a pleasure. See Ann Snitow, Christine Stansell, and Sharon Tompson, eds., *Powers of Desire: The Politics of Sexuality* (New York: Monthly Review Press, 1983), which sought "to integrate sexuality into the project of human liberation." Another collection that similarly tracked this debate was Carole Vance, ed., *Pleasure and Danger: Exploring Female Sexuality* (Boston: Routledge and Kegan Paul, 1984). Other valuable works that joined the debate over what was the "right kind of sex" were Morgan, "Politics of Sado-Masochism," in *Going Too Far*, 227–41; Bat-Ami Bar, "Feminism and Sadomasochism: Self Critical Notes," in Robin Ruth Linden and Darlene Pagano, eds., *Against Sadomasochism: A Radical Feminist Analysis* (East Palo Alto, Calif.: Frog in the Well, 1982), 72–82.

Feminism and sadomasochism. See Heresies, sex issue. Amber Hollibaugh, "Desire for the Future," in Vance, and Joan Nestle, *A Restricted Country* (London: Shebe, 1981); Kathleen Barry, "Sadomasochism: The New Backlash to Feminism," *Trivia* (Fall 1982): 77–92; Jessica Benjamin, "The Bonds of Love: Rational Violence and Erotic Domination," in Hester Eisenstein and Alice Jardine, eds., *The Future of Difference* (New Brunswick, N.J.: Rutgers University Press, 1985); Jessica Benjamin, "Master and Slave: The Fantasy of Erotic Domination," in *Powers of Desire*, 280–99; Johanna Heimholt, "From S/M, Feminist and Issues of Consent," in *Coming to Power*, Samois, ed. (Boston: Alyson Publications, 1981), 80–85; Gayle Rubin, "The Leather Menace: Comments on Politics and S/M," in *Coming to Power*, 192–227; Gayle Rubin, Deirdre English, and Amber Hollibaugh, "Talking Sex: A Conversation on Sexuality and Feminism," *Monthly Review 58* (July/August 1981): 43–62; Gayle Rubin, "Thinking Sex; Notes for a Radical Theory of the Politics of Sexuality," in Vance, *Pleasure*, 267–319; Diana Russell, "Sadomasochism: A Contra-Feminist Activity," in *Against Sadomasochism*, 176–83; Sally Roesch Wagner, "Pornography and the Sexual Revolution: The Backlash of Sadomasochism," in *Against Sadomasochism*, 23–44. Also see letters from readers to *Ms.* magazine in "Sex: Whose Revolution Is It?" in Mary Thom, ed., *Letters to Ms. 1972–1987* (New York: Holt, Rinehart, 1987), and "A Review of Current Work in the History of Sexuality," *Feminist Studies*; "Sexuality in History," the entire issue of *Radical History Review* (Spring/Summer 1979). For a good historical perspective on these sex debates, see Judith Walkowitz, "Male Vice and Female Virtue: Feminism and the Politics of Prostitution in Nineteenth-Century Britain," in *Powers of Desire*, 419–38. For a review essay on those writing for and against sadomasochism, see Ann Jones, "Fit to Be Tied," *Nation*, May 28, 1983. Also see a nuanced review of the struggle and feminist objections to sadomasochism in Leah Fritz, "Is There Sex After Sadomaschism?" in *Village Voice*, November 1, 1983, 24. In 1982, these various views collided at Barnard College's *Scholar and Feminist IX Conference*, "Toward a Politics of Sexuality." Each side claimed *the* correct view of sexuality. Some emphasized sexual crimes against women, citing rape, incest, pornography, and the sexual slavery industry. Others defended women's right to sexual freedom, opposed casting women as sexual victims, and supported the rights of prostitutes and sex workers to safe working conditions. See, for example, Varda Burstyn, ed., *Women Against Censorship* (Vancouver: Douglas & McIntyre, 1985); Andrea Dworkin, *Letters from a War Zone* (London: Secker and Warburg, 1988; Brooklyn, New York: Lawrence Hill Books, 1993).

CHAPTER SIX: PASSION AND POLITICS

See Charlotte Bunch, *Passionate Politics*; Robin Morgan, *Going Too Far*; Mary Thom, *Inside Ms.: 25 Years of the Magazine and the Feminist Movement* (New York: Holt, 1997); Carol Hanisch "The Personal Is Political," published in 1969, reprinted in *Feminist Revolution*; and Kathie Sarachild, "Program for Feminist Consciousness-Raising (1968)," in *Notes from the First Year*, APA. Vivian Gornick, "The Light of Liberation Is Blinding," in *The Village Voice*, December 10, 1970, 21; Ruth Rosen, "The Day They Buried Traditional Womanhood," in Peter Shafer, ed., *The Legacy: Vietnam in the American Imagination* (Boston: Beacon, 1990), 233–62; Amy Erdman Farrell, *Yours in Sisterhood: Ms. Magazine and the Promise of Popular Feminism* (Chapel Hill: University of North Carolina, 1998); Rozsika Parker and Griselda Pollock, eds., *Framing Feminism: Art and the Women's Movement 1970–1985* (London: Pandora Press, 1987); Gayle Kimball, *Women's Culture* (New Jersey: Scarecrow Press, 1981); Linda Nochlin, *Women, Art and Power* (New York: Harper and Row, 1988); Moira Roth, ed., *The Amazing Decade: Women and Performance Art in America 1970–80* (Los Angeles: Astro Arts, 1983); and *The Power of Feminist Art*, eds. Norma Broude and Mary Garrard (New York: Abrams, 1994).

CHAPTER SEVEN: THE POLITICS OF PARANOIA

FBI Women's Liberation Files, SL; *Hearings Before the Select Committee to Study Governmental Operations with Respect to Intelligence Activities of the United State Senate*, 94th Congress, 1st sess., vol. 6, November 18–19 and October 1, 3, 10, 11, 1975 (Washington: U.S. Government Printing Office, 1976); see Letty Cottin Pogrebin, "The FBI Was Watching," *Ms.*, June 1977. Works that discuss infiltration of this era, but not of the women's movement, include *The Cointelpro Papers*, and Brian Glick's *The War at Home* (Boston: South End Press, 1989), among many others. For material on Sagaris, see "An Analysis of Sagaris, Inc.," by the August 7th Survival Community," "Statement of the August 7th Committee," "The August 7th Survival Community Newsletter," all in APA. Also see "Our New Community," "Budget of Sagaris," "Sagaris: Table of Contents, Description, Self Criticism," all in Charlotte Bunch Papers, SL. Also see Carolyn Heilbrun,

The Education of a Woman: The Life of Gloria Steinem (New York: Ballantine, 1996) and Caroline Lazo, *Gloria Steinem: Feminist Extraordinaire* (New York: Lerner, 1998).

CHAPTER EIGHT: THE PROLIFERATION OF FEMINISM

Religion and spirituality. For those who challenged orthodox religion or created or rediscovered a spiritual tradition, see Mary Daly, *The Church and the Second Sex* (New York: Harper and Row, 1968), *Beyond God the Father: Towards a Philosophy of Women's Liberation* (Boston: Beacon Press, 1973), *Pure Lust: Elemental Feminist Philosophy* (Boston: Beacon Press, 1984); Carol Christ and Judith Plaskow, *Womanspirit Rising* (San Francisco: Harper, 1979); Carol P. Christ, *Diving Deep and Surfacing* (Boston: Beacon Press, 1995, 3d ed., originally published 1980), and Judith Plaskow and Carol P. Christ, *Weaving Visions* (New York: Harper-Collins, 1989), and Charlene Spretnak, *The Politics of Women's Spirituality: Essays on the Rise of Spiritual Power within the Feminist Movement* (Garden City, New York: Anchor, 1982).

Anne Carson, *Goddesses and Wise Women: The Literature of Feminist Spirituality 1980–92*, offers an annotated bibliography (Freedom, Calif.: Crossing Press, 1992).

Important works that influenced the growth of the movement include Paula Allen Gunn, *The Sacred Hoop: Recovering the Feminine in American Indian Traditions* (Boston: Beacon Press, 1996); Diana Bahr, *From Mission to Metropolis: Cupeno Indian Women in Los Angeles* (Norman: University Of Oklahoma Press, 1984); Starhawk, *The Spiral Dance: A Rebirth of the Ancient Religion of the Great Goddess* (New York: Harper and Row, 1979), *Dreaming the Dark: Magic, Sex and Politics* (Boston: Beacon Press, 1982), *The Fifth Sacred Thing* (New York: Bantam, 1993); Caroline Bynum, *Jesus As Mother: Studies in the Spirituality of the High Middle Ages* (Berkeley: University of California Press, 1982); Caroline Bynum, Stevan Harrell, and Paula Richman, eds., *Gender and Religion: On the Complexity of Symbols* (Boston: Beacon Press, 1986); Merlin Stone, *When God Was a Woman* (New York: Dial Press, 1976); Ginette Paris, *Pagan Meditations* (Dallas: Spring Publications, 1986).

Women's studies and feminist scholarship. The best general overviews can be found in Marilyn Boxer, *When Women Asked the Questions: Creating Women's Studies in America* (Baltimore: Johns Hopkins University, 1999); Ellen Dubois et al., eds., *Feminist Scholarship: Kindling in the Groves of Academe* (Chicago: University of Illinois Press, 1985), especially part 3, "The Response from the Disciplines"; and Christie Farnham, *The Impact of Feminist Research in the Academy* (Bloomington, Indiana:

Indiana University Press, 1987). For a good sense of how far feminist scholarship altered the disciplines by the mid-eighties, see Kris Montgomery, "The Story of Women's History Month: Reclaiming the Past, Rewriting the Future," in *Women Change America Gazette* (Sonoma: National Women's History Project, 1997), APA.

Working women. See early documents in Morgan, *Sisterhood*, and in Shapiro and Shapiro, *The Women Say*; see Denise D'Anne, "Working Women on Welfare," 64; Lynn O'Connor, Fred Garner, and Par Mialocq, "Office Politics," 45–51; Union WAGE, "Organizing Statement," 73; Nine to Five, "The Bill of Rights for Women Office Workers," 73; Union WAGE, "Purpose and Goals," 74; Karen Nussbaum, "We Have the Power of Women!" 71; Jesusita Novarro, "I Am a Working Mother," 72. Nancy Seifer, ed., *Nobody Speaks for Me: Self Portrait of Working Class Women* (New York: Simon and Schuster, 1976) is an important early work.

Young women responded to the women's movement during the 1980s and 1990s in a variety of ways. See the widely read Susan Bolotin, "Voices from the Post-Feminist Generation," *New York Times Magazine*, October 7, 1982, 28–31. Books by "Third Wave feminists" include Leslie Heywood and Jennifer Drake, eds., *Third Wave Agenda: Being Feminist, Doing Feminism* (Minneapolis: University of Minnesota, 1997) Paula Kamen, *Feminist Fatale: Voices from the "Twenty Something" Generation* (New York: Fine, 1991), Rebecca Walker, *To Be Real* (New York: Anchor, 1995), and Barbara Findlen, *Listen Up: Voices from the Next Feminist Generation* (New York: Seal, 1995) and Jennifer Baumgardner and Amy Richards, eds., *Manifesta: Young Women, Feminism, and the Future* (New York: Farrar, Straus & Giroux, 2000). In her bibliography, Paula Kamen cites a number of other articles and studies that document the acceptance by young women of ideas originally promoted by the women's movement, and their simultaneous rejection of being identified as a feminist. See "The 35 Million: A Preliminary Report on the Status of Young Women," *Institute for Women's Policy Research*, Washington, D.C. This report was released October 12, 1990. For conversations and interviews with young feminists, as well as the children of feminists, see Diane Salvatore, "Young Feminists Speak for Themselves," *Ms.*, April 1983, 43, 89, and "WAC TALK," a feature in *New Directions for Women*, January/February 1993, 19. Also see a collection titled *The Conversation Begins: Mothers and Daughters Talk About Living Feminism*, Christina Baker Kline, ed., (New York: Bantam, 1996); "Feminism Lures Young Allies," *New York Times* editorial, June 2, 1986. For a study of young women and their attitudes toward feminism, see Rose Glickman, *Daughters of Feminists* (New York: St. Martin's Press, 1993).

Older women. Patricia Huckle, *Tish Sommers, Activist and the Founding of the Older Women's League* (Knoxville, Tenn.: University of Tennessee Press, 1991), gives the single best history on the discovery of the "displaced homemaker." Other important feminist works on aging include Betty Friedan, *Fountain of Age* (New York: Touchstone, 1994); Erica Jong, *Fear of Fifty.*

African-Americans. Lee Rainwater and William L. Yancey, *The Moynihan Report and the Politics of Controversy* (Cambridge, Mass.: MIT Press, 1967), provides the background for the uproar that the *Moynihan Report* started. Celestine Ware, *Woman Power* (New York: Tower, 1970), was the earliest book to discuss and challenge the new feminist movement. Toni Cade, *The Black Woman* (New York: New American Library, 1970), offered the first essays that were widely debated. Some important articles that addressed the relationship between feminism and black women include Linda La Rue, "The Black Movement and Women's Liberation," in *The Black Scholar* 1:7 (May 1970); Charlayne Hunter, "Many Blacks Wary of 'Women's Liberation Movement,'" *New York Times*, November 17, 1970, 60; Angela Davis, *Angela Davis: An Autobiography* (New York: Random House, 1974); Gloria Hull, "My Life," APA; Toni Morrison, "Interview with Claudia Tate," in Claudia Tate, ed., *Black Women Writers at Work* (New York: Continuum, 1983), 117–31; from Third World Women's Alliance, "Black Women's Manifesto," n.d.; Linda La Rue, "Black Liberation and Women's Lib," *Transaction* (November–December 1970); Toni Morrison, "What the Black Woman Thinks About Women's Lib," *New York Times Magazine*, August 22, 1971; La-neeta Harris, "Black Women in Junior High Schools," in Tanner, *Voices*, 216. "The Sisters Reply," September 11, 1968, Mt. Vernon, N.Y., responding to "Birth Control Pill and Black Children," a statement by the Black Unity Party in Peekskill, N.Y., n.d.; Patricia Robinson, "Poor Black Women," n.d., all in Nancy Gray Osterud Collection, SL. For additional views, see Frances Beale, "The Double Jeopardy of Black Women" in "Documents from the Black Women's Liberation Movement," *Women's Liberation Movement*, in Documents from the Women's Liberation Movement, an On-Line Archival Collection, Duke University. For articles and manifestos that appeared as African-American women organized in the 1970s, see Michelle Wallace, "On the National Black Feminist Organization," June 1975, reprinted in Redstockings, *Feminist Revolution*, 174; and The Combahee River Collective, *The Combahee River Collective Statement: Black Feminist Organizing in the Seventies and Eighties* (New York: Kitchen Table: Women of Color Press, 1985 edition), pamphlet, APA.

For overall histories on black women, see Paula Giddings, *When and Where I Enter: The Impact of Black Women on Race and Sex in America* (New York: Bantam, 1984), and the collected essays in Darlene Clark Hine and Wilma King, eds., *We Specialize in the Wholly Impossible: A Reader in*

Black Women's History (Brooklyn, N.Y.: Carlson Publishing, 1995); Gloria Hull, Patricia Bell Scott, and Barbara Smith, eds., *All the Women Are White, All the Blacks Are Men and Some of Us Are Brave* (New York: Feminist Press, 1982); Nancie Caraway, *Segregated Sisterhood: Racism and the Politics of American Feminism* (Knoxville: University of Tennessee Press, 1986); Joyce Ladner, *Tomorrow's Tomorrow: The Black Woman* (New York: Doubleday, 1971); Gloria Joseph and Jill Lewis, *Common Differences: Conflicts in Black and White Feminist Perspectives* (New York: Anchor Books, 1981). The writer bell hooks has been extremely influential in offering theoretical challenges to assumptions held by white feminists. See bell hooks, *Ain't I a Woman: Black Women and Feminism; Feminist Theory: From Margin to Center* (Boston, South End Press, 1984), and *Talking Back: Thinking Feminist, Thinking Black* (Boston: South End Press 1989). For writing by Angela Davis, see *Women, Race and Class* (New York: Random House, 1981) and *Women, Culture and Politics* (New York: Random House, 1989). Other books that have informed and inspired are Audre Lorde, *Sister Outsider: Essays and Speeches* (Trumansburg, N.Y.: Crossing Press, 1984); Barbara Smith, ed., *Home Girls: A Black Feminist Anthology* (New York: Kitchen Table: Women of Color Press, 1983); Adrien Katherine Wing, ed., *Critical Race Feminism: A Reader* (New York: New York University Press, 1997); Kristal Brent Zook, "A Manifesto of Sorts for a Black Feminist Movement," *New York Times Magazine,* November 12, 1995, 86–89. Michelle Wallace, *Black Macho and the Myth of the Superwoman* (London: Verso, 1990 edition). Audre Lorde, "The Master's Tools Will Never Dismantle the Master's House," 1979, is a classic work reprinted in Moraga and Anzaldua. See bibliography in *Unequal Sisters,* pp. 585–590.

Chicanas. The best historical overview of Mexican-American women can be found in Vicki Ruiz, *Out of the Shadows: Mexican American Women in the Twentieth Century* (New York: Oxford, 1998). For important primary documents, see Alma M. Garcia, *Chicana Feminist Thought: The Basic Historical Writings* (New York: Routledge, 1997), and Martha Cotera, *The Chicana Feminist* (Austin, Information Systems Development, 1977). Important sources also include Nancy Nieto, "Macho Attitudes," *Hija de Cuauhtemoc* 1:1 (1971); Mirta Vidal, "Women: New Voice of La Raza" (New York: Pathfinder Press, 1971), reprinted in Chicanas Speak Out, DU. Segura and Pesquera, "Beyond Indifference and Antipathy: The Chicana Movement and Chicana Feminist Discourse," *Aztlan* (Fall 1988): 69–80; Adalijiza Sosa Riddell, "Chicanas and El Movimiento," *Aztlan* 5:1 (1974): 155–65; Mary Pardo, *MELA* (Philadelphia: Temple University Press, 1998); Gloria Anzaldua, *Borderlands: The New Mestiza* (San Francisco: Spinsters/Aunt Lute, 1987); Gretchen M. Bataille, Kathleen Mullen Sands, and Gloria Anzaldua, eds.; *Making Face, Making Soul: Creative* *and Critical Perspectives by Feminists of Color* (San Francisco: Aunt Lute Books, 1990); Gloria Anzaldua and Cherrie Moraga, eds., *This Bridge Called My Back: Writings by Radical Women of Color* (Watertown, Mass.: Persephone Press, 1981), which includes a number of documents by lesbians who felt they belonged nowhere. Carla Trujillo, ed., *Living Chicana Theory* (Berkeley: Third Woman Press, 1998), provides a range of important essays, as does Trujillo, *Chicana Lesbians: The Girls Our Mothers Warned Us About* (Berkeley: Third Woman Press, 1991).

Native American women. Among the hundreds of new works on Native America women, I found these particularly useful: Paula Gunn Allen, *As Long As the Rivers Flow: The Stories of Nine Native Americans* (New York: Scholastic, 1996); Theda Perdue, *Cherokee Women: Gender and Culture Change 1700–1835* (Lincoln: University of Nebraska Press, 1998); Carol Devens, *Countering Colonization: Native American Women and Great Lakes Missions* (1630–1900) (Berkeley: University of California Press, 1992); Margaret Jacobs, *Engendered Encounters: Feminism and Pueblo Culture 1879–1934* (Lincoln: University of Nebraska Press, 1999); Kathleen Donovan, ed., *Feminist Readings of Native American Literature: Coming to Voice* (Tucson: University of Arizona Press, 1998); Diana Meyers Bahr, *From Mission to Metropolis: Cupeno Indian Women in Los Angeles* (Norman: University of Oklahoma Press, 1993); Luana Ross, *Inventing the Savage: The Social Construction of Native American Criminality* (Austin: University of Texas Press, 1998); Sabine Lang, John L. Vantine, tr., *Men as Women, Women as Men: Changing Gender in Native American Cultures* (Austin: University of Texas Press, 1998); Ruth Roach Pierson and Nupur Chaudhuri, eds., *Nation, Empire, Colony: Historicizing Gender and Race* (Bloomington: Indiana University Press, 1998); Paula Gunn Allen, *Off the Reservation: Reflections on Boundary-Busting, Border-Crossing Loose Canons* (Boston: Beacon Press, 1998); Paula Gunn Allen, *The Sacred Hoop: Recovering the Feminine in American Indian Traditions* (Boston: Beacon Press, 1992); and Rayna Green, *Women in American Indian Society* (New York: Chelsea House, 1992). Gretchen M. Bataille, *American Indian Women, Telling Their Lives* (Lincoln: University of Nebraska Press, 1984); Elsie Allen, *Pomo Basketmaking: A Supreme Art for the Weaver*, Vinson Brown, ed. (Happy Camp, Calif.: Naturegraph Publishers, 1972); and Shirley Hill Witt, "Native Women Today: Sexism and the Indian Woman," in *Civil Rights Digest*, Spring 1974, are useful works for understanding American Indian women's relation to feminism. See also the bibliography in *Unequal Sisters*, pp. 599–605.

Asian-American women. A good collection of essays on Asian-American women is Sonia Shah, ed., *Dragon Ladies: Asian-American Feminists Breathe Fire* (Boston: South End Press, 1997), as is Elaine Kim and

Norma Alarcon, eds., *Writing Self/Writing Nation* (Berkeley: Third Woman
Press, 1994); Asian Women United of California, eds., *Making Waves: An
Anthology of Writing by and about Asian-American Women* (Boston: Bea-
con, 1989); Shirley Geok-lin Lim and Mayumi Tsutakawa, eds., *The For-
bidden Stitch: An Asian-American Women's Anthology*, (Corvallis, Oregon:
Calyx Book, 1989); Nobuya Tsuchida, ed., *Asian and Pacific American Ex-
periences: Women's Perspectives* (Minneapolis: University of Minnesota
Press, 1982); Eui-Young Yu and Philip H Phillips, eds., *Korean Women in
Transition: At Home and Abroad* (Los Angeles: California State Univ., Los
Angeles, 1987); Le Ly Hayslip, *When Heaven and Earth Changed Places:
A Vietnamese Woman's Journey from War to Peace* (New York: Doubleday,
1989); and see the bibliography in *Unequal Sisters*, pp. 590–593.

Other sources on minority women and feminism. Extensive bibliographies on minority women's history can be found in Ellen Carol DuBois
and Vicki L. Ruiz, eds., *Unequal Sisters: A Multicultural Reader in U.S.
Women's History* (New York: Routledge, 2000); Gloria Anzaldua and Cherrie Moraga, eds., *This Bridge Called My Back: Writings by Radical Women
of Color* (Watertown, Mass.: Persephone Press, 1981); and Alice Walker, *In
Search of Our Mothers' Garden* (San Diego: Harcourt Brace Jovanovich,
1983) is the source for writings about "womanism" instead of feminism.

The heartland and local community studies. Studies of local feminist communities are increasing rapidly. See Benita Roth, "The Fourth
World Is Born: The Separation of the Radical Women's Movement from the
New Left, 1968–1971," unpublished thesis, UCLA Department of Sociology, Spring 1989; Theresa Kaminski, "From Within and Without: Meanings of American Feminism in the 1960's and 1970's (Minneapolis)," paper
presented at 1993 Berkshire Conference, Vassar, New York; and "Still
Ain't Satisfied: Legacies of the 1970's Socialist Feminist Movement in
Minneapolis, St. Paul," n.d, unpublished dissertation, University of Min-
nesota, paper presented at same panel. Barbara Winslow, "The Struggle for
Abortion Reform in Washington State, 1967–1970," paper given to author
in 1993; Joanna Leslie Dyl, "Burn This and Memorize Yourself: The Col-
lectivists' Small Group as a Social Movement Organization in Women's
Liberation in the Bay Area," unpublished senior thesis, Department of
History, Stanford University; Judith Sealander and Dorothy Smith, "The
Rise and Fall of Feminist Organizations in the 1970's: Dayton as a Case
Study," *Feminist Studies* 12:2 (Summer 1986): 221–339, APA; Anne Pop-
kin, "Bread and Roses: An Early Moment in the Development of Socialist
Feminism," unpublished dissertation, Brandeis University, May 1978; and
Michelle Moravec, "In Their Own Times: Voices from Los Angeles,
1967–1976," master's thesis, UCLA, n.d. There are now a number of local

studies available. Barbara Winslow of Medgar Evers College is working on a study of Seattle Women's Liberation. Amy Kessleman at SUNY New Paltz is working on a study of New Haven. See Deborah Gerson, "Consciousness as Politics: Mobilization in Bay Area Women's Liberation, 1968–73," unpublished method paper, U.C. Berkeley Sociology Department; Nancy Whittier's study, *Feminist Generations* (of Columbus, Ohio) (Philadelphia: Temple University Press, 1995); Judith Ezekiel, "Une contribution à l'histoire du mouvement feministe Americain: l'etude du cas de Dayton, Ohio (1969–1980)," unpublished dissertation, Paris, 1987. For other scholars and students working on the women's movement, see *Women's Liberation Network Directory*, version 8/15/97, Web site: http://www.duke.edu/~ginnyd/wlrn.html. Also see "A Quiet Revolution: How life in one Wisconsin City has changed since the beginning of the Women's Movement," *Newsweek*, December 28, 1997.

Houston. For those interested in media studies and feminism, the press coverage of the Houston conference offers an especially interesting case study. The press coverage became increasingly respectful as reporters realized the significance of a government-sponsored meeting with a stated feminist agenda. For a range of examples, see Connie Skipitares, "Cleaver at Women's Session," *San Jose Mercury*, November 22, 1978, 28; Connie Skipitares, "Women Moving to Solidify their Gains," *San Jose Mercury*, November 1977, 1; Mildred Hamilton, "Women Endorse the ERA," *San Francisco Examiner*, November 20, 1977, 1; Merrill Shields with Lea Donosky, Lucy Howard, Elaine Sciolino, and Hall Bruno, "A Woman's Agenda," *Newsweek*, November 28, 1977, 57; Judith Anderson, "Gay, Abortion Planks Pass," *San Francisco Chronicle*, November 21, 1977, 1; Judith Anderson, "Women's Meeting Ends Abruptly," *San Francisco Chronicle*, November 22, 1977, 1; "What's Next for U.S. Women," *Time*, December 5, 1977, 18–26; Judith Anderson, "Houston Meeting: Was It Worth It," *San Francisco Chronicle*, November 24, 1977, 73; Anne Taylor Fleming, "That Week in Houston: It was said that the women's movement was in a state of disarray. The National Women's Conference proved otherwise," *New York Times Magazine*, December 25, 1977, 10–33; Bill Curry, "Multitude of Voices on Women's Issues," *Washington Post*, November 29, 1977, 1, 21, 32; Anna Quindlen, "Women's Parley Brings Action Over a Rights Agenda for Nation," *New York Times*, November 20, 1977, 1. For the official history of the Houston meetings, see National Commission on the Observance of International Women's Year, *The Spirit of Houston: An Official Report to the President, the Congress and the People of the United States* (Washington, D.C., March 1978); National Commission on the Observation of International Women's Year, *Declaration of American Women* (Washington, D.C.: IWY Commission, 1977).

CHAPTER NINE: SISTERHOOD TO SUPERWOMAN

For studies of media representations of the movement see Susan Douglas, *Where the Girls Are: Growing Up Female with the Mass Media* (Random House: New York, 1994); Gaye Tuchman, *Making News: A Study in the Construction of Reality* (New York: Free Press, 1978); Ella Taylor, *Prime Time Families: Television Culture in Postwar America* (Berkeley: University of California Press, 1989); Todd Gitlin, *Inside Prime Time* (Berkeley: University of California Press, 1983); Mary Anne Doane, et al., *Re-Vision: Essays in Feminist Film Criticism* (Frederick, Md.: University Publications of America, 1984).

Consumer feminism. See Elisabeth Cagan, "The Selling of the Women's Movement," *Social Policy* (May/June 1978); Scot Winoker, "Freud and Fashion; Tobacco Firms' Seduction of Women," *San Francisco Chronicle*, August 21, 1983, 6; "Brooke Shields Takes a Stand Against Smoking But the Government Didn't Want Her Message," *American Lung Association Bulletin* (June/July, 1981); Lawrence Wallack, "Mass Media Campaigns in a Hostile Environment: Advertising as Anti-Health Education," paper for Health Education and Media International Conference, March 24, 1981, Edinburgh, Scotland. David Reuben, *Any Woman Can! Love and Sexual Fulfillment for the Single, Widowed, Divorced, and Married* (New York: D. McKay, 1971).

Therapeutic feminism. The self-help books that best demonstrate the intersection between the women's movement and the human potential movement are: Dorothy Tennov, *Super Self: A Woman's Guide to Self-Management* (New York: Funk and Wagnalls, 1977); Dorothy Jongeward and Dru Scott, *Women As Winners: Transactional Analysis for Personal Growth* (Reading, Mass.: Addison-Wesley Publishing Company, 1976); Stanlee Phelps and Nancy Austin, *The Assertive Woman* (San Luis Obispo: Impact, 1975). Helen Gurley Brown, *Having It All* (New York: Pocket Books, 1982), is the best single description of the superwoman.

Film. Some films that addressed ideas of the women's movement were *A Woman under the Influence*, 1972; *Looking for Mr. Goodbar*, 1977; *Norma Rae*, 1979; *Nine to Five*, 1980; *Diary of a Mad Housewife*, 1970; *Alice Doesn't Live Here Anymore*, 1974; *Tootsie*, 1980; *Private Benjamin*, 1980; *Mr. Mom*, 1983; *Yentl*, 1983; *Silkwood*, 1983. Also see Janice Mendehall, *Films on the Women's Movement*; an annotated list of 90 films, mostly shorts, in Federal Women's Program Coordinator, General Service Administration, Washington, D.C., *Women and Film*, no. 2 (1972): 16; Lee Israel, "Women in Film: Saving an Endangered Species," *Ms.*, February 8, 1975, 51; Andrew Kopkind, "Hollywood—Under the Influence of Women," *Ramparts* (May 13, 1975): 56–60; R. McCormuck, "Women's Liberation Cinema," *Cineaste* (Spring 1972): 1–7; Linda Greene, "Politics of a Feminist Fantasy," *Jump Cut* 6 (March/April 1983): 14; Bosley Crowther, "Where Are the Women?" *New York Times*, January 23, 1966.

Feminist concerns with the new superwoman. See Arlie Hochschild, *The Second Shift* (Berkeley: University of California, 1989), and *The Time Bind* (New York: Viking, 1997), for how a stalled revolution affected women's lives. See also Joan Peters, *When Mothers Work: Loving Our Children Without Sacrificing Ourselves* (New York: Perseus, 1998) and Peggy Orenstein, *Flux: Women on Sex, Work, Kids, Love and Life in a Half-Changed World* (New York: Doubleday, 2000). A view that is harshly critical of the women's movement is Sylvia Hewlett, *A Lesser Life*.

Beyond backlash. Two important books are Susan Faludi, *Backlash: The Undeclared War Against American Women* (New York: Crown, 1991), and Juliet Mitchell and Ann Oakley, *Who's Afraid of Feminism? Seeing Through the Backlash* (New York: New Press, 1997).

See early attacks by Marabel Morgan, *The Total Woman* (New York: Pocket Books, 1973), and Midge Decter, *The New Chastity and Other Arguments Against Women's Liberation* (New York: Coward, McCann and Geoghegan, 1972). The term New Right was first used by Lee Edward in 1962 in proposing a conservative platform for Young Americans for Freedom. It became popular in 1975 when conservative Kevin Phillips began to associate the New Right with the efforts of Paul Weyrich, Howard Phillips, Richard Viguerie, and Terry Dolan, which is described in Rebecca Klatch, *Women of the New Right* (Philadelphia: Temple University Press, 1987). For a range of studies on the New Right and its relationship to feminism, see Allen Hunter, "In the Wings: New Right Ideology and Organization," *Radical America* 15 (Spring 1981): 112–28; Rosalind Pollack Petchesky, "Antiabortion, Antifeminism and the Rise of the New Right," *Feminist Studies* 7 (Summer 1981): 206–46; Barbara Ehrenreich, "The Social Issue Game: Family Feud on the Left," *Nation* 234 (March 13, 1982): 289, and Linda Gordon and Allen Hunter, "Sex, Family and the New Right: Anti-Feminism As a Political Force," *Radical America* 11–12 (November 1977–February 1978): 9–25, and David Frum, *How We Got Here: The Seventies* (New York: Basic, 2000). For women's opposition to feminism, see Andrea Dworkin, *Right Wing Women* (New York, 1983); Phyllis Schlafly, *The Power of the Positive Woman* (New York: Jove/HBJ, 1977); Lisa Cronin Wohl, "Phyllis Schlafly: The Sweetheart of the Silent Majority," *Ms.*, March 1974, 63, and the longer biography by Carol Festenthal, *The Sweetheart of the Silent Majority* (New York: Doubleday, 1981); Pamela Johnston Conover and Virginia Gray, *Feminism and the New Right: Conflict over the American Family* (New York: Praeger, 1983); Zillah Eisenstein, *Feminism and Sexual Equality: Crisis in Liberal America* (New York:

Monthly Review Press, 1984). Some of the best archival material on antifeminist sentiment can be found in a new collection called *Antifeminism in America: A Collection of Readings from the Literature of the Opponents to U.S. Feminism, 1948 to the Present*, edited with introductions by Angela Howard and Sasha Ranae Adams Tarrant (New York: Garland Press, 1997).

The ERA. The failure of the ERA to be ratified produced many different explanations. Some of the most important are Jane De Hart Mathew and Donald Mathew, "The Cultural Politics of ERA's Defeat," *Organization of American Historians Newsletter* 10:4 (November 1982): 13–15; Jane J. Mansbridge, *Why We Lost the ERA* (Chicago: University of Chicago Press, 1986), which emphasizes the lack of cohesive feminist organization around the ERA, and Mary Frances Berry, *Why the ERA Failed: Women's Rights and the Amending Process of the Constitution* (Bloomington: Indiana University, 1986), who suggests what preconditions were necessary to get an amendment ratified, such as consensus-building in all the states; Joan Hoff Wilson, ed., *The ERA and Right of Passage: The Past and Future of the ERA* (Bloomington: Indiana University Press, 1986), offers a collection of essays that examine everything from labor's objection to the ERA in the 1920s to the language used in the 1980s by opponents and proponents of the ERA. Also see "National Rallies Give Enthusiastic Sendoff to ERA Countdown Campaign," in *National Now Times*, July/August, 1981, 1, for a bittersweet reminder of the optimism that still could be mobilized just one year before the defeat. Possibly one of the most important and least remembered stories from the ERA battle involved a Mormon woman who refused to give up her struggle for passage of the amendment. For a popular review of her past and conversion to feminism, see Lisa Cronin Wohl, "A Feminist Latter-Day Saint: Why Sonia Johnson Won't Give Up on the ERA or the Mormons," *Ms.*, March 1980, 40.

Cultural wars. The literature on the cultural wars is vast. However, the majority of commentators have not recognized how deeply gendered—and racialized—are these cultural battles. For a sampling of some of the works that have responded to the Right's criticism of education, family, and religion, see Gerald Graff, *Beyond the Culture Wars: How Teaching the Conflicts Can Revitalize American Education* (New York: W. W. Norton, 1992), and *Curricular Reform and the Culture Wars* (New York: Garland, 1994); Henry Louis Gates, Jr., *Loose Canons: Notes on the Culture Wars* (New York: Oxford University Press, 1992); Todd Gitlin, *The Twilight of Common Dreams: Why America Is Wracked by Culture Wars* (New York: Metropolitan Books, 1995); James L. Nolan, ed., *The American Culture Wars: Current Contests and Future Prospects* (Charlottesville: University Press of Virginia, 1996); Lawrence Levine, *The Opening of the American Mind* (Boston: Beacon, 1997); Elayne Rapping, *Media-tions: Foray into the*

Culture and Gender Wars (Boston: South End Press, 1994); and Norma Broude and Mary D. Garrard, eds., *The Power of Feminist Art: The American Movement of the 1970s, History and Impact* (New York: Harry Abrams, 1996); and Robin Kelley, *Yo' Mama's Disfunktional! Fighting the Culture Wars in Urban America* (Boston: Beacon, 1998), which is one of the most insightful works on race and the culture wars.

Divorce and feminization of poverty. Although some social scientists by the 1990s found Lenore Weitzman's research to be overstated, her published numbers had by then become household words. Lenore J. Weitzman, *The Marriage Contract, Lovers and the Law* (New York: The Free Press, 1981). As women grew poorer, a number of writers addressed what Diana Pearce dubbed the new "feminization of poverty." Ruth Sidel, *Women and Children Last: The Plight of Poor Women in Affluent America* (New York: Viking, 1982); Andrew Hacker, *Two Nations: Black and White, Separate, Hostile, Unequal* (New York: Viking, 1992); Christopher Jencks, *Rethinking Social Policy: Race, Poverty, and the Underclass* (Cambridge, Mass:, Harvard University Press, 1992); Linda Gordon, ed., *Women, the State, and Welfare* (Madison: University of Wisconsin Press, 1990); Ken Auletta, *The Underclass* (New York: Random House, 1992); Diana Pearce, *Feminization of Poverty* (Washington, D.C.: Institute for Women's Policy Research, 1989); Ruth Sidel, *On Her Own: Growing Up in the Shadow of the American Dream* (New York: Viking, 1990); and Rochelle Lefkowitz and Ann Withorn, eds., *For Crying Out Loud: Women and Poverty in the United States* (New York: The Pilgrim Press, 1986).

Global feminism. One of the most useful books that describes the modern women's movement in the United States, Western Europe, and Japan is Monica Threlfall, ed., *Mapping the Women's Movement* (New York: Verso, 1996).

Women's rights as human rights. Some of the important historical works are Diana Russell and Nicole Van de Ven, eds., *The Proceedings of the International Tribunal on Crimes Against Women* (East Palo Alto, Calif.: Frog in the Well, 1984); Center for Women's Global Leadership, *Demanding Accountability: The Global Campaign and Vienna Tribunal on Violation of Women's Human Rights*, edited by Charlotte Bunch and Niamh Reilly, 1996. *Testimonies on the Global Tribunal on Violation of Women's Rights* includes full transcripts of the thirty-three testimonies given by women from twenty-five countries at the global tribunal, Vienna, June 1993; also published by the Center for Women's Global Leadership. Other publications that the center has published are important sources for the history of the global movement to redefine women's rights as human rights. *Gender Violence and Women's Human Rights in Africa* compiles the ideas and strategies of some of Africa's foremost women's human rights activists. The video, *The Vienna Tribunal: Women's Rights Are Human Rights*, is available from Women Make Movies, in New York. Also see Joanna Kerr, *Ours by Right: Women's Rights as Human Rights* (London: Zed, 1993), and Katarina Tomasevski, *Women and Human Rights* (London: Zed, 1993); *Women's Rights, Human Rights*, Julie Peter and Andrea Wolper, eds., (New York: Routledge, 1995); Roxanna Carrillo, *Battered Dreams: Violence Against Women as an Obstacle to Development* (New York: Unifem, 1992); *The Human Rights Watch Global Report on Women's Human Rights* (New York: Human Rights Watch, 1995); Marguerite Guzman Bouvard, *Women Reshaping Human Rights: How Extraordinary Activists Are Changing the World* (New York: Scholarly Resources, 1996).

Development. The purpose of the Grameen Bank was to provide small loans exclusively to the poor who possess no more than a half acre of land or assets not exceeding the value of one acre of cultivatable land. The bank loaned small amounts of money to village women, with which they could start small businesses. The records of the bank demonstrate that nearly all the loans were paid back rapidly and that the women were successful in gaining economic independence. For studies on this institution, see David Bornstein, *The Price of a Dream: The Story of the Grameen Bank and the Idea That Is Helping the Poor to Change Their Lives* (New York: Simon and Schuster, 1996); Helen Todd, *Women at the Center: Grameen Bank Borrowers After One Decade* (Boulder, Colo.: Westview Press, 1996); Abu N.M. Wahid, ed., *The Grameen Bank: Poverty Relief in Bangladesh* (Boulder: Westview Press, 1992); I.S.A. Baud and G. A. de Bruijne, eds., *Gender, Small-Scale Industry and Development Policy* (New York: International Women's Tribunal, 1993); Julia Moss, *Half the World, Half the Chance: An Introduction to Gender and Development* (New York: Oxfam, 1993); J. Ann Tickner, *Gender in International Relations: Feminist Perspectives on Securing Global Security* (New York: Columbia University Press, 1992). There is a huge literature on women and development now. I recommend the catalog *Women, Ink.: Books on Women and Development*, 777 United Nations Plaza, New York, New York 10017, for bibliographies and annotated lists of books I have used.

Global networks. On the creation of global networks, see Peggy Andres, *Sisters Listening to Sisters: Women of the World Share Stores of Personal Empowerment* (Westport: Bergen and Harvey, 1996); Amrita Basu, ed. *The Challenge of Local Feminism: Women's Movements in Global Perspective* (Boulder: Westview Press, 1995); and the many media and personal accounts from the UN conferences.

INDEX

FOR THE BEST IN PAPERBACKS, LOOK FOR THE (◐)

In every corner of the world, on every subject under the sun, Penguin represents quality and variety—the very best in publishing today.

For complete information about books available from Penguin—including Penguin Classics and Puffins—and how to order them, write to us at the appropriate address below. Please note that for copyright reasons the selection of books varies from country to country.

In the United States: Please write to *Penguin Group (USA), P.O. Box 12289 Dept. B, Newark, New Jersey 07101-5289* or call 1-800-788-6262.

In the United Kingdom: Please write to *Dept. EP, Penguin Books Ltd, Bath Road, Harmondsworth, West Drayton, Middlesex UB7 0DA.*

In Canada: Please write to *Penguin Books Canada Ltd, 90 Eglinton Avenue East, Suite 700, Toronto, Ontario M4P 2Y3.*

In Australia: Please write to *Penguin Books Australia Ltd, P.O. Box 257, Ringwood, Victoria 3134.*

In New Zealand: Please write to *Penguin Books (NZ) Ltd, Private Bag 102902, North Shore Mail Centre, Auckland 10.*

In India: Please write to *Penguin Books India Pvt Ltd, 11 Panchsheel Shopping Centre, Panchsheel Park, New Delhi 110 017.*

In the Netherlands: Please write to *Penguin Books Netherlands bv, Postbus 3507, NL-1001 AH Amsterdam.*

In Germany: Please write to *Penguin Books Deutschland GmbH, Metzlerstrasse 26, 60594 Frankfurt am Main.*

In Spain: Please write to *Penguin Books S. A., Bravo Murillo 19, 1° B, 28015 Madrid.*

In Italy: Please write to *Penguin Italia s.r.l., Via Benedetto Croce 2, 20094 Corsico, Milano.*

In France: Please write to *Penguin France, Le Carré Wilson, 62 rue Benjamin Baillaud, 31500 Toulouse.*

In Japan: Please write to *Penguin Books Japan Ltd, Kaneko Building, 2-3-25 Koraku, Bunkyo-Ku, Tokyo 112.*

In South Africa: Please write to *Penguin Books South Africa (Pty) Ltd, Private Bag X14, Parkview, 2122 Johannesburg.*